WAR CRIMES,
WAR CRIMINALS,
AND WAR CRIMES TRIALS

RECENT TITLES IN
BIBLIOGRAPHIES AND INDEXES IN WORLD HISTORY

Iran Media Index
Hamid Naficy, compiler

Serial Bibliographies and Abstracts in History: An Annotated Guide
David Henige, compiler

An Annotated Bibliography of the Holy Roman Empire
Jonathan W. Zophy, compiler

WAR CRIMES, WAR CRIMINALS, AND WAR CRIMES TRIALS

An Annotated Bibliography and Source Book

Compiled and edited by
Norman E. Tutorow

With the Special Assistance of Karen Winnovich

Bibliographies and Indexes in World History, Number 4

GREENWOOD PRESS
New York • Westport, Connecticut • London

LIBRARY OF CONGRESS CATALOGING-IN-PUBLICATION DATA

Tutorow, Norman E.
  War crimes, war criminals, and war crimes trials.

  (Bibliographies and indexes in world history,
ISSN 0742-6852 ; no. 4)
  Includes index.
  1. War crimes—Bibliography. 2. War criminals—
Bibliography. 3. War crime trials—Bibliography.
4. World War, 1939-1945—Atrocities—Bibliography.
I. Winnovich, Karen. II. Title. III. Series.
Z6464.W33T87   1986   016.3416'9   86-9985
[JX5419.5]
ISBN 0-313-24412-X (lib. bdg. : alk. paper)

Copyright © 1986 by Norman E. Tutorow

All rights reserved. No portion of this book may be
reproduced, by any process or technique, without the
express written consent of the publisher.

Library of Congress Catalog Card Number: 86-9985
ISBN: 0-313-24412-X
ISSN: 0742-6852

First published in 1986

Greenwood Press, Inc.
88 Post Road West, Westport, Connecticut 06881

Printed in the United States of America

The paper used in this book complies with the
Permanent Paper Standard issued by the National
Information Standards Organization (Z39.48-1984).

10 9 8 7 6 5 4 3 2 1

COPYRIGHT ACKNOWLEDGMENT

Material has been reprinted from *Historical Abstracts*, edited by Pamela R. Byrne, by permission of ABC-Clio, Inc., for entries 92, 150, 1052, 1110, 1246, 1617, 2165, 2166, 2304, 2500, 2653, 3099, 3218, 3600, 3607, 3608, 3610, 3875, and 4275.

ABOUT THE COMPILER

Norman E. Tutorow is a Historian and author of many books, pamphlets and articles. His books include *The Mexican-American War: An Annotated Bibliography* (Greenwood Press, 1981), and *Leland Stanford: Man of Many Careers*, and he has contributed articles to *Pacific Historian*, *The Quarterly Review*, and *American Neptune*.

Dedicated to the Memory of My Brother
VIRGIL W. TUTOROW, JR.

CONTENTS

FOREWORD	xvii
ACKNOWLEDGMENTS	xix
INTRODUCTION	3
1. Background	3
2. United Nations War Crimes Commission (UNWCC)	4
3. Overview of War Crimes Trials and Sentences	4
4. Nuremberg International Military Tribunal (IMT)	9
5. Nuremberg Military Tribunals (NMT)	11
6. International Military Tribunal for the Far East (IMTFE)	13
7. Sources and Depositories	17
8. Criticisms of War Crimes Trials	22
9. This Bibliography	23
End Notes	25
I. REFERENCE SECTION	31
A. BIBLIOGRAPHIES	31
B. GUIDES	40
C. INDEXES	42
D. REFERENCE WORKS	43
E. DOCUMENTS AND RECORDS BY NATION	43
1. General	43
2. France	44
3. Germany	44
4. Great Britain	44
5. Israel	44
6. Italy	44
7. Poland	44
8. United Nations	45
9. United States	45
a. General	45
b. Army	45
c. Department of State	46
d. NARS. General	47
e. NARS. Microfilm	47
f. NARS. Preliminary Inventories	48
g. NARS. Record Groups	49

            h. NARS. Special Lists   51
            i. Naval War College   51

    F. GENERAL WORKS ON ARCHIVES, LIBRARIES, AND OTHER
       DEPOSITORIES   52
        1. France   52
        2. Germany   52
        3. Great Britain   53
        4. Japan   53

II. GENERAL WORKS AND SUBSIDIARY TOPICS   54

    A. BACKGROUND WORKS   54
    B. PHILOSOPHICAL AND THEORETICAL WORKS   57
    C. INTERNATIONAL LAW   58
    D. INTERNATIONAL CRIMINAL COURT   60
    E. INTERNATIONAL CONFERENCES AND CONVENTIONS   62
    F. LAWS OF WAR   64
    G. SUPERIOR ORDERS AND MILITARY NECESSITY   70
    H. PRISONERS OF WAR   73
    I. HOSTAGES   76
    J. GUILT AND PERSONAL RESPONSIBILITY FOR WAR CRIMES   77
    K. RENUNCIATION OF WAR   82
    L. GENERAL WORKS ON WAR CRIMES TRIALS   83
    M. COMPARISONS OF TWO OR MORE TRIALS   83

III. EARLY WAR CRIMES, WAR CRIMINALS, AND WAR CRIMES TRIALS   89

    A. PRE-WORLD WAR I   89
        1. Ancient and Medieval   89
        2. Napoleonic   89
        3. American War for Independence   90
        4. American Civil War   90
        5. Turkey   92
        6. Greco-Bulgarian War   92
        7. Philippine Insurrection   92
    B. WORLD WAR I   93
        1. General Works on World War I   93
        2. War Crimes   95
            a. General Works on War Crimes   95
            b. Armenian-Turkish War Crimes   98
            c. Belgium   98
            d. France   99
        3. War Criminals   99
            a. General   99
            b. The Kaiser   101
        4. War Crimes Trials   102
            a. General   102
            b. Leipzig   103

IV. WORLD WAR II WAR CRIMES   105

    A. GENERAL WORKS   105
    B. DEFINITION OF WAR CRIMES   111
    C. WAR CRIMES AND WAR CRIMINALS   111
    D. ALLIED WAR CRIMES   111
    E. AGGRESSION AND AGGRESSIVE WAR AS WAR CRIMES   112
    F. COLLABORATION   114
    G. CRIMES AGAINST THE PEACE   114
    H. CRIMES AGAINST HUMANITY   114
    I. DEPORTATION, RESETTLEMENT, AND FORCED LABOR   119
    J. MEDICAL CRIMES   121
    K. ECONOMIC CRIMES: EXPLOITATION, PILLAGE, LOOTING   123

L. CRIMES AGAINST HOMOSEXUALS	123
M. CRIMES AGAINST GYPSIES	124
N. VICTIMS OF WAR CRIMES	124
O. WAR CRIMES BY AREA AND NATION WHERE COMMITTED	125
1. Asia	125
2. Belgium	127
3. Czechoslovakia	128
4. Denmark	129
5. France	129
6. Hungary	129
7. The Netherlands	130
8. Poland	130
a. General	130
b. Ghettos	133
c. Katyn Woods Massacre	135
9. Union of Soviet Socialist Republics	137
a. General	137
b. Series from the Soviet War News	141
10. Yugoslavia	144
V. WORLD WAR II WAR CRIMES: THE HOLOCAUST	145
A. GENERAL WORKS	145
B. DOCUMENTS	150
C. HISTORIES	151
D. ANTISEMITISM	153
E. GENOCIDE (FINAL SOLUTION, ENDLÖSUNG)	153
F. GENOCIDE CONVENTION	159
G. ECONOMIC PERSECUTION	160
H. RESCUE	160
I. RESISTANCE	161
J. SURVIVORS	163
K. PSYCHOLOGICAL ASPECTS	164
L. REVISIONIST WORKS	166
M. INTERNATIONAL MILITARY TRIBUNAL AND THE HOLOCAUST	167
N. BY AREA AND COUNTRY	167
1. Europe	167
2. Austria	169
3. Belgium	169
4. Bulgaria	169
5. Croatia	170
6. Denmark	170
7. France	170
8. Germany	171
9. Greece	172
10. Hungary	172
11. Italy	173
12. Lithuania	173
13. Macedonia	174
14. The Netherlands	174
15. Poland	174
16. Rumania	175
17. Slovakia	176
18. Thrace	176
19. Union of Soviet Socialist Republics	176
20. United States	176
21. Yugoslavia	177
VI. WORLD WAR II WAR CRIMES: CONCENTRATION CAMPS (KONZENTRATIONSLAGER, KZ, KL)	178
A. GENERAL	178
B. STUDIES OF TWO OR MORE CAMPS	183

C.	AUSCHWITZ	186
D.	BELZEC	192
E.	BERGEN-BELSEN	192
F.	BREENDONK	193
G.	BUCHENWALD	194
H.	CHELMNO	195
I.	COMPIÈGNY	195
J.	DACHAU	195
K.	DORA (NORDHAUSEN)	199
L.	DRANCY	200
M.	FLOSSENBURG	200
N.	GROSS-ROSEN	200
O.	GURS	200
P.	GUSEN	200
Q.	HOHENSTEIN	200
R.	ILAVA	201
S.	LE VERNET	201
T.	MAJDANEK	201
U.	MAUTHAUSEN	201
V.	NEUENGAMME	203
W.	NOVÁKY	203
X.	PAPENBURG	203
Y.	RADOM	203
Z.	RAVENSBRÜCK	203
AA.	RED CROSS	205
BB.	SACHSENHAUSEN (ORANIENBURG)	205
CC.	SALASPILS	205
DD.	SKARZYSKO (KAMIENNA)	205
EE.	SOBIBOR	206
FF.	STRUTHOF (NATZWEILER)	206
GG.	STUTTHOF (SZTUTOWO)	206
HH.	THERESIENSTADT (TEREZIN)	206
II.	TREBLINKA	207
JJ.	WESTERBORK	208

VII. WORLD WAR II WAR CRIMINALS 209
    A. BIOGRAPHICAL SECTION 209
        1. Biographies 209
        2. Autobiographies, Diaries, Memoirs, Reminiscences 221
        3. Correspondence, Other Writings, Speeches 226
    B. SPECIAL STUDIES 228
    C. PURSUIT, LOCATION, APPREHENSION 237
    D. AMNESTY, ASYLUM, CLEMENCY, PAROLE 241
    E. EXTRADITION 242
    F. CRIMINAL ORGANIZATIONS 243
        1. General 243
        2. Gestapo and Sicherheitsdienst 244
        3. Schutzstaffel 245
    G. PUNISHMENT 248

VIII. WORLD WAR II WAR CRIMES TRIALS IN ASIA 257

    A. GENERAL AND REFERENCE WORKS 257
    B. SPECIAL STUDIES 258
    C. WAR CRIMES TRIALS (NON-IMTFE) 259
        1. Australian 259
        2. British 259
        3. Double Tenth 259
        4. Masaharu Homma 260
        5. Khabarovsk 260
        6. Manila 261
        7. Shanghai 261
        8. Yasutake Sakakibara 261

			Contents xiii

```
            9. Yamashita Tomoyuki                           261
           10. Yokohama                                     264
           11. Comparisons of Two or More Trials            264
       D. IMTFE                                             265
            1. General Works                                265
            2. Documents                                    270
               a. General                                   270
               b. Indexes                                   271
               c. Indictments                               271
               d. Defense and Prosecution Records           271
               e. Prosecution Records                       272
               f. Witnesses                                 273
               g. Defense Records                           273
               h. Trial Proceedings                         274
               i. Verdicts, Sentences, Execution of Sentences  275
            3. Dissent                                      275
            4. Verdicts, Sentences, Execution of Sentences  277
            5. Amnesty and Early Release                    278
            6. Meaning and Significance of the IMTFE        279
            7. Later Evaluations                            279

IX. NUREMBERG INTERNATIONAL MILITARY TRIBUNAL               283

    A. GENERAL WORKS                                        283
    B. IMT, ALLIED, AND OTHER NON-CRIMINAL FIGURES          295
         1. Biographies                                     295
         2. Autobiographies                                 296
         3. Diaries                                         296
         4. Memoirs                                         297
    C. DOCUMENTS                                            297
    D. SPEECHES                                             304
    E. IMT AND INTERNATIONAL LAW                            305
    F. IMT AND INTERNATIONAL CONFERENCES AND CONVENTIONS    308
    G. PRINCIPLES AND PROCEDURES                            310
    H. LEGALITY, JUSTICE, AND JURISDICTION                  313
    I. GUILT AND RESPONSIBILITY                             317
    J. EX POST FACTO ASPECTS OF THE IMT                     321
    K. STATUTES OF LIMITATION                               322
    L. VERDICTS, SENTENCES, AND EXECUTION OF SENTENCES      325
    M. LATER EVALUATIONS AND CRITICISMS                     328
    N. SIGNIFICANCE OF THE IMT                              337
    O. THE UNITED NATIONS AND THE IMT                       341

X. AMERICAN MILITARY TRIBUNALS (NON-IMT)                    343

    A. GENERAL WORKS                                        343
    B. CONTROL COUNCIL TRIALS (12 "SUBSEQUENT PROCEEDINGS") 346
         1. General Works                                   346
         2. Trial Records                                   347
         3. Indexes to Trial Records                        350
         4. Specific Cases                                  351
              a. Case  1  Medical Case                      351
              b. Case  2  Milch Case                        352
              c. Case  3  Justice Case                      352
              d. Case  4  Pohl Case                         354
              e. Case  5  Flick Case                        355
              f. Case  6  Farben Case                       356
              g. Case  7  Hostage Case                      358
              h. Case  8  RuSHA Case                        359
              i. Case  9  Einsatzgruppen Case               359
              j. Case 10  Krupp Case                        360
              k. Case 11  Ministries Case                   361
              l. Case 12  High Command Case                 362
```

C. WORKS ON DE-NAZIFICATION PROCEEDINGS	363
D. SABOTEURS CASE	364
E. ALBERT BURY AND WILHELM HAFNER TRIAL	365
F. HADAMAR TRIAL	365
G. BORKUM ISLAND TRIAL	365
H. MALMÉDY TRIAL	365
I. BUCHENWALD/DACHAU TRIAL	367
J. MISCELLANEOUS	367

XI. ALLIED MILITARY TRIBUNALS AND NATIONAL TRIALS — 369

A. GENERAL WORKS	369
B. CONTROL COUNCIL LAW NO. 10	376
C. AUSTRIA	379
D. BELGIUM	379
E. CANADA	380
F. CZECHOSLOVAKIA	380
G. DENMARK	380
H. FINLAND	381
I. FRANCE	381
J. GERMANY	386
1. General	386
2. Hans Globke Trial, Berlin, 1963	389
3. Auschwitz Trials, Frankfurt am Main, 1963-1965	389
4. Bishop Matthias Defregger Trial, 1969	391
5. Miscellaneous Trials	391
6. Court Decisions Under Control Council Law No. 10	393
K. GREAT BRITAIN	398
1. General Works	398
2. Peleus Trial, Hamburg, 1945	399
3. Dulag-Luft Trial, Wuppertal, 1945	400
4. Belsen Trial, Lüneburg, 1945	400
5. Velpke Baby Home Trial, Brunswick, 1946	400
6. Von Falkenhorst Trial, Hamburg, 1946	400
7. Natzweiler Trial, Wuppertal, 1946	401
8. Stalag-Luft III Trial, Dachau, 1947	401
9. Von Manstein Trial, Hamburg, 1947	401
L. HUNGARY	402
M. ITALY	402
N. THE NETHERLANDS	403
O. NORWAY	403
P. POLAND	403
Q. RUMANIA	405
R. USSR	405

XII. ADOLF EICHMANN TRIAL — 408

A. GENERAL	408
B. BIOGRAPHICAL AND SPECIAL STUDIES	412
C. CRIMES	413
D. PURSUIT AND APPREHENSION	415
E. PROSECUTION	416
F. THE TRIAL	417
G. TRIAL DOCUMENTS	422
H. VERDICT	424
I. APPEAL	424
J. INTERNATIONAL LAW	425
K. LEGALITY AND JURISDICTION	426
L. PUBLIC AND PRESS REACTION	427
M. SIGNIFICANCE	428

XIII.	VIETNAM WAR AND WAR CRIMES TRIALS	429
	A. GENERAL WORKS	429
	B. INTERNATIONAL LAW	430
	C. LEGALITY AND JUSTICE OF AMERICAN INTERVENTION	431
	D. WAR CRIMES	433
	1. General	433
	2. Ben Suc	437
	2. My Lai	438
	3. Song My (Pinkville)	439
	4. Viet Cong War Crimes	440
	E. COVER-UP AND INVESTIGATION	441
	F. WAR CRIMES TRIALS	442
	1. General	442
	2. William Calley	443
	3. Howard B. Levy	444
	4. Ernest Medina	444
	5. Bertrand Russell (Stockholm) Tribunal	445
	G. CAMBODIA	446
XIV.	MISCELLANEOUS	448
	A. KOREAN WAR, 1950-1953	448
	B. ALGERIAN CIVIL WAR, 1954-1962	449
	C. PAKISTAN CIVIL WAR, BANGLADESH, 1972-1973	450
	D. MOZAMBIQUE MERCENARIES TRIAL, LUANDA, 1976	450
	E. EAST TIMOR	451
	F. DERING-URIS CASE	451
	G. BETH-DIN TRIAL	451
	H. AFGHANISTAN-SOVIET UNION WAR, 1980	451

APPENDICES   453

PART 1 INTERNATIONAL MILITARY TRIBUNAL - NUREMBERG   453

APPENDIX 1 THE LONDON AGREEMENT FOR THE PROSECUTION AND PUNISHMENT OF THE MAJOR WAR CRIMINALS OF THE EUROPEAN AXIS   453

APPENDIX 2 CHARTER OF THE NUREMBERG INTERNATIONAL MILITARY TRIBUNAL   455

APPENDIX 3 NUREMBERG IMT MEMBERS AND ALTERNATE MEMBERS OF THE TRIBUNAL   462

APPENDIX 4 NUREMBERG IMT DEFENDANTS AND DEFENSE COUNSELS   462

APPENDIX 5 NUREMBERG IMT CHARGES, VERDICTS, AND SENTENCES   463

      Figure 1. Counts of the Indictment   463
      Figure 2. Extracts from the Nuremberg IMT Indictment   463
      Figure 3. Table of Counts, Verdicts, and Sentences   464

APPENDIX 6 PRINCIPAL POSTS HELD BY NUREMBERG IMT DEFENDANTS   465

APPENDIX 7 NUREMBERG IMT OFFICIALS   467

      Figure 1. American Prosecution Team   467
      Figure 2. American Documentary Evidence Preparation Team   468
      Figure 3. British Prosecution Team   468
      Figure 4. French Prosecution Team   468
      Figure 5. Soviet Prosecution Team   468

xvi   Contents

PART 2 NUREMBERG MILITARY TRIBUNALS (NMT) (SUBSEQUENT CASES)   469

APPENDIX 8 NUREMBERG MILITARY TRIBUNALS   469

        Case 1. Medical Case   469
        Case 2. Milch Case   470
        Case 3. Justice Case   470
        Case 4. Pohl Case   471
        Case 5. Flick Case   471
        Case 6. Farben Case   472
        Case 7. Hostage Case   472
        Case 8. RuSHA Case   473
        Case 9. Einsatzgruppen Case   474
        Case 10. Krupp Case   475
        Case 11. Ministries Case   475
        Case 12. High Command Case   476

APPENDIX 9 NMT SUMMARY OF VERDICTS   477

PART 3 INTERNATIONAL MILITARY TRIBUNAL FOR THE FAR EAST (IMTFE) 478

APPENDIX 10 IMTFE PROSECUTING NATIONS   478

APPENDIX 11 IMTFE DEFENDANTS AND SENTENCES   478

APPENDIX 12 PRINCIPAL POSTS HELD BY IMTFE DEFENDANTS   479

APPENDIX 13 IMTFE COUNSELS   481

APPENDIX 14 IMTFE CHARGES, VERDICTS, AND SENTENCES   481

        Figure 1. Counts of the Indictment   481
        Figure 2. Table of Counts, Verdicts, and Sentences 482

PART 4 HOLOCAUST STATISTICS   483

APPENDIX 15 VARIOUS ESTIMATES OF JEWISH DEATHS   483

        Table 1. Anglo-American Committee   483
        Table 2. Lucy S. Dawidowicz   483
        Table 3. Gerald Fleming   484
        Table 4. Gerald Reitlinger   484
        Table 5. Jacob Lestchinsky   485
        Table 6. Raul Hilberg   485

APPENDIX 16 ABSORPTION OF JEWISH REFUGEES, 1933-1943   486

PART 5 MISCELLANEOUS APPENDICES   487

APPENDIX 17 EQUIVALENT RANKS OF THE UNITED STATES ARMY,
        THE GERMAN ARMY, AND THE WAFFEN-SS   487

APPENDIX 18 INTERNATIONAL WAR CRIMES TRIBUNAL (BERTRAND RUSSELL
        TRIBUNAL) (STOCKHOLM TRIBUNAL)   487

ABBREVIATIONS   489

GLOSSARY   493

JOURNALS AND OTHER PERIODICAL LITERATURE CONSULTED   501

INDEX OF AUTHORS, SUBJECTS, AND TOPICS   513

FOREWORD

For the scholar and the researcher bibliographies offer valuable tools and signposts in a mass of printed materials. For librarians and information specialists they provide useful shortcuts, and save expensive computer time by pinpointing exactly the reference that is needed. If a bibliography is logically arranged, carefully constructed, and reasonably complete, it is indeed a treasure.

Experienced historian and superbly qualified bibliographer Norman E. Tutorow has provided us with such a treasure in his bibliography War Crimes, War Criminals, and War Crimes Trials: An Annotated Bibliography and Source Book.

At the end of the Second World War the Allied powers with the help of military intelligence teams searched out German government, Nazi party, and military records assembled in so-called ministerial collecting centers. This material was to serve as basic documentation for the International Military Tribunal to be held at Nuremberg, and also provided some of the sources for the subsequent "successor" trials held by American, British, French, and Russian teams. This Nuremberg collection contained original documents, trial proceedings, staff evidence analyses, translations, working copies, personal dossiers of the accused, witness reports, and affidavits. Through the use of new and relatively inexpensive photocopy procedures and later through selective publication, this material became available to the scholarly community - to the historian, the political scientist, the lawyer, and researchers interested in sociology and psychology, who were suddenly able to study the records of the immediate past of a vanquished enemy. A whole generation of young scholars, many of them fresh from the battlefield and studying under the GI bill, was trained using these records.

To a more limited extent, due to the difficulties of language, this process also took place in the use of the documentation assembled for the International Military Tribunal for the Far East. The legal and ethical questions associated with the presumed right of the victors to try the vanquished in international military tribunals for war crimes, of which they themselves may also have been guilty, have been debated ever since.

In this carefully-constructed bibliography with annotations for the major publications, the author gives a survey of his sources, lists early war crimes trials, including those of World War I, and in Sections IV to XI deals with all aspects of World War II war crimes, both in Europe and in Asia. Sections V and VI put special emphasis on the Holocaust and on concentration camps. Sections XII to XIV deal with the post World War II period and include material on the Eichmann trial of 1961-1962 in Jerusalem, and the various trials associated with the war in Vietnam, including the Stockholm trial of 1967, presided over by Bertrand Russell.

It is particularly helpful that the 4500 references not only include monographs and government documents, but dissertations and periodical articles as well. The Appendix contains the text of the London agreement for the prosecution and punishment of the major war criminals of the European Axis as well as the Charter of the Nuremberg International Military Tribunal. The Appendix also lists the IMT defendants and their defense counsels, and gives the names of all the Allied prosecution teams, information that is difficult to locate. The same information is given for the participants in the International Military Tribunal for the Far East.

Finally, the whole work is rounded out by an index of both subjects and names.

This bibliography makes no claim to be exhaustive, but it can rightfully be considered as representative. By bringing together and arranging logically this vast variety of information on war crimes, war criminals, and war crimes trials, the author has performed a great service to the scholarly community.

Agnes F. Peterson
Hoover Institution, Stanford University
January 1986

ACKNOWLEDGMENTS

A bibliography is by its very nature a work of collaboration. Innumerable librarians, directors of special collections, archivists, family members, and friends contribute to this kind of endeavor by their tireless efforts and loyal support.

Many librarians have assisted me in my search for materials dealing with war crimes, war criminals, and war crimes trials, but none in greater measure than those at the Stanford University Library and the Hoover Institution on War, Peace and Revolution. In particular I wish to thank Agnes F. Petersen, Curator of the West European Collection, for writing the Foreword. I owe a debt of gratitude as well to a number of staff members and librarians for their much-needed and much-appreciated assistance, among them Galena Dotsenko, Diane L. Hill, Hilja Kukk, André Pierce, and Majorie Rauen.

Michael Anderson, Chief of the Archives Branch of the Federal Archives and Records Center, San Bruno, California, and John J. Slonaker, Chief, Historical Reference Section, United States Military History Institute, Carlisle Barracks, Pennsylvania, have contributed useful materials from their collections.

I give special thanks to Dr. Kurt Steiner, Professor of Political Science, Emeritus, Stanford University, and former Special Assistant to the Chief of the Trial Division, International Prosecution Section (IPS), and to Dr. Charles Burdick, Dean, School of Social Sciences, San José State University, for their invaluable contributions to the content and style of the Introduction.

A debt of gratitude is owing to the many who have assisted in the reading and rereading of the manuscript, for helpful suggestions in the editorial and proof-reading processes, and for countless laborious hours of checking card catalog entries of hundreds of books and articles. Chief among these supporters are Greg Grove, Ronald R. Mercik, Kirsten J. Nelson, Simon Srebrny, Harold W. Stombs, Brian H. Thompson, Tiffany Tom, and Darlene L. Tutorow. Bryan T. Winnovich and Darlene L. Tutorow are to be thanked as well for long-suffering.

Herman Weiss and Karin Weiss have offered much assistance with the German text, and Simon Srebrny helped with the German, French, and Polish.

I thank ABC-Clio Press, Santa Barbara, California, for permitting me to reproduce a number of historical abstracts of articles written in various eastern European languages.

My chief collaborator in this work has been Karen Winnovich, who formed and reformed the text repeatedly and handled the entire task of word-processing. She organized and edited the Index and ran all preliminary and final copy. I thank David L. Hunt for writing the computer program for the Index.

Despite the labors of these many, there remain errors of omission and commission for which I assume all responsibility.

Norman E. Tutorow
Portolá Valley, California

WAR CRIMES, WAR CRIMINALS, AND WAR CRIMES TRIALS

INTRODUCTION

1. Background

   Historians have tended to view wars simply in terms of causes and consequences, paying little regard to legal or moral considerations. They have traditionally classified them as simply offensive or defensive, but more recently they have begun to characterize them as just or unjust, legal or illegal, with Dutch scholar and statesman Hugo Grotius providing the bench mark for the latter concept. Despite the intentional destructiveness of war, man for centuries has attempted in some way or another to mitigate its barbarity by ordering its conduct by rules and codes. Some of these guidelines have found recent expression in the formulations of various Hague and Geneva conventions and in the pronouncements of numerous international conferences and agreements.

   The right of a sovereign nation to go to war has never been seriously questioned until recent times, and legal and moral responsibility has been of little or no concern: what mattered above all else was victory. It is inevitable that the formulation of rules of warfare should lead to increasing concern with the issues of legality and illegality, since rules are inevitably violated and violation implies some sort of responsibility and accountability. Since violation of law is a criminal act, a natural concomitant to legality and illegality is criminality.[1]

   International organizations dedicated to maintaining the peace - themselves a development of this century - have sought to discourage warfare, but have generally not attempted to prohibit nations from going to war. While the Covenant of the League of Nations, for example, did not consider war illegal, member nations were discouraged from resorting to war, though specific exceptions were made, particularly in cases involving self-defense. The League deftly avoided the sensitive issue of sovereignty in its proposal for collective response. Strict adherence to League provisions, though sanctioning or tolerating some wars, would undoubtedly have discouraged or even prevented others.

   In the years following World War I, various unsuccessful attempts were made to regulate, restrict, and discourage - if not outlaw -

warfare, and to try war criminals.[2] Among the international agreements made to realize these goals were the Kellogg-Briand Pact (The General Treaty for the Renunciation of War), which in 1928 still recognized the right of a nation to go to war in self-defense. There followed the Anti-War Treaty on Non-Aggression and Conciliation, signed in Rio de Janeiro on October 10, 1933, and the Act of Chapultepec of March 3, 1945. The United Nations Organization, created in 1945, provided another step in the direction of collective response to certain acts of war and to collective discouragement of resorting to war as a means of settling disputes between nations.

2. United Nations War Crimes Commission (UNWCC)

Long before the end of World War II, as crimes against prisoners of war and civilians, most notably Jews in occupied countries, were brought to the attention of the world, the United States, Great Britain, France, and the Soviet Union began planning post-war action against the Axis powers and set about compiling lists of war criminals. The policies of the Allied powers were implemented later by the United Nations War Crimes Commission (UNWCC), which was established on October 20, 1943, by the Allied representatives assembled at the Foreign Office in London.[3] The first official meeting of the Commission was held on January 11, 1944.[4]

The Commission was made up of representatives from Australia, Belgium, Canada, China, Czechoslovakia, Denmark, France, Greece, India, Luxembourg, the Netherlands, New Zealand, Norway, Poland, the United Kingdom, the United States, and Yugoslavia.[5] Immediately it set about formulating principles of international law and planning for the creation of postwar international tribunals to try war criminals. Its primary task was to collect, investigate, and record evidence of war crimes, and to report to the governments concerned all instances in which a *prima facie* case existed. The Commission had a small secretariat in London, but it worked mainly through committees and through a Far Eastern and Pacific Sub-Commission in Chungking.[6]

The Commission was assisted in its task by various national offices established by the member nations, offices which immediately began searching for war criminals. The national offices submitted to the Commission formal charges against suspected war criminals and a description of available evidence to substantiate the charges. After these charges were received, the Commission had to determine whether the accused should be arrested and prosecuted by the member governments. This made it necessary to identify and locate the accused and to plan for their later prosecution. The matter of evidence and witnesses became crucial, and, as it turned out, many refugees took an active part in gathering evidence and giving testimony. The Commission itself took no part in these arrests and prosecutions; in fact, most of the accused were never brought to trial.

These careful, long-range preparations led ultimately to the signing of the London Agreement, on August 8, 1945, but before any trials were conducted, widespread discussions were held in public and private regarding the legality of the projected trials.[7]

3. Overview of War Crimes Trials and Sentences

There is no complete list of the thousands of war crimes trials held following World War II. Among them were trials conducted by the International Military Tribunal at Nuremberg (IMT), the International Military Tribunal for the Far East (IMTFE) at Tokyo, the United States Military Tribunal at Nuremberg (NMT), United States Military Commissions sitting in various places in Europe and Asia, the General Military Government Court and Intermediate Government Court of the American Zone of Germany, British military courts sitting in various places in Europe and Asia, the French Permanent Military Tribunal sitting in various places in France, the French Court of Appeal and the General Military Government Tribunal of the French Occupation Zone of Germany, the Australian Military Court sitting at Rabaul, the Canadian Military Court sitting in Aurich, Germany, the Netherlands Temporary Court-Martial and Special Courts, the Norwegian Court of Appeal, the Supreme Court of Norway, the Chinese War Crimes Court, and the Supreme National Tribunal of Poland.[8]

The two international military tribunals tried a small number of major war criminals, while other tribunals tried so-called minor war criminals, among them financiers, industrialists, high government officials, police authorities, members of enemy armed forces, and other civilians.

Some enemy combatants accused of war crimes were tried by military tribunals, while most minor war criminals and civilians were tried by civil courts. These were either national courts of the nation that had apprehended the defendants or to which the defendants owed some sort of allegiance other than by citizenship. There were also a number of trials conducted by nations against their own citizens. In addition to the major trials, there were 2116 known military tribunal hearings, not including those conducted by the Soviet Union, Poland, and other Eastern Bloc nations, as well as hearings by German courts, other national courts, and the United States Supreme Court.[9]

Estimates vary on the total number of war crimes trials held. The United Nations War Crimes Commission, for example, reported on November 16, 1946, that as of October 31, 1946, a total of 1108 accused war criminals had been tried in Europe, 413 of whom had been sentenced to death, 485 imprisoned, and 210 acquitted. In the Far East 1350 had been tried, 384 of whom had been sentenced to death, 704 imprisoned, and 262 acquitted.[10] Before the Commission was phased out, it reported the total number of war crimes trials held - except those held in the Soviet Union and eastern European nations under Soviet control - as follows: American 809, British 524, Austrian 256, French 254, the Netherlands 30, Poland 24, Norway 9, Canada 4, and China 1.[11] The following is an estimate of the number of war crimes trials held by major Allied nations as of 1963:[12]

COUNTRY	NUMBER OF SENTENCES	DEATH SENTENCES
USA	1,814	450
UK	1,085	240
USSR	c. 10,000	?
WEST GERMANY	12,846	?

The United States held in all approximately 900 war crimes trials, involving more than 3000 defendants. About half these cases were tried in Germany. Of the defendants tried in Germany by the United States, 1380 were convicted and 241 acquitted. A total of 421 death sentences were handed down, many of which were commuted, and only 136 of the 194 life sentences were approved.[13]

6   Introduction

The second largest group of trials was conducted in Japan, with a few in Austria, Italy, the Philippines, China, and various Pacific islands. United States military courts sitting in the Philippines, China, the Pacific islands, and Japan conducted 474 trials, involving more than 1409 Japanese defendants.[14] In addition to the IMTFE proceedings in Tokyo, the United States conducted an important war crimes trial in Manila of General Yamashita Tomoyuki, commander of Japanese forces in the Philippines and Malaya. Hundreds of trials of less-well-known defendants were conducted by the United States Eighth Army in Yokohama.[15]

The United States War Crimes Branch, Manila, closed on January 1, 1947. Though Americans participated in the preparation for many of the remaining trials, the disposition of trials involving non-American victims became the responsibility of Filipino authorities. Final statistics of American trials conducted in the Philippines are as follows: cases tried, 97; defendants tried, 215; convictions, 195 (90.7%), acquittals, 20 (9.3%); death sentences, 92 (47.4% of those convicted).[16]

Final statistics for American trials conducted in the Far East are:[17]

	Yokohama	China	Manila	Pacific Islands	Total
Number of trials	319	11	97	47	474
Defendants tried	996	75	215	123	1,409
Convictions	854	67	195	113	1,229
Acquittals	142	8	20	10	180
Death sentences	51	10	92	10	163

In Lüneburg, Hamburg, and Italy, the British held 356 war crimes trials, involving more than 1000 defendants. At Lüneburg, Josef Kramer, Irme Grise, and forty-three others from the staff of Belsen and Auschwitz were tried.[18] Thirty were found guilty and eleven of the thirty were sentenced to death by hanging. In the Zyklon B case, Bruno Tesch and two others were tried for supplying concentration camps with Zyklon B pesticide to use to exterminate Jews. Tesch and one other defendant were hanged. In the Natzweiler case, Alphons Klein and five others were charged with killing four British women by lethal injection and for killing more than 100 Russians and Poles. One defendant was hanged and the rest were imprisoned.[19] In the Peleus trial, in Hamburg, the captain and four members of the crew of German U-Boat 852 were charged with murdering the survivors of the cargo ship Peleus as it was sinking.[20] Three were sentenced to death and the other two were sentenced to prison. The British also held trials in Rimini and Venice, and General Nikolaus von Falkenhorst, among others, was tried for the murder of British commandos in Norway. The last of the British trials, the highly controversial trial of Field Marshal Erich von Manstein, was held in Hamburg from August to December, 1949.

Statistics on British war crimes trials in the Far East are fairly complete: cases tried, 306; defendants, 920; number convicted, 811 (88.1%); acquitted, 107 (11.6%); death sentences, 279 (34.4% of the total number convicted); death sentences carried out, 265; life sentences, 55; unaccounted for or not tried, 3; results of two trials were not reported. Over 17% of those convicted had their sentences reduced or were released failing confirmation of sentences.[21]

Australian war crimes trials have come in for severe criticism, generally because of legal procedure rather than partiality or unfairness. Final statistics of the Australian trials are summarized below:

Place	Trials	Defendants	Acquitted	Convicted
Singapore	23	62	11	51
Morotai	25	148	67	81
Labuan	16	145	17	128
Wewak	2	2	1	1
Rabaul	188	390	124	266
Darwin	3	22	12	10
Hong Kong	13	42	4	38
Manus	26	113	44	69
TOTAL	296	924	280	644

Of the 644 prisoners convicted (69.5% of the total), 148 (23%) were sentenced to death and executed; 496 (77%) were imprisoned. The prison sentences were : life, 39; 25 years, 2; 11-24 years, 152; 10 years, 82; under 10 years, 22.[22]

Statistics on Dutch trials are as complete as those on the British. They held 448 war crimes trials; cases tried, 1038; convicted, 969 (93.4%); acquitted, 55 (5.3%); unaccounted for, 14 (1.3%); death sentences, 236 (23.3% of those convicted); life sentences, 28. Ten death sentences were commuted. The fate of 14 defendants is unclear, due to escape, release because of illness, or release because of insufficient evidence.[23]

It is unclear exactly when French trials in the Far East ended, but the final statistics reported are as follows: cases tried, 39; defendants, 230; convicted, 198 (86.1%); acquitted, 31 (13.5%); unaccounted for, 1; death sentences, 63 (31.8% of those convicted); death sentences carried out, 26; in absentia, 37.[24]

In many cases reports of trials and sentences in Europe as well as the Pacific vary and are inconsistent, but not nearly so much as reports of sentences served. Some discrepancies and inconsistencies result from reports of initial sentences that do not take into consideration later commutations. Other are based on errors of fact.[25] At any rate, the application of capital and lesser punishment was not as severe as the above sentences might suggest. In 1961 the Federal Ministry of Justice in Bonn reported that during the four and a half years in which the Allies exercised judicial power in Europe, they convicted 5025 people accused of war crimes, but that only 174 of them were still in prison in 1954.[26] Many of the death sentences imposed by the American Military Tribunal at Nuremberg were commuted to life imprisonment. Of the defendants given life sentences, a few were discharged, and several had their sentences reduced; in only a few cases were the original sentences actually carried out.[27]

In addition to war crimes trials conducted by foreign tribunals, there were thousands of denazification proceedings in Germany. On March 5, 1946, the three Länder (states) in the American Zone enacted a denazification law designed primarily not to punish Germans who had been Nazis, but to remove them from or keep them out of positions of postwar leadership. The accused were classified as either major offenders, offenders, lesser offenders, or followers.

8   Introduction

Major offenders were subject to immediate removal or permanent exclusion from public office, confiscation of property, and to a maximum of ten years in prison.[28]

Under this law, 13 million people in the American Zone of occupation had to register. Of them, approximately 3 million were found subject to classification under the denazification law. In all, 545 tribunals, employing 22,000 people, worked on this classification process. Despite amnesties granted by the Military Governor, over 930,000 defendants were eventually tried by denazification tribunals. Of them, 1549 were classified as major offenders, 21,000 as offenders, 104,000 as lesser offenders, and 475,000 as followers. Over 500,000 people were fined for various criminal offenses, 122,000 suffered restrictions on employment, 25,000 were subject to confiscation of property, 22,000 were declared ineligible to hold public office, 30,000 were required to perform special labor, and 9000 were given prison sentences.[29]

German courts prosecuted thousands of war criminals either not tried by the Allies or tried by them and acquitted. According to one account, West Germany alone prosecuted 12,982 defendants between 1945 and 1963. A German government publication reported on January 7, 1964, that in the American Zone alone 1814 people had been sentenced, 450 to death; in the British Zone 1085, 240 to death; and in the French Zone 2107, 104 to death. More than half those receiving the death sentence were actually executed.[30] A Japanese source reported that in all 5700 Japanese had been tried for war crimes and that 920 had been executed.[31]

Trials conducted by various occupational and national authorities are almost countless and records of them are not always easy to obtain. It is particularly difficult to secure reliable and verifiable information on those trials held by the Soviet Union, though much has been written about the famous Kharkov trial.[32] In carefully staged "show trials," Czechoslovakia tried and executed Karl H. Frank, Hanns Ludin, and Dieter Wisliceny, and Poland executed Joseph Bühler, Jürgen Stroop, and Rudolf Höß, among others.[33] We shall never know how many were tried or how many were executed without trial.

Many war criminals were tried for acts committed in concentration or extermination camps. There were seven so-called "parent cases" involving six concentration camps - Dachau, Mauthausen, Flossenburg, Nordhausen, Buchenwald, and Mühldorf - as well as 170 subsequent proceedings related to these trials.[34]

When Klaus Barbie was arrested in January of 1983, there were still 1671 cases involving war crimes in progress in German courts or prosecuting agencies. In February of that year there were eight jury hearings in progress in German cities, most of them relating to concentration camp offenses. From 1980 to 1981, West German prosecutors worked on 1367 war crimes cases, and seventeen jury trials ended in the conviction of twenty-two out of thirty-three defendants.

Of the nearly 88,000 war crimes cases opened in West Germany between 1945 and 1983, non-appealable sentences were imposed upon 6456 defendants, while acquittals were handed down in 79,638 cases - over 90% of the cases tried.[35]

4. Nuremberg International Military Tribunal (IMT)

In late 1944, Senators and Congressmen accelerated their activities for planning of the apprehension and prosecution of war criminals by introducing a number of resolutions calling for the President to establish a special commission to handle war crimes trials. President Harry S Truman responded with Executive Order 9547 of May 2, 1945, by which he appointed Supreme Court Justice Robert H. Jackson Representative and Chief Counsel for the United States in the preparation and prosecution of the Allied case against major Axis war criminals. On August 8, after consultation with the Control Council for Germany, Jackson signed an agreement with the representatives of the other three powers establishing an International Military Tribunal to try war criminals whose crimes were not committed against any particular Allied nation or which could not be identified with any particular geographical locality. All those charged by this tribunal were Germans accused of crimes committed in continental Europe.

A Charter for the Tribunal authorizing its organization and defining its jurisdiction and powers was annexed to the London Charter (agreement of August 8) and amended in only one minor detail two months later.[36] The IMT Charter gave the signatory nations the power to try and punish major war criminals for crimes committed either as individuals or as members of criminal organizations, as defined in the Charter. The circularity of having victors create a charter that gave them jurisdiction over areas of law contained in that selfsame charter was not lost on critics of war crimes tribunals.

Within the context of war crimes, the term crimes was not restricted in meaning to actions that violated the statutes of a legislative body, but rather encompassed actions committed that in a more general sense violated the laws and dictates of humanity. This lack of precise meaning has given rise to endless disputes about the legality of using ex post facto laws for the prosecution of war criminals.

Many legal as well as philosophical questions had to be answered, and, indeed, were answered. For example, if there were to be any sort of responsibility for war crimes, would this responsibility reside in the nation as a whole or in particular individuals? In addition, the complicated issue of punishment had to be worked out. Legal disputes ensued at Nuremberg as elsewhere about the problem of possible dual immunity from responsibility, accountability, prosecution, and punishment: If individuals could plead that their actions were acts of state and that they therefore were not personally accountable, and if states as sovereign powers were immune from prosecution, obviously there could be no accounting for so-called war crimes.

Article 7 of the Nuremberg IMT Charter rejected the act-of-state plea and held that international law was concerned not merely with the actions of sovereign states, but with the duties and liabilities of individuals as well. Crimes against international law could be committed only by specific individuals, not by abstract entities, and only by punishing these specific transgressors could international law be enforced.[37]

The plea of superior orders was likewise rejected by the Charter. If an order given were known to be a violation of civil or military law, both the person giving the order and the one executing it would be guilty of a crime, though the application of the principle could be mitigated in cases in which no moral choices were possible.[38] Two results of the Nuremberg IMT trial were that illegality was transformed into criminality, and that individuals were to be held personally responsible for their criminal actions.

Immediately after Jackson's appointment, the staff of the Office of the United States Chief Counsel, under the direction of Colonel Robert G. Storey, began collecting documentary evidence on which the accusations contained in the indictment could be based or supported. In fact, even before the war ended, the American and British armies had established special investigating teams, which followed closely behind the front lines, whose mission it was to obtain documentary evidence of various crimes of which Germans were being accused. The records thus collected were concentrated in a few document centers, and, as a consequence, the Office of the Chief Counsel soon found that it had more documentary material than it could handle. Its major task was to sift through and examine thousands of tons of records and to select only the most significant items for transmittal to Nuremberg for additional processing.

The administrative organization of the Office of the Chief Counsel was designed to facilitate the procurement and processing of evidence. At the top level were the Chief of Counsel and his personal staff, his associates, a Public Relations Officer, and an Executive Officer. Housekeeping duties, communications, and personnel activities were supervised by an Administration Office. The operating units consisted of an Interrogation Division, a Documentation Division, a Special Projects unit, and four committees, each of which specialized in compiling evidence relating to one of the four charges of the Nuremberg IMT indictment. Personnel in the Office of the Chief of Counsel were made available by various government departments and were carried on the payrolls of their respective agencies, while fiscal and personnel records relating to the employees in Nuremberg remained with the American Military Government organization.

On October 18, 1945, a committee of the Chief Counsels of the signatories - Robert H. Jackson for the United States, Attorney-General Sir Hartley Shawcross for Great Britain, General Roman A. Rudenko for the Soviet Union, and François de Menthon and Auguste Champetier de Ribes for France - signed and filed with the Tribunal, sitting at Berlin, an indictment setting forth the crimes of twenty-four people who would become the twenty-two Nuremberg defendants, as well as organizations to which they and others belonged.[39] The original twenty-four included Gustav Krupp, against whom charges were dropped, and Robert Ley, who committed suicide. The final twenty-two included Martin Bormann, who was never found but who was tried _in absentia_.[40]

Individually and collectively the defendants were charged with four counts: (1) common plan or conspiracy, (2) crimes against peace, (3) war crimes, and (4) crimes against humanity. The United States was responsible for presenting Count 1, Great Britain for Count 2, and France and the Soviet Union for Counts 3 and 4. The Soviet Union directed the prosecution of Counts 3 and 4 for crimes committed in the East, while France directed the case for crimes committed in the West.[41]

German defense attorneys were chosen from a list prepared by the Allied authorities, but a defendant could ask to be represented by an attorney not on this list. Some of the defense counsels selected had been members of the Nazi Party, while others had been anti-Nazi.[42]

The International Military Tribunal in Nuremberg held its first session on November 14, 1945, and its last on August 31, 1946, after 216 working days.[43] It held 403 open sessions and heard evidence from thirty-three witnesses for the prosecution and eighty for the defense, including nineteen defendants themselves. The testimony of 143 witnesses was given for the defense in the form of written answers to interrogatories, and 1809 affidavits were submitted by witnesses who agreed to testify in person if the defense required it. The tribunal heard twenty-two witnesses for accused organizations and then it appointed a commission to hear 100 witnesses for these organizations. There were 38,000 affidavits signed by 155,000 people filed for the leadership corps of the Nazi Party, 136,215 for the SS, 10,000 for the SA, 7000 for the SD, 3000 for the General Staff and High Command, and 2000 for the Gestapo. Most of these documents were read into the record.[44]

In all, twenty-two sentences were handed down: twelve death sentences (including Hermann Göring, who committed suicide, and Martin Bormann, who was never found), seven prison terms (three for life, two for twenty years, one for fifteen years, and one for ten years), and three acquittals.[45] The three acquitted, Hjalmar Schacht, Franz von Papen, and Hans Fritzsche, were later tried by German denazification courts and were found guilty of war crimes.[46]

5. Nuremberg Military Tribunals (NMT)

President Truman decided in January 1946 that the Office of Military Government in Germany would handle the remaining American trials of German war criminals. Consequently, on October 18, 1946, General Joseph T. McNary established a number of U.S. military tribunals in Nuremberg which held twelve trials within the next three years.[47] The Office of the Chief of Counsel, under Brigadier General Telford Taylor, handled the legal work.[48] These twelve "subsequent" Nuremberg trials lasted from October 26, 1946, to April 14, 1949, and in them 185 defendants, dubbed "second string" criminals, were indicted. Several were given death sentences which were later commuted, while others were given prison sentences, most of which were later reduced.[49] Several of those acquitted later faced German denazification tribunals. In all, 888 witnesses testified for the defense and 467 for the prosecution, while 375 defense attorneys and ninety-four prosecuting attorneys pleaded their respective cases.

The NMT trials were based on Allied Control Council Law No. 10, which was adopted by the four major Allied powers on December 20, 1945, and on Ordinance No. 7, which was released by the Commander of the United States Zone of Occupation in Germany on October 18, 1946, and amended on February 17, 1947.[50] This law, which authorized the Allies to arrest and try anyone suspected of war crimes, was preceded by three earlier Control Council laws which were designed to guarantee the administration of justice.[51] Among them were Control Council Law No. 1, which repealed a number of discriminatory and political laws adopted by the Nazis; Control Council Law No. 3, which dealt with fundamental principles of judicial reform; and Control Council Law No. 4, of October 30, 1945, which provided for the reorganization of the entire German judicial system. In West Germany, prosecution of war criminals remained the responsibility, under Control Council Law No. 10, of the Allied Courts until January 1, 1950, when Control Council Law No. 13, promulgated by the Allied High Commissioner on November 25, 1949, transferred these powers to the German judiciary.[52]

The Nuremberg Military Tribunal followed, in general, the guidelines laid down by the IMT, but there were several significant differences, including one involving the definition of what constituted crimes against the peace. The NMT extended criminality to include initiation of invasions which were not resisted, for example, those of Austria and Czechoslovakia. The defense attempted to prove that Austria had consented to her being occupied by Germany in 1938, that the occupation of Norway was justified on the ground that the German action was a defense against a planned British attack, and that the attack on the Soviet Union was justified on grounds of anticipated self-defense, since the Soviets, so the defense argued, were about to attack Germany.[53]

Another difference between the IMT Charter and Control Council Law No. 10 is that the latter was more stringent in the matter of membership in criminal organizations. Anyone who was a member of a criminal organization, as defined by the Nuremberg IMT Charter, was a war criminal under Control Council Law No. 10. This would have applied automatically to about two million Germans if it had not been ruled that the accused in question had to have had a personal knowledge of the criminal purposes or acts of the organization.[54] While the IMT tried only twenty-two major war criminals, thousands of Germans were brought to trial under Control Council Law No. 10. Under this law, the accused could be tried for crimes committed before as well as during the war, while IMT defendants could not be tried for any crimes against humanity committed before the declaration of war in 1939.

Another important difference between the two sets of trials was that the Nuremberg military tribunals were made up entirely of American judges. These trials had no international character whatsoever.

The NMT trials affirmed the IMT principle that individuals were subject to international law, a principle enunciated as follows in the *Einsatzgruppen Case*: "Nations can act only through human beings, and when Germany signed, ratified, and promulgated the Hague and Geneva Conventions, she bound each one of her subjects to their observance."[55] The NMT also affirmed the IMT principle that crime against the peace had a basis in international law, with the Kellogg-Briand Pact serving as the legal ground for this decision.[56]

The twelve NMT cases also confirmed the IMT judgment on war crimes and crimes against humanity, decisions based largely on various Hague and Geneva conventions.[57] And the NMT courts agreed with the IMT in rejecting the defense plea of superior orders.

In addition to the trials held in Nuremberg, the United States held a series of little-publicized, but much-criticized, trials in Dachau, conducted by military commissions or specially appointed military government courts.[58] These tribunals were made up of American officers, at least one of whom had to have had legal training or experience, as was required in a general court-martial. A majority of at least two-thirds was required for conviction. The defense attorneys in the Dachau trials were generally Americans, but many German attorneys were retained by the defendants or were officially assigned the task of assisting the American officers.

In the Dachau cases there were no indictments for crimes against the peace or against humanity; they dealt exclusively with conventional war crimes. The Dachau trials revived the tradition of having military tribunals try captured enemy nationals for violations of the laws of war. It was this that distinguished them from the NMT trials and explained why there were two sets of trials held by the Americans in the American Zone.[59] On trial were some members of the staffs of Mauthausen, Dachau, Flossenburg, and Buchenwald concentration camps, as well as German soldiers accused of murdering Americans at Malmédy during the Ardennes counteroffensive. Of the 1672 people tried, 1090 were ultimately sentenced, 426 to death.[60] Most of the sentences were later reduced; in fact, defendants sentenced to life imprisonment were generally released after seven years.

6. International Military Tribunal for the Far East (IMTFE)

The International Military Tribunal for the Far East (IMTFE) is the best known of the Pacific area war crimes trials, but - as is reflected in the above analysis of trial statistics - in terms of priority in time or number of defendants tried, it was overshadowed by other Asian trials.

The IMTFE had its origins in the Cairo Declaration of December 1, 1943, in which the United States, Great Britain, and China announced their intention to punish Japan for her aggressions.[61] The Potsdam Declaration of July 26, 1945, enlarged upon this determination, warning that stern justice was to be meted out to all war criminals, including those who mistreated prisoners of war.[62] The basic policy for the trial of Japanese war criminals was set forth in this declaration, which was accepted by Japanese representatives on September 2, 1945, as part of the instrument of surrender. As at Nuremberg, major offenders were to be prosecuted by an international agency before an international court. The IMTFE was set up by proclamation of General Douglas MacArthur, Supreme Commander for the Allied Powers (SCAP), on January 19, 1946.[63] In conjunction with the special proclamation, General Headquarters (GHQ) SCAP issued General Order No. 1, which officially set forth the charter of the tribunal. This charter, later amended and published as General Order No. 20, GHQ SCAP, April 25, 1946, outlined the Tribunal's constitution, jurisdiction, functions, and procedures. It called for a panel of between six and eleven members who were to be appointed by SCAP from nominations submitted by the nations which had signed the instrument of surrender, plus India and the Philippines.

The IMTFE was composed ultimately of members from eleven nations: Australia, Canada, China, France, India, the Netherlands, New Zealand, the Philippines, the Soviet Union, the United Kingdom, and the United States. Sir William Flood Webb of Australia was appointed president of the Tribunal. The other members were E. Stuart McDougall, Canada; Ju-Ao Mei, China; Henri Bernard, France; Lord William D. Patrick, Great Britain; Radhabinod Pal, India; Bernard Victor A. Röling, the Netherlands; Erima H. Northcroft, New Zealand; Delfin Jaranilla, the Philippines; Major General I.M. Zaryanov, the Soviet Union; and John P. Higgins, the United States. Higgins was succeeded in June 1946 by Major General Myron H. Cramer.

The Tribunal was empowered to try and punish Far Eastern war criminals who as individuals or as members of organizations were charged with crimes against the peace, conventional war crimes, and crimes against humanity. The Tokyo Charter did not contain any provision for trying criminal organizations, though it did provide for trying defendants either as individuals or as members of organizations. As it turned out, not a single Japanese organization was indicted.

Because a bench of twenty-two judges would have proven to be unwieldy, the IMTFE decided against having alternates, departing here from the procedure adopted at Nuremberg. Another difference was that at Nuremberg each of the signatories had the power to appoint a chief prosecutor, whereas in Tokyo the Chief of Counsel, who was appointed by President Truman, held this power.[64] Associate Counsels were appointed by the various member nations.

Several months before the proclamation establishing the IMTFE was issued, preliminary steps leading to the apprehension and detention of major criminals had already been undertaken by the Legal Section of SCAP. The International Prosecution Section (IPS) was established as a staff section of SCAP by Executive Order 9660 and announced in General Order No. 20, GHQ SCAP, on December 8, 1945.[65] The IPS was organized under the direction of Joseph B. Keenan, former assistant to the Attorney General of the United States, who occupied the positions of both Chief of Counsel and Chief of Section.

To facilitate its work, the IPS was organized into five major divisions. The most important of these was the Legal Division, under the direction of the Chief of Counsel. This division was made up of the Chief and the associate prosecutors of the ten other participating nations.[66] The duties of the Legal Division included the interrogation of suspects and the preparation and organization of evidence for presentation at the trial. The remaining divisions of the IPS were designed to provide support for the Legal Division. The Investigative Division collected information and evidence on suspected war criminals; the Document Division screened, analyzed, reproduced, and filed for future reference documentary evidence; the Language Division prepared translations of relevant documents into either English or Japanese or both, depending upon the circumstances; and the Administrative Division provided the necessary support for the section as a whole.[67]

The International Defense Panel (IDP) was intended as the counterpart of the IPS, and its organization roughly paralleled that of the IPS in being divided into Investigative, Language, Document, and Administrative divisions that supported the Legal Division. In preparation for the defense, the IDP was allowed free access to the facilities of the IPS, with the exception of those of the Legal Division. The IDP sought to aid Japanese defense lawyers in the preparation of their cases and to coordinate the defense as a whole through the machinery of its Evidence Committee, which reviewed and selected evidence, and, where several defendants shared a common interest in given issues, sought to provide the medium whereby the interested defense counsels could cooperate effectively in locating, preparing, and presenting the relevant evidence. This cooperation was severely limited by two early decisions, the first of which stated that no counsel, American or Japanese, would be heard unless he had been chosen by one of the defendants as his personal representative, while the second gave the Tribunal the right to disapprove of counsel. The IDP was weakened by the resignation of one Chief of Defense Counsel and some of his staff over a dispute involving the selection of counsel.[68]

The IMTFE held that its Charter was an expression of international law, and adopted the Nuremberg principle that individuals could be held responsible for actions which violated that law. The Tribunal insisted that the trial of war criminals did not imply a limitation of sovereignty.

The first meeting of the IMTFE, which was intended to be the first of several trials of Japanese war criminals, was held on April 29, 1946, in the auditorium of the Japanese War Ministry. At that time, the indictment against twenty-eight defendants was filed with the Tribunal.[69] The indictment contained some fifty-five separate counts divided into three groups.[70] Counts one to thirty-six charged the defendants generally with "crimes against peace" and specifically with conspiracy to wage aggressive warfare or warfare in violation of international laws and treaties, as set forth in Article 5a of the IMTFE Charter. Each act of war or aggression was set forth in the indictment as a separate count. Counts thirty-seven to fifty-two charged the defendants with the crimes of murder and conspiracy to commit murder, stating that they had conspired to kill civilians and members of the armed forces of certain nations by the initiation of unlawful hostilities in violation of the Hague Convention of 1899. Specific allegations included the attacks on Pearl Harbor and Hong Kong, the murder of prisoners of war in Japanese custody, the murder of civilians at Nanking, and the murder of members of the armed forces of the Soviet Union along the Mongolian border. Counts fifty-three to fifty-five charged the defendants generally with "conventional war crimes" and "crimes against humanity." The counts specifically accused the defendants of conspiracy to permit the armed forces of Japan to violate the laws and customs of war and of criminal failure to take adequate steps to secure observance of these laws and customs.

On May 3, 1946, the defendants were arraigned in open court and all pleaded not guilty. Before the trial ended, over two and a half years later, 419 witnesses had appeared in 818 court sessions covering 417 days, and 779 affidavits and depositions had been presented.[71]

In order to argue its case effectively, the prosecution divided its presentation into fourteen major phases. Phase One introduced the Tribunal to the governmental structure of Japan, in order to fix the responsibilities of the government and to link the defendants to acts of state. Phase Two portrayed the conditions prevailing in Japan during the period of the alleged conspiracy, to show the Tribunal the methods utilized by the defendants to seize power and exploit it for the purpose of waging aggressive war. The remaining twelve phases dealt with Japanese aggression, economic exploitation of occupied countries, economic mobilization for war, preparation of aggressive alliances, crimes against humanity, and complicity in criminal acts.[72]

The Tribunal heard the prosecution's case from June 4, 1946, to January 24, 1947. The defense then filed various motions for dismissal, arguing that the evidence presented had not proven the charges. The Tribunal rejected these motions, and from February 24, 1947, to January 12, 1948, the defense presented its case.[73] The IDP divided the defense into five general phases. Phase One elaborated on the prosecution's evidence relating to the Japanese government, while Phase Two, rejected by the Tribunal as irrelevant, discussed the state of international law at the time that the alleged crimes were committed. The evidence offered on this point dealt with various actions and pronouncements of other nations, including some of the prosecution powers, to show that aggressive war was not a crime under international law. In Phases Three to Five the defense denied that a conspiracy existed or that Japan's economic plans and policies had in any way been pursued in preparation for war. After the defense had presented its case, the prosecution was permitted to submit evidence in rebuttal. Final arguments lasted until April 16, 1948.[74]

The problem of translating oral and documentary evidence was almost insoluble; as a consequence, much of the Tribunal's time was spent attempting to render translations that would satisfy both the defense and the prosecution. The situation was partly remedied by the creation of a three-member Language Arbitration Board to settle such disputes.[75] This board was composed of one member appointed by the Tribunal and one each by the defense and the prosecution. The Tribunal not only required submission of documents to the board in advance of their actual presentation as evidence, but also required that potential witnesses submit a written deposition of their intended testimony. Once the question of translation was settled, the evidence could be presented to the court without further delay.

While the language difficulty was probably the major cause of the great length of the trial, it was not the only cause. The subject matter of the trial was unique in the history of jurisprudence. Tribunal members were called upon not only to consider questions of law, but also questions involving history, governmental procedures, and diplomatic relations. The Tribunal handed down its judgment between November 4 and November 12, 1948. In an opinion 1218 pages long and seven months in preparation, it rejected challenges to its own jurisdiction, issued findings of fact on the course of recent Japanese history, and rendered judgments and verdicts on the accused. Individual charges were considered against the defendants only with respect to ten of the fifty-five counts of the indictment. They were: Count 1, conspiracy; Count 27, waging war against China; Count 29, waging war against the United States; Count 31, waging war against Great Britain; Count 32, waging war against the Netherlands; Count 33, waging war against France; Count 35, waging war against the Soviet Union at Lake Khasan; Count 36, waging war against the Soviet Union at Nomohan; Count 54, ordering, authorizing, or permitting atrocities; and Count 55, disregard of duty to secure observance of and prevent breaches of the laws of war. Seven of the twenty-eight defendants were sentenced to death by hanging, sixteen to life imprisonment, one to twenty years imprisonment, and one to seven years imprisonment.[76] Verdicts were not handed down for three of the defendants, two of whom had died during the trial, while the third had been judged unfit to stand trial.

Most of the twenty-eight defendants were high officials, but they did not include the Emperor, or, in contrast to the Nuremberg IMT, any members of financial or industrial groups. No evidence was submitted to establish that the industrialists had conspired with the government or with military officials.[77] Another difference between the two IMTs was that in Nuremberg a distinction was made between a conspiracy to plan and prepare for and wage an aggressive war and the actual waging of such a war. The Tokyo Tribunal made no such distinction. A procedural difference between the two IMTs was that in Nuremberg four languages had been used, whereas in Tokyo only English and Japanese were used.

Ten days after the sentences were handed down, General MacArthur met with representatives of the Allied Nations to ask for comments that might assist him in reaching a decision concerning his review of the sentences. Since most of the representatives approved the sentences and because there were no technical reasons to warrant intervention, all were left standing.

Of special interest in the Tokyo trial were the separate and dissenting judgments of Justices Radhabinod Pal of India, Henri Bernard of France, and Bernard V.A. Röling of the Netherlands.[78]

Pal insisted that the so-called "law" concerning crimes against the peace amounted to ex post facto legislation; Röling, on the other hand, agreed that crimes against the peace were not "legal" crimes, but nevertheless thought that their perpetrators should be punished in order to protect the world from dangerous people.[79]

The seven prisoners sentenced to death were hanged on December 23, 1948. Six of the eighteen who received prison sentences died during their imprisonment and the other twelve served only part of their sentences. The Charter of the Tribunal had given SCAP authority to reduce the sentences at any time, and on March 7, 1950, a special SCAP directive authorized the reduction of sentences by two-thirds for good behavior and parole after fifteen years for prisoners with life sentences. General MacArthur used this authority only once, when former Foreign Minister Mamoru Shigemitsu was released on November 21, 1950.[80] Under Article 11 of the Treaty of Peace with Japan, signed at the San Francisco Peace Conference in September 1951, Japan accepted the judgments of the IMTFE and of the other Allied war crimes courts and agreed to carry out the sentences that had been imposed. In addition, Japan agreed that for those sentenced by the IMTFE, clemency, the reduction of sentences, or parole would not be granted except on the approval of a majority of the governments represented on the Tribunal and on the recommendation of Japan. Shortly after the end of the Allied occupation in 1952, the Japanese Ministry of Justice appealed for the parole of five prisoners who were suffering from ill health. Later, the Japanese government asked for and received the parole of other prisoners. Finally, on April 7, 1958, the Japanese Foreign Ministry announced the unconditional release of the ten surviving prisoners.[81]

7. Sources and Depositories

No other period in history has been so copiously documented as that between 1933 and 1945. The trials of war criminals and the actions of German and Japanese leaders before and during the war have led to compilations of materials that are now so vast in quantity that the researcher can find voluminous collections of finding aids and indices leading to materials available on almost any aspect of war crimes trials. Despite this unprecedented quantity of records, it is certain that many valuable and important documents were destroyed or lost. Furthermore, not all criminal acts were documented, and of those that were, only a relatively few documents were ever introduced before the various tribunals judging war criminals. There is considerable evidence that other documents were written with the intention of misleading readers, leaving the task of sorting, comparing, evaluating, and accepting or rejecting, to the historian, who knows all the while that he is subject to errors of judgment and mistaken conclusions because of misleading or missing documents.

The plethora of German records is due in part to the fact that German governmental departments kept lengthy, detailed records of their activities and to the fact that as the war was drawing to a close no order went out to destroy these records, many of which were incriminating. Frequently records were hidden rather than destroyed. The records of Alfred Rosenberg, for example, were found in an eighteen-inch thick false wall in an abandoned castle in eastern Bavaria. The documents in this find weighed several tons and included important letters involving Hitler, Göring, Goebbels, and even Vidkun Quisling. Found in another abandoned castle were 485 tons of Foreign Office records which contained many secret documents pertaining to pre-war plans of aggression.[82]

18 Introduction

Toward the end of the war the Reich Main Security Office (RSHA) moved its documents to Prague, where most of them were burned on the floor of the Prague headquarters, but many of this organization's records were recovered from copies sent to other agencies.[83]

IMT documents available to the researcher are almost endless in number. The official records of the Nuremberg IMT were published by the United States in forty-two volumes under the title Trials of War Criminals. The United States also published a collection of documents known as the "Red Series," having eight volumes, a two-volume supplement, and a volume of opinions. The proceedings of the Nuremberg IMT trial, but not the documents themselves, were published in twenty-three volumes by Great Britain. Proceedings as well as documents were also published in French and later in German. Although a printed version is not available, the Archives of the International Court of Justice has a thirty-nine-volume Russian transcript, partly typewritten and partly mimeographed.

The massive record collection for the Nuremberg IMT consisted of approximately 100,000 documents, of which about 10,000 were selected for use. The American staff assembled to handle these documents numbered 600 people with about that many again employed by the other powers. The verbatim transcripts of the Nuremberg IMT proceedings amount to 17,077 pages, and in Munich the Institut für Zeitgeschichte (IZG) alone has 9126 documents which had been submitted to the IMT. Each document is supplemented by a Staff Evidence Analysis (SEA) containing information on its origin. Similar analyses exist for documents that were not part of the 10,000 selected for use by the IMT.

Trial records themselves are also voluminous. For example, on the Nuremberg IMT alone, the records received by the National Archives from the Office of the United States Chief of Counsel for the Prosecution of Axis Criminality consist of photostatic copies of documents collected for use as evidence, actual trial proceedings, record copy and proof copy of Nazi Conspiracy and Aggression, microfilm copies of exhibits presented at the trial, and recordings of speeches, motion pictures made during the trial, photographs taken at the trial, and photographs submitted in evidence. The first group is the largest and contains photostatic copies of original documents collected by the American and British staffs, most of which were introduced in evidence and which constitute a part of the official records of the Tribunal.

The original records of the Nuremberg International Military Tribunal were deposited at the International Court of Justice, but copies are located in so many depositories that the researcher does not have to look far to find all the records of the trial.[84] An exact copy of the records was placed in the National Archives of the United States. Photostatic copies which have been put on display in a number of exhibits in the United States, together with photostats of British, French, and Soviet documents, have been deposited with the Departmental Records Branch of the Adjutant General's Office in Washington. See also various entries in this bibliography under the United Nations and various International Military Tribunal records and guides to records.

Before the Nuremberg IMT trial began, the following system was devised for coding documents:

C	Documents collected by the British Admiralty.
D	Documents of the British Prosecution.
M	Documents of the British Prosecution.
EC	Economics documents from several sources.
ECH	Economics documents from the Heidelberg Documents Center.
ECR	Economics documents from the Rosenheim Documents Center.
L	Documents collected in London.
PS	"Paris-Storey." The principal series of documents collected by the American prosecution. It was started in Paris under the direction of Colonel Storey, first Chief of the Documents Division. They were later extended greatly at Nuremberg.
R	Documents collected by the Office of Strategic Services (OSS), London Office.
RF	Documents introduced by the French prosecution.
TC	Documents dealing with international agreements (Hague conventions, Kellogg-Briand Pact, Versailles treaty, e.g.).
USSR	Documents introduced by the Soviet prosecution.

This bibliography contains a great number of documents and published works dealing with the judges of the "subsequent" Nuremberg Military Tribunals, all of whom were Americans. Several entries deal with the quantity, grouping, origin, history, administration, and final disposition of the records of the twelve trials, known as the "Green Series." The official records are in the possession of the United States, but mimeographed copies have been deposited at the headquarters of the United Nations, in the Bavarian State Archives in Nuremberg, the Institut für Zeitgeschichte in Munich, the Library of Congress, and the libraries of the Columbia University Law School and Harvard University Law School. The Institut für Zeitgeschichte alone has a collection of 31,224 documents relating to these trials. An important research source is the card catalogue, which contains approximately 180,000 cards covering 40,000 documents from the Nuremberg IMT trial and the twelve Nuremberg NMT trials.

The Nuremberg NMT documents are generally identified as follows:

NI	Nuremberg Industrialists. Documents dealing with German industry.
NIK	Documents prepared for the prosecution of the Krupp case.
NM	Nuremberg Miscellaneous. Documents concerning various Reich ministries.
NO	Nuremberg Organizations. Documents pertaining to the activities of the Nazi party.
NOKW	Nuremberg. Oberkommando der Wehrmacht. Documents pertaining to the high command of the German armed forces.
NP	Nuremberg Propaganda. Documents dealing with Nazi propaganda activities.

In addition to these main categories of documents processed in Nuremberg for submission to the various Tribunals, another series of documents was prepared by the Office of Chief of Counsel for War Crimes (OCCWC), the American prosecuting agency which prepared the material for the twelve "subsequent" trials. The most important of these documents are:

BB, BBH, BBT	Photostats of documents selected and processed by teams of the Berlin Branch of OCCWC, primarily from records in the custody of the Berlin Document Center and the Ministerial Document Branch.
SS	Photostats of documents pertaining to SS activities which were secured from records located in the Berlin Document Center.
WB	Photostats of documents covering activities of the German High Command which were obtained from the German Military Document Section of the Departmental Records Branch, NARS, Alexandria, Virginia.

Trial records of United States Military Government Courts have been deposited in the War Crimes Division of the Office of the Judge Advocate General. In Germany most of these documents are held in the <u>Justizministerien</u> of various <u>Länder</u>. In Poland the <u>Glowna Komisja</u> has the records of war crimes trials conducted by Polish tribunals.

The condensed record of the NMT was planned and published by the United States Department of the Army under the general direction of Colonel Edward H. Young, Chief, War Crimes Division, Office of the Judge Advocate General. The records were published in fifteen volumes. These cases required more than 1200 days of court proceedings. The mimeographed records of the proceedings exceed 330,000 pages, exclusive of hundreds of documents and briefs.[85] The set contains records of eighty-nine cases tried by various national and occupational authorities. A valuable source on some of these cases is the nine-volume work edited by Sir David Maxwell-Fyfe (Lord Kilmuir).[86] The trials reported in this set are a selection of those whose records are in the possession of the UNWCC. Only those deemed of great legal interest were selected, though most of them are important in the history of the war and of war crimes trials. In addition to the trials reported, many trials are included in the set which were not reported upon but which have been cited in various places.[87]

	Number of Trial Records Received	Number of Trials Reported Upon	Cited but not Reported Upon
United States	809	28	29
Britain	524	27	17
Australia	256	5	19
France	254	11	17
Netherlands	30	7	5
Poland	24	4	1
Norway	9	5	2
Canada	4	1	1
China	1	1	0
Greece	0	0	1
TOTAL	1,911	89	92

The cases listed in the <u>Law Reports</u> deal with criminals who fell within the first of the two categories of the Moscow Declaration of October 30, 1943, embracing individuals who committed crimes against the laws of war and whose offenses could be identified with particular locations.[88] These defendants were sometimes known as "minor war criminals," a term used to differentiate them from the defendants in the Nuremberg IMT. According to the Moscow Declaration, criminals in this category were to be returned to the scenes of their crimes and tried by the nation whose laws they had violated. They were charged with all varieties of crimes except the four charges against the Nuremberg IMT defendants.

In the cases reported in Law Reports, the prosecutions were conducted by military authorities, often with mixed panels, having officers of various nations, among them the United States, Great Britain, France, Greece, and the Netherlands, sitting together in judgment. At the Peleus trial, for example, Greek naval officers sat on the British military tribunal because the SS Peleus had been a Greek ship.[89]

The verdicts handed down did not explain the reasoning of the judges, making it almost impossible to identify precisely the grounds on which they based their decisions. The reports published in this set were prepared from shorthand and other notes taken at the hearings, from materials furnished to the Commission by the British Judge Advocate General, or from records supplied by the American representative on the Commission.

Many nations have deposited their trial records in the archives of the United Nations. In some cases copies of trial records have never been made, so the researcher may have to go to the archives of nations that had conducted various war crimes trials if he wishes to use original documents.

Holocaust records are almost without limit; consequently, several major archival collections have been assembled to house them, including that of the YIVO Institute for Jewish Research and the Franz Kursky Archives of the Jewish Labor Bund. Many published and unpublished materials are available at the Zionist Archives, the Leo Baeck Institute, and the Records Center of the American Jewish Committee, all in New York. A valuable depository of captured German records and records of criminal actions by Germans is in the Yiddish Scientific Institute (YIVO), in New York. Its collection of records of the German Ministry of Propaganda alone contains seventy folders. Many of the records of this collection have been described in print.[90] In addition to these depositories, Holocaust libraries across the world have amassed documents and published works in vast quantities.

IMTFE records are also voluminous. The IMTFE and SCAP published a number of important works. Some are IMTFE documents, others are background histories, and still others are useful index volumes to original documents. Some of these works have been reproduced as U.S. State Department publications. Prosecution and defense staffs gathered and presented 4336 exhibits, while 419 witnesses testified in court and 779 gave testimony in depositions or affidavits. The transcript of the proceedings filled 48,412 mimeographed pages in 113 volumes.[91] The foreign documents branch of the Central Intelligence Agency (CIA) removed 30,000 volumes of records from Japan following World War II. These records were deposited in the National Archives in May 1948 as Record Group 242.[92]

One of the greatest collections of war crimes materials in the world is in the Hoover Institution at Stanford University. Lists of processed records are available from the Library. Of considerable interest and value are the Himmler Files.[93] The personal files of Heinrich Himmler include detailed reports on the activities of

Einsatzgruppen in the eastern territories, and of the mass murder of Jews and others by the Gestapo, the SD, and the SS.

The collection of war crimes materials in the Library of Congress is extensive. Many of the Library's records are described in various issues of the Quarterly Journal of Current Acquisitions. The Library's records are filed under Main Collection, Film Division, Map Division, Microfilm Section, Aeronautics Division, Rare Books Division, Prints and Photographs Division, Music Division, and Newspaper Division. Many of these materials are filed by country.[94]

The National Archives of the United States contains a vast quantity of captured German materials, arranged in record groups that are described in this bibliography. These records include the Robert H. Jackson records, records of the Reich Culture Chamber, the Bormann Collection, NSDAP personnel files, records of the Reich Ministry for Public Enlightenment and Propaganda, records of the Reich Ministry for the Occupied Eastern Territories, and records of the Reichsführer SS. The National Archives of the United States and the American Historical Association published jointly the sixty-seven-volume set Guides to German Records Microfilmed at Alexandria, Virginia.

One of the greatest foreign depositories of war crimes materials is the Wiener Library, Institute of Contemporary History, in London. Another is the Centre de Documentation Juive Contemporaine, in Paris. In addition to an extensive collection of materials on the Nuremberg IMT trial, the center has the Rosenberg files, 300 documents from the RuSHA, documents of the German Foreign Office pertaining to Hungary, and a number of Gestapo records. The center sponsors the publication of Le Monde Juif and has sponsored the publication of a number of books and monographs.[95] Another major depository is the Netherlands State Institute for War Documentation.[96]

8. Criticisms of War Crimes Trials

Much has been written on the justice and injustice of the various war crimes trials. Some critics have defended the need for such trials, but would have preferred tribunals consisting of members of neutral and vanquished nations as well as victors.[97] Others deny the right of any nation to try soldiers or the industrial and political leaders of a defeated nation for the violation of what amounts to ex post facto or nonexistent laws, and they argue further that no laws defining war crimes existed until after World War II.

According to the Charter of the Nuremberg International Military Tribunal, "the planning and waging of aggressive war" was a crime, but the IMT was hard pressed to prove that it had not created ex post facto law. It insisted that the rules and principles of the Charter were not arbitrary measures laid down by victorious powers; rather, they were the expression of previously-recognized international law. Attention was therefore focused on every international pronouncement on the subject; however, even the American prosecutor admitted the lack of legal precedent for such principles and the ensuing trials.[98]

Standards of justice in the war crimes trials have been criticized by many who argue that the laws of no "civilized" country would permit the execution of a criminal on any capital charge with a jury divided three to one, as in the Nuremberg IMT, or, in the case of one Japanese defendant, six to five. In other words, war crimes justice was not the same as that afforded to ordinary criminals, in which case a unanimous decision by a jury was almost always required for death sentences.

Critics of the trials include many who object not merely to the alleged lowering of legal standards, but to the way the victors lowered themselves to the level of the criminals. One critic, for example, asserts that the American trials at Dachau represented an all-time low in Western concepts of justice and that brutality, torture, and cruelty were the order of the day.[99] Others argue that German domestic courts were much harder on war criminals than were tribunals consisting entirely of Allied members. Staunch defenders of Allied trials could point to the farcical post-World War I Leipzig trials that resulted from allowing the trial of war criminals by domestic courts in Germany.[100] That "victors' justice" was not universally approved is reflected in various disagreements among Allied judges that showed that many members of these tribunals were dissatisfied; in the Tokyo IMT, for example, dissenting opinions were written.

9. This Bibliography

An exhaustive bibliography on war crimes, war criminals, and war crimes trials is an impossibility. The number of documents dealing with the subject is so great that even a list of them would fill several volumes; the published works alone on the subject defy any adequate description in other than a multi-volume work that would necessitate collaboration by scholars competent in most of the major languages of the world. To abstract or describe them all would be virtually impossible.

I have tried to include in this bibliography most representative works on World War II published in English and some key works in German. A few books and articles in French, Dutch, Polish, Russian, Italian, Spanish, Finnish, and Japanese have been included that are particularly accessible to scholars, but no attempt has been made to search the literature of these languages, for even in them the volume of materials is overwhelming. If the scholar goes from the entries in the present work to their bibliographies alone, he will be inundated.

As background, I have included a few entries on earlier war crimes, war criminals, and war crimes trials, particularly those following World War I. To point to areas of need of further research by bibliographers and historians, I have touched briefly on war crimes and war crimes trials from a number of post-World War II wars and armed conflicts, but these sections do not deal in detail with the literature available. Appended to this work is a list of journals consulted. The purpose of this is to show users which journals have **not** been used.

By design, large bodies of literature on the laws of war, the various Hague and Geneva conventions, treatment of prisoners of war, treatment of civilians, and problems of the jurisdiction of military courts of occupational authorities have been omitted. Among the materials not covered at all or touched upon only briefly are unpublished manuscripts, memoirs and letters of soldiers, and newspaper reports and editorials. I have barely touched upon the literature of popular resistance movements, forced labor, the occupation of enemy territory, guerilla warfare and responses to such warfare, and various anti-war movements. The Holocaust and the spectacular trial of Adolf Eichmann have been treated in great detail by other bibliographers. Its literature is voluminous, so only the most important or seminal works are included here, particularly those works dealing with aspects of the Holocaust which resulted in trials.

Philosophical problems regarding collective guilt have been treated in great detail in war literature, but have been largely omitted here. Much of this literature deals with legal and philosophical arguments that were debated in considerable detail following World War II. The literature of war crimes themselves is so vast that I have had to omit most of what is, indeed, genuinely relevant as background material. The decision as to what to include and what to exclude is of course difficult and seemingly arbitrary. The compiler must guard against assembling a bibliography of warfare, or of the rules of warfare, and he must resist the temptation to list every war crime ever committed, particularly those that did not result in trials. Every act of cruelty perpetrated during a war could be construed as a crime, either against combatants, prisoners of war, or civilian noncombatants. The bibliographer is particularly tempted to compile a bibliography on German history, German institutions, and all the various German and Nazi organizations that committed war crimes, such as the SA, SD, SS, and Gestapo.[101]

This bibliography, then, makes no claim to being exhaustive. The key word to understanding its contents and approach is __representative__. I have used books, periodical articles, and government documents that could easily be supplemented by others, similar in scope in some cases, and complementary in others. It is primarily an American bibliography, but thousands more English-language works could still be added. The great volume of United States government documents has barely been sampled. The entries of U.S. government documents point to thousands more that the diligent researcher can easily uncover, though, again, the major and especially the seminal works are included here. Immigration and Naturalization Service Records, for example, contain thousands of entries dealing with loss of American citizenship and deportation of former Nazis who in some way had falsified their citizenship applications.

Just as many relevant documents and published works can be found among the government documents and in the archives of Belgium, Great Britain, France, Germany, the Netherlands, and Poland, to name but a few rich in accessible research materials. British and French government documents, though highly accessible to the scholar, have hardly been touched in this bibliography. Literally hundreds of thousand of documents as well as published works are available in Polish, Russian, Dutch, Italian, Czech, and Finnish.

I have tried to make each entry a self-contained unit that will easily lead the user to the source. For this reason, authors' names have been printed in full for each of their works entered consecutively. Journal entries have been identified without cumbersome and unnecessary Roman numerals. The system adopted in recent years by ABC-Clio has been used here, with some modification, with the year of publication followed by volume number, number of issue (sometimes date) within parentheses, with page numbers last; for example, 1945 2(3): 12-100. In cases where issue numbers have not been identified or do not exist, the volume number is followed by a colon and then by page numbers, for example, 1945 2: 12-100. In cases in which issue numbers are used without volume numbers, I have identified them as, for example, 1945 (1): 1-10. In some periodicals generally identified by dates rather than volume and issue numbers, I have identified articles by dates, followed by page numbers, as, for example, January 1, 1945: 1-10. I have avoided initials for journal titles, preferring rather to spell out the entire title with each entry. This avoids confusion resulting from several journals having the same initials. With widespread use of photoduplication in libraries, this system guarantees against a user finding that his duplicated page begins with an unidentified straight line indicating same author as before (which he may not have), an *ibid.*, whose earlier title he does not have, or a journal title lost in unrecognizable abbreviation.

In the important matter of orthography, many abbreviations used in this bibliography or contained in some entry titles are identified in an appended list of abbreviations. Spelling and editorial inconsistencies from various sources have generally been left intact, particularly in the matter of German "ss" which could have been "ß" or French titles with upper case nouns that are generally lower case in that language. Libraries are inconsistent in their use of German "von" and French "de" and "la" and similar forms in other languages. In this bibliography most entries are listed alphabetically by name, but users are advised to check under both forms. Index numbers in parentheses refer to page numbers.

END NOTES

1. There is an excellent treatment of this subject in the 26-page introduction to Wilbourn E. Benton and George Grimm (eds.). *Nuremberg: German Views of the War Trials* (Dallas: Southern Methodist University Press, 1970 edition).

2. See, for example, the literature of the abortive Leipzig trials.

3. For a sketch of the origins and functions of the UNWCC, see UNITED STATES. NATIONAL ARCHIVES AND RECORDS SERVICE. *Federal Records of World War II*. Volume 1, *Civilian Agencies* (Washington: NARS, 1950), Article 1794, p. 1059.

4. The UNWCC was dissolved in May 1948, *ibid.*

5. Over a dispute involving representation, the Soviet Union, demanding one vote for each of the Soviet Republics, refused to join the UNWCC and, indeed, formed its own. Philip R. Piccigallo. *The Japanese on Trial: Allied War Crimes Operations in the Fat East, 1945-1951* (Austin: University of Texas Press, 1979), p. 145.

6. UNITED STATES, NARS. *Civilian Agencies*, p. x. Also, R. John Pritchard and Sonia Magbanua Zaide (comps.). *The Tokyo War Crimes Trials* (New York and London: Garland, 1981), I, p. 4. Piccigallo, *The Japanese on Trial*, p. 101.

7. See Appendix 1.

8. Robert K. Woetzel. *The Nuremberg Trials in International Law* (London: Stevens & Sons, 1960), p. 218.

9. *Ibid.*, 230.

10. Quincy Wright. "The Law of the Nuremberg Trial," *American Journal of International Law* 1947 41(1): 38-72, especially p. 39, note 5.

26 Introduction

11. Maximilian Koessler. "American War Crimes Trials in Europe," *Georgetown Law Journal* 1950 39(1): 21-35, p. 21, note 18 cited.

12. Richard Harwood. *Nuremberg and other War Crimes Trials: A New Look* (Ladbroke, Southampton: Historical Review Press, 1978), p. 1.

13. Koessler. "American War Crimes Trials in Europe," p. 25.

14. Piccigallo. *The Japanese on Trial*, p. 48.

15. Robert E. Ward and Frank J. Shulman, et al. *The Allied Occupation of Japan, 1945-1952: An Annotated Bibliography of Western Language Materials* (Chicago: American Library Association, 1974), p. 341.

16. Piccigallo. *The Japanese on Trial*, p. 67.

17. *Ibid.*, p. 95.

18. Harwood, *Nuremberg and Other War Crimes Trials*, p. 1.

19. Willard B. Cowles. "Trials of War Criminals (Non-Nuremberg)," *American Journal of International Law* 1948 42(2): 299-319, pp. 311-313 cited.

20. *Ibid.*, pp. 301-303.

21. Piccigallo. *The Japanese on Trial*, p. 120. The author gives no explanation for the discrepancies between the totals listed here.

22. *Ibid.*, p. 139.

23. *Ibid.*, p. 183.

24. *Ibid.*, p. 208.

25. Discrepancies as well as errors are to be found in Jadwiga Gorzkowska and Elzbieta Zakowska. *Nazi Criminals before West German Courts* (Warsaw: Zachodnia Agencja Prasowa, 1965), pp. 15-17, which quotes directly from Hermann Langbein. *Im Namen des deutschen Volkes, Zwischenbilanz der Prozesse wegen nationalsozialistischer Verbrechen* (Vienna: Europa, 1963), p. 23. Whitney R. Harris. *Tyranny on Trial: The Evidence at Nuremberg* (Dallas: Southern Methodist University Press, 1954), pp. 544-545, is a more reliable source.

26. Gorzkowska and Zakowska. *Nazi Criminals*, pp. 14-15.

27. See Appendix 9.

28. Harris. *Tyranny*, p. 541.

29. *Ibid.*, pp. 541-542.

30. Eugene Davidson. *The Trial of the Germans: An Account of the twenty-two Defendants before the International Military Tribunal at Nuremberg* (New York: Macmillan, 1966), p. 30.

Introduction 27

31. Noboru Kojima. *Tokyo saiban*. 2 volumes (Tokyo: Chuo koron, 1971), II, p. 225.

32. Piccigallo. *The Japanese on Trial*, pp. 150-157.

33. Harwood. *Nuremberg and Other War Crimes Trials*, p. 1.

34. Koessler. "American War Crimes Trials in Europe," p. 33, note 74.

35. Brendan Murphy. *The Butcher of Lyon: The Story of Infamous Nazi Klaus Barbie* (New York: Empire Books, 1983), pp. 318-319.

36. See Appendix 2.

37. See Hans Ehard for an analysis of this truism. "The Nuremberg Trial Against the Major War Criminals and International Law," *American Journal of International Law* 1949 43(2): 223-245.

38. German soldiers in both world wars were taught not to obey orders they knew to be illegal. See Davidson. *The Trial of the Germans*, p. 20, for an analysis of the German, British, and American teachings on this subject.

39. See Appendix 5, Figure 3.

40. See Appendix 6.

41. See Appendix 5, Figures 1 and 2.

42. See Appendix 4.

43. Jacob Robinson. "The International Military Tribunal and the Holocaust: Some Legal Reflections," *Israel Law Review* 1972 7(1): 1-13, p. 1 cited.

44. Harris. *Tyranny*, p. ix. Wright. "The Law of the Nuremberg Trial," *passim*, p. 41 cited. Robert H. Jackson. "Nürnberg in Retrospect," *Canadian Bar Review* 1949 27(7): 761-781, p. 769 cited.

45. See Appendix 5, Figure 3.

46. Davidson. *The Trial of the Germans*, p. 29. In 1947 Von Papen was given a prison sentence of eight years, but he was freed in 1949. In the same year Fritzsche was sentenced to nine years, but he was pardoned in 1950. In 1948 Schacht was released from his imprisonment by a German appellate court.

47. See Appendix 8.

48. The Office of Chief of Counsel for war crimes was transferred to the Office of Military Government for Germany (United States) on October 24, 1946. Harris, *Tyranny*, p. 543. It was deactivated on June 20, 1949.

49. See Appendix 9.

50. The French Court at Rastatt (near Baden-Baden) also functioned under Control Council Law No. 10, but no British or Soviet courts operated under this law. The British, however, did set up a German tribunal to try individuals under Control Council Law No. 10.

51. Gorzkowska and Zakowska. *Nazi Criminals before West German Courts*, pp. 12-16.

52. German courts could prosecute war criminals under Control Council Law No. 10 if the accused were German citizens or were stateless, and then only with the permission of the occupation authorities. *Ibid.*, p. 11.

53. Wright. "The Law of the Nuremberg Trial," p. 66, note 110 cited.

54. See Francis B. Biddle's criticism of Law No. 10 in "The Nuremberg Trial," *American Philosophical Society Proceedings* 1947 41: 294-302, and in "Le Procès de Nuremberg," *Revue Internationale de Droit Pénal* 1948 19: 1-19

55. *U.S.* v. *Ohlendorf*, *Trials of War Criminals before the Nuremberg Military Tribunals under Control Council Law No. 10*, IV, pp. 460-461.

56. *U.S.* v. *Von Weizsäcker*, *ibid.*, XIV, pp. 319-322.

57. *U.S.* v. *Ohlendorf*, *ibid.*, IV, pp. 459-460, 470-471; *U.S.* v *Greifelt*, No. 8, *ibid.*, V, pp. 153-154.

58. Koessler. "American War Crimes Trials in Europe," pp. 18-112, *passim*. This article deals primarily with the Dachau trials.

59. *Ibid.*, p. 35.

60. Harris. *Tyranny*, pp. 540-541.

61. *U. S. Department of State Bulletin*, 1952, 23, 137ff. General Headquarters Supreme Commander for the Allied Powers, "General Orders No. 1," January 19, 1946, *U.S. Department of State Publication No. 2675*, pp. 5-10, and "General Orders No. 20," April 26, 1946, *ibid.*, pp. 11-16.

62. UNITED STATES. NARS. Preliminary Inventory No. 180, Record Group 238. Jarritus Wolfinger (comp.). *Preliminary Inventory of the Records of the International Military Tribunal for the Far East* (Washington: NARS, 1975), p. 1.

63. Ward and Shulman. *The Allied Occupation of Japan*, p. 341.

64. Piccigallo. *The Japanese on Trial*, p. 10.

65. Wolfinger. *Preliminary Inventory*, p. 2.

66. Justice Alan James Mansfield and Colonel Thomas Mornane, Australia; Brigadier Henry Grattan Nolan, Canada; Judge Che-chun Hsiang, China; Robert Oneto, France; Arthur S. Comyns-Carr, Great Britain; Govinda Menon, India; Justice W.G.F. Borgerhoff-Mulder, the Netherlands; Brigadier Ronald Henry Quilliam, New Zealand; Major Pedro López, the Philippines; and Minister S.A. Golunsky and Major General of Justice A.N. Vasilyev, the Soviet Union.

67. Wolfinger. *Preliminary Inventory*, p. 2.

68. *Ibid.*

69. See Appendix 11.

70. See Appendix 14, Figure 1.

71. Woetzel. "The Nuremberg Trials," p. 219. Wolfinger. *Preliminary Inventory*, p. 3.

72. Wolfinger. *Preliminary Inventory*, p 3.

73. See Appendix 13.

74. Ward and Shulman. *The Allied Occupation of Japan*, p. 341.

75. On this problem, see IMTFE. LANGUAGE ARBITRATION BOARD. *Index of Language Corrections Affecting Documents Admitted into Evidence and the Court Records of the International Military Tribunal for the Far East* (Tokyo: IMTFE, 1948).

76. See Appendices 11 and 14, Figure 2.

77. See Appendix 12.

78. Woetzel. *The Nuremberg Trials*, p. 232.

79. *Ibid*.

80. Wolfinger. *Preliminary Inventory*, p. 4.

81. *Ibid*.

82. Harris. *Tyranny*, p. viii.

83. *Ibid*., pp. viii-ix.

84. On this, see abstracts of the *Inventory of International Military Tribunal Archives Nürnberg as Transferred to International Court of Justice and various entries under the United Nations and the IMT*.

85. See Roger W. Barrett and William E. Jackson (eds.). *Nazi Conspiracy and Aggression* (Washington: GPO, 1946). See also August von Knieriem. *The Nuremberg Trials* (Chicago: Henry Regnery, 1959), p. xix.

86. This was a projected set of fifteen volumes, but only nine were published. Some bibliographies actually report all fifteen as published and give dates of publication and number of pages. The publisher, now in Glasgow, confirms that six of the fifteen volumes were never published. The volumes in this series are based on the official transcripts of the trials and on other authoritative sources. In most cases considerable portions of the transcripts are reproduced and the text of the most important documents are reproduced in full. An introductory chapter places each trial within its historical setting, states its legal basis, and points up the salient features of the case for both the prosecution and the defense. Photographs of the courtroom and other illustrations are included. Detailed descriptions of the abridged contents of these volumes are given in UNITED NATIONS WAR CRIMES COMMISSION. *Law Reports of Trials of War Criminals, Selected and Prepared by the United Nations War Crimes Commission* (London: HMPO, 1947-1949).

87. UNWCC. *Law Reports*, XV, pp. xvi.

88. See Quincy Wright's Foreword to *Law Reports of Trials of War Criminals*, UNWCC. *Law Reports*, I, pp. ix-xi.

89. Davidson. *The Trial of the Germans*, p. 5.

90. See, for example, an article by Bruno Blau. *Wiener Library Bulletin* 1951 5(1-2): 91.

91. Ward and Shulman. *The Allied Occupation of Japan*, p. 341.

92. Pritchard and Zaide. *The Tokyo War Crimes Trials*, p. viii.

93. These records are described in Gerhard L. Weinberg's *Guide to Captured German Documents* (New York: Columbia University Press, 1952), pp. 25-29.

94. *Ibid.*, pp. 30-60.

95. *Le Monde Juif*, formerly *Bulletin du Centre de Documentation Juive Contemporaine* (1946-1952), contains more than 60 entries of Nuremberg IMT documents, the largest published source of these documents next to *Trials of War Criminals*.

96. Weinberg. *Guide to Captured German Documents*, p. 64.

97. Ehard. "The Nuremberg Trial," p. 243.

98. Otto Kranzbühler. "Nuremberg Eighteen Years Afterwards," *De Paul Law Review* 1965 14(2): 333-347, pp. 338-342 cited.

99. Harwood. *Nuremberg and other War Crimes Trials: A New Look*, p. 1.

100. Sheldon Glueck. *War Criminals: Their Prosecution and Punishment* (New York: Knopf, 1944), *passim*, on Leipzig trials.

101. John R. Lewis. *Uncertain Judgment: A Bibliography of War Crimes Trials* (Santa Barbara: ABC-Clio, 1979).

I
REFERENCE SECTION

A. BIBLIOGRAPHIES

1 ALMOND, NINA, and RALPH HASSWELL LUTZ. *An Introduction to a Bibliography of the Paris Peace Conference*. Stanford: Stanford University Press, 1935. 32p. Collections of sources, source books, and archives publications. Hoover War Library Bibliographical Series No. 2. Concise listings, extensive annotations, author index.

2 AMICALE INTERNATIONALE DE NEUENGAMME. *Bibliographie der über Neuengamme erschienenen Bücher und Zeitschriften*. Hamburg: 1959. Part 1, books and articles, 7p. Part 2, documents and reports, 7p. Part 3, list of transports, 6p. Deals with Neuengamme concentration camp.

3 ARBEITSGRUPPE BIBLIOGRAPHIE DES INSTITUTS FÜR GESCHICHTE AN DER DEUTSCHEN AKADEMIE DER WISSENSCHAFTEN ZU BERLIN. *Jahresberichte für deutsche Geschichte*. New edition. Berlin: Akademie, 1952-present. Exhaustive bibliography covering all aspects of German history, with topical and author index. Topics on war criminals, World War II, and the Nuremberg IMT trial point to many valuable and useful books and articles.

4 AUFRICHT, HANS. *Guide to League of Nations Publications: A Bibliographical Survey of the Work of the League, 1920-1947*. New York: Columbia University Press, 1951. 682p. Lists and describes by subject the publications of the League of Nations and its various agencies. Index.

5 AUFRICHT, HANS. *War, Peace, and Reconstruction: A Classified Bibliography*. New York: Commission to Study the Organisation of Peace, [1943]. 56p. An annotated list on postwar planning, arranged by subject.

6 BALCH, EMILY GREENE. *Approaches to the Great Settlement: with a Bibliography of Some of the more Recent Books and Articles dealing with International Problems*. New York: B.W. Huebsch, for the American Union against Militarism, 1918. 351p. A bibliography of books and articles.

7 BAYLISS, GWYN M. *Bibliographic Guide to the Two World Wars*. London/New York: Bowker, 1977. Contains many entries on war crimes and related topics.

8 BEDNAREK, IRENA, and STANISLAW SOKOLOWSKI. *Fanfary i Werble*. Katowice: "Slask," 1972, pp. 550-552. Bibliography with 71 items dating from 1935-1963, with several entries on World War II, German war crimes, and the Nuremberg IMT trial.

9 BERNBAUM, JOHN A. "The Captured German Records: A Bibliographic Survey," *Historian* 1970 32(4): 564-575. An important survey of the published and unpublished finding aids to Nuremberg IMT materials, German Foreign Ministry documents, and records of the Nazi party and the German armed forces.

10 *Bibliothek des Instituts für Zeitgeschichte, München* [Library of the Institute for Contemporary History, Munich]. Boston: G.K. Hall, 1967. 5 volumes. Supplementary volume, 1973. Alphabetical listing of library holdings, with much on war crimes. Available in most major university libraries. The title page bears the English as well as the German title.

11 *Bibliothek des Instituts für Zeitgeschichte, München: Biographischer Katalog* [Library of the Institute for Contemporary History, Munich: Biographical Catalog]. Boston: G.K. Hall, 1967. Almost 16,000 entries. The title page bears the English as well as the German title.

12 *Bibliothek des Instituts für Zeitgeschichte, München, Erster Nachtragsband: Biographischer Katalog, Länderkatalog* [Library of the Institute for Contemporary History, Munich, First Supplement: Biographical Catalog, Regional Catalog]. Boston: G.K. Hall, 1973. Contains more than 12,000 entries The title page bears the English as well as the German title.

13 *Bibliothek des Instituts für Zeitgeschichte, München: Länderkatalog* [Library of the Institute for Contemporary History, Munich: Regional Catalog]. Boston: G.K. Hall, 1967. 2 volumes. Contains information on 284 cities, regions, and nations. The title page bears the English as well as the German title.

14 *Bibliothek des Instituts für Zeitgeschichte, München: Sachkatalog* [Library of the Institute for Contemporary History, Munich: Subject Catalog]. 6 volumes, Boston: G.K. Hall, 1967. 2 supplementary volumes, 1967 and 1973. The title page bears the English as well as the German title.

15 *Bibliothek des Johann Gottfried Herder-Instituts, Marburg/Lahn, Germany: Alphabetischer Katalog* [Library of the Johann Gottfried Herder Institute, Marburg/Lahn, Germany: Alphabetical Catalog]. 5 volumes. Boston: G.K. Hall, 1964. The title page bears the English as well as the German title.

16 BLANCHARD, CARROLL H., JR. *Korean War Bibliography and Maps of Korea*. [New York]: [Korean Conflict Research Foundation], 1964. 181p. 25 unpaged maps. Contains a section on atrocities.

17 BLAUSTEIN, ALBERT P. "Viet Nam: Current Legal Bibliography," *Law Library Journal* 1968 61(1): 20-22.

18 BLOOMBERG, MARTY, and HANS H. WEBER. *World War II and its Origins, a select annotated Bibliography of Books in English*. Littleton, Colorado: Libraries Unlimited, 1975. 311p. Contains

several chapters of voluminous background materials. Chapter 12, "War Crimes Trials" (pp. 272-289; entries 1558-1603), addresses itself to the subject at hand. 31-page index.

19 BRACHER, KARL DIETRICH, HANS-ADOLF JACOBSEN, and MANFRED FUNKE (eds.). Bibliographie zur Politik in Theorie und Praxis. Düsseldorf: Droste, 1976. 576p. 1982 edition, 252p.

20 BRAHAM, RANDOLPH L. The Eichmann Case: A Source Book. New York: World Federation of Hungarian Jews, 1969. 186p. This unannotated bibliography contains 1173 entries on Eichmann. The purposes of the book are to bring under one cover all the important references to periodical literature on the Eichmann case, to provide information and assistance to public and private agencies and scholars, and to serve as a guide in the preservation of the Churban record. The titles in languages other than French, German, Italian, and Spanish are given in English as well as in the originals. 12-page name index.

21 BRAHAM, RANDOLPH L. The Hungarian Jewish Catastrophe: A Selected and Annotated Bibliography. New York: YIVO Institute for Jewish Research, 1962. 86p.

22 BRENNECKE, GERHARD. Die Nürnberger Geschichtsentstellung. Quellen zur Vorgeschichte und Geschichte des 2. Weltkrieges aus den Akten der deutschen Verteidigung. Tübingen: Verlag der Deutschen Hochschullehrer Zeitung (Veröffentlichungen des Instituts für Deutsche Nachkriegsgeschichte), 1970. See Volume 5, pp. 401-412.

23 British National Bibliography. London: Council of the British National Bibliography, 1950-.

24 BRUCH, ELSA AUS DEM (comp.). "Bibliographie zu den Nürnberger Prozessen und ihrer Problematik," in Kurt Heinze, Karl Schilling, and Herman Maschke (eds.). Rechtsprechung der Nürnberger Militärtribunale. Sammlung der Rechtsthesen der Urteile und gesonderten Urteils begründungen der dreizehn Nürnberger Prozesse. Bonn: Girardet, 1952. pp. 333-343. Contains 271 items dating from 1944-1952 in English, French, German, Italian, and Spanish.

25 BRÜDIGAM, HEINZ. Wahrheit und Fälschung. Das Dritte Reich und seine Gegner in der Literatur seit 1945. Versuch eines kritischen Überblicks. Frankfurt am Main: Röderberg, 1959. 93p.

26 BURNS, RICHARD DEAN (comp.). Arms Control and Disarmament: A Bibliography. Santa Barbara: ABC-Clio, 1977.

27 BURNS, RICHARD DEAN, and MILTON LEITENBERG (comps.). The Wars in Vietnam, Cambodia, and Laos, 1945-1982: A Bibliographic Guide. Santa Barbara: ABC-Clio, 1984. 290p. General bibliography that deals with reference aids, Southeast Asia, Vietnam, the United States in Southeast Asia, American intervention in Vietnam, combat operations, war crimes, casualties, and opposition to the United States in Vietnam. 6202 entries, glossary, 22-page author index.

28 CARJEU, P.M. Projet d'une juridiction pénale internationale. Paris: A. Pedone, 1953. 119 items, dated 1890-1951, with some in English. There are 28 official documents and texts and 91 journal articles and books on international law, war crimes, Nazi crimes against humanity, the Permanent Court of International

Justice, war crimes trials, political repression, and political and international terrorism.

29 CARNEGIE ENDOWMENT FOR INTERNATIONAL PEACE. Bibliography, 1915-1957: Quincy Wright. New York: Carnegie Endowment for International Peace, 1957.

30 CARNEGIE ENDOWMENT FOR INTERNATIONAL PEACE. Responsibility for the World War. Miscellaneous Reading List, Number 25. Washington: Carnegie Endowment for International Peace, 1925.

31 CARROLL, BERENICE A., CLINTON F. FINK, and JANE E. MOHRAZ (comps.). Peace and War: A Guide to Bibliographies. Santa Barbara: ABC-Clio, 1983, 580p. Volume 16 of The War/Peace Bibliography Series, Richard Dean Burns (ed.). Chapter 34, "War Crimes, Atrocities, War Crimes Trials," pp. 488-496, contains 23 entries. Subject and author index.

32 CHEN, JOHN H.M. Vietnam: A Comprehensive Bibliography. Metuchen, New Jersey: Scarecrow, 1973. 314p.

33 CONOVER, HELEN F. (comp.). Current National Bibliographies. Washington: Library of Congress, General Reference and Bibliography Division, 1955.

34 CONOVER, HELEN F. (comp.). The Nazi State, War Crimes and War: A Bibliography. Washington: Library of Congress, 1945. 132p. A bibliography of titles from the Library of Congress card catalog, from a number of periodical indexes, and from the Interdepartmental Committee Lists. The focus is on German works, but many in English and French have been included. This work was compiled for the office of the Chief of Counsel for the Prosecution of Axis Criminality, and was organized in three sections: (1) Theory of War Crimes, (2) the National-Socialist State, and (3) War Atrocities. The entries cover events from World War I to publication in August 1945. Each entry carries the Library of Congress card catalog number. Contains works that treat in considerable detail war crimes, concentration camps, and the mistreatment of prisoners. The 2-page table of contents is helpful in locating topical entries, but the 16-page index is sketchy and incomplete and is therefore not as helpful as it could be in locating material hidden in the 1084 bibliographical entries.

35 DELUPIS, INGRID. A Bibliography of International Law. London: Bowker, 1975. 670p. Collates material from approximately 5000 books and journal articles. Includes war and armed conflicts among the subjects covered.

36 DENECKE, LUDWIG. Die Nachlässe in den Bibliotheken der Bundesrepublik Deutschland. 2nd, completely revised, edition. Boppard am Rhein: Boldt, 1981. 538p.

37 Deutsche Bibliographie. Das Deutsche Buch, Auswahl wichtiger Neuerscheinungen. Frankfurt am Main: Buchhändler-Vereinigung, 1950-.

38 Deutsche Nationalbibliographie und Bibliographie des im Ausland erschienenen deutschsprachigen Schrifttums. Leipzig: VEB Verlag für Buch- und Bibliothekswesen, 1931-.

39 Deutsches Bücherverzeichnis. Leipzig: VEB Verlag für Buch- und Bibliothekswesen, 1911-.

40 DEVOTO, ANDREA. Bibliografia dell'oppressione nazista fino al 1962. Florence: Olschki, 1964.

41 ENSER, ALFRED G.S. A Subject Bibliography of the First World War, Books in English, 1914-1978. London: Andre Deutsch, 1979. 485p. Contains entries on war crimes and war crimes trials.

42 ENSER, ALFRED G.S. A Subject Bibliography of the Second World War: Books in English, 1939-1974. Boulder, Colorado: Westview Press, 1977. 592p. Contains a few entries on the Warsaw uprising and 22 titles dealing with war crimes trials. All entries are abstracted elsewhere in this bibliography.

43 ERICKSON, RICHARD J. "Selected Bibliography Concerning the Laws of War Including the Law Applicable to Air Operations," Air Force Law Review 1974 16(Summer): 75-95.

44 FEIG, KONNILYN G. Hell on Earth: A Holocaust Bibliography. San Francisco: Multilith, 1981.

45 FEIG, KONNILYN G. The Voyage of the Damned: An Essayed Bibliography of the Holocaust. Portland: University of Maine, 1974.

46 FRIEDMAN, PHILIP, and JOSEPH GAR. Bibliography of Yiddish Books on the Catastrophe and Heroism. New York: Yad Vashem and Yivo Institute for Jewish Research, 1962. 330p.

47 FUNK, ARTHUR L., et al (comps.). A Select Bibliography of Books on the Second World War, in English, Published in the United States, 1966-1975. San Francisco: American Committee on the History of the Second World War, 1975. 33p.

48 FUNK, ARTHUR L. The Second World War: A Bibliography; A Select List of Publications appearing Since 1968. Gainesville: University of Florida Press, 1972. 32p.

49 GARSE, YVAN VAN. A Bibliography of Genocide, Crimes against Humanity, and War Crimes. Brussels/St. Niklaas: Studiecentrum voor Kriminologie en Gerechtelijke Geneeskunde, 1970. 155p. Lists 1750 books, pamphlets, and periodical articles relating principally to World War II, including materials in eastern as well as western European languages.

50 GARSE, YVAN VAN. Hungarian Literature on War Crimes and Crimes against Humanity. St. Niklaas: Information Retrieval System, 1970. Brussels: Studiecentrum voor Kriminologie en Gerechtelijke Geneeskunde, 1970. 16p. Unannotated.

51 GENDREL, MICHEL, and PHILIPPE LA FARGE. Éléments d'une bibliographie mondiale du droit pénal militaire, des crimes et délits contre la sureté de l'état et du droit pénal international. Paris: R. Pichon and R. Durand-Auzias, 1965. 216p. A bibliography of war crimes listed by topic and nation.

52 HANNIGAN, JANE A. (comp.). Publications of the Carnegie Endowment for International Peace, 1910-1967: Including International Conciliation, 1924-1967. New York: Carnegie Endowment for International Peace, 1971. 229p. Alphabetical arrangement of 1108 monographs issued by the Endowment from the journal International Conciliation. Detailed indexes of authors, corporate bodies, treaties, and subjects. Contains materials on both world wars.

53 HAAS, MICHAEL (comp.). *International Organization: An Interdisciplinary Bibliography*. Stanford: Hoover Institution Press, 1971. 944p.

54 HERRE, WYBO P. *International Bibliography of Air Law, 1900-1971*. Dobbs Ferry: Oceana Publications, 1972.

55 HERSCH, GISELA (comp.). *A Bibliography of German Studies, 1945-1971*. Bloomington: Indiana University Press, 1972. 603p.

56 HIRSCHBACH, FRANK. "Black Milk: The Treatment of Guilt in German Post War Literature," *Minnesota Review* 1963 3(2): 247-256.

57 KEHR, HELEN, and JANET LANGMAID (comps.). *The Nazi Era, 1919-1945: A Select Bibliography of Published Works from the early Roots to 1980*. London: Mansell, 1982. 621p. Contains 6523 entries, many of which deal with war crimes and war crimes trials. Chapter 8, "War Crimes," pp. 447-515, contains most of the pertinent entries, though there are others in chapters that deal with the criminal state, the road to war, and World War II. All relevant entries are abstracted in the present work.

58 KORMAN, GERD. "The Holocaust in American Historical Writing," *Societas* 1972 2(3): 251-270.

59 KOSICKI, JERZY, and WACLAW KOZLOWSKI. [Bibliography of Polish literature for the years 1944-1953 on Hitlerian war crimes]. Warsaw: Wydawnictwo Prawnicze, 1955. 179p. Contains 2296 items, in French, English, and German. Some have brief descriptive annotations. Organized into 14 categories, with authors and titles listed under each. Subjects covered include German aggression against Poland, persecution of the Polish population, extermination of the Jewish population, death camps and concentration camps, the treatment of prisoners of war, religious persecution, destruction and plunder of public and private property, and the Nuremberg IMT trial.

60 KRESLINS, JANIS A. *Foreign Affairs Bibliography: A Selected and Annotated List of Books on International Relations, 1962-1972*. New York/London: R.R. Bowker, 1976. 921p.

61 LASKA, VERA (comp.). *Nazism, Resistance, and Holocaust in World War II, a Bibliography*. Westport: Greenwood, 1983. 50p. Metuchen, New Jersey: Scarecrow, 1985. 183p. A bibliography of more than 1300 unnumbered entries arranged in 12 categories. Section 9, pp. 42-45, focuses on war crimes. Unannotated.

62 LEITENBERG, MILTON, and RICHARD DEAN BURNS. *The Vietnam Conflict: Its Geographical Dimensions, Political Traumas and Military Developments*. Santa Barbara: ABC-Clio, 1973. 164p.

63 LEWIS, JOHN R. (comp.). *Uncertain Judgment: A Bibliography of War Crimes Trials*. Santa Barbara: ABC-Clio, 1979. 251p. Volume 8 of the bibliographical series prepared by the Center for the Study of Armament and Disarmament. It contains 3352 unannotated entries. The organization is by general reference works, background issues, historical works, and subsidiary issues. The Introduction explains the rationale and organization of the work. Offers an 8-page table of contents in lieu of a topical or subject index. Unannotated. There is a 6-page chronology of war crimes, and an 8-page bibliographical essay which explains the format of the book.

64 MÖNNING, RICHARD (ed.). *Translations from the German, a series of Bibliographies, English, 1948-1964*. Göttingen: Vandenhoeck and Ruprecht, 1968. 509pages. "World War II," pp. 323-344, contains some entries on war crimes trials and related subjects.

65 MORTON, LOUIS (comp.). *Writings on World War II*. Washington: American Historical Association [Service Center for Teachers of History, Publication No. 66], 1967. 54p.

66 NEUMANN, INGE S. (comp.), and ROBERT A. ROSENBAUM (ed.). *European War Crimes Trials: A Bibliography*. New York: Carnegie Endowment for International Peace, 1951; reprinted, Westport: Greenwood, 1978. 113 lines. Mimeograph. Includes 746 items published between 1941 and 1950 in English, French, German, Italian, Dutch, Russian, and other European languages. Approximately two-thirds of the entries - those documents found in the New York area - have brief descriptive or critical annotations. Contains bibliographies, document collections, official records, reports, declarations, books, and journal articles on German war crimes and criminals as they relate to war crimes trials, international law, and jurisprudence. These materials deal with crimes against the peace and against humanity, hostages, genocide, quislings, extradition, guerrilla warfare, international penal codes, moral aspects of war, and the role of the United Nations in war crimes trials. The uneven quality and scope of the annotations make them of little value. The book suffers from having no subject or topical index, but it does have a 6-page author index.

67 NEW YORK PUBLIC LIBRARY. THE RESEARCH LIBRARY. *Subject Catalogue of the World War II Collection*. 3 volumes. Boston: G.K. Hall & Company, 1977-. More than 2100 pages of card catalog entries on World War II, listed alphabetically by author.

68 NEW YORK UNIVERSITY SCHOOL OF LAW LIBRARY STAFF. "Vietnam Bibliography," *New York University Law Review* 1970 45(4): 749-759. Contains bibliographies, entries from the *Congressional Record*, documents, books, and articles.

69 PAETEL, KARL O. "The Black Order: A Survey of the Literature on the SS," *Wiener Library Bulletin* 1959 12(3-4): 34-35.

70 PARRISH, MICHAEL. *The U.S.S.R. in World War II: An Annotated Bibliography of Books Published in the Soviet Union, 1945-1975, with an Addendum for the Years 1975-1980*. 2 volumes. New York: Garland, 1981. 388p., 907p. Volume 2, Section 15, pp. 537-543, contains books on war crimes.

71 PIEKARZ, MENDEL. [The Holocaust and its aftermath. Hebrew books published in the years 1933-1972]. 2 volumes. Jerusalem: Yad Vashem, 1974. 920p. In Hebrew.

72 PIEKARZ, MENDEL. [The Holocaust and its aftermath as seen through Hebrew periodicals. A bibliography]. Jerusalem: Yad Vashem, 1978. 492p. In Hebrew.

73 PIEKARZ, MENDEL (ed.). *The Jewish Holocaust and Heroism Through the Eyes of the Hebrew Press. A Bibliography*. Volume 1 (Joint Documentary Projects, Bibliographical Series No. 5). Series 1 was published in Jerusalem by Yad Vashem and in New York by YIVO in 1960.

74 PLISCHKE, ELMER. *American Foreign Relations: A Bibliography of Official Sources*. College Park, Maryland: Bureau of Governmental Research, College of Business and Public Administration, University of Maryland, 1955. 71p.

75 ROBINSON, JACOB, and PHILIP FRIEDMAN (comps.). *Guide to Jewish History under Nazi Impact*. New York: Yad Vashem Martyrs' and Heroes' Memorial Authority (Jerusalem), and YIVO Institute for Jewish Research (New York), 1960. 425p. Joint Documentary Projects, Bibliographical Series No. 1. Contains approximately 3700 entries, a few of which are abstracted briefly. The work is divided into 4 parts, consisting of 22 chapters. All entries from Chapter 14, "Crimes and Trials," pp. 176-221, are abstracted in the present work.

76 ROBINSON, JACOB, and MRS. PHILIP FRIEDMAN (comps.). *The Holocaust and after: Sources & Literature in English*. Jerusalem: Israel Universities Press, 1973. 353p. Yad Vashem Martyrs' and Heroes' Memorial Authority (Jerusalem) and YIVO Institute for Jewish Research (New York) - Joint Documentary Projects, Bibliographical Series, No. 12. This work contains 6638 entries dealing with the Holocaust. A few have been abstracted. The book is divided into 7 parts consisting of 32 chapters. All materials in Chapter 25, "Prosecution and Trial of War Crimes," pp. 182-186, and Chapter 30, "War Crimes Trials Reports," pp. 236-252, are included in the present work. The preface explains the nature and scope of the work and the origins and types of entries. Only works in English are included.

77 SACHAROFF, MARK. "Bibliography of Recent and Forthcoming Books on U.S. War Crimes in Indochina," *New Republic* 1971 164(1-2): 29, 31.

78 SAINSBURY, KEITH. *International History 1939-1970: A Select Bibliography*. London: Historical Association, 1973. 55p. Section 2, pp. 10-19, is devoted exclusively to World War II. Confined to English-language titles, with a short commentary.

79 SCANLON, HELEN L. (comp.). *War Crimes: A Selected List of Books and Articles defining War Crimes under International Law and discussing their Trial and Punishment, including Works on the International Criminal Court*. Washington: Carnegie Endowment for International Peace, 1945. 16p. This is Selected Bibliography 14, which contains 182 entries, most of which are abstracted in the present work. This work is distributed in mimeograph and is informally arranged, with no underlining or italicization of titles or distinction made between article and journal titles.

80 SCHAFFER, RONALD (comp.). *The United States in World War I: A Select Bibliography*. Santa Barbara: ABC-Clio Press, 1978.

81 SCHLACHTER, GAIL (ed.). *The Third Reich, 1933-1939: A Historical Bibliography*. Santa Barbara: ABC-Clio, 1984. 239p.

82 SCHORSCH, ISMAR. "German Anti-Semitism in the Light of Postwar Historiography," *Leo Baeck Institute Year Book* 1974 19: 257-271.

83 SCHUTTER, BART DE (comp.). *Bibliography on International Criminal Law*. Leiden: Sijthoff, 1972.

84 SCREEN, J.E.O. (ed.). *World Bibliographical Series*. 31 volumes. Santa Barbara: ABC Clio. 1981. 212p.

85 SIEKANOWICZ, PETER (comp.). Legal Sources and Bibliography of Poland. Library of Congress, Mid-European Law Project. New York: Praeger, 1964.

86 SMYTH, HOWARD MC GAW. "Some Italian Publications Regarding World War II," Military Affairs 1947 11(4): 245-253. An extensive and critical review of works on the war by Italian participants.

87 SPIER, HENRY O. (ed.). World War II in Our Magazines and Books: September 1939 to September 1945, A Bibliography. New York: Stuyvesant, 1945. 96p. Lists nearly 1500 books and journal articles on World War II, with emphasis upon American publications. Unannotated.

88 STACHURA, PETER D. The Weimar Era and Hitler, 1918-1933: A Critical Bibliography. Oxford: ABC-Clio, 1977.

89 STAPLETON, MARGARET L. The Truman and Eisenhower Years 1945-1960: A Selective Bibliography. Metuchen, New Jersey: Scarecrow Press, 1973. 221p. Unannotated list of 1932 books and articles relating to the United States in the postwar period. Covers the Yalta and Potsdam conferences and war crimes trials.

90 STEWART, WILLIAM J. The Era of Franklin Roosevelt: A Selected Bibliography of Periodical and Dissertation Literature 1945-1966. New York: Franklin D. Roosevelt Library, 1967. 175p. Annotated bibliography, 1 part of which deals with World War II. Author and subject indexes.

91 STRAUSS, HERBERT A. (ed.). Jewish Immigrants of the Nazi Period in the U.S.A. Volume 2. New York: K.G. Saur, 1981. 286p.

92 TARNOWSKA, MARIA. "Bibliografia Martyrologii Warmii, Mazur i Powisla w Latach 1939-45 [A Bibliography of Martyrology of Warmia, Masuria, and Powisla in the Years 1939-45]," Komunikaty Mazursko-Warminskie 1969 (104): 229-266. Bibliography of Polish martyrdom during World War II supplements materials collected by the Olsztyn branch of the Commission for the Investigation of Nazi Crimes from the Provincial State Archives at Olsztyn. Based on materials in various national and regional bibliographies of the Polish press. Covers victims of Nazi terror, personal memoirs of people who were held in prisons and camps, and concentration camps and extermination points in Olsztyn Province. Includes indices of authors, victims, and localities.

93 TREVOR-ROPER, HUGH R. "The Germans Re-appraise the War," Foreign Affairs 1953 31(2): 225-237. A survey of German historical writing on World War II.

94 UNITED NATIONS. INTERNATIONAL LAW COMMISSION. Bibliography on International Criminal Law and International Criminal Courts. A/CN. 4/28. June 6, 1950. Lake Success: United Nations, 1950.

95 UNITED STATES. LIBRARY OF CONGRESS. EUROPEAN AFFAIRS DIVISION. The United States and Post War Europe: A Bibliographical Examination of Thoughts Expressed in American Publications during 1948. Washington: Library of Congress, 1948. 123p. Consists of 417 annotated entries on the postwar situation in Europe and on American foreign policy. Confined to English-language materials, excluding official documents. Author index.

40 Reference Section

96   WAR BOOK CLUB, LONDON. *Register of Books Acquired 1914-1920*. 2 volumes. London: The Club, 1914-1920. Manuscript list of 1867 items, arranged by author and title.

97   WARD, ROBERT E., and FRANK J. SHULMAN, et al. *The Allied Occupation of Japan, 1945-1952: An Annotated Bibliography of Western Language Materials*. Chicago: American Library Association, 1974. 867p. Contains 2537 annotated entries published as a companion volume to a Japanese bibliography on the occupation, published in 1972. Entries 1011-1104 deal with war crimes trials.

98   WIENER LIBRARY. *Books on Persecution, Terror and Resistance in Nazi Germany*. London: Wiener Library (Catalogue Series, no. 1), 1949. 51p. 2nd edition, with Supplement, 1953. 23p. Lists books on war crimes and atrocities, but not on trials and legal problems. See following entry.

99   WOLFF, ILSE R. (ed.). *Persecution and Resistance under the Nazis*. 2nd edition. London: Vallentine, Mitchell, 1960. 208p. Wiener Library Catalogue Series No. 1. Detailed subject catalogue of the Wiener Library's holdings on the persecution of Jews and others. Includes 1943 books, pamphlets, and periodicals in a variety of European languages. Appendices list periodicals of Germans in exile and illegal anti-Nazi pamphlets and periodicals. Index. See previous entry.

100 ZIEGLER, JANET (comp.). *World War II: Books in English, 1945-1965*. Hoover Bibliographical Series, No. 45. Stanford: Hoover Institution Press, 1971. Lists 4519 books in English on the war. Some deal with war crimes trials. Unannotated.

B. GUIDES

101 AMERICAN HISTORICAL ASSOCIATION. COMMITTEE FOR THE STUDY OF WAR DOCUMENTS. *Supplement to the Guide to Captured German Documents*. Washington: National Archives, 1959. 69p. This is a supplement to Gerald L. Weinberg's work (which see). It brings up to date the listings of the Hoover Institution Library, the Library of Congress, the National Archives of the United States, and the YIVO Institute. It offers brief descriptions of the collections at the University of Pennsylvania Library and the Alderman Library of the University of Virginia.

102 COTTER, MICHAEL. *Vietnam: A Guide to Reference Sources*. Boston: G.K. Hall, 1977. 272p.3

103 GREAT BRITAIN. PUBLIC RECORD OFFICE. *The Second World War: A Guide to Documents in the Public Record Office*. London: HMSO, 1972. 303p. Basic guide to cabinet and departmental papers relating to World War II released in 1972. Contains short accounts of various wartime ministries, a list of major codenames, abbreviations, official histories, and a classified index.

104 INSTITUTE OF CONTEMPORARY HISTORY AND WIENER LIBRARY. *Guide to the Collection of Nuremberg Documents*. London: Institute of Contemporary History, 1969. 7p. A summary of the institute's holdings, with notes on Nuremberg documents held elsewhere.

105 *International Index to Periodicals: A Guide to Periodical Literature in the Social Sciences and Humanities*. New York: H.W. Wilson, 1907-.

106 KIMMICH, CHRISTOPH (ed. and comp.). German Foreign Policy, 1918-1945: A Guide to Research and Research Materials. Wilmington: Scholarly Resources, 1981. 293p.

107 LEWANSKI, RICHARD C. (comp.). Guide to Polish Libraries and Archives. New York: Columbia University Press, 1974. 209p.

108 LEWANSKI, RUDOLF J. (comp.), and RICHARD C. LEWANSKI (ed.). Guide to Italian Libraries and Archives. New York: Council for European Studies, 1979. 101p.

109 ROBINSON, JACOB, and YEHUDA BAUER (eds.). Guide to Unpublished Materials of the Holocaust Period. 6 volumes. Jerusalem: Hebrew University, 1970-1981. Both editors worked on the first 2 volumes; Bauer did the last four alone. Volume 3 (1975), 413p. Volume 4 (1977), 389p. Volume 5 (1979), 436p. Volume 3 lists the record groups in the Yad Vashem Archives and the record groups indexed within the volume and describes the record groups indexed. Index, pp. 81-413. 1-page bibliography. Volume 4 contains a list of new record groups in the Yad Vashem Archives, with the record groups indexed. Index, pp. 41-389. Volume 5 lists new record groups in the Yad Vashem Archives and record groups indexed in this volume, and describes the record groups indexed. Index, pp. 95-436. The 3 volumes described contain useful Introductions.

110 SEGALL, ARYEH (ed.). Guide to Jewish Archives. Jerusalem/New York: World Council on Jewish Archives, 1981. 90p.

111 THOMAS, DANIEL H., and LYNN M. CASE (eds.). Guide to the Diplomatic Archives of Western Europe. Philadelphia: University of Pennsylvania Press, 1959. Pages 339-340 contain a survey of UN holdings of UNWCC records.

112 UNITED NATIONS. COMMUNICATIONS AND RECORDS DIVISION. ARCHIVES SECTION. Guide to Records of the War Crimes Trials Held in Nürnberg, Germany, 1945-1949. Lake Success: United Nations, October 7, 1949. 4p. United Nations Archives Reference Guide, No. 7 (Revision No. 1). Mimeograph. Descriptive list of those records of the Nuremberg war crimes trials which have been transferred to the custody of the UN Archives. Most of the records described are available at major law libraries.

113 UNITED NATIONS. COMMUNICATIONS AND RECORDS DIVISION. ARCHIVES SECTION. Guide to the Records of the United Nations War Crimes Commission, London, 1943-1948. New York: United Nations, August 27, 1951. 14p. United Nations Archives Reference Guide, No. 19. A United Nations Archives reference guide which contains a history of the War Crimes Commission and its functions, a description of finding aids, and a list of records.

114 UNITED STATES. NATIONAL ARCHIVES AND RECORDS SERVICE. Guide to the National Archives of the United States. Washington: NARS, 1974. 884p. Contains many entries on war crimes and directions for finding the original documents in the holdings of the National Archives.

115 WEBB, HERSCHEL, with the assistance of MARLEIGH RYAN. Research in Japanese Sources: A Guide. New York: Columbia University Press, 1965.

42 Reference Section

116 WEINBERG, GERHARD L., and the WAR DOCUMENTATION STAFF (comps.). Guide to Captured German Documents. New York: Columbia University Press, 1952. This bibliography was prepared under the direction of Fritz T. Epstein under the auspices of the Human Resources Research Institute of the Air University, Maxwell Air Force Base, Alabama. It was published as Research Memorandum Number 2, Volume 1. This guide is the outgrowth of the War Documentation Project. It identifies the location and contents of a number of major depositories. Particularly valuable is a 5-page description of the documents held by the Hoover Library, a 31-page description of the holdings of the Library of Congress, and a 3-page description of materials held by the National Archives of the United States, as well as descriptions of the holdings of the Centre de Documentation Juive Contemporaine (Paris), the Netherlands State Institute for War-Documentation (Amsterdam), and the Yiddish Scientific Institute - YIVO (New York). All entries relating directly to war crimes, war criminals, or war crimes trials have been abstracted elsewhere in the present volume. Contains a 14-page index.

117 ZAWODNY, JANUSZK K. Guide to the Study of International Relations. San Francisco: Chandler, 1966. 151p.

C. INDEXES

118 BUCHANAN, WILLIAM W., and EDNA M. KANELY (comps.). Cumulative Subject Index to the Monthly Catalog of United States Government Publications. 14 volumes. Washington: Carrollton Press, 1972.

119 Index to Periodical Articles Related to Law. New York: Glenville Publications, 1959-.

120 MOSTECKY, VACLAV (ed.). Index to Multilateral Treaties: A Chronological List of Multi-Party International Agreements from the Sixteenth Century through 1963, with Citations to Their Text. Cambridge: Harvard University Press, Law School Library. 1965. 301p.

121 UNITED NATIONS. COMMUNICATIONS AND RECORDS DIVISION. ARCHIVES SECTION. Index to Minutes and Documents of the United Nations War Crimes Commission, 1945-1948. New York: United Nations, 1949. 108p. United Nations Archives Reference Guide, No. 11.

122 UNITED NATIONS. COMMUNICATIONS AND RECORDS DIVISION. ARCHIVES SECTION. Index to the Documents of the Research Office of the United Nations War Crimes Commission, 1944-1948. New York: United Nations, [no date given]. 17p. United Nations Archives Reference Guide, No. 12. Supplements No. 11, above.

123 UNITED NATIONS. COMMUNICATIONS AND RECORDS DIVISION. ARCHIVES SECTION. Index to War Crimes News Digest of the United Nations War Crimes Commission Research Office, Nos. XXV-XXXVI. New York: United Nations, January, 1950. 49p. United Nations Archives Reference Guide, No. 13.

124 UNITED NATIONS. DAG HAMMARSKJOLD LIBRARY. United Nations Documents Index. New York: United Nations, 1950-.

125 UNITED NATIONS. UNITED NATIONS WAR CRIMES COMMISSION (UNWCC). Alphabetical Index of War Criminals. 4 volumes. Covers Periodical Lists Numbers 1-40. Mimeograph.

Reference Section 43

126 UNITED NATIONS. UNITED NATIONS WAR CRIMES COMMISSION (UNWCC). Second Alphabetical Index of War Criminals, Suspects, and Material Witnesses. 4 volumes. Covers Periodical Lists Numbers 41-45 and 50-60. Mimeographed. Periodical Lists 46-49 contain the names of Japanese war criminals. There are 40,000 cards in the alphabetical card index.

D. REFERENCE WORKS

127 CENTRAL REGISTRY OF WAR CRIMINALS AND SECURITY SUSPECTS, BERLIN (CROWCASS). Consolidated Wanted Lists. 2 volumes and Supplement. Berlin: U.S. Army, Allied Control Authority, 1947.

128 CENTRAL REGISTRY OF WAR CRIMINALS AND SECURITY SUSPECTS. BERLIN (CROWCASS). Detention List. 11 volumes. Berlin: U.S. Army, Berlin Document Center, 1946-1948.

129 HACHWORTH, GREEN HAYWOOD (comp.). Digest of International Law. 8 volumes. Washington: GPO, 1940-1944.

130 SNYDER, LOUIS L. Encyclopedia of the Third Reich. New York: McGraw-Hill, 1976. 410p.

131 STOCKHORST, ERICH. Fünftausend Köpfe. Wer war was im Dritten Reich. Bruchsal/Baden: Blick und Bild, 1967. 461p.

132 TOTOK, WILHELM, ROLF WEITZEL, and KARL-HEINZ WEIMANN. Handbuch der bibliographischen Nachschlagewerke. Frankfurt am Main: Klostermann, 1977 edition. 367p. Relevant sources are included in the present work.

133 UNITED NATIONS. United Nations Treaty Series. 1070 volumes to date. New York: United Nations, 1946-.

134 UNITED NATIONS. UNITED NATIONS WAR CRIMES COMMISSION (UNWCC). List of War Criminals. 80 volumes. London: UNWCC, 1944-1948.

135 WHITMAN, MARJORIE (comp.). Digest of International Law. 15 volumes. Washington: GPO, 1963-1970.

136 WISTRICH, ROBERT. Who's Who in Nazi Germany. London: Weidenfeld and Nicolson, 1982. 359p. Contains approximately 350 vitas of people who were significant in the Third Reich, including actors, civil servants, industrialists, academicians, and artists. 4-page glossary, 1-page of comparative ranks in the German, SS, British, and American military services, 7-page bibliography.

137 WULF, JOSEPH. Aus dem Lexikon der Mörder. "Sonderbehandlung" und verwandte Worte in nationalsozialistischen Dokumenten. Gütersloh: Mohn, 1963. 111p.

E. DOCUMENTS AND RECORDS BY NATION

1. General

138 ISAACS, HAROLD ROBERTS (ed.). New Cycle in Asia: Selected Documents on Major International Developments in the Far East, 1943-1947. New York: Macmillan, 1947. 212p. Source of documents on the war and its immediate aftermath. Each group of documents is preceded by an outline of political events.

Reference Section

139 LAMBERT, MARGARET. "Source Materials made available to Historical Research as a Result of World War II," *International Affairs* 1959 35(2): 188-196. A survey of captured German, Italian, and Japanese archives.

140 LANGSAM, WALTER CONSUELO. *Historic Documents of World War II*. Princeton: Van Nostrand, 1958. 192p.

2. France

141 STEINBERG, LUCIEN. *Les Autorités allemandes en France occupée. Inventaire commenté de la collection de documents conservés au CDJC provenant des archives de l'Ambassade d'Allemagne, de l'Administration Militaire Allemande et de la Gestapo en France*. Paris: CDJC, 1966. 355p.

3. Germany

142 "A Treasure House of Documents: The International Tracing Service at Arolsen," *Wiener Library Bulletin* 1953 7: 29, 42. Describes documents relating to missing people who were incarcerated in Nazi concentration and labor camps.

143 JACOBSEN, HANS-ADOLF, and WERNER JOCHMANN (eds.). *Ausgewählte Dokumente zur Geschichte des Nationalsozialismus 1933-1945*. Bielefeld: Verlag Neue Gesellschaft, 1961.

4. Great Britain

144 WOODWARD, ERNEST L., and ROHAN BUTLER (eds.). *Documents on British Foreign Polity, 1919-1939*. First Series. 8 volumes. London: HMSO, 1947-1958.

5. Israel

145 BRAND, EMANUEL. "Materials from Trials of War Criminals being sent from West Germany to Yad Vashem," *Yad Vashem Bulletin* 1963 (31): 51-54. Original is in Hebrew.

146 FRAENKEL, JOSEF. "'Yad Vashem,' Israel's Memorial of the Persecution," *Wiener Library Bulletin* 1955 9: 16-. Describes the library and archival holdings relating to the Nazi persecution of Jews.

147 "Historical Archives in Jerusalem," *Wiener Library Bulletin* 1956 10: 27-. Surveys the documentary holdings of the Jewish General Archive.

148 ROSENKRANTZ, J. "The Wiesenthal Collection in the Yad Vashem Archives," *Yedi'ot Yad Vashem* 1957 12(January): 22-23. Original is in Hebrew.

6. Italy

149 CIANO, GALEAZZO. *L'Europa verso la catastrofa, 184 colloqui con Mussolini, Hitler, Franco, etc.* Milan: A. Mondadori, 1947. 722p. A collection of documents from the archives of the Palazzo Chigi which supplements the Ciano diaries.

7. Poland

150 BIEDA, TADEUSZ. "Zrodla Historyczne do Dziejow Okupacji Hitlerowskiej W Zbiorach Archiwalnych Wojewodztwa Rzeszowskiego

[Nazi Archival Documents in Rzeszow Province Archives]," Archeion 1976 64: 105-115. Describes the political value and significance of materials in the Rzeszow provincial archives in eastern Poland, which contain World War II German documents. Compares these to Polish documents which deal with German war crimes in the province.

151 BLUMENTHAL, NACHMAN. Dokumenty i Materialy. Lodz: Central Jewish Historical Commission of Poland, 1946. German documents. Volume 1, Obozy (camps); Volume 2, Akcje i Wysiedlenia (resettlement actions); Volume 3, Getto Lodzkie. Volumes 1 and 2 include survivor narratives in Polish.

8. United Nations

152 Inventory of International Military Tribunal Archives Nuernberg as Transferred to International Court of Justice. The Hague: [no publisher given], [no date given]. 409p. Mimeograph. Contains 28 boxes of written material and 9 boxes of transcriptions, 5259 items in all. The materials are filed under a variety of headings, among them prosecution and defense exhibits, transcripts, trial briefs, opening and closing statements, pleas, judgments, sentences, indictments, court records, and lists of various kinds.

153 UNITED NATIONS. INTERNATIONAL LAW COMMISSION (1ST SESSION). List of Documents. Doc. A/CN.4/10, April 11, 1949. Lake Success: United Nations, 1949.

9. United States

a. General

154 BROWN, DELMER M. "Instruction and Research: Recent Japanese Political and Historical Materials," American Political Science Review 1949 43(5): 1010-1017. Surveys materials at the University of California, Berkeley.

155 CAMPBELL, JOHN C. The United States in World Affairs, 1945-1947. New York/London: Harper & Brothers, 1947. 385p.

156 CONWAY, JOHN S. German Historical Source Material in the United States Universities. Pittsburgh: Council for European Studies, 1973. 23p. The product of a 1970 questionnaire sent to all major American universities in order to ascertain their holdings. Lists most National Archives microfilm records as well as university sources. Most of the records are not relevant to war crimes trials, but they do reflect on German actions that later were considered criminal.

157 DENNETT, RAYMOND, and ROBERT K. TURNER (eds.). Documents on American Foreign Relations. Volume 8, July 1, 1945 - December 31, 1946. Princeton: Princeton University Press, for the World Peace Foundation, 1948. 962p. Much on war crimes trials.

b. Army

158 UNITED STATES. ARMY. FAR EAST COMMAND, GENERAL HEADQUARTERS, MILITARY INTELLIGENCE SECTION, GENERAL STAFF. Memoirs: Supplement: Prince Saionji and the London Disarmament Treaty. Tokyo: [no publisher given], 1946.

c. Department of State

159 UNITED STATES. DEPARTMENT OF STATE. Documents on German Foreign Policy, 1918-1945, Series C. 5 volumes. Washington: GPO, 1957-1966.

160 UNITED STATES. DEPARTMENT OF STATE. Documents on German Foreign Policy, 1918-1945. Series D. 13 volumes. Washington: GPO, 1949-1964.

161 UNITED STATES. DEPARTMENT OF STATE. Documents on Germany, 1944-1971. Washington: Historical Office, Department of State, 1971. 897p. Updates 2 earlier documentary compilations which covered the periods 1944-1959 and 1944-1961.

162 UNITED STATES. DEPARTMENT OF STATE. Foreign Relations of the United States. Diplomatic Papers. 1942. 7 volumes. Washington: GPO, 1960-1963. Volume 1.

163 UNITED STATES. DEPARTMENT OF STATE. Foreign Relations of the United States. Diplomatic Papers. 1943. 6 volumes. Washington: GPO, 1963-1965. Volume 1, pp. 439-459, 513-749. Deals with the Cairo and Tehran conferences.

164 UNITED STATES. DEPARTMENT OF STATE. Foreign Relations of the United States. Diplomatic Papers. 1944. 8 volumes. Washington: GPO, 1966-1967. Volume 1. Deals with the Conference at Quebec.

165 UNITED STATES. DEPARTMENT OF STATE. Foreign Relations of the United States. Diplomatic Papers. 1945. 9 volumes. Washington: GPO, 1967-1969. Volume 2, European Advisory Council, Austria, Germany. Much on the Potsdam Conference.

166 UNITED STATES. DEPARTMENT OF STATE. Foreign Relations of the United States: Conferences at Malta and Yalta. Washington: GPO, 1945.

167 UNITED STATES. DEPARTMENT OF STATE. Foreign Relations of the United States. Diplomatic Papers. 1946. 11 volumes. Volume 1, The Far East. Washington: GPO, 1969-1972.

168 UNITED STATES. DEPARTMENT OF STATE. Foreign Relations of the United States. Diplomatic Papers. 1947. 8 volumes. Washington: GPO, 1972-1973.

169 UNITED STATES. DEPARTMENT OF STATE. Foreign Relations of the United States. Diplomatic Papers. 1948. 9 volumes. Washington: GPO, 1972-1975.

170 UNITED STATES. DEPARTMENT OF STATE. Papers Relating to the Foreign Relations of the United States: Japan, 1931-1941. 2 volumes. Washington: GPO, 1943.

171 UNITED STATES. DEPARTMENT OF STATE. Publications of the Department of State: October 1, 1929 to January 1, 1953. State Department Publication No. 5059. Washington: GPO, 1954.

172 UNITED STATES. DEPARTMENT OF STATE. The Axis in Defeat: A Collection of Documents on American Policy towards Germany and Japan. Washington: GPO, 1945. 118p. Covers major documents issued between 1941 and 1945, arranged under general policy, surrender, and occupation.

173 UNITED STATES. DEPARTMENT OF STATE. The Far Eastern Commission: Report by the Secretary General. State Department Publication No. 3420. Washington: GPO, 1949.

d. NARS. General

174 MORLEY, JAMES W. "Check List of Seized Japanese Records in the National Archives," Far Eastern Quarterly 1950 9(3): 306-333.

175 TAYLOR, TELFORD. "The Use of Captured German and Related Records in the Nürnberg War Crimes Trials," in Robert Wolfe (ed.). Captured German and Related Records: A National Archives Conference. Athens: Ohio University Press, 1974. pp. 92-100.

176 UNITED STATES. NATIONAL ARCHIVES AND RECORDS SERVICE. Federal Records of World War II. Volume 1, Civilian Agencies. Washington: NARS, 1950. 1073p. Volume 2, Military Agencies. Washington: NARS, 1951. 1061p. Section 1794 of Volume 1 has a brief essay on the United Nations War Crimes Commission. Both volumes contain useful information on the administration of records of war crimes trials and the present location of many documents, particularly those of the UNWCC.

e. NARS. Microfilm

177 UNITED STATES. NATIONAL ARCHIVES AND RECORDS SERVICE. Diary of Hans Frank. Microfilm of records described in NARS Preliminary Inventory 21. T992. Microfilm, 12 rolls.

178 UNITED STATES. NATIONAL ARCHIVES AND RECORDS SERVICE. German Documents among the War Crimes Records of the Judge Advocate Division, Headquarters, United States Army, Europe. Record Group 338: Records of the U.S. Army Commands, 1942-. T1021. Microfilm, 20 rolls.

179 UNITED STATES. NATIONAL ARCHIVES AND RECORDS SERVICE. Prosecution Exhibits Submitted to the International Military Tribunal. Microfilm of records described in NARS Preliminary Inventory 21. T988. Microfilm, 54 rolls.

180 UNITED STATES. NATIONAL ARCHIVES AND RECORDS SERVICE. Records of the U.S. Nuernberg War Crimes Trials: NG Series, 1933-1948. Record Group 238. T1139. Microfilm, 70 rolls.

181 UNITED STATES. NATIONAL ARCHIVES AND RECORDS SERVICE. Records of the U.S. Nuernberg War Crimes Trials: NI Series, 1933-1948. Record Group 238. T301. Microfilm, 164 rolls.

182 UNITED STATES. NATIONAL ARCHIVES AND RECORDS SERVICE. Records of the U.S. Nuernberg War Crimes Trials: NM Series, 1874-1946. Record Group 238. M936. Microfilm, 1 roll.

183 UNITED STATES. NATIONAL ARCHIVES AND RECORDS SERVICE. Records of the U.S. Nuernberg War Crimes Trials: NOKW Series, 1933-1947. Record Group 238. T1119. Microfilm, 47 rolls.

184 UNITED STATES. NATIONAL ARCHIVES AND RECORDS SERVICE. Records of the U.S. Nuernberg War Crimes Trials: NP Series, 1943-1946. Record Group 238. M942. Microfilm, 1 roll.

185 UNITED STATES. NATIONAL ARCHIVES AND RECORDS SERVICE. United States Trial Briefs and Document Books. Microfilm of records

described in NARS Preliminary Inventory 21. T991. Microfilm, 1 roll.

186 UNITED STATES. NATIONAL ARCHIVES AND RECORDS SERVICE. <u>U.S. Army Investigation and Trial Records of War Criminals: United States of America v. Jürgen Stroop, et al, March 29, 1945 - August 21, 1957</u>. M1095. Microfilm, 10 rolls. Washington: National Archives, 1982.

f. NARS. Preliminary Inventories

187 COLLIER, CLEVELAND E., et al (comps.). Preliminary Inventory. <u>Preliminary Inventory of the Seized Enemy Records in the Office of Military Archives</u>. Washington: NARS, 1965. 27p. Produced for staff use and not distributed as a National Archives publication. Documents described cover the period 1920-1945.

188 KIRCHMAN, CHARLES V., and GARRY D. RYAN (comps.). <u>Preliminary Inventory of the Textual Records of the International Military Tribunal for the Far East</u>. Record Group 238. NARS NM 62 1965. 5p. List of all IMTFE records in the holdings of the National Archives at Suitland, Maryland.

189 HALLEY, FRED G. (comp.). Preliminary Inventory No. 21, Record Group 238. <u>Preliminary Inventory of the Records of the United States Counsel for the Prosecution of Axis Criminality</u>. Washington: National Archives Publication 49-29, 1949. 182p. From Record Group 238: Records of the United States Counsel for the Prosecution of Axis Criminality. National Archives records described include photostats and processed documents, microfilm copies of documents, motion and still pictures, sound recordings, and various kinds of publications. The microfilms and exhibits include 930 American, 628 British, 1545 French, and 522 Soviet exhibits, American trial briefs, American documents, and Jodl documents. There are brief descriptions of 52 entries, each of which includes voluminous records, and 4 appendices. Identifies and in some cases describes in detail more than 3500 documents dealing with all aspects of German war crimes, the Nuremberg IMT trial, and related topics. The entries contain exhibit numbers, brief descriptions, the number of pages, the microfilm reel number, and microfilm frame numbers. No index.

190 HUFFORD, HAROLD E., and WATSON G. CAUDHILL (comps.). Preliminary Inventory No. 23, Record Group 46. <u>Preliminary Inventory of the Records of the United States Senate, 1789-1946</u>. Washington: NARS, 1950. 284p.

191 WOLFINGER, JARRITUS (comp.). Preliminary Inventory No. 180, Record Group 238. <u>Preliminary Inventory of the Records of the International Military Tribunal for the Far East</u>. Washington: NARS, 1975. 13p. The Introduction contains an historical synopsis of the IMTFE trial with a survey of various National Archives holdings of trial records. The appendix contains vitas of the 28. The following list covers most of the 22 annotated entries: (1) Minutes of the Proceedings, (2) Name and subject Index, (3) Name Index of Witnesses, (4) Transcript of Proceedings in Chambers, (5) the Court Journal, (6) Index to the Court Docket, (7) Name index to Witnesses in the Court Docket, (8) The Court Docket, (9) Court Papers, (10) Register of Court Exhibits, (11) List of Court Exhibits, (12) Court Exhibits, (13) List of Documents Rejected as Evidence by the Tribunal, (14) Rejected Exhibits, (15) Defense Documents, (16) Petitions Submitted to General Douglas MacArthur Requesting Review of the

Reference Section 49

Judgment and Sentences of the Tribunal, (17) Records Relating to General MacArthur's Review of the Judgment of the Tribunal, (18) Official Photographs, (19) Miscellaneous Records, and (20) Microfilm Copy of Selected IMTFE and IPS Records.

g. NARS. Record Groups

192 UNITED STATES. NATIONAL ARCHIVES AND RECORDS SERVICE. Record Group 59. General Records of the Department of States. <u>Records of the Department of State Special Interrogation Mission to Germany, 1945-1946</u>. M679. Microfilm, 3 rolls.

193 UNITED STATES. NATIONAL ARCHIVES AND RECORDS SERVICE. Record Group 107. Records of the Office of the Secretary of War. Records of the Office of the Assistant Secretary of War, 1917-1947. 60 linear feet. Some documents on war crimes are in the Modern Military Branch. Washington.

194 UNITED STATES. NATIONAL ARCHIVES AND RECORDS SERVICE. Record Group 111. Records of the Office of the Chief Signal Officer. Includes some films on war crimes trials in Germany and Japan

195 UNITED STATES. NATIONAL ARCHIVES AND RECORDS SERVICE. Record Group 153. Records of the Office of the Judge Advocate General (Army). Two files within this record group contain material on war crimes trials. The first, Records of the War Crimes Division, 1942-1951, 151 linear feet (in WNRC), contains case files for war crimes trials held by military commissions in Europe and the Mediterranean as well as trial records of the IMTFE. These include reports of Japanese atrocities in the Philippines and a law library file containing guides, handbooks, and other war crimes records. The second, Records of the International Affairs Division, 1943-1957, 336 linear feet, contains case files for investigations of war crimes trials held by military commissions in China, the Far East Command, and the European and Mediterranean theaters of operations, prisoner-of-war investigation reports, and case files of the Clemency and Parole Board for War Criminals. There are records on the Korean war which include historical reports of the War Crimes Division of the Judge Advocate Section in the Korean Communications Zone, case files for investigation of war crimes in Korea, and interrogation records of returned American prisoners following the prisoner exchange (Operation Big Switch) after the Korean armistice agreement.

196 UNITED STATES. NATIONAL ARCHIVES AND RECORDS SERVICE. Audiovisual Records, 1921-1949. Record Group 238. Contains 7108 items. Includes 5022 photographs of courtrooms, judges, prosecution and defense counsels, defendants, witnesses, and prisons connected with the Nuremberg IMT, U.S. military tribunals at Nuremberg, and the IMTFE. There are exhibits for the prosecution, consisting of photographs of the German destruction of the Warsaw ghetto, other German activities in Poland, and German activities at the Krupp works. Motion pictures (76 reels) used as evidence at the war crimes trials consist of films of concentration camps taken by American and Russian forces as they advanced through Germany. Also included are 2010 sound recordings, including the entire proceedings of the Nuremberg IMT.

197 UNITED STATES. NATIONAL ARCHIVES AND RECORDS SERVICE. National Archives Collection of World War II War Crimes Records. Record Group 238. This collection contains 1614 cubic feet of records

50   Reference Section

dating from 1900-1950. Most of them are on the 12 "subsequent" Nuremberg trials held under General Telford Taylor of the Office of the Chief Counsel for War Crimes and by the IMTFE in Tokyo. The major collections are described below, identified following their descriptive titles as (RG 238).

198 UNITED STATES. NATIONAL ARCHIVES AND RECORDS SERVICE. Records of the Advisory Board on Clemency for War Criminals, 1947-1950. Record Group 238. Contains 9 linear feet. This Board was established in the Office of the U.S. High Commissioner for Germany. The records include reports, correspondence, and petitions for clemency.

199 UNITED STATES. NATIONAL ARCHIVES AND RECORDS SERVICE. Records of the International Military Tribunal for the Far East, 1900-1948. Record Group 238. Contains 149 linear feet and 62 rolls of microfilm. Includes partially indexed transcripts of the proceedings, miscellaneous records, the court journal, indictments, motions, opinions, judgments, dissents, court exhibits, registers, rejected exhibits, defense documents, and a review of the sentences by General MacArthur.

200 UNITED STATES. NATIONAL ARCHIVES AND RECORDS SERVICE. Records of the Office of the Chief of Counsel for War Crimes, 1933-1949. Record Group 238. Contains 524 linear feet and 38 rolls of microfilm. Consists of correspondence and reports, interrogations, and other records of war crimes held by Allied military agencies. Executive Office records consist of administrative correspondence of the Publications Division, charts of German economic and political organizations (1933-1945), and records of the Nuremberg Military Post.

201 UNITED STATES. NATIONAL ARCHIVES AND RECORD SERVICE. Records of the Office of the U.S. Chief of Counsel for the Prosecution of Axis Criminality, 1933-1946. Record Group 238. Contains 401 linear feet and 107 rolls of microfilm. These records consist of documentary evidence and reference files, staff evidence analysis forms, transcripts of proceedings of the IMT, pretrial interrogations, U.S. trial briefs and document books (1945-1946), defense documents, American, Soviet, British, and French exhibits (1933-1946), transcripts of hearings in defense of organizations (May-August, 1946), and State Department dispatches (1933-1944). Also included are copies of the diaries of Hans Frank, kept while he was Governor General of Poland, partly on microfilm (1939-1945), those of Joseph Goebbels, also on microfilm (1942-1943), and microfilm copies (107 rolls) of the diaries and correspondence of General Alfred Jodl (1937-1945). There are the death books of the Mauthausen concentration camp (1939-1945), copies of the Four Power Agreement, the Charter of the IMT, opening addresses of Justice Jackson and the other three chief counsels, defense arguments, defendants' final pleas and statements, and judgments of the tribunal.

202 UNITED STATES. NATIONAL ARCHIVES AND RECORDS SERVICE. Records of the Office of the U.S. Commissioner, United Nations War Crimes Commission, 1943-1948. Record Group 238. Contains 6 linear feet. This 17-member Commission was established in London in October 1943 to prosecute Axis war criminals. It was dissolved in 1948. The records include minutes, reports, memoranda, correspondence, and issuances.

203 UNITED STATES. NATIONAL ARCHIVES AND RECORDS SERVICE. Records of Trials by U.S. Military Tribunals, Nuremberg ("Subsequent

Proceedings"), 1946-1949. Record Group 238. Contains 770 linear feet of transcripts and minutes in English and German of trial proceedings, prosecution and defense exhibits and documents, court records, lists of documents and witnesses, instructions, counsel statements and arguments, legal briefs, pleas, judgments, clemency petitions, administrative records, procedural correspondence, memoranda, reports, transcripts of executive and joint sessions, tribunal orders, correspondence relating to the 12 "subsequent" cases, daily bulletins of the Office of the Chief of Counsel for War Crimes, registers of transcripts of proceedings, and the documents and exhibits used as evidence.

204 UNITED STATES. NATIONAL ARCHIVES AND RECORDS SERVICE. Record Group 260. Records of the United States Occupation Headquarters, World War II. Records of the Office of Military Government for Germany (U.S.), 1944-1952. Contains 10,535 linear feet, 78 rolls of microfilm. Much on I.G. Farben and war crimes.

205 UNITED STATES. NATIONAL ARCHIVES AND RECORDS SERVICE. Record Group 331. Records of Allied Operational and Occupation Headquarters, World War II. Included in this record group are Records of General Headquarters, Supreme Commander for the Allied Powers (SCAP), 1945-1952, with a few dated as early as 1938. Contains 10,214 linear feet and 162 rolls of microfilm. Includes records of the Special International Prosecution Section (IPS), partly on 162 rolls of microfilm.

206 UNITED STATES. NATIONAL ARCHIVES AND RECORDS SERVICE. Record Group 338. Records of United States Army Commands, 1942-. Contains Judge Advocate Division war crimes correspondence and case files, 1945-1958, with indexes. Also included are records of War Criminal Prison No. 1 (Landsberg Prison), Munich District, Southern Area Command, consisting of personal name dossiers relating to the prosecution, execution, or release of war criminals.

h. NARS. Special Lists

207 MENDELSOHN, JOHN (comp.). Special List No. 38, Record Group 238. War Crimes Trials. Records of Case 2. United States of America vs. Erhard Milch, Nuernberg. Washington: NARS, 1975. 113p. Complete record of the trial, judgments, and documents. Appendix and index.

208 MENDELSOHN, JOHN (comp.). Special List No. 42, Record Group 238. War Crimes Trials. Records of Case 9. United States of America vs. Otto Ohlendorf, et al. Washington: NARS, 1978. 349p.

209 WOLFE, ROBERT (ed.). Captured German and Related Records: A National Archives Conference. Athens: Ohio University Press, 1974. 279p. A survey of the acquisition and organization of German documentary collections captured at the end of World War II and not deposited in the National Archives and other depositories. Contributors include several European archivists.

i. Naval War College

210 UNITED STATES. NAVAL WAR COLLEGE. International Law Documents, 1946-1947. Washington: GPO, 1948.

F. GENERAL WORKS ON ARCHIVES, LIBRARIES, AND OTHER DEPOSITORIES

1. France

211 BILLIG, JOSEPH (ed.). Alfred Rosenberg dans l'action idéologique, politique et administrative du Reich hitlérien; inventaire commenté de la collection de documents conservés en C.D.J.C. provenant des archives du Reichsleiter et ministre A. Rosenberg. Paris: CDJC, 1963.

212 MICHEL, H. "Les Principales Sources françaises de l'histoire de la Deuxième Guerre Mondiale," Revue Historique 1948 200(October-December): 206-219. A survey of French archives. Describes materials for studies of World War II, including records of war crimes.

213 WELSCH, ERWIN K. Libraries and Archives in France. New York: Council for European Studies, 1979. 146p.

2. Germany

214 BIBLIOTHEKSVERBAND DER DDR. Jahrbuch der Bibliotheken, Archive und Informationseinrichtungen der DDR. Leipzig: VEB Bibliographisches Institut, 1984. 385p. Various editions. In particular, see Volume 12, 1980-1982.

215 Dokumente und Materialien aus der Vorgeschichte des Zweiten Weltkrieges aus dem Archiv des Deutschen Auswärtigen Amtes 1937-38. Berlin: Ministerium für Auswärtige Angelegenheiten der UdSSR, [no date given].

216 "East Germany's Institute for Contemporary History," Wiener Library Bulletin 1954 8: 7.

217 GEBHARDT, WALTHER. (comp.). Spezialbestände in deutschen Bibliotheken. Bundesrepublik Deutschland einschl. Berlin (West). Berlin: Walter de Gruyter, 1977. 739p.

218 GENERALDIREKTION DER BAYERISCHEN STAATLICHEN BIBLIOTHEKEN. Handbuch der bayerischen Bibliotheken. Munich: K.G. Saur, 1983. 371p.

219 GIMBEL, JOHN. "The Origins of the 'Institut für Zeitgeschichte': Scholarship Politics and the American Occupation, 1945-1949," American Historical Review 1965 70(3): 714-731. The story of the background to the establishment of the Institute.

220 KAHN, DAVID. "Secrets of the Nazi Archives," Atlantic Monthly 1969 223(5): 50-56. A survey of the seizure of German official records at the end of World War II and their subsequent use by historians.

221 LULLIES, HILDEGARD. Verzeichnis der Bibliotheken in Berlin (West). Berlin: Heinz Spitzing, 1966. 301p.

222 PUCHNER, OTTO. „Der Bestand ‚Nürnberger Prozesse' im Staatsarchiv Nürnberg," Wehrwissenschaftliche Rundschau 1956 6(2): 93-97.

223 "The Arolsen Archives," Wiener Library Bulletin 1954 8: 31. A short description of services available.

224 VEREINIGUNG ÖSTERREICHISCHER BIBLIOTHEKARE (ed.). Handbuch österreichischer Bibliotheken. 2 volumes. Vienna: Österreichische Nationalbibliothek, 1961. Volume 1, 338p. Volume 2, 743p.

225 WELSCH, ERWIN K. (comp.). Libraries and Archives in Germany. Pittsburgh: Council for European Studies, 1975. 275p.

3. Great Britain

226 Keesing's Contemporary Archives. Volume 5. London: 1943-1946.

227 The Wiener Library: Its History and Activities, 1934-1945. London: Jewish Central Information Office, [1946]. 24p. Describes the foundation and growth of this library and its collection on Nazi Germany. Includes books, pamphlets, documents, newspaper clippings, and photographs.

4. Japan

228 UYEHARA, CECIL H. (comp.). Checklist of Archives in the Japanese Ministry of Foreign Affairs, Tokyo, Japan, 1868-1945: Microfilmed for the Library of Congress, 1949-1951. Washington: Library of Congress, Photoduplication Service, 1954.

229 YOUNG, JOHN (comp.). Checklist of Microfilm Reproductions of Selected Archives of the Japanese Army, Navy, and Other Government Agencies, 1868-1945. Washington: Georgetown University Press, 1959.

II
GENERAL WORKS AND SUBSIDIARY TOPICS

A. BACKGROUND WORKS

230 BERBER, FRIEDRICH [FRITZ] (ed.). Das Diktat von Versailles, Entstehung - Inhalt - Zerfall, eine Darstellung in Dokumenten. 3 volumes. Essen: Essener Verlagsanstalt [Deutsches Institut für Außenpolitik], 1939. General history in documents of the treaty of Versailles and German official reactions to it. Volume 2, pp. 1202-1220, deals with war guilt and war crimes.

231 EYCK, ERICH. Geschichte der Weimarer Republik. Erlenbach/Zurich: Eugen Rentsch, 1954-1962. 2 volumes. Published in English as A History of the Weimar Republic. Cambridge: Harvard University Press, 1962-1963. Volume 1 (492p.), Vom Zusammenbruch des Kaisertums bis zur Wahl Hindenburgs, discusses Germany's signing of the Treaty of Versailles with the stipulation that neither the acceptance of war guilt nor the obligation to extradite war criminals be binding. Deals with cases brought before the Supreme Court (Reichsgericht) on May 23, 1921, concerning the maltreatment of British prisoners of war and the sinking of a British hospital ship. 9 pages of notes, 8-page index of names. Volume 2 (624p.), Von der Konferenz von Locarno bis zu Hitlers Machtübernahme, does not deal specifically with war crimes. 15p. of notes, 11-page index.

232 GOERLITZ, WALTHER. Der deutsche Generalstab. Geschichte und Gestalt, 1657-1945. Frankfurt am Main: Verlag der Frankfurter Hefte, 1950. Published in English as History of the German General Staff, 1657-1945. New York: F.A. Praeger, 1953.

233 GORMAN, ROBERT N. "Military Courts and Military Government in Occupied Areas," Ohio Bar Association Report 1944 17(36): 479-486.

234 JACKSON, A.H. "Plundering in War and Other Depredations in Greek History from 800 B.C. to 146 B.C.," Ph.D. dissertation, Cambridge University, 1970.

235 LEMKIN, RAPHAEL. Axis Rule in Occupied Europe: Laws of Occupation, Analysis of Government, Proposals for Redress. Washington: Carnegie Endowment for International Peace, 1944. 674p. The texts of laws and decrees of the Axis Powers and of their

puppet regimes, issued for the governments of occupied territories and their military forces in Europe. Some chapters deal with the organization of the occupying powers of each country and the special measures adopted. Deals with war crimes and the Hague Conventions of 1899 and 1907.

236 LOEWENSTEIN, KARL. "Law and the Legislative Process in Occupied Germany. I," Yale Law Journal 1948 57(50; 724-760; "II," 57(6): 994-1022. 125 notes, 125 notes.

237 LOEWENSTEIN, KARL. "Reconstruction of the Administration of Justice in American-Occupied Germany," Harvard Law Review 1948 61(3): 419-467. 199 notes.

238 MASON, ALPHEUS THOMAS. "Extra-Judicial work for Judges: The Views of Chief Justice Stone," Harvard Law Review 1953 67(2): 193-216. Summarizes extra-judicial work that supreme court justices have been called upon to perform, and focuses upon the added burden placed upon the Supreme Court by Robert H. Jackson's leave of absence to serve as Chief American Prosecutor at Nuremberg. Chief Justice Harlan Stone's dislike for this use of judges was so strong that he refused to swear in Francis Biddle as a member of the panel of judges. Stone once referred to Jackson's duty on the war crimes tribunal as a "high grade lynching party in Nuremberg." Stone disapproved of non-judicial work; he objected on legal and political grounds to the trials in Nuremberg; and he resented the inconvenience and increased burden of work on the Supreme Court. Based on primary sources; 67 notes.

239 MAYER, S.L. (ed.). Signal: Hitler's Wartime Picture Magazine. London: Bison, 1976. Englewood Cliffs: Prentice-Hall, 1976. 188p. Contains a brief text with hundreds of pictures of all aspects of the European war. Short, illustrated treatment of the Katyn Woods massacre.

240 Militärstrafgesetzbuch in der Fassung vom 10. Oktober 1940-mit Einführungsgesetz und Kriegsstrafrechtsordnung. Berlin: Walter de Gruyter, 1943.

241 MOLTMANN, GÜNTER. Amerikas Deutschlandpolitik im zweiten Weltkrieg. Heidelberg: Winter, 1958.

242 MOLTMANN, GÜNTER. "Der Morgenthau Plan als historisches Problem," Wehrwissenschaftliche Rundschau 1955 5(1): 15-32. 49 notes.

243 MORGENTHAU, HENRY, JR. Germany Is Our Problem. New York: Harper and Brothers, 1945.

244 MOSLER, HERMANN. "Der Einfluß der Rechtsstellung Deutschlands auf die Kriegsverbrecherprozesse," Süddeutsche Juristen-Zeitung 1947 2(7): 362-370.

245 PAETZOLD, KURT O. Geschichte der NSDAP, 1920-45. Berlin (GDR): Deutscher Verlag der Wissenschaften, 1981. 429p.

246 RENAULT, LOUIS. "Dans Quelle Mesure le droit pénal peut-il s'appliquer à des faits de guerre contraires au droit des gens?" Revue Pénitentiaire de Droit Pénal 1915 42: 405-429.

247 RITTER, GERHARD. Karl Goerdeler und die deutsche Widerstandsbewegung. Stuttgart: Deutsche Verlags-Anstalt, 1954. Published

in English as *The German Resistance: Carl Goerdeler's Struggle against Tyranny*. New York: Praeger, 1959; London: G. Allen & Unwin, 1959. 330p. A history of the German resistance movements that seeks to avoid being a mere catalog of heroes by tracing the course of events against a background of international politics.

248 ROBIN, RAYMOND. *Des Occupations militaires en dehors des occupations de guerre*. Paris: 1913.

249 ROSENBERG, ALFRED. "Das Dritte Reich." Irregular pagination. This unpublished work is a rough, incomplete draft copy. Chapters do not appear in succession, with notes and outlines inserted throughout the manuscript. Book 1 is incomplete and Book 2 has been omitted entirely. Includes a mimeographed glossary of German terms. Footnotes to chapters appear occasionally. In Hoover Library.

250 ROSENMAN, SAMUEL I. *Working with Roosevelt*. New York: Harper and Row, 1952.

251 SCHNEIDER, HANS. "Das Ermächtigungsgesetz vom 24. März 1933," *Vierteljahrshefte für Zeitgeschichte* 1953 1(3): 197-221. Discusses Hitler's accession to power and how it was accomplished legally and constitutionally. 38 notes.

252 SHIRER, WILLIAM L. *A History of Nazi Germany: The Rise and Fall of the Third Reich*. New York: Simon and Schuster, 1960. 1245p. Published in German as *Aufstieg und Fall des Dritten Reiches*. Cologne/Berlin: Kiepenheuer & Witsch, 1961.

253 SNYDER, LOUIS LEO (ed.). *Hitler's Third Reich: A Documentary History*. Chicago: Nelson Halls, 1981.

254 STENZEL, ERNST. *Die Kriegsführung des deutschen Imperialismus und das Völkerrecht zur Planung und Vorbereitung des deutschen Imperialismus auf die barbarische Kriegsführung im Ersten und Zweiten Weltkrieg*. Berlin (GDR): Militärverlag der Deutschen Demokratischen Republik, 1973.

255 THOMAS, GEORG. *Geschichte der deutschen Wehr- und Rüstungswirtschaft (1918-1943/45)*. Boppard am Rhein: Harald Boldt, 1966.

256 TOYNBEE, ARNOLD J., and VERONICA TOYNBEE (eds.). *Hitler's Europe*. London/New York: Oxford University Press, 1954. 730p.

257 UNITED STATES. DEPARTMENT OF STATE. *Conference for the Conclusion and Signature of the Treaty of Peace with Japan*. State Department Publication No. 4392. Washington: GPO, 1951. 317p.

258 UNITED STATES. WAR DEPARTMENT. *The Statutory Criminal Law of Germany*. Pamphlet No. 31-122. Washington: War Department, 1946.

259 WEBER, WERNER, and WERNER JAHN. *Synopse zur Deutschlandpolitik: 1941-1973*. Göttingen: Schwartz, 1973. 107p.

260 WEGERER, ALFRED VON. *Die Widerlegung der Versailler Kriegsschuldthese*. Berlin: Reimar Hobbing, 1928. 237p. Published in English as *A Refutation of the Versailles War Guilt Thesis*. New York: Knopf, 1930. 386p. Critical of the "harmful" and "dangerous" Versailles precedent of assigning sole responsibility to one of the belligerents. Much useful background information on World War II and the thinking of Nazi leaders.

261 WULF, JOSEF. Die bildenden Künste im Dritten Reich. Gütersloh: Sigbert Mohn, 1963.

262 ZENTNER, KURT. Illustrierte Geschichte des Drittes Reiches. Munich: Südwest, 1965. 623p. Extensive pictorial history of the Third Reich. Covers the period leading up to the IMT trial at Nuremberg with only brief mention of the aftermath of World War II. 4-page chronology of events from 1918-1945, 6p. of biographical sketches of important people, 10-page index, 3-page bibliography, photographs, and facsimiles of documents.

263 ZIMMERMANN, LUDWIG. "Die Locarnoverträge als Versuch einer Lösung der Sicherheitsfrage," in Studien zur Geschichte der Weimarer Republik, Erlanger Forschungen. Series A, no. 6 Erlangen: Universitätsbund Erlangen, 1956.

B. PHILOSOPHICAL AND THEORETICAL WORKS

264 BOISSIER, PIERRE. "La Répression des 'petits' crimen de guerre," Revue Internationale de Droit Pénal 1948 19: 293-309. An examination of the procedures adopted by various European countries for the prosecution of so-called minor war criminals. It was necessary to abandon German law as the basis for the repression of war crimes. Three principles are examined: (1) The Anglo-Saxon procedure adopted by the United States, England, Denmark, the Netherlands, and Luxembourg, based largely on various Hague and Geneva conventions. (2) The French system, which deals with war crimes as a violation of French laws by a member of the enemy armed forces. (3) The Belgian law of June 20, 1947, which lay somewhere between the other two.

265 FREEMAN, ALWYN V. "War Crimes by Enemy Nationals Administering Justice in Occupied Territory," American Journal of International Law 1947 41(3): 579-610. The basic problem addressed is whether legislative and judicial action of a belligerent in violation of that part of the law of nations governing occupation of enemy territory constitutes a war crime on the part of civilian officials of the occupying state. Examines the legislative powers under the Hague Regulations, changes in judicial organization, and belligerent practices prior to World War I, during World War I, and during World War II. The major conclusion reached is that the action of a court rather than any alleged illegality in its inception should furnish the test of judicial criminality. Based on primary and secondary sources; 154 notes.

266 LAUTERPACHT, HERSCH. "The Subject of the law of Nations," Law Quarterly Review 1947 63(252): 438-460; 1948 64(253): 97-119. Following a technical discussion of the subject, particularly recent changes in substantive law, the author discusses the concept of crimes against humanity as developed at Nuremberg. 41 notes, 59 notes.

267 MOUTON, MARTINUS WILLEM. Oorlogsmisdrijven en het internationale recht. The Hague: A.A.M. Stols, 1947. 519p. Comprehensive historical and legal-theoretical treatment of the problem of war crimes and international law. Part 1 seeks to define war crimes. Part 2 is an historical survey of war crimes. Part 3 describes developments during World War II, particularly as a result of the work of the United Nations War Crimes Commission. Part 4 deals with the Nuremberg and Tokyo IMT trials. Special problems of international law are discussed in the remaining sections. The appendix contains a list of documents, books, and

articles. Reproduces the text of the Nuremberg IMT charter and other documents.

268 NISPEN TOT SEVENAER, CAREL MARIE OTTO VAN. L'Occupation allemande pendant la Dernière Guerre Mondiale. Considérations sur le caractère du pouvoir de la puissance occupante et de ses mesures selon les principes généraux du droit et selon la 4e convention de La Haye. The Hague: Martinus Nijhoff, 1946. 324p. Though this book does not address directly the problem of war crimes, it does discuss problems that came up in connection with war crimes trials and with German violations of the laws and conventions of warfare. 5-page bibliography, index.

269 RADIN, MAX. "International Crimes," Iowa Law Review 1946 32(1): 33-50. An essay on the historical development of the fundamental principles of criminals law in civilized countries. This development leads to the concept of international crime, defined as an attack on the world community. 13 notes.

270 UNITED NATIONS. Historical Survey of the Question of International Criminal Jurisdiction. Lake Success: United Nations, 1949.

271 WAKIN, MALHAM M. (ed.). War, Morality, and the Military Profession. Boulder, Colorado: Westview, 1979. 531p. Anthology of 31 essays. Those by General Telford Taylor on war crimes were taken from his Nuremberg and Vietnam: An American Tragedy. Undocumented; no bibliography, no index.

C. INTERNATIONAL LAW

272 BISHOP, WILLIAM W., JR. International Law, Cases and Materials. New York: Prentice-Hall, 1953.

273 BORCHARD, EDWIN M. "International Law and International Organization," American Journal of International Law 1947 41(1): 106-108.

274 BRIERLY, JAMES LESLIE. The Law of Nations: An Introduction to the International Law of Peace. Oxford: Clarendon, 1928. 6th edition. New York: Oxford University Press, 1963. 442p. Some remarks on the Nuremberg IMT and international law.

275 BRIGGS, HERBERT W. "New Dimensions in International Law," American Political Science Review 1952 46(3): 677-698. 79 notes.

276 "Criminal Justice," Revue Internationale de Droit Pénal 1925 2: 326-354; 1926 3: 492-515.

277 DONNEDIEU DE VABRES, HENRI. "La Codification du droit pénal international," Revue Internationale de Droit Pénal 1948 19: 21-35.

278 DUBOST, CHARLES. "Les Crimes des états et la coutume pénale internationale," Politique Étrangère 1946 11(6): 553-568.

279 ENGELSON, M. "L'Etablissement d'une paix durable par l'application d'un nouveau droit pénal international," Revue de Droit International de Sciences Diplomatiques et Politiques 1946 24 (2): 47-54; "Pour un Droit pénal international," Révue Internationale de Droit Pénal 1947 18: 208-214. Examines the role of international penal law in the establishment of a durable

peace. Purely legal solutions cannot bring peace; a proper social and economic order is necessary. 11 notes.

280 GUGGENHEIM, PAUL. "Der völkerrechtliche Schutz der Menschenrechte," Friedens-Warte 1949 49(4/5): 177-190. Surveys discussions of the problem of protecting human rights by international law, especially in connection with the United Nations and various war crimes trials. In the present state of the development of international law on this subject, it is advisable to determine a few general individual rights and leave to international and municipal jurisdictions more concrete and detailed norms.

281 HEFFTER, AUGUST W. Das europäische Völkerrecht der Gegenwart auf den bisherigen Grundlagen. 8th edition. Berlin: Schroeder, 1888. 505p.

282 HIGGINS, A. PEARCE, and C. JOHN COLOMBOS. The International Law of the Sea. 3rd edition. London: Longmans, Green, 1954.

283 KELSEN, HANS. Principles of International Law. New York: Rinehart, 1959.

284 KUNZ, JOSEF L. "The Problem of the Progressive Development of International Law," Iowa Law Review 1946 31(4): 544-560. 35 notes.

285 MOORE, WILLIAM HARRISON. The Act of State in English Law. London: J. Murray, 1906. 178p.

286 NORGAARD, CARL AAGE. The Position of the Individual in International Law. Copenhagen: Munksgaard, 1962.

287 PAPADATOS, PIERRE (PETER) A. Le Problème de l'ordre reçu droit pénal. Geneva: Droz, 1964. 175p. Part of the monograph series Travaux de droit, d'économie, de sociologie et de sciences politiques no. 27.

288 PHILLIPSON, COLEMAN. International Law and the Great War. London: T. Fisher Unwin, 1915. 407p.

289 REDLEY, ADOLPHUS G. "International Law at the Crossroads," South Atlantic Quarterly 1946 45(2): 165-175.

290 REEVES, JESSE S. "International Criminal Jurisdiction," American Society of International Law, Proceedings 1921 15: 62-69.

291 RIX, CARL B. "Human Rights and International Law," American Society of International Law, Proceedings 1949 43: 46-59. Undocumented.

292 ROXBURGH, RONALD F. "The Sanction of International Law," American Journal of International Law 1920 14: 26-37. 22 notes.

293 SARKER, LOTIKA. "The Proper Law of Crime in International Law," International and Comparative Law Quarterly 1962 11(April): 446-470. 101 notes.

294 SLOAN, F. BLAINE. "Comparative International and Municipal Law and Sanctions," Nebraska Law Review 1947 27(1): 1-29. Discusses the legality and effectiveness of civil and penal sanctions in international law. Suggests that sanctions be applied directly to individual offenders. 107 notes.

295 TOMBERG, VALENTIN. *Die Grundlagen des Völkerrechts als Menschheitsrecht*. Bonn: Schwippert, 1947. 195p.

D. INTERNATIONAL CRIMINAL COURT

296 BARCIKOWSKI, WACLAW. "Les Nations Unies et l'organisation de la répression des crimes de guerre," *Revue Internationale de Droit Pénal* 1946 17: 297-304. Discusses the need for an international penal code and court that would provide punishment for those guilty of preparing for war. Deals with the problems of structuring such a court and its relations to the United Nations.

297 BELLOT, HUGH HALE L. "A Permanent International Criminal Court," *International Law Association* 1922 1: 63-86.

298 BELLOT, HUGH HALE L. "Draft Statute for the Permanent International Criminal Court," *International Law Association*. Report of the Thirty-third Conference, September 8-13, 1924, in Stockholm. London: Sweet & Maxwell, 1925, pp. 75-111. Text of the draft statute, pp. 75-87. Discussion, pp. 87-111. Article 25 states that the jurisdiction of the court embraces all complaints or charges of violation of the laws and customs of war generally accepted as binding.

299 BELLOT, HUGH HALE L. "La Cour permanente internationale criminelle," *Revue Internationale de Droit Pénal* 1926 3: 333-337.

300 CALOYANNI, MÉGALOS A. "An International Criminal Court," *Transactions of the Grotius Society* 1928 14: 69-85.

301 CALOYANNI, MÉGALOS A. "Cour pénale internationale et code répressif des nations," *Revue de Droit International de Sciences Diplomatiques et Politiques* 1945 23: 219-227. 11 notes.

302 CALOYANNI, MÉGALOS A. "La cour criminelle internationale," *Revue Internationale de Droit Pénal* 1928 5: 261-264.

303 DONNEDIEU DE VABRES, HENRI. De l'Organisation d'une juridiction pénale internationale," *Revue Internationale de Droit Pénal* 1949 20: 1-8. Discusses the organization, competence, and functions of an international penal court. Stresses the need for establishing an international penal jurisdiction to prevent the inequities resulting from the conflict of national systems of law and to follow up the Nuremberg trials and derive from them the best possible results for justice and peace.

304 DONNEDIEU DE VABRES, HENRI. "La Cour permanente de justice internationale et sa vocation en matière criminelle," *Revue Internationale de Droit Pénal* 1924 1: 175-201.

305 FERENCZ, BENJAMIN B. *An International Criminal Court: A Step Toward World Peace - A Documentary History and Analysis*. 2 volumes. London: Oceana Publications, 1980. 538p. and 674p. Volume 1 deals with the road to war and the lessons of the 2 world wars. It contains a brief treatment of the IMTFE trial, footnotes, and more than 400 pages of documents. Volume 2 deals with genocide, an international criminal court, and the taking of hostages. It contains more than 500 pages of documents, an 18-page bibliography, and an 18-page index.

306 FINCH, GEORGE A. "Draft Statute of an International Criminal Court," *American Journal of International Law* 1952 46(1): 89-98. 15 notes.

307 LEVY, ALBERT G.D. "The Law and Procedure of War Crime Trials," American Political Science Review 1943 37(6): 1052-1081. Analyzes the failure of war crimes trials after World War I and discusses the Pact of Paris and its present significance. Traces the development of the movement for an international criminal court. Prefers this kind of court to an ad hoc military court. 78 notes.

308 LIANG, YUEN-LI. "The Establishment of an International Criminal Jurisdiction: The First Phase," American Journal of International Law 1952 46(1): 73-88. 71 notes.

309 PELLA, VESPASIEN V. "Draft for a Statute Establishing a Criminal Chamber on the Permanent Court of International Justice . . . . . Adopted by the International Association of Penal Law," Revue Internationale de Droit Pénal 1946 17: 230-248.

310 PELLA, VESPASIEN V. "Fonctions pacificatrices du droit pénal supranational et fin de système traditionnel des traités de paix," Revue Générale de Droit International Public 1947 51: 1-27. Historical survey of the new field of "supranational" penal law and a discussion of the establishment of an international criminal court or of a criminal chamber in the international court. An account of three different schools of thought on the subject of responsibility of states and individuals in international penal law.

311 PELLA, VESPASIEN V. La Guerre-crime et les criminels de guerre. Réflexions sur la justice pénale internationale, ce qu'elle est et ce qu'elle devrait être. Paris: A. Pedone, 1946. 208p. Advocates the codification of international penal law and the establishment of an international criminal court. Argues that the problems of war crimes and criminal (illegal) wars are the same and that only stable international institutions can ensure peace. Analyzes recent developments in international law, the work of the United Nations, and war crimes trials. Copious annotations.

312 PELLA, VESPASIEN V. "La Justice pénale internationale: Ce qu'elle est et ce qu'elle devrait être," Revue de Droit International de Sciences Diplomatiques et Politiques 1945 23(3): 84-139. An analysis of the London Agreement and the IMT Statute. Discusses the value of ad hoc justice versus the establishment of a permanent international criminal court, the problem of retroactivity in international penal law, and the penal responsibility of the state. Bibliographical footnotes. Heavily annotated.

313 PELLA, VESPASIEN V. "Plan for World Criminal Code," Revue Internationale de Droit Pénal 1946 17: 249-262. The plan was drawn up to serve as the basis for the work of the International Association of Penal Law, the Inter-Parliamentary Union, and the International Law Association.

314 PELLA, VESPASIEN V. "Towards an International Criminal Court," American Journal of International Law 1950 44(1): 37-68. Noting that the UN endorsed the principle of non-retroactivity in international criminal law, the author analyzes postwar developments in this law, particularly those associated with the Nuremberg and Tokyo IMT trials, in order to show the need for an international criminal court as a prerequisite to the codification of international criminal law. Comments on widespread skepticism regarding international criminal law and the danger

that the Nuremberg and Tokyo judgments would remain mere "pages of history" rather than precedents for change. 95 notes.

315 PHILLIMORE, WALTER G.P.F. "An International Criminal Court and the Resolutions of the Committee of Jurists," British Year Book of International Law 1922-1923 3: 79-86.

316 SOTTILE, ANTOINE. Les Criminels de guerre et le nouveau droit pénal international, seul moyen efficace pour assurer la paix du monde. Geneva: Independent Edition, 1946. 2nd edition. 47p. Pleads for a permanent international criminal court on the grounds that war is still the normal, and peace the abnormal, condition of mankind and that the only hope for the survival of civilization lies in the threat of criminal responsibility for the perpetrators of armed conflicts. Undocumented.

317 SOTTILE, ANTOINE. "The Problem of the Creation of a Permanent International Criminal Court," Revue de Droit International de Sciences Diplomatiques et Politiques 1951 29(4): 267-359. 91 notes.

318 UNITED NATIONS. COMMITTEE OF INTERNATIONAL CRIMINAL JURISDICTION, Draft Statute for an International Criminal Court, Report to the General Assembly on the Session held 1 August - 31 August 1951, with Annex I,A/AC48/4, 5 September 1951.

319 WEIS, GEORGE. "International Criminal Justice in Time of Peace," Transactions of the Grotius Society 1942 28: 27-63. A plan for an international criminal court and for the creation of a substantive criminal law for the protection of the peace. Discusses crimes against peace and common law, criminal law and international conventions, the Spa convention, and the movement for the creation of an international criminal law.

320 WRIGHT, QUINCY. "Proposal for an International Criminal Court," American Journal of International Law 1952 46(1): 60-72.

E. INTERNATIONAL CONFERENCES AND CONVENTIONS

321 COMMISSION ON THE RESPONSIBILITY OF THE AUTHORS OF WAR AND ON ENFORCEMENT OF PENALTIES. "Report," American Journal of International Law 1920 14(1): 95-154. Concludes that the war was premeditated by the Central Powers.

322 COWLES, WILLARD B. "The Dakin Index to the Proceedings of the Brussels Conference of 1874," American Journal of International Law 1949 43(3): 546-547.

323 FEIS, HERBERT. Between War and Peace: The Potsdam Conference. Princeton: Princeton University Press, [1960]. 367p. Published in German as Zwischen Krieg und Frieden. Das Potsdammer Abkommen. Frankfurt am Main: Athenäum, 1962. 381p.

324 FENWICK, CHARLES G. "The Implications of Consultation in the Pact of Paris," American Journal of International Law 1932 26(4): 787-789.

325 FORSYTHE, DAVID P. "The 1974 Diplomatic Conference on Humanitarian Law: Some Observations," American Journal of International Law 1975 69(1): 77-91. The 1974 Diplomatic Conference on the Reaffirmation and Development of International Humanitarian Law Applicable in Armed Conflicts is seen as a significant attempt to create new law for the protection of victims of

wars. The Conference failed to take action on extensive proposals by the International Committee of the Red Cross (ICRC) that were designed to supplement the Geneva Conventions of 1959. The reason why so little progress was made was the failure to adjust the ICRC approach to questions raised in recent UN debates. The author believes that this failure reflects the clash of the UN approach, backed by communist countries, and the ICRC approach, backed by most of the West. 32 notes.

326 FRANCE. MINISTRY OF FOREIGN AFFAIRS. Rapports et procès-verbaux d'enquête de la commission instituée en vue de constater les actes commis par l'ennemi en violation du droit des gens (décret du 23 septembre 1914). 9 volumes. Paris: 1915. Also published in 12 volumes, Paris: 1915-1919. The first report was issued separately as Le Libre rouge, and in English as German Atrocities in France. London: J. Causton & Sons, 1916. 46p.

327 MAHAN, ALFRED THAYER. "The Peace Conference and the Moral Aspects of War," North American Review 1899 149(October): 433-447.

328 MECHELYNCK, ALBERT (ed.). La Convention de la Haye concernant les lois et coutumes de la guerre sur terre, d'après les actes et documents des conférences de Bruxelles de 1874 et de La Haye de 1899 et 1907. Ghent: A. Hoste, 1915.

329 PARIS PEACE CONFERENCE. Report, Commission on Responsibility of the authors of the War and on Enforcement of Penalties. Oxford: Clarendon Press, 1919. London/New York: H. Milford, 1919. 82p. Carnegie Endowment for International Peace, Division of International Law, Pamphlet 32. Reprinted, without tables, in American Journal of International Law 1920 14 (1): 95-114. Discussed in Current History Magazine 1920 11(2): 380-384. Deals with the violation of the laws and customs of war. Reports on majority and dissenting opinions of American and Japanese members of the Commission of Responsibilities, Conference of Paris, 1919.

330 PICTET, JEAN S. "The New Geneva Conventions for the Protection of War Victims," American Journal of International Law 1951 45(3): 462-475. 15 notes.

331 SCHWELB, EGON. "The United Nations War Crimes Commission," British Year Book of International Law 1946 23: 363-376. Deals with the establishment of the Commission, legal statutes and organization, the original functions of the Commission, the examination of cases, the production of the lists of people accused of war crimes, the advisory functions of the Commission, and legal publications.

332 STONE, R. "The American-German Conference on Prisoners of War," American Journal of International Law 1919 13: 406-449.

333 UNITED NATIONS. COMMITTEE FOR THE PROGRESSIVE DEVELOPMENT OF INTERNATIONAL LAW AND ITS CODIFICATION. Disposition of Agenda Items and Check List of Documents. Doc. A/AC.10/57. 25 July 1947; Draft Proposal to Define the Principles Recognized in the Charter of the Nuremberg Tribunal and in the Judgment of the Tribunal and Draft Proposal for the Establishment of an International Court of Criminal Jurisdiction: Memorandum Submitted by the Delegate for France. Doc. A/AC.1021, 15 May 1949; Memorandum of the Subject of Genocide and Crimes against Humanity:

Submitted by the Representative of France. Doc. A/AC.10/29, 19 May 1947; Draft Texts Relating to the Principles of the Charter and Judgment of the Nuremberg Tribunal: Memorandum by the Delegate for France. Doc. A/AC.10/34, 27 May 1947; Proposals of the Delegation of Poland. Doc. A/AC.10/38. 2 June 1947; Draft Convention for the Prevention and Punishment of Genocide: Prepared by the Secretariat. Doc. A/AC.10/42, 6 June 1947; Draft Resolution of the Draft Convention on Genocide: Presented by the Delegation of the U.K. Doc. A/AC10/44, 6 June 1947; Report of the Committee on the Plans for the Formulation of the principles of the Nuremberg Charter and Judgment. Doc. A/AC.10/52, 17 June 1947; Letter from the Chairman of the Committee to the Secretary-General on the Draft Convention on Genocide. Doc. A/AC.10/55, 18 June 1947. Lake Success: United Nations, 1947.

334 UNITED NATIONS. GENERAL ASSEMBLY. Resolution 217A (III): Universal Declaration of Human Rights. Adopted at the 183rd plenary meeting, December 10, 1948. Official Records of the Third Session of the General Assembly, Part I, September 21 to December 12, 1948. Resolutions. Paris: 1948. pp. 71-77. Reprinted in International Organization 1949 3: 202-206.

335 UNITED NATIONS. INTERNATIONAL LAW COMMISSION. International Law Commission. Supplement No. 10 (A/925), No. 12 (A/1316), Lake Success: United Nations, 1949, 1950.

336 UNITED NATIONS. INTERNATIONAL LAW COMMISSION (1ST SESSION). Summary Records of Meetings. Docs. A/CN.4/SR.1-37, April 12 - June 9, 1949. Lake Success: United Nations, 1949.

337 WORLD VETERANS FEDERATION. International Conference on the later Effects of Imprisonment and Deportation. The Hague: November 20-25, 1961. 189p. With the participation of the government of the Netherlands, the International Committee of the Red Cross, . . . and the World Council for the Welfare of the Blind.

F. LAWS OF WAR

338 ADLER, GERALD J. "Targets in War: Legal Considerations," Houston Law Review 1970 8(1): 1-46. 251 notes.

339 AMOS, SHELDON. Political and Legal Remedies for War. London: Cassell, Petter, Galpin, 1880. 364p.

340 ARMOUT, W.S. "Customs of War in Ancient India," Transactions of the Grotius Society 1922 8: 71-88.

341 BALLIS, WILLIAM B. The Legal Position of War: Changes in its Practice and Theory from Plato to Vattel. The Hague: Nijhoff, 1937.

342 BASSIOUNI, M.C. "War Power and the Law of War," De Paul Law Review 1968 18(1): 188-201.

343 BAXTER, RICHARD R. "So-called 'Unprivileged Belligerency': Spies, Guerrillas, and Saboteurs," British Year Book of International Law 1951 28: 232-345.

344 BENTWICH, NORMAN. The Law of War in International Law. "Looking Forward." Pamphlet No. 2. London: Royal Institute of International Affairs, 1945.

345 BOISSIER, PIERRE. Völkerrecht und Militärbefehl. Ein Beitrag zur Frage der Verhütung und Bestrafung von Kriegsverbrechen. Stuttgart: K.F. Koehler, 1953. 162p.

346 BOWER, GRAHAM J. "The Law of War: Prisoners and Reprisals," Transactions of the Grotius Society 1915 1: 23-37.

347 BRAND, CLARENCE. Roman Military Law. Austin: University of Texas Press, 1968. 226p.

348 CASTRÉN, ERIK. The Present Law of War and Neutrality. Helsinki: Annales Academiae Scientiarum Fennicae, 1954. 630p. Contains brief remarks on the Nuremberg IMT.

349 COHEN, MARSHALL. "Taylor's Conception of the Laws of War," Yale Law Journal 1971 80(7): 1492-1500. 35 notes.

350 "Commission of Jurists to Consider and Report upon the Revision of the Rules of Warfare, General Report," American Journal of International Law, Supplement 1938 32(1): 1-56. General Report, The Hague, February 19, 1923. A general study of the rules of warfare.

351 DOWNEY, WILLIAM G., JR. "Revision of the Rules of Warfare," American Society of International Law, Proceedings 1949 43: 102-114.

352 DOWNEY, WILLIAM G., JR. "The Law of War and Military Necessity," American Journal of International Law 1953 47(2): 251-262. Touches on the Nuremberg IMT and the Yamashita trial in its discussion of the doctrine of military necessity. 39 notes.

353 DUNBAR, N.C.H. "Act of State and the Law of War," Juridical Review 1963 75: 246-273. 66 notes.

354 DUNBAR, N.C.H. "Maxim nullum crimen sine lege in Law of War," Juridical Review 1959 71: 176-196. 50 notes.

355 DUNBAR, N.C.H. "The Significance of Military Necessity in the Law of War," Juridical Review 1955 67(2): 201-212. 44 notes.

356 EDMUNDS, STERLING E. "The Laws of War: Their Rise in the Nineteenth Century and Their Collapse in the Twentieth," Virginia Law Review 1929 15(4): 321-349. 44 notes.

357 EDWARDS, CHARLES SCHAAR. "Law of War in the Thought of Hugo Grotius," Journal of Public Law 1970 19(2): 371-397. 70 notes.

358 FRIEDMAN, LEON. The Law of War: A Documentary History. 2 volumes. New York: Random House, 1972. 1764p.

359 FRIEDMANN, WOLFGANG. "International Law and the Present War," Transactions of the Grotius Society 1940 26: 221-233. Argues that most of the laws of warfare exist only on paper and that international law cannot survive without there being a power to enforce it.

360 GARCÍA-MORA, MANUEL R. "International Law and the Law of Hostile Military Expeditions," Fordham Law Review 1958 27(3): 309-331. 155 notes.

361 GARNER, JAMES W. International Law and the World War. 2 volumes. London: Longmans, Green, 1920.

362 GARNER, JAMES W. The German War Code: A Comparison of the German Manual of the Law of War with Those of the United States, Great Britain and France. Urbana: University of Illinois, 1918.

363 GRABER, DORIS APPEL. The Development of the Law of Belligerent Occupation. New York: Columbia University Press, 1949. 343p.

364 GREENSPAN, MORRIS. The Modern Law of Land Warfare. Berkeley: University of California Press, 1959. 724p.

365 HERSHEY, AMOS S. "The History of International Relations During Antiquity and the Middle Ages: International Law Impossible before the Rise of the Modern European State System," American Journal of International Law 1911 5(4): 901-933. Much on the treatment of prisoners of war and others unable to fight back and on the use of concealed weapons. 93 notes.

366 INTER-AMERICAN JURIDICAL COMMITTEE. Report on the International Juridical Status of Individuals as "War Criminals." Washington: Pan American Union, 1945. 15p. Rio de Janeiro: Inter-American Juridical Committee, 1945.

367 IVRAKIS, SOLON CLÉANTHES. Soviet Concepts of International Law, Criminal Law and Criminal Procedure at the International Conference on Military Trials. London: 1945. Cambridge, Massachusetts: 1950. 59p.

368 JACKSON, ROBERT H. "War Criminals and International Law: Judicial Proceedings Must Not Be Tied to Predetermined Policy," Saturday Review of Literature 1945 28(June 2): 7-8.

369 JENNINGS, W. IVOR. "The Rule of Law in Total War," Yale Law Journal 1941 50(3): 365-386. 3 notes.

370 KEEN, MAURICE H. The Laws of War in the Late Middle Ages. Toronto: University of Toronto Press. 1965.

371 KELLY, JOSEPH B. "A Legal Analysis of the Changes in War," Military Law Review 1961 13(July): 89-119.

372 KOROVIN, EUGENE A. "The Second World War and International Law," American Journal of International Law 1946 40(4): 742-755. The author was Professor of International Law at the University of Moscow and the Juridical Institute of the Ministry of Justice. An apology that sees the Soviet Union as the world's leading defender of oppressed peoples. According to the writer, the USSR contributed more to the destruction of Fascism than did any other country. The focus is upon recognition of national resistance movements in France, Yugoslavia, and Poland. Argues that absolute sovereignty of a state does not justify rampant nationalism. His examples of major postwar successes in democracy are Bulgaria, Rumania, Yugoslavia, Hungary, and Poland. Concludes that aggression is an international crime and that neutrality becomes a form of connivance. Undocumented.

373 KUNZ, JOSEF L. "The Chaotic Status of the Laws of War and the Urgent Necessity for their Revision," American Journal of International Law 1951 45(1): 37-61. 68 notes.

374 LACHS, MANFRED. "The Unwritten Laws of Warfare," Tulane Law Review 1945 20(1): 120-128. Shows how the unwritten laws of

warfare have been perverted in order to justify unlawful practices. Argues that the laws of warfare should be further codified and brought up to date. 16 notes.

375 LAUTERPACHT, HERSCH. "Rules of Warfare in an Unlawful War," in George A. Lipsky (ed.). Law and Politics in the World Community. Berkeley and Los Angeles: University of California Press, 1953.

376 MARIN, MIGUEL A. "The Evolution and Present Status of the Laws of War," Recueil des Cours 1957 92 (2): 629-754. 5-page bibliography.

377 MC CONNELL, JOHN R. "Can Law Impede Aggressive War?" American Bar Association Journal 1964 50(2): 131-135. Undocumented.

378 MILLER, RICHARD I. "Far Beyond Nuremberg: Steps toward International Criminal Jurisdiction," Kentucky Law Journal 1973 61: 925-930. 24 notes.

379 MOORE, JOHN NORTON. "Ratification of the Geneva Protocol on Gas and Bacterial Warfare," University of Virginia Law Review 1972 58(3): 420-509. 240 notes.

380 NURICK, LESTER, and ROGER W. BARRETT. "Legality of Guerrilla Forces under the Laws of War," American Journal of International Law 1946 40(3): 563-583. Surveys international law as laid down in various international agreements. There are some references to German practices during World War II. Concedes that it is difficult to determine when a disintegrating government still speaks for troops in the field. There is a reluctance to try as war criminals a large group of soldiers who continue to fight for reasons of patriotism. Examines cases from World War II in Europe and Asia, the Mexican War, the Philippine Insurrection, and the South African War. Based on primary and secondary sources, 91 notes.

381 NUSSBAUM, ARTHUR. "Just War - A Legal Concept?" Michigan Law Review 1943 42(3): 453-479. Detailed discussion of the concept of "just war" in the history of legal and political thought. Concludes that the concept is unacceptable from a legal point of view. The traditional doctrine of a "just war" is essentially religious. 136 notes.

382 PAGET, REGINALD T. „Soldat und Recht," Wehrwissenschaftliche Rundschau 1952 2(2): 41-50.

383 PARSONS, GEORGE R., JR. "International Law: Jurisdiction over Extraterritorial Crime: Universality Principle: War Crimes: Crime against Humanity: Piracy, Israel's Nazi and Nazi Collaborators (Punishment) Law," Cornell Law Quarterly 1961 46(2): 326-336.

384 PHILLIPS, C.P. "Air Warfare and Law: An Analysis of the Legal Doctrines and Policies," George Washington Law Review 1953 21(3): 311-335; (4): 395-422. Much on the Nuremberg IMT trial. 51 notes, 112 notes.

385 PHILLIPSON, COLEMAN. International Law and the Great War. London: T. Fisher Unwin, 1915. 407p. General history that deals systematically with German war crimes.

386 PROBST, H. Die Kriegsgefangenen nach modernem Völkerrecht. Munich: Wild, 1911.

387 "Project of an International Declaration Concerning the Laws and Customs of War, Adopted by the Conference of Brussels, August 27, 1874," American Journal of International Law 1907 1(Supplement): 96-103.

388 RENAULT, LOUIS. "De l'Application du droit pénal aux faits de guerre," Revue Générale de Droit International Public 1918 25(3): 5-29.

389 RÓHEIM, GÉZA. War, Crime and the Covenant. Monticello, New York: Medical Journal Press, 1945.

390 RÖLING, BERNARD V.A. "The Laws of War and the National Jurisdiction since 1945," Recueil de Cours 1960 100(2): 323-456.

391 SALDAÑA Y GARCIA RUBIO, QUINTILIANO, "La Justice pénal internationale," Recueil des Cours 1925 10(5): 227-429.

392 SCHENK, REINHOLD. Seekrieg und Völkerrecht. Die Maßnahmen der deutschen Seekriegsführung im 2. Weltkrieg in ihrer völkerrechtlichen Bedeutung. Cologne: Heymann, 1958.

393 SCHICK, FRANZ B. "International Criminal Law - Facts and Illusions," Modern Law Review 1948 11(3): 290-305. Attempts to create international criminal responsibility for political offenses and other acts of state. Concludes that before creating an international criminal law such as that enunciated at Nuremberg, it would be necessary to accept the principle of compulsory jurisdiction of an international court or agency over states in their disputes with one another. 82 notes.

394 SCHMID, JÜRG H. Die völkerrechtliche Stellung der Partisanen im Kriege. Zurich: Polygraphischer, 1956. 196p. Excellent general history of various underground and partisan movements in Europe, with much on measures of repression and war crimes. Copiously annotated; 5-page bibliography, 2-page list of documents.

395 SCHWARZENBERGER, GEORG. International Law and Totalitarian Lawlessness. London: Jonathan Cape, 1943. 162p. The first chapter discusses how the Nazis abused international law to further their aims. The next chapter defends the policies of the United States in the early part of the war. Chapter 3 analyses war crimes from the point of view of international customary and conventional law. Chapter 4 presents the author's thesis that only the presence of international law can deal with totalitarian lawlessness. Contains 9 appendices which deal with trials of war criminals before the German supreme court (the Leipzig trials), and German announcements in connection with the murder of Reinhard Heydrich. 51-page documentary appendix.

396 SPIROPOULOS, JEAN. "Draft Code of Offences against the Peace and Security of Mankind. Report of the International Law Commission," Revue Hellénique de Droit International 1950 3: 141-198.

397 STÖDTER, ROLF. Deutschlands Rechtslage. Hamburg: Rechts- und Staatswissenschaftlicher Verlag, 1948. 291p. Germany continues as a "person" in international law and Allied occupation is belligerent occupation. Defines the authority of the Allied

General Works 69

powers as territorial authority subject to international law and discusses occupation measures, many of which are in conflict with various Hague Conventions.

398 STONE, JULIUS. Legal Controls of International Conflict: Treaties on the Dynamics of Disputes and War-law. New York: Rinehart, 1959 edition. 903p.

399 STOWELL, ELLERY C. "Military Reprisals and the Sanctions of the Laws of War," American Journal of International Law 1942 36(4): 643-650. Discusses the value of specific provisions of the rules of warfare, showing that observance is generally to the advantage of both contestants. Some references to German occupation policies. 6 notes.

400 STRISOWER, LEO. Der Krieg und die Völkerrechtsordnung. Vienna: Manz, 1919.

401 SZURLEJ, S. "Nullum Crimen sine Lege," Studies in Polish and Comparative Law. London: Stevens, 1945. pp. 20-43.

402 TAYLOR, TELFORD. "The Concept of Justice and the Laws of War," Columbia Journal of Transnational Law 1974 13(2): 189-207.

403 THARP, PAUL A., JR. "The Laws of War as a Potential Legal Regime for the Control of Terrorist Activities," Journal of International Affairs 1978 32(1): 91-100. Recommends regulating terrorists by the laws of war. The complex traditions of extradition reveal problems in dealing with terrorists by treaties or by the concept of international crime as proposed by the United States. Although the compromise proposed by the Council of Europe is promising, the war crimes framework does not rely on criminal laws. It protects insurgents as well as the public.

404 UNITED NATIONS. INTERNATIONAL LAW COMMISSION (2ND SESSION). Draft Code of Offences against the Peace and Security of Mankind, Report by Spiropoulos. Document A/CN.4/25, April 26, 1950. Lake Success: United Nations, 1950.

405 UNITED STATES. CONGRESS. SENATE. Amelioration of the Condition of Wounded in Armies: Message from the President of the United States, Transmitting an Authenticated Copy of Convention Signed at Geneva on July 6, 1906. 59th Congress, 2nd Session. Washington: GPO, 1906.

406 UNITED STATES. DEPARTMENT OF THE AIR FORCE. Treaties Governing Land Warfare. AFP 110-1-3. Washington: GPO, 1958.

407 UNITED STATES. DEPARTMENT OF THE ARMY. The Law of Land Warfare: Department of the Army Field Manual F 27-10. Washington: GPO, 1956.

408 UNITED STATES. WAR DEPARTMENT. Rules of Land Warfare. Document No. 467. Washington: GPO, 1917.

409 UNITED STATES. WAR DEPARTMENT. Rules of Land Warfare . . .. Washington: GPO, 1940. 123p. (FM 27-10). Deals among other things with penalties for violating the laws of war.

410 UNITED STATES. WAR DEPARTMENT. Treaties Governing Land Warfare: Technical Manual TM-27-251. Washington: War Department, 1944.

411 VAN DYKE, JON M. "The Laws of War: Can They Ever Be Enforced?" Center Magazine 1971 4(July-August): 21-33.

412 WALTZOG, ALFONS. Recht der Landkriegsführung. Die wichtigsten Abkommen des Landkriegsrechts. Berlin: F. Vahlen, 1942.

413 WEHBERG, HANS. Das Beuterecht im Land- und Seekriege. Tübingen: J.C.B. Mohr, 1909. 135p. Published in English as Capture in War on Land and Sea. London: P.S. King and Son, 1911. 210p.

414 WILSON, GEORGE G. "The Guerilla and the Lawful Combatant," American Journal of International Law 1943 37(3): 494-495.

415 WINTHROP, WILLIAM W. Military Law and Precedents. 2d edition. Washington: GPO, 1920.

416 WRIGHT, QUINCY. "The Concept of Aggression in International Law," American Journal of International Law 1935 29(34): 373-395. 58 notes.

417 WRIGHT, QUINCY. The Role of International Law in the Elimination of War. Manchester: Manchester University Press, 1961.

418 WRIGHT, QUINCY. "The Status of Germany and the Peace Proclamation," American Journal of International Law 1952 46 (2): 299-308. Argues that after May 1945 Germany enacted legislation with the purpose of modifying the basic political, economic, and social structure of the country. Examines the question of whether international law permits the temporary exercise of sovereignty in conquered territories. Contains a few comments and various footnotes on the proposition that the United States did not maintain proper neutrality before war with Germany broke out. 28 notes.

G. SUPERIOR ORDERS AND MILITARY NECESSITY

419 AVINS, ALFRED. "Military Leadership and the Law," California Law Review 1959 47(5): 828-871. 176 notes.

420 BERGER, JACOB. "The Legal Nature of War Crimes and the Problem of Superior Command," American Political Science Review 1944 38(6): 1203-1208. Faced with the dangers inherent in admitting the defense of superior orders in war crimes trials, the author points to a way out of this difficulty by examining the similarity between war crimes and espionage trials. He elaborates on Paragraph 203 of the U.S. Rules of Land Warfare (1940). Discusses similarities between war crimes trials and espionage trials and the differences in defense.

421 BROWN, A.W. "Military Orders as a Defense in Civil Courts," Journal of the American Institute of Criminal Law and Criminology 1917 8(2): 190-210. 16 notes.

422 CORK, LORD. "Obedience to Lawful Commands," Journal of the Royal United Services Institution 1951 96(May): 258-262.

423 COSTE-FLORET, PAUL. "La Répression des crimes et le fait justificatif tiré de l'ordre supérieur," Recueil Dalloz 1945 1(278): 21-22.

424 DANIEL, AUBREY M., III. "The Defense of Superior Orders," University of Richmond Law Review 1973 7(3): 477-509. 69 notes.

425 DAUBE, DAVID. *The Defense of Superior Orders in Roman Law*. Oxford: Clarendon Press, 1956. 24p.

426 DE GIULIO, ANTHONY P. "Command Control: Lawful versus Unlawful Application," *San Diego Law Review* 1972 10(1): 72-107. 167 notes.

427 DINSTEIN, YORAM. *The Defence of "Obedience to Superior Orders" in International Law*. Leyden: A.W. Sijthoff, 1965. 278p. Treats the Leipzig trials and various aspects of the defense of superior orders in justification of the acts of individual soldiers. Reviews international law from 1919 to 1945 and repudiates the superior orders argument. Part 4 discusses the Nuremberg and Tokyo IMT trials as well as various national trials. 9-page bibliography, 11-page subject index, 2-page index of names.

428 DUKE, MARVIN L. "A Plea of Superior Orders," *Marine Corps Gazette* 1971 55(3): 34-39. Discusses war crimes in the Napoleonic wars, the American Civil War, World War II, and the war in Vietnam. Examines various national articles of war and the charter of the International Military Tribunal, and attempts to define war crimes. Undocumented.

429 DUNBAR, N.C.H. "Military Necessity in War Crimes Trials," *British Year Book of International Law* 1952 29: 442-452. 5 notes.

430 DUNBAR, N.C.H. "Some Aspects of the Problem of Superior Orders in the Law of War," *Juridical Review* 1951 63(3): 234-261. Published in French as "Quelques aspects du problème de l'obéissance aux ordres supérieurs en temps de guerre," *Le Droit au Service de la Paix* 1957 1: 24-47. 72 notes.

431 EHRENZWEIG, A. "Soldiers Liability for Wrongs committed on Duty under American and International Law," *Cornell Law Quarterly* 1944 30(2): 179-217. 224 notes.

432 FAULKNER, STANLEY. "War Crimes: Responsibilities of Individual Servicemen and of Superior Officers," *National Lawyers Guild Practitioner* 1974 31(3-4): 131-144. Undocumented.

433 FINCH, GEORGE A. "Superior Orders and War Crimes," *American Journal of International Law* 1921 15: 440-445. Deals with the acquittal of Karl Neumann, commander of a ship which sank the British hospital ship *Dover Castle*. Based on primary and secondary sources; 6 notes.

434 FUHRMANN, PETER. *Der höhere Befehl als Rechtfertigung im Völkerrecht*. Munich: A. Schubert, 1960; Berlin: C.H. Beck, 1963. 134p.

435 GREEN, L.C. "Superior Orders and the Reasonable Soldier," *Canadian Yearbook of International Law* 1970 8: 61-103. 121 notes.

436 GRENFELL, RUSSELL. "The Question of Superior Orders," *Journal of the Royal United Services Institution* 1951 96(May): 263-266.

437 HUGHES-MORGAN, SIR DAVID. "Disobedience to a Lawful Command," *Military Review* 1977 57(11): 69-75. Discusses the consequences of obedience to an unlawful military command. Present international law holds that obedience to an order does not necessarily excuse a person who has committed a war crime. English law has similar provisions, but under both systems of law the

question arises whether the soldier must be aware the order is illegal before he incurs criminal liability in obeying it. Concludes that the people who have been tried in the past for war crimes were the really serious offenders, and that a soldier must obey an order unless he is positive that it is illegal.

438 LEWY, GUENTER. "Superior Orders, Nuclear Warfare, and the Dictates of Conscience: The Dilemma of Military Obedience in the Atomic Age," American Political Science Review 1961 55(1): 3-23.

439 MILGRAM, STANLEY. Obedience to Orders. New York: Harper and Row, 1974.

440 MÜLLER-RAPPARD, EKKEHART. L'Ordre supérieur militaire et la responsabilité pénale du subordonné. Paris: A. Pedone, 1965. 281p.

441 PASTON, DAVID G. Superior Orders as Affecting Responsibility for War Crimes. New York: H.G. Publishing, 1946. 31p. The author was a colonel on the Judge Advocate General's staff during and after the war. He rejects the argument of superior orders, supporting his position by interrogation reports of Mauthausen camp officials and from the records of the Lienhart case before the Salzburg Military Tribunal.

442 POLLOCK, FREDERICK. "The Work of the League of Nations," Law Quarterly Review 1919 35(138): 193-198. Discusses criminal responsibility in the defense of superior orders. 1 note.

443 REDISH, MARTIN. "Military Law - Nuremberg Rule of Superior Oders - United States Court Martial Tribunal Admits Evidence of United States War Crimes in Vietnam in Support of Superior Orders of Defense," Harvard International Law Journal 1968 9(1): 169-181. 43 notes.

444 SACK, ALEXANDER N. "Punishment of War Criminals and the Defence of Superior Orders," Law Quarterly Review 1944 60(237): 63-68. Undocumented.

445 SACK, ALEXANDER N. "War Criminals and the Defense of Superior Order in International Law," Lawyers Guild Review 1945 5(1): 11-17. Traces the historical development of the concept, and shows that the so-called "Oppenheimer Rule" is not and never has been international law. Compares war crimes to piracy. 40 notes.

446 SIEGERT, KARL. Repressalie, Requisition und höherer Befehl. Ein Beitrag zur Rechtfertigung der Kriegsverurteilten. Göttingen: Göttinger Verlagsanstalt, 1953. 52p.

447 SMITH, H.A. "The Defence of Superior Orders," Journal of the Royal United Services Institution 1951 96(November): 617-619.

448 TALERICO, ANTHONY, JR. "Operation Justice," United States Naval Institute Proceedings. 1947 73(5): 509-521. Undocumented; 2 photographs.

449 TAUBENSCHLAG, RAFAEL [RAPHAEL]. "The Plea of Superior Orders, a Discussion of the Trial of War Criminals," New Europe 1945 5(2-3): 23-25.

450 UHLIG, HEINRICH. "Der verbrecherische Befehl," Das Parlament. Supplement B XXVII. Bonn: 1957.

451 VOLGER, T. "Zum Einwand des ,Handelns auf Befehl' im Völkerstrafrecht," Revue de Droit Pénal Militaire et de Droit de la Guerre 1968 7: 111-129.

452 WALTHER, HANS RUDOLF. "Das Problem des Handelns auf Befehl im Lichte der Nürnberger Prozesse," Doctor of Laws dissertation, Heidelberg University, 1950.

453 WEBER, HELLMUTH VON. "Die strafrechtliche Verantwortlichkeit für Handeln auf Befehl," Monatsschrift für Deutsches Recht 1948 2(February): 34-42.

454 WILNER, ALAN M. "Superior Orders as a Defense to Violations of International Criminal Law," Maryland Law Review 1966 26(2): 127-142. 76 notes.

455 WÜRTENBERGER, THOMAS. "Der Irrtum über die Völkerrechtsmäßigkeit des höheren Befehls im Strafrecht," Monatsschrift für Deutsches Recht 1948 2(September): 271-273. Deals with errors in regard to the lawfulness of acting on superior orders according to international law and the relation of this concept to penal law.

H. PRISONERS OF WAR

456 DATNER, SZYMON. Crimes Against POW'S. Responsibility of the Wehrmacht. Warsaw: Zachodnia Agencja Prasowa, 1964.

457 DILLON, J.V. "The Genesis of the 1949 Convention Relative to the Treatment of Prisoners of War," Miami Law Quarterly 1950 5(1): 40-63. 52 notes.

458 DUNN, J. HOWARD, and W. Hays Parks. "If I become a Prisoner of War," United States Naval Institute Proceedings 1976 102 (8/882): 18-27. The code of conduct for American soldiers taken as prisoners of war was an outgrowth of the Korean POW experience. This assessment of that code reveals that it has not stopped American soldiers from cooperating with the enemy. The articles of the code are discussed and assessed. Undocumented.

459 ESGAIN, ALBERT J., and WALDEMAR A. SOLF. "The 1949 Geneva Convention Relative to the Treatment of Prisoners of War: Its Principles, Innovations, and Deficiencies," North Carolina Law Review 1963 41: 537-596. 216 notes.

460 FEILCHENFELD, ERNST HERMANN. Prisoners of War. Washington: Georgetown University, School of Foreign Service, Institute of World Polity, 1948. 98p. A study of the legal status of prisoners of war by members of the Institute of World Polity, most of whom had been prisoners of war. Calls for a revision of Article 72 of the Geneva Convention and points out that unless war crimes trials are taken seriously by governments no convention would be taken seriously in the future. Topics covered include treatment of prisoners of war, war crimes, forced labor, atrocities, and reprisals.

461 FLORY, WILLIAM E.S. Prisoners of War: A Study in the Development of International Law. Washington: American Council of Public Affairs, 1942. 179p. Originally a Ph.D. dissertation, Duke University, 1941.

74 General Works

462 GARRETT, RICHARD. P.O.W. Newton Abbot: [Devon], 1981. 249p.

463 GLASER, STEFAN. "La Protection internationale des prisonniers de guerre et la responsabilité pour les crimes de guerre," Revue de Droit Pénal et de Criminologie 1951 31(May): 897-927.

464 HYDE, CHARLES C. "Concerning Prisoners of War," American Journal of International Law 1916 10(4): 600-602. On the Hague regulations of 1907.

465 "International Law - Prisoners of War - Criminal Responsibility." Canadian Bar Review 1945 23(5): 451-452. 3 notes.

466 JAWORSKI, LEON. "Military Trials of Prisoners of War," Texas Bar Journal 1944 7(8): 310-311, 330-332. Undocumented.

467 KELLY, JOSEPH B. "PW's as War Criminals," Military Review 1972 52(1): 91-96. Eleven Communist nations, including North Vietnam, appended a reservation to the United Nations prisoner of war convention of 1949, which allowed North Vietnam to treat American prisoners as war criminals, thus denying them international legal protection. The reasoning behind this policy is not considered valid by international lawyers, but little can be done to prevent the North Vietnamese from interpreting the code as they see fit. The term war criminal has been used increasingly since World War II, and has been expanded in meaning to include large numbers of enlisted men. The North Vietnamese consider anyone in opposition to them automatically guilty of "crimes against humanity." Discusses Nazi war crimes, the issue of war criminals, crimes against peace, and crimes against humanity. Based on government documents and private sources; 9 notes, 2 photographs.

468 KUNZ, JOSEF L. "Treatment of Prisoners of War," American Society of International Law, Proceedings 1953 47: 99-111.

469 KURTHA, AZIZ NOOMI. Prisoners of War and War Crimes. Karachi: Pakistan Herald Press, 1973. 177p. Contains the texts of the 1949 Geneva Convention and the Nuremberg IMT judgment, with commentary.

470 KURTHA, AZIZ NOOMI. "Prisoners of War, War Crimes, and the Geneva Conventions," Pakistan Horizon 1972 25 (1): 98-102. Relates the Geneva Conventions of 1949 to the 1971 war between India and Pakistan concerning the repatriation of sick and wounded prisoners and war crimes trials. Article 109 of the Convention requires that sick and wounded prisoners be repatriated as soon as they are fit to travel. India, after five months, had repatriated only a few prisoners. Based on a talk at a meeting of the Pakistan Institute of International Affairs, February 29, 1972. Undocumented.

471 LEVIE, HOWARD S. "Penal Sanctions for Maltreatment of Prisoners of War," American Journal of International Law 1962 56(2): 433-468. A general study, with much on mistreatment of prisoners of war by Germans during World War II. 139 notes.

472 LEWIS, GEORGE G., and JOHN MEWHA. History of Prisoner of War Utilization by the United States Army, 1776-1945. Washington: GPO, 1956. 278p.

473 MASCHKE, ERICH (ed.). Zur Geschichte der deutschen Kriegsgefangenen des Zweiten Weltkrieges. 22 volumes. Munich/Bielefeld: Ernst and Werner Gieseking, 1962-1974.

474 MASON, JOHN B. "German Prisoners of War in the United States," American Journal of International Law 1945 39(2): 198-215. 38 notes.

475 MASON, W. WYNNE. Prisoners of War. London: Oxford University Press, 1954.

476 "Massacre of the Prisoners. Illustrated," Newsweek 1950 36(August 28): 25.

477 MC GINNESS, JOHN R. "An International Bill of Rights for Prisoners of War," Cleveland-Marshall Law Review 1953 2(3): 158-165. 9 notes.

478 MOJONNY, GERARDO LUIGI. The Labor of Prisoners of War in Modern Times: An Appreciation on the Cause and the Effect of the German Conventions. Locarno: 1955.

479 "Question of Atrocities Committed by the North Korean and Chinese Communist Forces against United Nations' Prisoners of War in Korea," International Organization 1954 8(February): 70-72.

480 REITLINGER, GERALD. "The Truth about Hitler's 'Commissar Order,'" Commentary 1959 28(1): 7-18. 48 notes.

481 "Repressalien gegen Kriegsgefangene," Spruchgerichte 1948 1(March): 70-71.

482 SMITH, DELBERT D. "The Geneva Prisoner of War Convention: An Appraisal," New York University Law Review 1967 42(5): 880-914. 135 notes.

483 STREIM, ALFRED. Die Behandlung sowjetischer Kriegsgefangenen in "Fall Barbarossa:" eine Dokumentation unter Berücksichtigung der Unterlagen deutscher Strafverfolgungsbehörden und der Materialien der Zentralen Stelle der Landesjustizverwaltungen zur Aufklärung von NS-Verbrechen. Heidelberg/Karlsruhe: Müller, Juristischer Verlag, 1981. 442p.

484 STREIT, CHRISTIAN. Keine Kameraden. Die Wehrmacht und die sowjetischen Kriegsgefangenen 1941-1945. Stuttgart: Deutsche Verlags-Anstalt, 1978. 445p. A revision of the author's thesis, Heidelberg, 1977, which was presented under the title "Die sowjetischen Kriegsgefangenen als Opfer des nationalsozialistischen Vernichtungskrieges 1941-1945."

485 "The Employment of Prisoners of War in Germany," International Labour Review 1943 48(3): 316-323. 13 notes.

486 TROFIMENKO, G. Ich war in Deutschland gefangen. Zurich: Verlag der Partei der Arbeit, 1945. 85p. Written by a Soviet officer in a German "slave labor" camp.

487 UNITED NATIONS. GENERAL ASSEMBLY. Question of Atrocities Committed by the North Korean and Chinese Communist Forces against United Nations' Prisoners of War in Korea. General Assembly Resolution 804 (VIII) adopted December 3, 1953.

488 UNITED STATES. WAR DEPARTMENT. Enemy Prisoners of War. GPO, 1944. Army Technical Manual TM 19-500.

489 WERNER, GEORGES. "Les Prisonniers de guerre," Recueil des Cours 1928 21(1): 1-107. Heavily annotated.

490 WESTERMAN, GEORGE F. "International Law Protects PW's," Army Information Digest 1967 2(February): 32-39.

I. HOSTAGES

491 ANDLER, CHARLES PHILIPPE THÉODORE. "Frightfulness" in Theory and Practice as Compared with Franco-British War Usages. London: T.F. Unwin, 1916. 181p. Original is in French.

492 ARSENIJEVIC, DRAGO. Otages volontaires des SS. Paris: France-Empire, 1974. 363p.

493 ASCARELLI, ATTILIO. Le Fosse Ardeatine. Rome: Palombi, 1945. Rome: Canesi, 1965. 204p. Deals with German murder of hostages in Rome.

494 BRUNGS, BERNARD JOSEPH. "Hostages, Prisoner Reprisals, and Collective Penalties: The Development of International Law of War with Respect to Collective and Vicarious Punishment." 3 volumes. Ph.D. dissertation, Georgetown University, 1968. Abstracted in Dissertation Abstracts International 1969 29(7): 2774-A - 2775-A.

495 CRELINSTEN, RONALD D., and DENIS SZABO. Hostage-Taking. Lexington, Massachusetts: D.C. Heath, 1979. 160p. General treatment of hostage-taking, based on an international and interdisciplinary seminar held in Santa Margherita, Italy, in May 1970.

496 FATTIG, RICHARD C. "Reprisal: The German Army and the Execution of Hostages during the Second World War," Ph.D. dissertation, University of California at San Diego, 1980. 283p. Abstracted in Dissertation Abstracts International 1981 41(10): 4473-A.

497 Geisel- und Partisanentötungen im Zweiten Weltkrieg. Hinweise zur rechtlichen Beurteilung. Ludwigsburg: Zentrale der Landesjustizverwaltungen, 1968. 135p.

498 GINSBURGS, GEORGE. "Laws of War and War Crimes on the Russian Front during World War II: The Soviet View," Soviet Studies 1960 11(3): 253-285.

499 HAMMER, ELLEN, and MARINA SALVIN. "The Taking of Hostages in Theory and Practice," American Journal of International Law 1944 38(1): 20-33. A brief historical survey of the practice of hostage taking, followed by an analysis of various manuals of warfare and of the writings of international lawyers on the subject. The last part is an analysis of the German practice of hostage-taking during World War II. Much on other German atrocities. 82 notes.

500 KATZ, ROBERT. Death in Rome. London: Cape, 1967. 324p. Also published as Black Sabbath. A Journey through a Crime against Humanity. Toronto: Macmillan, 1969. Deals with hostages.

501 KUHN, ARTHUR K. "The Execution of Hostages," American Journal of International Law 1942 36(2): 271-274. Recommends that

severe punishment be meted out to those who ordered or carried out executions of civilians or hostages. 14 notes.

502 MELEN, ALEXANDER-CZESLAW. "La Question des otages à la lumière du droit," Revue de Droit International de Sciences Diplomatiques et Politiques 1946 24(1): 17-25. This article traces the history of hostage taking from ancient times and concludes that no one should be deprived of liberty and life except for a violation of the laws for which he is personally responsible. 24 notes.

503 NISPEN TOT SEVENAER, CAREL MARIE OTTO VAN. La Prise d'otages, examen de la licéite des pratiques modernes d'après le droit objectif et le droit des gens positif. The Hague: Martinus Nijhoff, 1949. 159p. Surveys the practice of hostage taking and shows the deterioration of the moral standards of law in this context. Discusses the provisions of army manuals on the taking of hostages. Defends the judgment of the American military court at Nuremberg.

504 PILLOUD, CLAUDE. "The Question of Hostages and the Geneva Conventions," Revue internationale de la Croix-Rouge [English Supplement] 1951 4(1393): 187-201.

505 UNITED NATIONS INFORMATION ORGANIZATION [OFFICE]. The Axis System of Hostages. London: HMSO, 1942.

506 UNITED STATES. DEPARTMENT OF STATE. "Execution of Hostages by the Nazis: Statement by the President," Department of State Bulletin 1941 5(122): 317. October 25, 1941. Contains warnings of retribution.

507 UNITED STATES. LIBRARY OF CONGRESS. Legislative Reference Service. Treatment of War Hostages and International Law. Washington: Library of Congress, 1942.

508 WRIGHT OF DURLEY, LORD. "The Killing of Hostages as a War Crime," British Year Book of International Law 1948 25: 296-310. A discussion of the German practice of killing hostages during World War II and international law relating to it. Discusses a number of legal precedents and specific trials. Concludes that the killing of hostages is contrary to the laws of war and is, therefore, murder.

509 YANG, LIEU-SHENG. "Hostages in Chinese History," Harvard Journal of Asiatic Studies 1952 15(December): 507-509.

J. GUILT AND PERSONAL RESPONSIBILITY FOR WAR CRIMES

510 ANGELL, ERNEST. "Sovereign Immunity - the Modern Trend,' Yale Law Journal 1925 35 (2): 150-168. 63 notes.

511 BARTLETT, C.A. HERESHOFF. "Liability for Official War Crimes," Law Quarterly Review 1919 35(April): 177-192. Undocumented.

512 BOOHAR, CHARLES W., JR. "Honorable Discharge: A Farewell to Responsibility for War Crimes," William and Mary Law Quarterly 1971 12(4): 878-894.

513 CARNEGIE ENDOWMENT FOR INTERNATIONAL PEACE. Report of the Commission on Responsibilities. Pamphlet No. 32. Oxford: Clarendon Press, 1919.

514 CHKHIKVADZE, V. "International Law Problems Bearing on the Responsibility of War Criminals," *International Affairs* 1972 (3): 49-56. The Nuremberg IMT trial established and confirmed the modern conception of international criminal law and prosecution by outlining the duty of countries to prosecute crimes encroaching on the principles of peace, freedom of nations, and basic human rights, providing definitions of such crimes, and by providing a precedent for the prosecution of war criminals. The principles established at Nuremberg led to the International Commission of Inquiry into American war crimes in Vietnam. Discusses eastern block adoption of legislative measures against war crimes and condemns statutory limitations on war crimes. Based largely on IMT records and United Nations Document A-7342. 15 notes.

515 COCKERHAM, WILLIAM C., and LAURENCE E. COHEN. "Obedience to Orders: Issues of Morality and Legality in Combat Among U.S. Army Paratroopers," *Social Forces* 1980 58(4): 1272-1288. Examines the attitudes of Army paratroopers on morality, legality, and compliance with orders from superiors. The soldiers agreed on questions regarding moral and legal conduct in combat. Those who were favorably disposed toward the army felt that all soldiers should participate in war regardless of their views on whether it was a just war. In general, those soldiers most committed to the military are more likely to obey commands, regardless of morality. Concludes that there is a good chance that the soldiers would act in a manner consistent with their attitudes when engaged in combat. Discusses the concept of an all volunteer army and the potential for another My Lai incident to occur. 4 notes. Bibliography.

516 COHEN, MARSHALL, THOMAS NAGEL, and THOMAS SCANLON (comps.). *War and Moral Responsibility*. Princeton: Princeton University Press, 1974. 182p.

517 DONNEDIEU DE VABRES, HENRI. "Les Limites de la responsabilité de personnes morales," *Revue Internationale de Droit Pénal* 1950 21: 339-351.

518 DURAND, CH. "La responsabilité internationale des états pour déni de justice," *Revue Générale de Droit International Public* 1931 38: 694-748. 37 notes.

519 FALK, RICHARD A. "Ecocide, Genocide, and the Nuremberg Tradition of Individual Responsibility," in Virginia Held, Sidney Morgenbesser, and Thomas Nagel (eds.), *Philosophy, Morality, and International Affairs*. New York: Oxford University Press, 1974.

520 FALK, RICHARD A. "War Crimes: The Circle of Responsibility," *Nation* 1970 210(3): 77-82.

521 FALK, RICHARD A., GABRIEL KOLKO, and ROBERT JAY LIFTON (eds.). *Crimes of War, a Legal, Political-Documentary, and Psychological Inquiry into the Responsibility of Leaders, Citizens, and Soldiers for Criminal Acts in Wars*. New York: Random House, 1971. 590p. Investigation into criminal aspects of the war in Vietnam. Discusses the declaration of St. Petersburg in 1868, the Hague Convention of 1907, the Versailles treaty of 1918, provisions of the Geneva Conventions on the Law of War in 1949, and the Genocide Convention of 1949. Reprints the Moscow Declaration on German atrocities, 1943; a statement by President Franklin Roosevelt on German war crimes, 1944; and the opening

statement at Nuremberg by Chief U.S. Prosecutor Robert H. Jackson, 1945. Discusses the Nuremberg judgment, the judgment in the Tokyo IMT trial, and the decision in the Eichmann case. Focuses on the Vietnam era, especially the My Lai massacre. 2-page bibliography, 12-page index.

522 FARRIN, A. "The Responsibility for Nazi Crimes," from War and the Working Class Information Bulletin 1943 111(October 2): 5-7, and Central European Observer 1943 20(18): 281-282.

523 FRANCE. MINISTRY OF WAR. Examen de la responsabilité pénale de l'Empereur Guillaume II. Paris: Imprimerie nationale, 1918. 26p.

524 FREEMAN, ALWYN V. "Responsibility of States for Unlawful Acts of their Armed Forces," Recueil des Cours 1955 88: 267-415.

525 FRIED, HANS ERNST [JOHN ERNEST]. The Guilt of the German Army. New York: Macmillan, 1942. 426p. Ph.D dissertation, Columbia University, 1942. Argues that the German army, with its guiding Prussian militarism, must share responsibility for the war and its excesses.

526 GARCÍA-MORA, MANUEL R. International Responsibility for Hostile Acts of Private Persons against Foreign States. The Hague: Nijhoff, 1962.

527 GIEBULTOWICZ, JÓZEF. [The responsibility of war criminals in the light of international law]. Warsaw: Spoldzielnia Wydawnicza "Czytelnik," 1945. 102p. Original is in Polish.

528 GLASER, STEFAN. "Culpabilité en droit international pénal," Recueil des Cours 1960 99: 467-593.

529 GLASER, STEFAN. "L'Acte d'état et le problème de la responsabilité individuelle," Revue de Droit Pénal et de Criminologie 1950 31: 1-17.

530 GLASER, STEFAN. "La Responsabilité de l'individu devant le droit international," Schweizerische Zeitschrift für Strafrecht 1949 64: 283-314.

531 GLASER, STEFAN. "Responsabilité pour la participation à une guerre-crime: Les soldats qui y prennent part encourent-ils une responsabilité pénale?" Revue de Science Criminelle et de Droit Pénal Comparé 1969 24(3): 593-622. Heavily annotated.

532 GÓMEZ GRAJALES, OCTAVIO. Los crímenes de guerra y la responsibilidad de los jefes de Estado. Mexico City: UNAM, 1947. 97p.

533 HALL, JEROME. "Nulla Poena sine Lege," Yale Law Journal 1937 47(2): 165-193. 93 notes.

534 HART, HERBERT L.A. Punishment and Responsibility: Essays in the Philosophy of Law. Oxford: Clarendon Press, 1968. 271p.

535 HERMES, FERDINAND A. "Collective Guilt," Notre Dame Lawyer 1948 23(4): 431-455. 40 notes.

536 HESSLER, CURT A. "Command Responsibility for War Crimes," Yale Law Journal 1973 82(6): 1274-1304. 85 notes.

537 HOSSBACH, FRIEDERICK. *Von der militärischen Verantwortlichkeit in der Zeit vor dem Zweiten Weltkriege*. Göttingen: Selbstverlag, 1948. 32p.

538 HOWARD, KENNETH A. "Command Responsibility for War Crimes," *Journal of Public Law* 1972 21(1): 7-22.

539 JESCHECK, HANS-HEINRICH. *Die Verantwortlichkeit der Staatsorgane nach Völkerstrafrecht. Eine Studie zu den Nürnberger Prozessen*. Volume 6. Bonn: Ludwig Röhrscheid, 1952. 420p.

540 KELSEN, HANS. "Collective and Individual Responsibility for Acts of State in International Law," *Jewish Yearbook of International Law* 1948 1: 226-239.

541 KELSEN, HANS. "Collective and Individual Responsibility in International Law with Particular Regard to the Punishment of War Criminals," *California Law Review* 1943 31(5): 530-571. A complete discussion of the problem, with specific suggestions for handling the punishment of war criminals. This punishment should be carried out by an impartial international organization to which both victors and vanquished would submit themselves. International law should be reformed to provide for the collective responsibility of states for the violation of international law by their agents. 45 notes.

542 KELSEN, HANS. *Peace Through Law*. Chapel Hill: University of North Carolina Press, 1944. 155p. Discusses individual responsibility under international law, punishment of offenses against that law, international criminal jurisdiction, and war guilt in both world wars. Undocumented; index.

543 KOMAROW, GARY. "Individual Responsibility under International Law: The Nuremberg Principles in Domestic Legal Systems," *International and Comparative Law Quarterly* 1980 29(1): 21-37.

544 KUNZ, JOSEF L. "*Bellum Justum et Bellum Legale*," *American Journal of International Law* 1951 45(3): 528-534. 16 notes.

545 LANDAU, A., and CZ. WASILKOWSKI. "The Responsibility for War Crimes in Polish Law," *Demokratyczny Przeglad Prawniczy* 1946 2(11-12): 27-37.

546 LEVY, ALBERT G.D. "Criminal Responsibility of Individuals and International Law," *University of Chicago Law Review* 1945 12(4): 313-332. Discusses the historical development of criminal responsibility in legal thought from Augustine to the present. Considers war crimes and the feasibility of inaugurating a world criminal law and court. 44 notes.

547 LÜDERS, KARL-HEINZ. „Zum Nürnberger Urteil. Strafgerichtsbarkeit über Angehörige des Feindstaats," *Süddeutsche Juristen-Zeitung* 1946 1(11/12): 216-218. According to German arguments, crimes under international law could not be committed by individuals, only by states. Since World War I, however, German courts have adopted the position of various international lawyers that members of a defeated nation may be tried by the victorious nation. This has led to the development of an international customary law. Author praises the Nuremberg judges for objectivity.

548 MÉRIGNHAC, ALEXANDRE G.J.A. "De la Responsabilité pénale des actes criminels commis au cours de la guerre 1914-1918," Revue de Droit International et de Législation Comparée 1920 1: 34-70.

549 PARKS, WILLIAM H. "Command Responsibility for War Crimes," Military Law Review 1973 62(Fall): 1-104.

550 PEPPERS, DONALD ALAN. "War Crimes and Induction: A Case for Selective Non-Conscientious Objection," Philosophy & Public Affairs 1974 3(2): 129-166. Describes the 4 classes of war crimes charged at Nuremberg IMT and the 3 traditional defenses: acts of state, superior orders, and duress. Attempts to develop a practical and credible legal philosophy that will support an argument against induction. An individual must contend that war crimes occur regularly in any war, that his being drafted would lead to his being ordered to commit war crimes, and that if he disobeyed such an order he could be prosecuted. The military laws of most nations state that a soldier has a positive duty not to commit war crimes, yet he can be punished for disobedience to orders. Examples are drawn for the Vietnam war to illustrate the arguments and principles presented.

551 PICCIOTTO, CYRIL M. "War Crimes," American Legal News 1916 2: 17-18. A discussion of the responsibility of states.

552 POLJOKAN, I. Les Responsabilités pour les crimes et délits de guerre. Paris: Jouve, 1923.

553 QUENEUDEC, JEAN PIERRE. La Responsabilité internationale de l'état pour les fautes personnelles de ses agents. Paris: Libr. Gen. de droit et de jurisprud., 1966. 277p. This is Volume 32 of Bibliothèque de Droit International.

554 ROUX, J.A. "A Propos des personnes morales. La Responsabilité pénal collectivités," Revue de Droit International de Sciences Diplomatiques et Politiques 1948 26(1): 38-52. Traces the concept of "legal person" in French law and its relation to modern penal law. 14 notes.

555 SACK, ALEXANDER N. "War Criminals and the Defense of Act of State in International Law," Lawyers Guild Review 1945 5(5): 288-300. Argues that individuals can be held personally liable for acts of state. Analyzes legal precedent to show that there is no written catalog of criminal "acts of state" and no pre-established plan for their punishment. Nor is there any reason for leaving such criminal acts unpunished or for having the accused "disposed of" without a judicial hearing. 134 notes.

556 SCHNEEBERGER, ERNST. "The Responsibility of the Individual under International Law," Georgetown Law Journal 1947 35(4): 481-489. 30 notes.

557 TALLOW, ADAMIN A. Command Responsibility: Its Legal Aspect. Manila: 1965. 472p. Originally a Ph.D. dissertation submitted to the University of Santo Tomas in the Philippines in 1958. A detailed study of command responsibility in connection with war crimes, particularly the responsibility a military officer has in maintaining strict discipline among his men. Discusses the nature of war crimes and war criminals, jurisdiction over war criminals, and command responsibilities as applied by war crimes tribunals in Nuremberg, Tokyo, and Manila. Includes the

dissenting opinions of Justice Pal and 2 others, the judgment in the Yamashita case, and the judgment of the Tokyo tribunal.

558 THORNEYCRAFT, E. *Personal Responsibility and the Law of Nations*. Leiden: Nijhoff, 1963.

559 WALD, GEORGE. "Corporate Responsibility for War Crimes," *New York Review of Books*, July 2, 1970: 4-6.

560 WASSERSTROM, RICHARD. "The Responsibility of the Individual for War Crimes," in Virginia Held, Sidney Morgenbesser, and Thomas Nagel (eds.). *Philosophy, Morality, and International Affairs: Essays edited for the Society for Philosophy and Public Affairs*. London: Oxford University Press. 1974.

561 WHARTON, J.F. "Germany: A Problem in Global Penology," *Saturday Review of Literature* 1945 28(July 28): 7-10.

562 WINNER, PERCY. "German Road Back: Inquiry into Guilt, Punishment and Expiation," *New Republic* 1945 112(23): 778-781.

K. RENUNCIATION OF WAR

563 BAILEY, SYDNEY D. *Prohibitions and Restraints in War*. London: Oxford University Press, 1972. 194p. Much on the theory and philosophy of war and criminal acts in war. Topics covered include just wars in international law, human rights in armed conflicts, various United Nations declarations on war, and reprints of the "Nuremberg principles." 6-page index.

564 BORCHARD, EDWIN M. "The Multilateral Treaty for the Renunciation of War," *American Journal of International Law* 1929 23(1): 116-120. Summarizes arguments on both sides of the issue.

565 LANSING, ROBERT L. "The Fallacy of 'Outlaw War,'" *Independent* 1924 113(August 16): 95-96.

566 SHOTWELL, JAMES T. *War as an Instrument of National Policy and its Renunciation at the Pact of Paris*. New York: Harcourt, Brace, 1929.

567 WHEELER-BENNETT, JOHN W. *Information on the Renunciation of War, 1927-1928*. London: George Allen and Unwin, 1928.

568 WRIGHT, QUINCY. "The Outlawry of War and the Law of War," *American Journal of International Law* 1953 47(3): 365-376. The first modern codification of the law of war, made during the American Civil War, applied primarily to civil strife. Discusses the Middle Age distinction between just and unjust wars and shows how this distinction applies to modern thinking between wars of aggression and wars of defense. Any law that is continually violated will lose its force. This is true as well of laws against war. Examines eight changes the outlawry of war has made in the law of war and its application. The Nuremberg finding that the claim that one must answer only to national law is not a defense against violating international law. Concludes that a clear understanding of the rules may deter aggression or suppress it when it appears. Based on primary and secondary sources; 42 notes.

L. GENERAL WORKS ON WAR CRIMES TRIALS

569 BRAND, G. "The War Crimes Trials and the Laws of War," British Year Book of International Law 1949 26: 414-427. 89 notes.

570 COWLES, WILLARD B. "Trial of War Criminals by Military Tribunals," American Bar Association Journal 1944 30(June): 330-333, 362.

571 EAGLETON, CLYDE. "A Plan for War Guilt Trials, Changing World 1943 15(7): 3.

572 GLUECK, SHELDON. "Trial and Punishment of the Axis War Criminals," Free World 1942 4(November): 138-146.

573 "Habeas-Corpus in Kriegsverbrecherprozessen," Archiv des Öffentlichen Rechts 1949 75: 225-228.

574 HOOVER, GLENN E. "The Outlook for 'War Guilt' Trials," Political Science Quarterly 1944 59(1): 40-48.

575 KLAFKOWSKI, ALFONS. "The Prosecution of Nazi Criminals as a Problem of International Law," Polish Western Affairs 1964 5(2): 266-274.

576 LONDON INTERNATIONAL ASSEMBLY. Reports on the Trial and Punishment of War Crimes, Being the Reports of Commission I of the L.I.A. under the Chairmanship of M. de Baer. London: 1943. 450p.

577 LUDWIG, EMIL, et al. "America's Town Meeting of the Air. How should the Axis War Criminals be tried?" Town Meeting 9(40): February 10, 1944.

578 MICHIE, ALLAN A. "How Will we Try the Axis War Criminals?" Readers Digest 1943 43(260): 57-60.

579 MUNRO, HECTOR A. "Plans for the Trial of War Criminals," Law Journal 1945 95(4121):5-7.

580 MUNRO, HECTRO A. "The Trial of Axis Crimes: Some Further Observations," Law Journal 1943 93(October 9): 323-324.

581 PATON, G.W. "The War Crimes Trials and International Law," Res Judicatae 1947 3(October): 123-132.

582 SCHÜTZE, HEINRICH ALBRECHT. Die Repressalie unter besonderer Berücksichtigung der Kriegsverbrecherprozesse. Bonn: Ludwig Röhrscheid, 1950. 106p.

583 SERAPHIM, HANS-GÜNTHER. "Nachkriegsprozesse und zeitgeschichtliche Forschung," in Mensch und Staat in Recht und Geschichte. Festschrift für Herbert Kraus. Kitzingen am Main: Holzner, 1954.

M. COMPARISONS OF TWO OR MORE TRIALS

584 APPLEMAN, JOHN ALAN. Military Tribunals and International Crimes. Indianapolis: Bobbs-Merrill, 1954. 421p. Westport: Greenwood Press, 1971. 421p. A comprehensive treatise on the war crimes trials which discusses the major trials held at Nuremberg and Tokyo and other lesser-known trials. The main

purpose of the book is to determine the legal right to conduct these proceedings.

585 AYMAR, BRANDT, and EDWARD SAGARIN. A Pictorial History of the World's Great Trials. From Socrates to Eichmann. New York: Crown Publishers, 1967.

586 AYMAR, BRANDT, and EDWARD SAGARIN. Laws and Trials that created History. New York: Crown Publishers, 1974. 214p. "The Nuremberg Trials," pp. 143-155, describes briefly the Nuremberg IMT trial. 8 illustrations, bibliography.

587 BAIRD, JAY W. (comp.). From Nuremberg to My Lai. Lexington, Massachusetts: Heath, 1972.

588 BISHOP, JOSEPH W., JR. "The Question of War Crimes," Commentary 1972 54(6): 85-92. A historical treatment of the development of the idea of war crimes. Outlines a few examples from ancient history, various 19th Century war crimes, and deals with the Hague Convention of 1907, the Geneva Convention of 1949, the war in Vietnam, and international law. Based on secondary sources; 1 note.

589 COOK, BLANCHE WIESEN. "American Justifications for Military Massacres from the Pequot Wars to Mylai," Peace and Change 1975 3(2-3): 4-20. Discusses American justification for war crimes against Indians, Filipinos, Vietnamese, and others from 1636 to the 1970s.

590 DICKLER, GERALD. Man on Trial, History-making Trials from Socrates to Oppenheimer. Garden City: Doubleday, 1962. 453p. Published in German as Dreizehn Prozesse, die Geschichte machten. Munich: Rutten and Loening, 1965. Chapter 10, "The Reichstag Fire Trial (1933)," pp. 201-231, has background material. Chapter 12, "The Nuremberg Trial (1945-1946)," pp. 323-374, discusses the uniqueness of the Nuremberg IMT trial in its purpose and methods. Many general aspects of the trial are covered, including historical background, the structure of the International Military Tribunal, courtroom procedures, and the four counts of the indictment. The mechanics of rationalization that made possible the atrocities committed under the Nazi regime are demonstrated by excerpts from the oral testimony of Erhard Milch, Hermann Göring, Joachim von Ribbentrop, Wilhelm Keitel, Hjalmar Schlacht, Baldur von Schirach, Fritz Sauckel, Arthur Seyss-Inquart, Franz von Papen, Albert Speer, and Konstantin von Neurath. Undocumented; 12-page bibliography, 14-page index to the entire book.

591 FALK, RICHARD A. "The Nuremberg Defense in the Pentagon Papers Case," Columbia Journal of Transnational Law 1974 13(2): 208-238.

592 HAMBURGER, ERNEST. "The Nuremberg Principles. 'Law Recognized by the Community of Nations,'" Wiener Library Bulletin 1961 15(2): 27. Touches on the Eichmann case, but focuses on Argentina's attitude to the Draft Covenant on Civil and Political Rights discussed in the United Nations on November 15, 1960.

593 HART, FRANKLIN A. "Yamashita, Nuremberg and Vietnam: Command Responsibility Reappraised," Naval War College Review 1972 25(1): 19-36.

594 HARWOOD, RICHARD. Nuremberg and other War Crimes Trials: A New Look. Ladbroke, Southampton: Historical Review Press, 1978. 70p. Revisionist treatment of the Nuremberg IMT and the defendants. Discusses Robert H. Jackson, the psychology of the defendants, witnesses, sentences, and executions. Treats briefly the trials at Manstein and Dachau as well as those by German and Italian courts. Brief criticism of the trials and appendices which deal with the Katyn Woods massacre, the bombing of civilians, and war crimes of Jews in Palestine. Charts list the various defendants of the IMT trials, with sentences. Contains a survey of statistics dealing with many of the trials. Lists IMT defense counsels. Undocumented; 38 photographs, 6 tables and charts.

595 HAUXHURST H.A., OWEN CUNNINGHAM, CHARLES F. WENNERSTRUM, and JAMES T. BRAND. "Forum on War Crimes Trials," American Bar Association, Proceedings [Section of International and Comparative Law] 1948: 30-47. Hauxhurst and Cunningham discuss war crimes trials in the Far East. Wennerstrum, commenting on the Nuremberg trial, insists that no victorious nation has the right to assign war guilt to the vanquished.

596 HELLER, MAXINE JACOBSON. "The Treatment of Defeated War Leaders," Ph.D. dissertation, Columbia University, 1965. 500p. Abstracted in Dissertation Abstracts International 1966 26:4786. This study deals with the treatment of war leaders after the Napoleonic Wars and World Wars I and II. It includes a discussion of the debates among the Allied powers concerning the possibility of war crimes trials in Tokyo and the fate of Hirohito. Concludes that in the case of Napoleon, Kaiser Wilhelm, and Hirohito, the victors sought to remove leaders who could conceivably precipitate further conflict.

597 HORSKY, CHARLES A. "Status of Prosecutions against German and Japanese War Criminals," Lawyers Guild Review 1946 6(2): 485-489.

598 KEMPNER, ROBERT M.W. "Les criminels à Nuremberg et à Jerusalem," Le Monde Juif 1961 16(24-25): 36-39.

599 KERNMAYR, ERICH [pseudonym, Erich Kern]. Deutschland im Abgrund; das falsche Gericht. Göttingen: K.W. Schütz, 1963. 359p. Last of a 3-volume work which deals with the post-World War II period. Contains much on various war crimes trials. Deals with the Katyn Woods massacre, Jews in the East, and the 12 "subsequent" Nuremberg trials. Bibliography, 30 photographs, index.

600 KRASKE, ERICH. "Klassisches Hellas und Nürnberger Prozeß," Archiv des Völkerrechts 1953 4(September): 183-189.

601 LAWRENCE, JAMES F. "Trial of Civilians by Military Tribunals under the Uniform Code of Military Justice," George Washington Law Revue 1953 21(6): 711-737. 115 notes.

602 LIPPERT, DAVID I. "The Eichman Case and the Nürnberger Trials," American Bar Association Journal 1962 48(8): 738-741.

603 MARIDAKIS, GEORGES S. "Un Précedent du procès de Nuremberg tiré de l'histoire de la Grèce ancienne," Revue Hellénique de Droit International 1952 5(July-December): 1-16. 2 notes.

604 MARTÍNEZ, JOSÉ AGUSTÍN. Los procesos penales de la postguerra (Documentos para la historia contemporánea. Madrid: Ediciones y

Publicaciones Españolas, 1955. 433p. Part 1 discusses post war national trials held in France. Part 2 reviews the trials of Tomoyuki Yamashita, Mamoru Shigemitsu, and Erich von Manstein. Discusses infractions of the Geneva Convention, the manufacture of Cyclon B gas, the Peleus trial, cooperation between the USSR and western democracies, victor's justice, and possible resistance to Hitler. Contains a chart of the verdict and sentences handed down by the Nuremberg IMT. Based on primary and secondary sources; 234 notes, no bibliography.

605 METCALF, LAWRENCE E., et al (eds.). War Criminals, War Victims: Andersonville, Nuremberg, Hiroshima, My Lai. Crises in World Order. New York: World Without War Publications, 1974. 62p. A pamphlet intended for high school use. Examines the complexities of applying international law to questions of individual rights and responsibilities. Includes various viewpoints, but offers no interpretations.

606 MIGNONE, A. FREDERICK. "After Nuremberg, Tokyo," Texas Law Review 1947 25(5): 475-490. 19 notes.

607 MURRAY, MICHAEL PATRICK. "A Study in Public International Law: Comparing the Trial of Adolf Eichmann in Jerusalem with the Trial of the Major German War Criminals at Nuremberg," S.J.D. dissertation, American University, 1973. 362p. Abstracted in Dissertation Abstracts International 1973 34(3): 3442-A.

608 POLEVOI, BORIS N. [The final reckoning: Nuremberg diaries]. Moscow: Progress Publishers, 1978. 325p. Translated by Janet Butler (Chapters 1-8) and Doris Bradbury (Chapters 9-29). Brief, but comprehensive account of the Nuremberg IMT trial taken from the notes of a Pravda correspondent. Traces the history of German war crimes trials from Leipzig following World War I through the handing down of the IMT verdict at Nuremberg. Most of the book deals with the course of the IMT trial, with considerable commentary on individual testimony. Undocumented; 48 pages of illustrations.

609 RENDULIC, LOTHAR. Glasenbach - Nürnberg - Landsberg. Ein Soldatenschicksal nach dem Krieg. Graz: L. Stocker, 1953. 222p. Deals throughout with individual responsibility for war crimes and with various aspects of the Nuremberg IMT and other war crimes trials. Memoirs, undocumented, no bibliography, no index.

610 [ROBINSON, NEHEMIAH]. The Prosecution of War Criminals Since the End of the War. A Brief Survey. New York: Institute of Jewish Affairs of the World Jewish Congress, 1961. 23p.

611 RÖLING, BERNARD V.A. "De processen van Nurenberg en Tokyo en die van Stockholm-Roskilde," Ars Aecqui 1968 7: 312-318.

612 RUFF, V.H. "Einheitliche Rechtsgrundlage. Zur abweichenden Rechtsprechung des Obersten Spruchgerichtshofes in Hamm und der Nürnberger Militärgerichte," Neue Juristische Wochenschrift 1948 1(8): 283-286.

613 RUHM VON OPPEN, BEATE (ed.). Documents on Germany under Occupation, 1945-1954. London/New York: Oxford University Press, 1955. 660p. Contains many documents and other entries on war crimes, war criminals, various tribunals, trials in the Soviet zone, and atrocities. Detailed chronological table of contents and index.

614 SNYDER, ORVILLE C. "It's not Law: The War Guilt Trials," Kentucky Law Journal 1949 38(1): 81-104. Deals with a series of war crimes trials whose verdicts were appealed to the United States Supreme Court. Examines the appeals and reasons given by the Court for refusing to hear the cases. In most cases the Court disclaimed jurisdiction on the basis that only the reviewing military authority had jurisdiction. It ruled later that the tribunal sentencing the prisoners was not a court of the United States, but was the agent of the Allied Powers. Examines the due process of law, standards of conduct, evidence, and the meaning of equality. Under these categories he examines the Yamashita case and the trials of Tojo and Göring. Concludes that the trials "do not look like due process" and that no decision of the Court lent any support to calling them legal. Based largely on Supreme Court cases and secondary sources; 124 notes.

615 SOLF, WALDEMAR A. "A Response to Telford Taylor's Nuremberg and Vietnam: An American Tragedy," Akron Law Review 1972 5(1): 43-68. 102 notes.

616 STOREY, ROBERT GERALD. Final Judgment? Pearl Harbor to Nuremberg. San Antonio: Naylor, 1968.

617 "Symposium: War Crimes Trials," University of Pittsburgh Law Review 1962 24(1): 73-154. A symposium which includes Dina Ghandy McIntyre. "The Nuremberg Trials," pp. 73-116. 164 notes. On the IMT: Elizabeth Heazlett. "Eichmann - International Law?" pp. 116-132. 77 notes; and Robert L. Birmingham. "The War Crimes Trials - A Second Look," pp. 132-154. 74 notes.

618 TAYLOR, TELFORD. "An Outline of the Research and Publication Possibilities of the War Crimes Trials," Louisiana Law Review 1949 9(4): 496-508. 5 notes. Deals with a variety of European war crimes trials.

619 TAYLOR, TELFORD. Nuremberg and Vietnam: An American Tragedy. Chicago: Quadrangle Books, 1970. 224p. Questions the legality of U.S. military action in Vietnam and Cambodia under the Nuremberg principles. Defines war crimes, laws of war, and the concept of military necessity. Examines the defense of superior orders, just and unjust wars, aggressive war in Vietnam, war crimes at Son My, and the punishment for crimes committed. 10 pages of notes, 6-page index.

620 TAYLOR, TELFORD. "Nuremberg and Vietnam: Who Is Responsible for War Crimes?" War/Peace Reports 1970 10: 3-10.

621 TAYLOR, TELFORD, et al [panelists]. "War Crimes, Just and Unjust Wars, and Comparisons between Nuremberg and Vietnam," Columbia Journal of Law and Social Problems 1971 8(1): 101-134.

622 "The Nuremberg Trials and Objection to Military Service in Vietnam," American Society of International Law, Proceedings 1969 63: 140-181. A symposium which includes Tom J. Farer. "The Nuremberg Trials and Objection to Serving in the Viet-Nam War," pp. 140-157; Benjamin Forman. "The Nuremberg Trials and Conscientious Objection to War: Justiciability under United States Municipal Law," pp. 157-164; with commentary by Telford Taylor, Robert K. Woetzel, and Hans E. Fried.

General Works

623 TRAININ, ARON NAUMOVICH. "From Nuremberg to Tokyo," *New Times* 1948 (12): 11-14. Expresses ideas similar to those of V. Berezhkov in an earlier article in the same periodical (which see). Compares the Nuremberg and Tokyo IMT trials and concludes that the Tokyo trial lacked the basic principles of justice found in the Nuremberg trial. The Tokyo trial was a case of "judicial tragedy."

624 UNITED STATES. CONGRESS. HOUSE OF REPRESENTATIVES. COMMITTEE ON THE JUDICIARY. *Official Accountability Act, Hearing before the Subcommittee on Courts, Civil Liberties, and the Administration of Justice*. 94th Congress, 2nd Session (February 2, 1976). Serial Number 66. 58p. Call Number Y4.J891: 9466. Hearing on House Resolution 8388. This hearing determined that one could not use the defense of action under higher orders to avoid criminal liability for war crimes. Discusses war crimes in Indochina, the Nuremberg IMT trial, the war in Vietnam, Ernest Medina, and William Calley.

625 WALKINSHAW, ROBERT B. "The Nuremberg and Tokyo Trials: Another Step toward International Justice," *American Bar Association Journal* 1949 35(April): 299-302, 362-363. These trials mark the recognition of a developing international "common law" against war crimes. Analyzes the place of the Nuremberg and Tokyo IMT trials in the evolution of international criminal law and discusses the legal basis for the establishment of the IMTFE, the method by which membership on the tribunal was determined, the manner of indicting the accused war criminals, difficulties resulting from having testimony in Japanese, and problems getting witnesses who could testify regarding events in China. The Tokyo trial is criticized on a procedural basis, but is viewed as the preferred method of punishing war criminals. 34 notes.

III
EARLY WAR CRIMES, WAR CRIMINALS, AND WAR CRIMES TRIALS

A. PRE-WORLD WAR I

1. Ancient and Medieval

626 BRAUER-GRAMM, HILDBURG. *Der Landvogt Peter von Hagenbach. Die burgundische Herrschaft am Oberrhein, 1469-74*. Göttingen: Musterschmidt,1957.379p.Trialof Peter von Hagenbach.

627 HEIMPEL, HERMANN. "Das Verfahren gegen Peter von Hagenbach zu Breisach, 1474," *Zeitschrift für die Geschichte des Oberrheins* 1942 55: 321-357.

628 HEIMPEL, HERMANN. "Peter von Hagenbach und die Herrschaft Burgunds am Oberrhein, 1469-1474," *Jahrbuch der Stadt Freiburg im Breisgau* 1942 5: 139-154.

629 NERLINGER, CHARLES. *Pierre de Hagenbach et la domination bourguignonne en Alsace, 1469-1474*. Nancy: Imprimerie de Berger-Leverault, 1890. 172p.

630 REUT-NICOLUSSI, EDUARD. "Kriegsverbrechen im peloponnesischen Krieg," *Österreichische Zeitschrift für öffentliches Recht* 1955 6(March): 490-500.

631 THUCYDIDES. *History of the Peloponnesian War*. Chicago/London: Great Books of the Western World. Volume 6. *Passim*. Excellent index, with much on theory and justice of warfare.

632 VAUGHN, RICHARD. *Charles the Bold: The Last of the Valois*. New York: Barnes and Noble, 1973.

633 WESTINGTON, MARS MC CLELLAND. *Atrocities in Roman Warfare to 133 B.C*. Chicago: University of Chicago Libraries (Private edition), 1938. 139p. Ph.D. dissertation, University of Chicago, 1938. Contains chapters on prisoners, spies, hostages, mutilation of the dead, and sacrilege. 2-page bibliography.

2. Napoleonic

634 BELLOT, HUGH HALE L. "The Detention of Napoleon Bonaparte," *Law Quarterly Review* 1923 39(154): 170-192.

635 STEWART, JOHN HALL. "The Imprisonment of Napoleon: A Legal Opinion by Lord Elton," *American Journal of International Law* 1951 45(3): 571-577.

3. **American War for Independence**

636 COIL, GEORGE L. "War-Crimes of the American Revolution," *Military Law Review* 1978 82(Fall): 171-198.

637 TREVELYAN, GEORGE OTTO. *The American Revolution*. New York: D. McKay, [1964]. 580p. Volume 5. Deals with the trial of Major John André in 1780.

4. **American Civil War**

638 ARENS, RICHARD. "Vicarious Punishment and War Crimes Prosecution: The Civil War or Alice through the Looking Glass," *Washington University Law Quarterly* 1951 1951(1): 62-84. 107 notes.

639 CHIPMAN, NORTON PARKER. *The Tragedy of Andersonville: Trial of Captain Henry Wirtz, the Prison Keeper*. San Francisco: Bancroft, 1911. 511p. The author was the Judge Advocate of the military court that tried Henry Wirz, "keeper" of the Confederate prison at Andersonville, Georgia, for war crimes. This book was written in response to a monument erected in memory of Wirtz by people who thought him innocent and the Union government guilty of the crimes with which he was charged. This reprinting of the evidence offered at the trial is designed to lay to rest any doubts as to his innocence. The 16 chapter heads describe in some detail their contents. Trial records and correspondence are quoted copiously, 33 illustrations.

640 DAVIS, GEORGE B. "Dr. Francis Lieber's Instructions for the Government of Armies in the Field," *American Journal of International Law* 1907 1: 13-25.

641 DYER, BRAINERD. "Francis Lieber and the American Civil War," *Huntington Library Quarterly* 1939 2(4): 449-465. 80 notes.

642 FUTCH, OVID L. *History of Andersonville Prison*. Gainesville: University of Florida Press, 1968.

643 GILMAN, DANIEL C. (ed.). *The Miscellaneous Writings of Francis Lieber*. 2 volumes. Philadelphia: Lippincott, 1881.

644 HALLECK, HENRY WAGER. "Military Tribunals and Their Jurisdiction: Historical Development of the Military Court - Conditions that Confronted the North during our Civil War," *American Journal of International Law* 1911 5(4): 958-967. Historical sketch of the jurisdiction of military tribunals, with emphasis on the American Civil war.

645 HESSELTINE, WILLIAM BEST. *Civil War Prisons: A Study in War Psychology*. Columbus: Ohio State University Press, 1930. 290p. New York: Frederick Unger, 1964.

646 HOLLS, FREDERICK WILLIAM. *Franz Lieber. Sein Leben und seine Werke*. New York: E. Steiger, 1884. 45p.

647 JONES, J. WILLIAM. *Confederate View of the Treatment of Prisoners, compiled from official Records and other Documents*. Richmond: Southern Historical Society, 1876. 213p. Publication as a single volume of two articles that appeared in the *Southern*

Historical Society Papers 1876 1(3) 113-221; (4): 225-330. Attempts to refute charges that the Confederate government had mistreated prisoners of a war. Detailed table of contents at the beginning of the first section outlines the material dealt with in both articles.

648 KELLOGG, ROBERT H. Life and Death in Rebel Prisons: giving a complete History of the inhuman and barbarous Treatment of our brave Soldiers by Rebel Authorities, inflicting terrible Suffering and frightful Mortality, principally at Andersonville, Ga., and Florence, S. C. Hartford: L. Stebbins, 1866. 423p. The author claims complete objectivity in this account of the place where "the climax of rebel barbarity was reached." Appendices contain several letters. 11 illustrations.

649 LASKA, LEWIS L., and JAMES M. SMITH. "'Hell and the Devil': Andersonville and the Trial of Henry Wirtz, C.S.A., 1865," Military Law Review 1975 68(Spring): 77-132.

650 MC ELROY, JOHN. Andersonville: A Story of Rebel Military Prisons, fifteen Months a Guest of the so-called Southern Confederacy, a private Soldier's Experience in Richmond, Andersonville, Savannah, Millen, Blackshear, and Florence. Toledo: D.R. Locke, 1879. 654p. Argues that the unparalleled cruelty and punishment inflicted upon Union captives was a result of 200 years of moral desolation and demonic values at work in the proslavery South. The 83 short chapters describe different aspects of life in Andersonville and various personal experiences of the author. 154 illustrations.

651 MC ELROY, JOHN. This was Andersonville, the true Story of Andersonville Military Prison as told in the personal Recollections of John McElroy, sometime Private, Co. L, 16th Illinois Cavalry. New York: McDowell, Obolensky, 1957. 355p. When McElroy's account first appeared in the Toledo Blade he received more than 3000 letters from former Andersonville prisoners endorsing his account. This "tale of unbelievable horror and human depravity" described the deeds and trial of Captain Henry Wirz, the first man sentenced to die for war crimes. McElroy is critical of both sides, including the "hoodlums, thieves, and murderers from the slums of New York" who were serving as Union prisoners in Andersonville. He makes a case against Wirz, Jefferson Davis, and General John H. Winder, the Prison Administrator. 64 notes, 24 photographs.

652 MORSBERGER, ROBERT E., and KATHARINE M. MORSBERGER, "After Andersonville: The First War Crimes Trial," Civil War Times Illustrated 1974 13(4): 30-41.

653 NYS, ERNEST. "Francis Lieber: His Life and Work," American Journal of International Law 1911 5: 84-117.

654 RUSS, WILLIAM A., JR. "Administrative Activities of the Union Army during the Civil War and after the Civil War," Mississippi Law Journal 1945 17(2): 71-89. 60 notes.

655 RUTMAN, DARRETT B. "The War Crimes and Trial of Henry Wirz," Civil War History 1960 6(2): 117-133. A Study of the activities of Henry Wirz (1822-1865) as commander of Andersonville Prison during the later stages of the American Civil War and his subsequent trial and execution as a war criminal. From a review of the contemporary press, the published trial records,

92 Early Trials

and the records and narratives of Andersonville Prison. Concludes that Wirz was convicted by post-war hysteria and the ambition of men in the Federal Government rather than by any evidence of his crimes.

656 SHEPARD, WILLIAM S. "One Hundredth Anniversary of the Lieber Code," *Military Law Review* 1963 21(July): 157-162.

657 UNITED STATES. CONGRESS. HOUSE OF REPRESENTATIVES. *Trial of Henry Wirz*. 40th Congress, 2nd Session, House Executive Document 23. Washington: GPO, 1868.

658 UNITED STATES. WAR DEPARTMENT. *Instructions for the Government of Armies of the United States in the Field*. General Order 100, April 24, 1863, by Francis Lieber. Washington: Department of War, 1863.

659 WHITE, LAURA A. "Atrocity Charges in the Civil War," *World Tomorrow* 1929 12(February): 67-70.

660 WILSON, THOMAS L. *Sufferings Endured for a Free Government; or, A History of the Cruelties and Atrocities of the Rebellion*. Philadelphia: King & Baird, 1865. 300p.

5. Turkey

661 AHMAD, FEROZ. *The Young Turks: The Committee of Union and Progress in Turkish Politics, 1908-1914*. Oxford: Clarendon, 1969.

6. Greco-Bulgarian War

662 BULGARIA. *Atrocités grecques en Macedoine pendant la guerre greco-bulgare*. Sofia: Imprimerie d'état, 1913.

663 TEMPERLEY, HAROLD. "The Bulgarian and Other Atrocities 1875-78, in the Light of Historical Criticism," *Proceedings of the British Academy* 1931 17: 105-146.

7. Philippine Insurrection

664 FARRELL, JOHN T. "An Abandoned Approach to Philippine History: John R.M. Taylor and the Philippine Insurrection Records," *Catholic Historical Review* 1954 39(4): 385-407.

665 MILLER, STUART C. "Our Mylai of 1900: Americans in the Philippine Insurrection," *Trans-Action* 1970 7(September): 19-28.

666 POMEROY, WILLIAM J. "Pacification in the Philippines, 1898-1913," *France-Asie* 1967 21(3): 427-446.

667 SCHIRMER, D.B. "Mylai was not the First Time," *New Republic* 1971 164(17): 18-21. On the Philippine insurrection.

668 UNITED STATES. CONGRESS. SENATE. *Affairs in the Philippine Islands*. 57th Congress, 1st Session. Senate Document 331. Washington: GPO, 1903.

669 UNITED STATES. CONGRESS. SENATE. *Charges of Cruelty to Natives of the Philippine Islands*. 57th Congress, 1st Session, Senate Document 20(5). Washington: GPO, 1901.

670 UNITED STATES. CONGRESS. SENATE. Trials of Court-Martial in the Philippine Islands in Consequence of Certain Instructions. 57th Congress, 2nd Session. Senate Document 213. Washington: GPO, 1903.

671 UNITED STATES. NATIONAL ARCHIVES AND RECORDS SERVICE. Microfilm Publications. Record Group 94. Pamphlet Accompanying M254. 643 rolls. Philippine Insurgent Records, 1896-1901, with Associated Records of the United States War Department, 1900-1906. Washington: NARS, 1967. 52p. Contains records captured by the United States Army during its suppression of the Philippine insurrection during the years 1899-1903, together with finding aids, translations, editorial matter, and other records. Tells the story of how these records were discovered, preserved, and microfilmed. The contents are identified by roll.

672 WELCH, RICHARD E., JR. "American Atrocities in the Philippines: The Indictment and the Response," Pacific Historical Review 1974 43(2): 233-253.

673 YOUNG, KENNETH RAY. "Atrocities and War Crimes: The Cases of Major Waller and General Smith," Leyte-Samar Studies 1978 12(1): 64-77. The September 1901 ambush of the American garrison at Balangiga, Samar, was the most reported incident of the Philippine insurrection. General Jacob H. Smith was assigned the task of pacifying Samar, and was given a battalion of Marines commanded by Major Littleton Waller. Smith's controversial statements and orders, plus Waller's sweep through the island, aroused antiimperialist outcries in the United States. Both men faced military trial. Smith, who admitted that he ordered Waller to turn Samar into a "howling wilderness," was reprimanded by the court while Waller was acquitted. Based on manuscript and published accounts of the trial and on Manila newspapers; 2 illustrations.

B. WORLD WAR I

1. General Works on World War I

674 CARNEGIE ENDOWMENT FOR INTERNATIONAL PEACE. Violations of the Laws and Customs of War: Report of the Majority and Dissenting Reports of the American and Japanese Members of the Commission on Responsibilities at the Conference of Paris, 1919. Oxford: Clarendon, 1919. Pamphlet No. 32.

675 DICKMANN, FRITZ. „Die Kriegsschuldfrage auf der Friedenskonferenz von Paris, 1919," Historische Zeitschrift 1963 197(1): 1-101. Copiously annotated.

676 EXNER, FRANZ. Krieg und Kriminalität in Österreich. Vienna: Hölder-Pichler-Tempsky, 1927. 219p.

677 FOLTZ, DAVID A. "The War Crimes Issue at the Paris Peace Conference, 1919-1920." Ph.D. dissertation, American University, 1978. 370p. Abstracted in Dissertation Abstracts International 1978 39(2): 1046-A.

678 FRAENKEL, ERNST. Military Occupation and the Rule of Law: Occupation Government in the Rhineland, 1918-1923. London: Oxford University Press, 1944. 267p. Prosecution of war criminals.

679 GERMANY. AUSWÄRTIGES AMT [FOREIGN OFFICE]. Greueltaten russischer Truppen gegen deutsche Zivilpersonen und deutsche Kriegsgefangene. Berlin: 1915. Published in English as Memorial on Atrocities Committed by Russian Troops upon German Inhabitants and German Prisoners.

680 GIBBONS, HERBERT ADAMS. The Blackest Page of Modern History: Events in Armenia in 1915: The Facts and the Responsibilities. New York/London: Putnam's Sons, 1916.

681 GREAT BRITAIN. FOREIGN OFFICE. Protocols and Correspondence between the Supreme Council and the Conference of Ambassadors and the German Government and the German Peace Delegation between January 10, 1920, and July 17, 1920, respecting the Execution of the Treaty of Versailles of June 28, 1919. London: HMSO, 1921. 178p. Misc. No. 15, 1921. Cmd. 1325. See table of contents for numerous documents concerning the punishment of war criminals.

682 LANSING, ROBERT (Committee Chairman). "Report of the Commission on the Responsibility of the Authors of the War and on Enforcement of Penalties," American Journal of International Law 1920 14(1): 95-154. On January 25, 1919, the Preliminary Peace Conference created a committee of 15 members to inquire into responsibility for World War I, breaches of the laws of war by the Germans and their allies, degree of responsibility borne by members of the armed forces, and possible creation of a tribunal to try the offenders. American Secretary of State Robert Lansing was appointed chairman. The committee concluded that: (1) the war was premeditated by the Central Powers and their allies Turkey and Bulgaria, (2) Germany and Austro-Hungary worked to nullify all conciliatory efforts made by the Entente, (3) German and Austro-Hungary violated Belgian neutrality, (4) the Central Powers carried on the war by barbarous and illegal methods in violation of the laws and customs of war, (5) there should be a commission established to compile a record of the Central Power violations of the laws of war, (6) all enemy violators of the laws of war, including heads of state, were liable for criminal prosecution for violating the neutrality of Belgium and Luxembourg, (7) penal sanctions should be created for the future to guarantee against Central Power "outrages," (8) all enemy nations must surrender for trial any criminals demanded by the Allies, and (9) all orders pertaining to the violation of the laws of war had to be turned over to the Allies. There follows a summary of the offenses committed by the Central Powers against the laws of war and the laws of humanity. Closes with a list of principles which should determine inhuman and improper acts of war and a statement of reservation by the Japanese. 69 notes.

683 LEPSIUS, JOHANNES. Deutschland und Armenien, 1914-1918. Sammlung diplomatischer Aktenstücke. Potsdam: Tempel, 1919.

684 MOOREHEAD, ALAN. Gallipoli. New York: Harper, 1956.

685 READ, JAMES MORGAN. "Atrocity Propaganda and the Irish Rebellion," Public Opinion Quarterly 1938 2(2): 229-244.

686 READ, JAMES MORGAN. Atrocity Propaganda, 1914-1919. New Haven: Yale University Press, for the University of Louisville, 1941. 319p. A history of Part VII (Penalties) of the Treaty of Versailles, which discussed war crimes and atrocities. A discussion of war guilt was begun in the same section and was carried

over into Section VIII. Topics discussed include French denunciation, Belgian deportations, English condemnation, notorious cases, and a day of reckoning. Copiously annotated; 14-page bibliography, 5 appendices, index.

2. War Crimes

a. General Works on War Crimes

687 BALLARD, F. Plain Truths versus German Lies: Documents. London: Kelly, 1915. 146p.

688 BELLOT, HUGH HALE L. "War Crimes: Their Prevention and Punishment," Transactions of the Grotius Society 1916 2: 31-55. 39 notes. Reprinted from Nineteenth Century and After 1916 80(September): 636-660.

689 BELLOT, HUGH HALE L. "War Crimes and War Criminals," Canadian Law Times 1916 36: 754-768.

690 BELLOT, HUGH HALE L. "War Crimes and War Criminals," Canadian Law Times 1917 37: 9-22.

691 BELLOT, HUGH HALE L. "War Crimes and War Criminals," Canadian Law Times 1916 36(November): 876-886.

692 BESIER, GERHARD. Krieg-Frieden-Abrüstung. Die Haltung der europäischen und amerikanischen Kirchen zur Frage der deutschen Kriegsschuld 1914-1933. Göttingen: Vandenhoeck & Ruprecht, 1982. 392p.

693 BRÜGEL, J.W. "Das Schicksal der Strafbestimmungen des Versailler Vertrages," Vierteljahrshefte für Zeitgeschichte 1958 6(3): 263-270.

694 COLBY, ELBRIDGE. "War Crimes," Michigan Law Review 1925 23(5): 482-511; (6): 606-634. 237 notes.

695 COLBY, ELBRIDGE. "War Crimes and their Punishment," Minnesota Law Review 1923 8(1): 40-46.

696 FEIN, HELEN. Imperial Crime and Punishment: The Massacre of Jallianwala Bagh and British Judgement, 1919-1920. Honolulu: University of Hawaii Press, 1977.

697 FENWICK, CHARLES G. "Germany and the Crime of the World War," American Journal of International Law 1929 23(4): 812-815.

698 German Atrocities: Official Book of the German Atrocities: Report of the Belgian, French and Russian Commissions of Enquiry. London: Pearson, 1915. 176p.

699 "German Atrocities on Record, with Authentic Illustrations," reprinted from The Field, The Country Gentleman's Newspaper (Supplement). 1915 125(3242): entire issue. 34p. Contains many documents and illustrations dealing with German atrocities in Belgium during World War I.

700 GIBBS, PHILIP. "War Crimes: The Average Point of View," Living Age 1920 304(3950): 710-711.

96 Early Trials

701 GREAT BRITAIN. COLONIAL OFFICE. Correspondence Relative to the Alleged Ill-Treatment of German Subjects Captured in the Cameroons. London: HMSO, 1915.

702 GREAT BRITAIN. COLONIAL OFFICE. Papers Relating to German Atrocities and Breaches of the Rules of War in Africa. London: HMSO, 1916.

703 GREAT BRITAIN. FOREIGN OFFICE. Evidence and Documents Laid before the Committee on Alleged German Atrocities, Presided over by the Right Honourable Viscount Bryce. London: HMSO, 1915.

704 GREAT BRITAIN. PARLIAMENT. Further Correspondence with the United States Ambassador Respecting the Treatment of British Prisoners of War and Interned Civilians in Germany. Sessional Papers, Cds. 8235, 8297. London: HMSO, 1916.

705 GREAT BRITAIN. TREASURY. Report of the Committee on Alleged German Outrages. London: HMSO, 1915. On the Bryce Report.

706 HILLIS, NEWELL D. German Atrocities. Their Nature and Philosophy: Studies in Belgium and France during July and August of 1917. New York: Fleming H. Revell, 1918. 160p. Deals with German atrocities, the Pan German empire scheme, what the Allies were fighting for, and illustrations that portray German war crimes.

707 JOSEPH, CHARLES MARIE [JOSEPH BÉDIER]. German Atrocities from German Evidence. Paris: A. Colin, 1917. 40p. Delegation propaganda authenticated by the French delegation to the Paris peace conference, 1919.

708 LE QUEUX, WILLIAM. German Atrocities: A Record of Shameless Deeds. London: Newnes, 1914. 128p.

709 Les Crimes des barbares. Leur atrocités sur terre, sur mer, et dans les airs. Montrouge: 1918.

710 MACCAS, L. German Barbarism: A Neutral's Indictment. London: Hodder and Stoughton, 1916. 228p.

711 MARSHALL, LOGAN. Horrors and Atrocities of the Great War. Philadelphia: Winston, 1915. 320p.

712 MC DONALD, JAMES GROVER. German "atrocities" and International Law. Chicago: Germanistic Society of Chicago, 1914. 16p.

713 MÉRIGNHAC, ALEXANDRE G.J.A. "De la sanction des infractions au droit des gens commises, au cours de la guerre européenne," Revue Générale de Droit International Public 1917 24: 5-56. Deals with the necessity of punishing war criminals.

714 MICHELON, CLAUDE. "Made in Germany:" A Compilation of German Atrocities Taken from Official Documents. Indianapolis: Bobbs-Merrill, 1918.

715 MIRMAN, LÉON, et al. Leur Crimes. Paris: Berger-Levrault, 1916. 116p. Published in English as Their Crimes. London: Cassell, 1917. 64p. The material in this book was gathered from reports issued by the French Commission of Enquiry, Germany's Violation of the Laws of Warfare (published by the French Ministry of

Foreign Affairs), 2 volumes containing 22 reports of the Belgian Commission, the reply to the German White Book of May 15, 1915, and notebooks found on wounded and captured German soldiers.

716 MORGAN, JOHN HARTMANN. German Atrocities: An official Investigation. London: Fisher Unwin, 1916. 235p. New York: E.P. Dutton, 1916. 192p. Chapter 2 first appeared in the June 1916 issue of Nineteenth Century and After.

717 Official Book of the German Atrocities Told by Victims and Eye-Witnesses. London: 1915.

718 PARLIAMENTARY RECRUITING SERVICE. The Truth about German Atrocities. London: 1915.

719 PIC, PAUL. "Violation systématique des lois de la guerre par les Austro-Allemandes. Les sanctions nécessaires," Revue Générale de Droit International Public 1916 23: 243-268.

720 Prisoners of War in the European War. Miscellaneous Reading List, No. 22. Washington: Carnegie Endowment for International Peace, Library, 1922.

721 Report on the Atrocities committed by the Austro-Hungarian Army during the first Invasion of Serbia. London: Simpkin Marshall, 1916. 204p.

722 REZANOFF, A.S. Les Atrocités allemandes du côté russe. Petrograd: W. Kirschbaum, 1915.

723 SARKISSIAN, ARSHAG O. Martyrdom and Rebirth. New York: Lydian, 1965.

724 SCHULZ, ERICH. Die Kriegsverbrechen. Eine international-strafrechtliche Studie über die Strafanspruchs- und Rechtswidrigkeitslehre, unter Berücksichtigung der Schuld- und Irrtumslehre. Berlin-Hohenschönhausen: Druck Lokalblattverlag, 1928. 132p.

725 STARR, MERRITT. "German Submarine Warfare Violates the Principles of International Law and Treaties Existing between Germany and the United States," Chicago Legal News 1918 51: 138.

726 STÜLPNAGEL, OTTO VON. Die Wahrheit über die deutschen Kriegsverbrechen. Berlin: Staatspolitischer Verlag, 1921. 470p. A defense of German war crimes, based on the argument that both sides were guilty of crimes and atrocities.

727 "The Crimes of Germany," The Field. [London]: 1916. 106p.

728 "The Treatment of War Crimes and Crimes Incidental to the War: The Experience of 1918-1922," Bulletin of International News 1945 22(3): 95-102; (5): 199-208; (6): 251-255; (7): 299-305. Deals with the punishment of traitors and violations of treaties and methods of punishment.

729 "War Crimes and their Punishment," Transactions of the Grotius Society 1923 8: xix-xxxi.

730 War on Hospital Ships. New York: Harper and Brothers, 1918. 47p. Eyewitness reports of German warfare on hospital ships. Contains British and German correspondence.

98 Early Trials

731 Where the German Army has Passed. London: Daily Chronicle, 1915. 66p.

b. Armenian-Turkish War Crimes

732 "Armenian Atrocities," Saturday Review [London] 1889 68(August 31): 230-231.

733 BEY, NAIM. The Memoirs of Naim Bey: Turkish Official Documents Relating to the Deportation and Massacres of Armenians. Aram Andonian (comp.). Newton Square, Pennsylvania: Armenian Historical Research Association, 1964.

734 BOYAJIAN, DICKRAN H. Armenia: The Case for a Forgotten Genocide. Westwood, New Jersey: Educational Book Crafters, 1972. 498p.

735 BRYCE, JAMES [Arnold J. Toynbee, ed.]. The Treatment of Armenians in the Ottoman Empire: Documents presented to Viscount Fallondon . . . with a Preface by Viscount Bryce, laid before the Houses of Parliament as an official Paper and published by Permission. London and New York: Hodder & Stroughton, 1916. 684p. Issued by the Foreign Office as Miscellaneous Report No. 31, 1916; Parliament. Papers by Command. Cd. 8325. 1915-1916.

736 DJEMAL, PASHA. Memories of a Turkish Statesman, 1913-1919. London: Hutchinson, [1922].

737 DYER, GWYNNE. "Turkish 'Falsifiers' and Armenian Deceivers: Historiography and the Armenian Massacres," Middle Eastern Studies 1976 12(1): 99-107. 8 notes.

738 KARAJIAN, SARKIS. "An Inquiry into the Statistics of the Turkish Genocide of the Armenians, 1915-1918," Armenian Review 1972 25(4): 3-44.

739 KAZARIAN, HAIGAZN K. "The Genocide of Kharpert's Armenians: A Turkish Judicial Document and Cipher Telegrams Pertaining to Kharpert," Armenian Review 1966 19(1): 16-23.

740 PICKTHALL, MARMADUKE. "Massacres and the Turks: The Other Side," Foreign Affairs 1920 (Special Supplement, July): xiv-xvi.

741 TOYNBEE, Arnold J. Armenian Atrocities: The Murder of a Nation. London/New York: Hodder & Stroughton, 1915. 119p. New York: Tankian Publishing Corp. 1975.

c. Belgium

742 ARCHER, WILLIAM. "The Germans in Belgium," Quarterly Review 1921 236(468): 190-205.

743 ASTON, GEORGE GREY. The Triangle of Terror in Belgium. London: J. Murray, 1918. 105p.

744 BELGIUM. COMMISSION D'ENQUÊTE SUR LA VIOLATION DES RÈGLES DU DROIT DES GENS, DES LOIS ET DES COUTUMES DE LA GUERRE. Rapports sur la violation du droit des gens en Belgique. 2 volumes. Paris: 1916. Published in English as Reports on the Violation of the Laws and Customs of War in Belgium. 2 volumes. London: 1915-1916.

745 BISSING, FRIEDERICH WILHELM FREIHERR VON. La Terreur en Belgique et dans la Prusse orientale. Monaco: Artistiques Réunies, 1915.

746 GRASSHOFF, RICHARD. The Tragedy of Belgium, an Answer to Professor Waxweiler. New York: G.W. Dillingham, 1915.

747 HEUVEL, J. VAN DEN. "De la Déportation des Belges en Allemagne," Revue Général de Droit International Public 1917 24: 261-300.

748 NOTHOMB, PIERRE. Les Barbares en Belgique. Paris: Perrin, 1915. 261p. Published in English as The Barbarians in Belgium. London: Jarrold & Sons, 1915. 254p.

749 TOYNBEE, ARNOLD J. The German Terror in Belgium: An Historical Record. New York: Doran, 1917. 212p. Discusses German ravages of Belgium and crimes of violence against civilians. 52 photographs. See Toynbee's German Terror in France.

d. France

750 FRANCE. MINISTRY OF FOREIGN AFFAIRS. Les Allemands à Lille dans le nord de la France. Paris: 1916. Published in English as The Deportation of Women and Girls from Lille. London: Hodder & Stoughton, for French Ministry of Foreign Affairs, 1916. 81pp.

751 FRANCE. MINISTRY OF FOREIGN AFFAIRS. Les Violations des lois de la guerre par l'Allemagne. Paris: 1915. Published in England as Germany's Violations of the Laws of War 1914-1915. London: William Heinemann, 1915. 343p. New York: G.P. Putnam's Sons, for the Ministry of Foreign Affairs, 1915. 346p. Describes in considerable detail the killing of prisoners, looting, rape, arson, murder, and the use of gas and burning liquids. Contains 121 reports of violations of the laws of war. This work is sometimes listed under the translator, J.O.P. Bland.

752 TOYNBEE, ARNOLD J. German Terror in France: An historical Record. New York: Doran. 1917. 220p. A continuation of German Terror in Belgium. Chapters in both books are numbered consecutively. 52 photographs.

3. War Criminals

a. General

753 "Aiding War Criminals to Escape," Literary Digest 1920 64(March 27): 30-31.

754 BEVAN, E.R. "Demand for the German War Criminals," Contemporary Review 1920 117(March): 305-316.

755 BOOTH, J.B. The Gentle Cultured German, the Roadhog of Europe. London: Grant Richards, 1915. 199p.

756 BREITSCHEID, RUDOLF. "The Punishment of the War Criminals," Nation 1921 113(2936): 397.

757 CADOUX. C.J. "The Punishing of Germany after the War of 1914-1918," Hibbert Journal 1945 43(January): 107-113.

758 GALLINGER, AUGUST. *The Countercharge: the Matter of War-Criminals from the German Side*. Munich: Süddeutsche Monatshefte, 1922. 146p. A sketch of the treatment of prisoners of war by France, England, Belgium, and Rumania. The French were sadists in their treatment of German prisoners of war.

759 GARNER, JAMES W. "Punishment of Offenders against the Laws and Customs of War," *American Journal of International Law* 1920 14: 70-94. 52 notes. Mostly on World War I, but much on general theory.

760 "German Criminals," *Independent and Weekly Review* 1920 101(February 21): 286-288.

761 "Germany's Elusive War-Criminals," *Literary Digest* 1920 64(February 21): 16-17.

762 GEYER, CURT. *Drei Verbrecher Deutschlands, ein Beitrag zur Geschichte Deutschlands und der Reparationsfrage von 1920 bis 1924*. Berlin: J.H.W. Dietz, 1924. 230p.

763 GREAT BRITAIN. WAR OFFICE. *Manual of Military Law, 1929, amendments (no. 12)*. London: HMSO, 1936. 95p. Some on the punishment of war criminals.

764 HARRISON, AUSTIN., and L. DUMONT-WILDEN. "Punishing the War Criminals," *Living Age* 1920 304(March 27): 751-762. Contains "The Punishment of War Guilt," by Austin Harrison, and "Germany and its War Criminals," by L. Dumont-Wilden.

765 KAUL, FRIEDRICH KARL. „Die Verfolgung deutscher Kriegsverbrecher nach dem Ersten Weltkrieg," *Zeitschrift für Geschichtswissenschaft* 1966 14: 19-32.

766 "Punishing War Criminals," *Current History* 1920 11(2): 373-380.

767 ROWLEY, LOUIS E. *War Criminals. Who were They? Why were They?* Lansing: [no publisher given], 1924. 35p.

768 "The Prosecution of German War Criminals," *Contemporary Review* 1920 117(March): 429. The text of the German law of December 13, 1919, directing the German public to initiate proceedings against German subjects accused of crimes or misconduct in occupied territories and elsewhere.

769 WILLIS, JAMES F. *Prologue to Nuremberg: The Politics and Diplomacy of Punishing War Criminals of the First World War*. Westport: Greenwood Press, 1982. 292p. (Contributions in Legal Studies, No. 20). Originally done as "Prologue to Nuremberg: The Punishment of War Criminals of the First World War," Ph.D. dissertation, Duke University, 1976. Abstracted in *Dissertation Abstracts International* 1977 37(7): 4529-A. This is an examination of the unsuccessful efforts to punish war criminals following World War I. Discusses the complex interrelationships between the politics and diplomacy of the war, the peace settlement, and the development of new concepts of international war crimes punishment. Describes the failure to implement international war crimes trials and traces the influences of this experience upon decisions to institute war crimes proceedings after World War II. Excerpts articles from the Treaty of Versailles (June 28, 1919), the Treaty of Saint-Germain-En-Laye (September 10, 1919), the Treaty of Neuilly-Sur-Seine (November 27, 1919), the Treaty of Trianon (June 4, 1920), and the Treaty

of Sèvres (August 10, 1920). 26-page bibliography, 16-page index, 11 illustrations.

770 WOLFF, THEODOR. "The War Criminals," Nation [London] 1920 26(March 13): 799-800.

771 WOOLSEY, THEODORE S. "Retaliation and Punishment," American Society of International Law, Proceedings 1915 9: 62-69.

b. The Kaiser

772 ERICKSON, OTTO. "A Judicial Reckoning for William Hohenzollern," Law Notes 1919 22(January): 184-189.

773 "Germany Debates Trying the Kaiser," Living Age 1920 304(3949): 626-635. A collection of 3 articles that appeared originally in the German press.

774 GREGORY, S.S. "Criminal Responsibility of Sovereigns for Willful Violations of the Laws of War," Virginia Law Review 1920 6(5): 400-421. 6 notes.

775 HANOTAUX, GABRIEL. "Les responsabilités de Guillaume II," Revue de Paris 1922 29: 485-490.

776 IRELAND, GORDON. "The Trial of Ex-Rulers," Tulane Law Review 1933 7(2): 279-285. 28 notes.

777 LARNAUDE, FERNAND, and ALBERT G. DE LA PRADELLE. "Examen de la responsabilité pénale de l'empereur Guillaume d'Allemagne," Journal du Droit International 1919 46: 131-159.

778 LEA, LUKE [William T. Alderson (ed.)]. "The Attempt to Capture the Kaiser," Tennessee Historical Quarterly 1961 20(3): 222-261. Undocumented.

779 LENER, SALVATORE. "Dal Mancato del Kaiser al Processo di Norimberga," Civiltà Cattolica 1946 47(March 2): 332-342.

780 LUDWIG, EMIL. Wilhelm der Zweite. Berlin: E. Rowohlt, 1926. 495p. Published in England as Kaiser Wilhelm II. London: G.P. Putnam's Sons, 1927. Republished in the United States as Wilhelm Hohenzollern: The Last of the Kaisers. New York: Blue Ribbon Books, 1932.

781 PIGGOTT, FRANCIS T. "Ex-Kaiser and His Officers, the Notes of the Allies to Holland and Germany" Nineteenth Century and After 1920 87(March): 537-554.

782 "Punishing War Criminals: Holland Refuses Extradition of ex-Kaiser - Allies Agree to Trial of 890 Others at Leipsic [sic]," Current History 1920 11(2): 375-384.

783 SCOTT, JAMES BROWN. "The Trial of the Kaiser," in Edward M. House (ed.). What Really Happened at Paris: The Story of the Peace Conference, 1918-1919. New York: Charles Scribner's Sons, 1921. 528p.

784 "Trial of Sovereigns for State and War Offences," Juridical Review 1931 43(2): 175-178.

785 VIERECK, GEORGE S. The Kaiser on Trial. New York: Greystone Press, 1937. 514p. A "suppositious" trial of the Kaiser which

advances detailed evidence for both sides. 6-page bibliography, 49-page appendix, index.

786 WILHELM II [Thomas R. Ybarra, ed.]. The Kaiser's Memoirs. New York: Harper and Brothers, 1922.

787 WILLIS, WILLIAM N. The Kaiser and His Barbarians, An Authoritative Record of the Crimes Committed by the Germans in France and Belgium in the Name of War; together with the Official Reports of the Commission of Enquiry Appointed by King Albert of Belgium. London: Anglo-Eastern, 1914. 64p.

788 WRIGHT, QUINCY. "The Legal Liability of the Kaiser," American Political Science Review 1919 13(1): 120-128. 40 notes.

4. War Crimes Trials

a. General

789 ADAM, GEORGE J. Treason and Tragedy: An Account of French War Trials. London: Cape, [1929]. 253p.

790 ADAMS, WILLIAM. "The American Peace Commission and the Punishment of Crimes Committed During War," Law Quarterly Review 1923 39(154): 245-251, 5 notes. A discussion of the legality of the trial of a sovereign by other powers.

791 CARSTEN, FRANCIS L. "The British Summary Court at Wiesbaden, 1926-1929," Modern Law Review 1944 7(4): 215-220. 45 notes.

792 FINCH, GEORGE A. "Jurisdiction of Local Courts to Try Enemy Persons for War Crimes," American Journal of International Law 1920 14(1-2): 218-223.

793 KAZARIAN, HAIGAZN K. "A Turkish Military Court Tries the Principal Genocidists of the District of Yozgat," Armenian Review 1972 25(Summer): 34-39.

794 KAZARIAN, HAIGAZN K. "The Genocide of Kharpert's Armenians: A Turkish Judicial Document and Cipher Telegrams Pertaining to Kharpert," Armenian Review 1966 19(Spring): 16-23.

795 KAZARIAN, HAIGAZN K. "The Massacres and Deportations at Papert: Findings of a Turkish Military Court," Armenian Review 1972 25(Autumn): 59-67.

796 KAZARIAN, HAIGAZN K. "Turkey Tries its Chief Criminals: Indictment and Sentence Passed Down by Military Court of 1919," Armenian Review 1971 24(Winter): 3-26.

797 SCOTT, JAMES BROWN. "The Execution of Captain Fryant," American Journal of International Law 1916 10(October): 865-877. 9 notes.

798 SLOOTEN, M. VAN. „Betrachtungen aus Anlaß des Prozesses Stenger-Crusius," Zeitschrift für Völkerrecht 1922-1923 12: 174-181.

799 TASJIAN, J.H. Turkey: Author of Genocide. Boston: Commemorative Commission on the Fiftieth Anniversary of the Turkish Massacres of the Armenians, 1965.

b. Leipzig

800 "Acquittals that convict Germany," Literary Digest 1921 70(4): 11.

801 BAILEY, GORDON W. "Dry Run for the Hangman: The Versailles-Leipzig Fiasco, 1919-1921. Feeble Foreshadow of Nuremberg." Ph.D. dissertation, University of Maryland, 1971.

802 BATTLE, GEORGE GORDON. "The Trials before the Leipsic [sic] Supreme Court of Germans accused of War Crimes," Virginia Law Review 1921 8(1): 1-26. Undocumented.

803 CLUENT, EDUARD. "Les criminels de guerre devant le Reichsgericht à Leipzig," Journal de Droit International 1921 48: 435-441.

804 "Der Leipziger U-Boot-Prozeß," Deutsche Rundschau 1921 189(November): 161-172. On the Dithmar-Boldt case.

805 GERMANY. Reichsgericht. Published in English as GREAT BRITAIN. PARLIAMENT. German War Trials. Reports of Proceedings before the Supreme Court in Leipzig. London: HMSO, 1921. 57p. Volume 12. Papers by Command 1450. Reprinted in American Journal of International Law 1922 16(October): 628-640, 674-724, and Supplement 1922 16(4): 195-197, as "Judicial Decisions Involving Questions of International Law: German War Trials." These are reports of the proceedings before the Supreme Court in Leipzig and include documents of the trials of a number of accused war criminals, a few of whom were convicted. Lists the results of 7 trials, including the Llandover Castle case, on which the Peleus case was based.

806 "Germany to Try Her Own War-Criminals," Literary Digest 1920 64(February 28): 19.

807 "How Two U-Boat Criminals Were Convicted: An Account of the Most Interesting Case That Has Come Before the German War Criminal Court at Leipsic [sic] - Conviction of Subordinate Officers Who Helped to Sink a Hospital Ship and Fired on the Helpless Survivors in Lifeboats," Current History 1921 14(6): 948-951.

808 MICHELSEN, ANDREAS HEINRICH (ed.). Das Urteil im Leipziger Uboots-Prozeß ein Fehlspruch? Juristische und militärische Gutachten. Berlin: Staatspolitischer Verlag, 1922. 62p.

809 MULLINS, CLAUDE. The Leipzig Trials: An Account of the War Criminal's Trials and a Study of German Mentality. London: H. F. and G. Witherby, 1921. 238p. The war crimes trials of Germans in Leipzig in 1921 consisted of 45 cases tried by the Criminal Senate of the Imperial Court of Justice of Germany. Reviews the Leipzig Court, the selection of cases, and preparations for the trials. There was no difference between the trials of war criminals and other defendants. Chapter 2 describes procedures concerning witnesses and the difficulties of holding the trials in Germany. Chapters 3 and 4 review various specific trials. Concludes with a comment on the sentences passed and results achieved. The author attributes the lenient sentences handed down to the principle that a subordinate is condemned for his own acts and is not wholly responsible. 4-page index. Undocumented.

810 MULLINS, CLAUDE. "War Criminals' Trials," Fortnightly Review 1921 116(September): 417-430.

811 SCHWERTFEGER, B. "Leipzig - das Brandmal des eigenen Landes," Militär-Wochenblatt 1921 106(September 3): 202-204.

812 "The Danger of the German Trials," Nation [London] 1920 26(February 7): 629-630.

813 "The Leipzig Trials," Living Age 1921 310(4020): 241-243.

814 "Trial of German Officers," Independent and Weekly Review 1920 101(February 14): 252-253.

815 WENDEL, HERMANN. "National Martyrs and Matters of Opinion," Living Age 1921 31(4030): 35-37.

IV
WORLD WAR II WAR CRIMES

A. GENERAL WORKS

816 AGUS, JACOB B. "Mass Crime and the Judeo-Christian Tradition: 1," Minnesota Review 1963 3(2): 205-219.

817 ALEXANDER, LEO. "Destructive and Self-Destructive Trends in Criminalized Society: A Study of Totalitarianism," Journal of Criminal Law and Criminology 1949 39(5): 553-564. 2 notes.

818 ALEXANDER, LEO. "The Molding of Personality Under Dictatorship: The Importance of the Destructive Drives in the Socio-Psychological Structure of Nazism," Journal of Criminal Law and Criminology 1949 40(1): 2-27. 11 notes.

819 ALEXANDER, LEO. "War Crimes: Their Social-psychological Aspects," American Journal of Psychiatry 1948 105(3): 170-177.

820 ALEXANDER, LEO. "War Crimes and their Motivation: The Socio-Psychological Structure of the SS and the Criminalization of a Society," Journal of Criminal Law and Criminology 1948 39(3): 298-326. The above 3 articles define war crimes and describe their social, criminal, and sociological implications. They conclude that the SS was a criminal organization.

821 "Allied Resolution on German War Crimes," Inter-Allied Review 1942 2(1): 2; 2(2): 32. Text of a resolution signed in London on January 14, 1942, by representatives of 9 occupied countries.

822 AMERICAN JEWISH COMMITTEE. To the Counsellors of Peace, Recommendations. New York: 1945. 110p. Deals with war crimes on pp. 102-110.

823 "An Official Nazi Report on the November (1938) Pogroms in Vienna," Yad Vashem Bulletin 1957 (2): 28.

824 BÍLEK, BOHUMIL. "In Dealing with War Crimes," Central European Observer 1945 22(1): 40. Summarizes the achievements of the United Nations War Crimes Commission.

825 CALDERÓN SERRANO, RICARDO. "Crímenes de guerra," Boletín Jurídico Militar 1949 15-17(March-April); 1951 (January-February): 1-378. Appended to each issue with separate numbers.

826 COHN, ERNST J. "The Problem of War Crimes Today," Transactions of the Grotius Society 1940 26: 125-151. Surveys the schemes for sanctions of war crimes elaborated during and after World War I and argues against amnesty of any kind for World War II war criminals.

827 DER GENERALSTAATSANWALT DER DDR UND MINISTERIUM DER JUSTIZ DER DDR. Die Haltung der beiden deutschen Staaten zu den Nazi- und Kriegsverbrechen. Eine Dokumentation. Berlin(GDR): Staatsverlag der DDR, 1965. 137p.

828 DEUTSCH, HAROLD C. "Nazi War Crimes and the German Collectivity," Minnesota Review 1963 3(2): 154-162.

829 Dokumenty i materialy po voprosam bor'by s voennymi prestupnikami i podzhigateliami voiny. Moscow: VIOA, 1949. 275p. A collection about war crimes.

830 Essays über Naziverbrechen, Simon Wiesenthal gewidmet. Amsterdam: Wiesenthal Fonds, [1973].

831 FARRIN, A. "The Responsibility for Nazi War Crimes," Central European Observer 1943 20(18): 281-282.

832 FRANCE. SERVICE D'INFORMATION DES CRIMES DE GUERRE. La Persécution raciale. Paris: Éditions Office Française, 1947. 292p.

833 GALBE, JOSÉ L. Crímenes y justicia de guerra (notas sobre patología del derecho penal). Havana: Jesús Montero (Biblioteca Jurídica de Autores Cubanos y Extranjeros), 1950, 318p. Lists 59 Spanish, French, and English books and official documents on German war crimes, political repression in Spain, and the Nuremberg IMT trial, written between 1929 and 1949.

834 GREAT BRITAIN. MINISTRY OF INFORMATION. A Catalogue of Crime: An Outline Indictment of German War Guilt, Criminal War Aims and Wartime Excesses. London: Ministry of Information, 1945. 71p.

835 HAAG, E. VAN DEN. "When is a Crime a War Crime?" National Review 1971 23(November 5): 1227-1232.

836 HERZOG, JACQUES-BERNARD. "Le Livre noir," République Française 1948 5: 270-276. Comment on the decree of September 30, 1947, creating a Comité du Livre Noir charged with preparing a publication which would give an account of enemy war crimes. Discusses the problem of documents. The projected work was never published.

837 HERZOG, JACQUES-BERNARD. "Les Principes juridiques de la répression des crimes de guerre," Schweizerische Zeitschrift für Strafrecht 1946 61: 277-304.

838 HOFFMAN, STANLEY. "War Crimes: Political and Legal Issues." Dissent 1971 18(6): 530-534.

839 HOFFMANN, GERHARD. Strafrechtliche Verantwortung im Völkerrecht. Zum gegenwärtigen Stand des völkerrechtlichen Strafrechts. Frankfurt am Main: Alfred Metzner, 1962. 211p.

Discusses war crimes, crimes against the peace, crimes against humanity, and the position of the Nuremberg principles in the context of international law. 8-page bibliography, 8-page index.

840 JÄGER, HERBERT. Verbrecher unter totalitärer Herrschaft. Studien zur nationalsozialistischen Gewaltkriminalität. Olten und Freiburg im Breisgau: Walter, 1967. 388p. Investigates the nature and cause of crimes committed during the Third Reich. Discusses the implications of the necessity of orders, the consciousness of illegality by criminals, war, and genocide. 7-page bibliography.

841 JANOWITZ, MORRIS. "German Reactions to Nazi Atrocities," American Journal of Sociology 1946 52(2): 141-146.

842 JOBST, VALENTINE III. "Is the Wearing of the Enemy's Uniform a Violation of the Laws of War," American Journal of International Law 1941 35(3): 435-442. 36 notes.

843 LANGBEIN, HERMANN. "La Justice allemande et les crimes nazis," Documents 1979 34(2): 19-28. Deals with trials of German war criminals, focusing on the number of defendants brought to trial, length of time involved in sentencing, and public opinion.

844 LÜTEM, ILHAM. "Some Controversial Aspects of War Crimes," Annals de la Faculté de Droit d'Istanbul 1952-1953 2: 146-169.

845 MANWELL, ROGER A., and HEINRICH FRAENKEL. Le Crime absolu. Paris: Stock, 1967. Published in English as The Incomparable Crime: Mass Extermination in the Twentieth Century; the Legacy of Guilt. New York: Putnam, 1967. 339p. 5 page bibliography.

846 MARCUS, ROBERT S. "Nazi Crimes to be Remembered," Congress Weekly, A Review of Jewish Interests 1948 (November 22): 10-13.

847 MENTHON, FRANCOIS E. DE. Frankreich verlangt Gerechtigkeit im Namen der Menschlichkeit. Rede des Generalstaatsanwalt F. de Menthon im Nürnberger Prozeß. [no publication data given]. Discusses French demands for justice for victims, the National Socialist teaching of race theory, military and diplomatic preparation for aggressive war, and the arguments of German propagandists. Deals with crimes against peace and crimes of war, including forced labor, economic pillage, and crimes against the individual and humanity. Defines war crimes as crimes against international and common law. Discusses individual and collective responsibility for crimes. Concludes with a dossier by M. Edgar-Faure on forced labor and economic plunder. Undocumented.

848 MÜLLER-PAYER, ALBERT. Die deutsche Sünde wider das Recht. Stuttgart: Franz Mittelbach, 1946. 109p.

849 PAXMAN, JEREMY. A Higher Form of Killing: The Secret Warfare. London: Chatto & Windus, 1982. 224p.

850 PFENNIGER, H.F. "Sind persönliche Kriegsrepressalien erlaubt?" Schweizerische Juristen-Zeitung 1964 60: 245-251.

851 REIK, OTTO E. "War Crimes - A Refutation of Objection," Kentucky Law Journal 1951 39(3): 317-326. 14 notes.

852 REIPERT, FRITZ. Kriegsmethoden und Kriegsverbrechen. Dokumente über die Kriegsführung der Plutokratien. Berlin: H.W. Rödiger, 1941. 174p.

853 RIGG, ROBERT B. "Where Does Killing End and Murder Begin in War?" Military Review 1971 51(March): 3-9.

854 ROBINSON, NEHEMIAH. "'The Others' and Their Fate," World Jewry 1961 (September): 13-14. A survey of Nazi crimes and trials of Nazis.

855 ROMASHKIN, P.S. Voennye prestupleniia imperializma [The war crimes of imperialism]. Moscow: 1953. Part of this study deals with German war crimes.

856 RÜCKERL, ADALBERT. Die Strafverfolgung von NS-Verbrechen: 1945-1978. Eine Dokumentation. Heidelberg and Karlsruhe: C.F. Müller, 1979. 148p. Published in English as The Investigation of Nazi Crimes, 1945-1978: A Documentation. 145p. Heidelberg: C.F. Müller, 1979. Contains background information on concentration camps and the "final solution" of the Jewish question. One section deals with the Nuremberg IMT and various American, British, French, and Russian war crimes trials. Separate chapters deal with war crimes investigations from 1945 to 1978, war crimes in Austria, the possibilities and limitations of such investigations, and the context of war crimes investigations in 8 northern and eastern European countries. Appendices contain statistical information, the fate of commanders of various concentration camps, and bibliographies on Einsatzgruppen A, B, C, and D.

857 RUSSELL, EDWARD F.L. [LORD RUSSELL OF LIVERPOOL]. The Scourge of the Swastika: A Short History of Nazi War Crimes. London: 1954. New York: Philosophical Library, 1954. 259p. General account of war crimes committed during World War II. Discusses Hitler's instruments of tyranny, war crimes on the high seas, and ill treatment and murder of prisoners of war and of civilians in occupied territory. Also deals with slave labor, concentration camps, and the "final solution" of the Jewish question. Includes bibliographical references, 5-page index, 29 photographs.

858 RÜTER-EHLERMANN, ADELHEID L., and C.F. RÜTER (comps.). Justiz und NS-Verbrechen: Sammlung deutscher Strafurteile wegen nationalsozialistischer Tötungsverbrechen, 1945-1966, Registerheft zum 1. Band, mit Hilfsmittelteil und Errataliste. Amsterdam: Amsterdam University Press (UPA), 1969. 97p. This is the index to volume 1 of the 22-volume set of trial records by the same title. Contains an introduction which explains the use of the register as a finding aid, a name index, place index, subject index, a register of laws, index of crimes charged, index of military units, and an index of publicized, judicial decisions.

859 RÜTER-EHLERMANN, ADELHEID L., and C.F. RÜTER (comps.) Volumes 1-5. These two were joined by H.H. FUCHS for Volumes 6-12. FUCHS, RÜTER, and IRENE SAGEL-GRANDE (comps.) did Volumes 13-21. All four worked on Volume 22. Justiz und NS-Verbrechen: Sammlung deutscher Strafurteile wegen Nationalsozialistischer Tötungsverbrechen 1945-1966. Amsterdam: UPA, 1968-1981. 22 volumes. German judgments rendered since the end of World War II until 1966 are covered in this series. Deals with all aspects of war crimes committed by Germany and her allies. The verdicts review in detail the evidence, defendants' motivations

and arguments offered in defense, and the local and historical circumstances of the crime. The collection is a result of collaboration between a number of Dutch and German scholars. Compiled at the Seminarium voor Strafrecht en Strafrechtspleging Van Hamel, University of Amsterdam. Each of the 616 cases examined here involved several defendants.

860 SANDMEL, SAMUEL. "Mass Crime and the Judeo-Christian Tradition II," *Minnesota Review* 1963 3(2): 220-227.

861 SAUER, WILHELM. "Zum Begriff der Verbrechensplanung," *Spruchgerichte* 1947 1(December): 57.

862 SAYRE, FRANCIS B. "Criminal Conspiracy," *Harvard Law Review* 1922 35(4): 393-427. 109 notes.

863 SCHICKEL, ALFRED. "Treatment of the Nazi Crimes in New German History Textbooks," *Patterns of Prejudice* 1974 8(2): 13-16, 21. Discusses current historiographic trends in West Germany regarding Adolf Hitler, German war crimes, and the anti-Semitism of the 1930s-1940s.

864 SELLING, LOWELL S. "Specific War Crimes," *Journal of Criminal Law and Criminology* 1944 34(2): 303-310.

865 SHEERIN, J.B. "War Crimes in High Places," *Catholic World* 1971 213(July): 163-164.

866 SIBLEY, MULFORD QUICKERT. "War Crimes, Morals, and Civilization," *Minnesota Review* 1963 3(2): 142-153.

867 SIBLEY, MULFORD QUICKERT. "War Crimes of World War II," *Minnesota Review* 1963 Special Issue (Winter): 141-262.

868 SNOW, EDGAR. "Here the Nazi Butchers Wasted Nothing," *Saturday Evening Post*, October 28, 1944: 18-21.

869 SPEYER, PAUL. "Les Crimes de guerre par omission," *Revue de Droit Pénal et de Criminologie* 1950 30(June): 903-943.

870 UNITED NATIONS INFORMATION ORGANIZATION [OFFICE]. *Religious Persecution*. London: HMSO, 1942. 23p.

871 UNITED NATIONS INFORMATION ORGANIZATION [OFFICE]. *War and Peace Aims: Extracts from Statements of United Nations Leaders. Special Supplement No. 1 to the United Nations Review*. New York: United Nations Information Office, January 30, 1943. 136p. Chapter 2, "Immediate Postwar Problems," deals with the prosecution of war criminals. Contains statements by Eduard Benes of Czechoslovakia, General Wladyslaw Sikorski (Prime Minister of the Polish government in exile), Franklin Roosevelt, Winston Churchill, Charles de Gaulle, Hubert Pierlot (Prime Minister of Belgium in exile), Vyacheslav M. Molotov, Adolf A. Berle, Jr., Sumner Wells, Stanislaw Stronski (Polish Minister of Information), Jan Masaryk (Vice-Premier and Foreign Minister of Czechoslovakia), Pieter Gerbrandy (Prime Minister of the Netherlands in exile), and Anthony Eden.

872 UNITED NATIONS INFORMATION ORGANIZATION [OFFICE]. *War and Peace Aims: Extracts from Statements of United Nations Leaders Special Supplement No. 3 to the United Nations Review*. New York: United Nations Information Office, April 30, 1944. 127p. Chapter 2, "Immediate Postwar Problems," contains extracts from

speeches of leaders of Great Britain, the United States, Belgium, the USSR, and Czechoslovakia dealing with prosecution of war criminals.

873 UNITED STATES. DEPARTMENT OF STATE. "Atrocities and War Crimes: Report from Robert H. Jackson to the President," Department of State Bulletin 1945 12(311): 1071-1078. June 10, 1945. On the legal and practical aspects of arrangements for war crimes trials.

874 UNITED STATES. DEPARTMENT OF STATE. "Crimes Against Civilian Populations in Occupied Countries," Department of State Bulletin 1942 7(165): 709-710. August 22, 1942. Statement on the subject by President Roosevelt, warning war criminals of postwar prosecution for their crimes.

875 UNITED STATES. DEPARTMENT OF STATE. "Declaration on German Hostilities," Department of State Bulletin 1943 9(228): 310-311. November 6, 1943. Reports by the US, UK, and USSR on atrocities committed by retreating German armies.

876 UNITED STATES. DEPARTMENT OF THE ARMY. OFFICE OF THE JUDGE ADVOCATE GENERAL. Report of the Deputy Judge Advocate for War Crimes, European Command, June 1944 to July 1948. 5 volumes. [no city given]: [no publisher given], 1948. 249p.

877 VEALE, FREDERICK J.P. War Crimes Discreetly Veiled. New York: Devin-Adair, 1959. 240p. Published in Spanish as El Crimen de Nuremberg. Barcelona: Editorial Ahr, 1955. Consists of independent sketches of 6 events in contemporary history dealing with war crimes. Discusses the myth of Stalin's murderous regime, the unjust indictment of German prisoners for the Katyn murders, the unsolved death of Mussolini as an act of murder by Communists. Relates the story of French doctor Marcel Petriot, who during both world wars abused his position to extort money. He was tried in Paris for the murder of 63 people. German Major Walter Reder was indicted by an Italian court for various crimes, among them the massacre of the civilian population of Marzabutta, Italy. His guilt is denied by the author. The case of General Bernhard Herman Ramcke, the Hangman of Brest, was tried by a French court on March 19, 1951; according to this author, for political reasons a verdict of innocent was impossible. Discusses the conviction of Admiral Erich Raeder. 39 notes, 3-page index, 16 photographs, 4 maps.

878 "War Crimes," Current Notes on International Affairs 1945 16 (October-November): 217-220.

879 "War Crimes," Solicitor 1942 9(2): 19-20.

880 "War Crimes - Moral, Political and Legal Problems," Round Table 1944 34: 121-129.

881 "War Crimes Issue: Nagging Questions," Newsweek 1969 74(December 8): 34-35.

882 WILKENS, E. N.S.- Verbrechen, Strafjustiz, deutsche Selbstbesinnung. Berlin: Lutherisches Verlagshaus Herbert Reuner, 1964.

883 WOETZEL, ROBERT K. "War Crimes by Irregular and Nongovernmental Forces," International Relations 1971 3(12): 995-1002, 1013. 38 notes.

884 WOLD, TERJE. "War Crimes, News of Norway [Washington] 1944 4(January 28): 5-8; United Nations Review 1944 4(3): 115-116. Address by the Norwegian Minister of Justice to the Manchester Reform Club.

885 WRONG, DENNIS H. "War Crimes and Politics," Dissent 1971 18(4): 327-329.

886 ZEMAN, ZBYNEK A.B. Nazi Propaganda. London: Oxford University Press, in association with the Wiener Library, 1964. 226p. An examination of the part played by the manipulation and control of public opinion in the National Socialists' capture and exercise of power in Germany, as well as of the manner in which Hitler's government employed propaganda in its bid for power abroad. Discusses the conquest of the masses, Jews and Communists, Nazi foreign broadcasting, an appeal to Austria, and propaganda in the war. Chart shows total broadcast time abroad daily from 1933-1939. Based on primary and secondary sources; 16-page index, 24-page bibliography, 18 photographs.

B. DEFINITION OF WAR CRIMES

887 ARONÉANU, EUGÈNE. La Définition de l'agression. Paris: Les Éditions Internationales, 1958. 405p. A general treatment of aggression, with occasional reference to the IMT trials at Nuremberg and Tokyo. 1854 notes, index, 19-page analytical table.

888 BENES, VACLAV. "The Question of the Definition of War Crimes," Central European Observer 1943 20(18): 282-283.

889 HAZARD, JOHN N. "Why Try Again to Define Aggression?" American Journal of International Law 1968 62(3): 701-710. 31 notes.

890 LACHS, MANFRED. War Crimes: An Attempt to Define the Issues. London: Stevens, 1945. 108p. Surveys international and municipal law and discusses the nature of the crimes, the identity of the criminals, and the question of jurisdiction and right of asylum. Contains a chapter on the trials of collaborators and another dealing with the case of the United Nations versus war criminals. Concludes with ten articles intended to define war crimes.

C. WAR CRIMES AND WAR CRIMINALS

891 HOFFMANN, J.R. "Nazi War Crimes and Criminals," Dicta 1946 23(1): 30-31.

892 MUNRO, HECTOR A. "War Crimes and Criminals," New Commonwealth 1943 8(May): 224-226.

893 PERGLER, CHARLES. "War Crimes and 'War Criminals,'" Journal of the Bar Association of the District of Columbia 1946 13(9): 385-392.

D. ALLIED WAR CRIMES

894 Allied War Crimes and Crimes against Humanity. Documents on World War II printed in German by Duerer-Verlag, whose monthly magazine Der Tag was banned in Germany and Austria, first by Allied occupation authorities and later by officials in both countries.

895 BARDÈCHE, MAURICE (general editor). "Crimes de guerre des alliés?" Défense de l'occident 1965 (49-50): 101p. [entire special number]. Paris: Défense de l'Occident, 1965. Part 1 deals with the crime of genocide. Part 2, crimes against humanity. Part 3, pillage and murder in occupied Europe. Part 4, the treatment of prisoners of war and disarmed troops. 3-page bibliography.

896 FAHEY, JAMES J. Pacific War Diary, 1942-1945. New York: Avon, 1963. Discusses atrocities committed by American soldiers against dead Japanese kamikazi pilots.

897 FALK, RICHARD A. "The Shimoda Case: A Legal Appraisal of the Atomic Attacks on Hiroshima and Nagasaki," American Journal of International Law 1965 59(4): 759-793. A case for damages suffered from the atomic bomb. Argues that the United States violated international law by using atomic weapons. 90 notes.

898 GALLERY, DANIEL V. Twenty Million Tons Under the Sea. Chicago: H. Regnery, 1956. 344p. Compares Allied and Axis war crimes at sea.

899 LA COSTE, RAYMOND. "Un Crime de guerre des alliés," Ecrits de Paris 1975 346: 5-15. The greatest war crime committed by Churchill and Anthony Eden was delivering millions of fleeing Russian refugees into the hands of Stalin.

900 "The Webling Incident," After the Battle 1980 (27): 30-33. Photographs of and conjectures on the incident of April 29, 1945, in which SS troops who surrendered were allegedly executed by U.S. troops of the 222nd Infantry Regiment, 42nd Division.

901 ZAYAS, ALFRED M. DE, with WALTER RABUS. Die Wehrmacht-Untersuchungsstelle. Deutsche Ermittlungen über alliierte Völkerrechtsverletzungen im Zweiten Weltkrieg. Munich: Universitas Langen-Müller, 1980. 477p. Detailed, heavily-documented study of allied violations of international laws of war. 20-page bibliography, 33 photographs, documents.

E. AGGRESSION AND AGGRESSIVE WAR AS WAR CRIMES

902 BELLONI, G.A. "Criminalità di Guerra," Guistizia Penale 1946 51(January): 1-8.

903 BISSCHOP, W.R. Criminality of War and its Prevention. London: Stevens, 1943. Read before the Grotius Society on May 5, 1943.

904 GABUS, ERIC. La criminalité de la guerre. Dissertation, University of Geneva. Geneva: Éditions Générales, 1953.

905 GLASER, STEFAN. "Constituye un crimen la guerra de agresión," Revista Española de Derecho Internacional 1953 6: 539-562. 53 notes.

906 GLASER, STEFAN. "Quelques Observations sur la prescription en matière de criminalité de guerre," Revue de Droit Pénal et de Criminologie 1965 45: 5-8. Much on statutes of limitation.

907 GOODHART, ARTHUR L. What Acts of War are Justifiable? Oxford Pamphlets on World Affairs No. 42. Oxford: Clarendon Press, 1940. 32p.

908 GROSS, LEO. "Criminality of Aggressive War," American Political Science Review 1947 41(April): 205-225.

909 KOHT, HALVDAN. Norway Neutral and Invaded. New York: Macmillan, 1941. 253p.

910 LEYRAT, P. DE. "Crime de la guerre et crimes de guerre," Cahiers du Monde Nouveau 1945 2(5): 557-606. The historical development of international law concerning war crimes culminating in the IMT Charter.

911 MANN, ERIC. Germany Prepares for War: The Case against Germany. Des Moines: Advertisers Press, 1944.

912 MURRAY, JOHN COURTNEY. "Remarks on the Moral Problems of War," Theological Studies 1959 20: 40-61.

913 NEUNER, ROBERT. "Criminal War and Criminal Warfare," New Europe 1942 2(November-December): 364-367.

914 POMPE, CORNELIUS A. Aggressive War: An International Crime. The Hague: Martinus Nijhoff, 1953. 382p. A study of the legal and philosophical implications of aggressive war as an international crime. Examines wars of aggression, evolution toward Nuremberg, punishment for waging aggressive war, and the implications of the Nuremberg principles. Copiously documented; 8-page bibliography, index.

915 POTTER, PITMAN B. "Offenses against the Peace and Security of Mankind," American Journal of International Law 1952 46(1): 101-102. 3 notes.

916 RADIN, MAX. "War Crimes and Crimes of War," Virginia Quarterly Review 1945 21(3): 497-516.

917 RÖLING, BERNARD V.A. "On Aggression, on International Criminal Law, on Criminal Jurisdiction," Nederlands Tijdschrift voor International Recht 1955 2(April): 167-196; 2(July): 279-289.

918 THOMAS, ANN VAN WYNEN, and A.J. THOMAS, JR. The Concept of Aggression in International Law. Dallas: Southern Methodist University Press, 1972. An SMU Law School Study which traces changing definitions of provocation, self-defense, and direct and indirect aggression.

919 WALDMANN, ALFRED. „Der Angriffskrieg als internationales Verbrechen nach den Nürnberger Entscheidungen ," Doctor of Laws Dissertation, Erlangen University, 1951. 126p.

920 WALDOCK, C.H.M. "Release of the Altmark's Prisoners," British Year Book of International Law 1947 24: 216-238.

921 WEERD, HARVEY A. DE. "Hitler's Plans for invading Britain," Military Affairs 1948 12(Fall): 142-148. Uses Nuremberg IMT trial documents and other captured documents to describe Hitler's intentions regarding the invasion of Great Britain.

922 YOKOTA, KISABURO. "War as an International Crime," in Dimitri S. Constantopoulos, Constantin Th. Eustathiades, and C.N. Fragistas (eds.). Grundprobleme des internationalen Rechts. Fundamental Problems of International Law. Problèmes fondementaux du droit international. Festschrift für Jean Spiropolous. Bonn: Schimmelbuch, 1957. 471p.

F. COLLABORATION

923 BOISSARIE, ANDRÉ. "Les Bases de la répression," Cahiers Politiques 1945 8(March): 12-20. Discusses the legislative basis of the French decrees concerning collaborators and maintains that these decrees are in complete accord with the principles of the French law.

924 BOSELLI, ALDO. I reati di collaborazione col tedesco invasore. Genoa: Societa Editrice Universale, 1946. 125pp. A discussion of legal theory and practice concerning crimes of collaboration with the Germans. Appendix contains the most important legislative decrees on the subject. 147p.

925 "Wartime Collaborators: A Comparative Study of the Effect of their Trials on the Treason Law of Great Britain, Switzerland and France," Yale Law Journal 1947 56(7): 1210-1233. A study of the modification of trial procedures and the substantive changes in the treason law instituted to punish wartime collaborators. Great Britain and Switzerland were able to avoid serious difficulties and popular criticism, while France found it necessary to proceed on a theory of criminality that was retroactive in nature. Footnotes contain information on individual trials and statistics. 137 notes.

G. CRIMES AGAINST THE PEACE

926 GARCÍA-MORA, MANUEL R. "Crimes against Peace in International Law: From Nuremberg to the Present," Kentucky Law Journal 1964 53(1): 36-55.

927 PELLA, V. VESPASIEN. "Le Code des crimes contre la paix et la sécurité de l'humanité (observation et réflexions)," Revue de Droit International de Sciences Diplomatiques et Politiques 1952 30(4): 337-354; 1953 31(2): 125-150; (3): 257-271; (4): 353-362; 1954 32(1): 3-11; (2): 111-118; (3): 231-240; (4): 351-360; 1955 33(1): 13-25; (3): 243-252; (4): 329-339; 1956 34(1): 33-47; (2): 161-172; (4): 372-385. 356 notes.

928 SCHAFER, MARK. Crimes against Peace. Ambilly: Les Presses de Savoie, 1952. 222p.

929 SCHICK, FRANZ B. "Crimes against Peace," Journal of Criminal Law and Criminology 1948 38(February): 445-465. A discussion of the legal and political difficulties inherent in the concept of crimes against peace. Analyzes the Nuremberg IMT Charter, the judgment, and statements of the prosecution, and then compares them to Allied policies and practices before the war.

H. CRIMES AGAINST HUMANITY

930 ARONÉANU, EUGÈNE. "La Guerre internationale d'intervention pour cause d'humanité," Revue International de Droit Pénal 1948 19: 173-244. World War II was an international denunciation of German violations of human rights. The war crimes trials and the establishment of the United Nations Commission on human rights are steps toward a truly international democratic order.

931 ARONÉANU, EUGÈNE. "Le Crime contre l'humanité," Nouvelle Revue de Droit International Privé 1946 13: 369-418. Published in German as Das Verbrechen gegen die Menschlichkeit. Baden-Baden: Schröder, 1947. 55p. Also published as part of an anthology (see following entry). Discusses the theory and

philosophy of war crimes, crimes against humanity, the Declaration of St. James, the Declaration of Moscow, Justice Robert H. Jackson, different categories of crimes charged at Nuremberg, international law, the limitation of state sovereignty, and definitions of various war crimes. Summarizes the evolution through which the theory of crimes against humanity had passed. Based on primary and secondary sources; 37 notes.

932 ARONÉANU, EUGÈNE. Le Crime contre l'humanité. Paris: Librairie Dalloz, 1961. 322p. An anthology of six essays, three of which had been published earlier in periodical form. The essays are "Le Crime contre l'humanité," "La Guerre internationale d'intervention pour crimes contre l'humanité," "Naissance et application de la loi internationale réprimant le crime contre l'humanité," "La Persécution crime clandestin ou crime contre l'humanité," and "Où en est la Répression des crimes contre l'humanité." This anthology contains an introduction and summary in English of "The Crime against Humanity" (pp. 73-77). Excellent summaries preceding the various essays take the place of an index and many of the entries contain summaries themselves. The appendix contains various declarations of President Franklin Roosevelt and Prime Minister Winston Churchill, and a number of French, Russian, American, and British documents. Several of the documents discuss war crimes, the problems of defining war crimes, the nature of the charges to be brought against war criminals, various principles of international law, the terms of the IMT, and Control Law 10, adopted December 20, 1945. 344 notes.

933 ARONÉANU, EUGÈNE. "Le Crime contre l'humanité et la juridiction penal international," Revue de Droit International de Sciences Diplomatiques et Politiques 1950 28(2): 229-246. 30 notes.

934 ARONÉANU, EUGÈNE. "Les Droits de l'homme et le crime contre l'humanité," Revue de Droit International de Sciences Diplomatiques et Politiques 1947 25(3): 187-196. Report presented to the international congress of democratic jurists. Brussels, July 1947. Discussion by the "first theoretician of the crime against humanity." Concludes that the IMT failed to set a precedent by declaring itself incompetent to judge international crimes of common law committed in time of peace. It is up to the Commission on Human Rights and the United Nations to establish the law in this matter.

935 ARONÉANU, EUGÈNE. "Les Nations Unies et le crime contre l'humanité," Revue de Droit International de Sciences Diplomatiques et Politiques 1948 26(3): 285-287.

936 ARONÉANU, EUGÈNE, "Responsabilités penales pour crime contre l'humanité," Revue de Droit International de Sciences Diplomatiques et Politiques 1948 26(2): 144-181. Discusses the evolution of the concept of crimes against humanity during the war and of the problem of responsibility. Copiously annotated.

937 BOISSARIE, ANDRÉ. "Rapport sur la définition du crime contre l'humanité présenté à la conférence d'unification du droit pénal (Brussels, 10 juil. 1947)," Revue Internationale de Droit Pénal 1947 18: 201-207. Defines the concept of crime against humanity and notes the independence of such crimes from a state of war. Stresses the need for codification of international penal law and for the creation of a criminal chamber in the International Court of Justice.

938 BRAND, JAMES T. "Crimes against Humanity and the Nürnberg Trials," *Oregon Law Review* 1949 28(2): 93-119. The author was Chief Justice of Military Tribunal No. 3. He discusses the legal bases of the concept of crimes against humanity and its application at Nuremberg, with special reference to the trial of members of the Reich Ministry of Justice. Relates the Nuremberg proceedings to the international movement for a bill of human rights. 30 notes.

939 BRITO, J.G. "Os crimes de guerra e contra a humanidade," *Revista Forense* 1951 135(May): 27-35.

940 BUSCH, RICHARD. „Das Verbrechen gegen die Menschlichkeit als Grundlage des Organisationsverbrechens," *Spruchgerichte* 1949 3(February-March): 56-60.

941 COHN, K. "Crimes against Humanity," *German Foreign Policy* 1967 6(February): 160-169.

942 DAUTRICOURT, JOSEPH Y. "Crime against Humanity - European Views on its Conception and its Future," *Journal of Criminal Law and Criminology* 1949 40(July-August): 170-175. Rejects the restrictive conception of crime against humanity as adopted in the judgment of the Flick case and contends that the interpretation adopted by the 8th Conference for the Unification of Penal Law (quoted in the judgment) was intended to be broader. Contrasts universal penal law with international penal law.

943 DAUTRICOURT, JOSEPH Y. "La Définition du crime contre l'humanité," *Revue de Droit International de Sciences Diplomatiques et Politiques* 1947 25(4): 294-313. Deals with the problem of defining crimes against humanity. Surveys the works of several writers who have dealt with this problem and then offers his own definition and explains how such crimes can be repressed.

944 DEL ROSAL FERNÁNDEZ, JUAN. *Acerca de los crimenes contra la humanidad.* Valencia: Collegio de Abogados, 1950. 23p.

945 FELDMANN, HORST. *Das Verbrechen gegen die Menschlichkeit.* Essen-Kettwig: West, 1948. 147p. A critical, legal study of the implications of permitting German courts to enforce the Allied-imposed law for the punishment of war criminals.

946 FERRINGER, NATALIE JEAN. "Crimes against Humanity: A Legal Problem in War and Peace," Ph.D. dissertation, University of Virginia, 1980. 332p. Detailed analysis of the subject, with much on the London Charter, the IMT Charter, and crimes against humanity in Vietnam, Bangladesh, Burundi, Biafra, South Africa, Northern Ireland, and the Soviet Union. Abstracted in *Dissertation Abstracts International* 1980 41(4): 1757-A - 1758-A.

947 GARCÍA-MORA, MANUEL R. "Crimes against Humanity and the Principle of Nonextradition of Political Offenders," *Michigan Law Review* 1964 62(6): 927-960. 172 notes.

948 GOLDSTEIN, ANATOLE. "Crimes against Humanity - Some Jewish Aspects," *Jewish Year Book of International Law* 1948 206-225. Discusses Allied policy towards Nazi persecution of Jews and points out that it was not until the London Agreement that the Allies decided to hold the Germans responsible for crimes committed against Jewish citizens. Control Council Law No. 10 went beyond the Charter in regarding crimes against humanity as independent and accessory crimes.

949 GRAVEN, JEAN. "La Définition et la répression des crimes contre l'humanité," *Revue* *de* *Droit* *International* *de* *Sciences* *Diplomatiques* *et* *Politiques* 1948 26(1): 1-32. Defines the concept of crimes against humanity and discusses problems of prosecution, such as the defense of superior orders. Questions whether an international penal court could function without an international police force.

950 GRAVEN, JEAN. "Les Crimes contre l'humanité," *Recueil* *des* *Cours* 1950 76(1): 433-607. Copiously annotated; 4-page bibliography.

951 HÄRTLE, HEINRICH. *Die* *Kriegsschuld* *der* *Sieger.* *Churchills,* *Roosevelts* *und* *Stalins* *Verbrechen* *gegen* *den* *Weltfrieden.* Göttingen: Schütz, 1966. 2nd edition. Preußisch Oldendorf: K.W. Schütz, 1971. 341p.

952 HEIDELMEYER, WOLFGANG. "Krieg und Nachkrieg: die UN-Grundsätze bei Kriegs- und Humanitätsverbrechen," *Vereinte* *Nationen* 1974 22(December): 176-179.

953 HERZOG, JACQUES-BERNARD. "Contribution à l'étude de la définition du crime contre l'humanité," *Revue* *Internationale* *de* *Droit* *Pénal* 1947 18: 155-170. Examines the sociological and juridical concepts of crimes against humanity. Defines such a crime as a breach of law committed in conformity with the criminal policy of the state. After discussing the Nuremberg IMT and a French law of August 18, 1944, the author characterizes the argumentation of the Nuremberg IMT as "incomplete," because it refused to consider acts committed before 1939. Contains a discussion of the literature on the subject.

954 HOLTZ, W. "Vom Sinne eines Begriffs ,Verbrechen gegen die Menschlichkeit,'" *Spruchgerichte* 1947 1: 62-66. Defines crime against humanity as the negation of the values pertaining to the concept as delineated by Christianity and humanism. Crimes against humanity were old crimes that could have been dealt with under existing law, but the concept of crime committed by an organization was new. Stresses the importance of preventative measures.

955 JAGUSCH, HEINRICH. "Das Verbrechen gegen die Menschlichkeit in der Rechtsprechung des Obersten Gerichtshofs für die Britische Zone," *Süddeutsche* *Juristen-Zeitung* 1949 4(9): 620-624. A survey of the decisions on the basis of Article 11 1c of Control Council Law No. 10.

956 LENER, SALVATORE. *Crimini* *di* *guerra* *e* *delitti* *contro* *l'umanita;* *lineamente* *di* *dottrina* *e* *spunti* *critici.* Rome: Edizioni "La Civiltà Cattolica," 1946. 3rd Edition, 1948. 159p.

957 LENER, SALVATORE. "Le Supreme barriere del diritto e i delitti contro l'umanità," *Civiltà* *Cattolica* 1946 47(June 15): 404-416.

958 LEVASSEUR, G. "Les Crimes contre l'humanité et le problème de leur prescription," *Journal* *de* *Droit* *International* 1966 93 (April-June): 259-284.

959 MERTENS, PIERRE. *L'Imprescriptibilité* *des* *crimes* *de* *guerre* *et* *contre* *l'humanité.* Brussels: Éditions de l'Université de Bruxelles, 1974. 230p.

960 MERTENS, PIERRE. "L'Imprescriptibilité des crimes de guerre et des crimes contre l'humanité," *Revue* *de* *Droit* *Pénal* *et* *de*

Criminologie 1970 51: 204-216. Much on the statute of limitations.

961 MEYROWITZ, HENRI. *La Répression par les tribunaux allemands des crimes contre l'humanité*. Paris: Pichor et Durand-Auzias, 1960. 514p.

962 MITTERMAIER, WOLFGANG. „Das Verbrechen gegen die Menschlichkeit," *Schweizerische Juristen-Zeitung* 1949 45(July 15): 213-218.

963 PAOLI, JULES. "Contribution à l'étude de crimes de guerre et de crimes contre l'humanité en droit pénal international," *Revue Générale de Droit International Public* 1941-1945 49(2): 129-165. Attempts to formulate natural and international theoretical bases of war crimes statutes. The thesis is that war crimes constitute an attack on a minimum juridical order of both nations concerned. This is the basis for prosecution of war criminals. Reviews attempts to prosecute war criminals after World War I.

964 QUINTANO RIPOLLÉS, ANTONIO. "Problemática de jurisdicción en la repression de la criminalidad contra la humanidad," *Revista de Derecho Internacional* 1948 54(September): 17-40.

965 RADBRUCH, GUSTAV. „Zur Diskussion über das Verbrechen gegen die Menschlichkeit," *Süddeutsche Juristen-Zeitung* 1947 2(Special Number, March): 131-136. Approves of the retroactivity of Control Council Law No. 10, arguing that retroactivity is frequently necessary in international law.

966 RESICH, ZBIGNIEW. "La Convention sur l'imprescriptibilitédes crimes de guerre et des crimes contre l'humanité," *Annuaire Polonais des Affaires Internationales* 1968 71: 58-69. Adopted by the United Nations on November 26, 1968.

967 ROLAND, M. "La Prescription de crimes contre l'humanité," *Revue de Droit Contemporain* 1964 11: 115-117.

968 SAUER, WILHELM. „Humanitäts- und Organisationsverbrechen - Zur Weiterbildung des Strafrechts," *Spruchgerichte* 1947 1(September): 6-9.

969 SCHAIBLE, RICHARD. „Die besonderen Tatsbestandsmerkmale des Verbrechens gegen die Menschlichkeit," *Spruchgerichte* 1947 1(November): 31-34.

970 SCHAIBLE, RICHARD. „War die Errichtung der Ghetti in den Ostgebieten ein Verbrechen gegen die Menschlichkeit?" *Spruchgerichte* 1948 2(October): 293-296.

971 SCHWELB, EGON. "Crimes against Humanity," *British Year Book of International Law* 1946 23: 178-226. Traces the development of the concept of crimes against humanity since the Hague Convention of 1907. Notes many restrictions of the concept adopted at Nuremberg.

972 SONTAG, ERNST. „Das Verbrechen gegen die Menschlichkeit," *Schweizerische Zeitschrift für Strafrecht* 1949 64: 201-209.

973 SOTTILE, ANTOINE. "La Prescription des crimes contre l'humanité et le droit pénal international," *Revue de Droit International de Sciences Diplomatiques et Politiques* 1965 43(1): 5-18.

974 TESAR, OTTOKAR. "Die naturrechtlichen Grundlagen der 'Crimes against Humanity,'" in Demetrios S. Constantopoulos and Hans Wehberg (eds.). Gegenwartsprobleme des internationalen Rechtes und der Rechtsphilosophie. Festschrift für Rudolf Laun. Hamburg: Girardet, 1953.

975 "Übersicht der Rechtsprechung des Obersten Gerichtshof für die britische Zone. Zum Verbrechen gegen die Menschlichkeit," Zentral-Justizblatt für die britische Zone 1948 2(November): 243-246.

976 UNITED STATES. DEPARTMENT OF STATE. "The United Nations: President Truman's Address to the General Assembly," Department of State Bulletin 1946 15(383): 808-812. November 3, 1946. Several remarks on the Nuremberg IMT trial and the continuing campaign against wars of aggression as crimes against humanity.

977 "Verbrechen gegen den Frieden, Kriegsverbrechen und Verbrechen gegen die Menchlichkeit verjähren nicht," Staat und Recht 1969 18: 4-25.

978 WIMMER, AUGUST. "Die Bestrafung von Humanitätsverbrechen und der Grundsatz 'nullum crimen sine lege,'" Süddeutsche Juristen-Zeitung 1947 2(3): 123-132. The principle nulla poena sine lege may be suspended if there is definite obligation for the state to apply a law retroactively. Argues that this is the case in crimes against humanity.

I. DEPORTATION, RESETTLEMENT, AND FORCED LABOR

979 ADLER, H.G. Der verwaltete Mensch. Studien zur Deportation der Juden aus Deutschland. Tübingen: J.C.B. Mohr (Paul Siebeck), 1974. 1076p. Excellent and exhaustive general history of Jewish deportations, though it does not address directly the problem of war crimes.

980 BILLSTEIN, AUREL. Fremdarbeiter in unserer Stadt 1939-1945. Kriegsgefangene und Deportierte "fremdvölkische Arbeitskräfte" am Beispiel Krefelds. Frankfurt am Main: Röderberg, 1980. 195p. On forced labor.

981 BOMERHAUSEN, CHRISTINE. Les Belges deportés à Dora et dans ses kommandos. Brussels: Université Libre de Bruxelles, 1978.

982 EVRARD, JACQUES. La Déportation des travailleurs français dans le IIIe Reich. Paris: Fayard, 1972. 460p.

983 FERENCZ, BENJAMIN B. Less than Slaves. Jewish forced Labor and the Quest for Compensation. Cambridge: Harvard University Press, 1979. 249p. Deals with I.G. Farben, Krupp, and Siemens.

984 FRIED, HANS ERNST [JOHN ERNEST] (comp.). The Exploitation of Foreign Labour by Germany. International Labour Office, Series C, No. 25. Montreal: International Labour Office, 1945. 286p.

985 FRIED, HANS ERNST [JOHN ERNEST]. "Transfer of Civilian Manpower from Occupied Territory," American Journal of International Law 1946 49(2): 303-331. A survey of German deportation policies and the international laws applicable to them, particularly the Hague regulations. Discusses the conditions under which German manpower could be recruited legally for reconstruction work in other countries.

986 GRANET, M. "La Déportation au procès international de Nuremberg," <u>Revue d'Histoire de la Deuxième Guerre Mondiale</u> 1954 4: 99-114.

987 GROSS, FELIKS. <u>The Polish Worker, a Study of a Social Stratum</u>. New York: Roy Publishers, 1945. Deals with forced labor. 274p.

988 HOMZE, EDWARD L. <u>Foreign Labor in Nazi Germany</u>. Princeton: Princeton University Press, 1967. 350p.

989 KANNAPIN, HANS-ECKHARDT. <u>Wirtschaft unter Zwang. Anmerkungen und Analysen zur rechtlichen und politischen Verantwortung der deutschen Wirtschaft unter der Herrschaft des Nationalsozialismus im Zweiten Weltkrieg, besonders im Hinblick auf den Einsatz und die Behandlung von ausländischen Arbeitskräften und Konzentrationslagerhäftlingen in deutschen Industrie- und Rüstungsbetrieben</u>. Cologne: Deutsche Industrieverlag, 1966. 334p. Deals with forced labor. Bibliography, tables.

990 KOEHL, ROBERT L. <u>RKFDV: German Resettlement and Population Policy, 1939-1945: A History of the Reich Commission for the Strengthening of Germandom</u>. Cambridge: Harvard University Press, 1957. 263p. Annotated bibliography.

991 KUCZYNSKI, JÜRGEN. <u>Istoriia uslovii truda v Germanii</u>. Moscow: [no publisher given]. 1949. Part of this study deals with the use of Russian slave labor in Germany during the war.

992 KULISCHER, EUGENE M. <u>The Displacement of Population in Europe</u>. Montreal: International Labour Office, 1943. London: King & Staples, 1943. Considerable data concerning Himmler's racial resettlements.

993 LANGE, HORST. <u>REIMAHG - Unternehmen des Todes. Der Aufbau der deutschen faschistischen Luftwaffe - Rolle des Gustloff-Konzerns - Verbrechen an ausländischen Zwangsarbeitern im unterirdischen Flugzeugswerk 'Reimahg' bei Kahla, 1944/1945</u>. Jena: Rat des Kreises, 1969. 164p. On forced labor.

994 "Mobilization of Foreign Labour in Germany," <u>International Labour Review</u> 1944 50(October): 469-480.

995 MOLDAWER, S. "The Road to Lublin," <u>Contemporary Jewish Record</u> 1940 (March-April): 119-133. Deals with the deportation of German Jews.

996 PFAHLMANN, HANS. <u>Fremdarbeiter und Kriegsgefangene in der deutschen Kriegswirtschaft 1939-1945</u>. Darmstadt: Wehr und Wissen Verlagsgesellschaft, 1968. 238p.

997 PROUDFOOT, MALCOLM J. <u>European Refugees, 1939-1952. A Study in Forced Population Movement</u>. Evanston, Illinois: Northwestern University Press, 1956.

998 RICHET, CHARLES, and ANTONIN MANS. <u>Pathologie de la déportation</u>. Monaco: A.D.I.F., 1958.

999 SIJES, B.A. <u>De arbeidsinzet: de gedwongen arbeid van Nederlanders in Duitsland, 1940-1945</u>. The Hague: Martinus Nijhoff, 1966. 730p. Summary in English. Illustrations, tables, diagrams, bibliography.

1000 "Soviet-Workers in Germany," International Labour Review 1943 47(May): 576-590.

1001 SPEEK, PETER. Foreign Workers in German War Efforts. Washington: GPO, 1942.

1002 "Too Much Lebensraum," Newsweek 1942 19(12): 37. Chart and commentary on German forced labor in various European countries.

1003 UNITED NATIONS. INFORMATION ORGANIZATION [OFFICE]. Slave Labour and Deportation. London: HMSO, 1944.

1004 UNITED NATIONS. RELIEF AND REHABILITATION ADMINISTRATION (UNRRA). Foreign Workers of Germany. A Report Based on Official German Sources. 2nd, revised edition, to November 1, 1944. UNRRA, European Regional Office, Displaced Persons Division, December 1944. 84p. Mimeographed. Deals with forced labor.

1005 VOS, JEAN DE [as related to Richard Baxter]. I was Hitler's Slave London: Quality Press, 1942. 122p. Deals with the forced labor of a Belgian worker.

1006 WEISSMANN KLEIN, GERDA. All But My Life. New York: Hill & Wang, 1957. 246p. On the life and forced labors of a young girl in German slave labor camps.

1007 ZENTRALE STELLE DER LANDESJUSTIZVERWALTUNGEN. Sonderbehandlung der in den deutschen Gebieten eingesetzten Zivilarbeiter und Kriegsgefangenen wegen Verstoßes die ihnen auferlegten Lebensführungsregeln. Ludwigsburg: [no publisher given], 196[?]. 53p. Deals with forced labor. Mimeographed.

J. MEDICAL CRIMES

1008 ALEXANDER, LEO. "Medical Science under Dictatorship," New England Journal of Medicine 1949 241(2): 39-47. 18 notes.

1009 BAEYER, WALTER VON. „Die Bestätigung der NS-Ideologie in der Medizin unter besonderer Berücksichtigung der Euthanasie," in Universitätstage, 1966, Nationalsozialismus und die deutsche Universität. Berlin: Walter de Gruyter, 1966.

1010 BATTAGLINI, ERNESTO, and G. VASSALLI (eds.). La Nuova Legislazione Penale. Milan: A. Giuffrè, 1946. 2 volumes. Collection of laws, ordinances, and statutes, including many on Fascism and war crimes.

1011 BAYLE, FRANCOIS. Croix gammée contre caducée; les expériences humaines en Allemagne pendant la deuxième guerre mondiale. Neustadt: Centre de l'Imprimerie Nationale, 1950. 1521p. Describes in detail medical services in Germany during World War 2, various medical experiments, medical exterminations, surgical experimentations, infectious diseases, and medical ethics. 9-page general conclusion summarizes the findings. Illustrated.

1012 BERNADAC, CHRISTIAN. Les médecins maudits. Les expériences médiales humaines dans les camps de concentration. Paris: Éditions France-Empire, 1967. 288p. On medical experiments.

1013 BOGUSZ, JÓZEF. "Closing Word," Przeglad Lekarski 1962 18(1): 54-55. Medical crimes committed by Germans. Includes information about the crimes and the names of several doctors.

1014 CATEL, WERNER. Grenzsituationen des Lebens. Beitrag zum Problem der begrenzten Euthanasie. Nuremberg: Glock and Lutz, 1962. 195p.

1015 German Medical War Crimes: A Summary of Information. London: World Medical Association, 1948. 15p.

1016 GREAT BRITAIN. ADVISORY COMMITTEE FOR THE INVESTIGATION OF GERMAN MEDICAL WAR CRIMES. Scientific Results of German Medical War Crimes: Report of an Enquiry by a Committee under the Chairmanship of Lord Moran. London: HMSO, 1949.

1017 GRUCHMANN, LOTHAR. "Euthanasie und Justiz im Dritten Reich," Vierteljahrshefte für Zeitgeschichte 1972 20(3): 235-279. 144 notes.

1018 HASE, HAMS CHRISTOPH VON (ed.). Evangelische Dokumente zur Ermordung der "unheilbar Kranken" unter der nationalsozialistischen Herrschaft in den Jahren 1939-1945. Stuttgart: Innere Mission und Hilfswerk der Evangelischen Kirche in Deutschland, [1964], 128p.

1019 HERMANN, ALFRED. Die Mordkiste von Hadamar. Eine Erzählung aufgrund authentischer Dokumente und wahrer Begebenheiten. Dortmund: Ruhr-Donau, 1961.

1020 HONOLKA, BERT. Die Kreuzelschreiber. Ärzte ohne Gewissen. Euthanasie im Dritten Reich. Hamburg: Rütten & Loening, 1961. 157p.

1021 IVY, ANDREW CONWAY. Report on War Crimes of a Medical Nature Committed in Germany and Elsewhere on German Nationals and the Nationals of Occupied Countries by the Nazi Regime during World War II. [no city given]: [no publisher given], [1945]. 22 lines.

1022 MANT, A.K. "Medical War Crimes in Nazi Germany," Saint Mary's Hospital Gazette 1961 27: 1-6.

1023 MENGES, JAN. "Euthanasie" in het Derde Rijk. Haarlem: Bohn, 1972. 188p. Summaries in English, German, and French.

1024 MENKES, G., R. HERMANN, and A. MIÈGE. Cobayes humains. Enquête de trois médecins suisses dans les bagnes nazis. Geneva: Éditions des Trois Collines, 1946. 90p.

1025 MITSCHERLICH, ALEXANDER, and FRED MIELKE. Death Doctors. London: ELEK, 1962.

1026 MITSCHERLICH, ALEXANDER, and FRED MIELKE. Wissenschaft ohne Menschlichkeit. Medizinische und eugenische Irrwege unter Diktatur, Bürokratie und Krieg. Heidelberg: Lambert Schneider, 1949. 307p.

1027 NIEDERMEYER, ALBERT. Éthique médicale. Vienna: Herder, 1954. A German doctor analyzes the pseudo-scientific aberrations which led the Germans to practice the liquidation of aliens.

1028 NOWAK, KURT. "Euthanasie und Sterilisierung im Dritten Reich. Die Konfrontation der evangelischen und katholischen Kirche mit dem "Gesetz zur Verhütung erbkranken Nachwuchses" und der "Euthanasie" Aktion. Göttingen: Vanderhoeck & Ruprecht, 1980. 221p. Enlarged version of a dissertation, Leipzig, 1971.

1029 SCHMIDT, GERHARD. Selektion in der Heilanstalt 1939-1945. Stuttgart: Evangelisches Verlagswerk, 1965. 151p.

1030 TERNON, YVES, and SOCRATE HELMAN. Histoire de la médecine SS; ou, Le Mythe du racisme biologique. Tournai: Castermann, 1969. 223p. Topics covered include fundamentals of SS medicine, SS medicine in concentration camps, the selection process for extermination in Auschwitz, sterilization, and methods of extermination. 5-page bibliography. Contains a number of documents as well as illustrations.

1031 TERNON, YVES, and SOCRATE HELMAN. Le Massacre des aliénés, des théoriciens nazis aux praticiens SS. Tournai: Castermann, 1971. Contains a number of documents as well as illustrations.

1032 TERNON, YVES, and SOCRATE HELMAN. Les Médecins allemands et le national-socialisme; Les Métamorphoses du darwinisme. Paris: Castermann, 1973. Studies the perversions and aberrations committed by Nazi doctors in the name of experimental medicine. Contains a number of documents and illustrations.

1033 URIS, LEON. QBVII. London: Corgi Books, 1971. 447p. Novel about medical experiments on Jews in concentration camps.

K. ECONOMIC CRIMES: EXPLOITATION, PILLAGE, LOOTING

1034 DOWNEY, WILLIAM G., JR. "Captured Enemy Property: Booty of War and Seized Enemy Property," American Journal of International Law 1950 44(3): 488-504. 68 notes.

1035 FAURE, EDGAR. "Le Travail obligatoire et le pillage economique," France Intérieure 1946 (April): 7-13. Dossier presented by Faure, delegate of the French Provisional Government at the Nuremberg IMT trial.

1036 FREEMAN, ALWYN V. "General Note on the Law of War Booty," American Journal of International Law 1946 40(4): 795-803. Discusses German violations. 35 notes.

1037 GREAT BRITAIN. FOREIGN OFFICE. Inter-Allied Declaration against Acts of Dispossession Committed in Territories under Enemy Occupation or Control. Cmd. 6418. London: HMSO, 1943.

1038 HEDIGER, ERNEST S. "Nazi Exploitation of Occupied Europe," Foreign Policy Reports 1942 18(6): 66-79. 60 notes.

1039 MIHAN, GEORGE. Looted Treasure: Germany's Raid on Art. London: Alliance Press, 1944. 94p.

1040 WOOLSEY, L.H. "The Forced Transfer of Property in Enemy Occupied Territory," American Journal of International Law 1943 37(9): 282-286.

L. CRIMES AGAINST HOMOSEXUALS

1041 HARTHAUSER, WOLFGANG. "Der Massenmord an Homosexuellen im Dritten Reich," in Willhart S. Schlegel, et al (eds.). Das grosse Tabu. Zeugnisse und Dokumente zum Problem der Homosexualität. Munich: Rütten und Loening, 1967. 164p.

1042 RECTOR, FRANK. The Nazi Extermination of Homosexuals. New York: Stein and Day, 1980. 189p. Discusses homosexual society from the sexual libertarianism that flourished in post-World War I Berlin through the extermination of an estimated 220,000 homosexuals by the National Socialists. Reviews the careers of notorious homosexual Nazi leaders including Ernst Röhm, who became SA Chief of Staff in 1931 and who ws ordered executed by Hitler in June 1934, and Dr. Walter Funk, who was appointed Reich Minister of Economics in 1938. Contains personal testimony by two prominent and anonymous homosexual survivors of the concentration camps. 161 notes, 7-page index, 4-page bibliography, 20 photographs.

1043 SCHULZE-WILDE, HARRY. Das Schicksal der Verfemten. Die Verfolgung der Homosexuellen im „Dritten Reich" und ihre Stellung in der heutigen Gesellschaft. Tübingen: Katzmann, 1969. 154p.

1044 STEAKLEY, JAMES D. The Homosexual Emancipation Movement in Germany. New York: Arno Press, 1975.

M. CRIMES AGAINST GYPSIES

1045 ADLER, MARTA. My Life with the Gypsies. London: Souvenir Press, 1960. 204p. Chapters 11 and 12 deal with Nazi persecution.

1046 DÖRING, HANS-JOACHIM. „Die Motive der Zigeuner-Deportation vom Mai 1940," Vierteljahrshefte für Zeitgeschichte 1959 7(4): 418-428. 38 notes.

1047 DÖRING, HANS-JOACHIM. Die Zigeuner im nationalsozialistischen Staat. Hamburg: Kriminalistik Verlag, 1964. 231p.

1048 KENRICK, DONALD, and GRATTAN PUXON. The Destiny of Europe's Gypsies. New York: Basic Books, 1972.

1049 NOVITCH, MIRIAM. Le Génocide des tziganes sous le régime nazi. Paris: Comité pour l'Erection du Monument en Mémoire des Tziganes assassinés à Auschwitz, [1965]. 29p. Also published in Italian.

1050 SIJES, B.A., et al. Vervolging van Zigeuners in Nederland 1940-1945. The Hague: Martinus Nijhoff, 1979. 189p. Summary in English.

1051 STEINMETZ, SELMA. Österreichs Zigeuner im NS-Staat. Vienna: Europa, 1966. 64p. With bibliography.

N. VICTIMS OF WAR CRIMES

1052 BARSKI, JÓZEF. "Zbrodnie Hitlerowskie Na Dzieciach [Nazi Crimes Against Children]," Biuletyn Zydowskiego Instytutu Historycznego w Polsce 1979 (4) [whole number 112]: 121-126. Reviews the findings of a conference on children during World War II, held in Warsaw on April 26-28, 1979. War crimes included violent abuse of children in concentration camps and ghettos, pseudoscientific experiments, robbery, removal of Polish children to Germany, and exploitation through heavy labor. Undocumented.

1053 BORWICZ, MICHEL. Écrits des condamnés à mort sous l'occupation nazie (1939-1945). [Paris]: Gallimard, 1973. 374p. In the form of an annotated anthology, this work is more an attempt to preserve the writings of the victims than a study of crimes committed against them. The writings, although of moral and even sometimes literary interest, deal little with the actual nature of the crimes. Chapter 8, "The Universe of the Concentration Camp," pp. 78-120, deals with specific crimes. Part 1 (Chapters 1-9) gives an historical, cultural, and political background to the victims' concentration camp writings, including an explanation of the means whereby such writings were preserved and made public. Part 2 (Chapters 10-16) deals with the writings themselves. Part 3 (Chapters 17-26) is all literary explication. Part 4 (Résumé and Conclusions) deals with the human-interest impact of the writings.

1054 BRINGMANN, FRITZ. Kindermord am Bullenhuserdamm. SS-Verbrechen in Hamburg 1945. Menschenversuch an Kindern. Frankfurt am Main: Röderberg, 1978. 64p.

1055 Children in Bondage. A Survey of Child Life in the Occupied Countries of Europe and in Finland. London: Longmans, Green, 1942. 136p. Conducted by the "Save the Children" Fund.

1056 CONWAY, JOHN S. The Nazi Persecution of the Churches, 1933-1945. New York: Basic Books, 1968.

1057 DIPLOMATIC CONFERENCE FOR THE DRAWING UP OF A NEW CONVENTION INTENDED TO PROTECT WAR VICTIMS, GENEVA, 1949. The Geneva Conventions of August 12, 1949. Geneva: International Committee of the Red Cross, 1949. 249p.

1058 SCHIRILLA, LÁSZLÓ. Wiedergutmachung für Nationalgeschädigte. Ein Bericht über die Benachteiligung von Opfern der Nationalsozialistischen Gewaltherrschaft. Munich: Chr. Kaiser, 1982; Mainz: Matthias-Grünewald, 1982. 156p. The story of reparations paid to victims of NS actions. 1-page bibliography, 9 appendices.

1059 UNITED STATES. DEPARTMENT OF STATE. "Geneva Conventions for Protection of War Victims," Department of State Bulletin 1955 33(837): 69-79. July 11, 1955. Statements by State Department officials on the conventions.

1060 UNITED STATES. DEPARTMENT OF STATE. Geneva Conventions of August 12, 1949, for the Protection of War Victims. State Department Publication No. 3938. Washington: GPO, 1950.

O. WAR CRIMES BY AREA AND NATION WHERE COMMITTED

1. Asia

1061 CHIANG, WEN-HSIEN. "Dohihara Kenji and the Japanese Expansion into China, 1931-1936," Ph.D. dissertation, University of Pennsylvania, 1969. 336p. Abstracted in Dissertation Abstracts International 1969 30(6): 2591-A - 2592-A. Studies the role of General Kenji in 4 particular events: the Nakamura incident, the Mukden incident, the abduction of Henry P'u-yi, and the North China autonomy scheme. Concludes that the IMTFE correctly judged Kenji guilty of conspiracy against China, but went too far in sentencing him to death. Based on Chinese, Japanese, and English sources.

1062 FALK, STANLEY L. **Bataan: The March of Death**. New York: W.W. Norton, 1962. 256p. In the spring of 1942, the Japanese 14th Army overran Bataan Peninsula on the island of Luzon and captured 78,100 American and Filipino troops. The evacuation was named the Death March, to convey the brutality and suffering inflicted upon captives. Based on American and Japanese army records, on the war crimes trial of Lieutenant General Masaharu Homma, who commanded the Japanese army in the Philippines and who was subsequently executed, on interviews with survivors, diaries, letters, and personal accounts. Appendices give Japanese army regulations for handling prisoners of war and a list of senior command and staff officials on Bataan. Undocumented; bibliographical note, 4-page index, 8 photographs.

1063 HSÜ, SHU-HSI (comp.). **A New Digest of Japanese War Conduct**. Shanghai: Kelly & Walsh, 1941. 273p.

1064 HSÜ, SHU-HSI. **War Crimes of the Japanese**. Shanghai: [no publisher given], 1938. pp. 169-170.

1065 HYDE, CHARLES C. "Japanese Execution of American Aviators," **American Journal of International Law** 1943 37(3): 480-482. The crews of two American planes were captured by the Japanese following a raid on Japan on April 18, 1942. They were tried by a military court tribunal and some were executed. The Japanese argued that the pilots had deliberately bombed civilian targets. The American government insisted that the Japanese used cruelty to extort false confessions from the crews and charged the Japanese with having violated the Geneva Convention with regard to treatment of prisoners of war. Based on primary and secondary sources; 9 notes.

1066 IWAMATSU, SHIGETOSHI. "A Perspective on the War Crimes," **Bulletin of the Atomic Scientists** 1982 38(2): 29-32. Written by an atomic bomb victim.

1067 POWELL, JOHN W. "Japan's Germ Warfare - The United States Cover-Up of a War Crime," **Bulletin of Concerned Asian Scholars** 1980 12(4): 2-17.

1068 RAGINSKIĬ, MARK. "Monstrous Atrocities of the Japanese Imperialists," **New Times** 1950 (2): 3-7. From evidence pre-sented at the IMTFE, the author accuses the Japanese of intending to use bacteriological weapons in World War II. Describes specific details of such a plan as revealed in the testimony of a number of former generals. Soviet intervention in Manchuria frustrated these plans.

1069 RUSSELL, EDWARD F.L. [LORD RUSSELL OF LIVERPOOL]. **The Knights of Bushido: A Short History of Japanese War Crimes**. London: Cassell, 1958. 335p. General survey of Japanese war crimes during World War II. Discusses the treatment of prisoners of war, the murder of captured allied air crews, forced labor on the Burma-Siam railway, and death marches, including Bataan (April 1942). Investigates conditions in civilian internment camps, war crimes on the high seas, cannibalism, vivisection, and mutilation. One chapter reports on the Kempei Tai, the Japanese army's military police under the War Ministry. Contains excerpts from its manual "Notes for the Interrogation of Prisoners of War," which outlines Kempei Tai methods of torture in Burma from 1943. Concludes with a chapter on the trials of Japanese war criminals and discusses the verdict handed down by the IMTFE on November 12, 1948, and presents biographical sketches of each major defendant. Contains a summary of British, American, and Australian trials of minor Japanese war criminals. Appendix contains some legal aspects of war crimes trials, including an analysis of the plea of superior orders. Contains reproductions of paintings and drawings by Leo Rawlings, who was captured in the fall of Singapore and held for over 3 years by the Japanese. Includes bibliographical references, 7-page index, 38 illustrations.

1070 SVESHNIKOV, I. "Japan's Undeclared Wars on the Soviet Union," New Times 1948 (46): 15-20. Asserts that the IMTFE proved beyond all doubt that the Japanese committed acts of aggression against the Soviet Union and the Mongolian People's Republic. Contains a detailed list of these acts.

1071 VASILYEV, A.N. "The Atrocities of the Aggressors Have Been Exposed," Soviet Press Translations 1950 5(July 1): 411-413. Abridged version of "Misdeeds of Aggressors have been Exposed," Current Digest of the Soviet Press 1950 2(19): 35. On the Khabarovsk trial and the criminal conduct of the Emperor of Japan.

1072 WOLF, STEWART, and HERBERT S. RIPLEY. "Reactions among Allied Prisoners of War subjected to Three Years of Imprisonment and Torture by thge Japanese," American Journal of Psychiatry 1947 104(3): 180-193. 22 notes.

1073 WULFFTEN PALTHE, P.M. VAN. "Neuro-psychiatric Experiences in Japanese Internment Camps in Java," Documenta Neerlandica et Indonesica de Morbis Tropicis 1950 2(2): 135-140.

2. Belgium

1074 ARDENNE, R. [pseudonym]. German Exploitation of Belgium. Washington: Brookings Institution, 1942. 65p. Pamphlet outlining the German occupation and exploitation of Belgium from May 1940. Analyzes the methods by which National Socialists attempted to reorganize the economic production of Belgium so as to make it contribute to the German war economy. Discusses requisition of commodities, regulation of industrial production, control over foreign trade, and financial institutions. The exploitation extended to the appropriation of food, means of transportation, property, and use of Belgian workers.

1075 BELGIUM. MINISTRY OF JUSTICE. WAR CRIMES COMMISSION. Les crimes de guerre commis pendant la contre-offensive de von Rundstedt dans les Ardennes, decembre 1944-janvier 1945. Liège: Georges Thone, 1948.

1076 BELGIUM. MINISTRY OF JUSTICE. WAR CRIMES COMMISSION. War Crimes ... The Destruction of the Library of the University of Louvain. Liège: 1946.

1077 BELGIUM. MINISTRY OF JUSTICE. Les Crimes de guerre commis sous l'occupation de la Belgique, 1940-1945: La Persécution antisémitique en Belgique. Liège: Thones, 1947.

1078 DAUTRICOURT, JOSEPH Y. "La Répression de l'incivisme en Belgique," Revue Internationale de Droit Pénal 1946 17: 133-154. Reviews the organization and general procedure adopted in Belgium to punish the crime of incivisme (lack of patriotism). Examines the penal law and its application to the crime, the results of the prosecutions, and the author's evaluation of the trials.

1079 DAUTRICOURT, JOSEPH Y. "Nature et compétence 'De lege ferenda' de la jurisprudence belge pour la répression des crimes de guerre," Revue de Droit Pénal Militaire et de Droit de la Guerre 1966 5: 63-82.

1080 FOX, GRACE E. Civil Rights in German Occupied Belgium and Northern France. Chicago: American Bar Association, Junior Bar Conference, 1941. 15p.

1081 GORIS, JAN ALBERT. Belgium in Bondage. New York: L.B. Fischer, 1943. 259p.

1082 WAUTERS, A. "Le répression des crimes de guerre en Belgique," Revue de Droit Pénal et de Criminologie 1946-1947 27: 431-435.

1083 WOLF, JULES. "La question des crimes de guerre en Belgique," Journal des Tribunaux 1946 61: 513-517.

3. Czechoslovakia

1084 BELINA, JOSEF. Czech Labour Under Nazi Rule, etc. London: Lincolns-Prager, 1943. 63p.

1085 CZECHOSLOVAKIA. "Declaration on the Punishment of War Criminals in Czechoslovakia," European Observer 1943 20(March 5): 78. Contains a list of war criminals as of February 19, 1943.

1086 CZECHOSLOVAKIA. German Crimes Against Czechoslovakia. Official Czech Reports. London: September 1945. 118p. Mimeograph.

1087 CZECHOSLOVAKIA. MINISTRY OF FOREIGN AFFAIRS. Czechoslovakia fights back: A Document of the Czechoslovak Ministry of Foreign Affairs. Washington: American Council on Public Affairs, 1943. 210p. Discusses the Germanization of Czechoslovakia, especially rural Bohemia and Moravia, the looting of Czechoslovakia, religious persecution, defiance and resistance between 1939 and 1941, and the reign of terror from 1941 to 1943. Alludes to crimes committed by Catholic priests, by President Joseph Tiso, and by Prime Minster Bela Tuka - all collaborators with the German minority in Slovakia. Discusses Czech cooperation with the United Nations and the recognition by the Allies of a Czech government in exile in London. 6-page index.

1088 CZECHOSLOVAKIA. MINISTRY OF FOREIGN AFFAIRS. DEPARTMENT OF INFORMATION. German Massacres in Occupied Czechoslovakia Following the Attack on Reinhard Heydrich. London: Czechoslovak Ministry of Foreign Affairs, Department of Information, 1942. 15p.

1089 MASTNY, VOJTECH. The Czechs under Nazi Rule: The Failure of National Resistance, 1939-1942. New York: Columbia University Press, 1971. 274p.

1090 Verbrecher in Richterroben. Dokumente über die verbrecherische Tätigkeit von 230 nazistischen Richtern und Staatsanwälten auf dem okkupierten Gebiet der tschechoslowakischen Republik, die gegenwärtig in der west-deutschen Justiz dienen. Prague: Orbis, 1960.

4. Denmark

1091 MELCHIOR, MARCUS. Darkness over Denmark. London: New English Library, 1973. 192p.

5. France

1092 HOFFMAN, STANLEY. "Collaborationism in France during World War II," Journal of Modern History 1968 40(2): 375-395.

1093 KEMPNER, ROBERT M.W. "Murder by Government," Journal of Criminal Law and Criminology 1947 38(September-October): 235-238. Describes the murder of French General Maurice Mesny, according to documentary evidence from the files of the German Foreign Office presented at Nuremberg as evidence in the case of the Gestapo.

1094 LE BRETHON, J. "À Propos d'un crime de guerre (Royan 1945), Écrits de Paris 1979 (394): 31-34. The author was a participant in the attack on April 15, 1945, by an armored division of General Jacques Le Clerc's army on Royan, a French seaside resort on the Gironde estuary. The attack was devoid of heroism, had no strategic purpose, killed only innocent civilians, and caused great damage. Undocumented.

1095 REY, FRANCIS. "Violations du droit international commises par les Allemands en France dans la guerre de 1939," Revue Générale de Droit International Public 1941-1945 49(2): 1-127. An account of the violations of international law committed by Germans in France. Deals with violations of the laws of war, violations of various Geneva conventions, crimes against humanity, and reparations.

1096 ROUSSET, DAVID. Le pitre ne rit pas. Paris: Éditions du Pavois, 1948. 263p. Deals with German war crimes in France and Eastern Europe and in various concentration camps.

6. Hungary

1097 CALE, RUTH. "The Kastner Case Closed," Congress Weekly, A Review of Jewish Interests 1958 (March 3): 5-7.

1098 DEAN, GIDEON. "The Kastner Affair," Reconstructionist 1956 21(20): 13-19. At Nuremberg Kastner testified in Becher's behalf, citing evidence of Becher's interventions on behalf of Jews.

1099 LAQUEUR, WALTER Z. "The Kastner Case. Aftermath of the Catastrophe," Commentary 1955 20(6): 500-511.

1100 "No Reason to Repent," Jewish Observer and Middle East Review 1960 (December 9): 3-4. Eichmann's doctored version of the Kastner affair.

1101 SHTRIGLER, MORDECAI. "The Kastner Case," Jewish Frontier 1955 (August): 10-16. The case of Reszö Kasztner (Rudolf Kastner).

1102 SLOAN, JACOB. "From the Trial of Rudolf Kastner," Reconstructionist 1958 (December 29): 29-31.

7. The Netherlands

1103 KEMPNER, ROBERT M.W. Edith Stein und Anne Frank. 2 von Hunderttausend. Die Enthüllungen über die N.S. Verbrechen in Holland vor dem Schwurgericht in München. Die Ermordung der nichtarischen Mönche und Nonnen. Freiburg-im-Breisgau: Herder, 1968. 189p.

1104 KLEFFENS, EELCO NICOLAAS VAN. The Rape of the Netherlands. London: Hodder & Stroughton, 1940. 253p.

8. Poland

a. General

1105 AUSSCHUSS FÜR DEUTSCHE EINHEIT. Eichmann: Henker, Handlanger, Hintermänner. Eine Dokumentation. Berlin (GDR): 1961, 93p.

1106 BADKOWSKI, ANTONI, et al. Les Problèmes de la sauvegarde de la paix et la liquidation des suites de guerre au point de vue du droit polonais. Geneva/Brussels: Polish War Crimes Investigation Office, 1947. 128p.

1107 Black Book of Poland. New York: American Jewish Black Book Committee, 1945.

1108 CYPRIAN, TADEUSZ, and JERZY SAWICKI. Nie Oszczedzać Polski. Warsaw: Iskry, 1959. 475p. Published in English as Nazi Rule in Poland, 1939-1945. Warsaw: Polonia, 1961. 262p. Presents the basic documentary material on war crimes committed in Poland from 1939-1945. Discusses National Socialist aggression and occupation in Poland, the Germanization of children, Hans Frank's diary, forced labor, public execution, and Auschwitz. Concludes with a commentary by the authors, who were prosecuting attorneys representing Poland at the Nuremberg IMT trial. Epilogue reviews the last day of the trial and final statements by the accused. 196 notes, 60 photographs. No bibliography.

1109 German Atrocities in Poland: Some Facts. London: Free Europe, [1940]. 36p.

1110 GOGUEL, RUDI. "Die Bedeutung der 'Reichsuniversität Posen' für die Germanisierungspolitik in Polen im Zweiten Weltkrieg," Wissenschaftliche Zeitschrift der Humboldt-Universität zu Berlin 1968 17(2): 189-195. The German University in Poznan, established after the defeat of Poland in 1939, became the center of progressive Germanization. Describes activities of the university, among them the use of the medical faculty for the disposal of executed Polish resistance fighters, as well as the close cooperation of the staff with the Gestapo and the SS. Based on primary and secondary sources; 53 notes.

1111 KLAFKOWSKI, ALFONS. The Nuremberg Principles and the Development of International Law. Warsaw: Zachodnia Agencja Prasowa, 1966. 56p. Discusses the Nuremberg principles as part of international law, affirmation of these principles by the United Nations, the principles in state practice, and the exclusion from the Nuremberg principles of any statute of limitations.

1112 KRAUSNICK, HELMUT. "Hitler und die Morde in Polen," Vierteljahrshefte für Zeitgeschichte 1963 11(2): 196-209. 59 notes.

1113 LAEUEN, HARALD. <u>Polnische Tragödie</u>. Stuttgart: Steingruben, 1955. 359p.

1114 MOLDAWER, S. "The Road to Lublin," <u>Contemporary Jewish Record</u> 1940 (March-April): 119-133.

1115 MUSZKAT, MARIAN. <u>Polish Charges Against German War Criminals</u>. Warsaw: The National Office for the Investigation of German War Crimes, 1948. 232p. Excerpts from 18 cases submitted to the UNWCC.

1116 MUSZKAT, MARIAN, TADEUSZ CYPRIAN, and GEORGES SAWICKI. <u>Le droit polonais au service de la paix dans la lutte contre les criminels de guerre. Rapport présentés au Congrès international des juristes-démocrates et à l'Association internationale de droit pénal</u>. Paris: Publications of the Polish Ministry of Justice, 1947. 58p.

1117 POLAND. CENTRAL COMMISSION FOR THE INVESTIGATION OF GERMAN CRIMES IN POLAND. <u>German Crimes in Poland</u>. Warsaw: Central Commission for the Investigation of German Crimes in Poland, 1946-1947. Volumes 1-3. New York: Howard Fertig, 1982. 2 volumes bound as 1. 271p. and 168p. (reprint of 1946-1947 English edition). Results of investigations of crimes committed by Germans in Poland between 1939 and 1945, reprinted from <u>Biuletyn Glownej Komisji Badania Zbrodni Niemieckich w Polsce</u> [Bulletin of the Central Commission for the Investigation of German Crimes in Poland]. Volume 1 discusses the extermination camps Auschwitz, Treblinka, and Kulmhof, public executions at Warsaw, German crimes during the Warsaw uprising, German law in incorporated territory, and German crimes against Soviet prisoners of war in Poland. Volume 2 deals with the Nazi occupation of Poland as revealed through Hans Frank's diaries and reports from cabinet meetings of the German government. Describes how the eviction of Poles by Germans from the area of Zamść was carried out. Discusses the liquidation of the Warsaw ghetto as revealed in German documents, experimental operations in the Ravensbrück concentration camp, and the extermination of patients with mental disorders. Includes statistics relating to mass execution and facsimiles of official German orders dispatched to Poland. 26 notes, 40 photographs.

1118 POLAND. CENTRAL COMMISSION FOR THE INVESTIGATION OF GERMAN CRIMES IN POLAND. <u>Verbrechen an polnischen Kindern 1939-1945. Eine Dokumentation. Anhang: "Dokumente deutscher Verwaltung im besetzten Polen</u>." Munich/Salzburg: Pustet; Warsaw: Polish Scientific Publishing House, 1973. 239p. Original is in Polish.

1119 POLAND. MINISTRY OF FOREIGN AFFAIRS. <u>German Occupation of Poland, Extract of Note addressed to the Allied and Neutral Powers</u>. New York: Greystone, [1944]. 240p. Addresses by Polish Minister of Foreign Affairs, Auguste Zaleski, on May 3, 1941. Discusses outrages against individuals, religion, Polish culture, and property. Appendices contain the laws and customs of war on land from the 4th Hague Convention. German documents include proclamations and ordinances of military authorities, legislative enactments concerning areas incorporated into the Reich, official communiqués, circulars, and articles from the German Press. Polish documents pertain to hostages, individual and collective murders, concentration camps, forced labor in the Reich, and expulsions and deportations. Based on primary sources; no bibliography.

1120 POLAND. MINISTRY OF INFORMATION. Bestiality Unknown in Any Previous Record of History. London: Polish Ministry of Information, 1942. 56p.

1121 POLAND. MINISTRY OF INFORMATION. The German Invasion of Poland: Polish Black Book containing Documents, authenticated Reports and Photographs. London: Hutchinson, for Polish Ministry of Information, [1941]. 128p. The first part of a collection of documents which constitutes the "Black Book of German Atrocities." Contains authenticated reports of the Polish campaign of September 1939. First issued in London in 1940. See following entry for examples of the kinds of documents found here.

1122 POLAND. MINISTRY OF INFORMATION. The German New Order in Poland. New York: Putnam's Sons, 1942. 615p. London: Hutchinson, for the Polish Ministry of Information, [1941]. 585p. The contents of the British and American editions are identical, including photographs, with only slight differences in pagination. This is the second volume of a set known as the Black Book, named after the "black record of German barbarism, based on documents which it contains." See Volume 1, previous entry. Part 1, "Massacres and Tortures," compares Belgium in 1914 to Poland from 1939-1941. Discusses the murder of the civilian population during military operations in Bydgoszcz, Poland, mass slaughters, tortures, and concentration camps. Covers arrests, house searches, and the raping of women. Contains an analytical table of German judicial sentences. Appendices contain an address by Winston Churchill in 1940 on the persecution of Poles under German occupation. Part 2, "The Expulsion of the Polish Population from its land," reviews colonization of Polish lands in history, the aims of the German migration plan, and the course and methods of deportation. Part 3, "The Persecution of the Jews and the Ghettos," contains a statistical survey of Polish Jewry. Discusses confiscation of property, the ghettos, and religious persecution. Parts 4 and 5 deal with pillage, economic exploitation and the Göring-Frank circular, a secret document of the German colonial system. Part 6 covers religious persecution of Catholics, Protestants, and the Orthodox Church. Appendices include Vatican radio responses to persecution. Part 7, "Humiliation and degradation of the Polish nation," reviews Hitler's prewar statements about Poland, official insults, and his attempts to destroy the nation. Part 8, "The Destruction of Polish culture," discusses the destruction of Polish cultural institutions and the press. Part 9 deals with violations of International Law. Discusses division of the occupied territory and the illegal recruitment of Polish citizens for military service. Appendices contain an essay on the laws and customs of war on land, decrees relating to the German administration of territories incorporated into the Reich, decrees relating to the German administration of the government, and a report on German atrocities compiled by the Polish Minister of Home Affairs. 17-page index.

1123 PRÄG, WERNER, and WOLFGANG JACOBMEYER (eds.). Das Diensttagebuch des deutschen Generalgouverneurs in Polen 1939-1945. Stuttgart: Deutsche Verlags-Anstalt, 1976.

1124 SCHADEWALDT, HANS (comp.). **Polish Acts of Atrocity against the German Minority in Poland**. 2nd edition. Berlin: Volk und Reich. New York: German Library of Information, 1940. 259p. Report by the German Foreign Office on the outrages perpetrated by Polish citizens upon the German minority in the first few days of World War II. Gives a German interpretation of relations between Poland and Germany before the outbreak of war. Contains reports of witnesses and medical examiners. 45p. of photographs and facsimiles of documents, particularly newspaper clippings. Includes bibliographical references.

1125 SZENDE, STEFAN. **Den siste Juden fran Polen** [The last Jew from Poland]. Stockholm: Bonniers, 1944. 316p. Published in English as **The Promise Hitler Kept**. London: Gollancz, 1945. Published in German as **Der letzte Jude aus Polen**. Zurich: Europa, 1945. Eyewitness report of extermination of Jews, by a Jew who escaped in 1943.

b. Ghettos

1126 BARKAI, MEYER. **The Fighting Ghettos**. Philadelphia: J.B. Lippincott, 1962. 407p.

1127 BERNSTEIN, J., et al. **Ghetto. Berichte aus dem Warschauer Ghetto 1939-1945**. Berlin: Union, 1966. 506p. First edition, 1955, in Yiddish.

1128 BLUMENTHAL, NACHMAN, and JOSEPH KERMISH. [Resistance and revolt in the Warsaw ghetto. A documentary history]. Jerusalem: Yad Vashem, 1965. 495p. Text in Hebrew, summary in English.

1129 BORWICZ, MICHEL (ed.). **L'Insurrection du ghetto de Varsovie**. Paris: Juillard, 1966. 251p.

1130 CIECHANOWSKI, JAN M. **The Warsaw Rising of 1944**. London/New York: Cambridge University Press, 1974.

1131 FRIEDMAN, PHILIP (ed.). **Martyrs and Fighters. The Epic of the Warsaw Ghetto**. New York: Praeger, 1954. 325p.

1132 FRIEDMAN, TUVIAH. **Der Bericht des SS-Generals Jürgen Stroop über den Aufstand der Warschauer Ghetto-Kämpfer**. Haifa: 1959. Mimeograph.

1133 GOLDSTEIN, BERNARD. **The Stars Bear Witness**. New York: Viking, 1949; London: Gollancz, 1950. 295p. A chronicle of the last hours of the Warsaw ghetto.

1134 HERSEY, JOHN. **The Wall**. New York: A.A. Knopf, 1951. 632p. Although written as a novel, this is in fact a very able synthesis of a number of survivor reports from the Warsaw ghetto.

1135 HILBERG, RAUL. "The Ghetto as a Form of Government," **Annals of the American Academy of Political and Social Science** 1980 450(July): 98-112. The ghetto was a captive city-state, totally subordinate to German authority while remaining a Jewish entity with traditions and expectations rooted in Jewish experience. For the incarcerated Jews, the ghetto was also a mirage, in that it instilled thoughts of normalcy and continuity in the Jewish community at a time when the Germans were preparing for deportations of the victims to death camps. 65 notes.

1136 KOHN, STANISLAW. "The Treblinka Revolt," in I. Cukierman and M. Bassok (eds.). Story of the Battle of the Ghettos. Israel: Hakibbutz Hameuchad, 1954.

1137 KRANNHALS, HANS VON. Der Warschauer Aufstand, 1944. Frankfurt am Main: Bernard & Graefe Verlag für Wehrwesen, 1962. 445p. Report on the 1944 resistance to the German occupation of Warsaw. Background material includes a discussion of the Polish army, underground movements in Poland, and the Katyn Forest massacre. Deals with German methods used to suppress the uprising. Appendices contain documents on the uprising, including letters and memorandum from military officials. 10-page bibliography, 13-page index.

1138 LITAI, CHAIM LAZAR. [Muranowska 7. The Warsaw ghetto rising]. Tel Aviv: Massada-P.E.C. Press, 1966. 341p. In Hebrew.

1139 LITTNER, JACOB. Aufzeichnungen aus einem Erdloch. Munich: H. Kluger, 1948. 147p. A Munich stamp-dealer's experience in the Galician ghetto of Zbaraz.

1140 MARK, BERNARD. Der Aufstand im Warschauer Ghetto. Entstehung und Verlauf. Berlin (GDR): Dietz, 1957; 3rd, enlarged edition, 1959. Original in Polish.

1141 MARK, BERNARD. Des Voix dans la nuit. La Résistance juive à Auschwitz-Birkenau. Paris: Plon, 1982. 362p.

1142 MARK, BERNARD (ed.). The Report of Jürgen Stroop concerning the Uprising in the Ghetto of Warsaw and the Liquidation of the Jewish Residential Area. Warsaw: Zydowski Instytut Historyczny, 1958. 124p. A description of the documents, with extensive photographs and photostatic materials concerning the uprising of the Warsaw ghetto. There is a new English version, The Stroop Report. London: Secker & Warburg, 1980.

1143 MEED, VLADKA. On Both Sides of the Wall. Memoirs from the Warsaw Ghetto. [Tel Aviv]: Ghetto Fighters' House, 1972. 343p. The original was published in 1948 in Yiddish. Published in 1968 in Hebrew.

1144 MICHAEL, H.A., et al. [First ghetto in revolt - Lachwa]. Jerusalem: The Encyclopedia of the Diaspora, 1957. 500p. In Hebrew.

1145 NESHAMIT, SARA. [The ghetto struggle]. Jerusalem: Ministry of Education and Culture, 1968. 200p. In Hebrew.

1146 NOVITCH, MIRIAM. La Révolte du ghetto de Varsovie. Documents inédits de la presse clandestine. Paris: Presses du Temps Présent, 1968. 142p.

1147 POLAND. POLISH EMBASSY IN THE UNITED STATES. Warsaw Accuses. [no city given]: Library of the Polish Embassy, [no date given]. 39 unnumbered pages. Contains 10 pages of text on the destruction of Warsaw, with 56 photographs.

1148 POLISH GOVERNMENT INFORMATION CENTER. "Under German Occupation," Polish Facts and Figures 1944 (6): 16-27. A pamphlet that deals with the loss of rights, the loss of property, the Warsaw ghetto, and Jews in the resistance and the underground.

1149 RINGELBLUM, EMANUEL. <u>Notes from the Warsaw Ghetto; the Journal of Emmanuel Ringelblum</u>. New York: McGraw-Hill, 1958. 369p. Published in German as <u>Ghetto Warschau. Tagebücher aus dem Chaos</u>. Stuttgart: Seewald, 1967. 254p. Originally published in Polish in 1952.

1150 SAKOWSKA, RUTA. [People in the quarter. Jews in Warsaw during the Nazi occupation (October 1939 - March 1943). Warsaw: Panstwowe Wyd. Naukowe, 1975. 398p. In Polish. Contains illustrations, maps, tables, and a bibliography.

1151 TENNENBAUM-BACKER, NINA. [A man and a fighter. Mordekhai Tennenbaum-Tamaroff, hero of the ghettoes]. Jerusalem: Yad Vashem, 1974. 282p. In Hebrew.

1152 TRUNK, ISAIAH. <u>Ghetto Lodz. A Historical and Sociological Study, including Documents, Maps, and Tables</u>. New York: Yad Vashem/Yivo Institute for Jewish Research, Joint Documentary Projects, 1962. 528p. In Yiddish, summary in English.

1153 TRUNK, ISAIAH. <u>Judenrat. The Jewish Councils in Eastern Europe unde Nazi Occupation</u>. New York: Macmillan, 1972. 664p.

1154 TUSHNET, LEONARD. <u>To Die with Honour; the Uprising of the Jews in the Warsaw Ghetto</u>. London: Citadel, 1965. 128p.

1155 UMADEVI (pseudonym). <u>All for Freedom: The Warsaw Epic</u>. Bombay: Padma 217p.

1156 WERSTEIN, IRVING. <u>The Uprising of the Warsaw Ghetto, November 1940 - May 1943</u>. New York: Norton 1968. 157p.

1157 WULF, JOSEF. <u>Das Dritte Reich und seine Vollstrecker. Die Liquidation von 500 000 Juden im Ghetto Warschau</u>. Berlin/Grunewald: Arani, 1961. 383p. Covers in detail the famous Stroop report and the destruction of the ghetto, and identifies most of the Germans who carried out the destruction. Based on primary documents; 49 photographs, index.

c. Katyn Woods Massacre

1158 ANDERS, WLADYSLAW. <u>The Crime of Katyn: Facts and Documents</u>. London: Polish Cultural Foundation, 1965. 278p. When the International Military Tribunal in Nuremberg pronounced its sentence in the fall of 1946 the Katyn crime was not mentioned among the atrocities. The author, Commander-in-Chief of Polish forces in the USSR from 1941, had been a prisoner of war in the Soviet Union. Traces the development of the investigation, including the refusal of the Soviet government to allow the Investigative Committee of the Red Cross to be sent to the scene, the publication of documents by Germans, and the Soviet Commission's communiqué of January 1944. Discusses missing prisoners-of-war in 1941-1943 before the discovery of mass graves, German and Soviet radio communiqués and reaction in London, propaganda campaigns, and the Polish government's statement. Contains the full text of the final report of the German police dated June 10, 1943, the report of the International Medical Commission, and testimony of Soviet witnesses. Contains personal memoirs of survivors and stories from the scene of the crime. Appendices contain newspaper and magazine reports pertaining to Katyn. Based on primary documents. 6-page index.

1159 BECKMANN, O. "Katyn - Moscow Fight against Historical Truth - The Coverup of a War Crime," Beiträge zur Konfliktforschung 1980 10(4): 137-163.

1160 Der Massenmord im Walde von Katyn. Ein Tatsachenbericht auf Grund amtlichen Unterlagen. Berlin: NSDAP, 1943. A 6-page pamphlet with 26p. of pictures.

1161 FITZ GIBBON, LOUIS. Katyn: A Crime without Parallel. New York: Charles Scribner's Sons, 1979. 285p. Torrance, California: Noontide Press, 1979. Account of the Katyn murders. The remains of 4253 Polish officers and intellectuals who vanished in 1940 were discovered in Russia in the Spring of 1943. A massacre of this scale could only be organized at the national level, leading the author to conclude that only the Germans or Soviets could have committed the crime. Contains official German documentary evidence, and the report of the International Military Commission, which in 1943 conducted an investigation at Katyn. Appendices contain General Wladyslaw Anders' statement on April 28, 1950, the 10th anniversary of the Katyn murder, Professor Sir Douglas Savory's speech in the House of Commons on November 6, 1952, the interim report of the U.S. Congressional Select Committee on July 2, 1952, an extract from the U.S. Congressional Record of Congressman Edward Joseph Derwinski's speech in the House of Representatives on May 14, 1962, and an incomplete list of Soviet officials and NKVD (Commissariat for Foreign Affairs) personnel involved in the Katyn massacres. List of 4143 victims identified as of June 7, 1943. 3-page bibliography, 5-page index, 44 photographs.

1162 GERMANY. AUSWÄRTIGES AMT [FOREIGN OFFICE]. Amtliches Material zum Massenmord von Katyn. Berlin: Zentralverlag der NSDAP, Franz Eher Nachf., 1943. 331p. A German study of the mass slaughter of Polish officers at Katyn Woods which attempts to establish Russian responsibility and guilt. 64 photographs.

1163 GERMANY. AUSWÄRTIGES AMT [FOREIGN OFFICE]. Bolschewistische Verbrechen gegen Kriegsrecht und Menschlichkeit, Dokumente zusammengestellt vom Auswärtigen Amt. Berlin: Deutscher Verlag, for the Foreign Office, 1941-1942. 2 volumes. A German study of the mass slaughter of Katyn Woods which attempts to establish Russian guilt. Volume 1 gives an overview of the atrocities committed by the Russian army during the first months of World War II. A collection of 159 documents pertaining to thousands of individual cases. Volume 2 contains official reports and the testimony of witnesses and reprints 150 documents as grounds for Hitler's so-called "counterattack" on the Soviet Union in 1941.

1164 Katyn. Ein ungesühntes Kriegsverbrechen gegen die Wehrkraft eines Volkes. Munich: Wehrwissenschaftlicher Verlag Walther de Bouché, 1952. 51p. A pamphlet.

1165 Khatyn'. Minsk: Belarus', 1970. 60p. A photo album of the Katyn Woods massacre which blames the Germans for the crime committed against polish prisoners of war. The text is in Russian and White Russian.

1166 MACKIEWICZ, JOSEF. The Katyn Wood Murders. London: World Affairs Book Club, [no date given].

1167 POLAND. POLISH GOVERNMENT IN EXILE. The Mass Murder of Polish Prisoners of War in Katyn. London: Polish Government in Exile [no publisher given], March 1946. 31p. Marked "Most Secret," and "Not for Publication." Based on a study entitled "Facts and Documents Concerning Polish Prisoners of War Captured by the U.S.S.R. in the 1939 campaign."

1168 POLAND. POLISH GOVERNMENT INFORMATION CENTER. "Under German Occupation," Polish Facts and Figures 1944 (2): 19-22. A pamphlet that presents Soviet evidence that the Germans massacred 11,000 Polish officers in August 1941.

1169 UNITED STATES. CONGRESS. HOUSE OF REPRESENTATIVES. The Katyn Forest Massacre. Hearings before the Select Committee to Conduct an Investigation of the Facts, Evidence and Circumstances of the Katyn Forest Massacre. 82nd Congress, 1st and 2nd Sessions, 1951-1952. 7 volumes. Washington: GPO, 1952.

1170 ZAWODNY, JANUSZK K. Death in the Forest. Notre Dame: University of Notre Dame Press, 1962. Published in German as Zum Beispiel Katyn: Klärung eines Kriegsverbrechens. Munich: Verlag Information und Wissen, 1972. 192p.

1171 ZAWODNY, JANUSZK K. "Katyn Forest Massacre: Morals in American Foreign Policy," Minnesota Review 1963 3(2): 228-236.

9. Union of Soviet Socialist Republics

a. General

1172 BESSIE, ALVAH CECIL. This is Your Enemy . . . A Documentary Record of Nazi Atrocities against Civilians and Soldiers of our Soviet Ally. New York: [no publisher given], 1942. 48p.

1173 DALLIN, ALEXANDER. German Rule in Russia, 1941-1945: A Study of Occupation Policies. London: Macmillan, 1957. 695p. 2nd English edition, Boulder, Colorado: Westview Press, 1981. 707p. Published in German as Deutsche Herrschaft in Rußland, 1941-1945: Eine Studie über Besatzungspolitik. Düsseldorf: Droste, 1958. Based on "German Policy and the Occupation of the Soviet Union, 1941-1944," Ph.D. dissertation, Columbia University, 1953. 347p. Abstracted in Dissertation Abstracts International 1956 16(12): 2539-2540. A comprehensive study of German civil and military rule in the occupied parts of the Soviet Union. Discusses Alfred Rosenberg's role as Reichsminister as well as conflicts between him and various civilian and SS leaders. Comments on the mistreatment of prisoners of war and of civilians as well as the misuse of labor. 1981 edition has a 13-page index and a 4-page glossary.

1174 Dokumenty obviniaiut. Moscow: Gospolitizdat, 1945. 392p. A collection of documents on German war crimes in Russia gathered by the Soviet commission of inquiry.

1175 GERMANY (FEDERAL REPUBLIC). SUPREME COURT. "Killing of Russian Slave Laborers by German Soldiers in 1945 - Murder Under Penal Code - No Defense Under International Law - No Defense of Superior Orders - Section 47, I, No. 2, Military Penal Code. Decision of the West German Federal Supreme Court, September 30, 1960, 4 St. R. 242/60, Straf- und Strafprozesserecht," Juristenzeitung 1962 17(1): 28-30. American Journal of International Law 1963 57(1): 139-140.

1176 GERMANY. REICHSMINISTERIUM FÜR DIE BESETZTEN OSTGEBIETE. Amtliches Material zum Massenmord von Winniza. Berlin: Zentralverlag der NSDAP, 1944. 282p. National Socialist publication intended to make Soviet atrocities known to the world. Investigates the finding of mass graves. Contains police records, a report of the the Murder Commission of Winniza, and a list of victims identified as of October 7, 1943. Also covers judicial aspects of the massacre and records of a German investigation conducted in 1943.

1177 GERNET, M.N. Prestupleniia gitlerovtsev protiv chelovechnosti. Moscow: Iurizdat, 1945. 28p. A catalog of crimes committed by Germans in Russia.

1178 KAMENETSKY, IHOR. Hitler's Occupation of Ukraine, 1941-1944; a Study of Totalitarian Imperialism. Milwaukee: Marquette University Press, 1956. 101p.

1179 KAPLANAS, O. Deviatyi fort obviniaet. Vilna: Gospolitnauchizdat, several editions between 1961 and 1970. 64p. This pamphlet was originally published in Lithuanian. It is about German war crimes committed against partisans and underground workers in Lithuania.

1180 KARPENKO, Z. Pod fashistskim igom. Kalinin: Gaz "Proletar pravda," 1945. 79p. A collection of crimes committed by Germans in the Kalinin oblast.

1181 Khar'kovshchina v gody Vel. Otech. voiny, Iiun' 1941-1943 g. Sb. dokumentov i materialov. Charkov: "Prapor," 1965. 428p. Documents about the German occupation of Charkov during the war, including partisan activity.

1182 Khronologicheskii spravochnik o vremennoi okkupatsii nemetsko-rumynskimi zakhvatchikami Izmail'skoi oblasti i osvobozhdenie ee Krasnoi Armiei (1941-1944 gg). Izmail: Pridunaiaskaia pravda, 1950. 98p. Deals with the German and Rumanian occupation of the Izmail oblast and their crimes.

1183 KONDRATES, Z. IX fort. Vilna: Gospolitnauchizdat, 1961. 56p. About crimes committed by Germans against communists and members of the underground in Lithuania.

1184 KRAUSNICK, HELMUT. "Kommissarbefehl und ,Gerichtsbarkeitserlaß Barbarossa' in neuer Sicht," Vierteljahrshefte für Zeitgeschichte 1977 25(4): 682-738. 283 notes. An analysis of the origins of the German Army's decree to liquidate Russian army political commissars and to limit the Army's jurisdiction in Soviet areas occupied by Germany. The German officer corps resisted the order limiting its power more than it did the extermination order. Based on recently opened army records at the German Federal Military Archive at Freiburg, the Institute of Contemporary History at Munich, and Nuremberg IMT trial documents; 283 notes.

1185 "Leningrad. Chrezvychainaia gos. kommissia po ustanovleniiu i rassledovaniiu zlodeianii nemets-fashist zakhvatchikov," Sbornik. Leningrad: Gospolitizdat, 1945. 40p. An account of German war crimes in the Leningrad area.

1186 LEVIT, S.E. "Nekotorye dannye o razorenii i ograblenii Moldavii nemetsko-rumynskimi okkupantami v 1941-1944 gg," Volume 2, pp. 6-27 of Uchenye zapiski. Kishinev: Mold n-i bazy AN SSR,

In-t istorii, 1949. Deals with crimes committed by German and Russian occupying forces in Moldavia during World War II.

1187 Maski sorvany. Tallin: Estgozidat, 1961. 168p. Deals with German war crimes committed in Estonia.

1188 Ne zabyvai Audrini. Riga: Liesma, 1968. 236p. A collection of documents and materials dealing with German war crimes in Latvia.

1189 NIKITIN, M.N. and P.I. VAGIN. The Crimes of the German Fascists in the Leningrad Region: Materials and Documents. London: Hutchinson, [1946]. 128p. Deals with the extermination and enslavement of Soviet citizens and the plunder of private and public property. Appendices contain lists of German crimes, names of 231 villages burned and destroyed, and the names of 481 Soviet citizens killed.

1190 Odessa v Vel. Otech. voiny Sovetskogo Soiuza. Odessa: Obl. izd., 1948, 1949, 1951. 3 volumes, 276, 292, 238p. A collection of documents and materials about Odessa during the war.

1191 PEISAKHOVICH. A.IA. Bor'ba trudiashchikhsia Beloruss SSR za vosstanovlenie nar, khoziaistva i kul'tury v gody Vel. Otech. voiny. Minsk: Kn.izd, 1959. 37p. A study of life in White Russia under German rule.

1192 Predat' zabveniiu Nikogda! Minsk: Golas Radzimy, 1965. 59p. Deals with German war crimes in White Russia.

1193 Prestupleniia nemetsko-fashistskikh okkupantov v Belorussii, 1941-1944. Minsk: Belarus, 1965. 463p. Deals with German war crimes in White Russia.

1194 Prestupnye tseli - prestupnye sredstva. Dokumenty ob okkupatsionnoi politike fashistskoi Germanii na territorii SSSR (1941-1944). Moscow: Gospolitizdat, 1963. 324p. Collection of documents and reports showing the predatory nature of the German occupation force in Russia. Contains a large number of pictures.

1195 RIASNOI, V.V., and IU.M. CHERNIAVSKII. Na sluzhbe d'iavolu. Moscow: Iurid. lit, 1969. 239p. A Soviet account of the activities of a major German war criminal, Oscar Dirlewanger, who was active in White Russia and Poland. Dirlewanger escaped to Egypt after the war and lived in safety under Nasser.

1196 ROMANOVSKII, V.F. "Prestypleniia germanskogo fashizma v Belorussii," pp. 331-337 of Volume 1, Vtoraia mirovaia voine, obshchie problemy . . . . Moscow: Nauka, 1966. 348p. Deals with German rule in White Russia, where more than 2 million civilians and prisoners of war were exterminated.

1197 ROMANOWSKI, WINCENTY. "'Other Germans' (Testimony on Grabe)," Yad Vashem Bulletin 1966 (19): 18-23. An account of Hermann Grabe's intensive efforts to save Jewish lives in the district of Volyhnia in 1942 and 1943. Reproduced from Kierunki, Warsaw-Krakow, 46/128 (November 16, 1958).

1198 ROSTOWSKI, DIETER. "SS-Verbrechen an Verwundeten der 2. Polnischen Armee Ende April 1945," Militärgeschichte 1980 19(4): 454-460. As wounded Polish soldiers were being transported to the rear, their convoy was attacked at the town of Horka on

April 26, 1945. Many of the wounded were killed and buried. Statements of six witnesses are appended. 24 notes.

1199 SSSR. Chrezvychainaia gos. kommissia. po ustanovleniiu i rassledovaniiu zlodeianii nemets-fashist zakvatchikov. Sbornik. Moscow: Gospolitizdat, 1945. 459p. The chief publication of the Soviet War Crimes Commission. Elderly German rear area and garrison commanders were hanged without formality, while people such as Erich Koch, Generals Manstein and Reinhardt, and other "deeply implicated" individuals such as Sepp Dietrich and the leadership of the Army Group Center were either not tried or were extradicted. Deals with Germans who tried to form anti-Soviet military units among former Soviet subjects. These were punished brutally.

1200 UNION OF SOVIET SOCIALIST REPUBLICS. Soviet Government Statements on Nazi Atrocities. London: Hutchinson, 1946. 320p.

1201 UNION OF SOVIET SOCIALIST REPUBLICS. LAWS AND STATUTES. "Decree of the Presidium of the Supreme Soviet of the USSR on the Formation of an extraordinary State Committee for the ascertaining and investigation of crimes committed by the German-fascist invaders and their associates and damage caused by them to citizens, collective farms, public bodies, state enterprises and institutions of the USSR," Information Bulletin [Special Supplement] 1943 (December): 155-157.

1202 UNION OF SOVIET SOCIALIST REPUBLICS. Narodnyi komissariat po inostraaaym delam. Note of V. M. Molotov, People's Commissar of Foreign Affairs of the USSR on the mass forcible abduction of peaceful Soviet Citizens to German-fascist slavery and on the responsibility for this crime of German authorities and private persons who exploit the forced labor. Information Bulletin 1943 (52): 1-9.

1203 UNION OF SOVIET SOCIALIST REPUBLICS. New Soviet Documents on Nazi Atrocities. London: Hutchinson, for New Soviet News, 1943. 128p. 48 illustrations.

1204 UNION OF SOVIET SOCIALIST REPUBLICS. PEOPLE'S COMMISSARIAT FOR FOREIGN AFFAIRS. We Shall not Forgive. The Horrors of the German Invasion in Documents and Photographs. Moscow: Foreign Languages Publishing House, 1942. 144p. The material contained here was used to illustrate the note of V. Molotov, People's Commissar of Foreign Affairs of the U.S.S.R., April 27, 1942.

1205 UNION OF SOVIET SOCIALIST REPUBLICS. Soviet Documents on Nazi Atrocities. London: Hutchinson, for "Soviet War News," 1942. 190p. Contains 200 photographs.

1206 UNION OF SOVIET SOCIALIST REPUBLICS. Statement of [October 14, 1942] the Soviet government regarding the responsibility of the "Hitlerite" invaders and their accomplices for the infamies committed by them in the occupied countries of Europe. Information Bulletin [Special Supplement] 1943 (December): 151-154.

1207 UTEVSKII, B.S. Prectupleniia gitlerovtsev protiv mirgnogo naseloniia. Moscow: Iurizdat, 1946. 48p. A catalog of German crimes in Russia.

1208 UTEVSKII, B.S. *Sudebnye protsessy o zlodeianiiakh nemetskofashistskikh na territorii SSSR*. Moscow: Iurizdat, 1946. 60p. An account of German crimes in Russia.

1209 UZHDAVINIS, V. *Tragediia sela Pirchiupis*. Vilna: Gospolitnauchizdat, 1963. 55p. A case of German war crimes in Lithuania during the occupation.

1210 VATIN, V. and P. GUMMEL'. *Na fashistskoi katogre*. Rostov: Rostizdat, 1946. 87p. A collection of testimonies of Soviet citizens from the Don area who were taken in slavery to Germany.

1211 VORONKOV, N.D. "K voprosu o posledstviiakh nemetskofashistskoi okkupatsii v Mogilevskoi oblasti," *Trudy* 1960 33: 3-23. A study of German crimes in the Mogilev oblast.

b. Series from the *Soviet War News*

>UNION OF SOVIET SOCIALIST REPUBLICS. The following 34 reports on war crimes reported by the U.S.S.R. are listed chronologically by date published in the *Soviet War News*.

1212 UNION OF SOVIET SOCIALIST REPUBLICS. Note sent on November 25, 1941, by V.M. Molotov, People's Commissar for Foreign Affairs, to all governments with which the U.S.S.R. had diplomatic relations, on "Appalling atrocities committed by the German authorities against the Soviet prisoners of war." *Soviet War News*, November 27, 1941. No. 120.

1213 UNION OF SOVIET SOCIALIST REPUBLICS. Note sent on January 6, 1942, by V.M. Molotov, People's Commissar for Foreign Affairs, to all governments with which the USSR had diplomatic relations, on "Wholesale robbery, despoliation of population and monstrous atrocities committed by German authorities in the invaded Soviet territories." *Soviet War News*, January 8, 1942. No. 153.

1214 UNION OF SOVIET SOCIALIST REPUBLICS. Note sent on April 27, 1942, by V.M. Molotov, People's Commissar for Foreign Affairs, to all governments with which the USSR had diplomatic relations, on "The monstrous villainies, atrocities and outrages committed by the German-Fascist invaders in the occupied Soviet areas, and on the responsibility of the German government and command for these crimes." *Soviet War News*, April 30, 1942. No. 246.

1215 UNION OF SOVIET SOCIALIST REPUBLICS. Declaration issued by the Soviet government on October 14, 1942, on the responsibility of the "Hitlerite" invaders and their accomplices for atrocities perpetrated in occupied countries of Europe. *Soviet War News*, October 16, 1942. No. 388.

1216 UNION OF SOVIET SOCIALIST REPUBLICS. Decree issued by the Supreme Soviet of the USSR on November 2, 1942, on the formation of the "Extraordinary State Commission for Ascertaining and Investigating crimes perpetrated by the German-Fascist invaders and their accomplices and the damage inflicted by them on citizens, collective farms, social organizations, State enterprises and institutions of the U.S.S.R." *Soviet War News*, November 5, 1942. No. 405.

1217 UNION OF SOVIET SOCIALIST REPUBLICS. Statement issued on December 19, 1942, by the Information Bureau of the People's Commissariat for Foreign Affairs of the USSR on the execution by "Hitlerite" authorities of the plan to exterminate the Jewish population in the occupied territory of Europe. Soviet War News, December 21, 1942. No. 443.

1218 UNION OF SOVIET SOCIALIST REPUBLICS. Note sent on May 11, 1943, by the People's Commissar for Foreign Affairs, V.M. Molotov, to all governments with which the USSR had diplomatic relations, on "The Forcible mass deportation into German-Fascist slavery of the Soviet citizens, and on the responsibility for these crimes of the German authorities and private individuals who exploited the forced labour of Soviet citizens in Germany." Soviet War News, May 13, 1943.

1219 UNION OF SOVIET SOCIALIST REPUBLICS. Communiqués issued by the Soviet Extraordinary State Commission for Ascertaining and Investigating crimes committed by the German-Fascist invaders and their accomplices. Protocol on the plunder by the German-Fascist invaders of Rostov Museum at Pyatigorsk. Soviet War News, June 28, 1943. No. 597.

1220 UNION OF SOVIET SOCIALIST REPUBLICS. Protocol on the poisoning by the German-Fascist invaders of patients in the Sapogov Hospital, Kursk Region. Soviet War News, June 28, 1943. No. 597.

1221 UNION OF SOVIET SOCIALIST REPUBLICS. Protocol on the torture and shooting by the German-Fascist invaders of Soviet citizens in Kupyansk, Kharkov Region. Soviet War News, June 28, 1943. No. 597.

1222 UNION OF SOVIET SOCIALIST REPUBLICS. Report on the gas massacre by the German-Fascist invaders in Krasnodar. Soviet War News, July 14, 1943. No. 611.

1223 UNION OF SOVIET SOCIALIST REPUBLICS. Report on the crimes committed by the German-Fascist invaders in the Stavropol Territory, Northern Caucasus. Soviet War News, August 7, 1943. No. 631.

1224 UNION OF SOVIET SOCIALIST REPUBLICS. Report on the atrocities committed by the German-Fascist invaders in Orel. Soviet War News, September 9 and 10, 1943. Nos. 659 and 660.

1225 UNION OF SOVIET SOCIALIST REPUBLICS. J.V. Stalin, "On the Great Patriotic War of the Soviet Union." Contains the Declaration by Roosevelt, Churchill and Stalin on the responsibility of the "Hitlerites" for the atrocities perpetrated by them, issued at the Moscow Conference (October 19 to 30, 1943). Soviet War News, November 3, 1943. No. 7052.

1226 UNION OF SOVIET SOCIALIST REPUBLICS. Report on destruction wrought by the German-Fascist invaders on the industry, municipal economy, and cultural-educational institutions of the Stalino Region of the Donbas. Soviet War News, November 16 and 17, 1943. Nos. 715 and 716.

1227 UNION OF SOVIET SOCIALIST REPUBLICS. Statements on the responsibility of the German-Fascist invaders for atrocities in Kharkov. Soviet War News, December 14, 1943. No. 738.

1228 UNION OF SOVIET SOCIALIST REPUBLICS. Report of Special Commission for Ascertaining and Investigating the circumstances of the shooting of Polish officer prisoners by the German-Fascist invaders in the Katyn Forest. Soviet War News, January 27, 28, and 31, and February 1, 1944. Nos. 774-777. Reprinted in booklet form as The Truth about Katyn, issued by Soviet War News.

1229 UNION OF SOVIET SOCIALIST REPUBLICS. Report on the atrocities committed by the German-Fascist invaders in Kiev. Soviet War News, March 1 and 3, 1944. Nos. 800 and 802.

1230 UNION OF SOVIET SOCIALIST REPUBLICS. Report on the directives and orders of the "Hitlerite" Government and German Military Command concerning the extermination of Soviet prisoners of war and civilians. Soviet War News, March 14, 1944. No. 810.

1231 UNION OF SOVIET SOCIALIST REPUBLICS. Report on the extermination by the German-Fascist invaders of Soviet people by infecting them with disease. Soviet War News, May 2, 1944. No. 848.

1232 UNION OF SOVIET SOCIALIST REPUBLICS. Report on the destruction and crimes perpetrated by the German-Fascist invaders in the town of Novgorod and the Novgorod district of the Leningrad Region. Soviet War News, May 8, 1944. No. 852.

1233 UNION OF SOVIET SOCIALIST REPUBLICS. Report on the destruction, plunder and crimes perpetrated by the German-Fascist invaders and their associates in the town of Rovno and in the Rovno Region. Soviet War News, May 9, 1944. No. 853.

1234 UNION OF SOVIET SOCIALIST REPUBLICS. Report on crimes committed by the German-Rumanian invaders in the town of Odessa and in the districts of the Odessa Region. Soviet War News, June 16, 1944. No. 885.

1235 UNION OF SOVIET SOCIALIST REPUBLICS. Report of the extermination of Soviet prisoners of war by the "Hitlerites" at the "Gross-Lazaret" at Slavuta, in the Kamenets-Podolsk Region. Soviet War News, August 5, 1944. No. 928.

1236 UNION OF SOVIET SOCIALIST REPUBLICS. Report on crimes committed by the Finnish-Fascist invaders and their associates on the territory of the Karelo-Finnish Soviet Socialist Republic. Soviet War News, August 21, 1944. No. 940. August 22, 1944. No. 941.

1237 UNION OF SOVIET SOCIALIST REPUBLICS. Protocol on the destruction and villainies committed by the German-Fascist barbarians in the Pushkin Reservation of the Academy of Sciences of the USSR. Soviet War News, August 31, 1944. No. 949.

1238 UNION OF SOVIET SOCIALIST REPUBLICS. Statement on the destruction by the German-Fascist invaders of monuments of art and architecture in the towns of Petrodvorets, Pushkin, and Pavlovsk. Soviet War News, September 5, 1944. No. 953.

1239 UNION OF SOVIET SOCIALIST REPUBLICS. Report of the Polish-Soviet Extraordinary Commission for the Investigation of crimes committed by the German-Fascist invaders in the extermination camp at Maidanek in the town of Lublin. Soviet War News, September 19, 1944. No. 965.

1240 UNION OF SOVIET SOCIALIST REPUBLICS. Report on crimes committed by the German-Fascist invaders in the city of Minsk. Soviet War News, September 22, 1944. No. 967.

1241 UNION OF SOVIET SOCIALIST REPUBLICS. Reports on Crimes committed by the German-Fascist invaders in the Esthonian Soviet Socialist Republic. Soviet War News, November 28 and 29, 1944. Nos. 1022 and 1023.

1242 UNION OF SOVIET SOCIALIST REPUBLICS. Report on crimes committed by the German-Fascist invaders on the territory of the Lvov Region. Soviet War News, December 29 and 30, 1944. Nos. 1046 and 1047.

1243 UNION OF SOVIET SOCIALIST REPUBLICS. Report on crimes perpetrated by the German-Fascist invaders in the Lithuanian Soviet Socialist Republic. Soviet War News. January 5, 1945. No. 1052.

1244 UNION OF SOVIET SOCIALIST REPUBLICS. Report on crimes committed by the German-Fascist invaders in the Latvian Soviet Socialist Republic. Soviet War News, April 17 and 18, 1945. Nos. 1134 and 1135.

1245 UNION OF SOVIET SOCIALIST REPUBLICS. Report on crimes committed by the German government in Oswiecim (Auschwitz). Soviet War News, May 17, 1945. No. 1158.

10. Yugoslavia

1246 LASIC, DUSAN. "Organizacija Policijsko-Obavestajne Sluzbe 'Nezavis ne Drzave Hrvatske' Ravnateljstvo Za Javni Red I Sigurnost [The Organization of the Police and Intelligence Force of the Independent State of Croatia: the Committee for Public Order and Safety]," Zbornik za Istoriju [Yugoslavia] 1972 6: 183-194. The Police and Intelligence Force of Croatia committed war crimes in Yugoslavia during World War II. Deals with the activities of the Force, with special reference to the wide powers of the Department of Public Order and Safety, which was under the control of the Ministry of Internal Affairs.

1247 YUGOSLAVIA. Exposé des crimes italiens contre Yougoslavie et ses peuples. Belgrade: Commission d'État pour la recherche des crimes de guerre, 1946. 201p. Published in English as Reports on Italian Crimes against Yugoslavia and its People. Belgrade: State Commission for the Investigation of War Crimes, 1946. 196p.

V
WORLD WAR II WAR CRIMES: THE HOLOCAUST

A. GENERAL WORKS

1248 ANGLO-AMERICAN COMMITTEE OF INQUIRY. Report on the Problems of European Jewry and Palestine. Lausanne, April 20, 1946. London: HMSO, [1946]. 30p. Cmd. 6808. Contains a detailed breakdown of the much-debated figure, produced by the World Jewish Congress, of 5,700,000 Jewish victims.

1249 ARENDT, HANNAH. The Jew as Pariah: Jewish Identity and Politics in the Modern Age. New York: Grove, 1978. 288p. Collection of writings on Jewish identity, culture, history, and politics. Part III, "The Eichmann controversy," pp. 225-277, contains essays on organized guilt, universal responsibility, collaboration, letters on the Eichmann case exchanged between Gershom Scholem and Hannah Arendt in 1963, and responses to Arendt's opinion of the Eichmann trial. 1-page bibliography of books by Hannah Arendt, 8-page index.

1250 BAR-NATAN, MOSHE. "Israel Relives the Holocaust," Jewish Frontier 1961 28(6): 4-6.

1251 BERGMANN, MARTIN S., and MILTON E. JUCOVY (eds.). Generations of the Holocaust. New York: Basic Books, 1982. 338p. A study of the way in which children of Holocaust survivors carry on the sufferings of their parents. Material from 30 Jewish survivor-families and analyses of children of Nazis went into making up this book. The study centers around how parents have passed along to their children many of their concentration camp experiences. Worse perhaps than the stories told are the products of their own imaginations as they try to fill the gaps in their parents' stories. Part I traces the backgrounds; Part II deals with the survivors' children; Part III deals with the persecutors' children; and Part IV examines the various theoretical and clinical aspects of the study. An excellent epilogue recaps the whole study. 10-page bibliography and 12-page index.

1252 BLATTER, JANET, and SYBIL MILTON. Art of the Holocaust. New York: Rutledge Press, 1981. 272p.

1253 BLAYNEY, MICHAEL S. "Herbert Pell, War Crimes, and the Jews," American Jewish Historical Quarterly 1976 65(4): 335-352. Herbert Claiborne Pell, a Harvard classmate of Franklin D. Roosevelt, was one of Roosevelt's political appointees. Pell was an early and vigorous denouncer of Nazi policies and his letters to the President stand in marked contrast to the restrained style and attitude of the State Department. His 1943 appointment to the United Nations War Crimes Commission led to increased conflict with the State Department, which did not agree with his definition of war crimes and atrocities. The question whether crimes against Jews came within the jurisdiction of the commission was an issue that divided Pell and the State Department, which wanted the Commission to serve only as a fact-finding body. With the President on his side, Pell was successful in his more vigorous plans for the Commission. In 1944 the State Department lobbied to have Congress stop funding Pell and his staff and in January 1945 Pell was dismissed. He became a hero to the American-Jewish community. 45 notes.

1254 BOYENS, ARMIN F.C. "The Ecumenical Community and the Holocaust," Annals of the American Academy of Political and Social Science 1980 450(July): 140-152. In most churches there were small minorities who took up the fight for the rights of the persecuted and who tried to help the refugees. In some instances churches resisted Hitler's policy of extermination by protesting publicly. This work for the rescue of Jews led to Christian-Jewish cooperation on national and international levels. 62 notes.

1255 CARMON, ARYE. "Problems in Coping with the Holocaust: Experiences with Students in a Multinational Program," Annals of the American Academy of Political and Social Science 1980 450(July): 227-236. A program on teaching the Holocaust has been developed in the United States, Germany, and Israel in order to overcome problems in coping with this unique theme in the classroom.

1256 CHARTOCK, ROSELLE, and JACK SPENCER (eds.). The Holocaust Years: Society on Trial. New York: Bantam Books, in cooperation with the Anti-Defamation League of B'nai B'rith, 1978. 295p. An anthology containing excerpts from 88 articles, essays, and books. The six section heads are: (1) What Happened? (2) Victims and Victimizers, (3) How and Why? (4) What does the Holocaust Reveal about the Individual and Society? (5) Aftermath, and (6) Could it Happen Again? Some of the writers whose works are excerpted are Lucy Dawidowicz, William L. Shirer, Viktor E. Frankl, Elie Wiesel, Thomas Hobbes, John Locke, Albert Speer, and Anne Frank. The front bibliography is useful, but confused and disordered. The 7-page bibliography is too sketchy to be of any value. Undocumented.

1257 CONFÉRENCE DES COMMISSIONS HISTORIQUES ET DES CENTRES DE DOCUMENTATION JUIFS. Les Juifs en Europe 1939-45. Paris: CDJC, 1947.

1258 CRAWFORD, FRED ROBERTS. "The Holocaust: A Never-Ending Agony," Annals of the American Academy of Political and Social Science 1980 450(July): 250-255. Forty percent of the American soldiers held in German concentration camps revealed severe emotional stress. From an original goal of 10 oral histories, the project entitled "Witness to the Holocaust" has expanded to almost 400 known witnesses and has completed interviews with 80. The experiences which these nurses, Red Cross workers, and United Nations Refugee Relief Agency (UNRRA) workers shared verify the nature of the concentration camp system and its impact on Jews and non-Jews during World War II. Undocumented.

1259 DAWIDOWICZ, LUCY S. Holocaust Reader. New York: Behrman House, 1976. 397p.

1260 DONAT, ALEXANDER. The Holocaust Kingdom, a Memoir. London: Secker and Warburg, 1965; New York: Holt, Rinehart and Winston, 1978. 361p. These memoirs of a Jewish publisher of a daily newspaper in Warsaw relives the experiences of a family during World War II. Describes life in the Warsaw ghetto before and after the resettlement. One chapter is devoted to the author's wife, Lena, who gives an account of life at the Maidanek concentration camp from a woman's perspective. Includes 3 maps depicting the journey through four countries, 9 death camps, the Warsaw ghetto before the resettlement, and the ghetto in 1943. Undocumented.

1261 DRINAN, ROBERT F. "The Christian Response to the Holocaust," Annals of the American Academy of Political and Social Science 1980 450 (July): 179-189. The reaction of Christians to the Holocaust can generally be described as mild, vague, and belated. While there are notable exceptions to the general ineffectiveness of the Church in showing its concern over rising antisemitism, it failed in any significant way to provide political or moral leadership. 52 notes

1262 ECKARDT, ALICE L., and A. ROY ECKARDT. "The Holocaust and the Enigma of Uniqueness: A Philosophical Effort at Practical Clarification," Annals of the American Academy of Political and Social Science 1980 450 (July): 165-178. This philosophical analysis seeks to foster understanding between representatives of diverse disciplines in their study of the Holocaust. 32 notes.

1263 EISENBERG, AZRIEL. Witness to the Holocaust. New York: Pilgrim Press, 1981. 647p. This anthology reprints approximately 200 testimonials on the Holocaust. The entries are classified under 27 major headings, among them: Germany goes Nazi, NSDAP, SS and Gestapo as a state within a state, Kristallnacht, destruction of Jewish books and treasures, deportation, death camps, extermination, children of the Holocaust, the Warsaw uprising, death marches, postwar Germany and the Jews, and lessons for mankind. Contains a 5-page list of works cited as well as readings at the ends of most chapters. Scholarly use of this otherwise excellent book is hampered by the absence of an index.

1264 FRIEDMAN, SAUL S. AMCHA: An Oral Testament of the Holocaust. Washington: University Press of America, 1979. 434p. A supplementary book of readings to be used with a number of major textbooks used in teaching the Holocaust. The term Amcha refers to the common people among the Jews. The interviews reprinted here, made between 1972 and 1976, include 6 from Germany, 3 from Austria, 9 from Poland, 1 from the Netherlands, 1 from Belgium, 5 from Hungary, 2 from Carpathia, and 1 from Rumania. 4-page glossary. Nearly every interview contains a bibliography.

1265 GLATSTEIN, JACOB, ISRAEL KNOX, and SAMUEL MARGOSHES (eds.). Anthology of Holocaust Literature. Philadelphia: Jewish Publication Society of America, 1969. 412p. This volume contains a valuable and useful introduction which explains its organization and its source of materials. It deals with Jewish uprisings and ghettos, children, and concentration and death camps. These topics include all or portions of 63 works by Jewish as well as non-Jewish writers. The 6-page glossary identifies a number of outstanding events and people related to the Holocaust, and the 6-page section on biography identifies 55 key figures. The 4-page acknowledgment lists the titles of all works excerpted.

1266 JEWISH BLACK BOOK COMMITTEE. WORLD JEWISH CONGRESS. The Black Book, the Nazi Crime Against the Jewish People. New York: Duell, Sloan and Pearce, for the Jewish Black Book Committee, 1946. 560p. Republished as Black Book of the Nazi Crime against the Jewish People. Atlanta: Nexus, 1982.

1267 KERNMAYR, ERICH [pseudonym, Erich Kern]. Die Tragödie der Juden, Schicksal zwischen Propaganda und Wahrheit. Preußisch Oldendorf: W. Schutz, 1979. 327p. Describes public reaction and antisemitism relating to the influx of Jews into Germany and Austria since the late 19th century. The National Socialist party responded to the xenophobia with increasingly severe measures. This book presents the alternatives offered to the Jewish question by the United States, England, Jewish organizations, National Socialists, and various European governments. Sociological data surrounding Jewish emigration and immigration includes population statistics of Jews in Europe. Discusses the Madagascar Project, the Wannsee Conference, and England's rejection of the Jews. Chapters on Chaim Weizman, President of the Jewish Agency, and Adolf Eichmann. 6-page index of names, 3-page bibliography, 10 pages of illustrations.

1268 LAQUEUR, WALTER. The First News of the Holocaust. New York: Leo Baeck Institute, 1979.

1269 LITTELL, FRANKLIN H. "Fundamentals in Holocaust Studies," Annals of the American Academy of Political and Social Science 1980 450(July): 213-217. Regular conferences on Holocaust studies began in 1970. The modern university, with its commitment to technology and its scant attention to ethics, is called into question by the Holocaust, since the death camps were planned, built, and operated by men and women, many of whom had a university education. Sees a great increase in international cooperation among Israelis, West Germans, and North Americans. 3 notes.

1270 MASSOW, A.W. "Der gelbe Stern," Spruchgerichte 1948 1(May): 136-137.

1271 MENDELSOHN, JOHN. Legalizing the Holocaust: The Early Phase, 1933-1939. The Holocaust. Volume 1. New York: Garland, 1982. 212p.

1272 PILCH, JUDAH (ed.). The Jewish Catastrophe in Europe. [New York]: American Association for Jewish Education, 1968. 230p. A textbook that deals with Jewish life in Europe between the two world wars, the "Jewish question" in the Third Reich, the Holocaust, and the literature of the Holocaust. End-chapter notes, 120 photographs, maps, excellent glossary.

1273 PINKUS, OSCAR. The House of Ashes. Cleveland: World, 1964. 243p.

1274 PINSON, KOPPEL S. (ed.). Yivo Annual of Jewish Social Science. Volume 8. New York: Yiddish Scientific Institute, 1953. This entire issue was devoted to the Holocaust.

1275 ROBINSON, JACOB. And the Crooked Shall be Made Straight. La Tragédie juive sous la croix gammée. Paris: CDJC, 1968. 470p.

1276 ROTH, JOHN K. "Holocaust Business: Some Reflections on Arbeit macht Frei," Annals of the American Academy of Political and Social Science 1980 450 (July): 68-82. Focuses on the principal extermination centers - Auschwitz-Birkenau, Belzec, Chelmno, Maidanek, Sobibor, and Treblinka - where countless Jews were killed. The Nazi system included some 1600 forced labor operations. Explores the links between industry, slave labor. and the Holocaust. 33 notes.

1277 ROTHCHILD, SYLVIA (ed.). Voices from the Holocaust. New York: New American Library, 1981. 456p. This anthology contains 34 entries under "Life Before the Holocaust," 30 entries under "Life During the Holocaust," and 28 entries under "Life in America."

1278 SCHATZKER, CHAIM. "The Teaching of the Holocaust: Dilemmas and Considerations," Annals of the American Academy of Political and Social Science 1980 450(July): 218-226. The literature of the schools has failed to deal with the problem of teaching the Holocaust. Publications dealing with teaching the Holocaust began appearing in the early 1960s and the late 1970s in Israel, Germany, the United States, and elsewhere. The object here is to bring students to an honest confrontation with the phenomenon of antisemitism and with the murder of European Jews. 19 notes.

1279 SCHULTZ, JOSEPH P., and CARLA L. KLAUSNER. From Destruction to Rebirth: The Holocaust and the State of Israel. Washington: American University Press, 1978.

1280 SHERWIN, BYRON L., and SUSAN G. AMENT (eds.). Encountering the Holocaust: An Interdisciplinary Survey. Chicago: Impact Press, 1980. 502p.

1281 STÖHR, MARTIN (ed.), in collaboration with ULRIKE BERGER, PETRA HELDT, HELMUT JUST, and PETER VON OSTENSACKEN. Erinnern, nicht vergessen. Zugänge zum Holocaust. Munich: Chr. Kaiser, 1979. 179p. An anthology which contains scores of quotations on various holocausts. Essays deal with various aspects of the Holocaust, among them isolation, exile, deportation, concentration camps, and mass murder. Works cited are listed in the 6-page bibliography and notes.

1282 SYRKIN, MARIE. "Diaries of the Holocaust," in Murray Mindlin and Chaim Bermant (eds.). Explorations. London: Barrie & Rockliff, 1967.

1283 UNITED NATIONS INFORMATION ORGANIZATION [OFFICE]. Persecution of the Jews. London: HMSO, 1942. 20p.

1284 WELLERS, GEORGE. Reply to the Neo-Nazi Falsification of Historical Facts concerning the Holocaust. Published as Part 2 (pp. 105-215) of Serge Klarsfeld (ed.) The Holocaust and the

Neo-Nazi Mythomania. New York: Beate Klarsfeld Foundation, 1978. A polemic attacking writers such as Paul Rassinier, who argue that gas chambers were not used for the systematic extermination of Jews and that the actual number of Jews killed was much lower than generally believed. Appendices contain the first unabridged publication of the two Korherr reports. 1-page bibliography.

1285 WORLD JEWISH CONGRESS. BRITISH SECTION. St James' Conference of the Allied Governments in London and Nazi Anti-Jewish Crimes: Documents Exchanged with the World Jewish Congress. London: British Section of the World Jewish Congress, 1942.

B. DOCUMENTS

1286 ARAD, YITZHAK, GUTMAN YISRAEL, and ABRAHAM MARGALIOT. Documents on the Holocaust: Selected Sources on the Destruction of the Jews of Germany and Austria, Poland, and the Soviet Union. Jerusalem: Yad Vashem (in cooperation with the Anti-Defamation League and Ktav Publishing House), 1981. Contains a collection of documents from the various areas listed in the title, including statements on Nazi ideology, Nazi policy towards the Jews, and Jewish response to persecution.

1287 BERG, MARY. Warsaw Ghetto. A Diary. New York: L.B. Fischer, 1945. 253p. Although only 15 when she left Warsaw, this witness was more objective than most. Also published in French, Italian and Hebrew.

1288 BLUMENTHAL, NACHMAN. [Conducts and actions of a judenrat. Documents from the Bialystock ghetto]. Jerusalem: Yad Vashem, 1962. 561p. In Hebrew; documents in Yiddish, summary in English.

1289 BLUMENTHAL, NACHMAN. [Documents from Lublin ghetto. Judenrat without direction]. Jerusalem: Yad Vashem, 1967. 395, 312, 30p. In Hebrew; translated from Polish, introduction in English.

1290 CZERNIAKOW, ADAM. Warsaw Ghetto Diary, 6-9-39 - 23.7.42. Jerusalem: Yad Vashem, 1968. 395p. Diary in Hebrew; introduction in English. 264p.

1291 HANNELL, SALOMEA. "Revolt," in Documents of Crime and Martyrdom. Cracow: Jewish Historical Commission of Cracow, 1945. Original is in Yiddish.

1292 HILBERG, RAUL. Documents of Destruction: Germany and Jewry, 1933-1945. London: W.H. Allen, 1972. 242p. A list of previously unpublished documents on the Holocaust. No index.

1293 NOAM, ERNST, WOLF-ARNO KROPAT, and KLAUS MORITZ (comps.). Justiz und Judenverfolgung. Schriften der Kommission für die Geschichte der Juden in Hessen I und II. 2 volumes. Noam and Kropat compiled Volume 1; Noam and Moritz, Volume 2. Volume 1, Juden vor Gericht, 1933-1945. Dokumente aus hessischen Justizakten. Wiesbaden: Kommission für die Geschichte der Juden in Hessen, 1975. 327p. Deals with trials of Jews under the National Socialist regime. Problems of administering justice arose because of the unwillingness of officials to adhere to traditional norms and legal concepts when prosecuting Jews. Discusses civil, occupational, and administrative tactics used to define "illegal" Jewish activity. Covers punitive action taken against the Jews as a group, including financial restrictions, deportation, bans against gatherings, control of political behavior, and regulations determining the given names of Jewish children. Each measure is described within a sociological context and is supported by legal documents from the government of the state of Hessen. 6-page bibliography, 3-page list of documents cited. Volume 2, NS-Verbrechen vor Gericht, 1945-1955. Wiesbaden: Kommission für die Geschichte der Juden in Hessen, 1978. 374p. Persecution of Jews as reflected by National Socialist policy and criminal proceedings. Discusses the reinstatement of the principles for a constitutional state into the legal system and the legal grounds for changing the penal code in reaction to National Socialist crimes. A section on documents contains SA records dating from 1933-1935, the November pogrom of 1938, and texts relating to Gestapo crimes (1942-1944). 5-page bibliography, 2-page register of court decisions from the state legislatures, 6-page index of names, and 2-page list of documents.

1294 RUBENSTEIN, RICHARD. After Auschwitz: Essays in Contemporary Judaism. Indianapolis: Bobbs-Merrill, 1966.

1295 STENDIG, JAKOB. "Execution in Plashow," in Documents of Crimes and Martyrdom. Cracow: Jewish Historical Commission of Cracow, 1945. Original is in Yiddish.

C. HISTORIES

1296 BAUER, YEHUDA. A History of the Holocaust. New York: Franklin Watts, 1982. 398p. The Holocaust is the watershed event in modern history. To approach the Holocaust from a literary, philosophical, or theological point of view, one must first know its history. This requires looking at Jewish history and antisemitism from ancient times to the present. Major sections analyze the problem of (1) Jewish identity, (2) liberalism, emancipation, and antisemitism, (3) World War I and its aftermath, (4) the Weimar Republic, (5) the evolution of Nazi Jewish policy from 1933-1938, (6) German Jewry from 1933-1938, (7) the beginning of the siege against Jews in Poland, (8) life in the ghettoes, (9) the "final solution," (10) West European Jewry from 1940-1944, (11) resistance, (12) rescue, (13) the last years of the Holocaust (1943-1945), and (14) aftermath and revival. Based on primary and secondary sources; 233 notes, 10-page bibliography, 18-page index.

1297 BAUER, YEHUDA. The Holocaust in Historical Perspective. Seattle: University of Washington Press, 1978. Attacks those who attempt to transform the Holocaust into a mystical experience. Essays on the Holocaust and American Jewry, Jew and Gentile, the aftermath of the Holocaust, and the mission of Joel Brand.

1298 BAUER, YEHUDA, and NATHAN ROTENSTREICH (eds.). The Holocaust as Historical Experience: Essays and a Discussion. New York: Holmes & Meier, 1981. 288p.

1299 CONWAY, JOHN S. "The Holocaust and the Historians," Annals of the American Academy of Political and Social Science 1980 450(July): 153-164. The Holocaust has been interpreted by historians largely according to the needs of their audiences. Jewish historians view it as the culminating tragedy of their people before the rebirth in statehood. German historians are more concerned with overcoming their guilt and therefore concentrate less on Jewish sufferings and more on Nazi rule.

Christian historians have sought to eradicate the long tradition of Christian prejudice against Jews. Historians of Nazism are divided into rival schools and have yet to reach any firm conclusions on topics such as the genesis of the "final solution." 34 notes.

1300 DAWIDOWICZ, LUCY S. *The Holocaust and the Historians*. Cambridge, Massachusetts/London: Harvard University Press, 1981. 187p. Historians have neglected the subject of how 6,000,000 Jews were murdered in Europe. Among the factors contributing to this neglect are national partisanship and a lack of interest in the fate of the Jews. This book tries to explain the factors of methodology and prejudice, politics and personality, and tradition and ideology in an attempt to explain why contemporary historians have neglected so important a subject. Major topics include the Holocaust according to English and American historians, German historians confront National Socialism, erasing the Holocaust in the USSR, Polish historical revisionism, and the Holocaust in Jewish history. All works examined are listed in the 33-page section on notes. 4-page index.

1301 DAWIDOWICZ, LUCY S. *The War against the Jews, 1933-1945*. New York: Holt, Rinehart and Winston, 1975. 460p. This book developed out of a course of studies at Yeshiva University. It directs itself to the questions of how it was possible for a modern state to carry out the systematic murder of a whole people for no reason other than that they were Jews, how it was possible for a whole people to allow itself to be destroyed, and how it was possible for the world to stand by without halting this destruction. Part I, "The Final Solution," addresses the first issue. Part II, "The Holocaust," the second. Appendix A deals with the Jews in Hitler's "mental world," antisemitism in modern Germany, anti-Jewish legislation, the SS as the instrument of the "final solution," and the annihilation camps. Appendix B is a table showing the number of Jews killed, arranged by country. Based on primary and secondary sources; 598 notes, 14-page bibliography, 10-page index, 4 maps.

1302 FOSTER, CLAUDE R., JR. "Historical Antecedents: Why the Holocaust?" *Annals of the American Academy of Political and Social Science* 1980 450(July): 1-19. Antisemitism, a necessary precursor to the Holocaust, has a long history and was usually based on political, economic, religious, or social prejudice. In the latter part of the nineteenth century, a violent racial antisemitism appeared that rejected assimilation as a solution to the "Jewish problem." The tensions among the Jews themselves - liberals versus orthodox and Zionists versus assimilationists, economic crises, the need to find a scapegoat for national humiliation, the identification of Jews with Marxists, and the swing to the political right led to the Holocaust. 81 notes.

1303 GILBERT, MARTIN. *Atlas of the Holocaust*. London: Michael Joseph, 1982. 256p. Contains 316 maps and 60 photographs depicting anti-Jewish violence and destruction of Jews in Europe from just before World War I to 1950. The author personally drew all the maps, a result of seven years' research.

1304 KORMAN, GERD (ed.). *Hunter and Hunted. Human History of the Holocaust*. New York: Viking, 1973. 320p.

D. ANTISEMITISM

1305 DAVIES, ALAN. "Racism and German Protestant Theology: A Prelude to the Holocaust," Annals of the American Academy of Political and Social Science 1980 450(July): 20-34. The success of racism in modern Europe had a great deal to do with the experience of military defeat and political collapse. German Protestant theology during the 19th century was slowly colored by romantic nationalistic ideas that eventually would open the door to racism. 67 notes.

1306 GADE, RICHARD F. A Historical Survey of Anti-Semitism. Grand Rapids: Baker Book House, 1981. 147p.

1307 GOLDSTEIN, ANATOLE. Survey of Events in Jewish Life in 1954. Part III. Anti-Semitism and War Crimes;. New York: World Jewish Congress, Institute of Jewish Affairs, 1955. 21p. Pages 15-21 deal with the treatment of war criminals in West Germany.

1308 KERR, HELEN (comp.). Prejudice: Racist-Religious-Nationalist. London: Vallentine, Mitchell (for the Institute of Contemporary Jewry), 1971. 385p. Wiener Library catalogue series No. 5. Most of the entries relate to antisemitism in German-occupied Europe during World War II.

1309 NOLTE, ERNST. „Eine frühe Quelle zu Hitlers Antisemitismus," Historische Zeitschrift 1961 192(3): 584-606. 61 notes.

E. GENOCIDE (FINAL SOLUTION, ENDLÖSUNG)

1310 ADLER, H.G. Der Kampf gegen die „Endlösung" der Judenfrage. Bonn: Bundeszentrale für Heimatdienst, 1958. 119p.

1311 AINSZTEIN, REUBEN. "Genocide," New Statesman 1981 101(2604): 68; (2605): 810. Pieter Menten, a Dutch art collector, was convicted of having committed mass murder while he was in the service of the Nazis.

1312 AINSZTEIN, REUBEN. "The Failure of the West," Jewish Quarterly 1966, 1967 14(4): 11-20.

1313 ALGAZY, JOSEPH. The Summary of the "Final Solution" and the Literature denying the Holocaust. Treatise presented to Tel Aviv University. 1979. 190p. Appendices contain the "Korherr File" and selected excerpts from anti-Holocaust literature.

1314 ARONSFELD, C.C. "The Nazi Design was Extermination, not Emigration," Patterns of Prejudice 1975 9(33): 20, 24.

1315 AUERBACH, HELLMUTH. „Die Endlösung - nicht perfekt geplant," Frankfurter Allgemeine Zeitung, June 12, 1974.

1316 „Augenzeugenbericht zu den Massenvergasungen," Vierteljahrshefte für Zeitgeschichte 1953 1(2): 177-194. 56 notes.

1317 BAUER, YEHUDA. "Genocide: Was it the Nazis' Original Plan? Annals of the American Academy of Political and Social Science 1980 450(July): 35-45. Nowhere is there any indication before 1939 that the Nazis planned the mass execution of Jews. The plan they did have was to evict all Jews from Germany. Several hundred thousand did leave; those left behind as well as the millions conquered as the Germans swept through Europe caused Hitler a problem. The last alternative was the "final solution," which took form after 1941 with the adoption of the Einsatzgruppen plan for the mass murder of Jews in Russia, mainly by machine gun, and the Wannsee plan for the mass murder of Jews in Poland in the gas ovens and the crematoria established at 6 death camps. 13 notes.

1318 BILLIG, JOSEPH. L'Allemagne et le genocide: Plans et réalisations Nazis. Paris: CDJC, 1950. 110p.

1319 BILLIG, JOSEPH [Serge Klarsfeld and Beate Klarsfeld, eds.]. La Solution finale de la question Juive. Essai sur ses principes dans le IIIe Reich et en France sous l'occupation. Paris: CDJC, 1977. 207p. Published in German as Die Endlösung der Judenfrage. Studie über ihre Grundsätze im III. Reich und in Frankreich während der Besatzung. Also issued with the slightly different title Die Endlösung der Judenfrage in Frankreich. Paris: CDJC, 1977. Serge Klarsfeld (ed.). The French edition contains 45 chapters, each of which deals with a different aspect of the "final solution." Major topics covered include the role of the SS and Gestapo, Eichmann and Hitler in the implementation of the "final solution," Kurt Lischka and Jews in France, and the role of Ernst Achenbach and Herbert Hagen. Contains a 1-page bibliography, brief biographical sketches of 30 people responsible for the "final solution" in France, and an index.

1320 BILLIG, JOSEPH. The Launching of the "Final Solution" of the Jewish Question. Published as Part 1 (pp. 1-104a) of Serge Klarsfeld (ed.). The Holocaust and the Neo-Nazi Mythomania. New York: Beate Klarsfeld Foundation, 1978. Examines Hitler's anti-Jewish actions, the "final solution," the Jewish question in the Gestapo and SD, various attempts to force Jewish migration, Eichmann's task force, Hitler's orders to Himmler on the matter, and gas chambers in the concentration camps. 1-page bibliography, 29p. of notes.

1321 BLUMENTHAL, NACHMAN. Slowa niewinne [Innocent words]. Cracow: Centralna Zydowska Komisya Historyczna w Polsce, 1947. 271p. German documents and survivor narratives in Polish. Volume 1 contains a glossary of Nazi vocabulary used to disguise the extermination campaign.

1322 BONTÉ, FLORIMOND. Six Millions de crimes. Paris: Éditions Sociales, 1964. 470p.

1323 BOWER, FRANCIS. "Genocide," Nineteenth Century and After 1945 138(November): 234-240. Notes that the Nuremberg IMT indictment defined the crime of genocide for the first time.

1324 BOYAJIAN, DICKRAN H. Armenia: The Case for a Forgotten Genocide. Westwood, New Jersey: Educational Book Crafters, 1972. 498p.

1325 BROWNING, CHRISTOPHER R. The Final Solution and the German Foreign Office. A Study of Referat D III of Abteilung Deutschland, 1940-1943. New York: Holmes & Meier, 1979. 276p. Deals with the evolution and background of German Jewish policy.

1326 BUND DER VERFOLGTEN DES NAZIREGIMES. Das „Wannsee-Protokoll" zur Endlösung der Judenfrage, und einige Fragen an die, die es angeht. Düsseldorf: Bundesvorstand des BVN, 1952. 26p.

1327 CLAUGHT, R. "The Crime of Genocide," American Journal of Economics and Sociology 1949 8: 351-365.

1328 COHN, NORMAN. Warrant for Genocide: The Myth of Jewish World Conspiracy and the Protocols of the Elders of Zion. New York: Harper & Row, 1967.

1329 EHRHARDT, HELMUT. Euthanasie und Vernichtung "Lebensunwerten" Lebens. Stuttgart: Enke, 1965. 58p.

1330 ESH, SHAUL. "Between Discrimination and Extermination (The Fateful Year 1938)," Yad Vashem Studies 1958 2: 79-93. 48 notes.

1331 FEIN, HELEN. Accounting for Genocide: National Responses and Jewish Victimization during the Holocaust. New York: Free Press, 1979. 468p. Detailed study that examines various 20th Century paths to genocide, national differences in Jewish victimization, the response of Christian churches to threats against Jews, various movements in nations outside the German orbit, and the Warsaw ghetto. 48p. of notes, 41-page bibliography.

1332 FLEMING, GERALD. Hitler und die Endlösung. Es ist des Führers Wunsch. Munich: Limes, 1982. 218p. Published in English as Hitler and the Final Solution. Berkeley: University of California Press, 1984. 219p.

1333 FRIEDLANDER, HENRY, and SYBIL MILTON (eds.). The Holocaust: Ideology, Bureaucracy, and Genocide. Millwood, New York: Kraus International Publications, 1980. 361p. Foreword by Lillian Tinter Silberstein, who organized the 1977 and 1978 conferences on the Holocaust in San Jose, California, under the auspices of the National Conference of Christians and Jews. Twenty-three participants contributed the 26 essays in this anthology. Major headings are: Before the Holocaust, the Setting of the Holocaust, the Professions in Nazi Germany and the Holocaust, anti-Nazi elites in occupied Europe from 1939-1945, the United States and the Holocaust, and the Aftermath. The Introduction cites a number of similar conferences treating the Holocaust which have produced other anthologies. The final essay points to a methodology of teaching the Holocaust. Contains a biographical sketch of each of the participants. 614 notes.

1334 "Germans impose Mass Death on Red Prisoners and Poles," Life 1942 12(8): 26-27. 10 photographs.

1335 GREEN, GERALD. Holocaust: A Novel of Survival and Triumph. New York: Bantam Books, 1978. 408p. A story of how some survived the Holocaust, even though 6,000,000 did not. This book tells the story of two families, one the "tormentor," the other the "victim." The book was the basis for a television program of the same title. Undocumented.

1336 GROBMAN, ALEX, and DANIEL LANDES (eds.). Genocide, Critical Issues of the Holocaust, a Companion to the Film "Genocide". Los Angeles: Simon Wiesenthal Center, 1983; Chappaqua, New York: Rossel Books, 1983. 501p. Documentary text from the film "Genocide" and essays pertaining to the Holocaust. Topics covered include "Nuremberg and other Trials," by Henry Friedlander, "World War II Nazis in the United States," by Martin Mendelsohn, and excerpts from testimony given at the Eichmann trial. Appendices contain documents on Reinhard Heydrich's policy concerning Jews in occupied territories, excerpts from a speech by Hans Frank on the extermination of the Jews, on problems of Jewish resistance, Hitler's ban on public reference to the "final solution of the Jewish question," excerpts from a speech by Heinrich Himmler before SS officers in Poznan, excerpts from notes on the extermination camp at Belzec, and evidence given at the Nuremberg IMT trial on Auschwitz. Contains a 19-page glossary, 10 maps, 5-page bibliography, 7-page general index.

1337 HEARST, ERNEST. "The British and the Slaughter of the Jews," Wiener Library Bulletin 1967 21(1): 32, 38; and 22(2): 30, 40.

1338 HILLGRUBER, ANDREAS. "Die ׳Endlösung' und das deutsche Ostimperium als Kernstück des rassenideologischen Programms des Nationalsozialismus," Vierteljahrshefte für Zeitgeschichte 1972 20(2): 133-153. 59 notes.

1339 HOROWITZ, IRVIN LOUIS. Genocide. New Brunswick: Transaction Books, 1976.

1340 HOUSEPIAN, MARJORIE. "The Unremembered Genocide," Commentary 1966 42(3): 55-61.

1341 JEWISH HISTORICAL INSTITUTE (WARSAW). Faschismus, Getto, Massenmord. Dokumentation über Ausrottung und Widerstand der Juden in Polen während des zweiten Weltkrieges. Berlin (GDR): Rütten und Loening, 1960. Also published as Faschismus - Getto - Massenmord. Frankfurt am Main: Röderberg, 1960.

1342 KOO, WELLINGTON, JR. "Some Aspects of the Work of the Legal Committee of the General Assembly during the Second Part of the First Session," American Journal of International Law 1947 41(3): 635-650. 66 notes.

1343 KUPER, LEO. International Action Against Genocide. London: Minority Rights Group, 1982. 17p.

1344 LACCONIA, A. "Le Délit de génocide et les droits de l'homme dans la sociéte," Revue de Droit Pénal et de Criminologie 1950 30(February): 489-492.

1345 LAQUEUR, WALTER. The Terrible Secret: Suppression of the Truth about Hitler's "Final Solution." London: Weidenfeld and Nicolson, 1980; New York: Penguin Books, 1982. 262p. Covers the period June 1941 to the end of 1942 and shows which nations already had knowledge of the mass murder of Jews, which was already underway by the end of 1941. Analyzes the problem from the perspective of the neutrals, the Allied powers, Poland, and the Vatican. 12p. of notes, 5 appendices, bibliographical note, index.

1346 LEMKIN, RAPHAEL. "Genocide - A Modern Crime," Free World 1945 9(4): 39-43. Premeditated murder, as planned and practiced by Hitler, must be brought within the scope and jurisdiction of international law.

1347 LEMKIN, RAPHAEL. "Genocide as a Crime under International Law," American Journal of International Law 1947 41(1): 145-151. Account of the development of the concept of genocide and report of the U.N. resolution declaring genocide a crime under international law.

1348 LEMKIN, RAPHAEL. Le Crime de génocide. Paris: La documentation Française, 1946.

1349 LEMKIN, RAPHAEL. "Le Crime de génocide," Revue de Droit International de Sciences Diplomatiques et Politiques 1946 24(4): 213-223.

1350 LEMKIN, RAPHAEL. "Le Génocide," Revue Internationale de Droit Pénal 1946 17: 371-386.

1351 LEMKIN, RAPHAEL. "Genocide," American Scholar 1946 15(2): 227-230.

1352 LENSKI, MORDECAI. "Who Inspired Hitler's Plans to Destroy the Jews," Yad Vashem Bulletin 1964 (4): 49-52.

1353 LEVIN, NORA. The Holocaust: The Destruction of European Jewry, 1933-1945. New York: Schocken, 1968, 1973. 768p. Emphasizes the rise of Hitler, the Nazi plan to destroy all European Jews, the military and political context of the Holocaust, and various forms of Jewish resistance. Part 1, "The Preparation," deals with Jews in Germany, Eichmann in Austria, the invasion of Poland, Reinhard Heydrich's order to destroy Jews, various Nazi ghettos, the Warsaw uprising, and the "final solution." Part 2, "The Deportations," examines deportations on a nation-to-nation basis, dealing with most European nations. Appendices estimate Jewish losses by nation. 26p. of notes, 57 photographs.

1354 MANVELL, ROGER A., and HEINRICH FRAENKEL. The Incomparable Crime: Mass Extermination in the Twentieth Century: The Legacy of Guilt. New York: G.P. Putnam's Sons, 1967. 339p. Analysis of the causes and effects of genocide as practiced by the Nazi regime. Examines the extent of knowledge in Germany of atrocities committed and the guilt of the German people. Discusses the surviving archives of the concentration camps, roots of anti-Semitism, and the operations of Hitler, Himmler, Heydrich, and Streicher. Describes the four major Action Groups (Einsatzgruppen), the administration of death camps, and the revelation of mass extermination. Concludes with a review of post-war trials. Appendices contain documents showing the attitude of the S.S., the awarding of medals to SS men serving in execution squads, a statement seeking instructions on how to loot a body, and a document listing technical improvements in vehicles used for gassing Jewish victims. 8 facsimiles of documents, 6-page bibliography, 7-page index.

1355 MC KELLER, PETER. "Responsibility for the Nazi Policy of Extermination," Journal of Social Psychology 1951 34(November): 153-163.

1356 MIAJA DE LA MUELA, ADOLFO. "El genocido, delito internacional," Revista Española de Derecho Internacional 1951 4(2): 363-408.

1357 MORSE, ARTHUR D. While Six Million Died: A Chronicle of American Apathy. New York: Random House, 1967. 420p. Focuses on bystanders rather than on the killers and their victims. To determine why "the United States and Britain stood by without doing anything," the author examines published literature as well as government documents which were denied to the public. 20p. of notes.

1358 MOSHEIM, BERTHOLD. "Die Arbeiten der Vereinten Nationen zur Frage der Rechte des Individuums und des Verbrechens der Genocide," Archiv des Völkerrechts 1949-1950 2: 180-193.

1359 MOSSE, GEORGE L. Toward the Final Solution: A History of European Racism. New York: Harper & Row, 1980.

1360 POLIAKOV, LÉON. Bréviaire de Haine. Paris: Calmann-Lévy, 1951. The first attempt at a comprehensive survey of the "final solution." Published in English as The Harvest of Hate. The Nazi Program for the Destruction of the Jews in Europe. New York: Holocaust Library, 1979. 350p.

1361 REICHMANN, EVA G. Die Flucht in den Haß. Die Ursachen der deutschen Judenkatastrophe. Frankfurt am Main: Europäische Verlagsanstalt, 1966. 324p.

1362 REITLINGER, GERALD. The Final Solution: the Attempt to exterminate the Jews of Europe, 1939-1945. New York: Beechhurst, 1953. 622p. London: Vallentine, Mitchell, 1953. 2nd, enlarged edition, South Brunswick, New Jersey: T. Yoseloff, 1961. 667p. Story of the persecution of the Jews in Europe from 1939-1945. Published in German as Die Endlösung - Hitlers Versuche der Ausrottung der Juden Europas - 1939-1945. Berlin: Colloquium, 1956. Part 1 discusses deportations, the ghettoes, the Madagascar project, and the gas chambers. Part 2 deals with the "final solution" in practice in European nations and the Soviet Union. Appendix I is a statistical summary of the "final solution." Appendix II outlines the fate of some participants in the "final solution" as of October 1952. 13-page chronology. 1-page bibliography, 28-page index.

1363 ROTHE, WOLF DIETER (comp.). Die Endlösung der Judenfrage. 1 volume to date. Frankfurt am Main: Bierbaum, 1974.

1364 SARTRE, JEAN-PAUL. On Genocide: And a Summary of the Evidence and the Judgments of the International War Crimes Tribunal. Boston: Beacon Press, 1968. 85p. Contains Sartre's essay as well as a summary of the evidence and the judgments of Bertrand Russell's war crimes tribunal. This work was adopted by the Tribunal as part of its findings.

1365 STILLSCHWEIG, KURT. "Das Abkommen zur Bekämpfung von Genocide," Friedens-Warte 1949 49: 93-104.

1366 TOKAYER, MARVIN, and MARY SWARTZ. The Fuga Plan: The Untold Story of the Japanese and the Jews during World War II. New York: Paddington Press, 1979.

1367 UNITED STATES. DEPARTMENT OF STATE. "Genocide: Report of the U.S. Representative on ECOSOC Committee," Department of State Bulletin 1948 18(466): 723-727. Report of June 6, 1948, with a definition and discussion of genocide.

1368 WUCHER, ALBERT. Eichmanns gab es viele. Ein Dokumentarbericht über die Endlösung der Judenfrage. Munich: Droemersche Verlagsanstalt, 1961. 286p.

1369 ZIMMELS, HIRSCH JAKOB. The Echo of the Nazi Holocaust in Rabbinic Literature. London: [private printing], 1975. 372p. New York: Ktav, 1977. 377p. Responses illustrating how Jews lived while confronting extermination.

F. GENOCIDE CONVENTION

1370 BRÜGEL, J.W. "Die Konvention zur Verhütung und Bekämpfung des Gruppenmordes," Europa-Archiv 1949 4(July 20): 2307-2312. 5 notes.

1371 CARLSTON, KENNETH S. "Should the United States ratify the Genocide Convention?" American Bar Association, Proceedings [Section of International and Comparative Law] 1949; 35-39. This article criticizes the Convention for failing to establish principles or rules whereby the crime of genocide could be punished in the Soviet Union. 4 notes.

1372 CARLSTON, KENNETH S. "The Genocide Convention: A Problem for the American Lawyer," American Bar Association Journal 1950 36(March): 206-209. 5 notes.

1373 DONNEDIEU DE VABRES, HENRI. "La Répression du génocide," Recueil Dalloz 1948: 145-148. Criticizes the draft of the Genocide Convention as a confused and confusing document, and asserts that the creation of an international penal jurisdiction must precede codification of the principles of the charter and judgment of the Nuremberg tribunal.

1374 DULLES, JOHN FOSTER. "International Criminal Law and Individuals - A Comment on the Principles involved in the Human Rights Covenant and Genocide Convention," American Bar Association, Proceedings [Sectional of International and Comparative Law] 1949: 23-25. Shows why the "law" of the Versailles Treaty could not cope with German armament and declares that only a law which operates on individuals, not upon states, can ensure respect for international agreements.

1375 FINCH, GEORGE A. "The Genocide Convention," American Journal of International Law 1949 43(4): 732-738. The convention met in Paris on December 9, 1948. Discusses the responsibility of a state for the violation of international law.

1376 "Genocide: A Commentary on the Convention," Yale Law Journal 1949 58(7): 1142-1160. Examines the relationship of the Genocide Convention to U.S. law and the problem of enforcement. Appendix contains the text of the Convention report.

1377 KUHN, ARTHUR K. "The Genocide Convention and State Rights," American Journal of International Law 1949 43(3): 498-501. Note on the participation of the United States in a genocide convention and on the elaboration of the concept of genocide in connection with the Nuremberg IMT trial.

1378 KUNZ, JOSEF L. "The United Nations Convention on Genocide," American Journal of International Law 1949 43(4): 738-746. A legal analysis of the Convention and its relation to the Nuremberg Charter.

1379 LANDSBERG, WILLIAM H. "Gruppenmord als internationales Verbrechen. Das ,Genocide'-Abkommen der Vereinten Nationen," Außenpolitik 1953 4: 310-321.

1380 PHILLIPS, O.L. "The Genocide Convention: Its Effect on Our Legal System," American Bar Association Journal 1949 35(August): 623-625. 10 notes.

1381 TURLINGTON, EDGAR. "The Genocide Convention Should be Ratified," *American Bar Association, Proceedings* [Section of International and Comparative Law] 1949: 26-34. Congress should have no hesitation in ratifying the Convention, since it aimed exclusively at mass extermination and not at discrimination against racial or other groups. Undocumented.

1382 UNITED NATIONS. DEPARTMENT OF PUBLIC INFORMATION. *The Convention on Genocide*. 2nd, revised edition. New York: United Nations, 1952.

1383 UNITED NATIONS. GENERAL ASSEMBLY. Resolution 260 (III): The Prevention and Punishment of the Crime of Genocide. (A) Adoption of the Convention on the Prevention and Punishment of the Crime of Genocide, and text of the Convention. (B) Study by the International Law Commission of the question of an international criminal jurisdiction. (C) Application with respect to dependent territory of the Convention on the Prevention and Punishment of the Crime Genocide. Adopted at the 179th plenary meeting, December 9, 1948. Official Records of the Third Session of the General Assembly, Part I, September 21 - December 12, 1948, Resolutions. Paris: 1948. pp.174-178. The text of the Convention is reprinted in *International Organization* 1949 3(February): 206-209.

G. ECONOMIC PERSECUTION

1384 KRAUS, OTA B., and ERICH KULKA. *Massenmord und Profit. Die faschistische Ausrottungspolitik und ihre ökonomischen Hintergründe*. Berlin(GDR): Dietz, 1963. 438p.

1385 MÜLLERHEIM, FRITZ. *Die gesetzlichen und außergesetzlichen Maßnahmen zur wirtschaftlichen Vernichtung der Juden in Deutschland 1933-1945*. Hamburg: 1952.

H. RESCUE

1386 FEINGOLD, HENRY L. "Failure to Rescue European Jewry: Wartime Britain and America," *Annals of the American Academy of Political and Social Science* 1980 450 (July): 113-121. During the Holocaust British leadership was unable to perceive that "the smoke of the chimney of the death camps meant that its own world was also aflame." Britain's rescue policy tended to serve as an adjunct to German plans for the destruction of European Jews. Far more than their American counterparts, British decision makers felt threatened by the Nazi ability to "dump" thousands, perhaps millions of Jews. The failure to attempt seriously the rescue of millions of Jews went beyond the exigencies of war. 8 notes.

1387 FEINGOLD, HENRY L. *The Politics of Rescue: The Roosevelt Administration and the Holocaust, 1938-1945*. New Brunswick, New Jersey: Rutgers University Press, 1970. 394p. Examines the political reaction of the Roosevelt administration to the Holocaust. Focuses on rescue and relief programs set up by the United States government and discusses deportation, resettlement, and the National Socialist plan to ship Jews to Madagascar. Reviews official U.S. reaction to the "final solution" and to other atrocities. 16-page bibliography, 28-page index.

1388 FLENDER, HAROLD. *Rescue in Denmark*. New York: Simon and Schuster, 1963. 281p.

1389 KIRCHHOFF, HANS. "What Saved the Danish Jews?" *Peace News*, November 8, 1963.

1390 MENDELSOHN, JOHN. "The Holocaust: Rescue and Relief Documentation in the National Archives," *Annals of the American Academy of Political and Social Science* 1980 450 (July): 237-249. The National Archives, a major center for the study of the Holocaust, has many records on the subject, yet no general finding aid exists. Researchers have explored the records of the killing and the destruction of nearly six million Jews, but have neglected records dealing with rescue and relief attempts. This article focuses on the latter topic by delineating where in the National Archives one may find such documentation. Foremost are the records of the War Refugee Board, which was created in early 1944 to provide avenues of rescue and relief to the Jews in Europe. Other records deal with the emigration of Jews from Germany, the Evian Conference, the subsequent Schacht-Rublee negotiations, the Haavara agreements on emigration to Palestine, and the trip to Havana and return of the *St. Louis*. 68 notes.

1391 PENKOWER, MONTY N. "Jewish Organizations and the Creation of the U.S. War Refugee Board," *Annals of the American Academy of Political and Social Science* 1980 450 (July): 122-139. The Anglo-American Alliance moved slowly in dealing with the Holocaust. Refusing the initial appeal of Jewish organizations that food and medical packages be dispatched to the ghettos of Europe, London and Washington argued that supplies would be diverted for the Germans' personal use or would be granted the Jews just to free the Third Reich from its "responsibility" to feed them. The subsequent plan of the World Jewish Congress to rescue Jews through the use of accounts in Switzerland received the approval of the U.S. Treasury in mid-1943, but the State Department and the British Foreign Office procrastinated. The persistence of Treasury Secretary Henry Morgenthau, Jr. and his staff in bypassing the State Department and ultimately confronting Franklin D. Roosevelt in January 1944, along with increasing calls from Congress and the public for a presidential rescue commission, resulted in the creation of the U.S. War Refugee Board. 43 notes.

1392 THOMAS, GORDON, and MAX MORGAN WITTS. *Voyage of the Damned*. New York: Stein and Day, 1974. The story of the *St. Louis*. 317p.

1393 VALENTIN, HUGO. "Rescue and Relief Activities in Behalf of Jewish Victims of Nazism in Scandinavia," *Yivo Annual of Jewish Social Science* 8: 224-234.

1394 YAHIL, LENI. *The Rescue of Danish Jewry, Test of a Democracy*. Philadelphia: Jewish Publication Society of America, 1969. 536p. Original is in Hebrew.

I. RESISTANCE

1395 BAUER, YEHUDA. *They Chose Life: Jewish Resistance and the Holocaust*. New York: American Jewish Committee, 1973.

1396 BRAUN, A.Z., and LEVIN DOV. "Factors and Motivations in Jewish Resistance," *Yad Vashem Bulletin* 1957 2: 4.

1397 GRUBSZTEIN, MEIR, et al (eds.). *Jewish Resistance during the Holocaust: Proceedings of the Conference on Manifestations of*

Jewish Resistance, Jerusalem, April 7-11, 1968. Jerusalem: Yad Vashem, 1971. 562p. This work was originally published in Hebrew, the language of most of the lectures. Among the topics covered are the Warsaw ghetto revolt, Jewish resistance, Jewish political activities against the German government, youth movements in the underground, participation of Jews in allied armies, and escape routes used during the war. Appendices and index.

1398 HANDLIN, OSCAR. "Jewish Resistance to the Nazis," Commentary 1962 34(5): 398-405.

1399 LASKA, VERA (ed.). Women in the Resistance and in the Holocaust. Westport: Greenwood Press, 1983. 330p.

1400 MARK, BERNARD. "Problems Related to the Study of the Jewish Resistance Movement in the Second World War," Yad Vashem Studies 1959 3: 41-65.

1401 NOVITCH, MIRIAM (ed.). Le Passage des barbares. Contribution à l'histoire de la déportation et de la résistance des Juifs grecs. [Paris]: Presses du Temps Présent, [1972], 141p.

1402 NYISZLI, MIKLOS. Auschwitz. A Doctor's Eyewitness Account. New York: Frederick Fell, 1960. 222p. London: Panther, 1962. Some critics doubt the existence of Nyiszli. Largely an account of the 12th Sonderkommando, which revolted, while the other 13 did not. Undocumented; 17 photographs.

1403 RYAN, MICHAEL D. (ed.). Human Response to the Holocaust: Perpetrators and Victims, Bystanders and Resisters. New York: Edwin Mellen, 1981. 278p. An anthology that contains essays on German concentration camps.

1404 SCHAPPES, MORRIS U. "Holocaust and Resistance," Journal of Contemporary Psychotherapy 1980 11(1): 61-69. Deals with Nazi malevolence in selecting Jewish holidays as dates for some of their most barbarous actions, U.S. official observance of the Holocaust, and the use of the term Holocaust. Because of extermination of two-thirds of the Jews of Europe the world Jewish population in 1979 was still 4 million less than in 1933. Discusses survivors, forgiveness, and the quality and extent of resistance.

1405 STEINBERG, LUCIEN. La Révolte des justes. Les Juifs contre Hitler, 1933-1945. Paris: Fayard, 1970. 605p. Bibliography. Published in English as Not as a Lamb. The Jews against Hitler. Farnborough: Saxon House, 1974.

1406 SUHL, YURI (ed.). They Fought Back: The Story of the Jewish Resistance in Nazi Europe. New York: Crown, 1967. 327p.

1407 SYRKIN, MARIE. Blessed is the Match, the Story of Jewish Resistance. New York: Knopf, 1947. 361p. London: Gollancz, 1948. 254p.

1408 SZNER, ZVI (ed.). Extermination and Resistance; Historical Records and Source Material. Israel: Ghetto Fighter's House, 1958. 196p.

1409 TRUNK, ISAIAH. Jewish Responses to Nazi Persecution: Collective and Individual Behaviour in Extremis. New York: Stein and Day, 1979. 371p. In 62 eyewitness accounts of physical and spiritual resistance to the Nazis, this book tells of the uprisings in the ghettoes, resistance in the camps, and the experiences of the Jewish partisans. Original is in Yiddish.

1410 WASSERSTEIN, BERNARD. **Britain and the Jews of Europe, 1939-1945.** Oxford: Clarendon Press, 1979.

1411 WASSERSTEIN, BERNARD. "The Myth of 'Jewish Silence,'" **Midstream** 1980 26(7): 10-15.

J. SURVIVORS

1412 DANIELI, YAEL. "Countertransference in the Treatment and Study of Nazi Holocaust Survivors and their Children," **Victimology: An International Journal** 1980 5(2-4): 355-367.

1413 DANIELI, YAEL. "Families of Survivors of the Nazi Holocaust: Some Long and Short Term Effects," in N. Milgram (ed.). **Psychological Stress and Adjustment in Time of War and Peace.** Washington: Hemisphere, 1980.

1414 DAVIDSON, SHAMAI. **Spheres of Psychotherapeutic Activity.** Jerusalem: Medical Department, Kuput Cholim Center, 1972.

1415 DINNERSTEIN, LEONARD. **America and the Survivors of the Holocaust.** New York: Columbia University Press, 1982. 409p.

1416 EISNER, JACK. **The Survivor.** New York: William Morrow, 1980. 320p. Personal narrative of a Jewish survivor of the Holocaust in Poland which tells the story of a teenager who escaped from the Warsaw ghetto, concentration camps, execution squads, and the gas chamber. The author was 13 years old when his terror began and 19 when it ended. Contains 2 maps of the Warsaw ghetto showing the original area of Jewish resettlement (November 1940) and the walled ghetto (September 1941). Undocumented, 23 photographs.

1417 EITINGER, LEO. **Concentration Camp Survivors in Norway and Israel.** The Hague: Martinus Nijhoff, 1972.

1418 EITINGER, LEO. "Concentration Camp Survivors in the Postwar World," **American Journal of Orthopsychiatry** 1962 32: 367-375.

1419 EPSTEIN, HELEN. **Children of the Holocaust: Conversations with Sons and Daughters of Survivors.** New York: G.P. Putnam's Sons, 1979. 348p. Based on memory and correspondence of several hundred survivors and children of survivors of the Holocaust. Focuses on the experiences of the author and many families with whom she came in contact. 2-page bibliography on the children of survivors.

1420 FURMAN E. "The Impact of the Nazi Concentration Camps on the Children of Survivors," in Volume 2, E. James Anthony and Cyrille Koupernik (eds.). **The Child in His Family.** New York: Wiley, 1973. 509p.

1421 "One Hundred Concentration Camp Survivors," **Israel Annals of Psychiatry** 1966 4: 78-90.

1422 RAKOFF, VIVIAN. "Long Term Effects of the Concentration Camp Experience," **Viewpoints Magazine** 1966 (March): 17-21. Citing case histories of adolescent offspring of concentration camp survivors, a psychiatrist wonders whether there were any survivors at all.

1423 RAKOFF, VIVIAN, J.J. SIGAL, and N.B. EPSTEIN. "Children and Families of Concentration Camp Survivors," *Canada's Mental Health* 1966 14(July-August): 14-26.

1424 RUSTIN, STANLEY. "The Legacy is Loss," *Journal of Contemporary Psychotherapy* 1980 11(1): 32-43. Understanding survivors involves understanding that the survivors and their offspring are not a homogeneous group. Numerous variables, such as the age of the survivor during the Holocaust period, the nature of the experiences, and the length of time the survivor was imprisoned, affect the survivor's reactions. Based on secondary sources; 20 notes.

1425 SHAPIRO. LEON, and JOSHUA STARR. "Recent Population Data Regarding the Jews of Europe," *Jewish Social Studies* 1946 8(2): 75-86. Statistics of Jewish survival in Europe. 15 notes.

1426 STEINITZ, LUCY Y., and DAVID M. SZONY (eds.). *Living after the Holocaust*. New York: Bloch, 1977. In 1975 *Response* magazine devoted an entire issue to children of survivors. This is a paperback publication of that issue.

1427 THORNE, LEON. *Out of the Ashes. The Story of a Survivor*. New York: Rosebern, 1961. 203p. From the ghettoes of Lemberg, Drohobycz, Sambor, and the labor camps Janover and Hyrawka.

1428 WORMSER-MIGOT, OLGA, and HENRI MICHEL. *La Tragédie de la déportation, 1940-1945; Témoignages des survivants des camps de concentration allemands*. Paris: Hachette, 1954. 511p.

K. PSYCHOLOGICAL ASPECTS

1429 BAEYER, WALTER RITTER VON, HEINZ HÄFNER, and KARL PETER KISKER. *Psychiatrie der Verfolgten. Psychopathologische und gutachtliche Erfahrungen an Opfern der nationalsozialistischen Verfolgung und vergleichbarer Extrembelastungen*. Berlin/Göttingen/Heidelberg: Springer, 1964. 397p. This psychological and psychiatric appraisal of the emotional disorders resulting from Nazi persecution is based on a statistical analysis made by 700 experts. Clinical data and psychological case studies of concentration camp inmates illustrate the effects of internment on a generation of survivors. Chapter 1 describes the causes of "national socialist terror" and discusses discrimination, the "final solution," adaptation to concentration camps, ghettos, and hideouts. Other chapters deal with the stresses of war, prisoner of war camps, and research conducted in Denmark, Norway, France, Great Britain, and the Netherlands on various aspects of these problems. Includes a 10-page bibliography, 71 tables, and name and subject indexes.

1430 BAROCAS, HARVEY A., and CAROL B. BAROCAS. "Separation-Individuation Conflicts in Children of Holocaust Survivors," *Journal of Contemporary Psychotherapy* 1980 11(1): 6-14. Examines the developmental conflicts of children of Holocaust survivors with emphasis on psychic trauma and second-generation survivor effects. Discusses depression, guilt, and aggression. Developmental failures may predispose these children to low self-esteem, narcissistic vulnerability, identity problems, and impairments in interpersonal relations. The need for further research and clinical investigations is emphasized to help develop preventive measures and attenuate the effects of the Holocaust on future generations. Based on secondary sources; 10 notes.

1431 BOYLE, KAY. *Breaking the Silence: Why a Mother tells her Son about the Nazi Era*. New York: Institute of Human Relations, 1962. 39p. Pamphlet published by the American Jewish Committee as a guide for parents to explain National Socialist atrocities to their children. Personal narrative of wartime experiences by a Jewish mother. 1-page bibliography.

1432 FEUERSTEIN, CHESTER W. "Working with the Holocaust Victims Psychologically: Some Vital Cautions," *Journal of Contemporary Psychotherapy* 1980 11(1): 70-77. Traces the evolution of the Holocaust as a subject of psychological research. Focuses on the special danger of diminishing or trivializing the Holocaust in the course of writing about aspects or elements of it. Based on secondary works; 9 notes.

1433 FRIEDMAN, PHILIP. "Some Aspects of Concentration Camp Psychology," *American Journal of Psychiatry* 1949 105(8): 601-605.

1434 FOGELMAN, EVA, and BELLA SAVRAN. "Brief Group Therapy with Offspring of Holocaust Survivors: Leaders' Reactions," *American Journal of Orthopsychiatry* 1980 50(1): 96-108.

1435 FOGELMAN, EVA, and BELLA SAVRAN. "Therapeutic Groups for Children of Holocaust Survivors," *International Journal of Group Psychotherapy* 1979 29(2): 211-235. Undocumented.

1436 GEVE, THOMAS. *Youth in Chains*. Jerusalem: Rubin Mass, 1958, 1981. 262p. Memoirs of a childhood in concentration camps.

1437 HOPPE, KLAUS. "Psychotherapy with Survivors of Nazi Persecution," in H. Krystak (ed.). *Massive Psychic Trauma*. New York: International Universities Press, 1968.

1438 JERUSCHALMI, ELIESER. *Das jüdische Märtyrerkind nach Tagebuchaufzeichnungen aus dem Ghetto von Schaulen 1941/44*. Darmstadt: Ökumenische Marienschwesternschaft, 1960. 64p. Original is in Hebrew.

1439 KARR, STEPHEN DAVID. "Second-Generation Effects of the Nazi Holocaust," Ph.D. dissertation, California School of Professional Psychology, Berkeley, 1973. 109p.

1440 KESTENBERG, JUDITH S. "Psychoanalyses of Children of Survivors from the Holocaust: Case Presentations and Assessment," *Journal of the American Psychoanalytic Association* 1980 28: 775-804.

1441 KUPER, LEO. *Child of the Holocaust*. London: Routledge & Kegan Paul, 1967. 283p.

1442 PAPANEK, ERNST, and EDWARD LINN. *Out of the Fire*. New York: Morrow, 1975. 299p. Deals with children.

1443 *Persecution of Jewish Youth under the Nazis. The Official Nazi Attitude as Shown in Decrees, Regulations, Official Handbooks, and the Press*. London: Jewish Central Information Office, [no date given]. Typescript.

1444 PRINCE, ROBERT M. "A Case Study of a Psychohistorical Figure: The Influence of the Holocaust on Identity," Journal of Contemporary Psychotherapy 1980 11 (1): 44-60. The Holocaust is a psychological event as well as an historical event, one that provides themes and metaphors around which personal identity is organized. Discusses the case history of a child of a Holocaust survivor who denies any reaction to her father's survivor status. Based on secondary sources; 4 notes.

1445 SHUVAL, JUDITH T. "Some Persistent Effects of Trauma: Five Years after the Nazi Concentration Camps," Social Problems 1957 5(3): 230-243. 12 notes.

1446 WIND, EMMANUEL DE. "The Confrontation with Death: Symposium on Psychic Traumatization through Social Catastrophe," International Journal of Psychoanalysis 1968 49(2-3): 302-305. Undocumented.

L. REVISIONIST WORKS

1447 ARONSFELD, C.C. "A Propos of a British 'Historical Review': Facts of the Holocaust," Patterns of Prejudice 1974 8(4): 11-16. 19 notes.

1448 BUTZ, ARTHUR R. Hoax of the Twentieth Century. London: Historical Review Press, 1976.

1449 Gaskammern oder Brutöfen. Der Schwindel von den sechs Millionen unschuldigen ermordeten Juden. Cairo: Informationsamt, 1961. 19p.

1450 GRIMSTADT, WILLIAM N. The Six Million Reconsidered. Is the "Nazi Holocaust" Story a Zionist Propaganda Ploy? Torrance, California: Noontide Press, 1979. 170p.

1451 HARWOOD, RICHARD E. Did Six Million Really Die? The Truth at Last. Surrey, England: Historical Review Press, 1977. 28p. Argues that the allegation that six million Jews died during World War II as a direct result of official German policy of extermination is unfounded. According to Heinrich Himmler's statistics and those of the World Centre of Contemporary Jewish Documentation in Paris, Jews numbered approximately 5,400,000 in Europe and Russia when the area of German occupation was at its greatest. Most of these Jews experienced death as a result of war. Harwood attributes the large estimates to atrocity propaganda which mushroomed in the aftermath of the war. 11 photographs, map of concentration and extermination camps.

1452 HEIMANN, GUIDO. „Die Lüge von den sechs Millionen," Der Weg 1954 7: 479-487.

1453 KULKA, ERICH. The Holocaust is being Denied. Tel Aviv: Committee of Auschwitz Camp Survivors in Israel, 1977.

1454 RASSINIER, PAUL. Debunking the Genocide Myth: A Study of the Nazi Concentration Camps and the alleged Extermination of European Jewry. Los Angeles: Noontide Press, 1978. 441p. A former concentration camp inmate himself, the author argues here as elsewhere against concentration camp "legends" pertaining to a Nazi conspiracy to exterminate all European Jews. This work embodies major portions of the author's Le Passage de la ligne, Le Mensonge d'Ulysse, Ulysse trahi par les siens, and Le Drame des Juifs européens. Documented; no bibliography.

M. INTERNATIONAL MILITARY TRIBUNAL AND THE HOLOCAUST

1455 ROBINSON, JACOB. "The International Military Tribunal and the Holocaust," Israel Law Review 1972 7(1): 1-13. The author was Legal Adviser to the Jewish Agency and the Israel Delegation, 1947-1957, and Consultant on Holocaust Research to the Memorial Foundation for Jewish Culture. Deals with the treatment of Jewish genocide in the Nuremberg IMT trial, wartime movements for the trial of war criminals, how the Allied powers agreed on war crimes trials, the four counts brought against the defendants, three of which dealt with the murder of Jews, the crimes of the Gestapo, the SD, Julius Streicher, and Wilhelm Frick, and the Eichmann trial. Concludes that people have a right to existence and continuity, and that this doctrine was given international acceptance with the execution of Eichmann. Based on primary and secondary sources; 38 notes.

1456 ROBINSON, JACOB. "The Jewish Tragedy in Nuremberg," Hadassah Magazine 1946 (December): 9-11, 30.

1457 ROBINSON, JACOB, and HENRY SACHS. The Holocaust: The Nuremberg Evidence. Volume 1. Jerusalem: Yad Vashem, 1976.

1458 WOLFE, ROBERT. "Putative Threat to National Security as a Nuremberg Defense for Genocide," Annals of the American Academy of Political and Social Science 1980 450 (July): 46-67. The Nuremberg trial of Otto Ohlendorf, SS group leader and Lieutenant General of Police, is discussed to illustrate the fact of genocide. A detailed study of his background suggests that the climate of humiliation and ethnocentrism in post-World War I Germany had a strong influence on him. He was educated in law and economics and became active in the Nazi Party in 1925, eventually leading Einsatzgruppe D in the Ukraine. His defense at the trial was that he believed Jews, as agents of the Bolsheviks, were a threat to German national security. Transcripts from his testimony include nearly verbatim quotations from some of Himmler's speeches. 102 notes.

N. BY AREA AND COUNTRY

1. Europe

1459 ADAM, UWE DIETRICH. Judenpolitik im Dritten Reich. Düsseldorf: Droste, 1972. 382p. General history, with chapters on the Wannsee Conference and the "final solution." Bibliography, subject and name indexes.

1460 Blackbook of Localities whose Jewish Population was exterminated by the Nazis. Jerusalem: Yad Vashem, 1965. 440p. A statistical record containing tables on the number of Jews who were to be killed under the provisions of the "final solution" and the number of localities by country actually emptied of their Jewish residents. Charts show the location and number of Jewish residents in 15 European countries.

1461 CARP, MATATIAS. Les Juifs en Europe. Paris: CDJC, 1947.

1462 HILBERG, RAUL. The Destruction of the European Jews. Chicago: Quadrangle, 1961. 788p. 3 volumes. New York: Holmes & Meier, 1985. 1273p.

1463 INSTITUTE OF JEWISH AFFAIRS. Hitler's Ten-Year War on the Jews. New York: 1943. Important articles by Josef Schechtmann, Boris Shub, and others on the condition of Jewry at the time of the German conquests. 311p.

1464 INSTITUTE OF JEWISH AFFAIRS. Jews in Nazi Europe. Baltimore: [Inter-American Jewish Conference], November 1941. Stencil copy of statistical data supplied to the Conference.

1465 JACKSON, ROBERT H. "The Jewish Case against the Nazis," Jewish Spectator 1946 (March): 7-10.

1466 JEWISH BLACK BOOK COMMITTEE. The Black Book: The Ruthless Murder of Jews by German-fascist Invaders throughout the temporarily occupied Regions of the Soviet Union and in the Death Camps of Poland during the War of 1941-1945. New York: Holocaust Library, 1981. 595p.

1467 KRIEGER, SEYMOUR (comp.). Nazi Germany's War against the Jews. New York: American Jewish Conference, 1947. 857p. A complete account of Germany's destruction of European Jewry as revealed in the evidence assembled at Nuremberg. Hundreds of pages of well-arranged documents are preceded by 2 chapters of text. An introductory chapter presents proposals by the American Jewish Conference for inclusion in the German peace treaty.

1468 MONNERAY, HENRI (ed.). La Persécution des Juifs dans les pays de l'est, présentée par la France à Nuremberg. Paris: CDJC, 1949. 356p.

1469 POLIAKOV, LÉON, and JOSEF WULF. Das Dritte Reich und die Juden. Dokumente und Aufsätze. Berlin/Grunewald: Arani, 1955. 457p.

1470 POLIAKOV, LÉON, and JOSEF WULF (eds.). Das Dritte Reich und seine Diener, Dokumente. Berlin/Grunewald: Arani, 1956. 510p. Chapter 1, "Foreign Affairs," contains documents dealing with Jews in Germany, Serbia, Croatia, Bulgaria, Greece, Rumania, Slovakia, Hungary, Denmark, and Switzerland. Chapter 2, "Justice," deals with Jews in Germany. Chapter 3, "Wehrmacht," contains documents on the position of Jews in Germany during World War II. All three chapters contain a large number of photographs.

1471 SCHEFFLER, WOLFGANG. Judenverfolgung im Dritten Reich 1933-1945. 2nd, enlarged edition. Berlin: Colloquium, 1960. 125p. Concise but fairly comprehensive history of Jewish persecution in the Third Reich. Opening commentary on the hatred of Jews throughout the course of history, with most of the account dealing with the period of World War II. Bibliography.

1472 SCHOENBERNER, GERHARD. Der gelbe Stern. Die Judenverfolgung in Europa 1933 bis 1945. Hamburg: Rütten & Loening, 1960. 223p. Published in English as The Yellow Star: The Persecution of the Jews in Europe, 1933-1945. London: Corgi, 1969. New York: Bantam, 1973. 287p. Mostly illustrations. One of the most graphic records of Jewish persecution during the Third Reich. 179 photographs, map, table of chronology.

1473 SEBBA, LESLIE. "The Reparations Agreements: A New Perspective." Annals of the American Academy of Political and Social Science 1980 45 (July): 202-212. In the wake of the Holocaust, a series of agreements was reached between the Federal Republic of Germany and representatives of the Jewish people regarding compensation for the suffering inflicted during the Holocaust. The agreements had many unusual features to which insufficient attention has been devoted in the existing literature. Examines the practical and ideological issues involved. 29 notes.

1474 STRAUSS, WALTHER. "Das Reichsministerium des Innern und die Judengesetzgebung. Aufzeichnungen von Bernhard Lösener," Vierteljahrshefte für Zeitgeschichte 1961 9(3): 262-313. 19 notes.

2. Austria

1475 FRAENKEL, JOSEF (ed.). The Jews of Austria. Essays on their Life, History and Destruction. London: Vallentine, Mitchell, 1967. 584p.

1476 ROSENKRANTZ, HERBERT. Verfolgung und Selbstbehauptung. Die Juden in Österreich 1938-1954. Vienna: Herold, 1978. 400p.

1477 WEINZIERL, ERIKA. Zu wenig Gerechte. Österreicher und Judenverfolgung 1938-1945. Graz: Styria, 1969. 208p.

3. Belgium

1478 SCHMIDT, EPHRAIM. L'Histoire des Juifs à Anvers (Antwerpen). Antwerp: Ontwikkeling, 1969. 291p.

1479 STEINBERG, LUCIEN. Le Comité de défense des Juifs en Belgique, 1942-1944. Brussels: Université de Bruxelles, 1973. 198p.

4. Bulgaria

1480 CENTRAL CONSISTORY OF JEWS IN THE PEOPLE'S REPUBLIC OF BULGARIA. Evrei zaginali v antifashistkata borba [Jews who perished in the struggle against Fascism]. Sofia: Central Consistory of Jews in the People's Republic of Bulgaria, 1958. 367p.

1481 CHARY, FREDERICK BARRY. The Bulgarian Jews and the Final Solution, 1940-1944. Pittsburgh: University of Pittsburgh Press, 1972. 246p.

1482 MÜNZ, MAX. "Die Verantwortlichkeit für die Judenverfolgungen im Ausland während der nationalsozialistischen Herrschaft. Ein Beitrag zur Klärung des Begriffes der "Veranlassung" . . . seines Verhältnisses zur Staatssouveränität und seiner Anwendung auf die Einwirkung des nationalsozialistischen Deutschlands auf nichtdeutsche Staaten 1933-1945 hinsichtlich der Rechtsstellung und Behandlung der Juden unter besonderer Berücksichtigung der Judenverfolgungen in Bulgarien, Rumanien und Ungarn." Frankfurt am Main: [Inaugural-Dissertation], 1958. 251p.

1483 NAINOVITCH, ISAK. "Who saved the Bulgarian Jews from the Death Camps?" Annual of the Social, Cultural, and Educational Association of the Jews of the People's Republic of Bulgaria [Sofia] 1966 1(1): 63-81.

1484 OLIVER, H.D. We Were Saved: How the Jews of Bulgaria Were Kept from the Death Camps. Sofia: Foreign Languages Press, 1967.

5. Croatia

1485 PARIS, EDMOND. <u>Genocide in Satellite Croatia, 1941-1945</u>. Chicago: American Institute for Balkan Affairs, [1960].

6. Denmark

1486 BERTELSEN, AAGE. <u>October '43</u>. New York: G.P. Putnam's Sons, 1954. 256p. The story of the extermination of Jews in Denmark and the rescue of thousands of them before deportation and extermination. Undocumented; 1 map.

7. France

1487 BILLIG, JOSEPH. <u>L'Institut d'étude des questions juives, officine française des autorités nazies en France. Inventaire commenté de la collection de documents provenant des archives de l'institut conservés au CDJC</u>. Paris: CDJC, 1974. 217p.

1488 <u>Judenverfolgung in Frankreich. Dokumente über die Verantwortlichkeit des Reiches für die Judenmaßnahmen im besetzten und unbesetzten Frankreich, insbesondere auch Algerien, Marokko, Tunis</u>. Frankfurt am Main: United Restitution Organization, 1959. 235p.

1489 LES FILS ET FILLES DES DEPORTÉS JUIFS DE FRANCE (FFDJF). <u>Le procès de Cologne</u>. New York: Beate Klarsfeld Foundation, [no date given; post 1980]. 43p. A collection of newspaper articles in English, French, and German covering the 1979 trial in Cologne of Herbert Hagen, Kurt Lischka, and Ernst Heinrichsohn for abetting the murder of 50,000 Jews by shipping them from France to Auschwitz. Serge Klarsfeld led the successful campaign against them. More than 100 photographs and illustrations.

1490 MONNERAY, HENRI [comp.]. <u>La Persécution des Juifs en France et dans les autres pays de l'ouest presentée par la France à Nuremberg</u>. Paris: CDJC, 1947. 426p. Collection of documents compiled by Henri Monneray, alternate at the Nuremberg IMT trial. Discusses charges brought by French representatives François de Menthon and Edgar Faure. Contains documents pertaining to the persecution of Jews in France, the Netherlands, Luxembourg, Denmark, and Norway. Part III contains excerpts from the interrogation of defendants Joachim von Ribbentrop, Alfred Rosenberg, Fritz Sauckel, Arthur Seyss-Inquart, and an examination of witnesses Helmut Knochen and Franz Straut. Concludes with a summation of the judgment at Nuremberg. Contains a chart of Jewish organization in Paris and the rest of France, and one giving Jewish population statistics in metropolitan Paris by age group. Based on primary documents; 19-page index, no bibliography, photocopies of 20 documents.

1491 POLIAKOV, LÉON. <u>L'Étoile jaune</u>. Paris: CDJC, 1949. 93p. Contains a score of letters on the German policy of requiring Jews to wear yellow stars to mark them as Jews.

1492 POLIAKOV, LÉON, and JACQUES SABILLE. <u>La Condition des Juifs en France sous l'occupation italienne</u>. Paris: CDJC, 1955. 191p. Published in English as <u>Jews Under the Italian Occupation</u>. Paris: CDJC, 1955. 1955. 208p. Based on German, Italian, and French documents abandoned when the Allies closed in on the Germans and Vichy French. These documents tell the story of how the Germans tried to force the Italians to enforce the strict, anti-Jewish policies adopted by the Germans.

1493 VORMEIER, BARBARA. Die Deportierung deutscher und österreichischer Juden aus Frankreich. La Déportation des Juifs allemands et autrichiens de France (1942-1944). The Deportation of German and Austrian Jews from France (1942-1944). Paris: Éditions la Solidarité, 1980. 120p. A study of the deportation, with text and titles in German, French, and English. Contains a 52-page list of those deported.

8. Germany

1494 ADLER, H.G. Die Juden in Deutschland. Von der Aufklärung bis zum Nationalsozialismus. Munich: Kösel, 1960. 177p. Published in English as Jews in Germany: From the Enlightenment to National Socialism. Notre Dame: University of Notre Dame Press, 1969. 152p.

1495 BALL-KADURI, K.J. "Berlin is 'Purged' of Jews: The Jews of Berlin in 1943," Yad Vashem Studies 1963 5: 271-316. 82 notes.

1496 BAUM, RAINER C. The Holocaust and the German Elite. Genocide and National Suicide 1871-1945. Totowa, New Jersey: Rowman and Littlefield, 1981. 374p.

1497 BILLIG, JOSEPH. Les Camps de concentration dans l'économie du Reich hitlérien. Paris: Presses Universitaires de France, 1973. 337p. Focuses on the SS and the German system of concentration camps. Chapters cover the creation of the camp system, economic and industrial output of the camps, and testimonies about working conditions in them. 6 pages of references to works cited, name and document index.

1498 DROBISCH, KLAUS, RUDI GOGUEL, WERNER MÜLLER, and HORST DOHLE. Juden unterm Hakenkreuz. Verfolgung und Ausrottung der deutschen Juden, 1933-1945. Frankfurt am Main: Röderberg, 1973. 437p.

1499 GÖPPINGER, HORST. Die Verfolgung der Juristen jüdischer Abstammung durch den Nationalsozialismus. Villingen: Ring, 1963. 156p.

1500 GROSS, LEONARD. The Last Jews in Berlin. New York: Simon and Schuster, 1982. 349p.

1501 HUTTENBACH, HENRY. The Destruction of the Jewish Community of Worms, 1933-1945. A Study of the Holocaust Experience in Germany. New York: The Memorial Commission of Jewish Victims of Nazism from Worms, 1981. 256p.

1502 KEMPNER, ROBERT M.W. Der Mord an 35000 Berliner Juden. Heidelberg: 1970.

1503 KREMERS, HEINZ. "The First German Church faces the Challenge of the Holocaust: A Report," Annals of the American Academy of Political and Social Science 1980 450 (July): 190-201. After 20 years of discussion about the relationship of Christians and Jews, the Evangelische Kirche im Rheinland, regional church of the Evangelische Kirche in Deutschland, passed a resolution asserting the responsibility of Christianity for the Holocaust, the election of Israel as the people of God, and the common vocation of Jews and Christians to be witnesses of God to the world and to each other. 35 notes.

1504 KURTH, GERTRUD M. "The Jew and Adolf Hitler," Psychoanalytic Quarterly 1947 16: 11-32. 5 notes.

1505 SAUER, PAUL (ed.). Dokumente über die Verfolgung der jüdischen Bürger in Baden-Württemberg durch das nationalsozialistische Regime 1933-1945. 2 volumes. Stuttgart: W. Kohlhammer, 1966. 346p., 414p. These 2 volumes contain 267 and 550 documents, respectively. Volume 2 has an index.

1506 WALK, JOSEPH. Das Sonderrecht für die Juden im NS-Staat. Eine Sammlung der gesetzlichen Maßnahmen und Rechtlinien. Inhalt und Bedeutung. Heidelberg: Müller, 1981. 452p.

1507 WEINREICH, MAX. Hitler's Professors. The Part of Scholarship in Germany's Crimes against the Jewish People. New York: Yivo Institute for Jewish Research, 1946. 291p.

9. Greece

1508 KABELI, ISAAC. "The Resistance of the Greek Jews." Yivo Annual of Jewish Social Science 1953 8: 281-288. 31 notes.

1509 MOLHO, MICHAEL (ed.). In Memoriam: 1940-1944. Hommage aux victimes Juives des Nazis en Grèce. Salonika: N. Nicolaïdes, 1948,

10. Hungary

1510 ABRAHAM, RANDOLPH L. The Destruction of Hungarian Jewry: A Documentary Account. 2 volumes. New York: Pro Arte for the World Federation of Hungarian Jews, 1963. 969p. This is a collection of documents compiled by the World Federation of Hungarian Jews. Volume 1 contains documents pertaining to the pre-occupation era (September 1940 - March 19,1944). They deal with the treatment of Hungarian Jews abroad, the proposed deportation from Hungary of Jews of foreign citizenship, the Jewish labor battalions, massacres, and German-Hungarian relations regarding the treatment of the Jewish question in Hungary. Volume 2 includes documents on the period March 19, 1944 - April 4, 1945. They deal with the occupation, the implementation of the "final solution," the reports of SS and police leaders, the treatment of Hungarian Jews abroad in 1944, and international reaction and intervention. Lists of documents are in English, while the documents themselves are in German. Table of German and English abbreviations, lists of German Foreign Office ranks and Wehrmacht and SS ranks and their U.S. equivalents. Glossary of organizations pertaining to Hungarian Jewry, 3-page bibliography, 10-page bibliographical index, 12-page general index, chart of the German Foreign Office, map of major ghettos, assembly centers, and routes, and a tabulation of losses of Hungarian Jewry.

1511 CARMILLY-WEINBERGER, MOSHE (ed.). [Memorial volume for the Jews of Cluj-Kolozsvar]. New York: 1970. 468p. In Hungarian, English, and Hebrew. The Hungarian section includes S. Samuel's "Our Way to Auschwitz" and Carmilly-Weinberger's "The Tragedy of Transylvanian Jewry."

1512 ECK, NATHAN. "The March of Death from Serbia to Hungary (September 1944), and the Slaughter of Cservenka (Story of a Survivor of a Death Pit)," Yad Vashem Studies 1958 2: 255-294. 75 notes. Includes the memoirs of Zalman Teichman describing his journey from Bor to Cservenka-Temesvar.

1513 KASTNER, RESZOE. Der Bericht des jüdischen Rettungskomitees aus Budapest, 1942-43. Geneva: [stencil copy], 1946.

1514 LAMBERT, GILLES. Opération Hazalah: Budapest 1944. Les jeunes sionistes face aux nazis et aux juifs de Hongrie. Paris: Hachette, 1972. 189p. Focuses on German brutalities and crimes against the Jews.

1515 LÉVAI, EUGENE [Lawrence P. Davis, ed.]. The Black Book on the Martyrdom of Hungarian Jewry. Zurich: Central European Times and Vienna Panorama Publishing Company, 1948. Original in Hungarian.

1516 PALASTI, LASZLO. [The death march to Bor]. Budapest: Gábor, 1945. 94p. Original in Hungarian.

1517 WEISSBERG, ALEXANDER. Desperate Mission: Joel Brand's Story [as told by Alexander Weissberg]. New York: Criterion, 1958. 310p. Published in German as Geschichte von Joel Brand. The original was in Hebrew. An examination of the destruction of European Jewry as told by a leader of the Jewish underground in Budapest. There is much on Brand's discussions with his own companions, with SS leaders, with delegates of the Jewish Agency in Constantinople, and with British officers in Cairo. Documentary appendix, index.

11. Italy

1518 CENTRO DI DOCUMENTAZIONE EBRAICA CONTEMPORANEA, MILANO. Ebrei in Italia: deportazione, resistenza. Florence: Giuntina, 1975. 61p.

1519 Judenverfolgung in Italien, den italienisch besetzten Gebieten und in Nordafrika. Dokumentensammlung. Frankfurt am Main: United Restitution Organization, 1962. 229p.

1520 MICHAELIS, MEIR. "The Attitude of the Fascist Regime to the Jews in Italy," Yad Vashem Studies 1960 4: 1-41. 106 notes.

12. Lithuania

1521 ARAD, YITZHAK. Ghetto in Flames: The Struggle and Destruction of the Jews in Vilna in the Holocaust. New York: Ktav, 1980. 50p. Revised translation of 1976 work done in Hebrew. Deals with persecutions in Lithuania.

1522 ARAD, YITZHAK. "The 'Final Solution' in Lithuania in the Light of German Documentation," Yad Vashem Studies 1976 11: 234-272. 69 notes.

1523 LEVIN, DOV. [They fought back. Lithuanian Jewry's armed resistance to the Nazis, 1941-1945]. Jerusalem: Yad Vashem, 1974. 267p. Text in Hebrew; summary in English.

1524 SEGALSON, M., J. RABINOWITZ, and J. SCHOCHET (comps.). Vernichtung der Juden in Litauen, aus den Jahren 1941-1945. Tel Aviv: 1959. 57p. A collection of mimeographed materials on the extermination of Jews in Lithuania, translated from 4 books on the subject in Hebrew and Yiddish.

13. Macedonia

1525 MATKOVSKI, ALEKSANDAR. "The Destruction of Macedonian Jewry in 1943," *Yad Vashem Studies* 1959 3: 203-255. 143 notes.

14. The Netherlands

1526 HARARI, JACOB. *Die Ausrottung der Juden im besetzten Holland. Ein Tatsachenbericht.* Tel-Aviv: Irgun Olej Merkas Europa, 1944. 100p.

1527 JONG, LOUIS DE. "Jews and Non-Jews in Nazi-occupied Holland," in Max Beloff (ed.). *On the Track of Tyranny: Essays Presented by the Wiener Library to Leonard G. Montefiore, on the Occasion of his Seventieth Birthday.* Freeport, New York: Books for Libraries Press, 1960, 1971. 232p.

1528 KOCHBA, ADINA (comp.), and RINA KALINOV (ed.). [Underground of the Zionist youth in occupied Holland]. Tel Aviv: Hakibbutz Hameuchad, 1969. 312p. In Hebrew.

1529 MINCO, MARGA. *Das bittere Kraut. Eine kleine Chronik.* Hamburg: Rowohlt, 1959. 74p. Published in English as *Bitter Herbs: A Little Chronicle.* London: Oxford University Press, 1960. The chronicle of the only survivor of a Dutch Jewish family.

1530 PRESSER, JACOB. *Ashes in the Wind. The Destruction of Dutch Jewry.* New York: Dutton, 1965. London: Souvenir Press, 1968. 556p. Original was published in Dutch in 1965.

1531 SIJES, B.A. *Studies over jodenvervolging.* Assen: Van Gorcum, 1974. 184p.

15. Poland

1532 APENSZLAK, JACOB, JACOB KENNER, ISAAC LEVIN, and MOSES POLAKIEWICZ (eds.). *The Black Book of Polish Jewry, an Account of the Martyrdom of Polish Jewry under the Nazi Occupation.* New York: The American Federation of Polish Jews in Cooperation with the Association of Jewish Refugees and Immigrants from Poland, [1943]. 343p.

1533 BLOOM, SOLOMON F. "Dictator of the Lodz Ghetto. The Strange History of Mordechai Chaim Rumkowski," *Commentary* 1949 7(2): 111-122.

1534 DABROWSKA, DANUTA, and ABRAHAM WEIN (eds.). *Poland. I. The Communities of Lodz and its Region.* Jerusalem: Yad Vashem, 1976. 285p.

1535 DU PREL, MAX FREIHERR (ed.). *Das deutsche Generalgouvernement Polen.* 2nd edition. Würzburg: Triltsch, 1942. 404p. A guidebook for German troops, containing some data on the Jewish situation in Poland, collected by officials of Governor Hans Frank's Ministry of the Interior.

1536 GUTMAN, YISRAEL. *The Jews of Warsaw 1939-43.* Brighton: Harvester, 1982. 287p. Deals with the 1943 revolt of the Warsaw ghetto. Gutman was a survivor of the revolt. This is a story of the ghetto and the development of the uprising. Based on primary sources.

1537 HERSHKOVITCH, BENDET. "The Ghetto in Litzmannstadt (Lodz)," Yivo Annual of Jewish Social Science 1950 5: 85-122. 16 notes.

1538 KUGELMASS, JACK, and JONATHAN BOYAKIN (eds.). From a Ruined Garden: The Memorial Books of Polish Jewry. New York: Schocken, 1983. 274p. Major topics include "our towns," townspeople, lifeways, events, legends and folklore, Holocaust, and return. Appendix 1 (pp. 223-264) is a bibliography of eastern European memorial books. Appendix 2 (pp. 265-275) is a geographical index and gazetteer.

1539 SILBERSCHEIN, A. (ed.). Die Judenausrottung in Polen. Geneva: 1944-1946. Stenciled reports.

1540 Stroop Bericht. Es gibt keinen jüdischen Wohnbezirk in Warschau mehr. Neuwied: Hermann Luchterhand, 1960. Published in English as The Stroop Report: The Jewish Quarter of Warsaw is no More. New York: Pantheon, 1979.

1541 TRUNK, ISAIAH. "Epidemics and Mortality in the Warsaw Ghetto, 1939-1942," Yivo Annual of Jewish Social Science 1953 8: 82-122.

1542 TUSHNET, LEONARD. The Pavement of Hell. New York: St. Martin's Press, 1972. 210p. On ghettos in Lodz, Warsaw, and Vilna.

1543 WELLS, LEON W. "Revolte a la 'Brigade de la Mort,'" Le Monde Juif 1961 16(24-25): 88-93.

1544 WELLS, LEON W. The Janowska Road. New York: Macmillan, 1973. Published later as The Death Brigade. New York: Schocken, 1946, 1980. New York: Macmillan, 1963. Holocaust Library, 1978. Memoir of a young Jewish boy about the murder of Jews in East Galicia, including the Janowska camp in Lvov (Lemberg) and its "death brigade." An account of the special command engaged in burning bodies.

1545 WULF, JOSEF. "Lodz. Das letzte Ghetto auf polnischem Boden," Schriftenreihe der Bundeszentrale für Heimatdienst. Bonn: Bundeszentrale für Heimatdienst, 1962. 84p.

16. Rumania

1546 GUTTMANN, T. Dokumentenwerk über die jüdische Geschichte in der Zeit des Nazismus. 2 volumes. Jerusalem: 1945. Volume 1 contains important narratives from Jassy and Czernowitz and 62 letters on the Nisko settlement. Volume 2 deals with massacres in Bochnia-Jasienica, narrative of Israel Weitz.

1547 Judenverfolgung in Rumänien. Dokumentensammlung. Frankfurt am Main: United Restitution Organization, 1959. 3 volumes. Mimeograph.

1548 LAVI, THEODORE. "Documents on the Struggle of Rumanian Jewry for Its Rights During the Second World War, (Part One)," Yad Vashem Studies 1960 4: 265-315. 127 notes.

1549 LAVI, THEODORE. "The Vatican's Endeavors on Behalf of Rumanian Jewry During the Second World War," Yad Vashem Studies 1963 5: 405-418.

1550 ROHWER, JÜRGEN (ed.). *Die Versenkung der jüdischen Flüchtlingstransporter Struma und Merkure im Schwarzen Meer (Februar 1942, August 1944). Historische Untersuchung.* Frankfurt am Main: Bernard & Graefe, 1965. 153p.

17. Slovakia

1551 KAMENEC, IVAN. "[The origin and evolution of Jewish labor camps and centers in Slovakia, 1942-1944]," *Nove Obzory* 1966 8: 38p. Summaries in German and Russian.

1552 LIPSCHER, LADISLAV. *Die Juden im slowakischen Staat 1939-1945.* Munich: Oldenbourg, 1979. 210p.

1553 ROTKIRCHEN, LIVIA. "Activities of the Jewish Underground in Slovakia," *Yad Vashem Bulletin* 1961 8-9: 28-30.

1554 ROTKIRCHEN, LIVIA. [The destruction of Slovak Jewry: A documentary history]. Jerusalem: Yad Vashem, 1961. Hebrew text, English summary.

1555 STEINER, FREDERIC. *The Tragedy of Slovak Jewry.* Bratislava: Documentation Centre, CUJCR, 1949. Mainly photographic material.

1556 VASEK, ANTON. *Die Lösung der Judenfrage in der Slowakei. Systematische Übersicht der antijüdischen Gesetzgebung.* Bratislava-Pressburg: Globus, 1942. 161p.

18. Thrace

1557 VASILEVA, NADEJDA SLAVI. "On the Catastrophe of the Thracian Jews," *Yad Vashem Studies* 1959 3: 295-302.

19. Union of Soviet Socialist Republics

1558 DEKER, NIKOLAI, and ANDREI LEBED (eds.). *Genocide in the U.S.S.R. Studies in Group Destruction.* New York: Scarecrow, 1958. First published in Germany by the Institute for the Study of the U.S.S.R.

1559 GARFUNKEL, L. [The Destruction of Kovno's Jewry]. Jerusalem: Yad Vashem, 1959. 330p. Deals with the Kovno ghetto. In Hebrew.

1560 SCHWARZ, SOLOMON M. *The Jews in the Soviet Union.* Syracuse: Syracuse University Press, 1951. 380p. Though concerned primarily with Soviet-Jewish relations, this work contains one chapter on Jews under Nazi occupation. Copiously annotated; index.

1561 WEST, BENJAMIN (ed.). [The destruction of Russian Jewry by the Nazis. 1941-1943]. Tel Aviv: Hozaat Archeon Haavodah-Hamakhlekah Ickheker Yahadut Russia, 1963. 291p. In Hebrew.

20. United States

1562 ADLER, SELIG. "The United States and the Holocaust," *American Jewish Historical Quarterly* 1974 64(1): 14-23. The United States government could have done more to mitigate the catastrophe that befell European Jews had it not made incorrect assumptions concerning the extent of the Holocaust. Measures taken lacked a sense of urgency because of political maneuvers. The measures that were taken came too late to save any considerable number of Jews. 23 notes.

1563 BAUER, YEHUDA. *American Jewry and the Holocaust: The American Jewish Joint Distribution Committee, 1939-45*. Detroit: Wayne State University Press, 1982. 522p.

1564 WYMAN, DAVID S. *The Abandonment of the Jews: America and The Holocaust, 1941-1945*. New York: Pantheon, 1984. 444p. The complete story of the relationship of the United States to the Holocaust. 71p. of notes, 12-page bibliography, index.

21. Yugoslavia

1565 ALKALAY, DAVID. "The Fate of the Jews of Yugoslavia," *Yad Vashem Bulletin* 1959 3-4(October): 18.

1566 LOWENTHAL, ZDENKO (ed.). *The Crimes of the Fascist Occupants and their Collaborators against Jews in Yugoslavia*. Belgrade: Federation of Jewish Communities of Yugoslavia, 1957. 245p. In English. Contains a foreword, summary, and text relating to photo-documentation. Based on documents collected by the Yugoslav State Commission for Investigation of War Crimes.

VI
WORLD WAR II WAR CRIMES: CONCENTRATION CAMPS
(Konzentrationslager, KZ, KL)

A. GENERAL

1567 ABEL, THEODORE. "The Sociology of Concentration Camps." Lecture given in Section IV b, "Concentration Camps and Persecution of Jews," of the congress "The Second World War in the West." This congress took place in Amsterdam, September 5-9, 1950, under the auspices of the National Institute for War Documents at Amsterdam. The Institute has the complete text.

1568 ADLER, H.G. "Selbstverwaltung und Widerstand in den Konzentrationslagern der SS," Vierteljahrshefte für Zeitgeschichte 1960 8(3): 221-236. 27 notes.

1569 AMERICAN ASSOCIATION FOR A DEMOCRATIC GERMANY. They Fought Hitler First. Report on the Treatment of German Anti-Nazis in Concentration Camps from 1933 to 1939. New York: The Association, [1945].

1570 ARNDT, INO, and WOLFGANG SCHEFFLER. "Organisierter Massenmord an Juden in nationalsozialistischen Vernichtungslagern," Vierteljahrshefte für Zeitgeschichte 1976 24(2): 105-135. 65 notes.

1571 ARONÉANU, EUGÈNE. Konzentrationslager. Tatsachenbericht über die an der Menschheit begangenen Verbrechen. [no publication information given]. A reprint in monograph form of Document F 321 of the Nuremberg International Military Tribunal. Major topics covered include witnesses, reports, and documents associated with the IMT as well as deportation, internment, administration and management of the camps, all aspects of life in the camps, work, sanitary conditions, medical experiments, executions, and release. Undocumented; 18-page list of types and location of prison camps, 97 photographs, mostly death camp scenes.

1572 BAKER, LILLIAN. The Concentration Camp Conspiracy - A Second Pearl Harbor. Lawndale, California: AFHA Publications, 1981. 350p.

1573 BALLMANN, HANS. Im KZ - Ein Tatsachenbericht aus dem Konzentrationslager. Backnang/Wüttemberg: Praktikus, 1945. In Dachau Museum Library.

1574 BARTHEL, KARL. Die Welt ohne Erbarmen. Bilder und Skizzen aus dem K.Z. Rudolstadt: Griefenverlag, 1946. 162p.

1575 BILLIG, JOSEPH. L'Hitlérisme et le système concentrationnaire. Paris: Presses Universitaires de France, 1967.

1576 BILLINGER, KARL. Schutzhäftling 880. Aus einem deutschen Konzentrationslager. Paris: Éditions du Carrefour, 1935. 196p. A novel published in English as All Quiet in Germany. London: Gollancz, 1935. 288p.

1577 BIRKENFELD, GÜNTHER. "Der NKWD-Staat," Monat 1950 2(18): 628-643.

1578 BROSZAT, MARTIN. Studie zur Geschichte der Konzentrationslager. Stuttgart: 1970.

1579 CHODOFF, PAUL. "Late Effects of the Concentration Campo Syndrome," Archives of General Psychiatry 1963 8(April): 323-333.

1580 COHEN, ELIE A. Het duitse concentratiekamp: een medische en psychologische studie. Amsterdam: H.J. Paris, 1952, 1954. 258p. Published in English as Human Behavior in the Concentration Camp. New York: Norton, 1953. 295p. A clinical, pathological study of the victims as well as the aggressors, based on an account of the behavior of prisoners, guards, and executioners at Auschwitz, by a Dutch psychologist whose wife and children were killed in the gas chambers but who himself survived. Describes mass extermination, gas chambers, the selection process, and the death march. Medical aspects of the concentration camp are documented by tables giving mortality rates and the structural hierarchy of hospital personnel. Lists the diseases contracted by prisoners and medical experiments inflicted on the inmates. Reviews the psychology of the SS and the prisoners, outlining qualities peculiar to each group. The 1952 edition contains a summary in English with a résumé in French. The 1954 edition contains summaries in English, Dutch, French, and German. Based on secondary sources; 204 notes, 11-page bibliography.

1581 COMMITTEE OF THE INTERNATIONAL RED CROSS. Documents sur l'activité de la Croix Rouge en faveur des civil . . . détenus dans les camps de concentration en Allemagne, 1939-1945. Serie II. Geneva: CIRC, 1947. 156p. Chapter 12 is a report on the camp at Dachau.

1582 DE VOTO, ANDREA. "Psicologia e psicopatologia dei Lager nazisti," Rivista di Psicologia Sociale 1962 9(2): 163-186.

1583 DES PRES, TERRENCE. The Survivor: An Anatomy of Life in the Death Camps. New York: Oxford University Press, 1976.

1584 DESCHNER, KARLHEINZ (ed.). Das Jahrhundert der Barbarei. Munich: Desch, 1966. 529p. Contains H.G. Adler, "Pogrome und Konzentrationslager. Die Judenverfolgung im 20. Jahrhundert," pp. 243-315, and Karlheinz Deschner, "Die Politik der Päpste," pp. 316-370.

1585 DEUTSCHKRON, INGE. ...Denn ihrer war die Hölle, Kinder in Ghettos und Lagern. Cologne: Wissenschaft und Politik, 1965, 1979. 158p. Dedicated to the children who suffered under the Third Reich. Based on the testimony and memoirs of witnesses. Includes poems and drawings by the children of the ghettos and internment camps. Undocumented, 32 illustrations.

1586 EITINGER, LEO. "Pathology of the Concentration Camp Syndrome," Archives of General Psychiatry 1961 5(4): 371-379.

1587 ELIACH, YAFFA, and BRANA GUREWITSCH (eds.). The Liberators. Eyewitness Accounts of the Liberation of Concentration Camps. Oral History Testimonies of American Liberators from the Archives of the Center for Holocaust Studies. New York: Center for Holocaust Studies, 1981. 57p.

1588 FEDERN, ERNST. "The Terror as a System: The Concentration Camp," Psychiatric Quarterly Supplement 1948 22)1): 52-86.

1589 FEIG, KONNILYN G. Hitler's Death Camps, the Sanity of Madness. New York/London: Holmes and Meier, 1981. 547p. Focuses on the 19 major concentration camps, as defined by Himmler, on the evolution of the system, and on the many phases of the process of dehumanization, destruction, and death. Dachau was the model for scientific experimentation, Ravensbrück for the fate of women, Chelmno for primitive killing, Treblinka for the disposal of people, and Buchenwald for the internal political system. Appendix 1 gives directions to the camps. Appendix 2 lists the camps and their commandants. Appendix 3 lists the fate of the commandants. 40p. of notes, 29-page bibliography, index.

1590 FÉNELON, FANIA. Playing for Time. New York: Atheneum, 1977. Concentration camp memoirs.

1591 FOSMARK, JOHANNES (ed.). Danske i tyske koncentrationsleire [Danes in German concentration camps]. Copenhagen: Nordisk Forlag, 1945. 231p.

1592 FRANCE. SERVICE D'INFORMATION DES CRIMES DE GUERRE. Camps de concentration (crimes contre la personne humaine). [Paris]: Office Français d'Édition, 1945. 251p. A study of German concentration camps, with a 49-page appendix listing their names, locations, and types. 95 photographs.

1593 FRANKL, VICTOR E. From Death Camp to Existentialism: A Psychiatrist's Path to a new Therapy. Boston: Beacon, 1959.

1594 GLICKSMAN, W. "Social Differentiation in the German Concentration Camps," Yivo Annual of Jewish Social Studies 1953 8: 123-150.

1595 Häftlings Nummernzuteilung in Konzentrationslagern. Arolsen: Internationaler Suchdienst des IRK, 1965.

1596 HAJŠMAN, JAN. The Brown Beast: Concentration Camp Europe under the Rule of Hitler. Prague: Orbis, 1948.

1597 HELWEG-LARSEN, PER, et al. Famine Disease in German Concentration Camps - Complications and Sequels with Special Reference to Tuberculosis, Mental Disorders and Social Consequences. Copenhagen: A. Munksgaard, 1952. 460p. Published in German as Die Hungerkrankheit in den deutschen Konzentrationslagern, in

Gesundheitsschäden durch Verfolgung und Gefangenschaft und ihre Spätfolgen. Frankfurt am Main: 1955.

1598 HOFFMANN, BEDRICH. [And who will kill you? The experiences and sufferings of priests in concentration camps.]. Presov: Spolecenske Podniky, 1946. 590p. In Slovak. Summary in Latin, English, French, Polish, and Russian.

1599 HOPPE, KLAUS. "The Psychodynamics of Concentration Camp Victims," Psychoanalytic Forum 1966 1(1): 76-85.

1600 HOREC, JAROMIR (ed.). [Children's diaries from concentration camps and ghettoes]. Prague: Nase Vojsko-SPB, 1961. 269p.

1601 INTERNATIONAL TRACING SERVICE. Catalogue of Camps and Prisons in Germany and German occupied Territories, September 1st, 1939 - May 8th, 1945. 2 volumes. Arolsen: 1949, 1950. Volume 1, 486p., Volume 2, 335p. and Supplement (1951), 126p. Particularly important information on Polish labor camps. Includes maps, charts, and information on ghettos. Deals with hundreds of camps. The English and German works (following entry) are different, though there is much overlapping.

1602 INTERNATIONAL TRACING SERVICE. Vorläufiges Verzeichnis der Konzentrationslager und deren Außenkommandos sowie anderer Haftstätten unter dem Reichsführer-SS in Deutschland und deutschbesetzten Gebieten (1933-1945). Arolsen: 1969. 612p. Includes the dates of founding and closing or capture of each camp, the number of inmates incarcerated, and the use and purpose of forced labor. German edition has "International Committee of the Red Cross" above the title.

1603 JUILLARD, E. Atrocités allemandes dans les camps de concentration. Lyon: 1947.

1604 KAMINSKI, ANDREJ. Konzentrationslager 1896 bis heute. Eine Analyse. Stuttgart: Kohlhammer, 1982. 289p.

1605 KANTOR, ALFRED. The Book of Alfred Kantor. New York: McGraw-Hill, 1971. Contains concentration camp drawings.

1606 KATZ, JOSEF. One Who came Back. [no city given]: Herzl Press and Bergen-Belsen Memorial Press, 1973. Describes the nightmarish journey on the Vistula River of Jews shipped back to Germany after its defeat.

1607 KAUTSKY, BENEDIKT. Teufel und Verdammte. Erfahrungen und Erkenntnisse aus sieben Jahren in deutschen Konzentrationslagern Zurich: Büchergilde Gutenberg, 1946.

1608 KLAUSNER, ISRAEL. [Extermination camps in Poland]. Jerusalem: Mass, [1947]. 267p. In Hebrew.

1609 KOGON, EUGEN. Der SS-Staat. Das System der deutschen Konzentrationslager. Munich: Karl Alber, 1946. 3rd edition. Published in English as The Theory and Practice of Hell, the German Concentration Camps and the System behind Them. New York: Farrar, Straus, [1950]. 307p. The author, a survivor of Buchenwald, presents a dispassionate account of all aspects of concentration camp life. Appendices contain a chart of prisoner markings and a plan of Buchenwald and of "Detail 99," a murder plant located in the Buchenwald stable. 7-page index.

1610 KOSSO EDWARD. Handbuch zum Entschädigungsverfahren. Munich: Oldenbourg, 1958. 228p. Deals with the number of concentration camp prisoners, Jewish identification marks and symbols, and forced labor in the concentration camps. Contains a lists of ghettos, a bibliography, and maps.

1611 KÜHNRICH, HEINZ. Wahrheiten über den deutschen Imperialismus. Der KZ-Staat. Rolle und Entwicklung der faschistischen Konzentrationslager, 1933 bis 1945. Berlin(GDR): Dietz, 1960.

1612 LANGBEIN, HERMANN. ... nicht wie die Schafe zur Schlachtbank. Widerstand in den nationalsozialistischen Konzentrationslagern 1938-1945. Frankfurt am Main: Fischer, 1981. 496p.

1613 LANGHOFF, WOLFGANG. Die Moorsoldaten. 13 Monate Konzentrationslager. Unpolitischer Tatsachenbericht. Zurich: Schweizer Spiegel, 1935. 327p. Published in English as Rubber Truncheon; being an Account of Thirteen Months Spent in a Concentration Camp. New York: E.P. Dutton, 1935. 279p.

1614 LINGENS-REINER, ELLA. Prisoners of War. London: Victor Gollancz, 1948. Published in German as Eine Frau im Konzentrationslager. Vienna: Europa, 1966. 44p.

1615 MATUSSEK, PAUL. Internment in Concentration Camps and Its Consequences. Berlin: Springer, 1975.

1616 Oni ne stali koleni. Minsk: Belarus', 1966. 347p. Collection of memoirs of prisoners held in German concentration camps in Lithuania.

1617 PAPPALETTERA, VINCENZO, and LUIGI PAPPALETTERA. "Nuovi documenti per un'indagine sulle SS e i kapos nei lager nazisti [New Documents regarding the SS and Overseers in Nazi Camps]," Movimento di Liberazione in Italia 1968 20(93): 82-92. The lax policy of the Allies and the reluctance of West Germany to pass retroactive laws allowed most SS members and concentration camp overseers guilty of torture and murder to live peacefully in Germany after the war. While a number of SS members and overseers were executed immediately following the liberation, some 120,000 German and Austrian Nazis are still free. Based on first-hand accounts, trial records, and secondary sources; 7 notes.

1618 PINGEL, FALK. Häftlinge unter SS-Herrschaft. Widerstand, Selbstbehauptung und Vernichtung im Konzentrationslager. Hamburg: Hoffmann & Campe, 1978. 336p. Bielefeld: 1976.

1619 POLAND. MINISTRY OF THE INTERIOR. Poles in German Concentration Camps. London: [no publisher given], [no date given]. 45p.

1620 "Portraits of a Death Camp," Life 1979 20(April): 8-10.

1621 ROUSSET, DAVID. L'Univers concentrationnaire. Paris: Éditions du Pavois, 1946. 187p. Published in English as The Other Kingdom. New York: Reynal & Hitchcock, 1947, and A World Apart. London: Secker & Warburg, 1951.

1622 SCHÄTZLE, JULIUS. Wir klagen an! Ein Bericht über den Kampf, das Leiden und das Sterben in deutschen Konzentrationslagern. Stuttgart: Kulturaufbau, 1946.

1623 SCHMID, RICHARD. Einwände. Kritik an Gesetzen und Gerichten. Stuttgart: Henry Goverts, 1965. 270p. Theoretical study, with some observations on German concentration camps in chapter titled "Justiz im Dritten Reich."

1624 SIMON, SAM. Handbook of the Mail in the Concentration Camps, 1933-1945, and Related Material: A Postal History. [no city given]: privately printed, 1973.

1625 STRIGLER, MORDCHAI. In die fabriken fun toit [In the factories of death]. Buenos Aires: Zentral-farband fun pojlishe Jidn in Argentine, 1948. 429p. In Yiddish.

1626 Studien zur Geschichte der Konzentrationslager. Schriftenreihe der Vierteljahrshefte für Zeitgeschichte. Stuttgart: Deutsche Verlags-Anstalt, 1970. 202p.

1627 TAS, J. "Psychical Disorders among Inmates of Concentration Camps and Repatriates," Psychiatric Quarterly 1951 25(4): 679-690.

1628 Témoignages Strasbourgeois. De l'université aux camps de concentration. Paris: 1947. Collection of narratives of deported professors and readers of Strasbourg University, including the Auschwitz experiences of the Jewish professors Mark Klein, Robert Levy, Jules Hofstein, and Robert Waitz.

1629 TIDY, HENRY LETHEBY. Inter-Allied Conference on War Medicine, 1942-1945. London: Staples, 1947. 531p. Convened by the Royal Society of Medicine. Section XII deals with German concentration camps and liberated and displaced people as well as medical experiments.

1630 TRISKA, JAN F. "Work Redeems: Concentration Camp Labor and Nazi German Economy," Journal of Central European Affairs 1959 19: 3-22.

1631 UNION FÜR RECHT UND FREIHEIT, PRAG. Deutsche Frauenschicksale. London: Malik, 1937. 254p. Women in German prison and concentration camps, including Moringen and Hohnstein.

1632 UNIVERSITÉ DE STRASBOURG. De l'Université aux camps de concentration. Témoignages strasbourgeois. Paris: Éditions "Les Belles Lettres," 1947. 549p.

1633 WILDE, H. Sozialpsychologische Erfahrungen aus dem Lagerleben. Zurich: 1946.

1634 WORMSER-MIGOT, OLGA. Le Système concentrationnaire nazi, 1933-1945. Paris: Presses Universitaires de France, 1968. 660p. An essay on the history of German concentration camps.

B. STUDIES OF TWO OR MORE CAMPS

1635 ALTMANN, ERICH. Im Angesicht des Todes. 3 Jahre in deutschen KZ-rn Auschwitz, Buchenwald, Oranienburg. Luxemburg: Luxemburgensia, 1947.

1636 BERNADAC, CHRISTIAN. Les Médecins de l'impossible. Paris: Éditions France-Empire, 1968. 444p. On concentration camps Natzweiler, Oranienburg, Mauthausen, Ebensee, Melk, Gusen, Dachau, Schörzingen, Allach, Ravensbrück, Salaspils, Neuengamme, Buchenwald, Groß-Rosen, Nordhausen, Auschwitz, Bergen-Belsen.

184 Concentration Camps

1637 BORNSTEIN, B. *Die lange Nacht. Ein Bericht aus sieben Lagern.* Frankfurt am Main: Europäische Verlagsanstalt, 1967. 243p. Deals with Grunheide, Markstadt, Groß-Rosen, Flossenburg, Leonberg, and Mühldorf.

1638 BURKHARD, HUGO. *Tanz mal Jude! Von Dachau bis Shanghai, Meine Erlebnisse in den Konzentrationslagern Dachau, Buchenwald, Getto Shanghai, 1933-1948.* Nuremberg: Richard Reichenbach, 1966.

1639 CARROUGES, MICHEL. *Le Père Jacques.* Paris: Éditions du Seuil, 1958. 321p. On Mauthausen, Neue Breme, and Gusen.

1640 DAUM, F. *Nettengamme - Sachsenhausen. F. 84.296.* Lille: 1968.

1641 DELARBRE, LÉON. *Dora, Auschwitz, Buchenwald, Bergen-Belsen, Croquis clandestin.* Paris: M. de Romilly, 1945. [80 unnumbered pages]. Book of pencil drawings.

1642 DWORZECKI, MARC. [Jewish camps in Estonia, 1942-1944]. Jerusalem: Yad Vashem, 1970. 402p. Hebrew text, summary in English.

1643 FARAMUS, ANTHONY CHARLES. *The Faramus Story. Being the Experience of A.C. Faramus.* London: Wingate, 1954. 178p. The story of a political prisoner in Buchenwald and Mauthausen.

1644 FONTENEAU, HOMÈRE. *Le Long Chemin: Buchenwald, Maidanek, Auschwitz, Mauthausen.* Baignes: Impremerie Poly-Imprim, 1979. 128p.

1645 GOSTNER, ERWIN. *1000 Tage im KZ.* Innsbruck: Wagner'sche Universitäts-Buchdruckerei, 1945.

1646 HEGER, HEINZ. *Die Männer mit dem rosa Winkel. Der Bericht eines Homosexuellen über seine KZ-Haft von 1939-1945.* Hamburg: Merlin, 169p. Deals with Sachsenhausen and Flossenburg.

1647 HILLER, KURT. *Leben gegen die Zeit.* Volume 1, *Logos.* Reinbek bei Hamburg: Rowohlt, 1969. 421p. "Kazett," pp. 226-294, deals with Brandenburg and Oranienburg.

1648 KAUFMANN, MAX. *Churb'n Lettland's. Die Vernichtung der Juden Lettlands.* Munich: Selbstverlag, 1947. Deals with the Riga Ghetto and Kaiserswald and Stutthof camps.

1649 *Konzentrationslager. Ein Appell an das Gewissen der Welt. Ein Buch der Greuel. Die Opfer klagen an.* Carlsbad: "Graphia," 1936. 254p. Deals with concentration camps at Dachau, Brandenburg, Papenburg, Königstein, Lichtenburg, Colditz, Sachsenburg, Moringen, Hohnstein, Reichenbach, and Sonnenburg.

1650 KRAUS, OTA B., and ERICH KULKA. [Night and fog]. Prague: Nase Vojsko-SPB, 1958. 431p. Sequel to [Factory of death]. Contains maps showing camps. See Entry 1705.

1651 LANGBEIN, HERMANN. *Die Stärkeren. Ein Bericht aus Auschwitz und anderen Konzentrationslagern.* Cologne: Bund, 1982. 292p.

1652 LANZMANN, CLAUDE. *Shoah: An Oral History of the Holocaust.* New York: Pantheon, 1985. 200p. The text of the film "Shoah." Not a history, as such, but deals with a number of concentration camps.

1653 LIGGERI, PAOLO. Triangolo Rosso. Dalle carceri di S. Vittore ai campi di concentramento e di eliminazione di Fossoli, Bolzano, Mauthausen, Gusen, Dachau. Marzo 1944 - Maggio 1945. Milan: Instituto "La Casa," 1963. Chapter 7 deals with Dachau from December 1944 to April 1945.

1654 LITTEN, IRMGARD. A Mother Fights Hitler. London: George Allen and Unwin, 1940. Heinz Litten was a young lawyer who was arrested for defending anti-Nazi defendants in the Berlin courts. His mother tells of her determined but vain efforts to obtain his release. Discusses encounters with Rudolf Diels, head of the Gestapo. Part 3 deals with Buchenwald and Dachau.

1655 MARSHALL, BRUCE. The White Rabbit. From the Story told by Wing-Comander F.F.E. Yeo-Thomas. London: Evans, 1952. 262p. The Gestapo in action against a British agent in France. Includes sections on Buchenwald, Gleina, and Rehmsdorf.

1656 MINNEY, RUBEIGH JAMES. I shall fear no Evil. The Story of Dr. Alina Brewda. London: Kimber, 1966. 223p. Deals with the Warsaw ghetto, Majdanek, Auschwitz, and Ravensbrück.

1657 MORCINEK, GUSTAV. Das Mädchen von den Champs-Élysées - Erzählungen aus Dachau und Auschwitz. Berlin: Union, 1965.

1658 NANSEN, ODD. Von Tag zu Tag. Hamburg: Hans Dulk, 1949. English edition Day after Day. London: Putnam, 1949. American edition From Day to Day. New York: Putnam, 1949. The original is in Norwegian. Diary of Fridtjof Nansen's son in Grini, Veidal, Sachsenhausen, and Neuengamme.

1659 NEURATH, PAUL MARTIN. "Social Life in the German Concentration Camps of Dachau and Buchenwald," Ph.D. dissertation, Columbia University, 1951. Abstracted in Dissertation Abstracts International 1952 12(1): 111.

1660 PIASENTE, PARIDE (ed.). Italian Servicemen Interned in Nazi Camps. Notes for the Study of a Less Known Aspect of the Second World War. Rome: Associazione Nazionale ex-Internati, 1972. 38p.

1661 RÜCKERL, ADALBERT (ed.). Nationalsozialistische Vernichtungslager im Spiegel deutscher Strafprozesse. Belzec, Sobibor, Treblinka, Chelmno. Munich: Deutscher Taschenbuch, 1977. 358p.

1662 SALVESEN, SYLVIA. Forgive - But Not Forget. London: Hutchinson, 1958. 234p. Original in Norwegian. The story of a member of the Norwegian resistance in Grini and Ravensbrück.

1663 SCHÄTZLE, JULIUS. Stationen zur Hölle. Konzentrationslager in Baden und Württemberg 1933-1945. Frankfurt am Main: Röderberg, 1980. 81p.

1664 Simone et ses compagnons présentés par leurs camarades de prisons et de camps. Paris: Éditions de Minuit, 1947. 193p. Deals with French martyrs of the resistance in Fresnes, Ravensbrück, and Theresienstadt.

1665 SMITH, SYDNEY. Wings Day, the Man Who Led the RAF's Epic Battle in German Captivity. London: Collins, 1968. 252p. Deals with Sachsenhausen, Dachau, and Flossenburg.

1666 UNITED STATES. CONGRESS. 79TH CONGRESS JOINT COMMITTEE ON CONDITIONS IN CONCENTRATION CAMPS IN GERMANY. "Atrocities and other Conditions in Concentration Camps in Germany." Report of the Committee requested by General Dwight D. Eisenhower through Chief of Staff General George C. Marshall. 79th Congress, 1st Session, Senate Document No. 47. Washington: GPO, 1945. 16p.

1667 VERMEHREN, ISA. Reise durch den letzten Akt. Ein Bericht. 10.2.44 bis 29.6.45. Hamburg: Wegner, 1948. 233p. Deals with a "Sippenhäftling" in Ravensbrück, Buchenwald, and Dachau.

1668 WALLNER, PETER. By Order of the Gestapo. A Record of Life in Dachau and Buchenwald Concentration Camps. London: Murray, 1941. 271p.

1669 WEINSTOCK, ROLF. "Das wahre Gesicht Hitlerdeutschlands." Häftling Nr. 59.000 erzählt von dem Schicksal der 10.000 Juden aus Baden, aus der Pfalz und aus dem Saargebiet in den Höllen von Dachau, Gurs-Drancy, Auschwitz, Jawischowitz, Buchenwald. Singen (Hohentwiel): Volksverlag, 1948. 185p.

1670 WEISS, RESKA. Journey through Hell. A Woman's Account of Her Experiences at the Hands of the Nazis. London: Vallentine, Mitchell, 1961. 255p. Deals with life in Auschwitz and Neumark concentration camps and in the ghettoes of Riga, Ponovez, and Shavli.

1671 WELLERS, GEORGE. L'Étoile jaune à l'heure de Vichy. De Drancy à Auschwitz. Paris: Fayard, 1973. 452p. Also includes Compiègne.

1672 WIESEL. ELIE. La Nuit. Paris: Éditions de Minuit, 1958. 179p. Published in English as Night. London: MacGibbon & Kee, 1960; New York: Avon, 1969. 127p. A memoir of Hungarian Elie Wiesel, a boy sent to Auschwitz and then to Buchenwald, where his parents and younger sister were killed. This experience destroyed his faith. Concludes with his deliverance from the death camp when the war ended.

C. AUSCHWITZ

1673 ADELSBERGER, LUCIE. Auschwitz. Ein Tatsachenbericht. Berlin: Lettner, 1956.

1674 ADELSBERGER, LUCIE. "Medical Observations in Auschwitz Concentration Camp," Lancet 1946 [Part 1] 250(March 2): 317-319.

1675 ADELSBERGER, LUCIE. "Psychologische Beobachtungen im Konzentrationslager Auschwitz," Schweizerische Zeitschrift für Psychologie und ihre Anwendungen 1947 6(2): 124-131. The author was a prisoner at Auschwitz, Ravensbrück, and Neustadt.

1676 ADLER, H.G., HERMANN LANGBEIN, and ELLA LINGENS-REINER (eds.). Auschwitz, Zeugnisse und Berichte. Frankfurt am Main: Europäische Verlags-Anstalt, 1962. 423p.; 1979 edition, 316p.

1677 AMÉRY, JEAN. Jenseits von Schuld und Sühne. Bewältigungsversuche eines Überwältigen. Munich: Szczesny, 1966. 159p. Published in English as At the Mind's Limits: Contemplations by a Survivor on Auschwitz and its Realities. Bloomington: Indiana University Press, 1980. 111p.

Concentration Camps   187

1678 BAUM, BRUNO. Widerstand in Auschwitz. Berlin/Potsdam: VVN-Verlag, 1949. 55p.

1679 BEZWINSKA, JADWIGA, and CZECH DANUTA (eds.). Amidst a Nightmare of Crime: Notes of Prisoners of Sonderkommando Found at Auschwitz. Auschwitz: Panstwowe Museum, 1973.

1680 BEZWINSKA, JADWIGA, and DANUTA CZECH (eds.). KL Auschwitz Seen by the SS: Höß, Broad, Kremer. 2nd edition. Auschwitz: Pantswowe Museum, 1978. 331p. Views of Auschwitz by Rudolf Höß, Perry Broad, and Johann Paul Kremer.

1681 BIER, JEAN-PAUL. Auschwitz et les nouvelles littératures allemandes. Brussels: l'Université de Bruxelles (Centre national des Hautes Études Juives), 1979. 232p.

1682 BOGUSZ, JÓZEF. Auschwitz, an Anthology on Inhuman Medicine. Warsaw: 1970-1974. Several volumes selected from the medical review Przeglad Lekarski.

1683 BROAD, PERRY. KZ Auschwitz - Reminiscences of an SS-Man. Auschwitz: Panstwowe Museum, 1965.

1684 BROSZAT, MARTIN. Rudolf Höß, Kommandant in Auschwitz. Munich: 1963.

1685 CASTLE, JOHN. The Password is Courage. London: Souvenir Press, 1954. 224p.

1686 CZECH, DANUTA. "Kalendarium der Ereignisse im Konzentrationslager Auschwitz - Birkenau," Hefte von Auschwitz 1959 2: 90-118; 1962 6: 43-87; 1964 8: 47-133. The series consists of a set of 10 small volumes published by the Staatliches Museum, Auschwitz, between 1959 and 1967.

1687 DEMANT, EBBO (ed.). Auschwitz "direkt von der Rampe weg:" Kaduk, Erber, Klehr, 3 Täter geben zu Protokoll. Reinbek bei Hamburg: Rowohlt, 1979. 142p.

1688 FÉNELON, FANIA, and MARCELLE ROUTIER. Sursis pour l'orchestre. Paris: Stock, 1976. Published in German as Das Mädchenorchester in Auschwitz. Frankfurt am Main: Röderberg, 1976, and in English as The Musicians of Auschwitz. London: Michael Joseph, 1977. 262p.

1689 FLEISCHNER, EVA (ed.). Auschwitz: Beginning of a New Era? New York: Ktav, 1977.

1690 FRANCE. SERVICE D'INFORMATION DES CRIMES DE GUERRE. Camps de concentration. Auschwitz et Birkenau. Paris: Édition Office, français d'édition, 1945. 53p.

1691 FRIEDMAN, PHILIP. Auschwitz. Buenos Aires: Sociedad Hebraica Argentina, 1952. 170p.

1692 FRIEDMAN, PHILIP. This was Oswiecim. London: United Jewish Appeal, 1946. 84p. Edited by the former chief of the Central Jewish Historical Commission of Poland. A history of Auschwitz which contains several important testimonies.

1693 GARLINSKI, JOZEF. Fighting Auschwitz: The Resistance Movement in the Concentration Camp. London: Friedmann, 1975. 327p. Published first in 1974 in Polish.

1694 GILBERT, MARTIN. *Auschwitz and the Allies*. New York: Holt, Rinehart and Winston, 1981. 368p. Deals with the "final solution," the operation of Auschwitz, and the eventual liberation of the camp. Contains biographical notes, index, 19 maps, and 34 photographs.

1695 HAFFNER, D. *Aspects pathologiques du camp de concentration d'Auschwitz-Birkenau*. Tours: 1946.

1696 HART, KITTY. *I am Alive*. London: Abelard-Schuman, 1961. A memoir of Auschwitz.

1697 HART, KITTY. *Return to Auschwitz: The Remarkable Story of a Girl who Survived the Holocaust*. New York: Atheneum, 1982. 178p. The story of a young Polish girl who survived the concentration camps. After spending her early years in the Lublin ghetto, she worked as a laborer inside Germany until identified as a Jew and subsequently sentenced to death. This book tells the story of day-to-day survival in Auschwitz, the degradation of the prisoners, the slave labor to which they were subjected, the savage dogs and SS women, starvation, and regular selections for the gas chambers. Following 18 months in Auschwitz and a forced march across Germany, she was finally rescued by American forces. She and her mother later made their home in England. Undocumented; index, 1 map, 15 photographs.

1698 HELLMAN, PETER. *The Auschwitz Album: A Book Based upon an Album Discovered by a Concentration Camp Survivor, Lili Meier*. New York: Random House, 1981. 167p. In 25 pages of text and 166 pages of photographs, this book tells the story of extermination camp Auschwitz II, or Birkenau. Much on how the story was put together and how the photographs were collected.

1699 HILBERG, RAUL. *Sonderzüge nach Auschwitz*. Mainz: Dumhahn, 1981. 276p.

1700 HÖSS, RUDOLF. *Kommandant in Auschwitz. Autobiographische Aufzeichnungen von Rudolf Höß*. Stuttgart: Deutsche Verlags-Anstalt, 1958, 2nd edition, 1961. Originally published as *Meine Psyche. Werden, Leben und Erleben*. Published in English as *Commandant of Auschwitz, Autobiography*. Cleveland: World, 1959, 1960, and in French as *Le Commandant d'Auschwitz parle*. Paris: Juillard, 1959, Published in 1972 in Polish. Höß wrote his autobiography in 1947. He traces his life from childhood in the country near Baden-Baden, his military career, beginning as a volunteer in the Red Cross during World War I, followed by a tour of duty in the Middle East with the Badische Dragoner Regiment 21. He served 6 years in the Brandenburg penitentiary for war crimes. Examines his development through the 1930s as a member of the SS guard detachment at the Dachau and Sachsenhausen concentration camps. Höß describes his reaction to prewar punitive measures taken against prisoners and assesses the condition of the various camps at that time. The conclusion of his career as commander came at the height of the war. Includes two essays written by Höß, one on the "final solution" and the other on Himmler's attitude toward concentration camps. Based on personal experiences and primary sources; 210 notes, 2-page name index.

1701 INTERNATIONAL AUSCHWITZ COMMITTEE. *Anthology*. Warsaw: 1970-1971. 3 titles in 7 volumes. *Inhuman Medicine*, 2 volumes, 274p., 261p. *In Hell They Preserved Human Dignity*, 3 volumes,

212p., 227p., 222p. It Did Not End in "Forty-five," 2 volumes, 211p., 262p.

1702 KA-TZETNIK 135633 [pseudonym of KAROL CETYŃSKI]. Piepel. London: Blond, 1961. 284p. Deals with a young Jewish boy in Auschwitz. Original in Hebrew.

1703 KAUL, FRIEDRICH KARL. Ärzte in Auschwitz. Mit Unterstützung von Winfried Matthäus im Rahmen der Arbeit des Instituts für zeitgenössische Rechtsgeschichte bei der Juristischen Fakultät der Humboldt-Universität zu Berlin. Berlin (GDR): VEB Verlag Volk und Gesundheit, 1968. 337p.

1704 KOSSAK, ZOFIA. [From the abyss]. Poznan: Naglowski, 1947, 259p. Auschwitz.

1705 KRAUS, OTA B., and ERICH KULKA. [Factory of death]. Prague: Orbis, 1956. 217p. Published in German as Die Todesfabrik. Berlin (GDR): Kongreß, 1958. 146p. Published in English as The Death Factory: Documents on Auschwitz. Oxford: Pergamon, 1966. 284p. Also published in Hebrew. Jerusalem: 1960. Published in Russian as Fabrika smorti. Moscow: Gospolitizdat, 1960. 295p. The fully documented story of Auschwitz. Original in Czech. See Entry 1650.

1706 KULKA, ERICH. "Auschwitz Condoned: The Abortive Struggle against the Final Solution," Wiener Library Bulletin 1968 22(1): 2-5.

1707 LANGBEIN, HERMANN (comp.). Der Auschwitz-Prozeß. Eine Dokumentation. 2 volumes. Frankfurt am Main: Europäische Verlagsanstalt, 1965. 1027p.

1708 LANGBEIN, HERMANN. Hommes et femmes à Auschwitz. Paris: Fayard, 1975.

1709 LANGBEIN, HERMANN. Menschen in Auschwitz. Vienna: Europa, 1972. Has a useful bibliography.

1710 LANGBEIN, HERMANN. . . . wir haben es getan. Selbstporträts in Tagebüchern und Briefen, 1939-1945. Vienna: Europa, 1964. 136p. Letters and diary entries of the leader of the international resistance organization at Auschwitz concentration camp. Includes statistical data on production rates of workers at Auschwitz, data on transports into Auschwitz, and facsimiles of pages from the author's diary. 1-page bibliography.

1711 LEITNER, ISABELLA. Fragments of Isabella: A Memoir of Auschwitz. New York: Crowell, 1978.

1712 LENGYEL, OLGA. Five Chimneys: The Story of Auschwitz. Chicago: Ziff-Davies, 1947. 213p. London: Panther, 1959. A memoir.

1713 LEVI, PRIMO. Se questo è un uomo. Turin: De Silva, 1947. 194p. Published in English as If this is a Man. New York: Onan Press, 1959. 205p. Paper edition with title Survival in Auschwitz. New York: Collier, 1961. Published in French as J'étais un homme. Paris: Buchet-Chastel, 1961. Published in German as Ist das ein Mensch? Erinnerungen an Auschwitz. Frankfurt am Main: Fischer, 1979. A report about an Italian Jewish chemist deported from North Italy to Auschwitz III (Monowitz) in February 1944. One of the best eyewitness accounts of life in a concentration camp.

1714 LEWINSKA, PELAGIA. Vingt Mois à Auschwitz. [no city given]: Nagel, 1945. Published in English as Twenty Months at Auschwitz. New York: Lyle Stuart, 1968. 155p. Personal narrative of an inmate at Auschwitz. Describes daily prison life. Undocumented.

1715 LICHTHEIM, GEORGE. "German Diary," Commentary 1964 38(3): 42-49. Discusses the Auschwitz trial and "The Deputy."

1716 MAYBAUM, IGNAZ. The Face of God after Auschwitz. Greenwood, South Carolina: Attic Press, 1965.

1717 MENASCHE, ALBERT. Birkenau, Auschwitz II. New York: 1947.

1718 MÍKULSKI, JAN (ed.). From the History of KL Auschwitz. Volume 2. Auschwitz: Panstwowe Museum, 1976. Deals with pharmacological experiments at Auschwitz.

1719 MÜLLER, FILIP. Sonderbehandlung. Drei Jahre in den Krematorien und Gaskammern von Auschwitz. Munich: Steinhausen, 1979. 287p. Published in English as Auschwitz Inferno. The Testimony of a Sonderkommando. London: Routledge & Kegan Paul, 1979. 180p. American edition published as Three Years in the Gas Chambers. New York: Stein and Day, 1979.

1720 NAPORA, PAUL EDWARD. Auschwitz. San Antonio: Naylor, 1967.

NETHERLANDS RED CROSS. Auschwitz. 6 volumes. The Hague: 1947-1953.

1721 NETHERLANDS RED CROSS. Auschwitz. 6 volumes. The Hague: 1947-1953. (1) Het dodenboek van Auschwitz. 19470. 20p.

1722 NETHERLANDS RED CROSS. Auschwitz. 6 volumes. The Hague: 1947-1953. (2) De deportatietransporten van Juli 1942, tot en met 24 Augustus, 1942. 1948. 52p.

1723 NETHERLANDS RED CROSS. Auschwitz. 6 volumes. The Hague: 1947-1953. (3) De deportatietransporten in de zg. Cosel-periode. 1952. 97p.

1724 NETHERLANDS RED CROSS. Auschwitz. 6 volumes. The Hague: 1947-1953. (4) De deportatietransporten in 1943. 1953. 70p.

1725 NETHERLANDS RED CROSS. Auschwitz. 6 volumes. The Hague: 1947-1953. (5) De deportatietransporten in 1944. 1953. 38p. Mimeograph.

1726 NETHERLANDS RED CROSS. Auschwitz. 6 volumes. The Hague: 1947-1953. (6) De afvoertransporten uit Auschwitz et omgeving naar het Noorden en het Westen, en de grote evacuatietransporten. 1952. 125p. Mimeograph.

1727 NEWMAN, JUDITH STERNBERG. In the Hell of Auschwitz: The Wartime Memoirs of Judith Sternberg Newman. New York: Exposition Press, 1963. The memoir of the experiences of a nurse in Auschwitz. Much on the sufferings of Jewish girls and women in the camp.

1728 NOVAC, ANA. J'avais quatorze ans à Auschwitz. Paris: Presses de la Renaissance, 1982. 237p. The original was in Hungarian. Autobiography of a young Hungarian girl which focuses on the horrors of Auschwitz. Undocumented; no bibliography, no index.

1729 NYISZLI, MIKLOS. Auschwitz. A Doctor's Eyewitness Account. New York: Frederick Fell, 1960. 222p. London: Panther, 1962. Some critics doubt the existence of Nyiszli. Largely an account of the 12th Sonderkommando, which revolted, while the other 13 did not. Undocumented; 17 photographs.

1730 NYISZLI, MIKLOS. "Le SS Obersturmfuehrer Docteur Mengele," Les Temps Modernes 1951 66(April): 1855-1886. Not a study of Mengele, but the unique story of five months' survival in one of the Auschwitz crematoria. The author was deported in May 1944, from Nagy-Varad (Oradea Mare), now Rumania. Some critics doubt the existence of Nyiszli.

1731 NYISZLI, MIKLOS. Médecin à Auschwitz. [Paris]: Fayard, 1958.

1732 PANSTWOWE MUSEUM. [From the history of KZ-Auschwitz]. 2 volumes. Auschwitz: 1967, 1976. 225, 299p. In Polish.

1733 PAWLECZYNSKA, ANNA. Values and Violence in Auschwitz: A Sociological Analysis. Berkeley: University of California Press, 1979.

1734 PERL, GISELA. I Was a Doctor in Auschwitz. New York: International University Press, 1948.

1735 PISAR, SAMUEL. Of Blood and Hope. London: Cassell, 1980. 316p. The author spent 3 years as a young boy in Auschwitz.

1736 POLIAKOV, LÉON. Auschwitz. Paris: René Julliard, 1964. Major topics covered include the "industry" of death, life at Auschwitz, Auschwitz and Germany, and Rudolf Höß, the commandant of the camp. Documented; 1 map, 7 photographs.

1737 ROEDER, M. Die Auschwitz Lüge. Möhrkirch: Kritik, 1973.

1738 ROZANSKI, ZENON. Mützen ab. Eine Reportage aus der Strafkompanie des KZ Auschwitz. Hannover: Verlag "das andere Deutschland," 1948. 96p. A brief treatment of events in Auschwitz, written by an inmate. One of the rare accounts that goes back as far as 1941.

1739 RUDNICKI, ADOLF (ed.). Lest We Forget. Warsaw: "Polonia" Foreign Languages Publishing House, 1955. 171p. An anthology that contains a number of short reports, essays, and articles dealing with Auschwitz. Glossary, no table of contents, list of papers included, no index.

1740 SCHLEUNES, KARL A. The Twisted Road to Auschwitz: Nazi Policy toward German Jews, 1933-1939. Urbana: University of Illinois Press, 1970.

1741 SEHN, JAN. Concentration Camp Oswiecim (Auschwitz-Birkenau). Warsaw: Wydawnictwo Prawnicze, 1957. 163p.

1742 SMOLEŃ, KAZIMIERZ (ed.). Selected Problems from the History of KL Auschwitz. 2 volumes. Auschwitz: Pantswowe Museum, 1967,

1976. 225p. An anthology of 9 entries written by 6 contributors. Heavily documented, illustrated.

1743 STÄGLICH, WILHELM. Der Auschwitz-Mythos. Legende oder Wirklichkeit. Eine Kritische Bestandsaufnahme. Tübingen: Grabert, 1979.

1744 SZMAGLEWSKA, SEWERYNA. Dymy nad Birkenau. Warsaw: "Czytelnik," 1967. 371p. Published in English as Smoke over Birkenau. New York: Holt, 1947.

1745 TENENBAUM, JOSEPH. "Auschwitz in Retrospect," Jewish Social Studies 1953 15(3): 203-236.

1746 The Camp of Disappearing Men: A Story of the Oswiecim Concentration Camp, based on Reports of the Polish Underground Labor Movement. New York: Polish Labor Group, 1944. 42p. Based on a pamphlet issued by the Polish underground labor movement.

1747 TRUCK, BETTY, and ROBERT PAUL TRUCK. Médecins de la honte. La Vérité sur les expériences médicales pratiquées à Auschwitz. Paris: Presses de la Cité, 1975. 188p.

1748 UNITED STATES. WAR REFUGEE BOARD. German Extermination Camps, Auschwitz and Birkenau. Washington: Office of the President, November 1944. Four stenciled narratives of Polish and Slovak internees who escaped. The most important document is that of an anonymous Slovak Jewish doctor who escaped to Hungary in April 1944. There is a French version in Camps de Concentration. Paris: Service d'information des Crimes de Guerre, 1945. The complete version exists only in stencil in Silberschein, Judenausrottung in Polen. Geneva: 1944, Part III.

1749 WELLERS, GEORGE. De Drancy à Auschwitz. Paris: CDJC, 1946. 58p.

1750 WILLIAMS, ROGER M. "Why Wasn't Auschwitz Bombed?" Commonweal 1978 55(23): 746-751.

1751 WIND, EDUARD DE. Endstation ... Auschwitz. Amsterdam: Republick der letteren, 1946. 195p.

1752 WYMAN, DAVID S. "Why was Auschwitz never Bombed?" Commentary 1978 65(5): 37-46.

1753 ZYWULSKA, KRISTINA. [I survived Auschwitz]. Warsaw: Polonia, 1956. Published in English as I Came Back. New York: Roy, 1951; London: Dobson, 1951. 246p. Experiences of a Polish "Aryan." In Polish.

D. BELZEC

1754 REDER, RUDOLF. Belzec. Cracow: Central Polish Historical Commission, 1946. 65p.

1755 TREGENZA, MICHAEL. "Belzec Death Camp," Wiener Library Bulletin 1977 39(41-42): 8-25.

E. BERGEN-BELSEN

1756 BISCHOFF, FRIEDRICH (ed.). Das Lager Bergen-Belsen: Dokumente und Bilder mit erläuternden Texten. Hannover: Verlag für Literatur und Zeitgeschehen, [1966]. 32p.

1757 BLOCH, SAM E. Holocaust and Rebirth: Bergen Belsen, 1945-1965. New York: Bergen-Belsen Press, 1965.

1758 COLLIS, ROBERT. Straight On: Journey to Belsen and the Road Home. London: Methuen, 1947.

1759 FASSINA, P.-G. "Bergen-Belsen," Revue d'histoire de la Deuxième Guerre Mondiale 1962 12(45): 1-43. 91 notes.

1760 GERMANY. LOWER SAXONY. MINISTRY OF THE INTERIOR. Das Lager Bergen-Belsen. Dokumente und Bilder. Hannover: Fackeltraeger, 1981.

1761 HARDMAN, LESLIE. The Survivors: The Story of the Belsen Remnants. London: Vallentine, Mitchell, 1958.

1762 HEARTFIELD, JOHN. Photomontages of the Nazi Period. New York: Universe, 1977. Much on Bergen-Belsen.

1763 HERZBERG, ABEL J. Kroniek der Judenvervolging. The Hague: Arnheim, Van Loghum, Slaterus, 1956. 254p. History of the fate of Dutch Jewry. Contains a valuable account of Bergen-Belsen.

1764 KAMPS, KARL. Johannes Maria Verweyen. Gottsucher, Mahner und Bekenner. Wiesbaden: Credo, 1955. 114p.

1765 KOLB, EBERHARD. Bergen-Belsen. Geschichte des „Aufenthaltslagers," 1943-1945. Hannover: Verlag für Literatur und Zeitgeschehen, 1962.

1766 LEVY-HASS, HANNA [Eike Geisel, ed.]. Vielleicht war das alles erst der Anfang. Tagebuch aus dem KZ Bergen-Belsen 1944-1945. Berlin: Rotbuch, 1979. 110p. Published in English as Inside Belsen. Sussex: Harvester, 1982, and Totowa, New Jersey: Barnes & Noble, 1982. 134p. Contains "A Belsen Diary, 1944-1945," an interview between Levy-Hass and Eike Geisel, estimated figures on the massacre of European Jews, and the geographical distribution of concentration camps in Germany.

1767 LUSTGARTEN, EDGAR. „Irma Grese," in The Business of Murder. London: Harrap, 1968.

1768 MOLLISON, P.L. "Observations on Cases of Starvation at Belsen," British Medical Journal 1946 Part 1(January 5): 4-8. An abstract of a report to DMS 21 Army Group.

1769 NAPORA, PAUL EDWARD. Death at Belsen. San Antonio: Naylor, 1967.

1770 SINGTON, DERRICK. Belsen Uncovered. London: Duckworth, 1946. 208p. Published in German as Die Türe öffnen sich. Authentischer Bericht über das englische Hilfswerk für Belsen mit amtlichen Photos und einem Rückblick von Rudolf Küstermeier. Hamburg: Kulturverlag, 1948.

F. BREENDONK

1771 CONSEIL D'ADMINISTRATION DU MÉMORIAL NATIONALE DU FORT DE BREENDONK. Un témoin. Le Fort de Breendonk. Brussels: 1961. 113p.

1772 MARBAIX, EDGAR. Breendonck-la-Mort. Brussels: De Myttenaere, 1944. 104p.

G. BUCHENWALD

1773 ALEXANDER, EDWARD. "Abba Kovner: Poet of Holocaust and Rebirth," *Midstream* 1977 23(8): 50-59. Literature on the Holocaust. Deals primarily with Buchenwald. 16 notes.

1774 ANTELME, ROBERT. *Die Gattung Mensch*. Berlin: Aufbau, 1949, 350p.

1775 APITZ, BRUNO. *Naked among Wolves*. Berlin: Seven Seas, 1960. Some on Buchenwald.

1776 *Bericht des Internationalen Lagerkomitees*. Weimar: Thüringer Volksverlag, 1949. 215pp. Other volumes were projected, but only this one was issued.

1777 *Buchenwald. Mahnung und Verpflichtung. Dokumente und Berichte*. Berlin (GDR): Kongreß, 1961.

1778 DALBY, LOUISE ELLIOTT. *Leon Blum*. New York: Yoseloff, 1963. This biography tells of a rather comfortable imprisonment at Buchenwald. Blum's diet was poor and he lacked privacy, but otherwise he suffered little.

1779 DEUTSCHE AKADEMIE DER KÜNSTE. *Das Buchenwald Denkmal*. Dresden: Verlag der Kunst, 1960. 94p. Pictorial work on the Buchenwald Memorial, which was unveiled on September 14, 1958. Fritz Cremer led the group of architects and sculptors which began work on the monument in 1952. Their purpose was to honor the 56,000 who were murdered at Buchenwald. Includes a biographical overview of the artists. Undocumented; 46p. of plates.

1780 DEUTSCHER, IRWIN. "Buchenwald, Mai Lai, and Charles Van Doren: Social Psychology as Explanation," *Sociological Quarterly* 1970 11(4): 533-540. 1-page bibliography.

1781 FOREMAN, PAUL B. "Buchenwald and Modern Prisoner-of-War Detention Policy," *Social Forces* 1959 37(4): 289-298. 29 notes.

1782 GREAT BRITAIN. PARLIAMENT. *Buchenwald Camp: The Report of a Parliamentary Delegation*. London: HMSO, 1945. (Comd. 6626).

1783 HEILIG, B. *Men Crucified*. London: Eyre and Spottiswoode, 1941. 402p. Published in German as *Menschen am Kreuz: Dachau-Buchenwald*. Berlin: Verlag Neues Leben, 1948.

1784 HEIMLER, EUGENE. *Concentration Camp*. New York: Pyramid, 1959. Memoir of Buchenwald.

1785 HEIMLER, EUGENE. *Night of the Mist*. London: Bodley Head, 1962. Memoir of Buchenwald.

1786 KAMIN, GERHARD (ed.). *Häftling Nr. 7188. Tagebuchnotizen und Briefe*. Munich: Desch, 1966. 128p. On Ernst Wiechert and KZ Buchenwald.

1787 KOLB, EBERHARD. *Konzentrationslager Buchenwald*. Weimar: Thüringer Volksverlag, 1949.

1788 KÜHN, GÜNTER, and WOLFGANG WEBER. Stärker als die Wölfe. Ein Bericht über die illegale militärische Organisation im ehemaligen Konzentrationslager Buchenwald und den bewaffneten Aufstand. Berlin(GDR): Militärverlag der DDR, 1977. 324p.

1789 Les enfants de Buchenwald. Geneva: Union O.S.S., 1946. 85p.

1790 MOULIS, MILOSLAV. [In the claws of Buchenwald]. Prague: Nase Vojsko-S. P.B., 1957. 122p. In Czech.

1791 POLLER, WALTER. Arztschreiber in Buchenwald. Bericht des Häftlings 996 aus Block 39. Hamburg: Phonix-Verlag Christen, 1947. 236p. 2nd edition, Offenbach am Main: Das Segel, [1960]. Published in English as Medical Block, Buchenwald. The Personal Testimony of Inmate 996. Block 36. New York: Lyle Stuart, 1961; and London: Corgi Books, 1965.

1792 STEINWENDER, LEONHARD. Christus im Konzentrationslager. Wege der Gnade und des Opfers. Salzburg: Müller, 1946. 134p. A Catholic priest in Buchenwald.

1793 THOMAS, JACK. No Banners. The Story of Alfred and Henry Newton. London: Allen, 1955. 346p. On Buchenwald.

1794 WEINSTOCK, EUGENE. Beyond the Last Path. New York: Boni and Goer, 1947. Memoir of Buchenwald.

1795 WILENSKY, M. (comp.). War Behind Barbed Wire. Reminiscences of Buchenwald ex-Prisoners of War. Moscow: Foreign Languages Publishing House, 1959. 155p. Original is in Russian.

H. CHELMNO

1796 BEDNARZ, L. Le Camp d'extermination de Chelmno sur le Ner. Traduit du Polonais. Éditions de l'Amitié Franco-Polonaise, 1955.

1797 BEDNARZ, WLADYSLAW. Oboz stracen w Chelmnie nad Nerem. Warsaw: Panstwowe Instytut Wyd., 1946. 74p. Published in German as Das Vernichtungslager zu Chelmno am Ner. Schwerin: Die Oberste Kommission für die Untersuchung der deutschen Verbrechen in Polen, 1949. 203p.

1798 POSPIESZALSKI, KAROL MARIAN. [German foresters on the extermination of Jews at Chelmno on the Ner], Przeglad Zachodni 1962 18(3): 85-104. Text in Polish and German.

I. COMPIÈGNY

1799 BERNARD, JEAN-JACQUES. Le Camp de la mort lente (Compiègne 1941-1942). Paris: A. Michel, 1944. 246p. Published in English as Camp of Slow Death. London: Gollancz, 1945. An account of the author's imprisonment.

1800 REES, JOSEPH. Titus Brandsma. A Modern Martyr. London: Sidgwick & Jackson, 1971. 192p. A Dutch theologian who was a victim of the Gestapo.

J. DACHAU

1801 ANTONI, E. KZ. Von Dachau bis Auschwitz. Faschistische Konzentrationslager 1933-1943. Frankfurt am Main: Röderberg, 1979. 144p.

1802 BEIMLER, HANS. Im Mörderlager Dachau - Vier Wochen in den Händen der braunen Banditen. Moscow/Leningrad: Verlagsgenossenschaft ausländischer Arbeiter in der UdSSR, 1933. Published in English as Four Weeks in the Hands of Hitler's Hell-Hounds - The Nazi Murder Camp of Dachau. London: Modern Books, 1933.

1803 BELLAK, GIORGINA, and GIOVANNI MELODIA (eds.). Donne e Bambini nei Lager Nazisti. Milan: Associazione Nazionale ex Deportati Politici nei Lager Nazisti, 1960.

1804 BERBEN, PAUL. Histoire du camp de concentration de Dachau, 1933-1945. Brussels: Comité International de Dachau, 1968. Published in English as Dachau, 1933-1945: The Official History. London: Norfolk Press, 1975. 300p. Published under the auspices of the Dachau Concentration Camp International Committee (C.I.D.), which represented tens of thousands of deportees who were exterminated as well as those who survived. Based on authentic documents and the evidence of survivors. Discusses the creation of Dachau, categories of prisoners, camp command and administration, medical experiments, and punishment and execution of prisoners. 34 appendices include 4 plans of the camp, 2 maps, and statistics on prisoners, including transfers between camps. Facsimile of the order transferring prisoner Heinrich Baumann to Dachau, principal distinguishing badges and abbreviations, a statement by the chief camp doctor at Dachau. Contains lists of members of the C.I.D. on April 30, 1945. 9-page list of works at the Dachau trial on November 2, 1945, 9-page list of works in the Museum Library at Dachau, 3p. of bibliographical information, 6-page index, 27 photographs.

1805 BETTELHEIM, BRUNO. "Returning to Dachau: The Living and the Dead," Commentary 1956 21(February): 144-151. Undocumented.

1806 BETTELHEIM, BRUNO. Surviving. New York: Knopf, 1979.

1807 CARLS, HANS. Dachau. Erinnerungen eines katholischen Geistlichen aus der Zeit seiner Gefangenschaft, 1941-1945. Cologne: Bachem, 1946. 218p.

1808 CHART, K.S. EDMUND. Spis Pomordowanych Polaków w Obozie Koncentracyjnym w Dachau. Dachau/Munich: Wyd. "Slowo Polskie," 1946.

1809 CHURCHILL, PETER. The Spirit in the Cage. London: Hodder and Stoughton, 1954. Memoir of Dachau.

1810 CRAWFORD, FRED ROBERTS. Dachau. Atlanta: Center for Research in Social Change, 1979.

1811 Dachau - Ein Tatsachenbericht in Bildern. Munich: Printed by Heinrich Wiegand, [no date given].

1812 Dachau. The Nazi Hell. From the Notes of a Former Prisoner at the Notorious Nazi Concentration Camp. London: Aldor, 1939. 216p. Abridged version Dachau. London: Wells Gardner, Darton, 1942. 158p. Original in German.

1813 DE CONINCK, L. "Les Conversations de Dachau," Nouvelle Revue Théologique 1945 67(5): 561-575.

1814 Die Toten von Dachau. Deutsche und Österreicher. Ein Gedenk- und Nachschlagewerk. Munich: Staatskommissariat für rassich, religiös und politisch Verfolgte in Bayern, 1947. 104p.

1815 DIMITMAN, ELI ZACHARY. Horror of Dachau. Reprinted in Report to America, from dispatch sent to the Chicago Sun, May 3, 1945.

1816 DISTEL, BARBARA, and RUTH JAKUSCH (eds.). Concentration Camp Dachau, 1933-1945. Munich: Lipp. Comité International de Dachau, 1978.

1817 ECKER, FRITZ. Die Hölle Dachau - Betrachtungen eines Gemarterten nach sieben Monaten Dachau, in Konzentrationslager - Ein Appell an das Gewissen der Welt. Karlsbad [now Karlovy Vary, Czechoslovakia]: Verlags-Anstalt Graphica, 1934.

1818 Elsässer und Lothringer in Dachau. Nr. 3 - Arbeitssklave. Metz: Éditions Le Lorrain [for the author], 1946.

1819 ELYASHIV, VERA. Deutschland, kein Wintermärchen - Eine Israeli sieht die Bundesrepublik. Chapter 5 is "Endstation Dachau." Vienna/Düsseldorf: Econ, 1964.

1820 FEUERBACH, WALTHER. Monate Dachau - Ein Tatsachenbericht. Lucerne: Rex, 1945.

1821 FOOT, MICHAEL R.D. SOE in France - An Account of the Work of the British Special Operations Executive in France (1940-1944). London: HMSO, 1966. Includes details of the fate of resistance agents in Dachau.

1822 GEDZIOROWSKI, TADEUSZ. Dachau. Warsaw: Ksiazka i Wiedza, 1961. Chapter 4, "Dachau."

1823 HAULOT, ARTHUR, and ALI KUCI. Dachau. Brussels: Éditions "Est-Ouest," 1945.

1824 HESS, P. SALES. Dachau - Eine Welt ohne Gott. Nuremberg: Sebaldus, 1948.

1825 HILLER, KURT. Köpfe und Tröpfe - Profile aus einem Vierteljahrhundert. Hamburg: Rowoldt, 1950. Chapter 7 deals with Dachau.

1826 HORNUNG, WALTER. Dachau - Eine Chronik. Zurich: Europa, 1936.

1827 JAHNKE, K.H. "Dachau: Erinnerung an Heinz Eschen," in Helmut Eschwege (ed.). Kennzeichen J. - Bilder, Dokumente, Berichte zur Geschichte der Verbrechen des Hitlerfaschismus an den deutschen Juden 1933-1945. Berlin(GDR): VEB, Deutscher Verlag der Wissenschaften, 1966. 66p.

1828 JOOS, JOSEPH. Leben auf Widerruf - Begegnungen und Beobachtungen im KZ Dachau 1941-1945. Olten: Otto Walther Agentur, 1946.

1829 KESSLER, LEO. The Iron Fist. London: 1977. A Jewish writer describes the torture trials of the Waffen-SS at Dachau in 1946. The torturers were also Jews.

1830 KUBY, ERICH (ed.). Das Ende des Schreckens. Dokumente des Untergangs Januar bis Mai 1945. Munich: Süddeutscher Verlag,

1957. The Dachau chapter deals with the last days of the concentration camp.

1831 KUNTER, ERICH. <u>Weltreise nach Dachau - Ein Tatsachenroman nach den Erlebnissen und Berichten des Weltreisenden und ehemaligen politischen Häftlings Max Wittmann</u>. Bad Wildbad: Edition Pan, 1947.

1832 KUPFER-KOBERWITZ, EDGAR. <u>Die Mächtigen und die Hilflosen. Als Häftling in Dachau. Geschrieben von 1942 bis 1945 im Konzentrationslager Dachau</u>. 2 volumes. Volume 1, <u>Wie es begann</u> [1941-1942], Bonn: Bundeszentrale fü Heimatdienst, 1956. 430p. Volume 2, <u>Wie es endete</u> [1943-1945]. Stuttgart: Friedrich Vorwerk, 1960. 263p. Based on secret diary notes.

1833 L'AMICALE DES ANCIENS DE DACHAU (ed.). <u>Annuaire des Anciens de Dachau</u>. Paris: Édité par l'Amicale des Anciens de Dachau, 1955.

1834 LENZ, JOHANN. <u>Christus in Dachau. Ein religiöses Volksbuch und ein kirchengeschichtliches Zeugnis</u>. Vienna: Published by the author, distributed by Libri Catholici, 1956. Published in English as <u>Christ in Dachau or Christ Victorious. Experiences in a Concentration Camp</u>. Mödling: Published by the author, printed by Missionsdruckerei St. Gabriel, 1960.

1835 MICHELET, EDMOND. <u>Die Freiheitsstraße - Dachau 1943-1945</u>. Stuttgart: Europa-Contact, Gesellschaft für Internationale Beziehungen, 1960.

1836 MORELLI, VALERIA. <u>I deportati italiani nei campi die sterminio 1943-1945</u>. Milan: Scuole Grafiche Pav. Artigianelli, 1965. Chapter 1 deals with Dachau.

1837 MOSTAR, HERRMANN. <u>Nehmen Sie Ihr Urteil an? Menschen vor dem Richter</u>. Frankfurt am Main: Ullstein, 1963.

1838 MUNCH, MAURUS. <u>Unter 2579 Priestern in Dachau. Zum Gedenken an den 25. Jahrestag der Befreiung in der Osterzeit 1945</u>. Trier: Zimmer, 1972. 189p.

1839 MUSIOL, TEODOR. <u>Dachau, 1933-1945</u>. Katowyce: Wyd. "Slask" [for] Instytut Slaski w Opolu, 1971. 469p. Summaries in English, Russian, French, and German.

1840 NEUHÄUSLER, JOHANN. <u>Wie war das im KZ Dachau? Ein Versuch der Wahrheit näher zu kommen</u>. Munich: Kuratorium für Sühnemal KZ Dachau, 1960. Published in English as <u>What Was It Like in the Concentration Camp at Dachau?</u> Munich: Dachau Museum, 1954.

1841 PASCOLI, PIETRO. <u>I deportati - pagine di vita vissuta</u>. Florence: La Nuova Italia Editrice, 1960. Chapter 8 deals with Dachau.

1842 RAND, E. <u>Témoignages sur Dachau</u>. Brussels: Michel-Ange, 1946.

1843 ROSENCHER, HENRI. "Medicine in Dachau," <u>British Medical Journal</u> 1946 Part 2(December 21): 953-955.

1844 ROST, NICO. <u>Goethe in Dachau - Literatur und Wirklichkeit</u>. [no city given]: Volk und Welt, 1945. 314p. Munich: Willi Weismann, [no date given]. Berlin: [no publisher given], 1948.

1845 ROST, NICO. Ich war wieder in Dachau. Frankfurt am Main: Röderberg, 1956.

1846 ROST, NICO. Konzentrationslager Dachau. Brussels: International Dachau Committee (Publisher). Munich: Spöcker, Deisenhofen (Printer), 1964.

1847 Rue de la liberté - Dachau 1943-1945. Paris: Éditions du Seuil, 1955.

1848 SANGUEDOLCE, JOSEPH. Résistance: de Saint Étienne à Dachau. Paris: Éditions Sociales, 1973.

1849 SCHMIDT, DIETMAR. Martin Niemöller. Hamburg: Ernst Rowohlt, 1959. One chapter on Dachau,

1850 SCHNABEL, REIMUND. Die Frommen in der Hölle - Geistliche in Dachau. Frankfurt am Main: Röderberg, 1966.

1851 SELZER, MICHAEL. Deliverance Day: The Last Hours of Dachau. New York: McGraw, 1978; London: Sphere Books, 1980. 251p.

1852 SIEGRIST, ETTOR. Dachau - Dimenticare sarebbe una colpa. Genoa: Stabilimenti Grafici Federico Reale, 1945.

1853 SMITH, MARCUS J. Dachau: The Harrowing of Hell. Albuquerque: University of New Mexico Press, 1972. 291p. The author was a medical officer sent into Dachau after its liberation. For 25 years he was unable to think of his experiences there, where he and others tried to reclaim the lives of 32,000 inmates. Largely the story of displaced people and of a team trained to feed, clothe, treat, and repatriate many of these people. 11p. of notes.

1854 STEINBOCK, JOHANN. Das Ende von Dachau. Salzburg: Österreichischer Kulturverlag, 1948.

1855 ZAK, JOEL, JOSEF LINDENBERGER, and JACOB SILBERSTEIN (eds.). Memorial Dates Yorzait of the Martyred Jews of Dachau. 2 volumes. New York: Jewish Labor Committee, 1947. Volume 1 deals with Jews born in Lithuania, Latvia, Estonia, and White Russia. Volume 2 deals with Jews born in Poland.

K. DORA (NORDHAUSEN)

1856 BARTEL, WALTER. "Rolle und Bedeutung des Mittelwerkes einschließlich des KL Dora - Mittelbau und die Funktion der SS bei der A 4 - Produktion." Berlin (GDR): 1968. "Gutachten" by a Professor Ordinarius of the Humboldt University, Berlin.

1857 CABALA, ADAM. Arsenal grobow. Cracow: Wyd. Literackie, 1968. 272p.

1858 MICHEL, JEAN, and LOUIS NUCÉRA. Dora. Dans l'enfer du camp de concentration ou les savants nazis préparient la conquête de l'espace. Paris: Lattès, 1975. 439p.

1859 PROSECUTION STAFF. A Booklet with a Brief History of the "Dora"-Nordhausen Labor Concentration Camps and Information on the Nordhausen War Crimes Case of the USA versus Arthur Kurt Andrae et al. Nuremberg: 1947.

1860 RASSINIER, PAUL. Le Mensonge d'Ulysse. 4th edition. Paris: La Librairie française, 1955. 330p. Published in German as Die Lüge des Odysseus. Wiesbaden: Priester, 1959; in Spanish as La mentira de Ulises. Barcelona: Acervo, 1962; in Italian as La menzogna di Ulisse. Milan: Le Rune, 1966. An attack on concentration camp literature by a former prisoner at Dora.

L. DRANCY

1861 DARVILLE, JACQUES, and WICHENE SIMON. Drancy la juive ou La deuxième inquisition. Cachan (Seine): Breger: [1945]. 127p.

M. FLOSSENBURG

1862 "Flossenberg (sic). The Story of One Concentration Camp," National Jewish Monthly 1945 (October): 46-49.

1863 MOLDAWA, MIECZYSLAW. [Concentration camp in Silesia]. Warsaw: Wyd. "Polonia," 1967. 182p. In Polish.

1864 WALLEITNER, HUGO. Zebra. Ein Tatsachenbericht aus dem Konzentrationslager Flossenburg. Bad Ischl: [private printing], [1948]. 191p.

N. GROSS-ROSEN

1865 HELLER, PAUL. "A Concentration Camp Diary," Midstream 1980 26(4): 29-36. A memoir of Groß-Rosen KZ, near Breslau.

1866 MOLDAWA, MIECZYSLAW. [Gross-Rosen. Concentration camp in Silesia]. Warsaw: Wyd. "Polonia," 1967. 182p. Contains illustrations, maps, tables, and diagrams. In Polish.

O. GURS

1867 CADIER, HENRI. Le Calvaire d'Israél et la solidarité chrétienne. Geneva: Éditions Labor et Fides, 1945. 144p. Concentration camp Gurs.

1868 ISOLANI, GERTRUD. Stadt ohne Männer. Roman. 2nd edition. Basel: Buchverlag, Baseler Zeitung, 1979. 336p. An account of concentration camp Gurs in which the author was interned.

1869 KREHBIEL-DARMSTADTER, MARIA [Walter Schmitthenner (ed.)]. Briefe aus Gurs und Limonesi, 1940-1943. Heidelberg: Lambert Schneider, 1970. 383p.

1870 SCHRAMM, HANNA. Menschen in Gurs. Erinnerungen an ein französisches Internierungslager 1940-1941. Worms: Heintz, 1977. 404p.

P. GUSEN

1871 BOUARD, MICHEL DE. "Le Kommando de Gusen," Revue d'Histoire de la Deuxième Guerre Mondiale 1962 12(45): 44-70. 27 notes.

1872 MARSÁLEK, HANS. Konzentrationslager Gusen. Vienna: Österreichische Lagergemeinschaft Mauthausen, 1968.

Q. HOHENSTEIN

1873 HACKEL, FRANZ. Von der Jugendburg Hohnstein zum Schutzhaft-Lager Hohnstein. Berlin/Potsdam: VVN, 1949. 51p.

R. ILAVA

1874 SANDOR, ELO. [Ilava]. Brno: Mir, 1947. 45p. Original is in Slovak.

S. LE VERNET

1875 FREI, BRUNO. Die Männer von Vernet. Ein Tatsachenbericht. Berlin(GDR): Deutscher Militärverlag, 1961. 324p.

1876 KOESTLER, ARTHUR. Scum of the Earth. London: Jonathan Cape, 1941. 255p.

T. MAJDANEK

1877 Communiqué de la commission extraordinaire polono-soviétique chargée d'établir les forfaits commis par les Allemands au camp de destruction de Maidanek a Lublin. Moscow: Éditions en Langues étrangères, 1944. 28p. Published in German as Die Hölle von Maidanek. Bericht der Außerordentlichen Polnisch-Sowjetrussischen Kommission zur Untersuchung der von den deutschen im vernichtungslager Maidanek in der Stadt Lublin begangenen Verbrechen. Zurich: Verlag der Partei der Arbeit, 1945. 46p.

1878 GRYN, EDWARD, and ZOFIA MURAWSKA. Majdanek Concentration Camp. Lublin: Wydawnictwo Lubelskie, 1966.

1879 LICHTENSTEIN, HEINER. Majdanek. Reportage eines Prozesses. Frankfurt am Main: Europäische Verlagsanstalt, 1979. 188p. Deals with the concentration camp at Majdanek (Lublin).

1880 MURAWSKA, Z. [Camp de concentration. Majdanek]. Lublin: 1966. Original is in Polish.

1881 SIMONOV, KONSTANTIN. Ich sah das Vernichtungslager. [no city given]: Verlag der sowjetischen Militärverwaltung in Deutschland, [1945]. 200p.

U. MAUTHAUSEN

1882 BARTOLAI, SANTE. Da Fossoli a Mauthausen. Memorie di un sacerdote nei campe di concentramento nazisti. Modena: Instituto storico della Resistenza, 1966. 108p.

1883 BAUM, BRUNO. Die letzten Tage von Mauthausen. Berlin: Deutscher Militärverlag, 1965. 156p. Description of conditions at Mauthausen, the uprising, and eventual liberation of prisoners. Biographical sketches of 30 survivors. Documentation includes the text of the plea of Franz Ziereis, commander of the camp, who was arrested by Americans on May 23, 1945, an essay by the brother of an inmate who escaped in February 1945, a list of prisoners, by nationality, and a tabulation of deaths. 1-page bibliography.

1884 BERNADAC, CHRISTIAN. Mauthausen. 2 volumes. Paris: Éditions France-Empire, 1974-1975. Volume 1, Les 186 marches (1974), 379p. Volume 2, Le Neuvième cercle (1975), 381p.

1885 BOUARD, MICHEL DE. "Mauthausen," Revue d'Histoire de la Deuxième Guerre Mondiale 1954 4(15-16): 39-80. Heavily annotated.

1886 CHOUMOFF, PIERRE SERGE. Les Chambres de gaz de Mauthausen. La Vérité historique établie . . . a la demande de l'Amicale de Mauthausen. Paris: Amicale des Déportés et Familles des Desparus du Camp de Concentration de Mauthausen, 1972. 95p.

1887 Concentration Camp Mauthausen, Sub-Commands. Arolsen: International Tracing Service, 1950.

1888 LE CHÊNE, EVELYN. Mauthausen, the History of a Death Camp. London: Methuen, 1971. 296p. Information obtained through interviews with former prisoners, from the archives of the French ministry of war, and documents from the Wiener Library. Examines the administration and camp organization, torture, methods of murder, and hygiene. Discusses medical practice, experimentation, euthanasia, corruption, forgery by prison officials, sports, and entertainment of inmates. Includes a 20-page chapter on statistics outlining the duration of stay in relation to execution, categories of prisoners according to social group, and mode of execution. Appendix 1 contains a translation of the Bullet Decree of 1944. Appendix 2 is a list of 818 known staff members of Mauthausen and its sub-camps. Contains a map of German concentration camps, a plan of Hartheim and Mauthausen, and graphs of monthly death statistics. Facsimile of an OSS, War Crimes section list of Mauthausen documents. 3-page bibliography, 4-page general index, 3-page index of names.

1889 MARSÁLEK, HANS. Die Geschichte des Konzentrationslager Mauthausen, Dokumentation. Vienna: Österreichische Lagergemeinschaft Mauthausen, 1974. 323p. Describes prison conditions, daily activities of inmates, quarters, nutrition, and clothing. Chapters on Nazi doctors and pseudoscientific experimentation. Includes mortality rates, "natural" and "unnatural" deaths, and statistics on illness within the camp. 20 photographs of the memorial at Mauthausen, 20 photographs of the camp, 32-page glossary of camp expressions, 2-page bibliography, 6-page index.

1890 MARSÁLEK, HANS. Mauthausen. Vienna: Max Ungar, 1958.

1891 MARSÁLEK, HANS. Mauthausen mahnt. Vienna: Mauthausen-Komitee des Bundesverbandes der österreichischen KZler, Häftlinge und politisch Verfolgten, Selbstverlag. 1950. 102p.

1892 Mauthausen. Paris: L'Amicale de Mauthausen, [no date given].

1893 ÖSTERREICHISCHE LAGERGEMEINSCHAFT MAUTHAUSEN (ed.). KL Mauthausen/Unterkunft Gusen. Vienna: 1968.

1894 RIET, VICTOR VAN. Mauthausen, 188 marches et la mort. Brussels: André de Rache, 1977.

1895 SACHAROW, VALENTIN. Aufstand in Mauthausen. Berlin (GDR): Volk und Welt, 1961. 241p.

1896 TILLARD, P. Mauthausen. Paris: Éditions Sociales, 1945.

1897 UNITED STATES. NATIONAL ARCHIVES AND RECORDS SERVICE. Mauthausen Death Books. Microfilm of records described in NARS Preliminary Inventory 21. T990. 2 rolls.

1898 WENGER, WILLO. *Fern und ewig leuchtet Frieden. Ein Erlebnis aus dem Zeitgeschehen nach Berichten sowie nach Aufzeichnungen eines zum Tode Verurteilten.* Zurich: Europa, 1947. 337p.

1899 WIESENTHAL, SIMON. *KZ Mauthausen. Bild und Wort.* Linz/Vienna: Ibis, 1946.

V. NEUENGAMME

1900 AMICALE DE NEUENGAMME. *Le Camp de concentration de Neuengamme et ces kommandos extérieurs.* Paris: Amicale de Neuengamme, 1967.

1901 FREUNDESKREIS. *Totenbuch Neuengamme.* Wiesbaden: Saaten-Verlag, [196-]. 573p. The text is in German, French, Flemish, Czech, Danish, Greek, Italian, Serbo-Croat, Dutch, Polish, Spanish, Russian, Hungarian, and English.

1902 GOGUEL, RUDI. *"Cap Arcona." Report über den Untergang der Häftlingsflotte in der Lübecker Bucht am 3. Mai 1945.* Frankfurt am Main: Röderberg, 1972. 156p. Bibliography.

1903 KERN, PAUL, et al. *Les Jours de notre mémoire, 1940-1945. Neuengamme. Quatre survivants témoignent.* Paris: Éditions La Pensée Universelle, 1975. 250p.

1904 LAGERGEMEINSCHAFT NEUENGAMME. *So ging es zu Ende ... Neuengamme Dokumente und Berichte.* Hamburg: 1960. 102p.

1905 MEIER, HEINRICH CHRISTIAN. *So war es. Das Leben im KZ Neuengamme.* Hamburg: Phönix-Verlag Christen, 1946. 126p.

1906 POEL, ALBERT VAN DER. *Ich sah hinter den Vorhang. Ein Holländer erlebt Neuengamme.* Hamburg: Robert Mölich, 1948. Published in Dutch in 1945.

W. NOVÁKY

1907 KAMENEC, IVAN. "[Jewish concentration and labor camps in Nováky]," *Horna Nitra* 1966 3: 51-67. In Czech.

X. PAPENBURG

1908 HINRICHS, KLAUS. *Staatliches Konzentrationslager VII. Eine Erziehungsanstalt im Dritten Reich.* London: Malik, 1936. 436p.

Y. RADOM

1909 AKS, SHAMMAI. [Grief is my song]. Los Angeles: [private printing], 1968. 104p. Includes an account of forced labor on armaments in Camp Radom. In Yiddish, with English preface. Some songs in English and Polish.

Z. RAVENSBRÜCK

1910 AMICALE DE RAVENSBRÜCK AND ASSOCIATION DES DÉPORTÉES DE LA RÉSISTANCE. *Les Françaises à Ravensbrück.* Paris: Gallimard, 1965. 347p.

1911 BERNADAC, CHRISTIAN. *Kommandos de Femmes-Ravensbrück.* Paris: Éditions France Empire, 1973.

1912 BERNADAC, CHRISTIAN. Le Camps des Femmes-Ravensbruck. Paris: Éditions France Empire, 1972.

1913 BORSUM, LISE. Kvindehelvedet Ravensbrück [Women's Hell - Ravensbrück]. Copenhagen: Christensen, 1947. 291p.

1914 CETYŃSKI, KAROL [Pseudonym, KA-TZETNIK 135 633]. [House of dolls]. Tel Aviv: [no publisher given], 1953. 315p. Added title page has Doll House, by Ka-Tzetnik 135 633. Published in the United States as House of Dolls. New York: Simon and Schuster, 1955. 245p. British publication, House of Dolls. London: Muller, 1956. 239p. A novel based on the diary of a girl forced into prostitution in a labor camp. In Hebrew.

1915 DE GAULLE, GENEVIÈVE. "La Condition des enfants au Camp de Ravensbrück." Revue d'histoire de la Deuxième Guerre Mondiale 1962 12(45): 71-82. 47 notes.

1916 DOBACZEWSKA, WANDA. Kobiety z Ravensbrück [Women of Ravensbrück]. Warsaw: Czytelnik: 1946. 169p.

1917 DUFOURNIER, DENISE. La Maison des mortes. Ravensbrück. Paris: Hachette, 1945. 220p. Ravensbrück, The Women's Camp of Death. London: George Allen & Unwin, 1948.

1918 HÁJKOVÁ, DAGMAR, et al. Ravensbrück. Prague: Nase vojsko, 1960.

1919 HERMANN, NANDA. Der gesegnete Abgrund. Schutzhäftling Nr. 6582 im Frauenkonzentrationslager Ravensbrück. Nuremberg: Glock & Lutz, 1948. 216p.

1920 KOMITEE DER ANTIFASCHISTISCHEN WIDERSTANDSKÄMPFER IN DER DEUTSCHEN DEMOKRATISCHEN REPUBLIK. Die Frauen von Ravensbrück. Berlin (GDR): Kongress, 1960.

1921 LA GUARDIA GLUCK, GEMMA [Samuel Loeb Schneiderman, ed.]. My Story. New York: McKay, 1961. 116p. Experiences at Ravensbrück.

1922 MACHLEID, WANDA (ed.). Experimental Operations on Prisoners of Ravensbrück Concentration Camp. Poznan: Wyd. Zachodnie, 1960. 58p.

1923 MAUREL, MICHELINE. Un Camp très ordinaire. Paris: Éditions de Minuit, 1957. 191p. Published in English as An Ordinary Camp. New York: Simon & Schuster, 1958; and Ravensbrück. London: Blond, 1958. Deals with Neubrandenburg, a branch of Ravensbrück.

1924 SAINT-CLAIR, SIMON. Ravensbrück. L'Enfer des femmes. Paris: J. Tallandier, 1945. Revised edition, Paris: Fayard, 1962.

1925 SYMONOWICZ, WANDA (ed.). Beyond Human Endurance. The Ravensbrück Women tell their Stories. Warsaw: Interpress, 1970. 181p. On medical experiments. Original is in Polish.

1926 TILLION, GERMAINE. Ravensbrück. Paris: Éditions du Seuil, 1973. 279p. Published in English as Ravensbruck: An Eyewitness Account of a Women's Concentration Camp. Garden City: Anchor/Doubleday, 1975. 256p. English edition has an index. Devoted to a camp located north of Berlin. Based on notes made from 1942-1945. The first part of the volume is more a personal account, while the second part is an historical study, based on documents drawn up by the SS for its own use. Major topics discussed include SS women, medicine by the SS, extermination within the camp, gas chambers, gas chambers at Mauthausen and Dachau, and a study of Buchenwald.

1927 ZORNER, G., et al (eds.). *Frauen-KZ Ravensbrück*. Berlin: VEB Deutscher Verlag der Wissenschaften, 1971.

1928 ZUMPE, L. "Die Textilbetriebe der SS im Konzentrationslager Ravensbrück. Eine Studie über ökonomische Funktion und wirtschaftliche Tätigkeit der SS," *Jahrbuch für Wirtschaftsgeschichte* Part 1. Berlin (GDR): Akademie, 1969.

AA. RED CROSS

1929 MILENTIJEVICH, ZORAN. [Jewish inmates of the camp "Red Cross"]. Nish: Narodni m'zej Nish, 1976. 36p. In Serbian, with summaries in English, French, and Russian.

BB. SACHSENHAUSEN (ORANIENBURG)

1930 BALLHORN, FRANZ. *Die Kelter Gottes. Tagebuch eines jungen Christen 1940-1945*. Münster: Regensburg, 1980. 132p. Deals with the Oranienburg-Sachsenhausen concentration camp.

1931 *Damals in Sachsenhausen. Solidarität und Widerstand im Konzentrationslager Sachsenhausen*. Berlin(GDR): Kongreß, [no date given].

1932 *Dokumente, Aussagen, Forschungsergebnisse und Erlebnisberichte über das ehemalige Konzentrationslager Sachsenhausen*. Berlin (GDR): Deutscher Verlag der Wissenschaft, 1974.

1933 SEGER, GERHART. *A Nation Terrorized*. Chicago: Teolly & Lee, 1935. 204p.

1934 SZALET, LEON. *Experiment "E." A Report from an Extermination Laboratory*. New York: Didier, 1945. 284p. On medical experiments.

1935 ULLMANN, EDUARD (ed.). *Sachsenhausen*. Berlin: VEB Deutscher Verlag, 1974.

1936 UTSCH, BERT. *Gestapo-Häftling 52478 aus dem KZ Oranienburg-Sachsenhausen*. Ottobeuren: [private printing], 1945. 154p.

1937 WEISS-RUETHELS, A. *Nacht und Nebel. Ein Sachsenhausen-Buch*. Berlin/Potsdam: VVN, 1949.

CC. SALASPILS

1938 SAUSNITISA, K. (ed.). [In the death camp of Salaspils. Collected reminiscences]. Riga: Latviskoe Gosudarstvennoe Isd., 1964. 386p. Original is in Russian.

DD. SKARZYSKO (KAMIENNA)

1939 FREY, HANS (comp.). *Die Hölle von Kamienna*. Berlin/Potsdam: VVN, 1949. 96p.

EE. SOBIBOR

1940 AINSZTEIN, REUBEN. Jewish Resistance in Nazi-Occupied Eastern Europe. New York: Barnes and Noble, 1974.

1941 NETHERLANDS RED CROSS INFORMATION BUREAU. Sobibor. The Hague: 1946. Deals with Dutch survivors of the death camp.

1942 NOVITCH, MIRIAM. Sobibor. Martyre et révolte. Documents et témoignages. Paris: Centre de Publ. Asie Orientale, 1978. 170p. Published in English as Sobibor: Martyrdom and Revolt. New York: Holocaust Library, 1980.

FF. STRUTHOF (NATZWEILER)

1943 ALLAINMAT, HENRY. Auschwitz en France. La Verité sur le seul camp d'extermination nazi en France - Le Struthof. Paris: Presses de la Cité, 1974. 243p.

1944 BAUDOIN, R. Atrocités du camp de Struthof (Bas Rhine): douze photographies horrifiantes; après les resultats d'une enquête de Monsieur Baudoin. Metz: E. Gangloff, [1945?]. 16p.

1945 Natzweiler-Struthof. [no city given]: Le Comité National pour l'Erection et la Conservation d'un Mémorial de Déportation au Struthof, [1964].

1946 VORLANDER, HERWART (ed.). Nationalsozialistische Konzentrationslager im Dienst der totalen Kriegsführung. Sieben württembergische Außenkommandos des KZ Natzweiler/Elsaß. Stuttgart: Kohlhammer, 1978. 305p.

GG. STUTTHOF (SZTUTOWO)

1947 DUNN-WASOWICZ, KRZYSZTOF. Stutthof. Warsaw: Panstwowe Instytut Wyd., 1946. 103p.

HH. THERESIENSTADT (TEREZIN)

1948 ADLER, H.G. Die verheimlichte Wahrheit. Theresienstädter Dokumente. Tübingen: J.C.B. Mohr (Paul Siebeck), 1958. 372p. Contains 241 documents dealing with all aspects of life, torture, and death at Theresienstadt. The Forward lists 15 sources of research materials; the Introduction outlines the history of the camp and contains a city plan of Theresienstadt in the summer of 1944. Name, place, and subject indexes.

1949 ADLER, H.G. Theresienstadt, 1941-1945, das Antlitz einer Zwangsgemeinschaft. Geschichte, Soziologie, Psychologie. Tübingen: J.C.B. Mohr, 1955. 773p.

1950 BAECK, LEO [Eric H. Boehm, ed.]. We Survived. New Haven: Yale University Press, 1949.

1951 BOR, JOSEF. The Terezin Requiem. New York: Alfred A. Knopf, 1963; London: Heineman, 1963. 83p. Published in German as Theresienstädter Requiem. Gütersloh: Mohn, 1966. The original is in Czech.

1952 Hier leben keine Schmetterlinge. Prague: Staatliches Jüdisches Museum, 1959. Published in English as I Never Saw Another Butterfly: Children's Drawings and Poems from Theresienstadt

Concentration Camp 1942-1944. New York: McGraw-Hill, [1964]. 80p. Artistic expressions of condemned children.

1953 JACOBSON, JACOB. Terezin, the Daily Life, 1943-45. London: Jewish Central Information Office, 1946. Report Number 6, for the month of March, in stencil.

1954 JEWISH COMMITTEE FOR THERESIENSTADT. Totenbuch Theresienstadt. I: Deportierte aus Österreich. Vienna: Jüdisches Komitee für Theresienstadt, 1971. 160p. A list of the names of Theresienstadt inmates, with dates of birth and death.

1955 KARNY, MIROSLAV. „Das Konzentrationslager Terezin (Theresienstadt) in den Plänen der Nazis," Ceskoslovensky Casopis Historicky 1974 22: 673-702.

1956 LEDERER, ZDENEK. Ghetto Theresienstadt. London: E. Goldston, 1953. 275p. New York: Howard Fertig, 1983. 275p.

1957 NOVAK, VACLAV. Terezin. Pamatnik Terezin: 1974.

1958 OPPENHEIM, RALPH. An der Grenze des Lebens. Theresienstädter Tagebuch. Hamburg: Rütten & Loening, 1961. 251p.

1959 PETROW, RICHARD. The Bitter Years. New York: William Morrow, 1974.

1960 ROSE, ANNA. Refugee. New York: Dial Press, 1977. A memoir of Theresienstadt.

1961 SALUS, GRETE. Eine Frau erzählt. Bonn: Bundeszentrale für Heimatdienst, 1958. 99p. Jewish survivor of Auschwitz, Oederan, and Theresienstadt.

1962 SCHMIEDT, SHLOMO. "Hehalutz in Theresienstadt - Its Influence and Educational Activities," Yad Vashem Studies 1968 7: 107-125. 27 notes.

1963 Terezin-Ghetto. List of Saved Persons and Introduction. Prague: Repatriation Department of the Ministry of Protection of Labor and Social Welfare, 1945. 541p.

1964 UTITZ, E. Psychologie des Lebens im Konzentrationslager Theresienstadt. Vienna: 1948.

II. TREBLINKA

1965 ALEXANDER, EDWARD. "The Incredulity of the Holocaust," Midstream 1979 25(1): 49-59.

1966 AUERBACH, RACHEL. [On the fields of Treblinka - A report]. Lodz: Centraina Zydowska Komisja Historyczna, 1947. 109p. In Yiddish.

1967 DONAT, ALEXANDER (ed.). The Death Camp Treblinka. New York: Holocaust Library, 1979.

1968 GROSSMAN, WASSILI. Die Hölle von Treblinka. London: I.N.G. Publications, 1945. 24p. Published in Spanish as El infierno de Treblinka. Buenos Aires: Congreso Judio Mundial, 1968.

1969 NOAKES, JEREMY, and GEOFFREY PRIDHAM (eds.). Documents on Nazism, 1919-1945. London: Jonathan Cape, 1974. Much on Treblinka.

1970 NOVITCH, MIRIAM. La Vérité sur Treblinka. Paris: Presses du Temps Présent, 1967. 134p.

1971 STEINER, JEAN-FRANCOIS. Treblinka, la révolte d'un camp d'extermination. Paris: Fayard, 1966. 395p. Published in English as Treblinka. New York: Simon and Schuster, 1967. 415p. Attempts to discover why the Jews allowed themselves to be "led to the slaughterhouse like sheep." Reconstructs the events at the Treblinka extermination camp and discusses individual and group attitudes of prisoners, the Committee of Resistance of Treblinka, and the uprising and subsequent destruction of the camp. Undocumented.

1972 WIERNIK, YANKEL. A Year in Treblinka. An Inmate Who Escaped Tells the Day-to-Day Facts of One Year of His Torturous Experience. New York: American Representation of the General Jewish Workers' Union of Poland, [1945]. 46p.

JJ. WESTERBORK

1973 MECHANICUS, PHILIP. Waiting for Death. A Diary. London: Calder & Boyars, 1968. Original was published in Dutch in 1964.

1974 MECHANICUS, PHILIP. Year of Fear. New York: Hawthorn Books, 1964. 267p. An account of the author's deportation on May 28, 1943, with fellow Dutch Jews to Westerbork, a transit camp, life at the camp, and the final deportation to Auschwitz, on October 9, 1944, where he was killed.

1975 PRESSER, JACOB. De nacht der Girondijnen. Amsterdam: Commissie voor de Propaganda van het Nederlandse Boek, 1957. 84p. Published in English as Breaking Point. Cleveland: World, 1958. Published in German as Die Nacht der Girondisten. Hamburg: Rowohlt, 1959. A novel about the Westerbork concentration camp.

VII
WORLD WAR II
WAR CRIMINALS

A. BIOGRAPHICAL SECTION

1. Biographies

1976 ABETZ, OTTO. Pétain et les Allemands. Paris: 1948.

1977 ABSHAGEN, KARL HEINZ. Canaris, Patriot und Weltbürger. Stuttgart: Union Deutsche Verlagsgesellschaft, 1949. 409p. Biography of Admiral Wilhelm Canaris, chief of the German secret service. Covers his years as a World War I naval officer and his rise to the top of the German secret service. Discusses the men surrounding Canaris, in particular his close personal relationship with Reinhard Heydrich, his fight for peace during the Spanish Civil War, his opposition to expanding the arena of World War II, and his attempts to keep sabotage to a minimum in the operations of the secret service during World War II. Some remarks on Polish concentration camps. 6-page index of names, 7 pages of illustrations.

1978 ACKERMANN, JOSEF. Heinrich Himmler als Ideologe. Göttingen: Musterschmidt, 1970. 317p. Chapter 4 deals with the "final solution," Chapter 6 with Himmler and the Germanization, depopulation, and enslavement of the East.

1979 ANDERS, KARL. Im Nürnberger Irrgarten. Nuremberg: Nest, 1948. 230p. Contains brief biographical sketches of each of the defendants at the Nuremberg IMT trial, emphasizing the impressions of their contemporaries. A table lists the 21 by name and birthday and the verdicts for or against them. Contains essays on the general staff, the criminal acts of National Socialist organizations, prosecution and defense counsels, and the judges on the IMT. Discusses war guilt and indictments. Undocumented; 2-page index.

1980 ANDRUS, BURTON C. The Infamous of Nuremberg. London: Leslie Frewin, 1969. 211p. American edition, I Was the Nuremberg Jailer. New York: Coward-McCann, 1969. 211p. In writing this book, Colonel Andrus, Commandant of the Nuremberg prison, used many files not previously made public because their contents were "too sensitive for public scrutiny." This is the record of how the commandant and his fellow jailers lived with the rule that until proven guilty their prisoners were presumed innocent. Contains many insights into the lives, values, and behavior of the prisoners, particularly Rudolf Hess and Hermann Göring. Discusses daily activities, meals, correspondence, and the mental health of prisoners. Reviews prison conditions, anti-suicide measures, medical checks, visitors, interviews, the guarding of prisoners, and Göring's suicide. 5-page index, 32 photographs.

1981 ARONSON, SHLOMO. Beginnings of the Gestapo System, the Bavarian Model in 1933. Jerusalem: Israel University Press, 1969. 76p. History of the Bavarian Political Police (BPP) through 1934. Discusses Heinrich Himmler's appointment as commander and the creation of the triangle SS-Police-Concentration Camp. Appendix contains a list of SS ranks and their U.S. Army equivalents. 209 notes, 6 photographs, no bibliography.

1982 BACH, JÜRGEN A. Franz von Papen in der Weimarer Republik. Aktivitäten in Politik und Presse 1918-1932. Düsseldorf: Droste, 1977. 354p. Much useful background information on Von Papen's early political career. Useful 20-page bibliography contains works that deal with his later career.

1983 BECK, EARL R. Verdict on Schacht: A Study in the Problem of Political Guilt. Tallahassee: Florida State University, 1955. 201p. Number 20 of the Florida State University Studies. Deals with various criticisms and evaluations of Schacht, and concludes that much of the postwar treatment of Schacht was colored by wartime passion. Schacht believed that American authorities were persecuting him and the Krupp empire so there would no longer exist in Germany any first-rate financial wizards who could pose a threat to them. Concludes that Schacht was not a great man, but was a near-great man who sought and served the welfare of his country as he saw it. 7-page bibliography, 9-page index.

1984 BEWLEY, CHARLES. Hermann Göring. Göttingen: Göttinger-Verlagsanstalt, 1956. Published in English as Hermann Goering and the Third Reich. New York: Devin-Adair, 1962.

1985 BEZYMENSKII, L[EV] A[LEKSANDROVICH]. Die letzten Notizen von Martin Bormann. Ein Dokument und sein Verfasser. Stuttgart: Deutsche Verlags-Anstalt, 1974. 344p.

1986 BEZYMENSKII, L[EV] A[LEKSANDROVICH]. [On the trail of Martin Bormann]. 2nd edition. Moscow: Izd. Politicheskoi Literatury, 1965. 190p. In Russian. Published in German as Auf den Spuren von Martin Bormann. Berlin(GDR): Dietz, 1965.

1987 BEZYMENSKII, L[EV] A[LEKSANDROVICH]. Po sledam Martin Bormann. Moscow: Politizdat, 1964. 127p. A Soviet intelligence officer's account of Martin Bormann and his escape. Written before his remains were found.

1988 BIRD, EUGENE K. Prisoner #7 Rudolf Hess: The Thirty Years in Jail of Hitler's Deputy Führer. New York: Viking, 1974. 270p. Written by the American director of Spandau. Covers the dramatic flight of Rudolf Hess to England in 1941, his testimony at the Nuremberg IMT trial, and his years in Spandau prison. This biography describes his character and analyzes contacts and correspondence during the latter years of his imprisonment. Undocumented; 17 photographs.

1989 BIRD, EUGENE K. The Loneliest Man in the World. London: Secker and Warburg, 1974. 270p. Published in German as Hess. Der "Stellvertreter des Führers" Englandflug und britische Gefangenschaft Nürnberg und Spandau. Munich: Desch, 1974. 310p.

1990 BONDY, LOUIS W. Racketeers of Hatred: Julius Streicher and the Jew-Baiters' International. London/Leicester: N. Wolsey, 1946. 268p.

1991 BRISSAUD, ANDRÉ. Canaris. London: Weidenfeld and Nicolson, 1973. Much on KZ Flossenburg.

1992 BROSS, WERNER. Gespräche mit Hermann Göring während des Nürnberger Prozesses. Flensburg/Hamburg: Christian Wolf, 1950. 315p. Diary entries of the assistant to Hermann Göring's attorney made from January 12 to July 21, 1946. Transcription of talks with Göring during the Nuremberg IMT trial. Contains remarks by Göring on various trial documents and court proceedings. Appendix (pp. 245-315) contains the interrogation of Göring used as preparation for the trial. Contains a 2-page facsimile of a questionnaire completed by Joachim von Ribbentrop and "edited" by Göring and a sketch by Göring of Hitler's strategic position against the USSR. Undocumented; 6 photographs.

1993 BROWNE, COURTNEY. Tojo: The Last Banzai. New York: Holt, Rinehart and Winston, 1967. 260p. Deals with Tojo's imprisonment and trial. The account is generally sympathetic, depicting Tojo as an honorable human being with a warrior's code of ethics.

1994 BUCHANAN, ROBERT H. "The Era of Erich Raeder, 1894-1943, Dreams of World Empire: A Study in Historical Continuity," Ph.D. dissertation, University of Colorado at Boulder, 1980. 606p. Abstracted in Dissertation Abstracts International 1981 41(8): 3685-A.

1995 BULLOCK, ALAN. Hitler: A Study in Tyranny. London: Odhams, 1952. Revised edition, New York: Harper and Row, 1964. 858p. Published in German as Eine Studie in Tyrannei. Düsseldorf: 1953.

1996 BUTLER, EWAN, and GORDON YOUNG. Marshal without Glory. London: Hodder and Stoughton, 1951. 287p. Biography of Hermann Göring. Chapter 18 (pp. 262-272) discusses his imprisonment and last year. Covers his brief examination in court at Nuremberg and his suicide by poisoning. 1-page bibliography, 9-page index, 18 photographs.

1997 BUTOW, ROBERT J.C. Tojo and the Coming of the War. Princeton: Princeton University Press, 1961. 584p. A general history that contains some discussion of war crimes.

1998 BYTWERK, RANDALL L. Julius Streicher: The Man Who Persuaded a Nation to Hate Jews. New York: Stein and Day, 1983. 236p.

1999 CALIC, EDOUARD. Reinhard Heydrich. Schlüßelfigur des Dritten Reiches. Düsseldorf: Droste, 1982. Published in English as Reinhard Heydrich: The Chilling Story of the Man who Masterminded the Nazi Death Camps. New York: William Morrow, 1985. 272p. Depicts a fairley well-balanced, all-around man driven by "pathological ambition." 4p. of notes, index.

2000 COLVIN, IAN G. Chief of Intelligence. London: Gollancz, 1951. 223p. American edition, Master Spy. New York: 1952. The story of Admiral Canaris.

2001 DAIM, WILFRIED. Der Mann, der Hitler die Ideen gab. Von den religiösen Verirrungen eines Sektierers zum Rassenwahn des Diktators. Munich: Isar, 1958. 286p.

2002 DESCHNER, GÜNTHER. Reinhard Heydrich, Statthalter der totalen Macht, Biographie. Esslingen am Neckar: Bechtle, 1977. 376p. Published in English as Heydrich: The Pursuit of total Power. London: Orbis, 1981. 351p. Describes Heydrich's career and his role in the formation of National Socialist policy. Remarks on the shift of blame onto Heydrich by the accused and the witnesses at the Nuremberg IMT trial. Based on primary and secondary sources; 10 photographs, 7-page bibliography, 7-page index of names.

2003 DIDIER, FRIEDRICH. Europa arbeitet in Deutschland, Sauckel mobilisiert die Leistungsreserven. Berlin: Zentralverlag der NSDAP, 1943. 128p. National Socialist publication honoring the contributions of European workers to the German war economy. Emphasizes the leadership quality of Fritz Sauckel, Gauleiter and chief of the National Socialist labor force. Discusses foreign industrial labor and agriculture. Undocumented. 153 photographs.

2004 DIELS, RUDOLF. Lucifer Ante Portas. Zwischen Severing und Heydrich. Zürich: Interverlag, 1950. Stuttgart: Deutsche Verlags-Anstalt, 1950. 450p.

2005 DÖNITZ, KARL. Die U-Bootswaffe 4th edition. Berlin: Mittler, 1943.

2006 Dr Karl Brandt: His Career, His Position as Reich Commissioner for Health and Medical Services, Medical Information, Notes on Dr. Morell. CCPWE 32/DI-17, 30 June 1945, Washington: NARS, Modern Military Records Division, 1945.

2007 DUFF, SHIELA GRANT. A German Protectorate: The Czechs under Nazi Rule. London: Macmillan, 1942.

2008 DUPAYS, PAUL. Grands Chefs du nazisme, chronique historique. Tribunal International de Nuremberg, mi-mars à mi-avril 1946. Paris: Éditions de la Critique, 1946.

2009 DUTCH, OSWALD. Hitler's Twelve Apostles. New York: Robert M. McBride, 1940.

2010 FEST, JOACHIM C. Das Gesicht des Dritten Reiches. Munich: R. Piper, 1963. 391p. 5-page bibliography, index. Published in English as The Face of the Third Reich: Portraits of Nazi Leadership. New York: Pantheon, 1970. 402p. Biographical sketches of 17 major Nazi leaders. Concludes that despite the dominant personality of Hitler and others a people must be in a condition to be led astray before totalitarian rule can be imposed. 6-page bibliography, 10-page index, 75 pages of annotations.

2011 FEST, JOACHIM C. Hitler. Eine Biographie. Frankfurt am Main/Berlin/Vienna: Ullstein, 1973. 1190p. Published in English as Hitler. New York: Harcourt Brace Jovanovich, 1974. 844p. Contains much background on Hitler and his policies. Though it does not deal directly with war crimes, there is some information on the "final solution." Bibliography, index of names.

2012 FISHMAN, JACK. The Seven Men of Spandau. New York: Rinehart, 1954. 276p. A study of the Nuremberg IMT trial of Rudolf Hess, Albert Speer, Walter Frank, Baldur von Schirach, Erich Raeder, Constantin von Neurath, and Karl Dönitz, the defendants who were sentenced to prison terms rather than to death. Traces briefly some of their post-prison careers.

2013 FOERSTER, WOLFGANG. Generaloberst Ludwig Beck. Munich: Isar, 1953.

2014 FORNDRAN, ERHARD, FRANK GOLCZWEWSKI, and DIETER RIESENBERGER (eds.). Nationalsozialistische Außenpolitik. Determinanten internationaler Beziehungen in historischen Fallstudien. Opladen: Westdeutscher Verlag, 1976.

2015 FRANK, KARL-HERMANN, Reinhard Heydrich, Ein Leben der Tat. Prague: 1944.

2016 FRISCHAUER, WILLI. Himmler, the Evil Genius of the Third Reich. London: Odhams Press, 1953. 269p.

2017 FRISCHAUER, WILLI. The Rise and Fall of Hermann Goering. Boston: Houghton Mifflin, 1951. 309p. Chapters 21, "Guilt Unique," pp. 281-292, and 22, "Death with a Smile," pp. 293-296, deal with the trial and death of Göring. Bibliography and index.

2018 FRITZSCHE, HANS [Hildegard Springer, ed.]. Hier spricht Hans Fritzsche. Zürich: Interverlag, 1948. Republished as Es sprach Hans Fritsche, nach Gesprächen, Briefen und Dokumenten. Stuttgart: Thiele, [1949]. 335p. Contains documents of the Nuremberg IMT trial.

2019 FRITZSCHE, HILDEGARD. Vor dem Tribunal der Sieger. Gesetzlose Justiz in Nürnberg. Oldendorf: Schultz, 1981.

2020 FUNK, WALTHER. Grundsätze der deutschen Außenhandelspolitik und das Problem der internationalen Verschuldung. Berlin: Junker und Dünnhaupt, 1938.

2021 FUNKE, MANFRED (ed.). Hitler, Deutschland und die Mächte. Materialien zur Außenpolitik des Dritten Reiches. Düsseldorf: Droste, 1976. 848p.

2022 GOLDHAGEN, ERICH. „Albert Speer, Himmler and the Secrecy of the Final Solution," Midstream 1971 17(8): 43-50. 23 notes.

2023 GÖRLITZ, WALTER (ed.). Generalfeldmarschall Keitel - Verbrecher oder Offizier? Göttingen: Musterschmidt, 1961. 447p. Published in English as The Memoirs of Field Marshall Keitel. New York: Stein & Day, 1966. 288p.

2024 GRABER, G.S. The Life and Times of Reinhard Heydrich. New York: David McKay, 1980. 245p. Traces Heydrich's working class origins, education, and service in the navy. Contains chapters on Lina von Osten, his wife, and on Heydrich's appointment by Heinrich Himmler to the position of organizer of the Sicherheitsdienst (Security Service of the SS). Discusses Heydrich's assault on the Jews, his emasculation of the German army, and his assassination. Undocumented; 3-page glossary of National Socialist terms, 9-page index, 14 photographs.

2025 GRIFFITHS, RICHARD. **Marshall Pétain: A Biography of Marshal Philippe Pétain of Vichy**. Garden City: Doubleday, 1972. 379p.

2026 GRITZBACH, ERICH. **Hermann Göring: Werk und Mensch**. Munich: Zentralverlag der NSDAP, Franz Eher Nachfolger, 1939. 369p. Published in English as **Hermann Goering: The Man and his Work**. London: Hurst & Blackett, 1939.

2027 GRUBER, ANDREAS (ed.). **Staatsmänner und Diplomaten bei Hitler. Vertrauliche Aufzeichnungen über Unterredungen mit Vertretern des Auslands**. 2 volumes. Frankfurt am Main: Bernard und Graefe, 1967-1970.

2028 GUDERIAN, HEINZ. **Panzer Leader**. London: Michael Joseph, 1952. 528p.

2029 HAFFNER, SEBASTIAN. **Anmerkungen zu Hitler**. Munich: Kindler, 1978. 204p. Published in English as **Meaning of Hitler**. New York: Macmillan, 1979. 165p. Summarizes the achievements, successes, and failures of Hitler, with a 30-page chapter on his crimes, which included mass murder, forced labor, and deportation. Undocumented.

2030 HAMSIK, DUSAN, and J. PRAZAK. **Eine Bombe für Heydrich**. Berlin(GDR): Buchverlag des Morgan, 1964. 364p.

2031 HART, S.T. **Alfred Rosenberg**. Munich: J.F. Lehmanns, 1933.

2032 HART, W.E. [pseudonym]. **Hitler's Generals**. London: Cresset, 1944. Garden City: Doubleday, 1944. 222p. Reviews the careers of Hitler's senior generals as background to the history of Germany's rearmament after 1919. Chapters deal with Colonel General Baron Werner von Fritsch, Grand Admiral Karl Doenitz, Admiral Erich Raeder, field marshals Karl Rudolf Gerd von Rundstedt, Erwin Eugen Johannes Rommel, Erhard Milch, Walther Heinrich, Alfred Herman von Brauchitsch, Wilhelm Keitel, and Fedor von Bock. Undocumented; 8-page index, 8 portraits. Also in Spanish and Italian.

2033 HEIBER, HELMUT. **Adolf Hitler**. Berlin: Colloquium, 1960. Published in English as **Adolf Hitler, a Short Biography**. London: O. Wolff, 1961. 192p.

2034 HEIBER, HELMUT. **Joseph Goebbels**. Berlin: Colloquium, 1962. 433p.

2035 HEINEMAN, JOHN L. "Constantin Freiherr von Neurath as Foreign Minister, 1932-1935, A Study of a Conservative Civil Servant and Germany's Foreign Policy," Ph.D. dissertation, Cornell University, 1965. 439p. Abstracted in **Dissertation Abstracts International** 1965 26(1-2): 336.

2036 HERZOG, ROBERT. **Besatzungsverwaltung in den besetzten Ostgebieten, Abteilung Jugend**. Tübingen: Institut für Besatzungsfragen, 1960. 119p. On Baldur von Schirach.

2037 HIMMLER, HEINRICH [Bradley F. Smith and Agnes F. Peterson, eds.]. **Heinrich Himmler. Geheimreden 1933 bis 1945, und andere Ansprachen**. Frankfurt am Main: Propyläen, 1974. 319p. Collection of the texts of speeches made between 1933 and 1945 by

Himmler. Contains an essay on Himmler as orator. 2-page chronology of important events, list of SS officer ranks and German army equivalents, 10-page index of Himmler's speeches, 4-page bibliography, 3-page index of names, 220 photographs.

2038 HOFFMAN, HEINRICH. Hitler Was My Friend. London: Burke, 1955. 256p.

2039 HOWARD, TONI. "Eight Eyes on Seven Faces: Report from Inside Spandau," Newsweek 1947 30(7): 32-33. 1 photograph.

2040 HUTTON, JOSEPH BERNARD [pseudonym]. Rudolf Hess: The Man and his Mission. London: David Bruce & Watson, 1970. 262p. New York: Macmillan, 1971. Biography of Hess which focuses on his career with the National Socialist party and his trial for war crimes. Discusses his function as deputy to Adolf Hitler and his flight to Scotland, and describes his behavior during the proceedings at Nuremberg, ranging from initial indifference to the deterioration of his mental condition. He was found guilty and sentenced to life imprisonment at Spandau. From 1954 to 1966, defendants Constantin von Neurath, Erich Raeder, Karl Dönitz, Walter Funk, Albert Speer, and Baldur von Schirach were released from Spandau prison. Only Hess remained. Includes a letter from Professor Julius Epstein of Stanford University to the Premier of the Soviet Union calling for his release, and a map of Spandau prison. Appendix contains Alfred Seidl's petition to the governments of the Allied forces in May 1966 calling for the release of Hess from prison. 6-page index, no bibliography, 19 photographs.

2041 IVANOV, MIROSLAV. L'Attentat contre Heydrich. Paris: Robert Laffont, [1972]. 317p. Published in English as Target: Heydrich. New York: Macmillan, 1973. 292p. When resistance movements began to gain momentum in Czechoslovakia in the early 1940s, Reinhard Heydrich was sent to thwart them. Reports on the events that provoked Czech patriots to assassinate Heydrich on May 27, 1942. The author, a Czech journalist, has pieced together eyewitness accounts, key documents, and original Nazi records of the acts that contributed to the uprising. Undocumented; 28 photographs.

2042 JACOBSEN, HANS-ADOLF (ed.). Karl Haushofer. Leben und Werk. 2 volumes. Boppard am Rhein: Harald Boldt, 1978.

2043 JANSSEN, GREGOR. Das Ministerium Speer. Deutschlands Rüstung im Krieg. 2nd edition. Berlin: Ullstein, 1969. 446p.

2044 JODL, LUISE. Jenseits des Endes. Leben und Sterben des Generaloberst Alfred Jodl. Vienna: 1976.

2045 KESSEMEIER, CARIN. Der Leitartikler Goebbels in den N-S Organen „Der Angriff" und „Das Reich." Münster: C.J. Fahle, 1967. 348p. Focuses on propaganda and the press by examining National Socialist publications from 1927-1945. Analyzes content, style, tactics, goals, and effects of two National Socialist newspapers. Reveals tensions between National Socialist goals and those of Great Britain, the United States, and the Soviet Union. Appendices contain tables of articles from Der Angriff and Das Reich, including lists of reprinted and translated articles as well as front pages from both. Based on primary and secondary sources; 11-page bibliography, 23 photographs.

2046 KIEHL, WALTER. *Mann an der Fahne. Kameraden erzählen von Dr. Ley.* 5th edition. Munich: Zentralverlag der NSDAP, 1940. 304p. Early biography of Robert Ley, head of the Deutsche Arbeitsfront. Account of his youth and early career through 1940. 61 photographs, including facsimiles of documents. Undocumented.

2047 LANG, JOCHEN VON. *Der Sekretär. Martin Bormann: Der Mann der Hitler beherrschte.* Stuttgart: Deutsche Verlags-Anstalt, 1977. 511p. Published in English as *The Secretary: Martin Bormann: The Man who Manipulated Hitler.* New York: Random House, 1979. 430p. Discusses Bormann's early years, his involvement in criminal activities with the radical right-wing organization Deutschvölkischfreiheitspartei, which was founded in 1922. Follows his development from unknown party member to Reichsleiter in the NSDAP. Describes his stance against Christians and Jews, his idolization of Hitler, and his view of Slavs as slaves. Deals with his role in the extermination of Jews as the "armchair assassin" and as the secret ruler beside Hitler. The Postscript is an essay by the author on "How I found Martin Bormann". Appendix contains Bormann's 1945 dental chart, a medical examination form, appointment notebook, and reports on skeleton finds on the Ulap fairground, Berlin, in the search for Bormann. 1-page index of people interviewed, 8-page bibliography, 11-page index of names, 42 photographs.

2048 LANGE, EITEL. *Der Reichsmarschall im Kriege, ein Bericht in Wort und Bild.* Stuttgart: Curt E. Schwab, 1950. 216p. Glorification of Hermann Göring's career during the years 1940-1945, with his criminal activity mentioned briefly in the foreword. 152 photographs. Undocumented.

2049 LATERNSER, HANS. *Verteidigung deutscher Soldaten. Plädoyers vor alliierten Gerichten.* Bonn: Rolf Bohnemeier, 1950. 344p. The author served as defense attorney for several German officers. Part 1, pp. 7-46, reviews the defense of the Generalstab and OKW before the Nuremberg IMT. Part 2, pp. 47-109, deals with the defense of Field Marshal Albert Kesselring before a British Military Tribunal in Venice. He was indicted for guerrilla warfare and the bombing of Rome in 1943. Contains text of the final statement by Kesselring after his sentencing to death on May 6, 1947. Part 3, pp. 111-239, deals with the defense of Field Marshal Wilhelm List and Field Marshal Maximilian von Weich before an American military tribunal at Nuremberg. Contains List's final statement at his trial. Part 4, pp. 241-337, deals with the defense of Field Marshal Wilhelm Ritter von Leeb before an American Military Tribunal at Nuremberg. Discusses armament, participation in aggressive war, war crimes and crimes against humanity, the Einsatzgruppen of the secret police and SD, conspiracy, and problems in the defense of von Leeb. Contains his final statement after his acquittal. Based on primary sources; 4-page index of names, no bibliography.

2050 LEASOR, THOMAS JAMES. *Rudolf Hess, The Uninvited Envoy.* New York: McGraw-Hill, 1962; London: G. Allen, 1962. 239p.

2051 LEE, ASHER. *Goering, Air Leader.* New York: Hippocrene Books, 1972; London: Duckworth, 1972. 256p.

2052 LERNER, DANIEL, ITHIEL DE SOLA POOL, and GEORGE K. SCHUELLER. *The Nazi Elite.* Stanford: Stanford University Press (Hoover Institution, Series B), 1951. 112p.

2053 MANNING, PAUL. **Martin Bormann, Nazi in Exile**. Secaucus, New Jersey: Lyle Stuart, 1981. 302p. Bormann was tried *in absentia* by the Nuremberg IMT and found guilty of war crimes and crimes against humanity. The author considers the trial an act of vengeance for the crime of racial extermination. He believes that Bormann lives today in Argentina as a manipulator in silent, gigantic struggles among worldwide industrial and financial powers. Discusses the history of the I.G. Farben corporation from the early 1930s to the present. Undocumented; 6-page index, 22 photographs and illustrations.

2054 MANSTEIN, ERICH VON. **Aus einem Soldatenleben 1887-1939**. Bonn: Athenäum, 1958. 359p.

2055 MANVELL, ROGER A., and HEINRICH FRAENKEL. **Doctor Goebbels. His Life and Death**. New York: Simon and Schuster, 1960. London: Heinemann, 1960. 306p.

2056 MANVELL, ROGER A., and HEINRICH FRAENKEL. **Heinrich Himmler**. London: Heinemann, 1965. 285p.

2057 MANVELL, ROGER A., and HEINRICH FRAENKEL. **Hermann Göring**. New York: Simon and Schuster, 1962. 401p.

2058 MANVELL, ROGER A., and HEINRICH FRAENKEL. **Hess: A Biography**. New York: Drake, 1973. London: MacGibbon and Kee, 1972. 256p.

2059 MC GOVERN, JAMES. **Martin Bormann**. New York: William Morrow, 1968. 237p. Discusses Bormann's conviction in 1924 for the murder of Walter Kadow, his appointment as Reichsleiter in 1933, his position as Chief of Staff to the Deputy Führer, as Secretary to the Führer, and as head of the Nazi Party Chancellery. Discusses Bormann's attempt to escape from Berlin on May 1, 1945, and his subsequent disappearance. Reviews the Nuremberg IMT decision to try Bormann *in absentia*, and letters allegedly written by Bormann to Adolf Eichmann in Jerusalem after the trial. Investigates CIA attempts made during the 1950s to locate Bormann in Latin America. Concludes with a 2-page essay on source material available about Bormann. 5-page bibliography, 5p. of notes, 5-page index, 11 photographs.

2060 MICHAELIS, MEIR. **Mussolini and the Jews**. Oxford: Clarendon, 1978.

2061 MICHALKA, WOLFGANG. **Joachim von Ribbentrop und die deutsche Englandpolitik, 1933-1940**. Munich: Fink, 1976.

2062 MOCZARSKI, KAZIMIERZ. **Gespräche mit dem Henker. Das Leben des SS-Gruppenführers und Generalleutnants der Polizei Jürgen Stroop aufgezeichnet im Mokotow-Gefängnis zu Warschau**. Düsseldorf: Droste, 1978. 426p. Published in English as **Conversations with an Executioner**. Englewood Cliffs: Prentice-Hall, 1981. 282p. Original is in Polish.

2063 MOLL, OTTO E. **Die deutschen Generalfeldmarschälle, 1939-1945**. 2nd edition. Rastatt: Pabel, 1962.

2064 MOSLEY, LEONARD. **Hirohito, Emperor of Japan**. Englewood Cliffs: Prentice-Hall, 1966.

2065 MOSLEY, LEONARD. **The Reichs Marshal: A Biography of Herman Goering**. Garden City: Doubleday, 1974.

2066 MURPHY, BRENDAN. *The Butcher of Lyon: The Story of Infamous Nazi Klaus Barbie*. New York: Empire, 1983. 336p. A critical, biographical study of Barbie from his career during World War II, when he was a young SS officer, to his arrest and imprisonment in January 1983. There is much information on his crimes and death sentence and on the status of war crimes trials in Germany in 1983. 9p. of bibliographical notes, 29 photographs, and index.

2067 NELTE, OTTO. *Die Generäle. Das Nürnberger Urteil und die Schuld der Generäle*. Hannover: Verlag des Anderen Deutschlands, 1947.

2068 OESTREICH, PAUL H.A. *Walther Funk, ein Leben für die Wirtschaft*. Munich: Zentralverlag der NSDAP, Franz Eher Nachfolger, 1940.

2069 OVEN, WILFRED VON. *Mit Goebbels bis zum Ende*. Buenos Aires: Dürer, 1949. Later published as *Finale Furioso: mit Goebbels bis zum Ende*. Tübingen: Graebert, 1974. 662p. Diaries of Joseph Goebbels, NS Propaganda minister. Reviews the final years, beginning in 1943, with a daily account of activities within the top echelon of Hitler's government. Reports on Goebbels as Gauleiter of greater Berlin, his trip to Nuremberg in June 1944, and the assassination attempt on Hitler in July 1944. Discusses the last weeks of Goebbels' life and his suicide by poisoning. Based on primary sources; 6-page index of names, 10 photographs, no bibliography.

2070 PADFIELD, PETER. *Dönitz, the Last Führer: Portrait of a Nazi War Leader*. New York: Harper & Row, 1984. 524p. The last chapter deals with Dönitz' trial and defense. Documented; bibliography, subject index, maps, and 34 photographs.

2071 PAILLARD, GEORGES, and CLAUDE ROUGERIE. *Reinhard Heydrich (protecteur de Bohême et Moravie). Le Violiniste de la mort*. Paris: Fayard, 1973. 316p.

2072 PAPEN, FRANZ VON. *Der Wahrheit. Eine Gasse*. Munich: Paul List, 1952. 677p. A general history of Germany from the Second Reich through the Nuremberg IMT trial. Chapters 31-34, pp. 602-666, deal with Von Papen's arrest, trial, and reflections. Index.

2073 PEILLARD, LÉONCE. *The Laconia Affair*. New York: Putnam, 1963. 270p.

2074 PENTZLIN, HEINZ. *Hjalmar Schacht. Leben und Wirken einer umstrittenen Persönlichkeit*. Berlin: Ullstein, 1980. Hjalmar Schacht was president of the Reichsbank during the Third Reich. Reviews the charges brought against him by the Nuremberg IMT, his acquittal on all four counts of the indictment, his arrest by German courts under the denazification law, and hearings in German national courts which lasted until September 1950 and which were reopened in the fall of 1952. Concludes with a statement on Schacht's fate and responsibility. Includes a poem about fate written by Schacht. 9p. of notes, 5-page index of names.

2075 PETERSON, EDWARD N. *Hjalmar Schacht. For and against Hitler*. Boston: Christopher, 1954.

2076 POTTER, JOHN DEANE. *The Life and Death of a Japanese General*. New York: New American Library, 1962. 191p. Also published under the title A Soldier Must Hang: The Biography of an Oriental General. London: F. Muller, 1963. 210p. On Yamashita Tomoyuki.

2077 PRESSEISEN, ERNST L. Germany and Japan: A Study in Totalitarian Diplomacy, 1933-1941. The Hague: Nijhoff, 1958.

2078 PRIEPKE, MANFRED. Die evangelische Jugend im Dritten Reich, 1933-1936. Hannover/Frankfurt am Main: Norddeutsche Verlagsanstalt O. Goedel, 1960.

2079 REES, JOHN R. (ed.). The Mind of Rudolf Hess. New York: W.W. Norton, 1948.

2080 REIMANN, VIKTOR. Dr. Joseph Goebbels. Vienna: Fritz Molden, 1971. 383p. Discusses Goebbels' development from "national Bolshevik" to a follower of Hitler, and from reichsminister to chancellor. Deals extensively with his years in Berlin and the final weeks before his death. 2-page essay on sources, 9p. of notes, 9-page index of names.

2081 RIBADEAU DUMAS, FRANCOIS. Les Damnés de Nuremberg, ou les possédés du nazisme. Paris: Pierre Belfond, 1977. 314p. A person-by-person study of the Nuremberg IMT defendants.

2082 RIESS, CURT. Joseph Goebbels, A Biography. Garden City: Doubleday, 1948. 368p. Published in German as Joseph Goebbels. Eine Biographie. Baden Baden: Dreiecks Verlagsbuch, 1950. 508p.

2083 ROSENBERG, ALFRED. Der Mythus des 20. Jahrhunderts. Eine Wertung der seelisch geistigen Gestaltenkämpfe unserer Zeit. Munich: Hoheneichen, 1930. 670p. Useful here only for background material on Rosenberg.

2084 SCHEEL, KLAUS. Krieg über Ätherwellen. NS-Rundfunk und Monopole 1933-1945. Berlin: Deutscher Verlag der Wissenschaften, 1970. 313p. An exhaustive history of the use of radio for the purpose of spreading Nazi propaganda. Bibliography, 55 documents, 31 photographs, index.

2085 SCHIRACH, BALDUR VON. HJ im Dienst. Berlin: Bernard und Graefe, 1940.

2086 SCHIRACH, BALDUR VON. Kriminalität und Gefährdung der Jugend. Berlin: 1941.

2087 SCHWARZWÄLLER, WULF. „Der Stellvertreter des Führers." Rudolf Hess, der Mann in Spandau. Vienna: Fritz Molden, 1974. 304p. Covers the early years of Hess through the peak of his career as the "high priest" of the Hitler cult, his flight to Scotland, and his imprisonment at Spandau. Discusses his indictment, trial proceedings, and his testimony in court. Based on primary and secondary sources; undocumented, 3-page bibliography, 6-page index of names, 28 photographs.

2088 SCHWENGLER, WALTER. Völkerrecht, Versailler Vertrag und Auslieferungsfrage. Die Strafverfolgung wegen Kriegsverbrechen als Problem des Friedensschlusses 1919/20. Stuttgart: Deutsche Verlags-Anstalt, 1982. 402p. Deals with classical international laws of war, the Versailles treaty, and German War guilt in World War I. 5 appendices, 22-page bibliography, index.

2089 SCHWERIN-KROSIGK, LUTZ GRAF VON. *Es Geschah in Deutschland. Menschenbilder unseres Jahrhunderts*. 3rd edition. Tübingen/Stuttgart: Rainer Wunderlich, 1952, 384p. Biographical vignettes of many major German leaders, including a number of IMT defendants, with some commentary on war crimes trials. Undocumented.

2090 SEMMLER, RUDOLF. *Goebbels, the Man Next to Hitler*. London: Westhouse, 1947. 234p. Semmler was a member of Goebbels' propaganda ministry. Contains his diary from December 31, 1940, when he met Goebbels, until April 17, 1945, when he disappeared. Contains much insight into Goebbels as well as other Nazi leaders and into the workings of the Nazi government. 12 photographs, appendix, index.

2091 SHIROYAMA, SABURO. *War Criminals: the Life and Death of Hirota Koki*. Tokyo/New York: Kodansha International, distributed by Harper, 1977. 301p. Hirota Koki was the only civilian charged and convicted by the Tokyo war crimes tribunal. He had served as ambassador, foreign minister, and prime minister. Hirota was executed with six Japanese army officers in 1948. Presents him as a civilian swept along with the militarism that engulfed Japan. During the war he accepted responsibility for not having done more to avoid war. Photographs, bibliography.

2092 SIEWERT, CURT. *Schuldig? Die Generäle unter Hitler*. Bad Nauheim: Podzun, 1968.

2093 SINN, DIETER. *Illegal. Das grosse Verbrecherlexikon*. Kassodo: 1976. 501p.

2094 SMITH, BRADLEY F. *Adolf Hitler: His Family, Childhood, and Youth*. Stanford: Hoover Institution, 1967. 180p. Attempts to consolidate all source materials available on Hitler's youth and to determine which events most marked his character and personality. Concludes that as a boy Hitler was not an evil genius. Deals with the period from birth in 1889 to 1913. The appendices deal with the change in Hitler's father's name from Schickelgruber to Hitler and Hitler's literary career and life in Vienna. Contains a 9-page bibliography and 3-page index.

2095 SMITH, BRADLEY F. *Heinrich Himmler: A Nazi in the Making, 1900-1926*. Stanford: Hoover Institution, 1971. 211p. Traces Himmler's family origins in northern Bavaria, his schooling at the Gymnasium, training as a soldier in Regensburg in 1917, and university studies in agriculture in Munich. Investigates the roots of Himmler's anti-Semitism. 3-page bibliography, 7-page index, 5 photographs.

2096 STEINERT, MARLIS G. *Twenty-three Days: The Final Collapse of Nazi Germany*. New York: Walker, 1969. Much on Dönitz.

2097 STEPHAN, WERNER. *Joseph Goebbels - Dämon einer Diktatur*. Stuttgart: Union Deutsche Verlagsgesellschaft, 1949. 311p.

2098 STEVENSON, WILLIAM. *The Bormann Brotherhood*. New York: Harcourt Brace Jovanovich, 1973.

2099 STRECKER, REINHARD (ed.). *Dr. Hans Globke*. Hamburg: [no publisher given], [no date given].

2100 SÜNDERMANN, HELMUT. *Tagesparolen. Deutsche Presseanweisungen 1939-1945. Hitlers Propaganda und Kriegsführung.* Leoni am Starnberger See: Druffel, 1973.

2101 THOMPSON, HAROLD KEITH, and HENRY STRUTZ (eds.). *Doenitz at Nuremberg: A Reappraisal, War Crimes and the Military Professional.* New York: Amber, 1976. 198p. A list of responses to the trial and imprisonment of Admiral Dönitz, begun on the occasion of his release from Spandau Prison in 1956. The responses fall generally into 3 categories: those who continued to maintain the legality of the Nuremberg trial, those who believed the trial was illegal but a necessary instrument of political policy, and those who believed the trial was an attempt to create a new body of international law. The book consists of brief statements on the subject made by writers, diplomats, journalists, lawyers, publishers, jurists, statesmen, military men, and entertainers. Many of the statements are in the form of letters or notes to Dönitz himself. Based on thousands of letters, briefs, and manuscripts. Contains 215 photographs of those making the statements. Index.

2102 TOLAND, JOHN. *Adolf Hitler.* New York: Doubleday, 1976. 1035p. One of the best biographies of Hitler, with much on various war crimes trials. 87p. of footnotes, 17-page bibliography, scores of photographs, index.

2103 TRUCK, BETTY, and ROBERT PAUL TRUCK. *Mengele, l'ange de la mort. La Vie diabolique du docteur Josef Mengele, médecin-chef du camp d'extermination d'Auschwitz.* Paris: Presses de la Cité, 1976. 248p.

2104 VOGELSANG, REINHARD. *Der Freundeskreis Himmlers.* Göttingen: Musterschmidt, 1972. 182p.

2105 WAITE, R.G. *The Psychopathic God: Adolf Hitler.* New York: Basic Books, 1977. 482p.

2106 WEIZSÄCKER, ERNST HEINRICH VON [Leonidas E. Hill, ed.]. *Die Weizsäcker-Papiere 1933-1950.* Frankfurt am Main: Propyläen, 1974. 684p. A political-military biography that contains a detailed treatment of Weizsäcker's trial and imprisonment for war crimes. "Nuremberg and Landsberg, 1947-1950," pp. 411-461, discusses his arrest and trial, his imprisonment, and the revision of the judgment against him. Copiously annotated; bibliography, appendices, index.

2107 WIGHTON, CHARLES. *Heydrich, Hitler's most evil Henchman*: London: 1962. Philadelphia: Chilton, 1962.

2108 WULF, JOSEF. *Martin Bormann, Hitlers Schatten.* Gütersloh: Sigbert Mohn, 1962. Published in French as *Martin Bormann. l'Ombre de Hitler.* Paris: Gallimard, 1963.

2109 WYKES, ALAN. *Himmler.* London: Pan Books, 1973. 159p.

2110 ZOLLER, ALBERT. *Hitler privat. Erlebnisbericht seiner Geheimsekretärin.* Düsseldorf: Droste, 1949.

2. Autobiographies, Diaries, Memoirs, Reminiscences

2111 BEST, S. PAYNE. *The Venlo Incident.* London/New York: Hutchinson, 1950. 260p. Personal reminiscences of Heydrich, Mueller,

Schellenberg, and others shed light on the Munich bomb incident. Contains a first-hand description of the evacuation of Dachau.

2112 DIETRICH, OTTO. 12 Jahre mit Hitler. Munich: Isar, 1955. 285p. Biography of Adolf Hitler written by the press chief of the Reich. Discusses anti-Semitism, "Crystal Night," war without political deliberation, methods of violence, and the German-Russian alliance. Much emphasis on National Socialist foreign policy and military strategy. Short segment on Göring's arrest and Himmler's death. No specific mention of war crimes. 5-page index of names.

2113 DÖNITZ, KARL. Mein wechselvolles Leben. Göttingen: Musterschmidt, 1968.

2114 DÖNITZ, KARL. 10 Jahre und 20 Tage. 2nd edition. Bonn: Athenäum, 1958. Frankfurt am Main: Athenäum, 1963. 490p. Published in English as Memoirs, ten Years and twenty Days. Cleveland: World, 1959. 500p. London: Weidenfeld and Nicolson, 1959. Memoirs of Admiral Karl Dönitz, who was sentenced to 10 years imprisonment by the Nuremberg IMT for crimes against peace and against the laws of war. Primary emphasis on military strategy and on Dönitz' role as admiral during the Second World War. Includes bibliographical references. 4-page index of names.

2115 FRANK, HANS. Das Diensttagebuch des deutschen Generalgouverneurs in Polen, 1939-1945. Stuttgart: Deutsche Verlags-Anstalt, 1975.

2116 FRANK, HANS. Im Angesicht des Galgens. Deutung Hitlers und seiner Zeit auf Grund eigener Erlebnisse und Erkenntnisse. Munich/Gräfelfing: Friedrich Alfred Beck, 1953. 479p. Autobiography of the former Reichsminister and Governor General of Poland, written in his Nuremberg cell. Contains some discussion of his own guilt. Documents and an index of names.

2117 FRITZSCHE, HANS. Das Schwert auf der Waage. Hans Fritzsche über Nürnberg. Heidelberg: K. Vowinckel, 1953. 271p. Published in English as The Sword in the Scales. London: Allan Wingate, 1953. 335p. Autobiography of Hans Fritzsche, who was acquitted by the IMT on October 1, 1946. His personal experiences as a defendant at the Nuremberg trial includes his observations on 19 defendants and his impressions of the prosecuting team and German witnesses. Discusses Baldur von Schirach's confession, Albert Speer, and Bormann. Fritzsche supported a trial for war atrocities but he concluded that the Nuremberg trial failed to live up to its aim to correct injustice. The victors sought to establish the guilt of Germany, but would break off a hearing wherever the deeds of the allies were introduced. Contains a facsimile of Fritzsche's certificate of acquittal. Undocumented.

2118 GISEVIUS, HANS BERND. Bis zum bitteren Ende. Zurich: Fritz und Wasmuth, 1946, revised edition, 1960. Published in English as To the Bitter End. Boston: Houghton Mifflin, 1947. 632p. London: Jonathan Cape, 1948. Gisevius was one of the few survivors who planned ways of doing away with Hitler. Deals with several major incidents in the history of the Third Reich and Gestapo politics. The epilogue discusses the national guilt of Germany.

2119 GOEBBELS, JOSEPH [L.P. Lochner, ed.]. The Goebbels Diaries, 1942-1943. New York: Doubleday, 1948. 566p.

2120 GOEBBELS, JOSEPH [Max Fechner, ed]. Wie konnte es geschehen: Auszüge aus den Tagebüchern und Bekenntnissen eines Kriegsverbrechers. 4th edition. Berlin: J.H.W. Dietz, [1946]. 136p. Excerpts from the diaries of Joseph Goebbels, Nazi Propaganda Minister.

2121 GOEBBELS, JOSEPH. Tagebücher 1945. Die lezten Aufzeichnungen. Hamburg: C. Hoffmann and Campe, 1977. Published in English as Final Entries 1945: The Diaries of Joseph Goebbels. New York: Avon, 1979. 453p. Hugh Trevor-Roper (ed.). Covers the period February 27 - April 9, 1945. The book contains an introduction by Hugh Trevor-Roper, a brief essay on the story of the 1945 Goebbels diaries, and an appendix written by Goebbels to Hitler's last will and testament. Scholarly use of this volume is augmented by its chronology and place and name indexes. Editorial footnotes identify scores of people whose names are not easily recognized. 22 photographs, 7 maps.

2122 GÖRING, EMMY. My Life with Goering. London: David Bruce and Watson, 1972.

2123 HAENSEL, CARL. Das Gericht vertagt sich, aus dem Tagebuch eines Verteidigers bei den Nürnberger Prozessen. Hamburg: Classen, 1950. Munich: Limes, 1980. 346p. Diary entries from March to August 1946 of a defense attorney at the Nuremberg IMT trial. Recounts courtroom activities, including attempts to avoid sensationalism. Covers the testimony of Hermann Göring, Rudolf Hess, Joachim von Ribbentrop, Wilhelm Keitel, Ernst Kaltenbrunner, Alfred Rosenberg, Hans Frank, and Alfred Jodl. Treats Hans Frank's diary, discussions with his attorney, and his admission of guilt in participating in the destruction of Jews. Undocumented; 4-page index of names, 5-page subject index, 16-pages of illustrations.

2124 HALDER, FRANZ. Kriegstagebuch. 3 volumes. Stuttgart: W. Kohlhammer, 1962-1964. Volume 1, Vom Polenfeldzug bis zum Ende der Westoffensive (14.8.1939 - 30.6. 1940). 1962. 391p. Volume 2, Von der geplanten Landung in England bis zum Beginn des Ostfeldzuges (1.7.1940 - 21.6.1941). 1963. 503p. Volume 3, Der Rußlandfeldzug bis zum Marsch auf Stalingrad (22.6.1941 - 24.9.1942). 1964. 598p. This work has been translated into Russian. It contains much background material on actions later prosecuted as war crimes, particularly in occupied areas and against Jews. Each volume contains a name index and Volume 3 has a subject index to all three volumes. Volume 1 has a foldout map of the Russian campaign. Volumes 1 and 3 contain organizational charts of the German army. Several appendices to Volume 2 show the military organization of the German army.

2125 HEIBER, HELMUT. „Aus den Akten des Gauleiters Kube," Vierteljahrshefte für Zeitgeschichte 1956 4(1): 67-92. 42 notes.

2126 HEYDRICH, LINA. Leben mit einem Kriegsverbrecher. Pfaffenhofen: Ludwig, 1976. 211p.

2127 HÖSS, RUDOLF [Joel E. Dimsdale, ed.]. "Excerpts from the Autobiography of Rudolf Hoess," in Survivors, Victims, and Perpetrators: Essays on the Nazi Holocaust. Washington: Hemisphere, 1980.

2128 KEITEL, WILHELM. The Memoirs of Field-Marshall Keitel. New York: Stein and Day, 1966. 288p.

2129 KERSTEN, FELIX. Totenkopf und Treue. Heinrich Himmler ohne Uniform. Aus den Tagebuchblättern des finnischen Medizinalrats. Hamburg: Robert Möhlich, 1952. 407p. Published in English as The Memoirs of Felix Kersten. Garden City: Doubleday, 1947; The Kersten Memoirs, 1940-1945. London: Hutchinson, 1956. New York: Macmillan, 1957. Kersten was Himmler's masseur and confidant.

2130 KESSELRING, ALBERT, Soldat bis zum letzten Tag. Bonn: Athenäum, 1953. Published in English as Kesselring: A Soldier's Record. New York: Morrow, 1953. 381p.

2131 KODAMA, YOSHIO. Shibafu wa fumaretemo. Tokyo: Shinyukan Shimbunsha, 1956. 250p. Published in English as Sugamo Diary. [no city given]: Radio Press, 1960. 275p. Diary written from Sugamo Prison from 1946-1948 by a suspect who helped establish the Liberal-Democratic Party in Japan. Discusses aspects of prison life, including adaptation, interaction and activities among prisoners, investigation and questioning, stone breaking labor, and Kodama's eventual release. Undocumented; contains 118 cartoons by the author illustrating daily prison life, 3 photographs.

2132 KODAMA, YOSHIO. Ware yaburetari. Tokyo: Kyoyusha & Tokyo Shuppansha, 1949. 303p. Published in English as I Was Defeated. Tokyo: 1959. 228p. Autobiography written while Kodama was in the Sugamo Prison outside Tokyo from late 1945 to late 1948. Discusses his version of Japanese nationalism and militarism. The author disapproves of Japanese conduct of the war, and places the blame on bureaucrats, militarists, and imperial court politicians. Criticizes American softness on communism.

2133 KRÜGER, KURT. I Was Hitler's Doctor. New York: Biltmore, 1941.

2134 PAPEN, FRANZ VON. Memoir. New York: E.P. Dutton, 1953.

2135 RAEDER, ERICH. Mein Leben. 2 volumes. Tübingen: Fritz Schlichtenmayer, 1956-1957. Published in English as My Life. Annapolis: United States Naval Institute, 1960. 430p.

2136 RIBBENTROP, JOACHIM VON [Annelies von Ribbentrop, ed.]. Zwischen London und Moskau, Erinnerungen und letzte Aufzeichnungen. Leoni am Starnberger See: Druffel, [1953]. 336p. Published in English as The Ribbentrop Memoirs. London: Weidenfeld and Nicolson, 1954.

2137 ROSENBERG, ALFRED. Letzte Aufzeichnungen. Göttingen: Plesse, 1955. 343p. Autobiography of Alfred Rosenberg. Chapter 11, "Abschied - Nürnberg," pp. 305-316, deals with his attitude toward the Nuremberg IMT trial and his continuing protest against the eastern policies of Bormann and Himmler.

2138 ROSENBERG, ALFRED [Serge Lang and Ernst von Schenck, eds.]. Porträt eines Menschheitsverbrechers, nach den hinterlassenen Memoiren des ehemaligen Reichsministers Alfred Rosenberg. St. Gallen: Zollikofer, 1947. 356p. Published in English as Memoirs of Alfred Rosenberg. Chicago: Ziff-Davis, 1949. 328p. Memoirs of Alfred Rosenberg, written primarily to aid in his defense and to justify himself before the world. In criticizing Joseph Goebbels, Heinrich Himmler, Martin Bormann, and

Adolf Hitler, Rosenberg tries to prove that the sickness of the Third Reich was caused by the betrayal of the philosophy of National Socialism. This version of the memoirs covers Rosenberg's youth, the early history of the party, and the foundations of a thousand-year Reich. Concludes with Rosenberg's political testament. This is the first text published which was based on the memoirs of a criminal sentenced to death at Nuremberg. Contains a 4-page Dramatis Personae of important Nazi characters mentioned by Rosenberg, a 6-page chronology from 1918-1946, and a list of abbreviations, no bibliography or index.

2139 SCHACHT, HJALMAR. Abrechnung mit Hitler. Hamburg/Stuttgart: Rowohlt, 1948. 47 oversize pages published in English as Account Settled. London: Weidenfeld & Nicolson, 1949. 327p. Discusses Schacht's opposition to the war, his imprisonment, the Nuremberg IMT trial, and his career after his acquittal.

2140 SCHACHT, HJALMAR. 76 Jahre meines Lebens. Bad Wörishofen: Kindler und Schiermeyer, [1953]. 689p. Published in English as My First Seventy-Six Years. London: Allen Wingate, 1955; and as Confessions of "The Old Wizard," The Autobiography of Hjalmar Horace Greeley Schacht. Cambridge: Riverside Press, 1955. 484p. Boston: Houghton Mifflin, 1956. 484p. Autobiography of the president of the Reichsbank under Adolf Hitler. Discusses his youth, his career in finance, his break with Hitler, his arrest by the Americans, and his arraignment and appearance before the Nuremberg and denazification tribunals. Proceedings by the Württemburg court took place at the end of April 1947 and lasted 20 days. He was sentenced to 8 years in a labor camp. New pro-ceedings opened before the Ludwigsburg Court of Appeals in August 1948 resulted in his acquittal. On September 2, 1948, Schacht was set free. He was subsequently confined for 5 months by the British and finally emerged from the "jungle of German postwar jurisprudence." 10-page index, 22 photographs.

2141 SCHELLENBERG, WALTER [Louis Hagen, ed.]. Memoiren. Cologne: Verlag für Politik und Wissenschaft, 1956. Published in English as The Schellenberg Memoirs. London: A. Deutsch, 1956. 479p. Schellenberg was a young SS officer when he served in the SD. He appeared as a witness at the Nuremberg IMT trial. His own trial began in January 1948 in the Wilhelmstraße Case. He was sentence to 6 years, running from June 1945. Discusses his post-imprisonment career and the circumstances surrounding the publication of his memoirs.

2142 SCHIRACH, BALDUR VON. Ich glaubte an Hitler. Hamburg: 1967.

2143 SCHIRACH, HENRIETTE VON. Der Preis der Herrlichkeit. Wiesbaden: Limes, 1956. 266p. Published in English as The Price of Glory. London: Frederick Muller, 1960. Reminiscences of the wife of Baldur Von Schirach.

2144 SPEER, ALBERT. Erinnerungen. Frankfurt am Main: Ullstein, 1969. 608p. 66p. of notes, index. Published in English as Inside the Third Reich. New York: Macmillan, 1970. 596p. 43p. of notes, index. Excellent background study of the Nazi state. Scores of references to the Nuremberg IMT trial.

2145 SPEER, ALBERT. Spandauer Tagebücher. Berlin: Propyläen, 1975. 671p. Published in English as Spandau: The Secret Diaries. New York: Macmillan, 1976. 468p. Year-by-year account of Speer's

20 years in prison. Much on war crimes and other war criminals.

2146 STEINBAUER, GUSTAV. Ich war Verteidiger in Nürnberg. Ein Dokumentenbeitrag zum Kampf um Österreich. Klagenfurt: Eduard Kaiser, 1950. 388p. The first part of the book deals with the Nuremberg IMT in general, but pp. 65-end treat in particular the case of Arthur Seyss-Inquart.

2147 SZILARD, LEO. "My Trial as a War Criminal," University of Chicago Law Review 1949 17(1): 79-86. Undocumented. Excerpt in Common Cause 1950 3(January): 294-297.

2148 UNITED STATES. NATIONAL ARCHIVES AND RECORDS SERVICE. War Diaries and Correspondence of General Jodl. Microfilm of records described in NARS Preliminary Inventory 21. T989. 2 rolls.

2149 WEIZSÄCKER, ERNST HEINRICH VON. Erinnerungen. Munich: Paul List, 1950. 391p. Published in English as Memoirs of Ernst von Weizsäcker. Chicago: Henry Regnery, 1951. 322p. London: Gollancz, 1951. 322p. Contains some discussion of his appearance at the Nuremberg IMT trial as a witness for Admiral Raeder and ends in 1948 with his own arrest for war crimes.

2150 WIESENTHAL, SIMON. "The Murderers Among Us," Saturday Evening Post 1967 240(4): 42-62; 240(5): 38-53.

2151 WIESENTHAL, SIMON. The Murderers among Us, the Simon Wiesenthal Memoirs. New York: McGraw-Hill, 1967. 340p. London: Heinemann, 1967. 312p. Published in German as Doch die Mörder leben. Munich: Droesner, 1967. Memoirs of Nazi hunter Simon Wiesenthal. Wiesenthal's distinction between war crimes and SS crimes is central to his mission. Discusses his participation in the trial of Adolf Eichmann, his work for the War Crimes Commission in Linz, and his views on denazification and neo-nazism. Includes a chapter on Martin Bormann, whom the author considers the only major war criminal still unaccounted for. Contains an authorization of Wiesenthal's confidential mission granted by the OSS in Austria and copies of other correspondence with U.S. agencies. 4-page glossary.

3. Correspondence, Other Writings, Speeches

2152 BORMANN, MARTIN [Hugh R. Trevor-Roper, ed.]. The Bormann Letters: The private Correspondence between Martin Bormann and his Wife from January 1943 to April 1945. London: Weidenfeld & Nicolson, 1954.

2153 DELFOSSE, ALPHONSE. "Treatment of War Criminals in the Postwar Period," News from Belgium 1943 3(December 11): 396-398. Speech broadcast on October 9, 1943.

2154 DESMOND, CHARLES S., PAUL A. FREUND, POTTER STEWART, and LORD SHAWCROSS. Mr. Justice Jackson: Four Lectures in his Honor. New York/London: Columbia University Press, 1969. 136p. The lecture by Lord Shawcross, "Robert H. Jackson's Contribution's during the Nuremberg Trial," pp. 87-136, sketches the historical background to the trial. The British government favored executive action rather than trials for war crimes. Discusses Jackson's appointment as Chief Counsel for the United States and cites 2 passages from Jackson's initial report to the President in June 1945. Discusses differences in philosophy at the London conference between the Americans and Russians, the indictment, and the legal basis of the proceedings. Based on primary and secondary sources; 46 notes.

2155 HALL, THOMAS VAN. "The Legal Speaking of Robert H. Jackson at the Nuremberg Trial of Major War Criminals," Ph.D. dissertation, Bowling Green State University, 1977. 201p. Abstracted in Dissertation Abstracts International 1978 38(11): 6397-A.

2156 HESS, ILSE. England-Nürnberg-Spandau, ein Schicksal in Briefen. Leoni am Starnberger See: Druffel, 1952. 175p. Published in English as Prisoner of Peace. London: Britons, 1954. 151p. Collection of letters from 1947 and 1951 between Rudolf Hess and his wife Ilse and others. 13-page foreword by Ilse Hess summarizes the flight of Hess to Scotland in 1941. Undocumented; 3 photographs.

2157 HESS, ILSE. Gefangener des Friedens, neue Briefe aus Spandau. Leoni am Starnberger See: Druffel, 1955. 195p. Collection of letters written from Spandau prison between 1947 and 1953 by Rudolf Hess. Sequel to letters previously published under the title England-Nürnberg-Spandau. Also contains an epilog by the publishers on the Hess case before the Nuremberg IMT. Facsimile of his letter of departure, written on November 4, 1940. Undocumented; 6 photographs.

2158 HITLER, ADOLF [Erhard Klöß, ed.]. Reden des Führers. Politik und Propaganda Adolf Hitlers, 1922-1945. Munich: Deutscher Taschenbuch, 1967. 335p. Contains a 17-page introduction to Hitler's speeches as well as a number of speeches that relate to German excesses and attitudes toward Jews and other "undesirables" during the years before and during World War II. 5-page bibliography, 4-page index.

2159 ROSENBERG, ALFRED. Der deutsche Ordensstaat. Ein neuer Abschnitt in der Entwicklung des nationalsozialistischen Staatsgedankens. Munich: Zentralverlag der N.S.D.A.P., 1934. 20p. Alfred Rosenberg pamphlet published by the National Socialist party. No. 6 in the series Hier spricht das neue Deutschland! Propaganda publication issued for distribution among the German populace in the mid-1930s. Discusses the German state and party aspirations of the NSDAP. Presents useful information background to Nazi excesses during the following 11 years. Undocumented.

2160 ROSENBERG, ALFRED. Race and Race History, and other Essays by Alfred Rosenberg. New York: Harper & Row, 1970. 204p. Selections from 5 of Rosenberg's works. Emphasizes his influence on the distortion of German thought. 8-page bibliography.

2161 ROSENBERG, ALFRED. Schriften und Reden. Munich: Hoheneichen, 1943. Published notes of Alfred Rosenberg prefaced by a 107-page introduction in Volume 1 dealing with his background, ideology, publications, and career. Volume 1, Schriften aus den Jahren 1917-1921 (624p.), contains the first notebooks (1917-1919), which include essays on Jews, Schopenhauer, philosophy and art, and religious instruction. 5 illustrations include a sketch by Rosenberg and a reproduction of one page of his handwritten manuscript. Includes bibliographical references.

B. SPECIAL STUDIES

2162 ABEL, THEODORE. "Is a Psychiatric Interpretation of the German Enigma Necessary?" American Sociological Review 1945 10(4): 457-464. 16 notes.

2163 ABRAHAMS, GERALD. Day of Reckoning. London: W.H. Allen, [1943]. 64p. A discussion of the necessity for and the machinery of punishing German war criminals.

2164 AINSZTEIN, REUBEN. "The Collector (Pieter Menten and Nazi Complicity) (Part 1)," New Statesman 1981 101(2604): 6-8. 2 photographs.

2165 ALEKSEEV, NIKOLAĬ SERGEEVICH. "Nesostoiatel'nost' Popytok Reabilitatsii Reabilitatskikh Voennykh Prestupnikov [The Failure of the Attempt to Rehabilitate Nazi War Criminals]," Sovetskoe Gosudarstvo i Pravo 1976 (1): 95-102. Exposes the newest attempts, especially those by West German lawyer G. Artzt, to exonerate those responsible for crimes committed against humanity during the Nazi era, in particular by narrowing the responsibility for crimes committed in the course of World War II and clearing the Wehrmacht of responsibility. In undertaking such an attempt, Artzt distinguishes between war crimes and Nazi crimes. He attempts to undermine the principles underlying the Nuremberg IMT trial, and deliberately identifies war crimes with military crimes so as to place war crimes beyond the Charter of the Nuremberg IMT. Crimes had been planned and committed not only at the theater of war, but in Germany itself, and in some cases against Germans. Such crimes are beyond the provisions of military law, Artzt contends, but they are justly provided for in the Charter of the Nuremberg IMT. 9 notes.

2166 ALEKSEEV, NIKOLAĬ SERGEEVICH. "Protiv 'Teorii,' Reabilitiruiushchikh Natsistskikh Prestupnikov [Against the 'theory' of Rehabilitating Nazi Criminals]," Sovetskoe Gosudarstvo i Pravo 1969 (8): 30-39. Discusses the international conference on questions relating to the prosecution of German war criminals held in Moscow on March 25-29, 1969. Arguments are offered in favor of calling off the hunt for war criminals on the grounds that the procedures of the Nuremberg IMT trial violated international law and that a statute of limitations ought to be observed. Moscow was particularly concerned because the Bonn statute under which war criminals were subject to prosecution was to expire on December 31, 1969. Based on Russian and German sources; 24 notes.

2167 ALEXANDER, FRANZ, and HUGO STAUB. „Der Verbrecher und seine Richter," in Psychoanalyse und Justiz. Frankfurt: Fischer, 1971.

2168 ALEXANDROV, G.N., and M.J. RAGINSKY (comps.). Internationale Konferenz zu Fragen der Verfolgung von Nazi- und Kriegsverbrechen: Moskau, 25. - 28. März 1969. Moscow: APN-Verlag, 1969.

2169 ALLEN, CHARLES R. Nazi War Criminals Living Among Us. New York: Jewish Currents, 1963. 42p. Originally published in Jewish Currents 1963 (January): 312; (February): 3-16; (March): 3-16. "Among us" here means in the United States and Canada.

2170 AMERICAN HISTORICAL ASSOCIATION. What Shall Be Done with War Criminals. GI Roundtable, EM11. Washington: War Department, 1944.

2171 ARCHIV, PETER (ed.). Spiegelbild einer Verschwörung. Die Kaltenbrunner-Berichte an Bormann und Hitler über das Attentat vom 20. Juli 1944. Stuttgart: Seewald, 1961.

2172 ARONÉANU, EUGÈNE. "Le Juge Jackson et la justice pénal internationale," Revue de Droit International de Sciences Diplomatiques et Politiques 1954 32(4): 361-372.

2173 ARZINGER, R. Rehabilitierung der faschistischen Kriegsverbrecher, eine Gefahr für den Frieden in Europa. Berlin: Kongreß, 1954.

2174 ASSMANN, KURT. "Der deutsche U-Bootskrieg und die Nürnberger Rechtsprechung," Marine-Rundschau 1953 50(1): 2-8. Biography of Dönitz.

2175 ASSMANN, KURT. "Großadmiral Dr. h.c. Raeder und der Zweite Weltkrieg," Marine-Rundschau 1961 58(1): 3-17.

2176 ASSMANN, KURT. "Hitler and the German Officer Corps," Proceedings of the United States Naval Academy 1956 82(639): 509-520. On Nuremberg defendants. Assmann was a retired German admiral. 11 notes.

2177 AZIZ, PHILIPPE, and DOMINIQUE FRETARD. Les Criminels de guerre. [Paris]: Denoël, 1974. 369p. Journalist Aziz argues that Nazis are still at large. In this volume he deals systematically with the "brigade of vengeance," Nuremberg (the hour of châtiment), the continuing search for Bormann, and various neo-nazis. Part 2 is a 153-page encyclopedia of war criminals and their collaborators. Contains a 3-page list of documents consulted and an 11-page bibliography.

2178 BAER, MARCEL DE. "No Peace for War Criminals," News from Belgium and the Belgian Congo 1944 4(February 19): 53-56. Discusses legal bases for war crimes. International agreements must be incorporated into the provisions of municipal law to make them effective, legal instruments. Concludes that it would be legal to punish Hitler, since war is a "continuous offense" that would continue after the enactment of the law.

2179 BAER, MARCEL DE. "The Attitude of Neutral Countries toward War Criminals," Message, Belgian Review 1943 25(November): 7-11.

2180 BAER, MARCEL DE. "The Treatment of War Criminals: A Lesson from the Past," Message, Belgian Review 1942 13(November): 18-22.

2181 BAER, MARCEL DE. "The Treatment of War Criminals: Suggestions for the Future," Message, Belgian Review 1942 14(December): 10-13.

2182 "Bericht aus der Forschung. Die Vernehmung von Generalfeldmarschall Keitel durch die Sowjets," Wehrwissenschaftliche Rundschau 1961 11(11): 651-662. This translation includes the original Russian title and publication information.

2183 "Bericht aus der Forschung. Die Vernehmung von Generaloberst Jodl durch die Sowjets," Wehrwissenschaftliche Rundschau 1961

11(9): 534-542. This translation includes the original Russian title and publication information.

2184 BERNADOTTE [OF WISBORG], FOLKE. The Curtain Falls. New York: A.A. Knopf, 1945. 154p. Deals with Count Bernadotte's negotiations with Himmler and Schellenberg to end the war and obtain the release of prisoners.

2185 BEYER, STANLEY J. "German War Criminals," New Republic 1950 123(20): 4. A letter on the pending release from prison of Carl Krauch and Walther Dürfeld.

2186 BOLLMUS, REINHARD. Das Amt Rosenberg und seine Gegner. Studien zum Machtkampf im nationalsozialistischen Herrschaftssystem. Stuttgart: Deutsche Verlags-Anstalt, 1970. 360p. Analyzes Rosenberg's basic ideology through his work Myth of the Twentieth Century. This study examines the relationship between the National Socialist Combat League for Culture and the NSDAP, the regulations pertaining to German theater groups, and Rosenberg's appointment in 1934 to supervise all spiritual and secular education and training for the National Socialist party. Describes the struggle for political power between Rosenberg, Joseph Goebbels, and Robert Ley, Rosenberg's influence on public cultural affairs, his stance against the churches, and his role in the formation of National Socialist occupational policy. Appendix I contains budget and personnel statistics of Rosenberg's command from 1937-1943. 16-page bibliography, 3-page list of abbreviations, and a 7-page index of names.

2187 BOOZER, JACK S. "Children of Hippocrates: Doctors in Nazi Germany," Annals of the American Academy of Political and Social Science 1980 450 (July): 83-97. One of the unexplored aspects of the years 1933-1945 is the conduct of doctors. Many of them proposed, carried out, and cooperated with medical experiments without the consent of subjects and with little promise of any contribution to medical science. Many also participated in research and other medical activities, such as euthanasia and mass sterilization, whose purposes had nothing to do with medical knowledge that would eventually save or improve life. A brief survey of what the Medical case and the Auschwitz trial revealed about the conduct of the doctors raises questions about the effectiveness of the Hippocratic oath against the power of the state. 46 notes.

2188 BRAILSFORD, HENRY N. "What to do with Germany (Part III): The Problem of the War Criminals," New Republic 1944 111(4): 100-101.

2189 Braunbuch. Kriegs- und Nazi Verbrecher in der Bundesrepublik. Berlin(GDR): Archivverwaltung der DDR, 1965.

2190 CARTON DE WIART, H. "Grands Criminels de guerre," Revue de Droit International de Sciences Diplomatiques et Politiques 1946 24(1): 41-43.

2191 CECIL, ROBERT. The Myth of the Master Race: Alfred Rosenberg and Nazi Ideology. New York: Dodd Mead, 1972. 266p. London: B.T. Batsford, 1972. Rosenberg supervised the ideological and intellectual indoctrination and education of the NSDAP after 1934. In 1941 he became head of the Ministry of Eastern Occupied Territories. Describes his Estonian background, his life in Russia, and his role in the birth of the NSDAP, and discusses the Munich Putsch, Germanic ideology, and the Jewish world conspiracy. Rosenberg's religious outlook is analyzed in a summary of his major work, Mythus (1930), which is as much an attack on Christian churches as it is on Jewry. Deals with Rosenberg's foreign policy, the struggle with England, and his views on education and elitism. Concludes with his trial in Nuremberg. Appendix contains a review of Rosenberg's posthumously published memoir. 6p. of notes, 8-page bibliography, 19 page index, and 18 photographs.

2192 COMMISSION ON THE TRIAL AND PUNISHMENT OF WAR CRIMINALS. "The Case against War Criminals [Conclusions]," Free World 1944 7(2): 184-190. Topics discussed include the need for justice, war crimes, heads of state as war criminals, an international court, and the surrender of war criminals.

2193 CONSTANTINOPLE, DEMETRIOS S. (ed.). "Quelques Aspects de la jurisprudence concernant les criminels de guerre. L'Exception des ordres reçus et autres moyens de défense similaires," C. Th. Eustathaides and C.N. Fragistas (eds.). Festschrift für R. Laun. Bonn: Schimmelbusch, 1957.

2194 COWLES, WILLARD B. "High Government Officials as War Criminals," American Society of International Law, Proceedings 1945 39: 54-68. Argues that there is a well-established basis in customary law for punishing civilian officials for their responsibility in war crimes. 70 notes.

2195 DEAN, GORDON. "Mr. Justice Jackson: His Contribution at Nuremberg," American Bar Association Journal 1955 41(10): 912-915. Undocumented.

2196 DEAN, VERA M., and ONA K.D. RINGWOOD. "What should be done with War Criminals?" Foreign Policy Reports 1943 18(22): 296. 5 notes.

2197 DIMSDALE, JOEL E. (ed.). Survivors, Victims, and Perpetrators: Essays on the Nazi Holocaust. Washington: Hemisphere Publishers, 1980. 474p. A 16-chapter anthology, with Chapter 15, "Personality Organization and Psychological Functioning of the Nuremberg War Criminals: The Rorschach Data," pp. 359-403, done by the editor.

2198 FAIRMAN, CHARLES. "Associate Justices of the Supreme Court," [Robert H. Jackson: 1892-1954] Columbia Law Review 1955 55(4): 445-487. 185 notes.

2199 FARNSWORTH, CLYDE. "A Sleuth with 6 million Clients," New York Times Magazine 1964 (February 2): 11, 45-47. Condensed in Jewish Digest 1965 (May): 5-10. On Simon Wiesenthal of the Jewish Documentation Center in Vienna.

2200 "Fat, Satisfied, Vulgar," Newsweek 1945 25(21): 54, 56. On Göring.

2201 GERECKE, HENRY F. "I Walked to the Gallows with the Nazi Chiefs," Saturday Evening Post 1951 224(9): 17-19. The chaplain at the Nuremberg prison tells of the repentance of some of the IMT defendants before they were executed. 8 photographs.

2202 GIESING, E. "Preliminary Interrogation Report (PIR) 4 June 1945, and Hitler as seen by his doctors, Consolidated Interrogation Report (CIR) 15 October 1945," Washington: NARS, Modern Military Records Division, 1945.

2203 GILBERT, GUSTAVE M. "Hermann Goering: Amiable Psychopath," Journal of Abnormal and Social Psychology 1948 43(April): 211-229.

2204 GILBERT, GUSTAVE M. The Psychology of Dictatorship: Based on an Examination of the Leaders of Nazi Germany. New York: Ronald Press, 1950. An elaboration on the conclusions and results described in Gilbert's Nuremberg Diary.

2205 GLASER, STEFAN. "La Convention de Genève et les criminels de guerre," Revue de Droit Pénal et de Criminologie 1952 32(February): 517-522.

2206 GLUECK, SHELDON. "Justice for War Criminals," American Mercury 1945 60(255): 274-280.

2207 GLUECK, SHELDON. What shall be done with War Criminals? Washington: GPO, 1944.

2208 GRAY, LESLIE B. "Handling the War Criminal," Nevada State Bar Journal 1946 11(1): 8-14.

2209 HARRIS, HENRY W. Problems of the Peace. Cambridge: University Press, 1944. 116p. Pages 87-95 deal with war criminals.

2210 HARROWER, MOLLY. "Rorschach Records of the Nazi War Criminals: An Experimental Study after Thirty Years," Journal of Personality Assessment 1976 40(4): 341-351. Rorschach records of 17 Nazis made in 1946 are subjected to an experimental procedure in which 8 Nazi records and 8 control records are evaluated by 10 Rorschach experts.

2211 HARROWER, MOLLY. "Were Hitler's Henchmen Mad?" Psychology Today 1976 10(2): 76-80. 8 photographs. Concludes that the defendants were similar to any average group of American citizens.

2212 HASSELBACH, HANS KARL VON. Hitler as seen by his Doctors. 01-CIR-2,15 October. 1945, Washington: NARS, Modern Military Records Division, 1945. See Entry 2225.

2213 HESTON, LEONARD L., and RENATE HESTON. The Medical Casebook of Adolf Hitler. New York: Stein and Day, 1980. 184p. A book that looks like a hospital medical chart. Hitler had major illnesses involving the gastrointestinal, nervous, and circulatory systems and was intermittently incapacitated by organic brain disease. Albert Speer, in the Introduction, agrees that the writers have correctly recognized changes in Hitler's behavior that were caused most likely by his use of various amphetamines. Amphetamine poisoning probably set in sometime in 1942, even though Hitler was taking these drugs as early as 1936. The book provides a medical chronology of Hitler's life, a systematic analysis of his various illnesses, and has an appendix which lists his physical examinations from 1923-1945, his laboratory and electrocardiographic examinations from 1935-1945, and his medical treatments from 1935-1945. 185 notes, 5-page bibliography, 3 appendices, 8-page index, 6 illustrations.

2214 JEROME, VICTOR JEREMY. "What of the War Criminals," Political Affairs 1945 24(2): 130-144. Published later as Chapter 5, "The Sword of Justice," pp. 73-95, of The Treatment of Defeated Germany. New York: New Century, 1945. 107p.

2215 KELLEY, DOUGLAS M. Twenty-Two Cells in Nuremberg: A Psychiatrist Examines the Nazi Criminals. New York: Greenberg, 1947. 245p.

2216 KEMPNER, ROBERT M.W. "Cross-Examining War Criminals," Yad Vashem Studies 1963 5: 43-68. Cross-examination of Göring, Heinrich Lammers, Edmund Veesenmayer, and Ernst Wilhelm Bohle. Also done in Hebrew.

2217 KESSEL, JOSEPH. Les Mains du miracle. Paris: Gallimard, 1960. 309p. Published in English as The Man with the Miraculous Hands. New York: Farrar, Straus & Cudahy, 1961. 235p. Published in German as Medizinalrat Kersten. Der Mann mit den magischen Händen. Munich: Nymphenburger, 1961.

2218 KLESSMANN, CRISTOPH. "Der Generalgouverneur Hans Frank," Vierteljahrshefte für Zeitgeschichte 1971 19(3): 245-260. 79 notes.

2219 KURLAND, PHILIP B. "Robert H. Jackson," in Volume 4 of Leon Friedman and Fred L. Israel (eds.). The Justices of the Supreme Court, 1789-1969: Their Lives and Major Opinions. 4 volumes. New York: Chelsea House, in Association with Bowker, 1969.

2220 LAQUEUR, WALTER. Die deutsche Jugendbewegung. Cologne: Wissenschaft und Politik, 1962. 279p.

2221 LEMKIN, RAPHAEL. "The Legal Case Against Hitler," Nation 1945 160(8): 205-207. 1 cartoon.

2222 LIDDELL HART, BASIL H. The German Generals Talk. New York: William Morrow, 1948. 308p.

2223 "Living Symbols," Newsweek 1965 66 (19): 53. Deals with Spandau prisoners.

2224 Livre brun. Les Criminels de guerre nazis en Allemagne occidentale. Dresden: R.D.A., [no date given].

2225 LOEHLEIN, W. Hitler as seen by his Doctors. 01/CIR/4, 29 November 1945, Annex III. Washington: NARS, Modern Military Records Division, 1945. See Entry 2212.

2226 LONDON INTERNATIONAL ASSEMBLY. The Punishment of War Criminals, Recommendations . . . . [no publisher given], [1944]. 32p.

2227 MAIER, K. Ist Schacht ein Verbrecher? Reutlingen: Die Zukunft, 1948. 47p.

2228 MANN, PEGGY. "The Dentist and the Bishop: 'I Knew the Man Was a Satan . . . ,'" Present Tense 1974 1(4): 29-35. Charles H. Kremer's efforts to expose Rumanian war criminal Bishop Valerian Trifa's role in the murder of Jews during World War II.

2229 MARTIENSSEN, ANTHONY K. Hitler and His Admirals. London: Secker and Warburg, 1948. New York: Dutton, 1949. 275p. This is an account of Hitler's relation to his admirals and the development of Nazi naval policy, based largely on captured German Naval Archives found at Schloß Tambach.

2230 MIALE, FLORENCE R., and MICHAEL SELZER. The Nuremberg Mind: The Psychology of Nazi Leaders. New York: Quadrangle/New York Times, 1975. 302p. One of the authors was a prison psychologist at the Nuremberg IMT trial. Presents the Rorschach records and interpretations of them for 16 of the defendants tried at Nuremberg. Records of the other six defendants, Karl Dönitz, Wilhelm Frick, Alfred Jodl, Robert Ley, Erich Raeder, and Julius Streicher were unavailable. Materials are intended as illustrative rather than a thorough integration of psychological data. Appendix A contains the Rorschach record of Adolf Eichmann. 4-page bibliography, 32 photographs of defendants.

2231 MUELLER, GENE A. "Wilhelm Keitel: Chief of the Oberkommando der Wehrmacht, 1938-1945," Ph.D. dissertation, University of Idaho, 1973. 248p. Abstracted in Dissertation Abstracts International 1973 34(2): 1217-A.

2232 MUNRO, HECTOR A. "The United States and War Criminals," Law Journal 1945 95(4149): 231-233.

2233 MUNRO, HECTOR A. "War Criminals and International Justice," Law Journal 1945 95(4142): 173-174.

2234 MUNRO, HECTOR A. "War Criminals and the Neutrals," Fortnightly Law Journal 1944 14(2): 24-27. 1 note.

2235 MUNRO, HECTOR A. "War Criminals and the Neutrals: The Position in International Law," New Zealand Law Journal 1944 20(3): 30-31; (4): 43-45. 1 note.

2236 MUSZKAT, MARIAN. "New Trends in 'Rehabilitating' Nazi War Criminals," Yad Vashem Bulletin 1965 16: 26-33.

2237 "Navy Department Participation in the Prosecution of War Criminals," Journal of Criminal Law and Criminology 1945 36(1): 39-40.

2238 OTTOLENGHI, GIACOMO. "Le Problème des criminels de guerre," Revue de Droit International de Sciences Diplomatiques et Politiques 1946 24(1): 1-16.

2239 POLLOCK, JAMES K. "Nazi War Criminals," Current History 1944 6(32): 304-310. Undocumented.

2240 POLYANSKY, N.N. "The Berlin Conference and the War Criminals," Information Bulletin 1945 5(90): 1-2.

2241 PRITT, DENIS N. "The Trial of War Criminals," Political Quarterly 1945 16(3): 195-204. Undocumented.

2242 PRITT, DENIS N. War Criminals. London: Labour Monthly, [no date given]. 32p. Discusses the history of war criminals and the "farcical" Leipzig trials. Short essays on the Declaration of St. James, the U.N. War Crimes Commission, and the Moscow declaration. Deals with legal questions concerning whether war itself is a crime as well as acts committed against the criminal's own nationals. Excerpts from the above appeared in Labour Monthly 1944 26(11): 332-338.

2243 REES, JOHN R. (ed.). *The Case of Rudolf Hess, a Problem in Diagnosis and Forensic Psychiatry by the Following Physicians in the Services who have been Concerned with him from 1941 to 1945. Henry V. Dicks (and others)*. London: Heinemann, 1947. 224p. New York: Norton, 1948. 224p.

2244 *Report on the International Juridical Status of Individuals as "War Criminals."* Washington: [no publisher given], 1945.

2245 SABBETHAI, K. [pseudonym]. "A Tzaddik in Nuremberg," *Jewish Frontier* 1946 13(10): 61-66. Deals with a staff member of the American prosecution staff in Nuremberg whose main task was to prepare the case concerning crimes against Jews.

2246 SCHÄTZEL, WALTER. "Das Recht des Kriegsverbrechers auf rechtliches Gehör," in *Festschrift für Wilhelm Sauer*. Berlin: W. de Gruyter, 1949.

2247 SCHMIDT, MATHIAS. *Albert Speer. Das Ende eines Mythos. Speers wahre Rolle im Dritten Reich*. Bern: Scherz, 1982. 301p. Deals with Speer's public career, his attitude toward the July 20, 1944, assassination attempt, his role in the Dönitz government, the Nuremberg IMT trial, his imprisonment at Spandau, and his role in the "final solution." Concludes that Speer was a shrewd, leading figure in the Third Reich. 37p. of notes, 12-page bibliography, index.

2248 SEABURY, PAUL. "Ribbentrop and the German Foreign Office," *Political Science Quarterly* 1951 66(4): 532-555. 31 notes.

2249 SELZER, MICHAEL. "On Nazis and Normality," *Psychohistory Review* 1977 5(4): 34-36. Questions the methodology and the conclusions of Molly Harrower in "Were Hitler's Henchmen Mad?" Concludes that war criminals were normal individuals. Based on secondary sources; 11 notes.

2250 SINCLAIR, UPTON. "What Shall be Done with Hitler?" *Free World* 1944 7(February): 121-124.

2251 STRUM, HARVEY. "Henry Stimson and the Nuremberg War Crimes Trials," *Mid-America* 1983 65(1): 3-13.

2252 SULLIVAN, JAMES D. "Jurisdiction of Commission Established to Try War Criminals," *Notre Dame Lawyer* 1946 21(3): 237-239. Deals with the Yamashita appeal, *Yamashita v. Styer, Commanding General, U.S. Army Forces, Western Pacific*. 66 Sup. Ct. 340, February 4, 1946.

2253 SUND, HARALD. "Les criminels de guerre en Norvège et la répression de leurs délits," *Revue de Droit Pénal et de Criminologie* 1947 27(May): 705-719.

2254 "Surrender and Trial of War Criminals: Committee Passes United Kingdom Resolution," *United Nations Weekly Bulletin* 3(8): 567-570.

2255 "These are the Top Nazi Criminals - Shall they go Free?" *Congress Weekly, A Review of Jewish Interests* 1954 21(April 5): 4-5. The reference is to Rudolf Hess, Walther Funk, Baldur von Schirach, Albert Speer, and Constantin von Neurath.

2256 THOMAS, W. HUGH. *The Murder of Rudolf Hess*. New York: Harper & Row, 1979. 224p. An account of the mission of Hess to

England on May 10, 1941, in search of peace, with a map of the route of his plane. Speculates on his mental condition during the Nuremberg trial and on his alleged murder. Questions whether the defendant was really Hess. Describes conditions at Spandau and defense attorney Alfred Seidl's attempts to appeal the conviction of Hess. 15 photographs, 3-page bibliography, 8-page index.

2257 TRAININ, ARON NAUMOVICH. "Judging the War Criminals," New Masses 1944 52(11): 3-6; 52(12): 10-12. Discusses the responsibility of Hitler's followers for crimes against international law and morality.

2258 TREVOR-ROPER, HUGH R. "Martin Bormann," Der Monat 1954 6(68): 168-176. 21 notes.

2259 UNITED NATIONS WAR CRIMES COMMISSION. Charges by the European and the United States Governments against German, Italian and Japanese War Criminals. 41 volumes. London: HMSO, 1944-1947.

2260 UNITED STATES. CONGRESS. HOUSE OF REPRESENTATIVES. COMMITTEE ON THE JUDICIARY. Alleged Nazi War Criminals, Hearings before the Subcommittee on Immigration, Citizenship, and International Law. 95th Congress, 2nd Session. 2 volumes. Part 1 (August 3, 1977), Serial Number 9539, 233p., and Part 2 (July 1921, 1978), Serial Number 39, 210p. U.S. Government Documents call number Y4.J89/1:9539. Hearings to review the admission into the United States of alleged German war criminals. Reviews various Executive Branch investigations of war criminals, including the Government Accounting Office report of May 15, 1970, entitled "Widespread Conspiracy to obstruct Probes of alleged Nazi War Criminals not supported by Evidence: Controversy may continue." Appendices include correspondence and various documents on the exclusion of Nazis from the United States.

2261 UNITED STATES. DEPARTMENT OF STATE. "Execution of Death Sentences of German War Criminals Withheld," Department of State Bulletin 1951 24(610): 412. March 12, 1951. The U.S. Supreme Courts asked the State Department to delay the execution of 7 German war criminals.

2262 VAMBERY, RUSTEM. "Criminals and War Crimes," Nation 1945 160 (20): 567-568.

2263 WARREN, EARL. "John J. Parker," New York University Law Review 1958 33(5: 649-651.

2264 WATKINS, H.E. "A Great Judge and a Great American: Chief Judge John J. Parker, 1885-1958," American Bar Association Journal 1958 44(5): 448-449. Undocumented.

2265 "What to do with Japan?" Free World 1944 7(3): 232-245. Round table. participants were Burnet Hershey, S.R. Chow, John Goette, Randall Gould, Garrett Graham, W.L. Holland, Andre Guibault, and George Woodhead. Discusses various proposals for punishing Japanese war criminals without destroying Japan and the Japanese people. Free World contains scores of articles on this subject.

2266 "Why Blush for the Bill of Rights?" Saturday Evening Post 1944 217(23): 108. A brief comparison of the Russian and Anglo-American conceptions of what a war criminal is.

2267 WIENER, JAN G. The Assassination of Heydrich. New York: Grossman, 1969. 177p. Deals with the German occupation of Czechoslovakia, Czech resistance, and Heydrich's assassination and reprisals. Based on recollections of participants, miscellaneous documents, and German reports. 32 photographs.

2268 WOLD, TERJE. "War Criminals, Quislings, and their Accomplices," News of Norway 1944 (September 29): 145-147.

2269 YOUNG, GEORGE. "War Criminals," Contemporary Review 1942 162(August): 77-81.

2270 ZANDER, JENS-PETER. Das Verbrechen im Kriege, ein Völkerrechtlicher Begriff. Ein Beitrag zur Problematik des Kriegsverbrechens. Würzburg: 1969.

C. PURSUIT, LOCATION, APPREHENSION

2271 "A New Hunt for Old Nazis," Newsweek 1980 96(1): 84. A brief account of current Nazi trackers.

2272 ALLEN, CHARLES R. "Our Government 'Replies' to Charges. State Department and Immigration Service Evade Issue of Nazi War Criminals Among Us," Jewish Currents 1963 (May): 36-38.

2273 ANDERSON, JACK. "Nazi War Criminals in South America," Parade 1960 (November 13): 6-9.

2274 "Belated Push to deport former Nazis: More than three Decades after World War II, the U.S. is stepping up its Pursuit of hundreds accused of Torture and Mass Murder," U.S. News and World Report 1980 88(33): 11.

2275 BENAMI, SHADDAI. "Dead Nazis Who Are Still Alive. Israel's Mystery Man Hunts them in the Foreign Legion," Jewish Digest 1962 (December): 78-80.

2276 BLIGH, DAVID BEN-MORDECHAY. "They Hunt Nazis," Congress Weekly, A Review of Jewish Interests 1957 (May 13): 11-12. Discusses the activities of an all-Jewish platoon of "search police" founded by Dr. Lidya Torabin-Ofratti.

2277 BLUM, HOWARD. Wanted! The Search for Nazis in America. New York: Quadrangle/New York Times, 1977. 256p. Story of Sergeant Tony DeVito's search for 59 Nazi war criminals living in the United States. Describes his work for the immigration service, and attempts to uncover confirming evidence and connections to war criminals within the United States. Undocumented.

2278 BRAND, EMANUEL. "Nazis in the Service of Nasserism," Yad Vashem Bulletin 1967 (21): 18-21.

2279 BROCKDORFF, WERNER. Flucht vor Nürnberg. Pläne und Organisation der Fluchtwege der NS-Prominenz im „Römischen Weg." Munich/Wels: Weisermühl, 1969. 286p.

2280 CERMAK, JOHN F., JR. "The Effect of Government Knowledge on Denaturalization Proceedings: A Return to illegal Procurement?" American University Law Review 1981 30(2): 519-546. 208 notes.

2281 COHEN, ROBERT A. "United States Exclusion and Deportations of Nazi War Criminals: The Act of October 20, 1978," New York

University Journal of International Law and Politics 1980 13(1): 101-133. Discusses the workability and constitutionality of recent changes in the Immigration and Nationality Act of 1952, which was amended in 1978. The law was designed to exclude and deport former Nazi war criminals.

2282 "Denaturalization of Nazi War Criminals: Is there sufficient Justice for those who would not dispense Justice?" *Maryland Law Review* 1981 40(1): 39-89. Fedorenko v. United States, 101 Supreme Court 737 (1981). Immigration and Nationality Act, 8 U.S.C. 1451. 249 notes.

2283 EDELMAN, MAURICE. "Will the War Criminals Escape?" *New Republic* 1945 112(8): 259-260.

2284 "Ex-Nazis in Egypt," *National Jewish Monthly* 1963 (May): 14, 49.5

2285 FUZ, G.C. "Justice Denied: Shielding Nazi Murderers of Postal Employees in Danzig," *Nation* 1967 205(October 23): 386.

2286 HAUSNER, GIDEON. "Nazi War Criminals in Hiding in Arab States," *The Records of the General Assembly of the United Nations* A/PV/1538 1967 (June 27): 42-56. Mimeograph.

2287 HEIMAN, LEO. "A Who's Who of the World's Top Nazis. Where They Are Now and What They Are Doing," *Jewish Digest* 1967 (February): 75-80.

2288 HEIMAN, LEO. "843 Down . . . 12,000 to Go," *National Jewish Monthly* 1962 76(6): 12-13, 41. Deals with the Nazi war crimes investigation group of the Israeli Police HQ, and Eytan Lieff, head, who was succeeded by G. Lengsfelder.

2289 HEIMAN, LEO. "He Hunts Nazis," *Jewish Digest* 1958 (March): 30-40. Deals with the career of Tuvia(h) Friedman(n).

2290 HEIMAN, LEO. "We'll find Bormann," *National Jewish Monthly* 1961 (September): 13, 55-57.

2291 "Holocaust Unforgotten: Should Germany Stop Chasing Its Mostly Septuagenarian Nazi War Criminals? Good Arguments both Ways; but, on Balance, Probably Not," *Economist* 1979 270(7067): 14, 17.

2292 HOLZBERG, BRYAN. "Cleveland Trial Relives Treblinka," *National Law Journal* 1981 3(25): 10. Deals with John Demjanjuk, accused Nazi Guard.

2293 "In Pursuit of the Criminals," *Wiener Library Bulletin* 1961 15(2): 25.

2294 "In Pursuit of the Criminals: Another List of Prosecutions," *Wiener Library Bulletin* 1962 16(1): 4. Lists of Germans and Austrians recently prosecuted for war crimes. Lists names, positions, crimes, and sentences.

2295 "In Quest of the Guilty Ones. The Search for War Criminals Continues," *World Jewry* 1963 (March-April): 8-9.

2296 JACOBS, MONTY. "Wanted by Yugoslavia," *Congress Weekly, A Review of Jewish Interests* 1958 (March 31): 11-13. On Ante Pavelic and Andrija Artukovic.

2297 KLAIDMAN, STEPHEN. "The Nazi Hunters: Justice, Not Vengeance," Present Tense 1977 4(2): 21-26. Examines the motivations and activities of Nazi hunters from 1947 to 1977, including Shirley Korman, Vincent A. Schiano, Anthony DeVito, Wayne Perlmutter, Bessy Pupko, and Charles R. Allen, Jr. Discusses litigation against suspected war criminals and reviews policies and actions of the United States Immigration and Naturalization Service, the Department of Justice, Congress, the National Council of Churches, and the World Jewish Congress. Based on primary and secondary sources; 5 photographs.

2298 KOHN, ALAN. "U.S. Seeks to Jail L.I. Man suspected of Nazi War Crimes," New York Law Journal 1981 185(July 31): 1.

2299 LEIGH, MONROE. "Revocation of Naturalization - Illegal Procurement - Concealment of Prior Service as a Nazi Prison Guard," American Journal of International Law 1981 75(3): 669-671.

2300 LEVY, ALAN. Wanted: Nazi Criminals at Large. New York: Berkly, 1962. 175p.

2301 LINKLATER, ISABEL HILTON, and NEAL ASCHERSON. The Fourth Reich: Klaus Barbie and the neo-Fascist Connection. London: Stoughton, 1984. 352p. The complete story of the pursuit, detection, and apprehension of the "Butcher of Lyon." Bibliography, 22 photographs, index.

2302 MAILMAN, STANLEY. "Naturalizing a Treblinka Guard," New York Law Journal 1981 185(42): 1-2.

2303 "On the Track of the Guilty: War Crimes Charges and Sentences," Wiener Library Bulletin 1964 18(1): 21. A list of war criminals, trials, and sentences.

2304 PILICHOWSKI, CZESLAW. "Zasady Norymberskie a Sprawa Scigania I Karania Hitlerowskich Zbrodniarzy Wojennych (1945-1971) [The Nuremberg findings and the problem of tracking down and punishing Nazi war criminals, 1945-1971]," Sprawy Miedzynarodowe 1971 24 (11): 28-49. Discusses legal standards and international declarations on the prosecution of Nazi war criminals since 1939 and the role of the Glowna Komisja Badan Zbrodni Hitlerowskich w Polsce [Chief Investigation Commission for Nazi Crimes in Poland (GKBZHwP)]. The commission prevented West Germany's parliament from introducing a statute of limitations on Nazi war crimes. Based on published Polish and German official documents and articles; 76 notes.

2305 PINTER, ISTVÁN, and LÁSZLO SZABÓ (eds.). Criminals at Large. Budapest: Pannonia, 1961. 330p.

2306 PLAUEN, E.O. Der Galgentanz, eine Moritat unseres Jahrhunderts. La danza de la horca. Buenos Aires: Dürer, 1952. 69p. Special issue of the magazine Der Weg. Text and cartoons reprinted from Das Reich, Berlin, 1940-1944. Text in German and Spanish. Deals with escaped war criminals.

2307 ROBINSON, NEHEMIAH. "The Fate of Hitler's Confederates. The Lesser Nazis and What Happened to Them," Jewish Digest 1963 (April): 21-24.

2308 RYAN, ALLAN A., JR. Quiet Neighbors: Prosecuting Nazi War Criminals in America. San Diego: Harcourt Brace Jovanovich,

1984. 386p. The story of the search for and prosecution of Nazis who migrated to the United States and assumed new identities. Discusses the role of the United States Office of Special Investigation. Illustrated, annotated.

2309 SALOMON, MICHEL. "Tracking Nazi War Criminals. A Conversation with Simon Wiesenthal," Midstream 1967 13(9): 19-27.

2310 SZABÓ, LADISLAO. Hitler estavivo. Nuevo Berchtesgaden en el Antártico. Buenos Aires: Edition El Tabano, 1947. 167p. Deals with escaped war criminals.

2311 UNITED STATES. CONGRESS. HOUSE OF REPRESENTATIVES. COMMITTEE ON THE JUDICIARY. Illegal Aliens. 450p. February 4, 26, March 5, 12, 13, 19, 1975. U.S. Government Documents call number Y4.J89/1:94-8. The March 19, 1975 entry, pp. 335-365, deal with INS problems with Nazi war criminals.

2312 UNITED STATES. CONGRESS. HOUSE OF REPRESENTATIVES. COMMITTEE ON THE JUDICIARY. Immigration and Naturalization Service Oversight. 55p. April 3, June 25, 1974. Call number Y4.J89/1:93-97. Discusses undesirable aliens and naturalized citizens living in the United States.

2313 UNITED STATES. CONGRESS. HOUSE OF REPRESENTATIVES. COMMITTEE ON THE JUDICIARY. Oversight of INS Programs and Activities, Hearings before the Subcommittee on Immigration, Citizenship, and International Law. 95th Congress, 1st and 2nd Sessions March 9, 23, 1977, and February 8, 9, and March 9, 1978. Serial Number 26. 467p. U.S. Government Documents call number Y4.J89/1:95/26. Brief discussion of progress and reasons for delay in recently instituted programs for the prosecution of German war criminals.

2314 UNITED STATES. CONGRESS. HOUSE OF REPRESENTATIVES. COMMITTEE ON THE JUDICIARY. Review of Immigration Problems, Hearings before the Subcommittee on Immigration, Citizenship, and International Law. 94th Congress, 1st and 2nd Sessions (June 11, 12, December 10, 1975; July 28, 1976). Serial No. 62. 159p. U.S. Government Documents call number Y4.J89 1: 94-92. Contains some discussion of the investigation of alleged Nazis living in the United States.

2315 UNITED STATES. GENERAL ACCOUNTING OFFICE. Widespread Conspiracy to Obstruct Probes of Alleged Nazi War Criminals not Supported by Available Evidence. Washington: GAO, 1978. 62p.

2316 UNITED STATES. IMMIGRATION AND NATURALIZATION SERVICE (INS). Oversight of INS Policies and Legal Issues. 99p. August 3, 1978. U.S. Government Documents call number Y4.J89/1:95/59. Contains material on INS Special Litigation Unit prosecution of alleged Nazi war criminals.

2317 UNITED STATES. IMMIGRATION AND NATURALIZATION SERVICE (INS). Overview of INS Enforcement and Service Programs, Including the development of automated files and identification cards. Much on Nazi war criminal investigation. Washington: INS, March 29, 1979.

2318 "United States Sifts Ex-Nazi Scientists for Possible War Criminals," Nature 1979 282(5736): 220.

2319 „Wer ist Organisationsverbrecher?" Spruchgerichte 1948 2(July): 202-205.

2320 WINTER, JAMES. "The Case Against Dr. Horst Schumann. Infamous Nazi Surgeon Still Eludes Justice," World Jewry 1964 (November-December): 8.

2321 WRIGHT, ROBERT A.W. "That the Guilty Shall Not Escape, a Far-reaching Plan has been Devised to find and bring War Criminals to Justice," New York Times Magazine, May 13, 1945: 6, 34-35. The Chairman of the United Nations War Crimes Commission outlines the procedure to be followed by the Commission.

2322 YOUNG, ROWLAND L. "Citizens . . . denaturalization," American Bar Association Journal 1981 67(April): 489-490. Federenko v. United States. 101 S. Ct (January 21, 1981).

D. AMNESTY, ASYLUM, CLEMENCY, PAROLE

2323 GROSSMANN, KURT R. "Amnesty for the Nazi 'Little Men,'" Congress Weekly, A Review of Jewish Interests 1947 14(June 10): 9-10. Discusses the implications involved in the fact that the United States granted amnesty to 80,000 "lesser" Nazis.

2324 LACHS, MANFRED. "Crimes de guerre - délits politiques," Revue de Droit International de Sciences Diplomatiques et Politiques 1945 23(1-2): 10-20.

2325 MORGENSTERN, FELICE. "Asylum for War Criminals, Quislings and Traitors," British Year Book of International Law 1948 25: 382-386. Gives an account of recent practices concerning the right to asylum. Notes that traitors are no longer treated as political offenders and are not necessarily granted asylum.

2326 POLLAK, STEPHEN W. "Political Asylum. Cairo," World Jewry 1959 (January): 17. Cairo had become a political asylum for a number of former Nazis, including Johannes von Leers (Osman Amin von Leers), Louis Heiden (Louis al-Hadj), Leopold Gleim (Colonel al-Naher), and Bernhard Bender (Colonel Ben-Salem).

2327 PRZYBYLSKI, PETER. "Bonn's Concealed Amnesty for Nazi and War Criminals: A Menace to European Security," German Foreign Policy 1969 8(4): 243-256. 43 notes.

2328 ROTH, ANDREW. "The Release and Rehabilitation of Nazi War Criminals," Nation 1951 172(4): 69-70.

2329 ROTH, S.J. "Where Interpol is Wrong," World Jewry 1961 (September): 4-5. Deals with asylum for and extradition of Nazi war criminals.

2330 "Shape of Things," Nation 1951 172(6): 117-118. Deals with High Commission John J. McCloy's "wholesale" clemency for Nazi war criminals.

2331 UNITED STATES. DEPARTMENT OF STATE. "Answer to Soviet Protest on MacArthur Clemency Circular: Text of U.S. and Russian Notes," Department of State Bulletin 23(575): 60-61. July 10, 1950. The United States rejected the Soviet request that the Supreme Commander for the Allied Powers (SCAP) not consider parole or clemency for some war criminals.

2332 UNITED STATES. DEPARTMENT OF STATE. "Attitudes of Neutral Governments Regarding Asylum to War Criminals," Department of State Bulletin 1945 12(294): 190-192. February 11, 1945. Deals with the attitudes of Argentina, Ireland, Portugal, Spain, Sweden, and Switzerland.

2333 UNITED STATES. DEPARTMENT OF STATE. "Parole and Clemency Board for War Criminals Appointed," Department of State Bulletin 1953 29(749): 599-600. On the creation of the board by the U.S. High Commissioner for Germany

2334 UNITED STATES. DEPARTMENT OF STATE. "Procedures for Clemency and Parole for War Criminals," Department of State Bulletin 1953 29(743): 391. 3 notes.

2335 UNITED STATES. DEPARTMENT OF STATE. "Stay of Executions of German War Criminals Lifted," Department of State Bulletin 1951 24(622): 907.

2336 "Will War Criminals find Asylum?" Jewish Comment 1943 (24): 1-3.

E. EXTRADITION

2337 "An Unsolved Problem in War Crimes," American Perspective 1947 1(20): 112-116. Comments on the failure of certain countries to extradite collaborators and war criminals, and asks for clearer definitions of the terms asylum, extradition, treason, and war crimes. 13 notes.

2338 DURDENEVSKY, V. "The Question of Surrender of War Criminals by Italy," Information Bulletin 1946 6(49): 427.

2339 "Extradition of War Criminals," Law Journal 1945 95(4172): 459. Short note on the problem and definition of "an offense of a political character." Discusses 2 precedents for the extradition of war criminals, one from 1891 and the other from 1894.

2340 GARCÍA-MORA, MANUEL R. "War Crimes and the Principle of Non-Extradition of Political Offenders," Wayne Law Review 1963 9(2): 269-293. 134 notes.

2341 GREEN, L.C. "Political Offenses, War Crimes and Extradition," International and Comparative Law Quarterly 1962 11(April): 329-354.

2342 INTERNATIONAL SOCIETY OF MILITARY LAW AND THE LAWS OF WAR. Quatrième Congrès International: Madrid, 9-12 mai 1967. 2 volumes. Brussels: Société internationale de droit pénal militaire et de droit de la guerre, 1969. Deals with the extradition of war criminals.

2343 LERSNER, KURT VON. „Die Auslieferung der deutschen Kriegsverbrecher," in Zehn Jahre Versailles. Heinrich Schnee and Hans Draeger (eds.). 3 volumes. Berlin: Brückenverlag, 1929-1930. Volume 1, pp. 545-619. Volume 3, Karl C. von Loesch and Max Hildebert Boehm (eds.), was published under the title Grendzdeutschland seit Versailles.

2344 MUSZKAT, MARIAN. [A study on the extradition of Nazi war criminals]. Warsaw: Ministry of Justice, 1950. In Polish.

2345 MUSZKAT, MARIAN. "[Extradition of war criminals]," Wojskowy Przeglad Prawniczy 1947 2-3: 246-263. In Polish.

2346 NEUMANN, ROBERT G. "Neutral States and the Extradition of War Criminals," American Journal of International Law 1951 45(3): 495-508. 69 notes.

2347 "Policy on Surrender of War Criminals Reaffirmed," United Nations Weekly Bulletin 1947 3(20): 624-626.

2348 "Surrender and Trial of War Criminals: Committee Passes United Kingdom Resolution," United Nations Weekly Bulletin 1947 3(18): 567-570.

2349 UNITED NATIONS. GENERAL ASSEMBLY. Resolution 3(I): The Extradition and Punishment of War Criminals. Adopted at the 32nd plenary meeting, February 13, 1946. Resolutions Adopted by the General Assembly during the First Part of its First Session, from January 10 to February 14, 1946. London: 1946.

F. CRIMINAL ORGANIZATIONS

1. General

2350 ARTZT, HEINZ. Mörder in Uniform. Organisationen, die zu Vollstreckern nationalsozialistischer Verbrechen wurden. Munich: Kindler, 1979. 205p. Deals mainly with the SS and its departments.

2351 BECKER, WALTER. „Die Lüge als Tatbestandsmerkmal bei Organisationsverbrechen," Spruchgerichte 1948 2(September): 257-261.

2352 BREETZKE, E. „Vom Unrecht bei dem Organisationsdelikt," Spruchgerichte 1949 3(February-March): 51-56.

2353 COMMITTEE OF ANTI-FASCIST RESISTANCE FIGHTERS IN THE GERMAN DEMOCRATIC REPUBLIC. IG-Farben, Auschwitz, Mass Murder. Berlin(GDR): 1964.

2354 „Der Zwang zur Mitgliedschaft beim Organisationsverbrechen," Spruchgerichte 1949 3(February-March): 47-51.

2355 DREHER, EDUARD. „Die Entwicklung der Strafzumessungsprobleme in der Rechtsprechung zum Organisationsverbrechen," Spruchgerichte 1949 3(January): 7-11.

2356 HAENSEL, CARL. „Hauptprobleme des Organisationsverbrechens," Spruchgerichte 1948 2(April): 100-104. Considers the problem of superior orders as well as ignorance of the nature of the organization as a defense for war crimes.

2357 JERUSALEM, FRANZ. „Die allgemeine Rechtslehre und die Konstruktion des Organisationsverbrechens," Spruchgerichte 1948 2(September): 261-262.

2358 JERUSALEM, FRANZ. „Zum Begriff des Organisationsverbrechens," Spruchgerichte 1948 2(May): 129-130.

2359 JOHANNY, KARL. Der Tatbestand des Kriegsverbrechens und moderner Kleinkrieg unter Berücksichtigung der Legitimität seiner Teilnehmer. Würzburg: 1966.

2360 KIRCHNER, CARL. "Die Unteilbarkeit des Schuldspruchs beim Organisationsverbrechen," Spruchgerichte 1949 3(January): 3-7.

2361 KIRCHNER, CARL. "Tateinheit und Tatmehrheit beim Organisationsverbrechen in der Rechtsprechung des Obersten Spruchgerichtshofes," Spruchgerichte 1948 2(November): 305-307.

2362 KREBS, ALBERT. Tendenzen und Gestalten der NSDAP. Stuttgart: Deutsche Verlags-Anstalt, 1959.

2363 MAYER, HELLMUTH. "Die materielle Gerechtigkeit der Strafen für die Mitgliedschaft in den verbrecherischen Organisationen," Spruchgerichte 1947 1(October): 17-19.

2364 MEYER-ABICH, FRIEDRICH. "Vom Unrechtsgehalt des Organisationsverbrechens," Spruchgerichte 1947 1(September): 2-5.

2365 MITTELBACH, HANS. "Das Verfahren gegen Angehörige verbrecherischer Organisationen," Zentral-Justizblatt für die Britische Zone 1947 1(October): 71-74.

2366 MITTELBACH, HANS. "Die Bestrafung der Zugehörigkeit zu verbrecherischen Organisationen," Zentral-Justizblatt für die Britische Zone 1947 1(August): 33-36.

2367 RADANDT, HANS. Kriegsverbrecherkonzern Mansfeld. Die Rolle des Mansfeld-Konzerns bei der Vorbereitung und während des zweiten Weltkriegs. Berlin: Tribüne, 1957. 292p. Detailed analysis of the operation, finance, and products of this company as they related to the German war effort.

2368 SONTAG, ERNST. "Das Organisationsverbrechen des neuen deutschen Strafrechts," Schweizerische Zeitschrift für Strafrecht 1949 64: 65-71.

2369 "Unrechtsbewußtsein, Gruppenkriminalität und Paragraph 128 des Strafgesetzbuches," Spruchgerichte 1947 1(September): 10-11.

2370 WEBER, HELMUTH VON. "Die allgemeinen Lehren des Strafrechts in ihrer Anwendung auf das Organisationsverbrechen," Spruchgerichte 1948 2: 193-199.

2371 WERNER, WOLFHART. "Das Unrechtsbewußtsein des Organisationsangehörigen. Eine Erwiderung auf den Artikel Dr. H. Mittelbachs," Spruchgerichte 1948 2(August): 233-234.

2372 WERNER, WOLFHART. "Der Tatbestand des Organisationsverbrechens," Spruchgerichte 1947 1(December): 59-61.

2. Gestapo and Sicherheitsdienst

2373 CRANKSHAW, EDWARD. Gestapo. Instrument of Tyranny. London: Putnam, 1956. 275p. New York: Viking, 1956. General history of Nazism and the development of the Gestapo and the SD, with biographical sketches of Heinrich Himmler and Reinhard Heydrich. Discusses Gestapo methods of torture, the Jewish question, and the "final solution." Describes the procedure for mass extermination by the commandos and contains a chapter on the Night and Fog Decree of 1942, which altered measures to be taken against offenders, including civilians in occupied areas. Sentences of life at hard labor were replaced by the death penalty or deportation. At Auschwitz more Jews were gassed than at any other camp. Includes a glossary of Nazi and

Gestapo organizations and equivalent military ranks. Based on primary and secondary sources; 278 notes, 6 illustrations, 11-page index, and 4-page bibliography.

2374 DELARUE, JACQUES. *Histoire de la Gestapo*. Paris: Fayard, 1962. 473p. Published in German as *Geschichte der Gestapo*. Düsseldorf: Droste, 1964. Published in English as *The Gestapo, a History of Horror*. New York: William Morrow, 1964. 384p. Discusses the birth of the Gestapo (1933-1934), its methods under Himmler (1934-1936), preparation for the invasion of Austria (1936-1939), the Gestapo at war (1940), atrocities in France (1940-1944), and the collapse of the Gestapo (1944). Appendices contain a chart of the internal structure of the Reich Security Main Office (RSHA), and the text of the second Oberg-Bousquet Agreement between the Germans and the French. French edition contains a 6-page bibliography. English edition contains a 4-page bibliography, 14-page index, and 47 photographs.

2375 DESROCHES, ALAIN. *La Gestapo. Atrocités et secrets de l'inquisition nazie*. Paris: Vecchi, 1972.

2376 SCHNEIDER, PETER. "Rechtssicherheit und richterliche Unabhängigkeit aus der Sicht des SD," *Vierteljahrshefte für Zeitgeschichte* 1956 4(4): 399-422. 17 notes.

2377 ZIPFEL, F. *Gestapo und Sicherheitsdienst*. Berlin/Grunewald: Arani, 1960. Volume 3 of Joseph Wulf (ed.). *Das Dritte Reich*.

3. Schutzstaffel

2378 ALEXANDER, LEO. "Sociopsychologic Structure of the SS," *Archives of Neurology and Psychiatry* 1948 59(May): 622-634.

2379 BUCHHEIM, HANS. "Die SS in der Verfassung des Dritten Reiches," *Vierteljahrshefte für Zeitgeschichte* 1955 3(2): 127-157. Discusses the structure and organization of the SS. In no sense was it a homogeneous organization composed of members having the same rights and duties. Major topics include the origins of the SS, the SS and the police, the Waffen-SS, and the national commissioner for the consolidation of German nationhood. Contains in its 62 notes a valuable bibliography of primary works, including many documents used in the Nuremberg IMT trial.

2380 "Dokumente des Verbrechens der Waffen-SS. Geheimbefehle und Protokolle aus der Kriegszeit entdeckt," *Neues Deutschland* 1956 (September 25): 2.

2381 "Genügt die Kenntnis eines Angehörigen der Waffen-SS von der Pflicht der Juden zum Tragen des Judensterns zu einer Verurteilung wegen Organisationsverbrechens?" *Spruchgerichte* 1947 1(December): 69-70.

2382 GRUNBERGER, RICHARD. *Hitler's SS*. London: Delacorte Press and George Weidenfeld and Nicolson, 1970.

2383 HAUSSER, PAUL. *Waffen-SS im Einsatz*. Göttingen: Plesse, 1953. 270p.

2384 HOETTL, WILHELM [pseudonym, Walter Hagen]. *Die geheime Front. Organisation, Personen und Aktionen*. Zurich: Europa, 1950; Linz/Vienna: 1950. Published in English as *The Secret Front* -

The Story of Nazi Political Espionage. London: Weidenfeld & Nicolson, [1953]; New York: Praeger, [1954]. An account of the workings of the foreign intelligence organization of the SD. Hagen, as Lt. Col. Willy Hoettl, was Chief of Bureau 6 of the RSHA. Contains much on Himmler, Heydrich, Müller, and Schellenberg.

2385 HÖHNE, HEINZ. Der Orden unter dem Totenkopf. Die Geschichte der SS. Gütersloh: Mohn, 650p. Published in English as The Order of the Death's Head: The Story of Hitler's SS. New York: Coward-McCann, 1978. 690p.

2386 KEMPNER, ROBERT M.W. SS im Kreuzverhör. Munich: Rütten und Loening, 1964. 304p. Analyzes the proceedings against the Schutzstaffel (SS), focusing on the crimes committed by organizations. Covers the Einsatzgruppen trial and testimony of its major defendant, Otto Ohlendorf. Discusses arguments of the defense, including military necessity, the reasoning behind mass torture, the murder of civilians, and superior orders. One section deals with the WVHA (SS Economic and Administration Department) under Oswald Pohl. Discusses the function of the organization, medical experiments, euthanasia, treatment of concentration camp inmates and Jews, Pohl's testimony and connection with the Reichsbank. Another section covers the trial of the SS-Rasse- und Siedlungshauptamt (RuSHA), the Race and Settlement Administrative Department. Discusses the abduction of foreign children, abortions of workers in the eastern zones, punishment for sexual relations with Germans, and deportation and separation of families. Contains a list of participants at the Conference on Evacuation on January 30, 1940. Other chapters discuss cross-examination and hearings of high SS officials, including Reichsminister Hans Heinrich Lammers, Otto Dietrich, and SS leaders of the "Crystal Night" and Röhm-Putsch. Based on primary sources; 10-page index, no bibliography.

2387 KOEHL, ROBERT L. "The Character of the SS," Journal of Modern History 1962 34(3): 275-283. 48 notes.

2388 KOMITEE DER ANTIFASCHISTISCHEN WIDERSTANDSKÄMPFER IN DER DEUTSCHEN DEMOKRATISCHEN REPUBLIK. SS im Einsatz. Eine Dokumentation über die Verbrechen der SS. Berlin (GDR): Kongreß, 1957, 1964. 646p.

2389 KRAUSNICK, HELMUT, HANS BUCHHEIM, MARTIN BROSZAT, and HANS-ADOLF JACOBSEN. Anatomie des SS-Staates. Olten/Freiburg im Breisgau: Walker, 1965. Published in English as Anatomy of the SS State. New York: Walker, 1968. 614p. Statements by 4 German historians who were members of the prosecution in a series of trials at Frankfurt am Main in 1963 of minor Nazi war criminals for crimes committed at Auschwitz. Part 1, "The Persecution of the Jews," discusses the "final solution," Nuremberg laws, and social Darwinism. Part 2, "The SS-instrument of Domination," traces the history of the SS, the Gestapo, and the SD. Part 3, "Command and Compliance," deals with the ideology and mentality of the SS. Part 4, "The Concentration Camps 1933-1945," reviews arrest operations and use of concentration camp labor. Part 5, "The Kommissarbefehl and mass executions of Soviet Russian prisoners of war," contains excerpts from Document No. 12, directing the execution of political commissars and other Soviets. Appendices contain a 36-page glossary, and a table comparing U.S., British, and German army ranks, as well as German police, NSDAP, and SS ranks, 17-page Dramatis

Personae, 4-page chronology of events, 4-page bibliography, 8-page index.

2390 LITTLEJOHN, DAVID. The Patriotic Traitors. Garden City: Doubleday, 1972. Contains a general discussion of foreign volunteers who fought on the German side in units of the Waffen-SS. Some were assigned to other duties, such as guarding concentration camps. Littlejohn mentions, for example, that while the bulk of the Dutch and Flemish SS volunteers were transferred to the Waffen-SS after June 22, 1941, some of them were retained in Holland where they guarded the concentration camps at Westerbork, Vught, and Amersfoort.

2391 NEUSÜSS-HUNKEL, ERMENHILD. Die SS (Schriftenreihe des Instituts für Wissenschaftliche Politik in Marburg/Lahn, Nr. 2). Hannover/Frankfurt am Main: Norddeutsche Verlags-Anstalt, 1956. 143p. Describes the creation, organization, management, and actions of the SS. Contains organizational charts, 12p. of notes, 2-page bibliography, no index.

2392 PAETEL, KARL O. „Die SS: Ein Beitrag zur Soziologie des Nationalsozialismus," Vierteljahrshefte für Zeitgeschichte 1954 2(1): 1-33. Provides insights into the composition and philosophy of the SS and the mentality of its members and leaders. 80 notes.

2393 PAETEL, KARL O. "The Reign of the Black Order," in The Third Reich. New York: International Council for Philosophy and Humanistic Studies and UNESCO, 1955.

2394 PREUSS, ERICH. Bilanz des SS-Konzerns - Ein dokumentarischer Tatsachenbericht. Munich: Philipp Rauscher, 1951.

2395 REITLINGER, GERALD, The SS: Alibi of a Nation, 1922-1945. London: William Heinemann, 1956; Englewood Cliffs: Prentice Hall, 1981. 502p. Gives an account of what has been called the Nazi Praetorian Guard, from 1923, before the founding of the SS, until its destruction in 1945. The SS is depicted as a tyrannical expression of bureaucracy in politics. The book concerns itself largely with the administration and internal rivalries of the Nazi state and how the system worked in both peace and war. It includes a study of the field divisions of the SS, an analysis of the Gestapo, and a look at the rival agencies within the German military intelligence system. Discusses concentration camps and death camps and contains a 20-page Dramatis Personae which identifies more than 250 major figures mentioned in the book. Based on original German documents, including captured files of the SS leadership; 6-page bibliography, 3 maps, 16-page index.

2396 SCHNABEL, REIMUND. Macht ohne Moral. Eine Dokumentation über die SS. Frankfurt am Main: Röderberg, 1957. 582p. General history of the SS. The whose major chapters deal with terror in Germany, concentration camps, terror in Europe, the end of the war, and the postwar period. The last chapter deals with the SS in the Nuremberg IMT trial. 12-page list of documents used, 5-page bibliography, index.

2397 STEIN, GEORGE H. The Waffen SS: Hitler's Elite Guard at War, 1939-1945. Ithaca: Cornell University Press, 1966. 330p. Published in German as Geschichte der Waffen-SS. Düsseldorf: 1967.

2398 SYDNOR, CHARLES W. *Soldiers of Destruction. The SS Death's Head Division, 1933-1945*. Princeton: Princeton University Press, 1977. Much on KZ Stutthof.

2399 THOMPSON, LARRY. "Lebensborn and the Eugenics Policy of the Reichsführer-SS," *Central European History* 1971 4(1): 54-77.

2400 ZACHAKEL, FRIEDRICH. *Waffen-SS im Westen. Ein Bericht im Bildern*. Munich: Franz Eher, 1941.

2401 "Zur Deutung des Organisationsverbrechens," *Deutsche Rechts-Zeitschrift* 1948 3(6): 201-202.

2402 "Zur Kenntnis der SS-Mitglieder von der Judenverfolgung durch ihre Organisationen," *Spruchgerichte* 1948 2(August): 228-230.

2403 "Zur strafrechtlichen Beurteilung der SS Formation SD," *Spruchgerichte* 1948 2(November): 319-321.

G. PUNISHMENT

2404 ALEXANDROWICZ, IGNACY. "Punishment of War Criminals," *New Europe and World Reconstruction* 1943 3(78): 39-41. Suggests actions to be taken by the Allies.

2405 AMERICAN JEWISH CONFERENCE. *Statement on Punishment of War Criminals*. New York: [The Conference], [1944]. 3p. Introduced by Samuel Dickstein and reprinted in the *Congressional Record*, 79th Congress, 1st Session, Volume 91 (Appendix), Part 10, January 9, 1945, p. A76.

2406 AMERICAN LABOR PARTY. "Statement by the American Labor Party on the Punishment of War Criminals." Introduced by Vito Marcantonio and reprinted in the *Congressional Record*, 79th Congress, 1st Session, Volume 91 (Appendix), Part 10, March 1, 1945, p. A932.

2407 ANDERSON, C. ARNOLD. "The Utility of the proposed Trial and Punishment of Enemy Leaders," *American Political Science Review* 1943 37(6): 1081-1100. Argues against the trial of German war criminals by anyone other than their own countrymen. The proposed proceedings were likely to miss the point, which should have been the prevention of the recurrence of war crimes. Compares the problems of the post-war world to those of the reconstruction period following the American Civil War. 37 notes.

2408 BAER, MARCEL DE. "The Punishment of War Criminals," *Belgium* 1942 3(September): 332-337.

2409 BARRY, JOHN V. "The Trial and Punishment of Axis War Criminals" *Australian Law Journal* 1943 17(2): 43-49. 9 notes.

2410 BARTOLOMEO CARLOMAGNO, ROBERTO. *El castigo de los criminales de guerra*. Córdova, Argentina: Imprenta de la Universidad, 1949. 76p.

2411 BASSO, A. "Criminali di Guerra e Collaborazionisti," *Stato Moderno* 1946 3(October 5): 435-437.

2412 BAYER, THEODORE. "Punishment of War Criminals," *Soviet Russia Today* 1945 13(10): 29-30.

2413 BENES, VÁCLAV. "The Problem of the Punishment of War Criminals," Headway in War-time 1943 44(May): 8-9, 14.

2414 BENES, VÁCLAV. "The Punishment of War Criminals," Spirit of Czechoslovakia 1944 5: 22-23.

2415 BIAL, LOUIS C. Vergeltung und Wiedergutmachung in Deutschland. Ein Beitrag zu den Fragen der Bestrafung der Naziverbrecher und der Wiedereinsetzung der Naziopfer in ihre Rechte. Havana: Editorial Lex, 1945. 83p. Asserts that the standard for the legality of Nazi laws should be the eternal principles of human morality. Argues that the crime of starting a war could be punished under existing laws. A main point in the argument is that the validity of international law was recognized in the Weimar constitution, and that German law to the contrary was illegal. Restitution of property must be made. Discusses legal technicalities of restitution.

2416 CREEL, GEORGE. "The Punishment," Collier's 1944 114(15): 50-51. Discusses procedure to be followed in connection with the punishment of war criminals.

2417 CREEL, GEORGE. War Criminals and Punishment. New York: Robert M. McBride, 1944. 303p. Hitler was the embodiment of the German people and Nazism was a perfect expression of the German mind. Chapter 8, "The Leipzig travesty," pp. 122-137, discusses the study of the Inter-Allied Commission on offenses against laws and customs of war. Reviews specific cases in post-World War I war crimes trials. Chapter 9, "Pledges of punishment," pp. 138-150, reviews the steps taken as early as 1941 for prosecuting National Socialist criminals, with a statement by Franklin Roosevelt. On January 13, 1942, a declaration on war crimes and war criminals was signed by representatives of Belgium, Czechoslovakia, Greece, Luxembourg, the Netherlands, Norway, Poland, and Yugoslavia. Chapter 10, "National trials," pp. 151-163, discusses the assumption that each ravaged country had the right to deal with war criminals as it deemed fit without interference from others. Covers the Kharkov trials in the USSR, a U.S. military commission's trial of 8 German saboteurs who landed on Long Island and in Florida in 1942, and a death sentence handed down by a Polish tribunal against an employee in the Warsaw Public Health Department for aiding the Gestapo. Chapter 11, "International trials," pp. 164-177, discusses intentions of the United Nations to seek justice for war crimes. Cites historical precedents for international courts having jurisdiction over criminal activity. Appendix I deals with Japanese war crimes. Appendix II reprints articles from the Hague Convention of 1907. Undocumented; 11-page index.

2418 Crimes and Punishment: A Pictorial Encyclopedia of Aberrant Behavior. 10 volumes. [no city given]: BPC Publishing Company, 1974. Volume 10, pp. 61-82, surveys a number of atrocities committed in earlier wars and then focuses on those perpetrated during World War II. Some of the atrocities examined were those committed at Katyn Wood, where thousands of Poles were killed by Russians, and the murder of the entire village of Oradour-sur-Glane in France. Several of the soldiers involved in this massacre were French, impressed into the military service of Germany. In January 1953, 21 former members of Der Führer Regiment were tried for their part in the massacre. Fourteen of them were French. Owing to a French amnesty law, none of the death and prison sentences was ever executed. The second section, "Justice at Nuremberg," is a 9-page examination of the trial, with photographs of most of the defendants. On October 16, 1946, 10 of the 22 defendants were hanged. Göring's body (he had committed suicide) was added to the others and all were taken secretly to Munich, where they were cremated and their ashes scattered in the River Isar. Undocumented; 51 photographs.

2419 DANIEL, J. Le Problème du châtiment des crimes de guerre d'après les enseignements de la deuxième guerre mondiale. Cairo: R. Schindler, 1946. 282p. Compact study of war crimes. Part 1 is an historical survey up to 1945. A war crime is defined as a punishable act constituting a violation of international law committed during hostilities and injurious either to the community of nations or to an individual. Part 2 rejects the notion of collective responsibility, but also rejects pleas of superior orders and acts of state.

2420 DESMOND, CHARLES S. "Prosecution of Axis War Crimes," New York State Bar Association Bulletin 1944 67: 362-367.

2421 EAGLETON, CLYDE. "Punishment of War Criminals by the United Nations," American Journal of International Law 1943 37(3): 495-499. Stresses the importance of having war criminals punished by the United Nations rather than by individual states. Discusses problems of the selection of rules to be enforced and the application of principles. 5 notes.

2422 EWING, ALFRED C. "The Ethics of Punishing Germany," Hibbert Journal 1945 43(January): 99-106.

2423 FINCH, GEORGE A. "Retribution for War Crimes," American Journal of International Law 1943 37(1): 81-88. Summarizes the state of international discussion of war crimes. Draws attention to the remarks of the British Lord Chancellor on October 7, 1942, and the Conference at St. James' Palace on January 13, 1942.

2424 FRANKLIN, MITCHELL. "Sources of International Law Relating to Sanctions against War Criminals," Journal of Criminal Law and Criminology 1945 36(September): 153-179. Shows how Article 50 of the 1907 Hague Convention must be interpreted to provide the basis for collective penalties to be imposed on war criminals. The defense of superior orders must be rejected. Discusses the basis of the punishment of particular crimes in light of French and German legal theory and positive law.

2425 GLASGOW, GEORGE. "Punishment of the Guilty," Contemporary Review 1944 166(944): 114-122.

2426 GLUECK, SHELDON. "Germany and War Guilt," New Republic 1944 110(8): 243-244.

2427 GLUECK, SHELDON. "Punishing the War Criminals," New Republic 1944 109(21): 706-709.

2428 GREAT BRITAIN. FOREIGN OFFICE. Punishment for War Crimes. The Interallied Documents Signed at St. James' Palace, London, 13 January, 1942, and Relative Documents. 2 volumes. London: HMSO, 1942. On the St. James' Conference.

2429 GREAT BRITAIN. HOUSE OF COMMONS. Parliamentary Debates, 5th Series. Volumes 383-392. London: HMSO, 1942-1943. Deals with

Jews, German barbarities, and various statements on the investigation of war crimes and the punishment of war criminals.

2430 GREAT BRITAIN. HOUSE OF LORDS. *Parliamentary Debates*. 5th Series. Volumes 124-135. London: HMSO, 1942-1945. Contains many debates on the punishment of war criminals.

2431 ROS, ANDRÉ. "Le Châtiment des crimes de guerre," *Cahiers Politiques* 1945 9(April): 49-58.

2432 GROSS, LEO. "The Punishment of War Criminals: The Nuremberg Trial," *Nederlands Tijdschrift voor International Recht* 1955 2(October): 356-374; 1956 3(January): 10-24.

2433 GROSSMANN, KURT R. "No Crime shall go Unpunished," *Knickerbocker Weekly* 1944 4(17): 28-29.

2434 HOBZA, ANTONÍN. [Survey of the international law of war. Supplement: The punishment of war criminals]. Prague: Vsehrd, 1946. 172p. In Czech.

2435 HUDES, TED. "Crime without Punishment - Nazi Killers and Kindly Courts," *American Zionist* 1966 (February): 21-23. Discusses the responsibility of men who replaced the Nazis and then failed to punish them.

2436 HULA, ERICH. "Punishment for War Crimes," *Social Research* 1946 13(1): 1-23. Discussion of the negotiations leading to the London Agreement and of the Nuremberg IMT proceedings. Argues that the trial did not apply the law, that the court was merely an agency for the victors, and that the proceedings were overlong and pedantic. 37 notes.

2437 HYDE, CHARLES C. "Punishment of War Criminals," *American Society of International Law, Proceedings* 1943 37: 39-46. Discusses some of the problems in punishing war criminals, such as obtaining the necessary evidence and organizing a competent international court. Recommends a court made up of neutral judges.

2438 INTER-ALLIED INFORMATION COMMITTEE. LONDON. *Punishment for War Crimes: The Inter-Allied Declaration Signed at St. James' Palace London on 13th January, 1942, and Relative Documents*. London: HMSO, 1942. 16p. Published by various agencies.

2439 INTER-ALLIED INFORMATION COMMITTEE. LONDON. *Punishment for War Crimes (2): Collective Notes Presented to the Governments of Great Britain, the U.S.S.R., and the U.S.A. and Relative Correspondence*. London: HMSO, 1942. 40p.

2440 INTERNATIONAL COMMITTEE FOR PENAL RECONSTRUCTION AND DEVELOPMENT. *Report on Rules and Procedure Relating to Punishment of War Crimes Committed in the Course of and Incidental to the Present War*. London: Cambridge University Press, 1943.

2441 INTERNATIONAL CONFERENCE ON PROSECUTION OF NAZI CRIMINALS, MOSCOW, 1969. *War Criminals Must Be Punished . . . . Main Documents*. Moscow: Novosti Press Agency Publishing House, 1969.

2442 JASZAI, DEZSO. "On the Preclusion of Proscription of War Crimes and of Certain Punishments Inflicted for Them," *Hungarian Law Review* 1965 (1): 5-10.

2443 LAUTERPACHT, HERSCH. "The Law of Nations and the Punishment of War Crimes," British Year Book of International Law 1944 21: 58-95. A theoretical discussion of certain legal aspects of war crimes trials. The author affirms the right under international law to punish war criminals, and then looks at four major problems: (1) the surrender of war criminals to victors, (2) legal limitations on the right to punish war criminals, (3) possible safeguards of impartiality and legal equality between the victor and the vanquished, and (4) extradition.

2444 LELEWER, GEORG. "Punishment of War Criminals," Central European Observer 1943 20(18): 283-284.

2445 LOEB, WALTER. "Punishment of War Criminals," Free Europe 1942 6(79): 170.

2446 LONDON INTERNATIONAL ASSEMBLY. COMMISSION ON THE TRIAL AND PUNISHMENT OF WAR CRIMINALS. "[Conclusions]," Free World 1944 7(2): 184-190. Deals with heads of state as war criminals, an international criminal court, and the surrender of war criminals. Contains a list of war criminals.

2447 MANNER, GEORGE. "The Legal Nature and Punishment of Criminal Acts of Violence Contrary to the Laws of War," American Journal of International Law 1943 37(3): 407-435. Discusses the January 13, 1942, resolution adopted in London by eight governments in exile and the free French National Committee to punish Germans guilty of war crimes committed in violation of the Fourth Hague Convention of 1907. The signatory governments were Belgium, Czechoslovakia, Greece, Luxembourg, the Netherlands, Norway, Poland, and Yugoslavia. Major topics examined are war crimes and jurisdiction over war crimes. Concludes that offenses against the laws of war are actually crimes against the municipal law of belligerent states, which have jurisdiction over war crimes committed by captured enemies in their territories. The decision to bring charges against the Germans is an act of international policy rather than a question of law. The documentation traces legal and philosophical arguments on the laws of nations and the laws of war, arguments repeated endlessly at the end of World War II in preparation for the Nuremberg IMT trial. 107 notes.

2448 MYERSON, MOSES HYMAN. Germany's War Crimes and Punishment: The Problem of Individual and Collective Criminality. Toronto: Macmillan, 1944. This book was completed in January 1944, before many of Germany's war crimes were known. Discusses the principle of war crimes and recommends trials and punishments. Insists that the punishments handed down have the dignity of legal judgments.

2449 NATIONAL LAWYERS GUILD (NATIONAL EXECUTIVE BOARD). "The Punishment of War Criminals," Lawyers Guild Review 1944 4(6): 18-23. Report adopted by the Executive Board of the National Lawyers Guild on December 16, 1944, in Washington. Takes the position that the punishment of war criminals is a war measure in the same sense as is military action. Rejects the invention of "new crimes," but also denies any validity to immunity from punishment because of acts of state or higher orders. 52 notes.

2450 PEPPER, CLAUDE D. "Punishment of War Criminals: A Major War Aim," Free World 1944 8(1): 72-74.

2451 PIUS XII, POPE. "An International Code for the Punishment of War Crimes," St. John's Law Review 1953 28(1): 1-18. A translation of a address delivered in French to the Sixtieth International Congress on Penal Law, October 3, 1953.

2452 "Punishment of War Crimes," Inter-Allied Review 1942 2(October 15): 233-236. Statements on the subject by Allied leaders.

2453 RADIN, MAX. The Day of Reckoning. New York: Knopf, 1943. 144p. A dramatic description of the imaginary trial of Hitler and associates on charges of murder. Described as a "searching discourse on the nature of law" which examines the legal grounds on which Nazi actions could be adjudged war crimes.

2454 ROWSON, S.W.D. "Punishment of War Criminals," Law Quarterly Review 1944 60(239): 225-226. Note on the revision of Chapter XIV, Paragraph 443, of the British Manual of Military Law concerning superior orders and the rules of warfare.

2455 SANKEY, JOHN S. "War Criminals: Should They be Tried?" Fortnightly 1943 159(January): 1-8.

2456 STRANSKY, JAROSLAV. "The Inter-Allied Conference on War Crimes and the Problem of Retribution," New Commonwealth Quarterly 1942 7(4): 250-257.

2457 TAFT, DONALD R. "Punishment of War Criminals," American Sociological Review 1946 11(August): 439-444. Argues that the punishment of war criminals would increase the probability of another world war. The principles of domestic criminology generally apply to the field of international behavior, and where they do not apply there is even less effective punishment in the international field.

2458 "The Punishment of the War Criminals," Information Bulletin 1945 5(28): 2-3. Criticism of the United Nations War Crimes Commission and survey of arrests and trials.

2459 UNITED NATIONS. COMMITTEE ON HUMAN RIGHTS. Question of the Punishment of War Criminals and Persons who have Committed Crimes against Humanity. Document No. 1969. E/CN.4/1010. November 24, 1969. New York: United Nations, 1969.

2460 UNITED NATIONS. INFORMATION ORGANIZATION [OFFICE]. Germany's Record and World Security. New York: United Nations, [1944]. 32p. Deals with the punishment of war criminals.

2461 UNITED NATIONS INFORMATION ORGANIZATION [OFFICE]. Punishment for War Crimes: The Inter-Allied Declaration signed at St. James' Palace, London, January 13, 1942, and Relative Documents. London: HMSO, 1942. 16p. Also in Punishment for War Crimes. New York: United Nations Information Office, 1943. 64p.

2462 UNITED NATIONS INFORMATION ORGANIZATION [OFFICE]. Punishment for War Crimes. New York: United Nations Information Office, 1942. 64p. Contains the inter-allied declaration signed at the Palace of St. James, London, on January 13, 1942, and related documents. Among the latter are various speeches, correspondence, and memoranda on Japanese atrocities. Almost identical in contents to 2 volumes published under the same title containing 16p. and 40p. These were published in French in 2 volumes under the title *Le Châtiment des crimes de guerre,* same pagination.

2463 UNITED NATIONS INFORMATION ORGANIZATION [OFFICE]. *War Crimes and the Punishment of War Criminals. Information Paper No. 1.* London: United Nations Information Organization, Reference Division, 1945. 15p.

2464 UNITED NATIONS. SECRETARY GENERAL. *Question of Punishment of War Criminals and of Persons who have committed Crimes against Humanity, Report of the Secretary General.* New York: United Nations, Economic and Social Council, 1967. 39p. The United Nations Economic and Social Council resolution 1158 (XLI) of April 5, 1966, urged all states to take any measures necessary to prevent the application of statutory limitations to war crimes and crimes against humanity, and to continue their efforts to ensure the arrest, extradition, and punishment of war criminals and to make available to other states any documents in their possession relating to such crimes. Contains the text of the Secretary General's note inviting governments to inform him of the measures they had adopted and to furnish materials for a draft convention on the nonapplicability of statutory limitation to war crimes. Contains the replies of 18 governments as of January 16, 1967. 3-page index of legal definitions of war crimes and crimes against humanity and of various measures taken by individual countries. Addendum 1-8 (128p.) contains replies of 25 governments received subsequent to January 16, 1967. Each is followed by a 1-page index. Based on primary sources; no bibliography.

2465 UNITED NATIONS. SECRETARY GENERAL. *Question of Punishment of War Criminals and of Persons who have committed Crimes against Humanity, Report of the Secretary General.* New York: United Nations, General Assembly, 1968. 47p. (Session 23). Comments by 25 governments on the U.N. Secretary General's preliminary draft convention on the non-applicability of statutory limitation on war crimes and crimes against humanity as of August 16, 1968. Annex contains the text of the draft convention. Based on primary sources; no bibliography.

2466 UNITED NATIONS. SECRETARY GENERAL. *Question of the Punishment of War Criminals and of Persons who have committed Crimes against Humanity, Note by the Secretary General.* United Nations: Economic and Social Council, 1969. 53p. Replies from 37 governments which had not previously submitted information on matters concerning war crimes and crimes against humanity. Part I contains information pertaining to the arrest, extradition, and punishment of war criminals. Part II contains information concerning the criteria for determining compensation to the victims of war crimes. Part III comments on the general observations in paragraphs 405-412 of the Secretary General's study. Based on primary sources; no bibliography or index.

2467 UNITED NATIONS. SECRETARY GENERAL. *Question of the Punishment of War Criminals and of Persons who have committed Crimes against Humanity, Report of the Secretary General.* United Nations: General Assembly, 1970. 26p. Responses submitted by 22 governments concerning measures taken in the implementation of a resolution calling for an investigation of war crimes and crimes against humanity. Contains the draft resolution recommended by the Economic and Social Council for adoption by the General Assembly.

2468 UNITED STATES. ARMY FORCES IN THE EUROPEAN THEATER. GENERAL BOARD. War Crimes and Punishment of War Criminals: Study Number 86. [no publication information given]. 16p. Copy in United States Army Military History Research Collection, Carlisle Barracks, Pennsylvania.

2469 UNITED STATES. CONGRESS. HOUSE OF REPRESENTATIVES. COMMITTEE ON FOREIGN AFFAIRS. Apprehension and Punishment of War Criminals; Report to Accompany House Resolution 39, which was to declare government policy in relation to the apprehension and punishment of war criminals, submitted by Luther H. Johnson, April 24, 1945. 79th Congress, 1st Session, House Report 442. Washington: GPO, 1945. 1p.

2470 UNITED STATES. CONGRESS. HOUSE OF REPRESENTATIVES. COMMITTEE ON FOREIGN AFFAIRS. Punishment of War Criminals: Hearings before the Committee on Foreign Affairs. 79th Congress, 1st Session, on House Joint Resolution 93. Washington: GPO, 1945. 126p. Requests that the President appoint a commission to cooperate with the United Nations War Crimes Commission or any other agency of the United Nations in preparation of plans for the punishment of war criminals. March 22 and 26, 1945.

2471 UNITED STATES. DEPARTMENT OF STATE. "Punishment of War Criminals," Department of State Bulletin 1945 12(293): 154-155. February 4, 1945. Also in United Nations Review 1954 5(March 15): 108-109. Statement by Acting Secretary of State Joseph Grew calling for public discussion of the punishment of war criminals.

2472 VEDOVATO, GIUSEPPE. "La punizione dei crimini di guerra," Rivista di Studi Politici Internazionali 1945 12: 141-178.

2473 VERMEYLEN, PIERRE. "The Punishment of Collaborators," Annals of the American Academy of Political and Social Sciences 1946 247(September): 73-77. A survey of the Belgian government on the repression of collaboration with the enemy.

2474 WALN, NORA. "Crime and Punishment," Atlantic Monthly 1946 177(1): 43-47.

2475 "War Criminals must face Punishment, say Churchmen," News of Norway [Washington] 1943 3(November 19): 173-174.

2476 WARREN, CHARLES. [Remarks on Punishment of War Criminals] American Society of International Law, Proceedings 1943 37: 51-53.

2477 "What Treatment for War Criminals?" Information Service [Federal Council of Churches of Christ in America] 1945 24(April 28): 1-4.

2478 WHITE, THOMAS R. "War Crimes and their Punishment," Yale Review 1943 32(June): 706-720.

2479 WILDING-WHITE, A.M. "Punishing War Criminals: What is the Applicable Law?" Law Journal 1945 95(4161): 331-332.

2480 WORLD JEWISH CONGRESS. EXECUTIVE COMMITTEE. "Punishment of War Criminals, a Statement of Policy adopted by the World Jewish Congress Executive Committee," Jewish Comment 1944 2(19): 1-4.

2481 WORLD JEWISH CONGRESS. INSTITUTE OF JEWISH AFFAIRS. *The Prosecution of War Criminals since the End of the War: A Brief Survey*. New York: World Jewish Congress, 1961.

2482 WRIGHT, QUINCY. "War Criminals," *American Journal of International Law* 1945 39(2): 257-285. A theoretical discussion of the legal principles applicable to the punishment of war criminals. There were 3 main categories: offenses against the laws of war, against the laws of peace, and against universal law. Discusses problems in applying different systems of law to war criminals. Argues that the war crimes trials did not rest on *ex post facto* law. 134 notes.

VIII
WORLD WAR II
WAR CRIMES TRIALS IN ASIA

A. GENERAL AND REFERENCE WORKS

2483 BAERWALD, HANS. *The Purge of Japanese Leaders under the Occupation*. Berkeley: University of California Press, 1959. 111p.

2484 BURNS, RICHARD DEAN, and EDWARD M. BENNETT (eds.). *Diplomats in Crisis: United States-Chinese-Japanese Relations, 1919-1941*. Santa Barbara: ABC-Clio, 1974. 346p.

2485 LEWE VAN ADUARD, EVART JOOST. *Japan: From Surrender to Peace*. New York: Praeger, 1954.

2486 MOODY, SAMUEL B., and MAURY ALLEN. *Reprieve from Hell*. New York: Pageant, 1961. 213p.

2487 MORTON, LOUIS. *The Fall of the Philippines*. Washington: GPO, 1953.

2488 PICCIGALLO, PHILIP R. "In the Shadow of Nuremberg: Trials of Japanese in the East, 1945-1951." Ph.D. dissertation, City University of New York, 1977. 424p. Abstracted in *Dissertation Abstracts International* 1977 38(1): 441-A - 442-A.

2489 PICCIGALLO, PHILIP R. *The Japanese on Trial: Allied War Crimes Operations in the East, 1945-1951*. Austin: University of Texas Press, 1979. 292p.

2490 SEBALD, WILLIAM J., and RUSSELL BRINES. *With MacArthur in Japan: A personal History of the Occupation*. New York: W.W. Norton, 1965. 318p. Chapter 8, "War Crimes Trials," pp. 151-176, is a brief overview of MacArthur and the trial of Japanese war criminals. Annotated, illustrated, index.

2491 UNITED NATIONS. SECRETARY GENERAL. Report on the *Activities of the Far Eastern Commission*. Washington: GPO, 1947. Appendix 39, p. 98.

2492 UNITED STATES. ARMY FORCES, PACIFIC. *Regulations Governing the Trial of War Criminals (in the Pacific and China Theaters: September 24, 1945 - December 27, 1946)*. [no city given]: U.S.

Army Forces, Pacific, 1945-1946. A collection of mimeographed bulletins regarding regulations for the trial of war criminals in the Pacific. The documents date from September 24, 1945, to December 27, 1946 and were issued either by General Headquarters, U.S. Army Forces, Pacific, or later by General Headquarters, SCAP. Each bulletin sets forth official policies on war crimes trials, including the establishment of military commissions, their jurisdiction and membership, prosecution powers, procedures, conduct of trials, rights of the accused, submission of evidence, judgment, and sentences. Available at the Army Library, the Pentagon, Washington.

2493 UNITED STATES. CONGRESS. HOUSE OF REPRESENTATIVES. COMMITTEE ON INTERNATIONAL RELATIONS. Volume 7 of Selected Executive Sessions Hearings of the Committee, 1943-1950. United States Policy in the Far East, Part I. Washington: GPO, 1976. U.S. Government Documents call number Y4. In816: H62. Focuses on American assistance to China and the Philippines, with comments on the costs and effects of war crimes trials, with particular reference to those held under the auspices of the Nuremberg IMT.

2494 UNITED STATES. DEPARTMENT OF STATE. Occupation of Japan. State Department Publication No. 2671. Washington: GPO, 1946. 173p.

B. SPECIAL STUDIES

2495 "Bring the War Criminals to Justice," New Times 1950 6(February 8): 3-5. Accuses the Japanese of planning biological warfare and demands that all Japanese war criminals, including Hirohito, be brought to justice. The United States blocked this "expression of justice."

2496 HANAYAMA, SHINSHO. The Way of Deliverance; three Years with the Condemned Japanese War Criminals. New York: Scribners, 1950. 297p. London: Victor Gollancz, 1955. 297p. Diary of a Buddhist chaplain in Sugarmo prison, 1946-1948. The author was chaplain to the accused Japanese war criminals and was with them during the trial. Discusses the final hours before the execution of Buddhist prisoners. Includes poems and excerpts from letters of the 27 condemned prisoners and biographical sketches obtained from talks with many of them. Appendix I contains a list of prisoners, with age, rank, time and mode of execution, and next of next of kin. Appendix II contains poems by Kaichi Hirate and Kunio Yoshizawa, written following their death sentences. Undocumented.

2497 JACKSON, WILLIAM E. "Putting the Nuremberg Law to Work," Foreign Affairs 1947 25(July): 550-565.

2498 "Joseph Keenan Meets the Press," American Mercury 1950 70 (April): 456-460. A "Meet the Press" interview of Joseph Keenan. He states that the Emperor should not have been tried, since he sincerely desired peace, that there was no evidence on the use of bacteriological warfare by the Japanese, and that war crimes trials were justified on the ground that they were murder trials, not trials for the punishment of a defeated enemy.

2499 "Justice Demands International Trial of Japanese War Criminals," Information Bulletin 1950 10(4): 112-113. This Pravda editorial of February 4, 1950, demands that high Japanese officials be brought to trial for conducting bacteriological warfare against China and the Soviet Union.

2500 SAKUDA, KEIICHI. "Reconciliación con la muerte. Análisis de algunos escritos de criminales de guerra Japoneses," Revista de Psicoanalisis, Psiquiatria y Psicologia 1966 (4): 7-25. A revised version of "Life and Death: The Views of Japanese War Criminals - An Analysis of Posthumous Letters of the Century," Psychologia [University of Kioto, Japan] 1964 7(3-4): 127-142. Reviews forms of reconciliation with death, among them death as an atonement and death as a sacrifice, and discusses the Japanese concept of courage. The little sense of guilt revealed by the prisoners is related to the vindictive nature of the tribunals, inadequate understanding of Japanese military practices, errors in legal proceedings, and maltreatment during detention. Based on secondary sources; 10 notes.

2501 "The Guilty: Hideki Tojo" Collier's 1944 113(February 5): 60.

C. WAR CRIMES TRIALS (NON-IMTFE)

1. Australian

2502 DICKINSON, GEORGE. "Japanese War Trials," Australian Quarterly 1952 24(2): 69-75. The author was an Australian army lawyer who defended Japanese war criminals. He criticizes the Australian war crimes court for modifying rules of evidence so that unfair and irrelevant evidence was introduced. Concludes that war crimes trials ought to be conducted by neutrals. 1 note.

2. British

2503 PRITCHARD, R. JOHN. "Lessons from British Proceedings against Japanese War Criminals," Human Rights Review. 1978 3(2): 104-121. British proceedings in the trials of Japanese war criminals provide better precedents than did British military courts held in Europe. These trials provide guidelines for future British efforts to regulate the treatment and punishment of enemies. Many important questions are raised, among them: "What scale of sanctions should be applied by a country against persons involved in the maltreatment of common criminals, political prisoners, or prisoners of war during a period of conflict?" Discusses why the Japanese trials were held and lists 10 classes of offenses perpetrated by the Japanese.

2504 SLEEMAN, COLIN (ed.). Trial of Gozawa Sadaichi and Nine Others. London: William Hodge, 1948. 245p. Volume 3 of Maxwell-Fyfe, (see Introduction). The verbatim report of the trial of 10 Japanese officers and men charged with mistreating more than 500 Indian troops. The prisoners were placed under the control of a special Japanese unit called the "Gozawa Butai." This group was responsible for brutal treatment of prisoners, with beatings, starvation, and inhuman labor assignments. [Not in UNWCC, Law Reports].

3. Double Tenth

2505 MALLAL, BASHIR (ed.). The Double Tenth Trial: War Crimes Court in re Lt. Sumida Haruzo and Twenty Others. Singapore: Malayan Law Journal Office, 1947. 652p. The trial was held from March 18 to April 15, 1946, in Singapore by a military court of the Singapore District.

2506 SLEEMAN, COLIN, and S.C. SILKIN (eds.). Trial of Sumida Haruzo and Twenty Others (The "Double Tenth" Trial). London: William Hodge, 1951. 324p. Volume 8 of Maxwell-Fyfe, (see Introduction). Trial held March 18 - April 15, 1946, at Singapore before a British war crimes court. The trial derives its name from the date October 10, 1943, the anniversary of the establishment of the Republic of China, when the Kempei Tai in Singapore staged a search of the Changi Internment Camp, which housed more than 3000 European civilians. Lt. Col. Sumida Haruzo, Chief of the Singapore Kempei Tai, and 20 other officers and enlisted men were tried for mistreating and torturing 57 civilians at Changi jail, 15 of whom died. [Not in UNWCC, Law Reports].

4. Masaharu Homma

2507 HANSON, JOHN FREDERICK. "The Trial of Lieutenant General Masaharu Homma," Ph.D. dissertation, Mississippi State University, 1977. 231p. Abstracted in Dissertation Abstracts International 1978 38(7): 4326-A - 4327-A.

2508 UNITED STATES. NATIONAL ARCHIVES AND RECORDS SERVICE. World War II Records Division, Alexandria, Virginia. United States of America vs. Masaharu Homma, before the Military Commission convened by the Commanding General, United States Army Forces Western Pacific. This is one of the most important collections of war crimes materials in the National Archives. It contains transcripts and exhibits of the war crimes trial of General Homma, which was held in Manila in early 1946. A copy is on file in the World War II Records Division, National Archives, Alexandria, Virginia. The record of the trial includes important statements by Americans and Filipinos who participated in or witnessed the death march as well as statements by Japanese who were connected with the event. The collection includes 30 volumes of testimony and an additional 400 or more separate statements.

5. Khabarovsk

2509 Materials on the Trial of Former Servicemen of the Japanese Army, Charged with Manufacturing and Employing Biological Weapons. Moscow: Foreign Languages Publishing House, 1950. 535p. Khabarovsk trial, Russia, 1949. Provides considerable documentation on the trial of Japanese charged with waging biological warfare. The trial was held in Khabarovsk from December 25 to 30, 1949. The proceedings showed how Japanese units in Manchuria began preparations for biological warfare as early as 1931, and how they subjected crops, cattle, Chinese and Soviet citizens, and American prisoners of war to germs which produced plague, anthrax, typhoid, and cholera. Documents on these activities were given to Joseph B. Keenan, but he did not use them at the Tokyo trial, thus allegedly saving some criminals from their just punishment.

2510 MAYEVSKY, V. "Monstrous Crimes Committed by Japanese Barbarians," Information Bulletin 1950 10(3): 93. Recounts the trial and conviction in Khabarovsk of Japanese army officers for planning and engaging in biological warfare. Refers specifically to actions of officers of detachments 100 and 731 of the Kwantung Army in Manchuria.

2511 RAGINSKIĬ, M. "Khabarovskij process nad japonskimi vrjennimi presteysnikami," Sovetskoe Gosudarstvo i Pravo 1950-1951 3: 8-25.

2512 "Trial of Former Japanese Soldiers Charged with Preparing and using Bacteriological Weapons," Current Digest of the Soviet Press 1950 2(1): 21-27. This series of articles gives detailed summaries of the trial in Khabarovsk of several Japanese soldiers accused of preparing to undertake bacteriological warfare against the Soviet Union. Includes cross-examinations of the defendants, a speech by state prosecutor L.N. Smirnov, and the concluding speeches of the defendants. These articles appeared in full in the December 26-31, 1949, issues of Pravda and Izvestia.

2513 "Trial of the Japanese Agents," Information Bulletin 1946 6(60): 23. A Moscow correspondent describes the trial of 8 "White Guard" Russians who had served in the Japanese intelligence service. They were convicted by the Military Collegium of the Supreme Court of the USSR on charges of espionage and sabotage, primarily in Manchuria. Sentences were death for 6, 20 years for 1, and 15 years for the last.

2514 U.S.S.R. MILITARY TRIBUNAL [PRIMORYA MILITARY AREA]. Materials on the Trial of Former Japanese Servicemen Charged with Manufacturing and Employing Bacteriological Weapons. Moscow: Foreign Languages Publishing House, 1950. 535p. The original was in Russian.

6. Manila

2515 HESSEL, EUGENE A. "Let the Judges do the Hanging!" Christian Century 1949 66(34): 984-986. A discussion of war crimes trials in Manila which lists a series of problems that made it difficult to arrive at justice, including the lapse of time since the crimes were committed, the vindictive nature of the prosecution, and the problem of pinpointing responsibility. The author defends Ichinose Haruo and points to what he considers overwhelming evidence that he was innocent.

7. Shanghai

2516 "Shanghai Execution," Life 1947 23(2): 34-35. Two Japanese war criminals were driven through the city in a truck and shot before a jeering crowd. 4 photographs.

8. Yasutake Sakakibara

2517 SUPREME COMMANDER OF THE ALLIED POWERS (SCAP). Documents of the war crimes trials, Tokyo, 1946-1948. Some issued by SCAP and others by the United States Eighth Army. [Tokyo: 1945-1946]. Various pagination. Documents on the trial of Yasutake Sakakibara for atrocities committed while serving as a guard at a Japanese prisoner of war camp.

9. Yamashita Tomoyuki

2518 DALY, JAMES J.A. "The Yamashita Case and the Martial Courts," Connecticut Bar Journal Part I 1947 21(2): 136-158; Part II (3): 210-229. 94 notes.

2519 FAIRMAN, CHARLES. "The Supreme Court on Military Jurisdiction: Martial Rule in Hawaii and the Yamashita Case," Harvard Law Review 1946 59(6): 833-882. 138 notes.

2520 FELDHAUS, J. GORDON. "The Trial of Yamashita," South Dakota Bar Journal 1946 15(2): 181-193. Also in Current Legal Thought 1947 13(August): 251-262. A brief biography of Yamashita, stressing his war-time activities and responsibilities. Describes the charges brought against Yamashita and the main points of his trial. Argues that the trial was unfair and lists 5 grounds upon which the defense attempted to appeal the death sentence. Undocumented.

2521 FUQUA, ELLIS E. "Judicial Review of War Crimes Trials," Journal of Criminal Law and Criminology 1946 37(1): 58-64. Also in Illinois Law Review 1946 40(March-April): 546-553. Condemns Allied trials of war criminals, using the case of General Yamashita as an example of a trial by an improperly constituted tribunal. Based on primary sources; 49 notes.

2522 GANOE, JOHN T. "The Yamashita Case and the Constitution," Oregon Law Review 1946 25(3): 143-158. 18 notes.

2523 "General Tomoyuki Yamashita vs. Lieutenant General Wilhelm D. Styer," United States Supreme Court Records. Lawyers' edition. 327: 499-545 (October 1945 term). The text of the case of General Yamashita, argued before the Supreme Court of the United States.

2524 GUY, GEORGE F. "The Defense of Yamashita, Wyoming Law Journal 1950 4(3): 153-180. Undocumented.

2525 KATONA, PAUL. "Japanese War Crime Trials," Free World 1946 12(November): 37-40. Following a description of war crimes trials, following World War I, the author concentrates on the trial of General Yamashita Tomoyuki, which took place before either international military tribunals and was thus the first major war crimes trial of World War II. Outlines the proceedings of the trial and concludes that Yamashita was not proven guilty of the charges against him, but was convicted for other reasons. Deals with ex post facto legislation and individual responsibility for acts performed in the capacity of an official of the state.

2526 KUHN, ARTHUR K. "International Law and National Legislation in the Trial of War Criminals - the Yamashita Case," American Journal of International Law 1950 44(3): 559-562. Discusses the legality of the Yamashita trial from the standpoint of international law. 9 notes.

2527 LAEL, RICHARD L. The Yamashita Precedent: War Crimes and Command Responsibility. Wilmington, Delaware: Scholarly Resources, 1982. 165p. Deals with the proceedings against Japanese general Tomoyuki Yamashita in 1946, the first war crimes trial that charged a commanding officer with failure to exercise adequately his command responsibility when no conclusive evidence linked him directly to the violations. Discusses war in the Philippines war crimes policymaking in Europe and the Far East. Focuses primarily on the principle of command responsibility in connection with Yamashita's actions in the Philippines and the precedent set for future war crimes cases.

Includes charts of the Japanese command structure as of December 1944 and January 1945, and a map of the locations of Philippine atrocities. 11-page bibliography, 7-page index.

2528 LIM, M. "Yamashita and Homma Trials - Highlights," Philadelphia Law Journal 1947 22(January): 4-12.

2529 "Manila Infamies," Newsweek 1945 26(217): 52-53. On Yamashita.

2530 REEL, ADOLF FRANK. "Even His Enemy," Ohio Bar Association Report 1946 19(10): 163-175. One of General Yamashita's defense attorneys discusses his trial and conviction and his reason for appealing the case to the Supreme Court of the United States. He presents at length the dissenting opinions of 2 justices of that court and argues that Yamashita was condemned to death without due process of law. Homma's trial was conducted in the same way. Address to the Ohio Bar Association, May 16, 1946.

2531 REEL, ADOLF FRANK. The Case of General Yamashita. Chicago: University of Chicago Press, 1949. 324p. Discusses the case against General Tomoyuki Yamashita, Commander of the Fourteenth Army Group, Imperial Japanese Army, for permitting atrocities against the United States and its allies, particularly the Philippines. Covers the general's arraignment, the Military Commission serving as the prosecution, legal ethics, the Palawan Incident, and the hanging of Yamashita on February 23, 1946. Appendices contain the majority opinion of the United States Supreme Court, delivered by Chief Justice Harlan Stone, as well as 2 dissenting opinions. This book became so controversial that SCAP prepared a work to correct the "gross misrepresentations" of Reel's account, published in 1950 as The Case of General Yamashita: A Memorandum (no. 1024). Reel's work was published in Japanese under the title Yamashita saiban. 2 volumes. Tokyo: Nihon Kyobunsha, 1952. It was barred from publication during the years of occupation. 53 notes, no bibliography or index.

2532 "Sober Afterglow," Time 1949 54(19): 26-27. Deals with the case of General Yamashita.

2533 SULLIVAN, JAMES D. "Jurisdiction of Commission Established to Try War Criminals," Notre Dame Lawyer 1946 21(3): 237-239. Deals with the Yamashita appeal, Yamashita v. Styer, Commanding General, U.S. Army Forces, Western Pacific. 66 U.S. Sup. Ct. 340, February 4, 1946.

2534 SUPREME COMMANDER ALLIED POWERS (SCAP). The Case of General Yamashita: A Memorandum by Courtney Whitney, Chief, Government Section. Tokyo: SCAP, 1950. 82p. Brigadier General Courtney Whitney prepared this memorandum for SCAP in order to defend the legality of the trial and conviction of General Yamashita Tomoyuki, who was convicted by an American military commission in Manila in 1945. Intended primarily to rebut arguments advanced by Captain Adolf F. Reel, one of 5 members of the defense team, in his controversial book The Case of General Yamashita.

2535 United States of America vs. Tomoyuki Yamashita, before the Military Commission Convened by the Commanding General, United States army Forces, Western Pacific [Proceedings]. 34 volumes. in 14. Manila: 1945.

2536 WRIGHT, QUINCY. "Due Process and International Law," _American Journal of International Law_ 1946 40(2): 398-406. By a 6 to 2 decision the United States Supreme Court sustained the decision of a military tribunal appointed by General Douglas MacArthur which sentenced General Yamashita for failing to prevent atrocities by troops under his command in the Philippines. Since the commission was established by the United States, the defendant was found to be deserving of protection under the due process clause of the Fifth Amendment. Asserts that the Fifth Amendment clearly was not intended to apply to courts exercising jurisdiction over the enemy. The article looks in depth at 6 questions raised by the court's decision and concludes that due process was accorded the defendant to the extent that Japan had insufficient ground for asserting that Yamashita had been denied justice. Though such cases may result in "arbitral decisions," it is a field that can be developed by precedents, of which this is clearly one. Based largely on court cases; 16 notes.

10. Yokohama

2537 LYMAN, ALBERT. "A Reviewer Reviews the Yokohama War Crimes Trials," _Journal of the Bar Association of the District of Columbia_ 1950 17(6): 267-280. Undocumented.

2538 MILLER, ROBERT W. "War Crimes Trials at Yokohama," _Brooklyn Law Review_ 1949 15(2): 191-209. 46 notes.

2539 SPURLOCK, PAUL E. "The Yokohama War Crimes Trials: The Truth About a Misunderstood Subject," _American Bar Association Journal_ 1950 36(May): 387-389, 436-437. Spurlock, former reviewer of the records and sentences of the Yokohama trials for the American Eighth Army, describes the process of punishing lesser Japanese war criminals. He reviews the work of the War Crimes Branch for the Pacific Theater, the creation of the Eighth Army Military Commission, the Legal Section of SCAP, prosecution and defense procedures, and trial methods,

2540 SUPREME COMMANDER ALLIED POWERS (SCAP). _Non-Military Activities of the Occupation of Japan_. Tokyo: SCAP, 1952. Monograph 5, "Trials of Class 'B' and 'C' War Criminals." Refers to evidence in the trial of General Tamura.

11. Comparison of Two or More Trials

2541 TAYLOR, LAWRENCE. _A Trial of Generals: Homma, Yamashita, MacArthur_. South Bend: Icarus, 1981. 233p. Account of the trials of Japanese generals Masaharu Homma and Tomoyuki Yamashita at Manila under the direction of General Douglas MacArthur. Book 1 outlines war crimes committed under the command of General Homma, including the Bataan death march and mistreatment in prison camps. Although Homma apparently knew nothing about the atrocities with which he was charged, as even the prosecutors admitted, it was concluded that he should have known. Book 2 discusses the operations of General Yamashita, who was only "vaguely aware" of the mistreatment of prisoners under his jurisdiction in the Philippines. Book 3 deals with the prosecution for war crimes. Discusses General MacArthur's creation of the IMTFE. A second military prosecuting agency was set up for the prosecution of minor criminals. The War Crimes Branch of the U.S. General Headquarters of the Army Forces in the Pacific based branches in Yokohama and Manila. The trials in Manila lacked the procedural safeguards and strict rules applied by the IMTFE. Discusses MacArthur's selection of a tribunal and his personal drafting of the criminal procedures to be followed in conducting the trial. Includes excerpts from testimony at the trial. 4-page bibliography, 4-page index, 30 photographs.

2542 "Two Japanese War Criminals," New Republic 1946 114(8): 269. An editorial comment on the procedures of the military tribunal established to try 2 Japanese war criminals. Points out that the U.S. Supreme Court had 2 dissenting opinions on the appeals of General Yamashita and General Homma. The dissenting justices argued that procedures were sloppy and that they denied the accused adequate time to prepare their defenses.

2543 UNITED STATES. SUPREME COURT. "Judicial Decisions in re Yamashita [and] in re Homma," American Journal of International Law 1946 40(2): 432-482. A collection of the official decisions and the dissenting opinions regarding the Yamashita and Homma cases.

D. IMTFE

1. General Works

2544 ALLEN, LAFE FRANKLIN. "Japan's Militarists Face the Music," American Foreign Service Journal 1947 24(August): 14-17, 41-44. Describes the proceedings of the IMTFE and the American determination to permit the prosecution and defense to express their opinions. The role of Chief Prosecutor Joseph B. Keenan is highlighted and prosecution arguments are outlined. Discusses defense preparation and legal tactics used to challenge the punishment of Japanese for violating international law.

2545 BASU, K.K. "Tokio Trials," Indian Law Review 1949 3: 25-30.

2546 BOUDKEVITCH, S.L. "Tirée du procès des grands criminels de guerre de Tokyo," La Vie Internationale 1968 9: 126-130; 11: 128-136.

2547 BOYD, CARL. "Exaltation and Hindsight: Tojo's 'Reflections Upon Parting with Lieutenant Colonel Kenworthy, a Man Bearing the Spirit of an Ancient Samurai,'" Montclair Journal of Social Science and Humanities 1974 3(2): 79-96. Examines a document written by Hideki Tojo. Based on a paper presented to the 7th Annual Bloomsburg State College [Pennsylvania] History Conference, in 1974.

2548 BROWN, ALLAN ROBERT. "The Role of the Emperor in Japan's Decision to go to War: the Record of the International Military Tribunal for the Far East," M.A. thesis, Stanford University, 1957. 120p. Chapter 2, "The International Military Tribunal for the Far East," pp. 9-16, surveys the creation of the records of the IMTFE.

2549 BROWN, BRENDAN FRANCIS. "Red China, the Tokyo Trial, and Aggressive War," Louisiana Bar Journal 1956 3(January): 145-159.

2550 CHO, SUNG YOON. "The Tokyo War Crimes Trial," Quarterly Journal of the Library of Congress 1967 24(4): 309-318.

2551 COMYNS-CARR, ARTHUR S. The Tokyo War Crimes Trial," Far Eastern Survey 1949 18(10): 109-114. An account of the IMTFE written by a member of the British prosecution staff at the

Tokyo trial. The author's intent is to draw attention to certain points without expressing an opinion on them. Compares this trial to that in Nuremberg. Discusses the pleas of the defendants, the tribunal's decision regarding the treatment of prisoners of war, and possible responsibility on the part of Hirohito.

2552 Criminal Conspiracy in the Japanese War Crimes Trials. Washington: [no publisher given], May 23, 1946. 407p. This memorandum, prepared for Joseph B. Keenan, Chief of Counsel for the United States for the IMTFE, deals with the early development of the law of criminal conspiracy, various legal cases that contributed to the development of the law, and theories of criminal conspiracy in the United States, England, France, China, Japan, and the Soviet Union. Concludes that the conspiracy doctrine held by the IMTFE, as adopted largely from the Nuremberg IMT, was consistent with the principles of justice generally held world wide. Contains essays on the common law of criminal conspiracy, federal statutes on criminal conspiracy, state statutes on criminal conspiracy, and a compilation of foreign laws on the subject. Heavily annotated. Appendices list the defendants as well as the 13-page indictment against them.

2553 FIXEL, ROWLAND WELLS. Trial of Japan's War Lords. [no city given]: [no publisher given], 1959. 247p.

2554 FOX, GALEN C. "The Nomonhan Conflict in the Tokyo International War Crimes Trial." M.A. thesis, University of Oregon, 1965. 130p.

2555 GOLUNSKY, S. "The Trial of the Japanese War Criminals," New Times 1947 18(May 1): 6-10. Discusses the organization and conduct of the Tokyo trial, with emphasis on the defendants and the prewar and wartime events discussed during the trial. The 28 defendants are divided into 5 groups: statesmen, military leaders, diplomats, economic officials, and ideologists of Japanese aggression.

2556 HORWITZ, SOLIS. The Tokyo Trial. New York: Carnegie Endowment for International Peace, 1950. International Conciliation 1950 (465): 473-584. The entire issue is an analysis of the IMTFE. Discusses the origin and authority of the trial, the charter of the tribunal and trial machinery, the defendants and the indictment, the trial itself, the judgment and sentences, and the dissenting and concurring opinions. Contains several appendices. The author was a member of the prosecution team.

2557 HYDER, ELTON M., JR. "The Tokyo Trial," Texas Bar Journal 1947 10(2): 136-137, 166-167.

2558 "International Military Tribunal for the Far East," International Organization 1947 1(1): 176. A summation of the nature and scope of the IMTFE, including particulars such as the provisions for the selection of members of the tribunal, the kinds of war criminals tried, a list of the defendants, and a list of prosecuting nations. 1 note.

2559 INTERNATIONAL MILITARY TRIBUNAL FOR THE FAR EAST (IMTFE). Special Studies, 1-21. [Tokyo]: [1947].

2560 "International Military Tribunal for the Far East: The Judges and Prosecutors," <u>New Zealand Law Journal</u> 1946 22(9): 119. Contains a list of judges and prosecutors at the IMTFE.

2561 "Jap War Criminals Await Trial," <u>Life</u> 1945 19(20): 29-33. A brief introductory essay and a series of photographs taken at the prison camp for accused war criminals on Omori Island. Pictured are Tojo, Suzuki, and several members of the Japanese cabinet at the time of the attack on Pearl Harbor.

2562 KEENAN, JOSEPH BERRY. <u>Our Relations in the Far East as They Appear in the International War Crimes Trials in Tokyo</u>. [no city given]: [no publisher given], 1946. 44p.

2563 KEENAN, JOSEPH BERRY, and BRENDAN FRANCIS BROWN. <u>Crimes against International Law</u>. Washington: Public Affairs Press, 1950. 226p. This work on the United States and the Tokyo war crimes trial is based up statements made at the trial by Joseph Keenan, Chief Counsel for the United States, and upon memoranda by Dr. Brendan Brown, his judicial consultant. Focuses on the law of the Tokyo case, rather than on atrocities committed. Argues that the charter afforded a fair trial at all stages of the proceedings. Discusses the Potsdam Declaration and the law of the charter, the IMTFE, aggressive war as an international crime, crimes against humanity, and individual responsibility under international law. Appendix I is an essay on genocide and international law presented by Brendan Brown to the Subcommittee on Genocide of the Senate Foreign Relations Committee on January 25, 1950. Appendix II is a memorandum by Eleanor Bontecons issued on September 25, 1946, concerning the question of replacement of a member of the IMTFE during the trial. Appendix III discusses the legal and sociological position of General Douglas MacArthur as Supreme Commander for the Allied Powers in the Pacific. Appendix IV presents rules of procedure of the IMTFE. Based on primary and secondary sources; 28p. of notes, 7-page bibliography, 4-page index.

2564 KOJIMA, NOBORU. <u>Tokyo Saiban</u>. 2 volumes. Tokyo: Chuo koron, 1971. Discusses Japanese war crimes trials and a list of 260 people originally slated for prosecution at Tokyo.

2565 "Le Nuremberg d'Extrême-Orient. Le Procès des criminels de guerre japonais s'est ouvert à Tokio," <u>Revue de Droit International de Sciences Diplomatiques et Politiques</u> 1946 24(1): 142-143.

2566 LIU, JAMES T.C. "The Tokyo Trial," <u>China Monthly</u> 1947 8(7): 242-245, 247. Focuses on the presentation of the preliminary defense and discusses the opening arguments of the defense, which were published in the U.S. Army newspaper <u>Stars and Stripes</u> on the day before the arguments began. Most of the article summarizes and comments on the defense presentation. Liu challenges Japanese contentions that the trial proceedings were illegal and that Japanese aggressions were acts of self-defense. 2 photographs.

2567 MARKOV, M. "The Approaching Trial of Major Japanese War Criminals," <u>New Times</u> 1946 8(April 15): 7-10. Reprinted in <u>Information Bulletin</u> 1946 6(46): 403-405. Argues for just and speedy punishment of war criminals, criticizes Americans for keeping the Emperor as titular head of the Japanese people, discusses prominent officials who should have been tried, and criticizes the manner in which the trial was conducted.

2568 MC AFEE, B. "The Tokio War Crimes Trials," *Annuaire de l'Association des Auditeurs et Anciens Auditeurs de l'Académie de Droit International de la Haye* 1958 28: 39-49.

2569 MC KENZIE, WALTER I. "The Japanese War Crimes Trials," *Michigan State Bar Journal* 1947 26(5): 16-21.

2570 MEEK, FRANK E. "[War crimes' trials in the Pacific]," *Idaho State Bar Proceedings* 1947 21: 36-42.

2571 MINEAR, RICHARD H. *Victors' Justice: The Tokyo War Crimes Trial*. Princeton: Princeton University Press, 1971. 229p. The author's purpose was to demolish the credibility of the Tokyo trial and its verdict. The book is largely a result of the effect on him of the Vietnam war. Even though objecting to the "victors' justice" of the Tokyo trials, Minear favored war crimes trials of men such as Lieutenant William Calley. He admits that his book is "political scholarship" and that none of his essential research demanded use of any foreign language. Minear's treatment covers the "lofty and low" motives of the war crimes trials, as well as the charter, indictment, and judgment of the Tribunal. He examines various problems of international law and legal process as well as those involving the Soviet Union, overall conspiracy, the Axis alliance, and Pearl Harbor. Concludes that the foundation of the trials in international law was shaky and that the legal process was seriously flawed. Based on secondary sources; 372 notes, 5 appendices, including a list of the defendants, verdicts, and sentences, 4-page bibliographical note, 13-page index.

2572 MIWA KAI, and PHILIP B. YAMPOLSKY. *Political Chronology of Japan, 1885-1957*. New York: Columbia East Asian Institute Studies No. 5, 1957. Reference book on Japanese cabinet positions and members.

2573 "Observations on the Trial of War Criminals in Japan," *External Affairs* 1949 1(2): 12-23. Presents a comprehensive, chronological history of the establishment of the IMTFE and an assessment of the historical value of the material presented by the prosecution and the defense. Contains information on each of the defendants.

2574 QUENTIN-BAXTER, R.Q. "The Task of the International Military Tribunal at Tokyo," *New Zealand Law Journal* 1949 25(7-10): 133-138. Under the Pact of Paris, the military tribunals could justly punish the leaders of Germany, Japan, and other nations for launching aggressive wars. Approves of the Nuremberg and Tokyo precedents for punishing subordinates as well as leaders.

2575 RAGINSKIĬ, MARK, and S.L. BOUDKEVITCH. "Les Crimes ne doivent pas se répéter. Vingt Ans après le procès de Tokyo," *La Vie Internationale* 1968 8: 97-103.

2576 RAGINSKIĬ, MARK, and S. ROZENBLIT. *Mezhdunarodnyi protsess glavnykh iaponskikh voennykh prestupnikov*. Moscow: 1950. 460p. Soviet version of the war crimes trials held in Tokyo.

2577 "Remember?" New Republic 1946 115(December 30): 895. Brief editorial on the trial of Tojo and 15 other accused war criminals demonstrates that Japanese people crowded the spectators' gallery in order to study the criminals themselves. The trials supplied a complete and objective account of Japanese wartime aggression. SCAP was encouraged to see the events of 1931-1945 as an aberration in Japanese history that should be forgotten as quickly as possible.

2578 RÖLING, BERNARD V.A. "The Tokyo Trial and the Development of International Law," Indian Law Review 1953 7(1): 4-14.

2579 SCHROEDER, PAUL W. The Axis Alliance and Japanese-American Relations, 1941. Ithaca: Cornell University Press, 1958. 245p. The epilogue contains a brief analysis of the Tokyo war crimes trial. Annotated, bibliography, index.

2580 SMALL, MELVIN. Victors' Justice: The Tokyo War Crimes Trial. Princeton: Princeton University Press, 1971. 229p.

2581 SUPREME COMMANDER FOR THE ALLIED POWERS. INTERNATIONAL PROSECUTION SECTION. Tokyo War Crimes Trials, Japanese Officials, 1927-1945. Tokyo: IMTFE, c.1947. 4p. Contains the names of the members of the 17 cabinets formed between April 20, 1917, and August 16, 1945. Identifies many high military members of the cabinet

2582 SUTTON, DAVID NELSON. "The Trial of Tojo," Virginia State Bar Association Proceedings 1949 60: 223-246. 54 notes.

2583 SUTTON, DAVID NELSON. "The Trial of Tojo: The Most Important Trial in All History?" American Bar Association Journal 1950 36(February): 93-96, 160-165. Examines the legal basis of the IMTFE and its composition and functioning. Discusses why the 28 defendants were selected and points out many difficulties arising out of differences between Japanese and Anglo-American legal systems. Concludes that the IMTFE charter was based on international law, that aggressive war is an international crime, and that national self-defense must be adjudicated before an impartial tribunal. 42 notes.

2584 TAKAYANAGI, KENZO. Kyokuto saiban to kokusaiho. Tokyo: Yuhikaku, 1948. Includes English text under the title The Tokio Trials and International Law: Answer to the Prosecution's Arguments on International Law Delivered at the International Military Tribunal for the Far East on 3 and 4 March 1948. Tokyo: Yuhikaku, 1948. 137p. The author was a defense counsel at the Tokyo war crimes trial. He studied at London's Middle Temple, Harvard, Northwestern, and the Tokyo Imperial University. Consists of Takayanagi's 2 lengthy addresses before the Tokyo tribunal in the winter of 1948. He argued against Joseph B. Keenan's assertion that the conspiracy charged against the defendants was known to and recognized by most civilized nations. He called the doctrine of conspiracy a dangerous product of English legal theory. He won over Pal of India and Webb of Australia to his way of thinking.

2585 "The International Military Tribunal for the Far East," Current Notes on International Affairs 1948 19(5): 231-241. Reports on the character and work of the IMTFE between January 19, 1946, and April 16, 1948, when the defense and prosecution rested. Summarizes the prosecution and defense phases of the trial.

2586 "Trial of Japanese Executioners," Oklahoma Bar Association Journal 1946 17(31): 1269-1272.

2587 TSAI, PAUL CHUNG-TSENG. "Judicial Administration of the Laws of War: Procedures in War Crimes Trials," LL.D. dissertation, Yale University, 1957. This analysis of war crimes trials procedures concludes with a formulation of standards for such trials. Much on the proceedings of the IMTFE.

2588 UEMATSU, KEITA. Kyokuto, Kokusai Gunji Saiban. Tokyo: Jimbutsu oraisha, 1962.

2589 UNITED STATES. DEPARTMENT OF STATE. "Apprehension, Trial, and Punishment of War Criminals in the Far East," Department of State Bulletin 1947 16(409): 804-806. May 4, 1947. Statement of U.S. policy on the subject.

2590 UNITED STATES. DEPARTMENT OF STATE. "Trial of Japanese War Criminals," Department of State Bulletin 1949 20(513): 569-571. Reprints recommendations of the Far Eastern Commission (FEC) to member governments in regard to the termination of war crimes proceedings.

2591 VASILYEV, A.N. "On Rapid Trial and Punishment of War Criminals (On the Results of the Tokio Trials)," Current Digest of the Soviet Press 1949 1(25): 11-15. A condensed translation of an analysis of the IMTFE which first appeared in the March 1949 edition of Sovetskoye gosudarstvo i pravo, pp. 40-49. Focuses on delaying tactics of the defense and inherent weaknesses of the Anglo-American court system, which together caused the trial to last more than 2 years.

2592 VASILYEV, A.N. "The Tokyo Trial of the Chief Japanese War Criminals," Soviet Press Translations 1948 3(7): 195-202. A 2-part article with appeared first in Pravda, January 19, and February 20, 1948. It reports the speech of Vasilyev, chief prosecutor for the Soviet Union at the Tokyo war crimes trial. Examines aggressions of Japan from the turn of the century to the end of World War II.

2593 WADSWORTH, LAWRENCE W., JR. "Short History of the Tokyo War Crime Trials: With special Reference to some Aspects of Procedure." Ph.D. dissertation, American University, 1955. 367p. Contains chapters on the origins of the Tokyo trial, the establishment of the tribunal as well as its powers and functions, the indictment, the cases for the prosecution and defense, court procedure and conduct of the trial, and the judgment and sentences.

2594 "Wages of Infamy: Japan's War Trials," Newsweek 1948 32(November 22): 35-36.

2. Documents

a. General

2595 INTERNATIONAL MILITARY TRIBUNAL FOR THE FAR EAST (IMTFE). LANGUAGE ARBITRATION BOARD. Index of Language Corrections Affecting Documents Admitted into Evidence and the Court Records of the International Military Tribunal for the Far East. Tokyo: 1948.

2596 SUPREME COMMANDER FOR THE ALLIED POWERS. INTERNATIONAL PROSECUTION SECTION. *International Military Tribunal for the Far East, Established at Tokyo, January 19, 1946*. State Department Publication No. 2765. Washington: GPO, 1947. 16p. Contains the official text of 3 documents relating to the IMTFE, a special proclamation to establish the the tribunal, issued by General MacArthur, on January 19, 1946; the charter of the tribunal, issued as SCAP General Order No. 1, January 19, 1946; and the amended charter of the tribunal, issued as General Order No. 20, April 26, 1946.

2597 UNITED STATES. DEPARTMENT OF STATE. "Charter of the International Military Tribunal for the Far East," *Department of State Bulletin* 1946 14(360): 890, 907.

2598 UNITED STATES. DEPARTMENT OF STATE. "Trial of Far Eastern War Criminals, Special Proclamation: Establishment of an International Military Tribunal for the Far East, Charter of the Tribunal," *Department of State Bulletin* 1946 14(349): 361-364. Consists of General MacArthur's proclamation on the establishment of the IMTFE and the charter of the tribunal.

2599 UNITED STATES. DEPARTMENT OF STATE. *Trial of Japanese War Criminals*. Department of State Publication No. 2613. Washington: GPO, 1946. 104p. Government documents pertaining to Japanese war criminals include the text of Unites States Chief Counsel Joseph B. Keenan's opening statement at the Tokyo trial, the charter of the IMTFE, and the text of the indictment. Appendices contain a summary of the principal matters and events on which the prosecution relied in support of the counts of the indictment, a list of articles of treaties violated by Japan, a list of official assurances violated by Japan, and a statement of individual responsibility for crimes set out in the indictment.

2600 "War Crimes: Greatest Trial in Tokyo," *Time* 1948 51(1): 24-25.

b. Indexes

2601 MAXON, YALE CANDEE. *Index to Documents, by Phrase and Subject* [of the International Military Tribunal for the Far East] *Documents 1 to 2969 and 4000 to 4095*. [Tokyo]: 1947.

c. Indictments

2602 UNITED STATES. DEPARTMENT OF STATE. "Trial of Far Eastern Criminals," *Department of State Bulletin* 1946 14(359): 846-848, 853. Consists of 2 items relating to the war crimes trials: a statement by Joseph Keenan on the indictment, and a document summarizing the indictment and listing the defendants and their former positions.

d. Defense and Prosecution Records

2603 INTERNATIONAL MILITARY TRIBUNAL FOR THE FAR EAST (IMTFE). *Tokyo War Crimes Trials, Documents, Exhibits for the Defense: Index*. Exhibit Nos. 2283-3915 . Tokyo: IMTFE, February 26, 1947 - April 16, 1948. This index contains a list of 1411 defense exhibits and 222 prosecution exhibits accepted as evidence. They are arranged according to order in which they were accepted. In addition to exhibit numbers, the index includes the title and the original number of the document and the pages of the Proceedings at which it is cited as evidence or for purposes of identification.

e. Prosecution Records

2604 INTERNATIONAL MILITARY TRIBUNAL FOR THE FAR EAST (IMTFE). Analysis of Documentary Evidence. IPS Document No. 0012. 27 volumes. Tokyo: IMTFE, 1947. Contains much basic information on Documents 1-4100, which were prepared by the IPS. Lists authors, dates, and locations of the original documents.

2605 INTERNATIONAL MILITARY TRIBUNAL FOR THE FAR EAST (IMTFE). Chronological Summary (of Evidence). IPS Document No. 0001. Tokyo: IMTFE, 1947. Oral and documentary evidence presented by the prosecution up to December 10, 1946, are summarized here in chronological order, beginning with the Tanaka cabinet in 1928 and ending with the Suzuki cabinet in 1945. Gives page references in the Proceedings.

2606 INTERNATIONAL MILITARY TRIBUNAL FOR THE FAR EAST (IMTFE). Decision of Imperial Conferences, Cabinet Meetings, and other Conferences and Meetings which appear in the Prosecution's Evidence. IPS Document No. 0004. Tokyo: IMTFE, 1947. 283p. Includes the arguments and the decisions agreed upon at various imperial conferences and meetings. Organized chronologically and limited to testimony and documents submitted by the prosecution. Gives Exhibit numbers and page numbers in the Proceedings.

2607 INTERNATIONAL MILITARY TRIBUNAL FOR THE FAR EAST (IMTFE). General Index of the Record of the Prosecution's Case. IPS Document No. 0005. Tokyo: IMTFE, 1947. 101p. The record of the prosecution's case reported on pages 1 to 16,997 of the Proceedings, presented between May 3, 1946, and January 31, 1947. Divides the treatment into 14 phases of the case. Includes entries of related names, places, and institutions, and lists pertinent pages in the Proceedings.

2608 INTERNATIONAL MILITARY TRIBUNAL FOR THE FAR EAST (IMTFE). Prosecution Documents Which Were Either Not Offered or Were Rejected. United States Library of Congress Microfilm, Law-133.

2609 INTERNATIONAL MILITARY TRIBUNAL FOR THE FAR EAST (IMTFE). Tokyo War Crimes Trials: Documents, Exhibits for the Prosecution. (Exhibit Numbers 1-2282). 22 volumes. Tokyo: IMFTE, 1947. The prosecution, working with the International Prosecution Section of SCAP, prepared over 12,000 documents to support its case. Of these, 2282 were presented before the court and were accepted as exhibits for the prosecution during the period May 4, 1946 to January 24, 1947. The records listed here by exhibit number include decisions of Allied conferences, imperial ordinances, Japanese memoranda, diaries, memoirs, books, and affidavits. The documents vary in length from one to several hundred pages.

2610 INTERNATIONAL MILITARY TRIBUNAL FOR THE FAR EAST (IMTFE). Tokyo War Crimes Trials, Documents, Exhibits for the Prosecution: Index. Tokyo: IMTFE, (May 4, 1946 - January 24, 1947). 322p. A total of 2282 prosecution exhibits accepted in evidence by the IMTFE are indexed here. They are described in the Proceedings, on pp. 105-16,259. Lists exhibits by number, provides information concerning numbers originally given by the prosecution, and gives the pages in the <u>Proceedings</u> for evidence and identification.

2611 INTERNATIONAL MILITARY TRIBUNAL FOR THE FAR EAST (IMTFE). <u>Tokyo War Crimes Trials, Index of Documents Not Specifically Linked to One or More of the Defendants</u>. Tokyo: IMTFE, May 26, 1947. 17p. This working list of prosecution documents is grouped according to 8 topics. It was prepared for the purpose of evaluating files material only, and is not as complete as <u>Index to Documents (by Phase and Subject)</u>. The topics are: materials on the Japanese government, constitution, and army; propaganda and internal politics; ultranationalist societies; China, collaboration with Germany and Italy; France, Thailand, the Netherlands, and Portugal; the Soviet Union; preparations for war against the United States and Great Britain; and documents dealing with class "B" and class "C" offenses. This index does not include any documents which appeared in <u>Revised Index of Documents by Defendants</u>, German documents numbered between 4000 and 4100, or documents numbered between 4100 and 11,900.

2612 INTERNATIONAL MILITARY TRIBUNAL FOR THE FAR EAST (IMTFE). <u>Tokyo War Crimes Trials, Index to Documents (by Phase and Subject)</u>. Tokyo: IMTFE, March 20, 1947. 20p. An index under 13 main headings with detailed subheadings of prosecution documents 1-2669, and 4000-4095. They pertain to all phases of the prosecution's case. Some of the major headings are: the functions of offices held by defendants, military aggression in Manchuria, military aggression in China, preparations for war, relations with various European and Asian nations, relations with the United States and Great Britain, and relations with the Netherlands and Portugal.

2613 INTERNATIONAL MILITARY TRIBUNAL FOR THE FAR EAST (IMTFE). <u>Tokyo War Crimes Trials, Numerical List of IPS Documents Introduced as Court Exhibits</u>. Tokyo: IMTFE, December 9, 1947. 32p. This is intended primarily as a cross-reference to the 2-volume <u>Index of Exhibits</u>. This list contains all IPS documents placed in evidence to the end of November 1947. The last prosecution document given is No. 8279, which is exhibit No. 1901.

f. Witnesses

2614 INTERNATIONAL MILITARY TRIBUNAL FOR THE FAR EAST (IMTFE). <u>Tokyo War Crimes Trials, Index of Witnesses</u>. Tokyo: IMTFE, 1948. 34p., 117p. The names of witnesses who testified for the prosecution or defense between June 17, 1946, and February 10, 1948, are indexed in this volume. The witnesses are listed in alphabetical order, with the names of people who directed the testimony. Lists the names of people who cross-examined the witnesses and the page numbers in the <u>Proceedings</u> where the testimony is recorded.

g. Defense Records

2615 INTERNATIONAL MILITARY TRIBUNAL FOR THE FAR EAST. (IMTFE). <u>Affidavit of Tojo. Individual Defense</u>. Tokyo: IMTFE, 1947. Defense Document 3000.

2616 INTERNATIONAL MILITARY TRIBUNAL FOR THE FAR EAST (IMTFE). <u>General Index of the Record of the Defense Case</u>. IPS Document

No. 0008. Tokyo: IMTFE, 1947. 152p. The defense case was divided into 6 "phases": general problems, Manchuria and Manchukuo, China, the Soviet Union, the Pacific War, and individual defense. This index is to statements and testimonies referring to the first 4 of these. This material was read before the tribunal by several defense counsels between February 24 and June 19, 1947. It is cited in the Proceedings on pages 17,004-24,758. Cross-referenced to the Proceedings.

2617 INTERNATIONAL MILITARY TRIBUNAL FOR THE FAR EAST (IMTFE). Rejected Defense Documents. United States Library of Congress Microfilm, Law-128.

2618 INTERNATIONAL MILITARY TRIBUNAL FOR THE FAR EAST (IMTFE). Tokyo War Crimes Trials. Addendum to Revised Index of Documents by Defendants. Tokyo: IMTFE, May 23, 1947. 7p. A sequel to the Revised Index of Documents by Defendants (1947), of April 14, 1947.

2619 INTERNATIONAL MILITARY TRIBUNAL FOR THE FAR EAST (IMTFE). Tokyo War Crimes Trials. Documents, Exhibits for the Defense. (Defense Documents Numbers 1-3088). 23 volumes. Tokyo: IMTFE, 1948. These documents were presented in court between January 27, 1947 and February 10, 1948. They are arranged according to defense document numbers rather than exhibit numbers. Not all of them were accepted as court exhibits. The documents include affidavits, sworn depositions of the defendants, memoirs, excerpts of past remarks, political and military records, telegrams, treaties, and reports.

2620 INTERNATIONAL MILITARY TRIBUNAL FOR THE FAR EAST (IMTFE). Tokyo War Crimes Trials, Revised Index of Documents by Defendants. Tokyo: IMTFE, April 14, 1947. 46p. A revision of the Index to Documents (by Defendants), issued on March 15, 1947. It includes a list of the numbers of all documents prepared for the defense of each of the 28 accused. The documents are arranged by defense document number, and, for those introduced as evidence, by exhibit number as well.

h. Trial Proceedings

2621 DULL, PAUL S., and MICHAEL TAKAAKI UMEMURA. The Tokyo Trials: A Functional Index to the Proceedings of the International Military Tribunal for the Far East. Ann Arbor: University of Michigan Press, 1957. An index and guide to the 50,000 pages of evidence taken at the IMTFE. Unlike the Nuremberg proceedings, those of the IMTFE were mimeographed but never printed.

2622 INTERNATIONAL MILITARY TRIBUNAL FOR THE FAR EAST (IMTFE). Narrative Summary of the Record. Tokyo: IMTFE, 1947. 6000p. This digest of the Proceedings (1946-1948) was prepared by the IPS to assist both the prosecution and the defense in preparing their summaries. The compilation of this summary was discontinued with page 37,167 of the Proceedings and does not cover that section of the defense case covered on pp. 37,168 to 38,947.

2623 INTERNATIONAL MILITARY TRIBUNAL FOR THE FAR EAST (IMTFE). Record of Proceedings, 1946-1948. Library of Congress Microfilm, 1964. International Military Tribunal for the Far East. 36 reels.

2624 INTERNATIONAL MILITARY TRIBUNAL FOR THE FAR EAST (IMTFE). 113 volumes. <u>Tokyo War Crimes Trials, Proceedings</u>. (818 Sessions). Tokyo: IMTFE, 1948. Available on microfilm (36 reels) from the Photoduplication Service, Department C-2, Library of Congress. (See following Entry). The official record of the tribunal, covering 818 sessions in 417 days between May 3, 1946, when the indictment was read and April 16, 1948, when the summations for the prosecution and defense were completed. The record does not include the proceedings of the last 7 sessions conducted in November 1948, when the judgment was read. These volumes contain a variety of materials, including a copy of the indictment, a discussion of the legal basis of the tribunal's jurisdiction, debates on legal technicalities, testimony of witnesses, a record of exhibits presented, arguments about evidence, testimony regarding Japanese attitudes towards war, material on military aggression against China, records of Japan's relations with other countries, material on the political role of the military, cabinet responsibility, and a discussion of individual responsibility.

2625 INTERNATIONAL MILITARY TRIBUNAL FOR THE FAR EAST (IMTFE). <u>Transcript of Proceedings: 7 January and 1 October, 1947</u>. United States Library of Congress Microfilm, Law-134. Microfilm records of IMTFE documents.

2626 PRITCHARD, R. JOHN, and SONIA MAGBANUA ZAIDE (comps.) [Donald Ameron Watt, Project Director]. <u>The Tokyo War Crimes Trials</u>. New York/London: Garland, 1981. 22 volumes. Volume 1, <u>Pre-Trial Documents, Transcript of the Proceedings in Open Session</u> (pages 1-2097), has a 17-page introduction, 6p. of notes, a 16-page preface, and a 4-page guide to the trial, and contains pre-trail documents on the establishment of the IMTFE, the Charter, a discussion of the appointment of members to the tribunal, and rules of procedure of the tribunal. It also lists the 11 accuser nations, the 28 defendants, and the 55 counts with which they were charged. Appendices list the members of the tribunal, gives a summary of the events and actions upon which the indictments were based, lists the articles of treaties and official assurances violated by Japan, and makes a statement regarding individual responsibility for crimes set out in the indictment. Most of Volume 1 and all of Volumes 2-22 contain the original proceedings of the trial itself.

i. Verdicts, Sentences, Execution of Sentences

2627 INTERNATIONAL MILITARY TRIBUNAL FOR THE FAR EAST (IMTFE). <u>Judgment of the International Military Tribunal for the Far East</u>. Tokyo: IMTFE, 1948. 1218p., 130p. The 10 chapters of the majority judgment of the tribunal are printed here. The judgment begins with a description of the establishment, jurisdiction, and proceedings of the tribunal. Japan became a member of the civilized community of nations by joining the League of Nations and later violated many of the laws of war adopted by the League. Contains many documents, but no index. The judgment was read into the <u>Proceedings</u> (pp. 48, 415-449, 858), and was later published by a number of institutions, including the United States War Department (1948, 7 volumes).

3. <u>Dissent</u>

2628 BERNARD, HENRI. <u>Memorandum. Dissenting Judgment</u>. Tokyo: IMTFE, 1948. 23p. Dissenting opinion of the French justice which criticizes the judicial procedures adopted for the trial and the sentences imposed. Argues that the defendants were not given adequate opportunity at the preliminary examination to obtain and organize evidence for their defense. Charges that dissenting opinions were ignored when the judgment was prepared.

2629 JARANILLA, DELFIN. Separate Opinion Concurring, The Majority Judgment. Tokyo: IMTFE, 1948. The author was the Philippine justice on the IMTFE. He defends the legality of the tribunal and is particularly critical of Pal. There is also a Japanese edition.

2630 PAL, RADHABINOD. Dissenting Opinion of Judgement and Decision of the International Military Tribunal for the Far East in the Case of the United States of America, the Republic of China, et al. against Araki Sadao, Dohihara Kenji, et al. Tokyo: IMTFE, 1948. 12 volumes. Pal questions the fundamental existence of a tribunal composed only of victorious powers and insists that the jurisdiction of the tribunal could not possibly extend to wars waged by Japan before 1941. Pal advocated acquitting all the defendants. Discusses in detail his 7-part dissent, his attitude toward President Truman's use of the atomic bomb, how his opinion was received in the rest of the world, and where it was published and how it was treated by scholars.

2631 PAL, RADHABINOD. International Military Tribunal of the Far East: Dissentient Judgment. Calcutta: Sanyal, 1953. 701p. Published in part in Japanese as Nihon muzairon. Tokyo: Nihon shobo, November 11, 1952. Minority legal opinion arguing against the concept of war crimes trials as conceived by the IMTFE. Part 1 (pp. 1-105) deals with the legal basis for the trial, the jurisdiction of the Tribunal, the law upon which the indictment was based, the charter definition of war crimes, and victor's justice. Part 2 (pp. 109-135) analyzes the definitions of aggressive war since the Paris Conference of 1936. Part 3 (pp. 139-173) raises questions concerning the rules of evidence and the examination of witnesses. Considers the inconsistency of the court with regard to inadmissible evidence. Part 4 (pp. 177-189) examines the Manchurian Incident, preparation of Japan for aggressive war, and the cumulative effect of evidence concerning conspiracy. Part 5 (pp. 577-582) investigates the scope of the IMTFE's jurisdiction. Part 6 (pp. 585-596) analyzes war crimes of murder and conspiracy in relation to the civilian population of Japanese occupied territories and in relation to prisoners of war. Part 7 (pp. 697-701) presents Justice Pal's recommendation that each of the accused be found not guilty. Based on primary sources; 54 photographs, no bibliography.

2632 RÖLING, BERNARD V.A. Opinion of Mr. Justice Röling, Member for the Netherlands. Tokyo: IMTFE, 1948. 249p. Minority opinion that argues that the jurisdiction of the IMTFE was restricted to the Pacific war and that the judgment concerning other wars in the Far East were outside this jurisdiction. Objects to the concepts of "crimes against peace" and "responsibility for war" on the ground that such concepts cannot be defined. Several IMTFE defendants should have been acquitted. A detailed justification of the author's assertions is included.

4. Verdicts, Sentences, Execution of Sentences

2633 ALLEN, LAFE FRANKLIN. "Judgment Day in Tokyo," Military Government Journal 1949 2(Fall): 7-8, 12. Briefly summarizes the proceedings of the IMTFE and the sentences handed down, and criticizes the tribunal for not trying the Emperor. Concludes that the trial was fair. Expresses the hope that the trial will convince the Japanese people that international lawlessness does not pay.

2634 COMYNS-CARR, ARTHUR S. "The Judgment of the International Military Tribunal for the Far East," Transactions of the Grotius Society 1949 34: 141-151. Compares the legal aspects of the Nuremberg and Tokyo IMT trials; the second recounts and comments on information discovered in the course of the Tokyo trial regarding events leading up to the war in the Pacific.

2635 "International Military Tribunal for the Far East," International Organization 1949 3(1): 184-186. Discusses the specifics of the November 1948 verdict against 28 Japanese war criminals. Lists the defendants, the charges against them, and the sentences handed down. Includes an explanation of why 2 of the 11 members of the tribunal presented minority judgments exonerating the defendants. 1 note.

2636 KUDRYAVTSEV, V. "Verdict against Japanese Militarism," Soviet Press Translations 1949 4(3): 70-71. This article appeared originally in the December 3, 1948, issue of Trud. It comments on the Tokyo (IMT) trial and outlines the 25 verdicts handed down, which are regarded as a triumph for the advocates of peace. Criticizes those who refuse to punish war criminals still at large.

2637 "Major Japanese War Criminals: International Tribunal's Findings," Current Notes on International Affairs 1949 20(3): 330-345. Discusses the findings of the IMTFE on several counts of the indictment, the verdicts, and the sentences. Includes separate opinions of the president of the tribunal and the dissenting opinions of the Indian, French, and Dutch judges, with some commentary on appeals to the United States Supreme Court.

2638 Prigover Tokiiskogo Mezhdunarodnogo Tribunala. Moscow: Gospolitizdat, 1950. Deals with the verdict of the Japanese war criminals at the IMTFE.

2639 RILEY, WALTER LEE. "The International Military Tribunal for the Far East and the Law of the Tribunal as Revealed by the Judgment and the Concurring and Dissenting Opinions." Ph.D. dissertation, University of Washington, 1957. 218p. Abstracted in Dissertation Abstracts International 1958 18(2): 1481. Evaluates the Tokyo war crimes trial as one of the most monstrous developments in the history of international law, basing his judgment on the decision of the tribunal to declare aggressive war a crime under international law and to charge those who initiated it with individual responsibility. There was no legal precedent for this. Trial by joint or several military jurisdictions would have been more acceptable.

2640 RÖLING, BERNARD V.A., and C.F. RÜTER (eds.). The Tokyo Judgment: The International Military Tribunal for the Far East (I.M.T.F.E.) 29 April 1946 - 12 November 1948. 3 volumes.

Amsterdam: University Press BV, 1977. Volume 1 (515p.) contains an introduction by Röling, the judgment of the IMTFE, the separate opinion of the president, the dissenting opinion of the member from France, and the concurring opinion of the member from the Philippines. The 12-page table of contents serves as an index. Volume 2 (629p.) contains the judgment of the member from India and the opinion of the member from the Netherlands. The 6-page table of contents serves as an index. Volume 3 contains annexes A and B belonging to the IMTFE and an index.

2641 "Sentence Japanese War Criminals," Christian Century 1948 65(47): 1262. An editorial that welcomed the handing down of the IMTFE sentences as another precedent in holding responsible those men who start wars. Hirohito should have been convicted as well as other war criminals.

2642 "The Verdict Pronounced by the International Military Tribunal for the Far East on the 25 Japanese War Crimes Suspects, November 12, 1948 (Excerpt)," Contemporary Japan 1948 17(July-December): 416-433. This is excerpted from the much longer official verdicts pronounced by the IMTFE. Summarizes briefly the wartime careers of the defendants and lists the charges against them.

2643 WEBB, WILLIAM F. Webb's Judgment. Tokyo: IMTFE, 1948. 658p. A separate statement filed by the Australian justice and the president of the tribunal stresses that the tribunal was a military court of the Allied powers and that the charter of the tribunal constituted a part of international law. Gives a detailed account of his reasoning with respect to each of the 25 verdicts handed down.

5. Amnesty and Early Release

2644 "General Douglas MacArthur's Review of the War Crimes Sentences Issued on November 24, 1948," Contemporary Japan 1948 17(7-12): 433-434. MacArthur's official statement on his responsibility to review IMTFE sentences. He could find no technical omission or commission that would warrant any reduction of the sentences.

2645 "Have We Lost the Peace? Japanese Convicted in War Crime Trials," Christian Century 1949 66(28): 838-839. Deals with a decision by the United States Supreme Court that held that convicted war criminals had the right to appeal their convictions through the federal court system. The decision came 6 months after 7 Japanese were hanged following a denial on technical grounds of their right to appeal to the Supreme Court. This is seen as an indication that "morally" the victorious powers had "lost the peace."

2646 "Note of Soviet Government to U.S. Government," Current Digest of the Soviet Press 1950 2(20): 33. On clemency. This note of May 11, 1950, reproduced here in full from the May 13, 1950, issues of Pravda and Izvestia, criticizes the SCAP circular of March 7, 1950, stating that all war criminals then serving sentences in Japan could be released before the expiration of their sentences. The Soviet government asserts that this would be a violation of international law, since it annuls the verdict of the IMTFE.

2647 "Note of the Soviet Government to the Government of USA," Information Bulletin 1951 11(5): 153. On clemency. This note of
February 12, 1951, protests the decision by SCAP to release
Shigemitsu Mamoru from prison prior to the completion of his
sentence. According to the Soviet government, the Far Eastern
Commission made no provision for the early release of Japanese
war criminals.

2648 "Soviet Government's Note to U.S. Government," Current Digest
of the Soviet Press 1950 2(35): 20. A note which appeared
first in Pravda, August 28, 1950, which criticizes SCAP for
allowing Japanese war criminals to be released before the
expiration of their sentences. Argues that MacArthur had ex-
ceeded his powers and had violated the charter of the IMTFE.

2649 UNITED STATES. DEPARTMENT OF STATE. "Board of Clemency for
Japanese War Criminals," Department of State Bulletin 1952
27(690): 408-409. September 15, 1952. Board established by
President Truman to advise and recommend on the matter of
parole for some Japanese war criminals. Contains the text of
the executive order.

2650 UNITED STATES. DEPARTMENT OF STATE. "Japanese War Criminals
Board," Department of State Bulletin 1952 27(696): 659. Public
Release 794, October 9, 1952.

6. Meaning and Significance of the IMTFE

2651 LIU, JAMES T.C. "The Tokyo Trial: Second Look," China Monthly
1947 8(August): 279-280. Sympathizes with the indifference
felt by most Japanese and Americans toward the IMTFE trial.
The length and complexity of the trial made it boring and
difficult to understand. He praises the trial for establishing
definitions of aggression and international morality and for
the light its vast documentation shed on the history of the
war.

2652 SOLOW, HERBERT. "'A Rather Startling Result': The Net of the
Tokyo-Nürnberg Tribunals is a Loss for U.S. Politics in the
Orient and for World Order," Fortune 1949 39(4): 158, 160,
162, 164. A critical account of the Nuremberg and Tokyo IMT's
which asserts that the net result of these 2 trials was a loss
for American politics in the Far East and for world order in
general.

2653 VASILYEV, A.N., and M. RAGINSKIĬ. "Urok Agressoram (K 30-
Letiiu Vyneseniia Prigovora Mezhdunarodnym Voennym Tribunalom
V Tokio Glavnym Iaponskim Voennym Prestupnikam [The Lesson to
the Aggressors: 30 Years of Passing Sentence of the International Military Tribunal in Tokyo on Japanese War Criminals],"
Sovetskoe Gosudarstvo i Pravo 1978 (11): 40-45. Describes
the trials of Japanese war criminals before the IMTFE, the
organization and activities of the tribunal, and the sentences
imposed. Lists the defendants, traces the diplomatic background to the trials, and discusses the cooperation of Japanese and American lawyers. 7 notes.

7. Later Evaluations

2654 "A 'Dead Man' Speaks," Life 1948 24(4): 87-91. Criticizes the
personnel of the IMTFE for abandoning the cause of promoting
democracy among the Japanese people in favor of personal

feuding, noting the animosity between Joseph Keenan and Tribunal President Sir William Webb.

2655 "Advocate of Plague," *Current Digest of the Soviet Press* 1950 2(9): 28-29. American prosecutor Joseph B. Keenan is accused of seeking to protect Emperor Hirohito from prosecution for his wartime activities. Keenan rejected reports by the Soviets that the Japanese were planning to wage biological warfare and rejected the so-called "irrefutable proof" of this presented at the Khabarovsk trial. The article asserts that Keenan was biased against the Soviet Union and was supporting the Emperor and other war criminals to use them in new "barbarous aggression." This article first appeared in *Izvestia*, February 23, 1950.

2656 BEREZHKOV, V. "The Tokyo Trial," *New Times* 1948 5(January 28): 6-9. Complains about the 2-year-long IMTFE trial, the domination of the trial by MacArthur and his appointees, and the whitewashing tactics of the American defense. Discusses American collusion with Japanese militarist leaders.

2657 BERGAMINI, DAVID. *Japan's Imperial Conspiracy*. New York: Morrow, 1971. 1239p. Challenges the contention that Japan's military activities during the 1930s were not within Hirohito's control. Discusses why and how the Japanese Emperor would easily have been convicted by the IMTFE.

2658 BLAKENEY, BEN BRUCE. "International Military Tribunal, Argument for Motions to Dismiss," *American Bar Association Journal* 1946 32(August): 475-477, 523. Contains arguments for dismissing charges against General Umeza and all other IMTFE defendants on the basis of lack of jurisdiction. Argues that war had never before been considered a crime, but rather a national policy based on force. Argues against *ex post facto* laws.

2659 BLEWETT, GEORGE F. "Victor's Injustice: The Tokyo War Crimes Trial," *American Perspective* 1950 4(3): 282-292. Blewett was the defense attorney for Tojo. Criticizes the double standard in the application of laws by the victorious to the vanquished.

2660 IENAGA, SABURO. "Bias in the Guise of Objectivity," *Japan Interpreter* 1977 11(3): 271-278. Argues that the vision of the Indian justice Radhabinod Pal was blurred by his ideological commitments and that he rendered a dangerous judgment which would have made heroes out of the men who plunged Japan into the disastrous war. Criticizes Pal's willingness to let Japan off so easily. Part of a literary debate with Richard H. Minear. 4 notes.

2661 "Ill-starred Defenders of War Criminals," *Current Digest of the Soviet Press* 1950 2(11): 22-23. A Soviet note of February 1, 1950, to the governments of the United States, Great Britain, and China proposing the creation of an international military tribunal for this trial of a group of Japanese war criminals, including Hirohito. Criticizes the United States for opposing the plan. An abridgement of an article which appeared originally in *Izvestia*, March 10, 1950

2662 IRELAND, GORDON. "Uncommon Law in Martial Tokyo," *Year Book of World Affairs* 1950 4: 50-104. Argues that the IMTFE *could* not apply international law and *did* not apply common law. Analyzes the creation of the tribunal, the charter, the trial, the judgment, separate opinions, the sentences, courtroom proceedings, jurisdiction, and appeals to the Supreme Court of the United States. Lists 10 serious violations of common law, including changes of judges, absence of participating judges from some sessions, failure of the French and Russian judges to understand the language in which the trial was conducted, failure to warn defendants that their statements cound be used against them, admission of hearsay evidence, and admission of evidence by affidavit. Concludes that the real "crime" was in being defeated in the war.

2663 KAJIMA, MORINOSUKE. *Modern Japan's Foreign Policy*. Rutland, Vermont: Tuttle, 1969. 327p. Chapter 5, "The Need to Reexamine 'Tokyo Trial,'" written in 1959, argues for a review of the verdicts and minority opinions of the Tokyo trial and criticizes the verdicts which held Japan solely responsible for the war in the Pacific.

2664 MARKOV, M. "Falsification of History at the Tokyo Trial," *New Times* 1948 17(April 21): 7-11. Questions the accuracy of reports about prewar and wartime activities of Japan and Germany that were revealed at the Tokyo trial. Attempts to show an extensive and intimate cooperation between the 2 countries throughout the war.

2665 MARKOV, M. "Mamoru Shigemitsu and his Patrons, *Current Digest of the Soviet Press* 1951 3(24): 11-12. Appeared first in *Literaturnaya gazeta*, June 7, 1951. Argues that MacArthur freed the former Japanese foreign minister before he had served his complete sentence because the State Department needed his services. Critical of SCAP for being easy on war criminals, a symbol of "Wall Street's policy in Japan."

2666 MINEAR, RICHARD H. "In Defense of Radha Binod Pal," *Japan Interpreter* 1977 11(3): 263-271. Argues that Radhabinod Pal, the Indian justice at the Tokyo war crimes trial, was a man of courage who possessed insight into the inherent unfairness of a victor's justice. Part of a literary debate with Ienaga Saburo. Undocumented.

2667 RAGINSKIĬ, MARK, and S. ROZENBLIT. "What People Expected of the International Tribunal in Tokyo," *Soviet Press Translations* 1948 3(July 15): 421-425. This article first appeared in *Pravda*, on June 2, 1948, just prior to the conclusion of the Tokyo trial. Argues that, contrary to the American position, Japan was an aggressor against the Soviet Union, despite their neutrality pact. Because of this, the Soviet Union demanded severe punishment of all Japanese aggressors.

2668 RAMA RAO, T.S. "The Dissenting Judgment of Mr. Justice Pal at the Tokyo Trial," *Indian Yearbook of International Affairs* 1953 2: 277-291. Examines Pal's dissenting judgment. Pal insisted that the IMT could not go beyond existing rules of international law and create new laws that could then be applied retroactively. Concludes that the only crime in the international sphere is that of losing a war.

2669 RÖLING, BERNARD V.A. "The Tokyo Trial in retrospect," in Yamaguchi Susumu (ed.). *Buddhism and Culture: Dedicated to Dr. Daisetz Teitaro Suzuki in Commemoration of His Ninetieth Birthday*. Kyoto: Nakano Press, 1960. Reviews the principal weaknesses of the Tokyo trial, the most important of which was the absence of neutrals on the bench, and discusses the character of both international military tribunals. Concludes that the motivation for their establishment was valid, which justified their creation.

2670 UNITED STATES. DEPARTMENT OF STATE. "U.S.S.R. Motives on Trying Emperor of Japan Question," *Department of State Bulletin* 22(554): 244. February 13, 1950. The Soviet Union suggested reopening war crimes trials and trying Hirohito. China later agreed.

IX
NUREMBERG INTERNATIONAL MILITARY TRIBUNAL

A. GENERAL WORKS

2671 ALBRECHT, R.G. <u>Defense</u> <u>Record</u>. Nuremberg: 1946. On the Nuremberg IMT.

2672 ALDERMAN, SIDNEY S. "Background and High Lights of the Nuremberg Trial," <u>I.C.C.</u> <u>Practitioners'</u> <u>Journal</u> 1946 14(2): 99-113. The author relates his experiences as assistant to Robert H. Jackson and describes the relations among the staff members of the 4 prosecution teams.

2673 ALDERMAN, SIDNEY S. "Negotiating the Nuremberg Trial Agreements, 1945," in Raymond Dennett and Joseph E. Johnson (eds.). <u>Negotiating</u> <u>with</u> <u>the</u> <u>Russians</u>. Boston: World Peace Foundation, 1951. 310p. Chapter 3, pp. 49-98, focuses primarily upon American-Soviet negotiations. Concludes that negotiations with the Soviet Union are possible only if the aims of both parties are the same.

2674 ALEXANDER, EVA V. "Trials of War Criminals," <u>Women</u> <u>Lawyers</u> <u>Journal</u> 1946 32(March): 28-29, 49-52.

2675 AMAUDRUZ, G.A. <u>UBU</u> - <u>Justicier</u> <u>au</u> <u>premier</u> <u>procès</u> <u>de</u> <u>Nuremberg</u>. Paris: Les Actes des Apôtres, 1949. 179p.

2676 BARDÈCHE, MAURICE. <u>Nuremberg</u> <u>ou</u> <u>la</u> <u>Terre</u> <u>Promise</u>. [Paris]: Édition des Sept Couleurs, 1948. 270p.

2677 BARDÈCHE, MAURICE. <u>Nuremberg,</u> <u>het</u> <u>beloofde</u> <u>land</u>. Antwerp: Dauperta, 1951.

2678 BAUER, FRITZ. <u>Die</u> <u>Kriegsverbrecher</u> <u>vor</u> <u>Gericht</u>. Zurich/New York: Europa, 1945. 237p.

2679 BERTRAND, CHARLES-AUGUSTE. "Les Procès de Nuremberg," <u>Revue</u> <u>du</u> <u>Barreau</u> <u>de</u> <u>la</u> <u>Province</u> <u>du</u> <u>Québec</u> 1948 8(9): 477-488.

2680 BIDDLE, FRANCIS B. "Nuremberg: The Fall of the Supermen," <u>American</u> <u>Heritage</u> 1962 13(5): 65-76. 11 photographs.

2681 BROWNE, WALDO. "The Nuremberg Trial," New Republic 1945 113(26): 871-872. Correspondence on the IMT trial.

2682 CALVOCORESSI, PETER. Nuremberg: The Facts, the Law and the Consequences. London: Chatto and Windus, 1947. 176p. New York: Macmillan, 1948. 176p. Explains the purpose, procedure, function, and consequences of the Nuremberg IMT trial as well as aggressive war, war crimes, and crimes against humanity. Summarizes the cross-examination of the major war criminals, with emphasis on Göring's confrontation with Robert H. Jackson. Excerpts from portions of the Nuremberg Charter that deal with indicted organizations. Presents an extract from the final prosecution speech delivered by General Telford Taylor concerning the case against the military. Concludes with an essay on the legal, judicial, and historical consequences of the Nuremberg trial. Appendices contain the Agreement of London and the Charter of the IMT, tables of charges, verdicts and sentences, the dissenting opinion of Soviet Major General I.T. Nikitchenko on Hjalmar Schacht, a table of principal posts occupied by the accused, defense council and cabinet ministers of the Third Reich, an account of the destruction of the Warsaw ghetto in 1943, the 1938 reorganization of the German machinery of command and some of its practical consequences, the military leadership of Germany as defined by the indictment, and the conclusion of General Telford Taylor's closing speech against the military leadership of Germany. Includes bibliographical references.

2683 CARTIER, RAYMOND. Les Secrets de la guerre dévoilés par Nuremberg. Paris: A. Fayard, [1946]. 318p.

2684 CONOT, ROBERT E. Justice at Nuremberg. New York: Harper and Row, 1983. 593p. Tells the story of the Nuremberg trial in a vivid, dramatic narrative. Part 1, pp. 1-28, "Crime and Punishment," examines the origins of the concept of an international trial and the organization of the tribunal. Part 2, pp. 29-96, "Interrogation and Indictment," deals with the imprisonment of the accused at Nuremberg and preparation of the case. Discusses the documentation division, the judges, the attorneys for the defense, the prosecution, Gustav Krupp's inability to stand trial, Robert Ley's suicide, and Hess and Göring. Part 3, pp. 97-326, "Prosecution," discusses conspiracy, the Röhm Purge, OSS chief William Donovan's conflict with chief prosecutor Robert Jackson, the rape of Czechoslovakia, Kristallnacht, the Moscow Pact, euthanasia, Einsatzgruppen, slave labor, the "final solution," medical experiments, the "Night and Fog" decree, and war crimes. Part 4, pp. 327-478, "Defense," presents the testimony of the defendants and their witnesses. Analyzes the character of the 22 major war criminals and traces the development of the proceedings. Discusses the Katyn Forest massacre and the case against organizations. Part 5, pp. 479-523, "Judgment," examines the deliberations of the judges, their verdicts, and the aftermath. Contains a map of principal concentration camps and extermination installations, a chart of the structure of the SS and police, and a diagram of the courtroom. 6-page bibliography, 9-page index, 31 photographs.

2685 COOPER, Robert W. Der Nürnberger Prozeß. Krefeld: Scherpe, 1947. Published in English as The Nuremberg Trial. Harmondsworth/New York: Penguin, 1947. 301p. The author, a Times of London correspondent, quotes extensively from the Nuremberg

IMT trial documents to show the full weight of the case against the accused. Undocumented.

2686 CROUCHET, R. Le Procès de Nuremberg: Les Criminels Nazis devant leurs Juges. Charleroi/Paris: Dupuis, 1946: Paris: Hachette, 1947.

2687 DAVIDSON, EUGENE. The Trial of the Germans: An Account of the Twenty-Two Defendants before the International Military Tribunal at Nuremberg. New York: Macmillan, 1966. 636p. One of the best early histories of the Nuremberg trial. Most of the book is a biographical analysis of the defendants, but the author's main concern is with the problem of guilt, mass murder, and aggression, the crimes with which most of the defendants were charged. The trial had to take place for political and psychological reasons, and though there was considerable fairness and legal form reflected throughout, there remained room for doubt in many individual cases. A scholarly work, with a 21-page bibliography, an 18-page index, 46 photographs, and 1278 footnotes.

2688 DEUTSCHES RUNDFUNKARCHIV. Tondokumente zur Zeitgeschichte: Nürnberger Prozeß (1945-1946). Frankfurt am Main: 1971. 63p.

2689 DODD, THOMAS J. "The Nuremberg Trial," Journal of Criminal Law and Criminology 1947 37(January): 357-367; and Pennsylvania Bar Association Quarterly 1947 18(2): 138-152.

2690 DONATI, A. "Il proceso di Norimberga e il diritto penale internazionale," Stato Moderno 1945 2(December 20): 350-351.

2691 DONNEDIEU DE VABRES, HENRI. "Le Procès de Nuremberg," Revue de Science Criminelle et de Droit Pénal Comparé 1947 2: 171-183.

2692 DONNEDIEU DE VABRES, HENRI. "Le Procès de Nuremberg (exposé fait le 27 février 1947 à la conférence du Jeune Barreau)," Revue de Droit Pénal et de Criminologie 1946-1947 27: 480-490.

2693 DONNEDIEU DE VABRES, HENRI. Le Procès de Nuremberg. Le Statut du Tribunal Militaire International, les debats, les chefs d'accusation, le jugement. Paris: Domat Montchrestien, 1947. 284p.

2694 DUNN, BENJAMIN J. "Trial of War Criminals," Australian Law Journal 1946 19(11): 359-361. 4 notes.

2695 DUPAYS, PAUL. Au Palais de Nuremberg, chronique historique. Au Tribunal International Militaire, mi-avril-mai 1946. Paris: Éditions de la Critique, 1952. 144p.

2696 DUPAYS, PAUL. Au Temple de Thémis, chronique historique: Justice à Laneberg à Nuremberg, mi-mars à mi-avril 1946. Paris: Éditions de la Critique, 1946.

2697 DUPAYS, PAUL. Justice chronique historique. Tribunal International de Nuremberg, mi-juin à mi-octobre, 1946. Paris: Éditions de la Critique, 1952. 158p.

2698 DUPAYS, PAUL. Ne fais pas à Autrui... chronique historique: Tribunal International de Nuremberg, janvier-mars, 1946. Paris: Éditions de la Critique, 1952.

2699 EHRENBURG, ILYA. "History's Morality: The Nuremberg Trial," Information Bulletin 1945 5(127): 1-3, 7.

2700 EHRENBURG, ILYA. "The Nuremberg Trial," Answer 1946 4(April-May): 11-12, 16.

2701 ELIASBERG, WLADIMIR C. "War Trials," Journal of Criminal Law and Criminology 1945 36(2): 85-86. Focuses on the trial of criminal organizations.

2702 FALK, RICHARD A. "The Nuremberg Tradition," Intercom 1971 13(1): 29-32.

2703 FERNÁNDEZ DE LA MORA, GONZALO. "Las aporias de Nuremberg," Arbor 1951 18(64): 537-562. 50 notes.

2704 FRANCO SODI, C. Racismo, antiracismo y justicia penal. El Tribunal de Nuremberg. Mexico City: Botas, 1946.

2705 GALLAGHER, RICHARD. Nuremberg: The Third Reich on Trial. New York: Avon, 1961. 255p. Chapter titles include "Day of Reckoning," "War in our Time," "The Grandest Larceny," "The Medical Experiments," "POW Atrocities," and the epilogue "Day of Judgment." Brief, popular history of the Nuremberg IMT trial as gleaned from the major trial records. Undocumented.

2706 GENTON, J. "Le Tribunal Militaire International. Compétence réelle. Les Solutions données par le statut du 8 aout 1945," Revue de Droit Pénal et de Criminologie 1947-1948 28: 477-561.

2707 GOUTEL, ERIC DE, FRANCIS MERCURY, PIERRE NOUAILLE, and LUCIEN VIÉVILLE (comps.). Le Procès de Nuremberg... Paris: Les amis de l'histoire, F. Beauval, 1969.

2708 GRAVEN, JEAN. En Assistant au procès des criminels de guerre. Les Enseignements de Nuremberg. Geneva: Georg, 1945.

2709 GREEN, L.C. "Trials of War Criminals," Solicitor 1947 14(7): 160, 162.

2710 GREGORY, TAPPAN. "The Nuremberg Trial," Connecticut Bar Journal 1947 21(1): 2-20. A report on the author's visit to Nuremberg in March 1946.

2711 GREGORY, TAPPAN. "The Nuremberg Trials," Illinois Bar Journal 1946 34(10): 469-482.

2712 GRUNDINSK, ULRICH. „Das Formalrecht des Nürnberger Strafverfahrens," Doctor of Laws dissertation, Erlangen University, 1949.

2713 HAENSEL, CARL. „Nürnberger Probleme," Deutsche Rechts-Zeitschrift 1946 1(3): 67-69.

2714 HAHNENFELD, G. „Die Herkunft der in dem Nürnberger Urteil gegen die sogenannten Hauptkriegsverbrecher angewandten allgemeinen Lehren des Strafrechts," Doctor of Laws dissertation, Frankfurt, 1949.

2715 HALPERN, BEN. "The Nuremberg Trial," Jewish Frontier 1946 (January): 30-32.

2716 HARRIS, WHITNEY R. "The Nuremberg Trial," State Bar Association Journal of California 1947 22(2): 97-121. Brief survey of the trial, judgment, and executions.

2717 HARRIS, WHITNEY R. Tyranny on Trial: The Evidence at Nuremberg. Dallas: Southern Methodist University Press, 1954. The author was a naval attorney who assisted Jackson in the prosecution of the Nuremberg IMT defendants. Most of the material was drawn from the official transcript of the proceedings of the IMT, the 8-volume work prepared by the Office of the United States Chief of Counsel for the Prosecution of Axis Criminality, and the record of the negotiations conducted by Robert H. Jackson, who contributed the Introduction to this volume. The major sections deal with background materials, the war itself, war crimes, and crimes against humanity. Contains 1064 notes, a 10-page bibliography, a 16-page index, 43 photographs, and lists of the members of the prosecution, the defense, and the defendants.

2718 HÄRTLE, HEINRICH. Freispruch für Deutschland. Unsere Soldaten vor dem Nürnberger Tribunal. Göttingen: K.W. Schütz, 1956. 345p.

2719 HAUSER, ERNEST O. "The Backstage Battle at Nuremberg," Saturday Evening Post 1946 218(29): 18, 19, 137.

2720 HERZOG, JACQUES-BERNARD. "Les Organisations nationales-socialistes devant le Tribunal de Nuremberg," Revue de Droit Pénal 1946 17: 343-359. States the defense and prosecution points of view, and gives an account of the judgment in the case of Nazi organizations. Discusses the problem of collective guilt and reviews the probable consequences of this trial for other trials in the 4 zones of occupation.

2721 HERZOG, JACQUES-BERNARD. Nuremberg. Un Échec fructueux? [no city given]: [no publisher given], 1974. 209p. Contains an historical background to the Nuremberg IMT trial as well as a section on the trial itself. Discusses the repression of war crimes, the jurisdiction of international law over war criminals, the IMT, preparations for the trial, debates, and various crimes with which the defendants were charged. Contains a list of 21 works by the author on the subject of the Nuremberg trial, and a 25-page general bibliography. Heavily documented.

2722 HEYDECKER, JOE J., and JOHANNES LEEB. Der Nürnberger Prozeß. Bilanz der Tausend Jahre. Cologne/Bonn: Kiepenheuer and Witsch, 1958; 2nd edition. 1959. 612p. Published in English as The Nuremberger Trials. London: William Heinemann, 1962. 379p. A later, German edition was published by Kiepenheuer in 1979 as The Nürnberger Prozeß: neue Dokumente, Erkenntnisse und Analysen. 584p. An attempt to make materials of the Nuremberg IMT trial accessible to a broad public. Covers the period from 1945, when the search for war criminals began, until 1947, when many of them were imprisoned at Spandau. The English edition has been shortened considerably. Both editions deal with the search for war criminals, the road to Nuremberg, the beginning of the IMT trial, the major defendants, the verdicts, and the execution of the sentences. The authors see this as the first attempt to write a history of the IMT based entirely on original documents. The German edition contains 50 photographs, 3-page subject index, 7-page name index, 8-page chronological table, and 9-page bibliography. The English version contains 13 photographs, 3-page bibliography, 15-page index.

2723 HUBER, JOHN. "The International Military Tribunal at Nuremberg," Labor and Nation 1945 1(December): 7-11.

2724 JACKSON, ROBERT H. "Nuremberg Trial of the Major Nazi Leaders," New York State Bar Association Bulletin 1947 70: 147-158.

2725 JACKSON, ROBERT H. "Nurnberg," Common Cause 1950 3(January): 284-294.

2726 KAHN, LEO. Nuremberg Trials. New York: Ballantine, 1972. 159p. Illustrated history of the Nuremberg IMT trial. Deals with the accumulation of evidence, the opening of the trial, key documents, the question of responsibility, and the implications of the trial. 145 photographs and illustrations.

2727 KEESHAN, ANNE (Text), and CHARLES W. ALEXANDER (Photographs). Justice at Nuremberg: A Pictorial Record of the Trial of Nazi War Criminals by the IMT at Nuremberg, Germany, 1945-46. [Chicago]: Marvel, 1946. 188p. Contains pictures of the principal events and personalities involved with the Nuremberg IMT trial. Photographed by Charles W. Alexander, director of photography for the trial. A running account of the proceedings, beginning with the negotiations which resulted in the four power agreement and charter. Portrays the prosecution staffs, the tribunal, the defendants, and the security arrangements. Undocumented; 120 photographs.

2728 KEMPNER, ROBERT M.W. "Rassegna dei processi di Norimberga," Rivista di Studi Politici Internazionali 1950 17(January-June): 66-88.

2729 KEMPNER, ROBERT M.W. "Übersicht über die Nürnberger Prozesse," Archiv des Völkerrechts 1950 2: 237-243.

2730 KRANZBÜHLER, OTTO. "Nürnberg als Rechtsproblem," in Um Recht und Gerechtigkeit. Festgabe für Erich Kaufmann. Stuttgart: W. Kohlhammer, 1950.

2731 LATERNSER, HANS. Plädoyer vor dem internationalen Militärgerichtshof zu Nürnberg. Nuremberg: Wilhelm Muhler, 1946.

2732 LAWRENCE, GEOFFREY [Baron Oaksey]. "The Nuremberg Trial," International Affairs 1947 23(April): 151-159.

2733 LAZARD, DIDIER. Le Procès de Nuremberg. Récit d'un témoin. Paris: Les Éditions de la Nouvelle France, 1947. 335p.

2734 "Le Procès de Nuremberg: Les Grands Criminels de guerre," Revue de Droit International de Sciences Diplomatiques et Politiques 1945 23(3): 278-286.

2735 LENER, SALVATORE. "Diritto e politica nel processo di Norimberga," Civiltà Cattolica 1946 97(July 20): 92-106.

2736 "Les Procès des Grands Criminels de Guerre à Nuremberg," Revue de Droit International de Sciences Diplomatiques et Politiques 1946 24(2): 112-137.

2737 LIND, JAKOV. "Nazis on Trial - Pages from a Journal," *Commentary* 1965 4(39): 69-72.

2738 LUNAU, HEINZ. *The Germans on Trial*. New York: Storm, 1948. 180p.

2739 MARTÍNEZ, JOSÉ AGUSTÍN. *El juicio de Nuremberg*. Havana: J. Montero, 1949.

2740 MASER, WERNER. *Nürnberg: Tribunal der Sieger*. Düsseldorf: Econ, 1977. 368p. Published in English as *Nuremberg, A Nation on Trial*. New York: Scribner's, 1979. Discusses preparations for holding the Nuremberg trial, and reviews the evidence, the limits of responsibility of non-military defendants, and the judgment. Raises questions concerning the legality of the IMT and its rules of procedure. Describes the Nuremberg court prison and lists its house rules as issued on September 11, 1945. 13-page bibliography, 21-page index, 20 photographs.

2741 MAYDA, GIUSEPPE. *Il processo di Norimberga*. Milan: A. Mondadori, 1972.

2742 MC CONNELL, G.R. "The Trial of War Criminals at Nuremberg," *Wyoming Law Journal* 1946 1(1): 3-12.

2743 MC INTYRE, DINA GHANDY. "The Nuernberg Trials," *University of Pittsburgh Law Review* 1962 24(1): 73-116. 166 notes.

2744 MENDELSSOHN, PETER DE. "America's Case at Nuernberg," *Nation* 1945 161(24): 652-654.

2745 MERLE, MARCEL. *Le Procès de Nuremberg et le châtiment des criminels de guerre*. Paris: A. Pedone, 1949. 185p. Traces the precedents established in World War I for treating acts committed during a war as crimes of war. Discusses the Nuremberg IMT trial in the context of international law, the statute of the tribunal, the legality of the tribunal, and the trial itself. Documented; 7-page bibliography.

2746 MONTERO, MARIO. "El Tribunal de Nuremberg, *Revista Peruana de Derecho Internacional* 1948 8(28): 128-145.

2747 MORRIS, JAMES. "Major War Crime Trial in Nürnberg," *North Dakota Bar Briefs* 1949 25(April): 97-109.

2748 MUNRO, HECTOR A. "Nuremberg and Law Enforcement," *New Commonwealth* 1948 9(May): 101-103.

2749 NAMIER, LEWIS BERNSTEIN. *In the Nazi Era*. London: Macmillan, 1952. 204p. Passing comments on the Nuremberg IMT trial. Some annotation, index.

2750 NEAVE, AIREY M.S. *Nuremberg: A Personal Record of the Trial of Major Nazi War Criminals*. London: Hodder & Stoughton, 1978. 348p. American edition, *On Trial at Nuremberg*. Boston: Little, Brown, 1979. 348p. Based on notes made during the Nuremberg IMT trial and on the author's memorandum of October 24, 1945, to the General Secretary of the IMT. Discusses Neave's investigations for the British War Crimes Executive and the nature of criminal organizations. A general account of the Nuremberg IMT trial and a personal record of how Neave viewed the Nuremberg defendants as he delivered the indictment. Some secondary documentation; 36 photographs, 14-page index. The appendix is a table of verdicts handed down.

2751 NEAVE, AIREY M.S. "The Trial of the S.S. at Nuremberg," *Revue Internationale de Droit Pénal* 1946 17: 277-290.

2752 OCCHI, ADAMO DEGLI. *Il processo di Norimberga*. Rome: Rizzoli, 1947. Volume 17, 350p., Volume 18, 357p. The complete story of the Nuremberg IMT in Italian. Based on IMT documents.

2753 PANNENBECKER, OTTO. "The Nuremberg War-Crimes Trial," *De Paul Law Review* 1965 14(2): 348-358. Pannenbecker was Chief Counsel for Wilhelm Frick, German Minister of the Interior. Since the IMT dealt with war crimes against other nations, crimes against non-Jewish German people were ignored. Discusses problems arising out of differences in Anglo-Saxon and Continental legal systems. The Nuremberg trial has been called the foundation of a new international law, but this has not proven to be the case. Its principles regarding the outlawry of war were not incorporated into the charter of the United Nations. Even though the Soviet Union conspired with Hitler to conquer and divide Poland, Soviets later sat in judgment as both judge and accomplice. Examines the organizations which the prosecution tried to label criminal and the problems involved in finding all members guilty of what an organization had done. Concludes that Frick's conviction was just, based on the evidence presented. Though the trial did not establish a new international law, it served as a warning. Undocumented.

2754 PARKER, JOHN J. "The Nuremberg Trial," *Journal of the American Judicature Society* 1946 39(December 4): 109-115.

2755 PARKER, JOHN J. "The Nuremberg Trial," *Kentucky State Bar Journal* 1947 11(3): 157-165, 185. 16 notes.

2756 PASKINS, BARRIES, and MICHAEL DOCKRILL. *The Ethics of War*. London: Duckworth, 1979. 332p. Chapter 6, Section 5, "Judgment on Individuals; the Nuremberg Trial," pp. 262-276, examines the Nuremberg IMT trial within the context of judgment against individuals, with focus on the justice or accuracy of the 4 counts of the indictment.

2757 PELCKMANN, HORST. *Plädoyer für die "SS" Schutzstaffel der NSDAP gehalten vor dem Internationalen Militärgerichtshof, Nürnberg*. Nuremberg: 1946. 87p.

2758 PHELEGER, HERMANN. "The Nuremberg Trials," *California State Bar Proceedings* 1946 19(September 24-28): 72-80.

2759 POLEVOI, BORIS N. *Niurenbergskie dnevniki*. Moscow: Sov. Rossiia, 1972. 238p. Published in German as *Nürnberger Tagebuch*. Berlin(GDR): Volk und Welt, 1971. Account of the trial of the major German war criminals.

2760 POLIAKOV, LÉON (comp.). *Le Procès de Nuremberg*. Paris: Julliard, 1971.

2761 POLTORAK, ARKADII IOSIFOVICH. "Nazi Generals before the Nuremberg Tribunal," *International Affairs* 1975 (9): 88-98. Discusses the USSR's role in bringing about the Nuremberg IMT trial. Reviews the testimony of German generals and field marshals at the trial. The preventive-war argument put forth by the German general staff is countered with evidence of intentional preparation for aggressive war. German generals defended Plan Barbarossa as a measure against an attack by the Soviet Union. It allowed for punitive measures against Soviets on orders from the commander of any German battalion. The German army command depended not only on purely military efforts but also on "brutal, sinister, and criminal means." Field Marshal Erich von Manstein testified that a legitimate military war was conducted by soldiers; the ideological war was waged by Hitler alone. Concludes that the knowledge that such heinous crimes were being committed implies a moral responsibility which overrides military orders. Undocumented.

2762 POLTORAK, ARKADII IOSIFOVICH. Niurnbergskii Epilog. Moscow: Izd. Ministerstva Oborony SSSR, 1965. 550p. Published in English as The Nuremberg Epilogue. Moscow: Progress Publishers, 1971. 477p. A general treatment of the Nuremberg IMT, containing detailed examination of Hermann Göring, Joachim von Ribbentrop, Wilhelm Keitel, Alfred Jodl, Ernst Kaltenbrunner, and Hjalmar Schacht. Deals in less detail with scores of other war criminals and gives a brief sketch of the other IMT defendants. Undocumented; no bibliography, no index, 33 photographs.

2763 POLYANSKY, N.N. "The Soviet Prosecution's Case at Nuremberg," New Times 1946 4(February 15): 3-6.

2764 PRZYBYLSKI, PETER. Zwischen Galgen und Amnestie. Kriegsverbrecherprozesse im Spiegel von Nürnberg. Berlin: Dietz, 1979. 205p.

2765 PÜSCHEL, WILHELM. Der Niedergang des Rechts im Dritten Reich. Reutlingen: Verlag "die Zukunft," 1947. 125p. General discussion of the loss of personal and legal rights by Germans under Hitler, with some commentary on the Nuremberg IMT trial.

2766 RAPPAPORT, EMIL S. "Le Troisième Nuremberg," Revue de Droit International Sciences de Diplomatiques et Politiques 1946 24(2): 44-46. The "third" Nuremberg was the Nuremberg of the IMT.

2767 RAUSCHENBACH, GERHARD. Der Nürnberger Prozeß gegen die Organisationen. Grundlagen, Probleme, Auswirkungen auf die Mitglieder und strafrechtliche Ergebnisse. New edition. Volume 13. Bonn: Ludwig Röhrscheid, 1954. 151p. A brief history of the case against organizations, the trial, the judgment, and the members of criminal organizations. Heavily annotated, with appendices containing 6 Nuremberg IMT documents on criminal organizations. Short bibliography, no index.

2768 RINGSTED, H.V. "Nazi Terror in Denmark as Exposed at the Nuremberg Trial," Danish Foreign Office Journal 1946 2(July): 11-115.

2769 ROME, M.E. "Trials at Nuremberg," Maryland State Bar Association Report 1946 51: 183-195.

2770 RUBIN, Eli. Nuremberg Trial: Germany before her Judges. London: Transatlantic Authors, 1945. 48p.

2771 SAUREL, LOUIS. Le Procès de Nuremberg. 2nd, revised edition. Paris: Rouff, 1967.

2772 SAWICKI, JERZY. From Nuremberg to the New Wehrmacht. Warsaw: Polonia, 1957. 460p. Published in German as Als sei Nürnberg nie gewesen... Die Abkehr von den völkerrechtlichen Prinzipien der Nürnberger Urteile. Berlin(GDR): Zentralverlag, 1958. The original was published in Polish in 1955. Topics covered include General Telford Taylor's secret report, the Krupp corporation, IG Farben, German war guilt, and the Nuremberg IMT and Spandau. Argues that West German revisionist literature attempts to rehabilitate war criminals to prepare for renewed imperialist aggression against Europe. Light documentation; no bibliography, index.

2773 SCHMIDT, PAUL. Der Statist auf der Galerie 1945 bis 1950. Kommentare, Vergleiche. Bonn: Athenäum, 1951. 307p. An excellent general treatment of the course of German affairs between 1945 and 1950. See in particular Chapter 3, "Alliiertes Nürnberger Recht 1946," pp. 82-132.

2774 SCHÖNBORN, ERWIN. Soldaten verteidigen ihre Ehre. Frankfurt am Main: Bierbaum, 1974.

2775 SEARS, CHARLES B. "The International Military Tribunal," New York State Bar Association Bulletin 1948 71: 196-204.

2776 SHAPIRO, WILLIAM E. (project editor). Trial at Nuremberg. New York: Franklin Watts, 1967. 66p. By the staff of CBS News, based on the television news series "The Twentieth Century." Deals briefly with the crimes of Germany, preparations for the IMT trial, the indictment, the defendants, the trial itself, the prosecution arguments, the defense, and verdicts and sentences. 51 photographs and illustrations, index. Undocumented.

2777 SIMON, S. La Galérie des monstres. A Nuremberg, dans les coulisses du plus grand procès de l'histoire. Nancy: Vagner, 1947.

2778 SMIRNOV, LEV NIKOLAEVICH. "Der Nürnberger Hauptkriegsverbrecherprozeß - eines der bedeutsamsten Ergebnisse der Zerschlagung der deutschen Imperialismus im zweiten Weltkrieg," Neue Justiz 1960 14(8): 290-292.

2779 SMITH, BRADLEY F. Reaching Judgment at Nuremberg. New York: Basic, 1977. 349p. Tells the story of the Nuremberg trial "from the bench," since much of the story is based on new materials that chronicle the decisive role of the judges. Examines the setting for the Nuremberg trial, and pays particular attention to what is called "the Road to Nuremberg," the London Conference, and the indictments. Goes on to examine the trial itself and each of the defendants in the order in which they appeared at the trial. The judges tried to act as judges, yet they were incapable of transcending the views of their own time and society. The whole proceeding proved that war crimes tribunals have little of value to offer in dealing with the transition from war to peace. Contains 2 indices, 1 of which charts the verdicts of all the defendants on each of the 4 counts as well as their sentences. The second gives a partial list of the members of the prosecution and defense teams. 9-page index, 2-page bibliography, 894 notes which include sources not listed in the bibliography, 7 photographs.

2780 SMITH, BRADLEY F. The American Road to Nuremberg: The Documentary Record, 1944-1945. Stanford: Hoover Institution Press,

1982. 259p. Documents include the Moscow Declaration (November 1, 1943), a statement on war criminals submitted by the American Jewish Conference to Secretary of State Cordell Hull (August 25, 1944), a report by Assistant Secretary of War John McCloy of a telephone conversation with War Secretary Stimson (August 28, 1944), telephone conversations between Stimson and the Judge Advocate General, Major General Myron C. Cramer (September 5, 1944), and memoranda between the chiefs of various branches of the U.S. government. Also contains 19 documents dealing with the establishment of a prosecution system within the U.S. Army's occupation program for Germany and the "Implementing Instrument" for the punishment of war criminals intended for review by the Big Three. 3-page bibliography, 5-page index.

2781 SMITH, BRADLEY F. The Road to Nuremberg. New York: Basic, 1981. 303p. A report on American policy decisions during World War II which led to the development of a plan for prosecuting major war criminals. Based primarily on the summary memoranda of legal draftsmen. Discusses preparation for the treatment of postwar Germany, the genesis of a trial plan, the Morgenthau plan, and Secretary of War Henry Stimson's support of a war crimes program. Examines the impact on war crimes policy of the Malmédy killings of 70 American prisoners in Belgium, and the conferences at Yalta (February 1945) and London (April 1945). 4-page bibliography, 13-page index.

2782 SMITH, WILLIS. "The Nuremberg Trials," American Bar Association Journal 1946 32(July): 390-396. Description of a visit to the IMT court room and a discussion of the indictment and the conduct of the trial.

2783 SOBOTKER, H. RODRÍGUEZ VON. "El castigo de los criminales de guerra," Revista de Derecho Internacional 1947 52(September): 23-46.

2784 SPAIN, IAN. "Trials of War Criminals," Australian Law Journal 1946 20(5): 171-173.

2785 STEPHENS, ROBERT GRIER, JR. "Aspects of the Nuremberg Trial," Georgia Bar Journal 1946 8(3): 262-267; 8(4): 375-383; 9(1): 57-65. 53 notes.

2786 STÖCKER, JAKOB. Vor dem Tribunal des Weltgerichts. Auf daß Gerechtigkeit werde! Streiflichter zum Nürnberger Prozeß. Hannover: "Das andere Deutschland," 1946. 39p. Discusses the system of the Nuremberg IMT, the robbery of art treasures, crimes of organizations, Göring, and eye witnesses at the trial.

2787 STOREY, ROBERT GERALD. "The Nuremberg Trials," Tennessee Law Review 1946 19(5): 517-525.

2788 SÜSKIND, W.E. Die Mächtigen vor Gericht. Nürnberg 1945/46 an Ort und Stelle erlebt. Munich: Paul List, 1963. Brief, general coverage of the Nuremberg IMT.

2789 SWEARINGEN, VICTOR C. "Nuremberg War Crimes Trials," Kentucky State Bar Journal 1947 12(1): 11-20.

2790 TAYLOR, TELFORD. "The Nuremberg Trials," Columbia Law Review 1955 55(4): 488-525.

2791 "The Chalice of Nuremberg," Time 1945 46(24): 25-28.

2792 "The Nuremberg Trials," International Review 1946 19(July): 99-100.

2793 "The Nürnberg Confusion," Fortune Magazine 1946 34(6): 120-121, 256-260, 263-264.

2794 THORPE, GERALD L. "The Nuremberg Trials: Considerations and Suggestions," Intercom 1971 13(1): 33-47.

2795 TORGERSEN, ROLF N. "Nürnberg processen," Tidsskrift for Rettsvitenskap 1946 59: 344-357. Published in English as "The Nuremberg Trials," Norseman 1946 4(November-December): 391-399.

2796 UNITED NATIONS. SECRETARY-GENERAL. "Nuremberg Tribunal, History and Analysis," Lake Success: United Nations, 1949. Memorandum submitted by the Secretary-General.

2797 UNITED STATES. DEPARTMENT OF STATE. "Cooperation with the United States Chief of Counsel for the Prosecution of Axis Criminality," Department of State Bulletin 1945 13(314): 40. July 1, 1945. Report of Joseph Grew, Acting Secretary of State, on State Department cooperation with Robert H. Jackson.

2798 UNITED STATES. DEPARTMENT OF STATE. "Fascism on Trial at Nürnberg," Department of State Bulletin 1946 14(346): 250-256. February 17, 1946. A discussion by Harold Judson and others of the historical significance of the Nuremberg IMT trial. A broadcast sponsored jointly by the State Department and Robert H. Jackson's staff.

2799 UNITED STATES. DEPARTMENT OF STATE. "Our Military Government Policy in Germany," Department of State Bulletin 1945 13(323): 310-318. National Broadcasting Company (NBC) broadcast which deals in places with war crimes trials. Features State Department, U.S. Army, and War Department officials.

2800 UNITED STATES. DEPARTMENT OF STATE. "Prosecution of Major Nazi War Criminals: Report from Francis Biddle to President Truman," Department of State Bulletin 1946 15: 954-957. November 24, 1946. On the need to draft an international criminal code.

2801 VAMBERY, RUSTEM. "The Nürnberg Novelty," Fortune Magazine 1945 32(December): 140-141.

2802 WALL, EDGAR. Il processo di Norimberga. Milan: Lucchi, 1946. 245p.

2803 WALSH, WILLIAM F. "The Evidence at Nuremberg," Congress Weekly, A Review of Jewish Interests 1946 (March 1): 13-14.

2804 WASSERSTROM, RICHARD (ed.). War and Morality. Belmont, California: Wadsworth, 1970. 136p. Several articles in this anthology deal with war crimes and related topics, particularly those on the Nuremberg IMT judgment and the plea of superior orders. 1-page bibliography.

2805 WHEELER-BENNETT, JOHN W. The Nemesis of Power: The German Army in Politics, 1918-1945. London: Macmillan, 1961. Much on the Nuremberg IMT.

2806 WIART, H. CARTON DE. "Grands Criminels de guerre," *Revue de Droit International de Sciences Diplomatiques et Politiques* 1946 24(2): 41-43. Praises the establishment of the IMT, contrasting it to the failure after World War I to deal with war criminals.

2807 WOLF, J. *Les Fondements du Tribunal Militaire International. Considération sur le procès de Nuremberg*. Brussels: Larcier, 1946.

2808 WOLF, ROBERT B. "The Trial at Nuremberg," *Case and Comment* 1946 51(4): 23-26.

2809 WRIGHT, QUINCY. "The Nuernberg Trial," *Journal of Criminal Law and Criminology* 1947 37(6): 477-478.

2810 WRIGHT, QUINCY. "The Nuremberg Trials," *Chicago Bar Record* 1946 27(2): 201-219.

B. IMT, ALLIED, AND OTHER NON-CRIMINAL FIGURES

1. Biographies

2811 ALZINGER, JOSEPH ADOLPHE [pseudonym, Josse Alzin]. *Ce petit moine dangereux - Le Père Titus Brandsma*. Paris: Bonne Presse, 1954; Published in Spanish as *Ese Frailecito Peligroso - Padre Tito Brandsma*. Madrid: Ediciones Carmelitanas, 1956; and in English as *A Dangerous Little Friar - Father Titus Brandsma*. Dublin: Clonmore and Reynolds, 1957.

2812 ARNON, JOSEPH. "The Passion of Janusz Korczak," *Midstream* 1973 19(5): 32-53. Biographical sketch of the renowned author, doctor, and teacher written by one of his students. Discusses his journey to Treblinka with 200 orphans in his care. Their journey was related to the destruction of the Warsaw ghetto. Before dying he wrote a ghetto diary which described that episode. An eye witness described his last moments of life.

2813 BARDENS, DENNIS. *Lord Justice Birkett*. London: R. Hale, 1962. 288p. A biography of Judge Birkett.

2814 BOWKER, ARCHIBALD EDGAR. *Behind the Bar*. London: Staples, 1948. 323p.

2815 GERHART, EUGENE C. *America's Advocate: Robert H. Jackson*. Indianapolis: Bobbs-Merrill, 1958. 545p.

2816 HYDE, H. MONTGOMERY. *Lord Justice: The Life and Times of Lord Birkett of Ulverston*. New York: Random House, 1965.

2817 "John J. Parker: Senior Circuit Judge - Fourth Circuit," *American Bar Association Journal* 1946 32(December): 856-859, 901-903.

2818 MASON, ALPHEUS THOMAS. *Harlan Fiske Stone, Pillar of the Law*. New York: Viking, 1956.

2819 MASTERS, ANTHONY. *The Summer that Bled. The Biography of Hannah Senesh*. London: Michael Joseph, 1972. 349p.

2820 SENESH, HANNAH. *Her Life and Diary*. London: Vallentine, Mitchell, 1971. 257p. Published in Hebrew in 1945.

2821 SHORTIS, F.C. *Father Brandsma - Carmelite - Educator - Journalist - Nazi Victim*. Melbourne: Australian Catholic Truth Society Record, 1956.

2822 TREECE, PATRICIA. *A Man for Others: Maximilian Kolbe Saint of Auschwitz. In the Words of Those who Knew Him*. San Francisco: Harper and Row, 1982. 198p. The biography of a Catholic priest who substituted himself for an Auschwitz prisoner who was condemned to death. 8-page bibliography.

2823 YOUNG-BRUEHL, ELISABETH. *Hannah Arendt: For Love of the World*. New Haven: Yale University Press, 1982. 616p.

2. Autobiographies

2824 BIDDLE, FRANCIS B. *In Brief Authority*. Garden City: Doubleday, 1962. 494p. Biddle's memoirs of the Nuremberg IMT. Book 4, "The Nürnberg Trial," pp. 367-487, deals with various aspects of the trial, from the organization of the tribunal to the handing down of sentences.

2825 PIGGOTT, FRANCIS S.G. *Broken Thread: An Autobiography*. Aldershot: Gale & Polden, 1950. 424p. Autobiography of a former British military attaché in Tokyo contains comments, notes, and documents on the Tokyo trial.

2826 WAINWRIGHT, JONATHAN MAYHEW. *General Wainwright's Story: The Account of Four Years of Humiliating Defeat, Surrender, and Captivity*. Garden City: Doubleday, 1946. 314.

3. Diaries

2827 CIANO, GALEAZZO [Hugh Gibson, ed.]. *The Ciano Diaries, 1939-1943, the Complete, Unabridged Diaries of Count Galeazzo Ciano, Italian Minister of Foreign Affairs, 1936-1943*. Garden City: Doubleday, 1946. 584p. Ciano's diaries were smuggled out of Italy by his wife after his execution. Ciano entered the Italian diplomatic service immediately after graduating from the University of Rome. He married Mussolini's daughter, Edda, and became Italian Minister for Foreign Affairs. Describes his attempts to change the course upon which Mussolini had embarked and to establish better relations between Italy and the Western powers. Only brief mention of his sentence. Undocumented.

2828 FRANK, ANNE. *Het achterhuis. Dagboekbrieven van 12 Juni 1942 - 1 Augustus 1944*. Amsterdam: Uitg. Contact, 1947. 253p. Published in German as *Das Tagebuch der Anne Frank*. Heidelberg: Schneider, 1950 (several editions until 1979). Published in English as *The Diary of a Young Girl*. London: Constellation, 1952. Published in over 50 other languages.

2829 GILBERT, GUSTAVE MAHLER. *Nuremberg Diary*. New York: Farrar, Straus, 1947, 471p. Diary of a prison psychologist at the Nuremberg IMT trial. This study includes a brief statement by 20 of the defendants, obtained by the author immediately following the handing down of verdicts. Appendix I contains extracts from the judgment of individual defendants. Appendix II is a chronology of the rise and fall of Germany from 1919-1945. Undocumented; 9-page index.

2830 HASSELL, ULRICH VON. *The Von Hassell Diaries, 1938-44: The Story of the Forces against Hitler inside Germany as Recorded* by Ambassador Ulrich von Hassell, a Leader of the Movement. New York: Doubleday, 1947. 400p.

2831 HENDRY, TERESSA. "Was Anne Frank's Diary a Hoax?" American Mercury 1967 103(485): 26-28. Answers in the affirmative.

2832 KAPLAN, CHAIM A. Scroll of Agony. The Warsaw Diary of Chaim A. Kaplan. London: Hamish Hamilton, 1966. 329p. Contains maps of the Warsaw ghetto.

2833 KORCZAK, JANUSZ. Ghetto Diary. New York: Schocken, 1978.

2834 ZYLBERBERG, MICHAEL. A Warsaw Diary, 1939-1945. London: Vallentine, Mitchell, 1969. 220p. The author survived by means of false papers.

4. Memoirs

2835 KALNOKY, INGEBORG, with ILONA HERISKO. The Guest House: A Nuremberg Memoir of Countess Kalnoky. Indianapolis: Bobbs-Merrill, 1974. 248p. The "Guest Book" kept by Countess Kalnoky contains a list of guests she met in Nuremberg while the IMT trial was underway. Recounts the travels and travails of this German-born lady who married a Hungarian and lived ten years in Hungary. Much on the persecution of her and her husband by the Gestapo. Deals with the author's experiences as a witness at the trial and her relationship to other witnesses. 21 photographs.

2836 KELLEY, DOUGLAS M. 22 Männer um Hitler. Erinnerungen des amerikanischen Armeearztes und Psychiaters am Nürnberger Gefängnis. Bern: 1947.

2837 KORDT, ERICH. Wahn und Wirklichkeit. Stuttgart: Union Deutsche Verlagsgesellschaft, 1948. 430p. A study of German policy since the end of World War II in Europe. Draws on personal experiences and memoirs. Reviewers accuse the author of many flagrant errors.

2838 LIPPE, VIKTOR VON DER. Nürnberger Tagebuchnotizen, November 1945 bis Oktober 1946. Frankfurt am Main: F. Knapp, 1951.

2839 MAXWELL-FYFE, DAVID (EARL OF KILMUIR). Political Adventure: The Memoirs of the Earl of Kilmuir. London: Weidenfeld and Nicolson, 1964. 356p.

2840 SANDBERG, MOSHE. My Longest Year. In the Hungarian Labour Service and in the Nazi Camps. Jerusalem: Yad Vashem, 1968. 114p. Original published in Hebrew in 1966.

C. DOCUMENTS

BARRETT, ROGER W., and WILLIAM E. JACKSON (eds.). Nazi Conspiracy and Aggression. Washington: GPO, 1946. 8 volumes. Known as the "Red Series." Sometimes this set is catalogued under the editors, sometimes under U.S. CHIEF OF COUNSEL FOR THE PROSECUTION OF AXIS CRIMINALITY, occasionally under INTERNATIONAL MILITARY TRIBUNAL, and at other times under the title. To add to the confusion, it is listed variously as having 8, 10, or 11 volumes. There are 8 volumes in the major set, a two-volume supplement, and sometimes associated with it a small volume titled <u>Nazi Conspiracy and Aggression, Opinion and Judgment</u>.

This is a collection of documents and materials used by the Americans and British for the prosecution at the Nuremberg International Military Tribunal. The documents are not a part of the trial records, but were used to prepare the case for the prosecution. Many of these documents were never read into the record and therefore appear in complete form only in this set. All documents are in English.

2841 BARRETT, ROGER W., and WILLIAM E. JACKSON (eds.). <u>Nazi Conspiracy and Aggression</u>. Volume 1. 1116p. Contains the agreement by the United States, France, Great Britain, and the Soviet Union for the prosecution and punishment of the major war criminals of the European Axis, the Charter of the Nuremberg IMT, the Protocol of October 6, 1945, Indictment No. 1, the opening address for the United States by the U.S. Chief of Counsel, as well as motions, rulings, and explanatory material relating to Robert Ley, Gustav Krupp, Martin Bormann, Ernst Kaltenbrunner, Julius Streicher, and Rudolf Hess. Contains essays prepared by the prosecution on the organization of the Nazi party and state, means used by the Nazi conspirators to gain control of the German nation, economic aspects of the conspiracy, and the launching of wars of aggression. Also discusses the slave labor program, illegal use of prisoners of war, concentration camps, the persecution of Jews, and the plunder of art treasures.

2842 BARRETT, ROGER W., and WILLIAM E. JACKSON (eds.). <u>Nazi Conspiracy and Aggression</u>. Volume 2. 1099p. Contains documents on the criminality of groups and organizations and describes the law under which Nazi organizations were accused of being criminal. Explains the criminal nature of the Nazi Party Leadership Corps, the Reich Cabinet, the Sturmabteilung (SA), the Schutzstaffeln (SS), the Geheime Staatspolizei (Gestapo), the Sicherheitsdienst (SD), and the General Staff and High Command of the Armed Forces. Includes essays on the individual responsibility of the defendants and presents biographical data on the principal officials of the German government, the Nazi party, and the heads of the Armed Forces. Also contains code names and words used by the German High Command for operations during the war, and data concerning the capture of defendants. Glossary of common German and Nazi titles, designations, and terms, with their official abbreviations. Table of commissioned ranks in the German Army, Navy, and SS, with their equivalents in the American military forces.

2843 BARRETT, ROGER W., and WILLIAM E. JACKSON (eds.). <u>Nazi Conspiracy and Aggression</u>. Volume 3. 1003p. Contains more than 1000 letters, documents, circulars, and official reports relating to the prosecution of the major war criminals at Nuremberg. Includes letters between Bormann and Rosenberg, Sauckel and Rosenberg, a file of papers on Case Green (the plan for the attack on Czechoslovakia), top secret orders from Hitler on Barbarossa, a secret thesis from the Academy of German Law, January 1940, on resettlement, and directives concerning the administration of occupied eastern territories.

2844 BARRETT, ROGER W., and WILLIAM E. JACKSON (eds.). <u>Nazi Conspiracy and Aggression</u>. Volume 4. 1107p. Translation of nearly 1000 documents pertaining to the operations of the National

Socialist regime. Includes police regulations, laws, orders, and decrees relating to the activities of Jews. Reproduces a report on a conference at the Ministry of Economics regarding the use of Belgian and Dutch capital investments in southeastern European enterprises, orders eliminating Jews from German economic life, reprint of the book The Poisonous Mushroom, published in 1938, concerning Jews, a preliminary report on Germany's crimes against Norway, prepared by the Royal Norwegian Government, diary entries, telegrams, and stenographic reports.

2845 BARRETT, ROGER W., and WILLIAM E. JACKSON (eds.). Nazi Conspiracy and Aggression. Volume 5. 1107p. Contains almost 1000 documents, including extracts from many National Socialist publications, and the text of speeches made by IMT defendants during the war years. Also includes affidavits by members of the SS and other organizations attesting to atrocities committed. Contains correspondence between the Foreign Ministry and German envoys, a 1937-1938 OKW directive for the unified preparation for war, orders establishing concentration camps, and memoranda on rearmament.

2846 BARRETT, ROGER W., and WILLIAM E. JACKSON (eds.). Nazi Conspiracy and Aggression. Volume 6. 1120p. Contains hundreds of documents, including orders concerning the employment of Germans in Jewish households, marriages of German men in occupied territories of the Netherlands, an exchange of letters between von Papen, Hitler, and Hindenburg, a certificate accompanying a human skin exhibit, a letter from Kaltenbrunner (June 30, 1944) concerning forced labor of Jews in Vienna, and extracts from war diaries of military officials.

2847 BARRETT, ROGER W., and WILLIAM E. JACKSON (eds.). Nazi Conspiracy and Aggression. Volume 7. 1116p. Contains hundreds of affidavits, speeches, and letters pertaining to Nazi conspiracy and aggression, speeches by Gustav Krupp, a file of circulars from the inspector of concentration camps, and from the chiefs of the Security Police and SD relating to procedure in cases of unnatural death of Soviet prisoners of war, letters concerning financial matters within the occupied zones, and a communiqué of the Polish-Soviet Extraordinary Commission for Investigating Crimes committed by Germans in the Majdanek extermination camp.

2848 BARRETT, ROGER W., and WILLIAM E. JACKSON (eds.). Nazi Conspiracy and Aggression. Volume 8. 1090p. Contains speeches by Julius Streicher, records of interviews with Rudolf Hess, a letter to Rosenberg enclosing secret reports from Kube on German atrocities in the east (June 18, 1943) found in Himmler's personal files, articles from the Hague Convention and Versailles Treaty, and excerpts from the British Blue Book and Polish White Book. Also contains affidavits by Otto Ohlendorf, head of one of the Einsatzgruppen, Generaloberst Franz Halder, and Vice-Admiral Leopold Bürkner. Contains 19 charts, including one depicting totalitarian control of propaganda and education, another on the organization of German business, and other organizational charts and maps. Concludes with an index of the thousands of documents reproduced in the set.

2849 BARRETT, ROGER W., and WILLIAM E. JACKSON (eds.). Nazi Conspiracy and Aggression. Supplement A. [Volume 9]. 1947. 1391p. Contains the rules of the Nuremberg IMT and the closing addresses of the representatives of the United Kingdom, the

United States, France, and the Soviet Union. Continues the series of documents contained in the 8 main volumes of the set. Includes lists of exhibit numbers assigned by the IMT to documents presented by the United States and Great Britain. Index to the hundreds of documents presented in this volume.

2850 BARRETT, ROGER W., and WILLIAM E. JACKSON (eds.). <u>Nazi Conspiracy and Aggression, Supplement B</u>. [Volume 10]. 1948. 1713p. Contains excerpts from interrogations conducted by the prosecution, a defense motion challenging the jurisdiction of the tribunal, an argument on the law of the case by Dr. Hermann Jahrreiss on behalf of the defense counsels, and the final arguments and pleas by the counsel of each defendant. Also contains the texts of pre-trial interrogations of defendants and an index of principal people referred to in the interrogations.

2851 BARRETT, ROGER W., and WILLIAM E. JACKSON (eds.). <u>Nazi Conspiracy and Aggression, Opinion and Judgment</u>. [Volume 11]. 1947. 190p. Part 1, pp. 1-166, contains a summary of the judgment of the Nuremberg IMT. Discusses the charter provisions, the common plan of conspiracy and aggressive war, violations of international treaties, war crimes and crimes against humanity, and the accused organizations and individuals. Part 2, pp. 166-188, is a review of the dissenting opinion. Discusses the acquittal of Hjalmar Schacht, Franz von Papen, and Hans Fritzsche. Examines the sentence of Rudolf Hess, and the judgments regarding the Reich Cabinet General Staff and High Command, and the OKW. Part 3, pp. 189-190, lists the sentences.

2852 FRANCE. MINISTRY OF INFORMATION. <u>Accord du 8 août 1945 Statut du Tribunal Militaire International, articles et documents</u>. Nouvelle Serie no. 348. Paris: Ministry of Information, 1945.

2853 FRANCE. MINISTRY OF INFORMATION. <u>Service de recherche des crimes de guerre ennemis. Le Procès de Nuremberg. L'Accusation alliée</u>. Paris: Office français d'Édition, 1946.

2854 FRANCE. MINISTRY OF INFORMATION. <u>Service de recherche des crimes de guerre ennemis. Le Procès de Nuremberg. L'Accusation française</u>. 2 volumes. Paris: Office français d'Édition. 1946.

2855 GREAT BRITAIN. WAR OFFICE. <u>Regulations for the Trial of War Criminals: Royal Warrant, June 14, 1945</u>. London: War Office, 1945.

2856 GSOVSKI, VLADIMIR. "New Material on War Crimes Trials in Nuremberg," <u>Library of Congress Information Bulletin</u> 1950 9(32): 14-15.

2857 HOLZHAUSEN, RUDOLF. „Die Quellen zur Erforschung der Geschichte des ‚Dritten Reiches,'" <u>Archivalische Zeitschrift</u> 1950 46: 196-206. A discussion of the documents of the Nuremberg trial and the records of the German government and the Nazi Party which are in the custody of the United States.

2858 INTERNATIONAL MILITARY TRIBUNAL (IMT), NUREMBERG. <u>Documents Constituting Basic Authority War Crimes Trials</u>. Nuremberg: IMT Secretariat, 1947.

2859 INTERNATIONAL MILITARY TRIBUNAL (IMT), NUREMBERG. In Nürnberg wird gerichtet! Anklageschrift des Internationalen Militärgerichtshofes gegen die 24 nazistischen Kriegsverbrecher. Görlitz: Hoffmann & Reiber, 1946. 47p.

2860 INTERNATIONAL MILITARY TRIBUNAL (IMT), NUREMBERG. American edition: Trial of the Major War Criminals before the International Military Tribunal, Nuremberg, 14 November 1945 - 1 October 1946. 42 volumes. Nuremberg: IMT, 1947-1949. British edition: The Trial of German Major War Criminals: Proceedings of the International Military Tribunal sitting at Nuremberg, Germany, 20th November, 1945 to 1st December, 1946. Condensed edition, published in 21 volumes. London: HMSO, 1946. French edition: Procès des grands criminels de guerre devant le Tribunal militaire international, Nuremberg, 14 novembre 1945 - 1er octobre 1946. 41 volumes. Paris: Imprimerie Nationale, 1947-1949. German edition: Der Prozeß gegen die Hauptkriegsverbrecher vor dem Internationalen Militärgerichtshof, Nürnberg, 14. November 1945 bis 1. Oktober 1946 42 Volumes. Nuremberg: IMT, 1947-1949. These are the official publications of the Nuremberg IMT trial. It was originally intended that the proceedings would be printed in English, French, Russian, and German, and that the documents would be printed in the original language in which they were introduced. The proceedings of the IMT were recorded in full by stenographic notes, and a recording of all oral proceedings was made. Volume 1 (367p.) contains basic, offical, pretrial documents together with the Tribunal's judgment and sentence of the defendants. Lists members and alternate members of the Tribunal, officials of the General Secretariat, the prosecution and defense counsels, and the defendants. Discusses the establishment of the IMT, gives the rules of procedure, and lists the texts of all indictments and the pleas of the defendants. Contains a number of motions on behalf of various defendants as well as answers to the motions. Discusses possible medical examination for Rudolf Hess. Contains the Charter of the IMT, the London Agreement of August 8, 1945, and the minutes of the opening session of the Tribunal at Berlin on October 18, 1945. Volumes 2-23 contain the proceedings of the IMT. Volume 23 (732p.) and Volume 24 are indexes to volumes 1-22. Part 1 (Volume 23, pp. 1-70) is a chronological index recording the development of the trial. Part 2 (Volume 23, pp: 7-732) is a subject index, and Part 3 is a document index preceded by a short explanation of its use. Part 4 is a name index, which contains a mall index for each defendant. Volumes 25-42 contain reprints of the documents admitted as evidence. All English, French, and German documents are reproduced in their original language; all documents originally in Russian are reprinted in English and German translation. Any document not in one of these 4 languages is published in the language in which it was introduced in court. All documents are reproduced in full unless otherwise stated. These volumes contain thousands of original documents, charts, tables, and photographs.

2861 JACKSON, ROBERT H. "Report to the President from Justice Robert H. Jackson, Chief of Counsel for the United States in the Prosecution of Axis War Criminals, June 7, 1945," American Journal of International Law, Supplement 1945 39(3): 178-190.

2862 JACKSON, ROBERT H. The Nürnberg Case, as presented by Robert H. Jackson, Chief of Counsel for the United States, together with other Documents. New York: Knopf, 1947. 268p. Contains a preface by Jackson, his June 7, 1945, report to President Harry Truman, the four-power agreement for trials, the Charter of the IMT, the opening statement for the United States, delivered November 21, 1945, the law under which various organizations were accused of being criminal, Jackson's closing address, delivered July 26, 1946, and excerpts from the cross-examinations of Hermann Göring, Hjalmar Schacht, Albert Speer, and Erhard Milch.

2863 KÖHLER, FRITZ (comp.). Geheime Kommandosache. Aus den Dokumenten des Nürnberger Prozesses gegen die Hauptkriegsverbrecher. Berlin: Kongreß, 1956. 191p.

2864 LA GERMONIÈRE, PAUL (ed.). Le Procès de Nuremberg, avec le Texte officiel intégral de jugements portés contre les 22 accusés grands criminels de guerre. Lyon: Publicité Éditions Générales, 1946. 130p.

2865 MENDELSOHN, JOHN. "Trial by Document: The Problem of Due Process for War Criminals at Nuernberg," Prologue 1975 7(4): 227-234. The Nuremberg IMT trial pioneered the use of voluminous documents as court evidence against large groups of defendants. To convict officials who gave orders but did not execute them personally, the prosecution relied heavily on German records. The defendants were treated fairly, considering the intense hatreds engendered by World War II. The prosecution enjoyed easier access to documents in the early cases, and case procedures were disadvantageous to SS defendants. Based on primary and secondary sources; 31 notes, 6 photographs.

2866 MENDELSOHN, JOHN. "Trial by Document: The Use of Seized Records in the United States Proceedings at Nuernberg," Ph.D. dissertation, University of Maryland, 1974. 238p. Abstracted in Dissertation Abstracts International 1975 35(9): 6068-A - 6069-A.

2867 MENDELSSOHN, PETER DE. The Nuremberg Documents: Some Aspects of German War Policy, 1939-1945. London: Allen and Unwin, 1946. 291p. A collection of the most important Nuremberg documents, compiled by the New Statesman. Deals with German military planning from 1937-1940, German-Italian relations from 1937-1943, plans for the invasion of Britain, German-Spanish relations from 1937-1943, German-Soviet relations from 1939-1941. Contains a summary of the documents.

2868 MONNERAY, HENRI. "La Preuve documentaire et testimoniale au procès de Nuremberg," Revue Générale de Droit International Public 1948 52(January-June): 20-49. Discusses some of the procedures adopted at Nuremberg, particularly on the presentation of evidence, the admissibility of testimony and documents, and the rules followed in the trial of organizations. 108 notes.

2869 NIEBERGALL, FRED. "Brief Survey Concerning the Records of the War Crimes Trials held in Nürnberg, Germany," Law Library Journal 1949 42(2): 87-90.

2870 NIEBERGALL, FRED. "The Documents of Nuremberg," Wiener Library Bulletin 1949 3(March): 9.

2871 Niurnbergskii protsess. Sbornik materialov. Moscow: Iurizdat, 1955-1956. 2 volumes. 654, 598p. A selection of Nuremberg IMT documents.

2872 Niurnbergskii protsess nad glavnymi nemetskimi voennymi prestupnikami. Moscow: Gosiurizdat, 1957-1962. 10 volumes. Russian translation of the proceedings of the Nuremberg IMT.

2873 OSCAR, FRIEDRICH (OLMES). Über Galgen wächst kein Gras. Die fragwürdige Kulisse der Kriegsverbrecherprozesse im Spiegel unbekannter Dokumente. Brunswick: Erasmus, 1950.

2874 PANNENBECKER, OTTO (ed.). Geheim! Dokumentarische Tatsachen aus dem Nürnberger Prozeß. Düsseldorf: Bastion, 1947. 223p. Contains letters and other documents on the preparation for and direction of World War II, on occupied areas, on the treatment of Jews, on the SD and Gestapo, on the management of concentration camps, and on justice in the Third Reich.

2875 ROBERTS, ADAM, and RICHARD GUELFF (eds.). Documents on the Laws of War. Oxford: Clarendon Press, 1982. 498p. Chapter 16, "1946 Judgment of the International Military Tribunal at Nuremberg. Extracts on Crimes against International Law," pp. 153-156, describes briefly the charges against the Nuremberg IMT defendants.

2876 SCHNEIDER, ROLF. Prozeß in Nürnberg (Ein Dokumentarstück). Mit einem Anhang. Auszüge aus dem „Nürnberger Tagebuch" von G.M. Gilbert. Frankfurt am Main: Fischer, 1968.

2877 SERAPHIM, HANS-GÜNTHER. „Der Index der amtlichen deutschen Ausgabe des Prozesses der Hauptkriegsverbrecher," Europa Archiv 1950 5(May 20): 3028-3031.

2878 SERAPHIM, HANS-GÜNTHER. „Die Dokumentenedition der amtlichen deutschen Ausgabe des Verfahrens gegen die Hauptkriegsverbrecher," Europa-Archiv 1950 5(September 5): 3307-3310.

2879 STEINIGER, P.A. (comp.). Der Nürnberger Prozeß. Aus den Protokollen, Dokumenten und Materialien des Prozesses gegen die Hauptkriegsverbrecher vor dem Internationalen Militärgerichtshof. 2 volumes. 5th edition. Berlin: Deutscher Verlag der Wissenschaften, 1962. Volume 1, 318p., Volume 2, 611p. A thorough study of the IMT. Examines crimes under the 4 charges on a nation-to-nation basis. Copiously documented, documents, photographs, index.

2880 STIPP, JOHN L. (ed.). Devil's Diary: The Record of Nazi Conspiracy and Aggression. Yellow Springs, Ohio: Antioch Press, 1955. 236p. A condensation of Roger W. Barrett and William E. Jackson (eds.). Nazi Crimes and Aggression.

2881 UNITED STATES. DEPARTMENT OF STATE. "Final Report to the President from Supreme Court Justice Jackson," Department of State Bulletin 1946 15(382): 771-776. October 27, 1946. This report and President Truman's reply have been published in various forms and have been abstracted elsewhere.

2882 UNITED STATES. DEPARTMENT OF STATE. "Reply of President Truman to Justice Jackson," Department of State Bulletin 1946 15 (382): 776. October 27, 1946. Truman's reply to Robert H. Jackson's final report.

2883 UNITED STATES. DEPARTMENT OF STATE. Trial of War Criminals: 1. Report of Robert H. Jackson to the President; 2. Agreement Establishing an International Military Tribunal; 3. Indictment. Report. State Department Publication No. 2420. Washington: GPO, 1945. 89p.

2884 UNITED STATES. NATIONAL ARCHIVES AND RECORDS SERVICE. Records of the United States Nuernberg War Crimes Trials Interrogations, 1946-1949. Washington: NARS, 1977.

2885 VICAR, G. Le Livre noir. 100 documents prodigieux sur le plus grand procès de l'histoire. Paris: Éditions du Bateau Irre, 1946.

2886 WIENER LIBRARY. Catalogue of Nuremberg Documents. London: Wiener Library, 1961. 139p. The main catalog lists prosecution documents in serial order. Defense documents are arranged alphabetically under defendant, and 2 appendices list the defendants with their original sentences and later reductions and gives a list of testimonies. Supplement No. 1 (1962, 13p.) lists documents which deal with the Holocaust. Supplement No. 2 (1962, 37p.) lists summaries of interrogations, and Supplement No. 3 (1963, 133p.) is a key to documents in prosecution records.

2887 WIENER LIBRARY. List of Nuremberg Documents dealing with the Persecution of Jews. London: Wiener Library, 1967. 231p. Typescript.

D. SPEECHES

2888 Exposés introductifs de M. le Juge Jackson, Sir Hartley Shawcross et le Général R. Rudenko: Introduction de M. Champetier de Ribes. Paris: Office français d'Édition, 1946. IMT documents.

2889 INTERNATIONAL MILITARY TRIBUNAL (IMT), NUREMBERG. The Trial of German Major War Criminals by the International Military Tribunal Sitting at Nuremberg, Germany (Commencing 20th November, 1945): Speeches of the Chief Prosecutors for the United States of America, the French Republic, the United Kingdom of Great Britain and Northern Ireland and the Union of Soviet Socialist Republics, at the Close of the Case against the Individual Defendants. London: HMSO, 1946.

2890 INTERNATIONAL MILITARY TRIBUNAL (IMT), NUREMBERG. The Trial of German Major War Criminals by the International Military Tribunal Sitting at Nuremberg, Germany (Commencing 20th November, 1945): Speeches of the Prosecutors for the United States of America, the French Republic, the United Kingdom of Great Britain and Northern Ireland and the Union of Soviet Socialist Republics at the Close of the Case against the Indicted Organisations. London: HMSO, 1946.

2891 JACKSON, ROBERT H. Opening Address for the United States. [Washington]: War Department, Bureau of Public Relations, [no date given]. 29p. Opening address for the U.S. by Robert H. Jackson at the Nuremberg IMT. Department document announcing the case against 22 individual defendants and six National Socialist organizations. Jackson discusses the consolidation of Nazi power, the battle against the working class and the churches, crimes against the Jews, terrorism and preparation for war, aggression, war crimes, crimes against peace, the law of individual responsibility, political, police, and military organizations, and the responsibility of the tribunal. Undocumented.

2892 JACKSON, ROBERT H. <u>The Case against the Nazi War Criminals, opening Statement for the United States of America and other Documents</u>. New York: Knopf, 1946. 217p. Contains the opening address for the United States before the International Military Tribunal at Nuremberg as presented by Robert H. Jackson, Chief Counsel for the United States. Appendix I contains the text of an agreement by the United States, France, the United Kingdom, and the Soviet Union for the prosecution of the major war criminals. Appendix II is the text of the indictment of the four powers against 22 Nuremberg defendants and six criminal organizations. Appendix A contains a statement of individual responsibility, Appendix B a statement of criminality of groups and organizations, and Appendix C the charges and particulars of violations of international treaties and agreements perpetuated by the defendants in the course of planning, preparing, and initiating the war. Undocumented; 4 photographs.

2893 RUDENKO, ROMAN A. <u>Die Gerechtigkeit fordert für alle Hauptkriegsverbrecher nur eine Strafe, die Todesstrafe. General Rudenkos Schlußrede in Nürnberg</u>. Berlin: Tägliche Rundschau, 1947. 63p. A defendant-by-defendant analysis showing why each should be condemned to death.

2894 RUDENKO, ROMAN A. <u>Die Gerechtigkeit nehme ihren Lauf! Die Reden des sowjetischen Hauptanklägers R.A. Rudenko im Nürnberger Prozeß der deutschen Hauptkriegsverbrecher</u>. Berlin: Verlag der Sowjetischen Militärverwaltung in Deutschland, 1946. 229p. Discusses the meaning and significance of the Nuremberg IMT trial, war crimes committed by Germans, the defendants, and criminal organizations.

2895 SHAWCROSS, HARTLEY. <u>Nürnberg. Die Rede des englischen Hauptanklagevertreters</u>. Hamburg: Phoenix, 1946. 61p.

2896 <u>The Trial of German Major War Criminals by the International Military Tribunal Sitting at Nuremberg. Opening Speeches of the Chief Prosecutors</u>. London: HMSO, 1946. 171p.

E. IMT AND INTERNATIONAL LAW

2897 BIDDLE, FRANCIS B. "The Nürnberg Trial," <u>American Philosophical Society Proceedings</u> 1947 91(3): 294-302. 18 notes. <u>Virginia Law Quarterly</u> 1947, p. 679. "Le procès de Nuremberg," <u>Revue Internationale de Droit Pénal</u> 1948 19: 1-19. Discusses the nature of the Nuremberg IMT trial and misconceptions concerning it. Describes the results of the proceedings as a step toward preventing wars of aggression by establishing the principle of individual responsibility. Nuremberg is the cradle of a new discipline: interstate penal law, as defined by A. Sottile.

2898 BOWER, ROBERT J. "The Nuremberg Trial and its Place in International Law," M.A. thesis, Stanford University, 1947. 201p. An attempt to portray the Nuremberg IMT in its relations to international law. Discusses the establishment of the IMT, whether the "Nuremberg law" was <u>ex post facto</u>, and acts of state. Bibliography.

2899 CALOYANNI, MÉGALOS A. "Memorandum on International Criminal Legislation and Peace," Revue Internationale de Droit Pénal 1946 17: 305-332. Discusses developments in the theory of international law since World War I and recent developments in the practice of international law, including the Nuremberg IMT trial. Recommends that the Security Council take up the problem of international crime and attempt a systematic codification of penal law.

2900 CHALUFOUR, A. "Le Procès de Nuremberg et le droit international," Annuaire de l'Association des Auditeurs et Anciens Auditeurs de l'Academie de Droit International de La Haye 1958 28: 26-38.

2901 DONNEDIEU DE VABRES, HENRI. "Le Jugement de Nuremberg et le principe de légalité des délits et des peines," Revue de Droit Pénal et de Criminologie 1947 27(July): 813-833.

2902 DONNEDIEU DE VABRES, HENRI. Le Procès de Nuremberg devant les principes modernes du droit international. Paris: Sirey, 1947. Deals with the principles of international penal law as derived from war crimes trials.

2903 DONNEDIEU DE VABRES, HENRI. "Le Procès de Nuremberg devant les principes modernes du droit pénal international," Recueil des Cours 1947 70: 477-582. Copiously annotated. 3-page bibliography.

2904 EHARD, HANS. "The Nuremberg Trial Against the Major War Criminals and International Law," American Journal of International Law 1949 43(2): 223-245. Originally published in Süddeutsche Juristen-Zeitung 1948 3(7): 353-368. A German viewpoint of the Nuremberg IMT trial which was published with the blessing of Robert H. Jackson, not because he agreed with it, but because he thought it an intelligent and scholarly viewpoint that raised criticism of the trial to a more profitable level. Ehard was Minister-President of Bavaria. The text is an address to a meeting of lawyers in Munich on June 2, 1948. Deals with the formal basis of the trial and the legal problems involved and then draws certain general conclusions as to the legality, alternatives to, and long-range results of the trial. Lists specific crimes under each of the four indictments brought against the defendants. Argues that war criminals would have been tried as fairly and more legally before German courts and criticizes the IMT for not allowing Germans or even neutrals to participate in the trial. Regardless of its illegal character and the many shortcomings of the trial, it was a guidepost for the further development of the law of nations. Based on the official records of the trial; 49 notes.

2905 FINCH, GEORGE A. "The Nuremberg Trial and International Law," American Journal of International Law 1947 41(1): 20-37. Enlarged and annotated version of an address delivered in Atlantic City, New Jersey, October 29, 1946, before the Section of International and Comparative Law of the American Bar Association, by the Chairman of the Committee on Punishment of War Criminals. The author's comments are limited to the Nuremberg indictment and judgment. He defends the legality of the proceedings and the justification of the four charges brought against the Nuremberg defendants. Based largely on secondary sources; 37 notes.

2906 GLASER, STEFAN. "Les Lois de Nuremberg et le droit international: En marge de l'ouvrage du Dr. H.H. Jescheck 'Die Verantwortlichkeit der Staatsorgane nach Völkerstrafrecht,'" Schweizerische Zeitschrift für Strafrecht 1953 68: 321-359.

2907 HARDING-BARLOW, M. "International Law and the Nuremberg Trial," South African Law Journal 1948 65(August): 375-386.

2908 HYDE, CHARLES C. International Law Chiefly as Interpreted and Applied by the United States . . . 2nd edition. Boston: Little, Brown, 1945. 3 volumes. Arrangements for the prosecution and punishment of people charged with violations of the laws of war, particularly Volume 3, pp. 2409-2415.

2909 JACKSON, ROBERT H. "The Trials of War Criminals: An Experiment in International Legal Understanding," American Bar Association Journal 1946 32(June): 319-321.

2910 KELSEN, HANS. "Sanctions in International Law under the Charter of the United Nations," Iowa Law Review 1946 31(May): 499-543.

2911 KELSEN, HANS. "The Legal Status of Germany According to the Declaration of Berlin," American Journal of International Law 1945 39(3): 518-526. Argues that the legal status of German war criminals was different from that of all other war criminals and that they could be tried under the legislative, executive, and judicial powers of the occupying powers. 5 notes.

2912 LAUER, LAWRENCE. "The International War Criminal Trials and the Common Law of War," St. John's Law Review 1945 20(1): 18-24. 28 notes.

2913 LINDBERG, HUGO. En Dag i Nürnberg. Stockholm: Wahlström and Widstrand, 1946. 85p. Brief exposition of the fundamental laws governing the trial. Most of the book is devoted to Rudolf Höß, Commander of Auschwitz, who, in the author's estimation, typified German readiness to obey authority blindly.

2914 MALÉZIEUX, R. "Le Statut international des criminels de guerre," Revue Générale de Droit International Public 1941-1945 49(2): 167-180. Analyzes the legal bases of the Nuremberg IMT trial and the Control Council and their functions in the prosecution of war criminals. Also considers the legal bases of the proceedings against so-called minor war criminals, pointing out the international character of the statutes governing the trials of those prosecuted under local jurisdiction. Discusses the United Nations War Crimes Commission. 21 notes.

2915 PAL, RADHABINOD. Crimes in International Relations. Calcutta: University of Calcutta, 1955.

2916 SCHICK, FRANZ B. "Law or Politics for the Maintenance of Peace," Juridical Review 1947 59(1): 50-69. Discusses the conflict between the Charter of the UN and the Charter of the Nuremberg IMT, showing that the former affirms the principle of collective responsibility and the latter that of individual responsibility. Demands that these viewpoints be reconciled. 31 notes.

2917 SCHICK, FRANZ B. "War Criminals and the Law of the United Nations," University of Toronto Law Journal 1947 7(1): 27-67. Compares the legal principles of the Nuremberg IMT trial to the relevant chapters of the UN Charter and finds that the intention of the victorious powers to establish the legal principle of individual criminal responsibility for violations of international law was not carried out in the UN Charter. 138 notes.

2918 SOTTILE, ANTOINE. "Les Criminels de guerre et le nouveau droit pénal international, le seul moyen pour assurer la paix du monde," Revue de Droit International de Sciences Diplomatiques et Politiques 1945 23(4): 228-250.

2919 STIMSON, HENRY L. "The Nuremberg Trial: Landmark in Law," Foreign Affairs 1947 25(2): 179-189. Sees the Nuremberg trial as a great accomplishment and comments on the fairness of the proceedings

2920 TRAININ, ARON NAUMOVICH. "Le Tribunal militaire international et le procès de Nuremberg," Revue Internationale de Droit Pénal 1946 17: 263-276. An account of the events leading to the establishment of the IMT in Nuremberg and a description of its functions. The author maintains that there are no laws in international affairs, only conventions and agreements. Principles of national law cannot be applied in international situations.

2921 TRUYOL Y SERRA, ANTONIO. "Crímenes de guerra y derecho natural," Revista Española de Derecho Internacional 1948 1(2): 45-73. 35 notes.

2922 TUSHINS, J.W. "Notes on International Law, the Nuremberg Trials of World War II Criminals," Law Society Quarterly 1946 12 (November): 321-326.

2923 "War Crimes and International Law," Fortnightly 1945 158(October): 228-233.

2924 WOETZEL, ROBERT K. The Nuremberg Trials in International Law. London: Stevens, 1960. New York: Praeger, 1960. 287p. The 1962 edition contains a postlude on the Eichmann case. A scholarly study that concludes that the Nuremberg trial had both a legal character and a legal basis. Discusses some historical precursors to the trial as well as individual responsibility under international law.

2925 YRIGOYEN, JAIME. El proceso de Nuremberg y el derecho internacional. Lima: 1955.

F. IMT AND INTERNATIONAL CONFERENCES AND CONVENTIONS

2926 ALBRECHT, A.R. "War Reprisals in the War Crimes Trials and in the Geneva Conventions of 1949," American Journal of International Law 1953 47(4): 590-614. 108 notes.

2927 ALFARO, RICARDO. Report on the Question of International Criminal Jurisdiction. Doc. A/CN.4/15, 3 March 1950. Lake Success: United Nations, 1950. 46p. Mimeograph.

2928 "Allied Conference on German War Crimes, London, 1942," Inter-Allied Review 1942 2(February): 32-35. On speeches and statements made at the conference.

2929 BARRY, JOHN V. "The Moscow Declaration on War Crimes," Australian Law Journal 1943 17(8): 248-250. On the Moscow Declaration on atrocities, November 1, 1943. 9 notes.

2930 DICKINSON, EDWIN D., GEORGE A. FINCH, and CHARLES CHENEY HYDE (eds.). "Report of the Sub-committee on the Trial and Punishment of War Criminals," American Journal of International Law 1943 37(4): 663-666.

2931 GREAT BRITAIN. FOREIGN OFFICE. Report of the Crimea Conference, February 11, 1945. Cmd. 6598. London: HMSO, 1946.

2932 GROH, FRANZ. Das Recht der Kriegsgefangenen und Zivilpersonen nach den Genfer Konventionen vom 12. August 1949. Hamburg: Forschungsstelle für Völkerrecht und ausländisches öffentliches Recht der Universität Hamburg, 1953.

2933 HEBREW UNIVERSITY, JERUSALEM. Symposium on War Crimes, Crimes against Humanity, and Statutory Limitations, Jerusalem, May 28, 1968. Jerusalem: Hebrew University, 1968. Publication No. 15 of the Institute of Criminology.

2934 INTER-ALLIED INFORMATION COMMITTEE. LONDON. Issued 9 pamphlets under the general heading "Conditions in Occupied Territories." Those dealing with war crimes are No. 3, Religious Persecution, August 12, 1942. 23p. No. 6, Persecution of the Jews, December 18, 1942. 20p. No. 7, Women Under Axis Rule, November 30, 1943. 19p. No. 8, Slave Labour and Deportation, August 24, 1944. 24p.

2935 JACKSON, ROBERT H. Report of Robert H. Jackson, United States Representative to the International Conference on Military Trials, London, 1945. Washington: GPO, 1949. 441p. State Department Publication 3080. A documentary record of the negotiations of the United States, France, Great Britain, and the Soviet Union which culminated in the agreement and charter of the International Military Tribunal. Presents a formal statement of the principles of law agreed upon for the trial of German war criminals. Lists 63 documents, including a complete roster of the representatives and their assistants. Contains the text of the Nuremberg charter.

2936 LACHS, MANFRED. "War Crimes - Political Offenses," Juridical Review 1944 56(April): 27-41. Comment on the Moscow Declaration. War criminals cannot be treated as political offenders.

2937 MAYNARD, J.A. "Crimes et criminels de guerre: problème etudié par une groupe de Juristes aux Etats-Unis," Revue Internationale de Droit Penal 1946 17: 333-342. Describes the composition and work of the International Lawyers Committee on War Crimes, established under the auspices of the École Libre des Hautes Études in February, 1945.

2938 SANDSTRÖM, EMIL. Report on the Question of International Criminal Jurisdiction. Doc. A/CN.4/20, 30 March 1950. Lake Success: United Nations, 1950. 17p. mimeograph.

2939 SCHLÖGEL, ANTON. Die Genfer Rotkreuz-Abkommen vom 12. August 1949. 3rd edition. Mainz: Verlagsanstalt Hüthig und Dreyer, 1955.

2940 SILVERGATE, JESSE. "The Role of the UN War Crimes Commission in Developing the Nuremberg Conspiracy Doctrine," Studies in

History and Sociology 1971 3(2): 1-13. The United Nations War Crimes Commission was given the task of preparing reports and recommendations for subsequent trials at Nuremberg. Discusses collective responsibility, aggressive war, and the definition of war crimes. 44 notes.

2941 STREBEL, HELMUT. "Die Genfer Abkommen vom 12. August 1949 - Fragen des Anwendungsbereichs," *Zeitschrift für ausländisches Öffentliches Recht und Völkerrecht* 1950 13(February): 118-145. 48 notes.

2942 UNITED NATIONS. INTERNATIONAL LAW COMMISSION. *Historical Survey of the Question of International Criminal Jurisdiction. Memorandum Submitted by the Secretary-General.* Document A/CN.4/7/Rev.1. Lake Success: United Nations, 1949. 147p. Contains an introduction, a consideration of international criminal jurisdiction before the creation of the UN as well as within the UN, and appendices.

2943 UNITED NATIONS. INTERNATIONAL LAW COMMISSION. "Report of the International Law Commission Covering its Third Session 16 May - 27 July 1951, with Draft Code of Offences against the Peace and Security of Mankind." Document A/CN.4/48, 30 July 1951.

2944 UNITED STATES. DEPARTMENT OF STATE. "Toward Revision of the Geneva Convention," *Department of State Bulletin* 1948 19(October 10): 464-465.

2945 UNITED STATES. DEPARTMENT OF STATE. "Tripartite Conference at Berlin," *Department of State Bulletin* 1945 13(August 5): 153-161. On the Potsdam Conference.

G. PRINCIPLES AND PROCEDURES

2946 BALAZS, ANDRÉ. "Die rechtliche Begründung des Nürnberger Urteils," *Friedens-Warte* 1946 46(6): 369-375. An abstract of the judgment, with emphasis on the parts of particular interest to the international lawyer. 30 notes.

2947 "Commission formulates Nuremberg Principles," *United Nations Weekly Bulletin* 1950 9(August 1): 108-110.

2948 CRAMER, MYRON C. "Military Justice and Trial Procedure," *American Bar Association Journal* 1943 29(July): 368-371.

2949 DESCHEEMAEKER, JACQUES. "Le Tribunal Militaire International des Grands Criminels de Guerre," *Revue Générale de Droit International Public* 1946 50: 210-311. Discusses the organization, jurisdiction, and procedures of the Tribunal and the origins and precedents of the judgment. *Le Tribunal militaire international des grands criminels de guerre.* Paris: Éditions A. Pedone, 1947. Extract from above. 161 notes.

2950 FERENCZ, BENJAMIN B. "Nürnberg Trial Procedure and the Rights of the Accused," *Journal of Criminal Law and Criminology* 1948 39(2): 144-151. 57 notes.

2951 GELBERG, LUDWIG. "Die Nürnberger Prinzipien und das moderne Völkerrecht," *Demokratie und Recht* 1978 6(2): 177-187.

2952 GORMLEY, W. PAUL. "The Procedural Status of the Individual before Supranational Judicial Tribunals, Part II," *University of Detroit Law Journal* 1964 41(4): 405-446. 276 notes.

2953 HUGUENEY, LOUIS. "Le Procès de Nuremberg devant les principes modernes de droit pénal international," *Revue Internationale de Droit Pénal* 1948 19: 277-280. Summary of a lecture by Donnedieu de Vabres at the Academy of The Hague in June 1948. He rejected the notion of conspiracy and had little enthusiasm for the new concept of crimes against humanity.

2954 JESSUP, PHILIP C. "The Crime of Aggression and the Future of International Law," *Political Science Quarterly* 1947 62(1): 1-10. Urges the strengthening of the Nuremberg precedent in order to control war. Discusses the endorsement of the IMT Charter by the United Nations and the adoption of the resolution on genocide. An international criminal law court should be organized.

2955 KAUFMAN, MARY M. "The Individual's Duty under the Law of Nurnberg: The Effect of Knowledge on Justiciability," *Lawyers Guild Practitioner* 1968 27(1): 15-21.

2956 KENNY, JOHN P. *Moral Aspects of Nuremberg*. Washington: Pontifical Faculty of Theology, Dominican House of Studies, 1949. 168p. Deals with the philosophical bases of the Nuremberg IMT trial. Since international law arose from scholastic philosophy, Thomistic principles are proposed as a sound basis for an international tribunal. The deficiencies of the tribunal resulted from a false notion of international right.

2957 KLAFKOWSKI, ALFONS. [The German occupation of Poland in the light of international law]. Poznan: Instytut Zachodn, 1946. 196p.

2958 KOZHEVNIKOV, F.I. [The Soviet state and international law, 1917-1947]. Moscow: 1948. 376p. In Russian. Deals with contemporary developments in international law, particularly the Nuremberg principles. The author praises the recognition of the existence of crimes against humanity and personal responsibility for aggressive war. The Nuremberg IMT judgment is the first example of international justice over war criminals.

2959 LIPPERT, DAVID I. "Codification of the Nurnberg Principles," *Los Angeles Bar Bulletin* 1953 28(5): 157-158, 166-175. 45 notes.

2960 MORGAN, JOHN HARTMANN. *The Great Assize: An Examination of the Law of the Nuremberg Trials*. London: J. Murray, 1948. 44p. The author was vice-chairman of the British War Crimes Committee of 1918-1919. He is critical of several theories underlying the Nuremberg IMT trial. Except for violations of the laws of warfare, there is no valid legal precedent or positive international law to deal with the crime of conspiracy, crimes against humanity, or aggressive war.

2961 O'BRIEN, WILLIAM V. "The Nuremberg Principles," in James Finn (ed.). *A Conflict of Loyalties*. New York: Pegasus, 1968. 287p.

2962 SCHILLING, KARL, and KURT HEINZE. *Die Rechtsprechung der Nürnberger Militärtribunale*. Bonn: Schilling, 1952.

2963 SOHN, LOUIS B. "Formulation of the Nuremberg Principles by the International Law Commission," *American Bar Association Journal* 1950 36(June): 505-508.

2964 SPIROPOULOS, JEAN. "Formulation of the Nürnberg Principles," Revue Hellénique de Droit International 1951 4: 129-162.

2965 TRAININE, ARON NAUMOVICH. "Court Procedure at Nuremberg," Soviet News 1945 1330(December 21): 2.

2966 TRAININE, ARON NAUMOVICH. "La Procédure à Nuremberg," Revue de Droit International de Sciences Diplomatiques et Politiques 1946 24(2): 77-81.

2967 UNITED NATIONS. COMMITTEE ON THE PROGRESSIVE DEVELOPMENT OF INTERNATIONAL LAW AND ITS CODIFICATION. Report on the Plans for the Formulation of the Principles of the Nuremberg Charter and Judgment. 1947. A/AC.10/52 (mimeograph). Published as "Report of the Committee on the Progressive Development of International Law and its Codification on the Plans for the Formulation of the Principles of the Nuremberg Charter and Judgment," American Journal of International Law, Supplement 1947 41: 26-27.

2968 UNITED NATIONS. GENERAL ASSEMBLY. The Formulation of the Principles Recognized in the Charter of the Nuremberg Tribunal and in the Judgment of the Tribunal: Adopted at the 123rd Plenary Meeting, November 21, 1947: Official Records of the Second Session of the General Assembly, Resolutions, 16 September-29 November 1947. Res. 177 (2). Lake Success: United Nations, 1948.

2969 UNITED NATIONS. INTERNATIONAL LAW COMMISSION (1ST SESSION). Report of the International Law Commission Covering its First Session, April 12 - June 9, 1949. General Assembly, Official Records: Fourth Session, Supplement No. 10 (Doc. A/925). Lake Success: United Nations, 1949. 10p. Chapter 3 is entitled "Formulation of the Nuremberg Principles and Preparation of a Draft Code of Offences against the Peace and Security of Mankind." Chapter 4 is "Study of the Question of International Criminal Jurisdiction."

2970 UNITED NATIONS. INTERNATIONAL LAW COMMISSION (2ND SESSION). Formulation of the Nürnberg Principles: Report by J. Spiropoulos. Doc. A/CN.4/22, April 12, 1950. Lake Success: United Nations, 1950. 41p. Mimeograph.

2971 UNITED NATIONS. INTERNATIONAL LAW COMMISSION (2ND SESSION). Report of the International Law Commission, Covering its Second Session 5 June - 29 July 1950. General Assembly, Official Records: Fifth Session, Supplement No. 12 (Doc. A/1316). Lake Success: United Nations, 1950. 22p. Part 3 deals with the formulation of the Nuremberg principles, Part 4 with the question of international criminal jurisdiction, and Part 5 with offenses against the peace and security of mankind. Also published as "Report of the International Law Commission Covering its Second Session, June 5 - July 29, 1950," American Journal of International Law, Supplement 1950 44(4): 125-134. Part III: Formulation of the Nuremberg principles. 20 notes.

2972 UNITED NATIONS. "Plans for the Formulation of the Principles of the Nuernberg Charter and Judgment," Yearbook of the United Nations 1947-1948: 214-215. Lake Success: United Nations, 1949, 1950.

2973 VAMBERY, RUSTEM. "The Law of the Tribunal," Nation 1946 163 (October 12): 400-401.

2974 WOETZEL, ROBERT K. "Comments on the Nuremberg Principles and Conscientious Objection, with Special Reference to War Crimes," Catholic Lawyer 1970 16(Summer): 257-263.

2975 WORTLEY, B.A. "Keeping the Peace," Law Quarterly Review 1947 63(250): 188-207. Holds that the principles of international law were legitimately enforced at Nuremberg. 68 notes.

2976 WRIGHT, QUINCY. "The Law of the Nuremberg Trial," American Journal of International Law 1947 41(1): 38-72. This comprehensive analysis of the Nuremberg trial concludes that the trial was a step forward in the development of international criminal law. Major topics covered include the origin of the trial, the charter and the trial itself, criticisms of the trial, the jurisdiction of the IMT, the procedure of the trial, application of the law, offenses against the law of nations, ex post facto aspects of the trial, war crimes and crimes against humanity, crimes against peace, and acts of state. Based on primary and secondary sources; 127 notes.

2977 WRIGHT, QUINCY. "War Crimes under International Law," Law Quarterly Review 1946 62(January): 40-52. Analyzes the 4 counts of the indictment in light of both positive and common international law.

2978 ZOUREK, J. "Les principes de Nuremberg, étape décision dans l'évolution du droit international," Revue de Droit Contemporain 1961 8(2): 107-128.

H. LEGALITY, JUSTICE, AND JURISDICTION

2979 APRIL, NATHAN. "An Inquiry into the Juridical Basis for the Nuernberg War Crimes Trial," Minnesota Law Review 1946 30(5): 313-331. Criticizes the Nuremberg proceedings, arguing that the illegal IMT was not constituted under the laws of the various nations whom it purported to represent. Counts 2 and 4 of the indictment were not juridically-cognizable offenses. Count 3 stated no case and Count 4 was not substantiated. Suggests trial by military commissions.

2980 ARNDT, ADOLF. "Das Befreiungsgesetz ist kein Strafgesetz," Süddeutsche Juristen-Zeitung 1948 3(2): 110. Note criticizes the Katzenberger article on the relationship of the Nuremberg judgment to the Befreiungsgesetz. Argues that the latter law was a German law, not a penal law, and that the interpretation given it by the Nuremberg court and the members of the military government was incorrect.

2981 BAXTER, RICHARD R. "The Municipal and International Law Basis of Jurisdiction over War Crimes," British Year Book of International Law 1951 28: 382-393.

2982 BERNAYS, MURRAY C. "Legal Basis of the Nürnberg Trials," Survey Graphic 1946 35(January): 4-9; (November): 390-391.

2983 BERNAYS, MURRAY C. "Nuremberg: Its Justification and Lessons," West Virginia Bar Association Report 1946 62: 68-83. 3 notes.

2984 BRIERLY, JAMES LESLIE. "The Nature of War Crimes Jurisdiction," Norseman 1944 2(May-June): 166-172.

2985 CARNEGIE, A.R. "Jurisdiction over Violations of the Laws and Customs of War," British Year Book of International Law 1963 39: 402-424.

2986 COLAS, RAYMOND. "La Compétence des juridictions militaires dans la répression des crimes de guerre," Revue de Science Criminelle et de Droit Pénal Comparé 1967 22(3): 482-493. 27 notes.

2987 CONLEN, WILLIAM J., ROBERT H. JACKSON, and WALTER LIPPMANN. "The Legal Basis for Trial of War Criminals," Temple Law Quarterly 1946 19(3): 133-235. Jackson's address, pp. 135-143, is found also in the American Bar Association Journal 1945 31(June): 290-294. The preface to this milestone article was contributed by William J. Conlen. Jackson's contribution - "The Rule of Law Among Nations" - is a reprint of an address delivered to the American Society of International Law, Washington, April 13, 1945. This address deals with the necessity that courts be independent of political considerations and that the trial of war criminals be a trial in fact as well as form. Jackson was unwilling to enter the controversy as to what to do with war criminals, but if it were decided to execute them, this should be done not as a judicial act, but as a military or political act. He was not in principle opposed to war crimes trials, but he criticized "farcical judicial trials" that carried out political policy without any genuine judicial process. "Justice Jackson's Report to President Truman on the Legal Basis for Trial of War Criminals" is reprinted on pp. 144-156. Lippmann's article is an endorsement of Jackson's views on the necessity of trying war criminals. This article contains the text of many primary documents, among them: "Agreement for the Establishment of An International Tribunal," pp. 160-161, "Charter of the International Military Tribunal," pp. 169-171, "Indictment Against Major Nazi War Criminals," pp. 172-210. Appendix A delineates the specific charges against the defendants, pp. 211-222; Appendix B is a statement of criminality of groups and organizations, pp. 223-226; Appendix C is a list of charges and particulars of violations of international treaties, agreements, and assurances caused by the defendants in the course of planning, preparing for, and initiating the war, pp. 227-235. Undocumented.

2988 COWLES, WILLARD B. "Universality of Jurisdiction over War Crimes," California Law Review 1945 33(2): 177-218. Finding the origin of the law governing war crimes in the laws of brigandage and piracy, the author presents an account of the development of the laws of brigandage in international legal thought and practice, citing ten cases where jurisdiction has been assumed by military tribunals when the victims were not nationals of the punishing states. Concludes that every independent state has jurisdiction over war criminals in its custody regardless of the nationality of the victim or the place where the offense was committed. 156 notes.

2989 ECER, BOHUSLAV, [The main provisions of the substantive law of the Nuremberg trial], Pravnik 1946 85(1-2): In Czech.

2990 ERHARD, HANS. "The Nuremberg Trial against the Major War Criminals and International Law," American Journal of International Law 1949 43(2): 223-245. 49 notes.

2991 FORBES, GORDON W. "Some Legal Aspects of the Nuremberg Trial," Canadian Bar Review 1946 24(7): 584-599. 1 note.

2992 FORMAN, BENJAMIN. "The Nuremberg Trials and Conscientious Objection to War: Justiciability under United States Municipal Law," Proceedings of the American Society of International Law 1969 63: 157-164. 32 notes.

2993 GLAHN, GERHARD VON. The Occupation of Enemy Territory: A Commentary on the Law and Practice of Belligerent Occupation. Minneapolis: University of Minnesota Press, 1957. 350p. 28-page bibliography.

2994 GLUECK, SHELDON. "By What Tribunal Shall War Offenders be Tried?" Harvard Law Review 1943 56(7): 1059-1089. Examines 4 types of tribunals by which war criminals might be tried: (1) ordinary criminal courts, (2) military tribunals, (3) a joint military tribunal, and (4) an international criminal court created for the specific purpose of trying war criminals. 88 notes.

2995 GLUECK, SHELDON. "By What Tribunal Shall War Offenders be Tried?" Nebraska Law Review 1945 24(2): 143-181. 189 notes.

2996 GLUECK, SHELDON. The Nuremberg Trial and Aggressive War. New York: A.A. Knopf, 1946. 121p. Reproduces the author's article "The Nuernberg Trial and Aggressive War," Harvard Law Review 1946 59(3): 396-446. Argues that "aggressive war" is unlawful and criminal. Deals with acts of state, individual responsibility, and the legacy of the Nuremberg IMT proceedings. Appendix B, "Official Pronouncements on the Treatment of War Criminals," and Appendix E, "Alleged Acts of Aggression on the Part of Russia and the United States," are especially useful. 154 notes.

2997 GLUECK, SHELDON. War Criminals: Their Prosecution and Punishment. New York: Knopf, 1944. 250p. Defining war crimes as violations of the rules of warfare and of the principles of criminal law generally observed in civilized states, the author urges the trial and punishment of war criminals by an international criminal court composed of representatives of the United Nations, possibly including neutrals and exiled jurists. Discusses the "debacle" of justice at the close of World War I, the liability of heads of state, the plea of superior orders, and acts of state.

2998 GLUECK, SHELDON. "War Criminals - Their Prosecution and Punishment: The Record of History," Lawyers Guild Review 1945 5(1): 1-10. 29 notes.

2999 GOLDMAN, HARVEY A. "Jurisdictional Problems Related to the Prosecution of Former Servicemen for Violations of the Law of War," Virginia Law Review 1970 56(5): 947-967. 120 notes.

3000 GOODHART, ARTHUR L. "The Legality of the Nuremberg Trials," Juridical Review 1946 58(1): 1-19. A detailed defense of the Nuremberg IMT trial on the basis of positive international law and common sense. 17 notes.

3001 GRAVEN, JEAN. "De la Justice internationale à la paix (les enseignements de Nuremberg," Revue de Droit International de Sciences Diplomatiques et Politiques 1946 24(3): 183-212; 1947 25(1): 3-17. The first article deals with the legality of the

Nuremberg IMT proceedings, which demonstrate the feasibility of an international criminal court. An appendix contains notes on trials of war criminals by military tribunals, occupation courts, and popular national tribunals. The second article considers formal objections to the Nuremberg trial. The author finds no difficulty in justifying the prosecution of criminals for the violation of the laws of warfare and for crimes against humanity, but he does find difficulty with the concept of conspiracy and crimes against the peace. Concludes that the Germans acted outside any system of law and compares the role of the judge in international penal law to that of the judge in common law. 19 and 61 notes.

3002 GREGORY, TAPPAN. "Murder is Murder and the Guilty can be Punished," *American Bar Association Journal* 1946 32(September): 544-549. Analysis of the legal basis of the indictment and trial. Stresses the fairness of the proceedings.

3003 IVRAKIS, SOLON CLEANTHES. "Nürnberg: Confusion and Catharsis: An Inquiry into Some of the Legal and Philosophical Issues of the Trial," M.A. thesis, Cambridge University, 1950.

3004 JACKSON, ROBERT H. "Law under which Nazi Organizations are accused of being criminal," *Temple Law Quarterly* 1946 19(4): 371-389. Discusses the thoroughness with which Nazi organizations imposed their will on the German people as well as those of occupied countries. This is all background for the author's defenses for condemning, indicting, and trying organizations. Jackson argues that every form of government has treated some organizations as criminal. The six organizations indicted as criminal were chosen because they were the ultimate repositories of all Nazi power. Jackson argues that innocent or passive citizens would not have been unjustly tried as members of these organizations. Undocumented.

3005 JAFFE, SIDNEY E. "Natural Law and the Nürnberg Trials," *Nebraska Law Review* 1946 26(1): 90-95. Natural law alone can justify the entire conduct of the Nuremberg trials. 6 notes.

3006 KATZENBERGER, K. "Das Korps der politischen Leiter im Urteil von Nürnberg," *Neue Juristische Wochenschrift* 1948 1(10): 371-375. 20 notes.

3007 KEMPSKI, JÜRGEN VON. "Krieg als Straftat," *Merkur* 1947 1(1): 28-40. A study of the legal and philosophical bases of the Nuremberg IMT judgment. Attempts to define "outlawry of war" in terms of positive international and natural law.

3008 KUHN, ARTHUR K. "International Criminal Jurisdiction," *American Journal of International Law* 1947 41(2): 430-433. Comments on advances made in international law as a result of World War II and on the conditions for organizing an international criminal jurisdiction. 6 notes.

3009 LANDE, ADOLF. *The Legal Basis of the Nurenberg Trial*. New York: The Library, Interim International Information Service, 1945. Deals with personal, local, and substantive jurisdiction, why war crimes trials were not left to German courts, the responsibility of heads of state, pleas of superior orders, acts of state, and retroactivity of criminal law.

3010 LENER, SALVATORE. Diritto e politica nelle sanzione contre el fascismo e nelle epurazione dell'amministrazione. Rome: Edizione "La Civiltà Cattolica," 1946. 94p. The acts of the fascist rulers are subject to penal jurisdiction only when they are intrinsically unjust from the point of view of penal law.

3011 LEONHARDT, HANS. "The Nuremberg Trial: A Legal Analysis," Review of Politics 1949 11(4): 449-476. 114 notes.

3012 LUND, T.G. "The Legal Procedure at the Nuremberg Trials," Fortnightly Law Journal 1946 16(3): 41-43. Author comments on the "conspicuous" fairness of the procedure.

3013 MUNRO, HECTOR A. "The Trial of Axis War Criminals: The Question of Procedure," Law Journal 1943 93(4047): 251-252. Also published in Fortnightly Law Journal 1943 13(8): 119-122.

3014 NARTATEZ, M.C. "Right of Military Occupant to Establish Courts in Occupied Territory," Philadelphia Law Journal 1949 24 (June): 182-185.

3015 NERONE, F. REGAN. "Legality of Nuremberg," Duquesne University Law Review 1965 4(1): 146-162. 75 notes.

3016 PAOLINI, F. A dieci anni dal processo di Norimberga la sua giustificazione. Bologna: Cappelli, 1956.

3017 PAULSON, STANLEY L. "Classical Legal Positivism at Nuremberg," Philosophy and Public Affairs 1975 4(2): 132-158. At the Nuremberg IMT trial the defense counsel offered three main defenses, dealing with acts of state, superior orders, and ex-post-facto law. All were subsequently rejected. The radical difference in philosophical perspectives on the nature of law is seen as the key factor in the dispute between the defense on one side and the prosecution and tribunal on the other over the relevance of doctrines of classical legal positivism. Concludes that there are noncontingent lines between the doctrines of legal positivism and the Nuremberg defenses.

3018 SCHAICK, F.L. VAN. "War Trials and Future Peace," Editorial Research Reports 1948 (September 7): 611-627. Deals with the trial of war criminals after World War II, the legality of the Nuremberg trial, and the effect of the trials on future peace.

3019 SCHICK, FRANZ B. "New Crimes? Legal Bases of the Nuremberg Trials," Free World 1946 11(2): 39-42. 1 photograph.

3020 STOREY, ROBERT GERALD. "Legal Aspects of the Trial of Major War Criminals at Nuremberg," Louisiana State Bar Association Journal 1946 5(October): 67-81.

3021 UNDERHILL, L.K. "Justification of Military Tribunals in the United States over Civilians," California Law Review 1924 12(2): 75-98; 12(3): 150-178. 144 and 283 notes.

I. GUILT AND RESPONSIBILITY

3022 ANSPACHER, JOHN. "The German Guilt," in Arthur Settel (ed.). Das ist Germany. Frankfurt am Main: W. Metzner, 1950. 373p. Published in English as This is Germany. New York: William Sloan Associates, 1950.

3023 ARENS, RICHARD. "Nuremberg and Group Prosecution," Washington University Law Quarterly 1951 1951(3): 329-357. 113 notes. Critical of group sanctions.

3024 ARNDT, ADOLF. "Just Peace," Süddeutsche Juristen-Zeitung 1948 3(1): 1-14. A discussion of whether Allied policy is designed to assure a just peace. Argues that the concept of collective guilt is based on the incorrect assumption that the war was a war of intervention only and that the principles of the Potsdam Declaration did not constitute a basis for a just peace. 28 notes.

3025 BOYENS, ARMIN. "Das Stuttgarter Schuldbekenntnis vom 19. Oktober 1945 - Entstehung und Bedeutung," Vierteljahrshefte für Zeitgeschichte 1971 19(4): 374-397. Describes the origin, enactment, meaning, and foreign and domestic reception of the declaration of guilt of the Council of Evangelical Churches in Germany on October 19, 1945. Traces the growing awareness among German churchmen of war crimes. Based on documents in the archives of the World Council of Churches in Geneva and on secondary works; 82 notes.

3026 BURG, J.G. [pseudonym]. Schuld und Schicksal. Europas Juden zwischen Henkern und Heuchlern. Munich: Damm, [1962]. 370p.

3027 CAMPBELL, ROBYN MOORE, JR. "Military Command Liability for Grave Breachers of National and International Law," Ph.D. dissertation, Duke University, 1974. 350p. Abstracted in Dissertation Abstracts International 1974 34(12): 7855-A.

3028 CRAIG, GORDON A. "Army and National Socialism, 1933-1945; The Responsibility of the Generals," World Politics 1949 2(3): 426-438. 20 notes.

3029 ECER, BOHUSLAV. "Accomplices of Hitler: The Criminal Responsibility of the German Financial and Industrial Leaders according to the Soviet Criminal Law," Labour Monthly 1945 27(3): 146-150.

3030 ECKERT, J. Schuldig oder entlastet? Munich: Rechts- und Wirtschaftsverlag, Dr. Gruber, 1947. 206p.

3031 FISCHLSCHWEIGER, HAGEN. "Zum Problem der Kollektivhaftung," Juristische Blätter 1951 73: 30-34.

3032 FOERTSCH, HERMANN. Schuld und Verhängnis. Stuttgart: 1951.

3033 FRASER, LINDLEY. Germany between Two Wars: A Study of Propaganda and Warguilt. London: Oxford University Press, 1945. 184p. Rejects German arguments of self defense and focuses on the nation's collective war guilt. Undocumented; index.

3034 GRENFELL, RUSSELL. Unconditional Hatred: German War Guilt and the Future of Europe. New York: Devin-Adair, 1953. 273p. Published in German as Bedingungsloser Haß? Die deutsche Kriegsschuld und Europas Zukunft. Tübingen: F. Schlichtenmayer, 1954. 281p.

3035 HAENSEL, CARL. "Zum Nürnberger Urteil: Schuldprinzip und Gruppenkriminalität," Süddeutsche Juristen-Zeitung 1947 2(1): 19-25.

3036 HAMEROW, THEODORE S. "Review Essay: Guilt, Redemption, and Writing German History," American Historical Review 1983 88(1): 53-72. Bibliographical essay which examines a number of post World War II works. Some recent writers have seen the Germans as victims of their neighbors, rather than as oppressors. Predicts that the cycle of indictment and apologia, of guilt and redemption, may be coming to an end as sober, judicious understanding of what happened emerges. Recent works show a more temperate approach to Germany's recent past and show a nation whose people find the deeds of the 1930s and 1940s incomprehensible. Based on secondary sources; 36 notes.

3037 HERMES, FERDINAND A., "The 'War Guilt' of the German People," American Journal of Economics and Sociology 1944 3(2): 201-216. The Nazi minority, not the entire German nation, was guilty. 34 notes.

3038 HIGH, STANLEY, et al. "Should the German People Be Held Responsible for the Crimes of Their Nazi Leaders?" Town Meeting 1945 11(7): 3-21.

3039 JASPERS, KARL. Die Schuldfrage, ein Beitrag zur deutschen Frage. Zurich: Artemis, 1946. 96p. Published in English as The Question of German Guilt. New York: Dial Press, 1947. 123p. Attempts to define national guilt. Regards the punishment of war criminals as exoneration for the guilt of individual Germans. Reviews the purpose of the Nuremberg IMT and its implications for the German people. The leaders are condemned; the people as a whole are not.

3040 JASPERS, KARL. La Culpabilité allemande. [Paris]: Édition de Minuit, 1948.

3041 KOROVIN, EUGENE A. Kratkii Kurs Mezhduriarodnogo prava Moscow: Military-Juridical Academy, Workers and Peasants Red Army, 1944. 112p. Short course in International Law. Part 2, The Law of War. A state like Hitler's Germany, with its organized violation of all treaties and customary international law, cannot claim protection in international conventions when punishment is at issue. Personal responsibility for violation of the laws of war must be the basis of contemporary international law.

3042 LESSNER, ERWIN, et al. "Should all Germans be punished for Nazi Crimes and Atrocities," Town Meeting 1944 10(35): 3-22.

3043 MC CAULEY, JAMES. "Punish only - the Guilty," Catholic World 1945 161(June): 240-247.

3044 MORTON, LOUIS. "From Fort Sumter to Poland: The Question of War Guilt," World Politics 1962 14(2): 386-392.

3045 PHLEGER, HERMAN. "Nuremberg Eyewitness Says War Guilt Trial Handled Fairly," Commonwealth, Official Organ of the California Commonwealth Club 1946 22(April 22): 73-74, 77-78.

3046 SAUER, WILHELM. "Zum Begriff der Kollektivschuld," Deutsche Rechts-Zeitschrift 1947 2(2): 48.

3047 SCHINDLER, R. Das Wesen der Volksehre. Zugleich ein Beitrag zur Frage der Kollektivschuld. Münster: Rechts- und Staatswissenschaftliche Dissertation, 1948.

3048 SCHOLZ, HEINRICH. "Zur deutschen Kollektiv-Verantwortlichkeit," Frankfurter Hefte 1947 2(4): 357-373. On the collective responsibility of Germans.

3049 "Settling the Issue of War Guilt, Conclusive Verdict against Nazis," U.S. News and World Report 1946 21(15): 24-25.

3050 "Should Judicial Respect Be Accorded to Nazi Acts of State?" Columbia Law Review 1947 47(6): 1061-1068. 54 notes.

3051 SOCIÉTÉ EGYPTIENNE DE DROIT INTERNATIONAL. Le Procès de Nuremberg. La Responsabilité individuelle dans la perpetration des crimes contre la paix: Aperçu opinions juridiques actuelles. Alexandria: Imprimerie Al-Basir, 1946.

3052 TOUZALIN, H. DE. "Réflexions à propos du délit d'appartenance sur un essai d'unification des règles de répression en matière d'infractions aux lois et coutumes de la guerre," Revue de Droit Pénal Militaire et de Droit de la Guerre 1965 4(1): 133-158. The summary is in English.

3053 TRAININ, ARON NAUMOVICH. "Criminal Responsibility for Propaganda of Aggression," Voks Bulletin 1949 58: 13-26.

3054 TRAININ, ARON NAUMOVICH. Hitlerite Responsibility under Criminal Law. London/New York: Hutchinson, [1945]. 108p. Published in Moscow in 1944. Discusses the war for the "Fatherland" and the problem of international criminal responsibility, German crimes in World War I, and the Treaty of Versailles. Deals with the crimes of the "Hitlerites" against peace and complicity in international crime. Concludes with remarks on mutual aid by states in the struggle against international crime. Appendix contains Soviet evidence of Nazi atrocities. 5p. of authoritative statements, reports, and documents on the subject published in English. 49 notes.

3055 TRAININ, ARON NAUMOVICH. "The Responsibility of Hitler Germany for the Crimes and Damage caused by Aggression," Voks Bulletin 1943 (8): 5-14.

3056 VERMEIL, EDMOND. "Karl Jaspers et sa conception de la responsabilité allemande," Revue d'Histoire de la Deuxième Guerre Mondiale 1952 2(7): 1-12.

3057 VOGT, HANNAH. Schuld oder Verhängnis? Zwölf Fragen an Deutschlands jüngste Vergangenheit. Frankfurt am Main: Diesterweg, 1961. 251p. Published in English as The Burden of Guilt: A Short History of Germany, 1914-1945. New York: Oxford University Press, 1964. 97p.

3058 WEBER, HELLMUTH VON. "Die strafrechtliche Verantwortlichkeit für Handeln auf Befehl," Monatsschrift für deutsches Recht 1948 2(February): 34-42.

3059 WRIGHT, QUINCY. "International Law and Guilt by Association," American Journal of International Law 1949 43(4): 746-755. Discusses in detail the notion that advanced systems of criminal law accept the principle that guilt is personal. Though unpopular groups are often held collectively guilty, there has been steady progress toward universal acceptance that guilt is personal. Argues against the proposition that the Nuremberg judgment advanced the notion of guilt by association. World War II marked important progress toward general recognition that the crimes of an aggressive war should be blamed on those who start the war, not on the state in general. Even liability of those belonging to "criminal organizations" was limited to those who were voluntary members and who knew it was engaged in criminal activities. Based on secondary sources; 42 notes.

J. EX POST FACTO ASPECTS OF THE IMT

3060 GAULT, P.F. "Prosecution of War Criminals," Journal of Criminal Law and Criminology 1945 36(3): 180-183. Criticizes war crimes trials as arbitrary, a consequence of ex poste facto law. Advocates trials by military commission.

3061 GREWE, WILHELM GEORG, and OTTO KÜSTER. Nürnberg als Rechtsfrage, eine Diskussion. Stuttgart: Ernst Klett, 1947. 111p. A report on 3 meetings of the Stuttgarter Privat-Studiengesellschaft. Includes the text of a lecture by Grewe, a criticism by Küster, and the ensuing discussion. Grewe analyzes the Nuremberg indictment and rejects crimes against peace and crimes against humanity as violating the principle nulla poena sine lege. He seeks to show that Nuremberg principles anticipated a world order that was far from being realized.

3062 HOFMANNSTHAL, EMILIO VON. "War Crimes not tried under Retroactive Law," New York University Law Quarterly Review 1947 22(1): 93-99. Denies that the war crimes trials were made under retroactive law. Cites the Kellogg-Briand pact as an international law that covered the trials and also cites some national laws that are retroactive. 41 notes.

3063 IRELAND, GORDON A. "Ex Post Facto from Rome to Tokyo," Temple Law Quarterly 1947 21(1): 27-61. 113 notes.

3064 KARANIKAS, DÉMÈTRE I. "Le Principe de la non-rétroactivité des lois pénales après la guerre," Revue Hellénique de Droit International 1950 3(January-March): 136-140. 9 notes.

3065 KELSEN, HANS. "The Rule Against ex post facto Laws and the Prosecution of the Axis War Criminals," Judge Advocate Journal 1945 2(3): 8, 46.

3066 ROUX, J.A. "A Propos de la Non-Rétroactivité de la loi pénale," Revue de Droit International de Sciences Diplomatiques et Politiques 1947 25(2): 179-186. Discusses the problem of avoiding retroactivity in law and the equally important principle that just and necessary punishment be meted out for heinous crimes. 3 notes.

3067 SMEAD, ELMER E. "The Rule against Retroactive Legislation: A Basic Principle of Jurisprudence," Minnesota Law Review 1936 20(7): 775-797. 66 notes.

3068 WECHSLER, HERBERT. "The Issues of the Nuremberg Trial," Political Science Quarterly 1947 62(1): 11-26. Asserts that the question of retroactivity is a secondary one and explores some of the issues on which historical judgments on the trial will probably be based. Raises the questions of whether it was wise to institute punitive proceedings at all, what effectiveness the punishment may have, and the extent to which the London Charter employed the concept of individual responsibility.

Concedes the "inequality" of the war crimes trials, but maintains that the Nuremberg IMT trial was necessary to build a world of just law.

3069 WRIGHT, QUINCY. "The Nuremberg Trial," <u>Annals</u> <u>of</u> <u>the</u> <u>American</u> <u>Academy</u> <u>of</u> <u>Political</u> <u>and</u> <u>Social</u> <u>Science</u> 1946 246(July): 72-80. Comments on some legal issues in connection with the Nuremberg IMT trial. Cites the Henfield case of 1793 on the <u>ex</u> <u>post</u> <u>facto</u> question.

K. STATUTES OF LIMITATION

3070 ALEXANDROV, G. "The Legal Position," <u>New</u> <u>Times</u> 1979 13(March): 24-25.

3071 ARONSON, SHLOMO. "The Last Judgment. Report," <u>Israel</u> <u>Magazine</u> 1969 1(10): 5-7. In favor of abolishing the statute of limitations.

3072 "As You Were," <u>Newsweek</u> 1969 73(May 19): 48. German reactions to a proposal to extend the statute of limitations.

3073 BAKER, JACK. "Amnesty for Nazis," <u>Anti-Defamation</u> <u>League</u> <u>Bulletin</u> 1965 (January): 3, 8.

3074 BAUM, PHIL. "Time and War Crimes," <u>Congress</u> <u>Weekly,</u> <u>A</u> <u>Review</u> <u>of</u> <u>Jewish</u> <u>Interests</u> 1968 (November 25): 4-5. Against the statute of limitations.

3075 BAUMANN, J. <u>Der</u> <u>Aufstand</u> <u>des</u> <u>schlechten</u> <u>Gewissens.</u> <u>Ein</u> <u>Diskussionsbeitrag</u> <u>zur</u> <u>Verjährung</u> <u>des</u> <u>NS-Gewaltsverbrechens</u>. Bielefeld: Ernst und Gieseking, 1965.

3076 BENJAMIN, D. „Über die Nichtverjährung von Nazi- und Kriegsverbrechen," <u>Neue</u> <u>Justiz</u> 1964 18(18): 545-549.

3077 BEZYMENSKII, LEV. "'Statute of Limitations' again?" <u>New</u> <u>Times</u> 1978 41(October): 10-11. Deals with the prosecution of German war criminals.

3078 BLIGH, DAVID. "War Crimes: Statute of Limitations on Austrian State TV," <u>Reconstructionist</u> 1965 (January 8): 7-14.

3079 "Bonn may extend Statute on War Criminals," <u>Christian</u> <u>Century</u> 1965 82(10): 292-293.

3080 BRACHMANN, BOTHO. „Kriegsverbrechen und Verbrechen gegen die Menschlichkeit sind unverjährbar," <u>Archivmitteilungen</u> 1969 19(1): 6-8. The 1968 socialist constitution of the German Democratic Republic states that the statute of limitations on war crimes and crimes against humanity cannot be dismissed. Notes the results of the punishment of war crimes in East Germany, where 3115 people were sentenced as war criminals, 2426 as denunciants, 901 as members of the Gestapo and Nazi police, and 668 as members of the Nazi state system. In contrast to those sentenced in East Germany, there are many war criminals still free in West Germany. 17 notes.

3081 CLAUSNITZER, MARTIN. "The Statute of Limitations for Murder in the Federal Republic of Germany," <u>International</u> <u>and</u> <u>Comparative</u> <u>Law</u> <u>Quarterly</u> 1980 29(April): 473-479. 34 notes.

3082 CYPRIAN, TADEUSZ. "Zur Nichtverjährbarkeit von Verbrechen gegen das Völkerrecht," Staat und Recht 1969 18: 25-28.

3083 Die Bestrafung der Nazi- und Kriegsverbrecher. Gebot der Menschlichkeit und Sicherung des Friedens. Dokumente und Materialien zur Verabschiedung des Gesetzes über die Nichtverjährung von Nazi- und Kriegsverbrechen in d.7. Sitzung d. Volkskammer der DDR vom 1.9.1964. Berlin(GDR): Staatsverlag der DDR, 1964. Deals with the statute of limitations on war crimes trials.

3084 ERMACORA, F. "Die Verjährung von Kriegsverbrechen und Verbrechen gegen die Menschlichkeit vor Organen der Vereinten Nationen," Österreichische Zeitschrift für öffentliches Recht 1967 17: 27-44.

3085 FAWCETT, J.E.S. "A Time Limit for Punishment of War Crimes?" International and Comparative Law Quarterly 1965 14(April): 627-632. 9 notes.

3086 JASPERS, KARL. Die Schuldfrage. Für Völkermord gibt es keine Verjährung. Munich: Piper, 1979. 201p. Written between 1945 and 1968.

3087 JASPERS, KARL, AND RUDOLF AUGSTEIN. "No Statute of Limitations for Genocide. A Conversation with Karl Jaspers," Midstream 1966 12(2): 3-18.

3088 ARAGEZYAN, KAREN. "Statute of Limitations: The Debate," New Times 1979 13(March): 22-24.

3089 KAUL, FRIEDRICH KARL. "Und Wiederum: Verjährung nazistischer Kriegsverbrechen," Neue Justiz 1966 20(11): 340-341.

3090 LAKSHMANAN, R. "Convention on the Non-Applicability of Statutory Limitations to War Crimes and Crimes against Humanity: A Critique," Indian Journal of International Law 1969 9(April): 221-230.

3091 LEKSCHAS, J. "Zum Problem der Verjährung von Kriegs-und Naziverbrechen," Staat und Recht 1964 13: 1187-1203.

3092 LERNER, NATHAN. "Convention on the Non-Applicability of Statutory Limitations to War Crimes," Israel Law Review 1969 4(4): 512-533.

3093 MARKOV, KIRILL. "Whom Professor Jacobsen is Shielding," New Times 1979 19(May): 26-27. Comments on the debate in West Germany over whether to abolish the statute of limitations for premeditated murder.

3094 MILLER, ROBERT H. "The Convention of the Non-Applicability of Statutory Limitations to War Crimes and Crimes against Humanity," American Journal of International Law 1971 65(3): 476-501. 143 notes.

3095 MUSZKAT, MARIAN. "Twenty Years after Nuremberg. The Struggle to Abrogate the Statute of Limitations for Crimes against Humanity," Yad Vashem Bulletin 1967 21(November): 3-10.

3096 PALEY, JEFFREY. "Nazi Crimes and the Statute of Limitations," New Republic 1965 152(10): 6-7.

3097 PILICHOWSKI, CZESLAW. No Time-Limit for these Crimes. Warsaw: Interpress Publishers, 1980. 187p. Deals with Germany's policies in Poland, her treatment of prisoners of war, slave labor camps, prisons and detention centers, Polish women in German prisons, the massacre of Jews, German concentration and extermination camps, and the legal foundations for the punishment of German war criminals. 27p. of notes, 10 appendices.

3098 PRITT, DENIS N. "Nazi War Crimes: Prosecution or Statutory Limitation," New World Review 1969 37: 46-51.

3099 REGENT-LECHOWICZ, MARIA. "Moralno-Prawne Aspekty Nieprzedawnienia Scigania I Karania Hitlerowskich Zbrodni Wojennych I Zbrodni Przeciw Ludzkości [Moral and Legal Aspects of the Nonlimitation on Prosecution and Punishment of Nazi War Crimes and Crimes against Humanity]," Panstwo i Prawo 1979 34(10) [whole no. 494]: 4-17. The Polish Deputy Minister of Justice argues here that West Germany is open to moral and legal censure for not accepting the 1968 United Nations resolution on the nonapplication of statutory limitations to war crimes and crimes against humanity. Discusses statutes under which war criminals were prosecuted, particularly in the Federal Republic of Germany, and examines the moral and legal implications under international law of these prosecutions. Since January 1, 1950, the courts of the Federal Republic have had full jurisdiction over war criminals. War crimes are treated as ordinary crimes, punishable under the criminal code of the nation. Contains summaries in English, French, and Russian. 33 notes.

3100 RUSSE, HERMANN JOSEF. "Le Refus de la prescription c'est savoir assumer le passe Nazi," Documents 1979 34(3): 45-53. The author, a deputy in the Bundestag, analyzes the motion he introduced for the refusal of applying to Nazi war criminals the statute of limitations which was to expire on December 31, 1979.

3101 SCHOENBAUM, DAVID L. "Nazi Murders and German Politics," Commentary 1965 39(6): 72-77. A report on the political background of the Bundestag debates in March 1964, which resulted in an extension of the statute of limitations for 4 years.

3102 SCHOENBAUM, DAVID L. "Time Runs Out on Germany's War-Crimes Trials," Reporter 1965 32(March 11): 30-32. Deals with the furor in Germany and the rest of the world over the decision not to extend the statute of limitations for war crimes beyond May 8, 1965.

3103 "Semifinal Solution," Newsweek 1969 73(18): 44. On West German decision on the statute of limitations.

3104 "Shifting the Guilt," Time 1969 93(May 2): 24-25.

3105 STOOP, BERT. "Unfinished War?" Christian Century 1965 82(6): 166 Deals with Nazi criminals and West Germany's 20-year statute of limitations.

3106 UNITED STATES. IMMIGRATION AND NATURALIZATION SERVICE. Extension and Revision of the Export Administration Act of 1969. Part 2. 259p. May 1-4, 7-9, 1979. U.S. Government Documents call number Y4.F76/1:Ex7/5/pt.2. Includes a transcript (p. 79) of favorable committee vote on unrelated House Resolution 106, urging West Germany to abolish or extend the statute of limitations on war crimes.

3107 VOGEL, ROLF (ed.). *Ein Weg aus der Vergangenheit. Eine Dokumentation zur Verjährungsfrage und zu den NS-Prozessen.* Frankfurt am Main: Ullstein, 1969. 223p. Complete analysis of the problem of the statute of limitations regarding war crimes trials.

3108 WIESENTHAL, SIMON (ed.). *Verjährung.* Frankfurt am Main: Europäische Verlagsanstalt, 1965.

3109 "Yad Vashem and the Statute of Limitations in West Germany," *Yad Vashem Bulletin* 1965 16: 2-5.

L. VERDICTS, SENTENCES, AND EXECUTION OF SENTENCES

3110 BADER, KARL S. "Umschau - zum Nürnberger Urteil," *Deutsche Rechts-Zeitschrift* 1946 1(5): 140-142. Deals primarily with the Nuremberg IMT, with much on need for trials under Control Council Law No. 10.

3111 BAYLES, WILLIAM. *Seven Were Hanged.* London: 1945.

3112 BERNSTEIN, VICTOR H. *Final Judgment: The Story of Nuremberg.* New York: Boni and Gaer, 1947. 289p. Republished *The Holocaust - the Final Judgment.* Indianapolis: Bobbs-Merrill, 1980. 289p. Analyzes the successes and failures of the Nuremberg IMT trial with respect to National Socialist crimes, using documents from German sources that became available only one year prior to publication. Discusses aggression, genocide, concentration camps, and collective guilt. Appendix contains extracts from the indictment and from Article 6 of the Charter, lists of organizations and individuals indicted, a brief career history of the indicted, and the final judgment against each. 9-page document index, 5-page general index.

3113 BOSCH, WILLIAM J. *Judgment on Nuremberg: American Attitudes toward the major German War-Crime Trials.* Chapel Hill: University of North Carolina Press, 1970. 272p. Ph.D. dissertation, University of North Carolina Press, 1965. 689p. This is an investigation of American attitudes on legal, political, psychological and ethical issues in the Nuremberg trial. Raises the question of the IMT's legality and deals with the composition of the court, victor's justice, the nature of the verdicts, and the effects of the trial on the future. Discusses American policy makers and the war crime trials, and the views of the American public, of lawyers, and of behavioral scientists. 26-page bibliography, 6-page index.

3114 CARJEU, P. *Le Jugement du Tribunal Militaire de Nuremberg.* Paris: Institut de Criminologie, 1951.

3115 *Das Siegertribunal.* Coburg: Nation Europa Verlag, 1976.

3116 "Die gesetzesgleiche Wirkung des Nürnberger Urteils," *Spruchgerichte* 1948 2(December): 332-338.

3117 EMMET, CHRISTOPHER. "Verdict on Nuremberg," *Commonweal* 1946 45(6): 138-141. 2 notes.

3118 GREAT BRITAIN. FOREIGN OFFICE. Parliament, Papers by Command. Cmd. 7627. Miscellaneous No. 12. Judgement of the International Military Tribunal for the Trial of the major German War Criminals (with the Dissenting Opinion of the Soviet Member), Nuremberg 30th September and 1st October, 1946. London: HMSO, 1946. 149p.

3119 GUTZWILLER, MAX. "Um das Urteil von Nürnberg," Schweizer Rundschau 1946 46: 687-692.

3120 HAZAN, EDOUARD TAWFIK. "Étude critique du jugement de Nuremberg," Revue de Droit International pour le Moyen-Orient 1951 1(May): 33-42; 1952 2(January): 173-186.

3121 HUBBERT, CECIL F. "Nuremberg - Justice or Vengeance?" Military Government Journal 1948 1(5): 11-14.

3122 INTERNATIONAL MILITARY TRIBUNAL (IMT), NUREMBERG. Das Urteil von Nürnberg; vollständiger Text. Munich: Nymphenburger Verlaghandlung, 1946. 208p. On cover, as subtitle, Grundlage eines neuen Völkerrechts. Düsseldorf: L. Schwann, [1947]. 191p. Baden-Baden: Arbeitsgemeinschaft "Das Licht," 1946. 210p. 3rd edition, München: Deutscher Taschenbuch Verlag, 1961. 299p. German text of the Nuremberg IMT proceedings from September 30 and October 1, 1946. Lists members of the Court of Justice at the IMT, the staff of the General Secretariat, representatives for the allied defense, defense attorneys, and defendants. Table of the sentences of the 22 defendants. Notes cite variations and deletions from the original English text.

3123 "International Military Tribunal (Nuremberg), Judgment and Sentences," American Journal of International Law 1947 41(1): 172-333.

3124 JACOBY, GERHARD. "The Verdict of Nuremberg," Jewish Frontier 1946 13(11): 32-35

3125 JANECZEK, EDWARD J. Nuremberg Judgment in the Light of International Law. Geneva: Imprimeries Populaires, 1949. 142p. Thesis, University fo Geneva, 1949.

3126 "Judgment of the International Military Tribunal Against Major Nazi War Criminals and Criminal Organizations," Philippine Law Journal 1947 22(4): 175-204; 22(5): 244-292; 22(6): 331-412. Undocumented.

3127 KARSTEN, THOMAS L., and JAMES H. MATHIAS. "The Judgment at Nuremberg," New Republic 1946 115(16): 512.

3128 KIRCHNER, CARL. "Das Nürnberger Urteil und der Par. 267 Abs 1 Strafprozeßordnung," Spruchgerichte 1948 2(July): 199-200.

3129 KRAMARZ, H. "Täter und Teilnehmer im Urteil des Internationalen Militärgerichtshofs zu Nürnberg," Doctor of Laws dissertation, Erlangen University, 1952.

3130 KRAUS, HERBERT. Gerichtstag in Nürnberg. Hamburg: Gesetz und Recht, 1947. 25p.

3131 KRAUS, HERBERT. Vorbemerkung zu "Das Urteil von Nürnberg 1946." Munich: 1961.

3132 LA FARGE, JOHN J. "Judgment," America 1946 76(October 12): 29.

3133 "Le Verdict de Nuremberg," Revue de Droit International 1946 24: 260-264.

3134 LEVENTHAL, HAROLD, et al. "The Nuernberg Verdict," Harvard Law Review 1947 60(6): 857-907. An analysis of the verdict and of the Tribunal's (IMT) position in the light of prosecution and defense evidence. Argues that there are limitations on using this case as a precedent for future cases. In the future a strong United Nations rather than a penal code is needed to prevent war. 212 notes.

3135 MANN, ABBY. Judgment at Nuremberg. New York: New American Library, 1961.

3136 MARTIUS, GEORG. "Das Nürnberger Urteil vom 30. September - 1. Oktober 1946 in völkerrechtlicher Beziehung," Neue Justiz 1947 1(4/5): 91-98. Sees the declaration of aggressive war as the greatest of war crimes and the Hague regulations as binding international law. 29 notes.

3137 "Nazi Leaders Hang for War Crimes," Lutheran Outlook 1946 15(October): 294-295.

3138 "Nazi Leaders Sing their Swan Song," Life 1946 21(12): 40-41.

3139 NEUMANN, FRANZ. Das Nürnberger Juristenurteil. Hamburg: 1948.

3140 "Nuremberg: Last Laugh," Newsweek 1946 28(18): 45-47.

3141 "Nuremberg: The Acquitted," Newsweek 1946 28(16): 57-58.

3142 REUTER, PAUL. "Le Jugement du Tribunal militaire de Nuremberg," Recueil-Dalloz [Chronique] 1946 20(39-40): 77-80.

3143 ROBINSON, JACOB. "The Nuremberg Judgment," Congress Weekly, A Review of Jewish Interests 1946 13(October 25): 6-8.

3144 SCHICK, FRANZ B. "War Crimes and the Problem of an International Criminal Court," Canadian Yearbook of International Law 1942: 67-88.

3145 SCHUSTER, GEORGE N. "Hanging at Nuremberg: The Truth Was Not Allowed to Emerge," Commonweal 1946 45(November 15): 110-113.

3146 SCHWARZENBERGER, GEORG. "The Judgment of Nuremberg," Year Book of World Affairs 1948 2: 94-124. Discusses the organization and jurisdiction of the Nuremberg IMT and the law applied by the tribunal. Argues that within the framework of the Charter, the IMT merely extended the range of municipal jurisdiction and assimilated jurisdiction in crimes under the Charter to jurisdiction in war crimes under international customary law. 95 notes. Based on "The Judgment of Nuremberg," Tulane Law Review 1947 21(3): 329-361.

3147 SERAPHIM, HANS-GÜNTHER. "Die Erschliessung der Nürnberger Prozeßakten," Archivar 1975 28(November): 417-422.

3148 TEITGEN, M. "Le Jugement de Nuremberg," Revue de Droit International de Sciences Diplomatiques et Politiques 1946 24(3): 161-173. Discusses the contribution of the Nuremberg IMT judgment to the progress of international law. Examines the decisions on Nazi organizations and the rulers of the Third Reich, with special reference to the cases of those acquitted.

3149 UNITED STATES. DEPARTMENT OF STATE. "The Nürnberg Judgment, a Summary," State Department Bulletin 1947 16(392): 9-19. January 5, 1947. State Department Publication No. 2727. Washington: GPO, 1947. Focuses on the reasoning of the Tribunal, rather than on the verdict.

3150 VERCEL, MICHEL C. Les Rescapés de Nuremberg: Les "seigneurs de la guerre" après le verdict. Paris: Albin Michel, 1966. 250p. Deals with the 10 "rescapés" of Nuremberg. Lists interviews and archives consulted. 1-page bibliography, 13 photographs, appendix.

3151 WALSH, MOIRA. "Judgment at Nuremberg," America 1962 106(January 20): 542-544.

3152 "We Furnish the Hangman," Ave Maria 1946 64(November 7): 580-581.

3153 "World Judgment on Persecutors," America 1946 76(October 26): 93-95.

3154 WRIGHT, QUINCY. "Legal Positivism and the Nuremberg Judgment," American Journal of International Law 1948 42(2): 405-414. Comments made on international law depend more on the theory of law held by the commentator than on the events themselves. That is why positivistic jurists with their 19th Century philosophy have been critical of events such as the Nuremberg IMT trial. Positivism assumes that the state is the only subject of international law and that Germany did not give its consent to the trial. Positivism pushed to its logical extreme would make international law impossible. A new, dynamic concept of international law makes it easy to justify war crimes trials. Positivists reject the statement in the Nuremberg Charter that individuals have duties that transcend national obligations. The crimes with which the defendants were charged were not "acts of state" and therefore they were personally responsible for them. The Nuremberg Tribunal manifested more that the prejudice of victors; it reflected the overwhelming opinion of the world. Based on secondary sources; 23 notes.

M. LATER EVALUATIONS AND CRITICISMS

3155 ALEXANDROV, GEORGII N. "Looking back to Nuremberg . . . Notes of a Soviet Prosecutor," New Times 1965 43(October 27):16-19; 44(November 2): 20-23; 46(November 15): 16-19; 47(November 24): 28-31. 7 illustrations.

3156 AMCHAN, MORRIS. "Nuremberg Revisited," Federal Bar Journal 1971 30(3): 242-253.

3157 ASCHENAUER, RUDOLF. Zur Frage einer Revision der Kriegsverbrecherprozesse. Nürnberg: Selbstverlag, 1949. 80p. Contains excerpts from periodical articles, congressional records, and American court records. Advocates the establishment of a superior court of appeals for war crimes trials which would be neutral and objective and have the power to review, reverse, and modify judgments handed down. The author contends that there have been war crimes trials in which recognized principles of law and procedure have not been violated. Part I analyzes the basic legal principles and procedures of the Nuremberg and Dachau trials. Part 2 discusses obstacles to an objective review of the trials and points to ways to overcome them.

3158 BEHLING, KURT, "Nürnberger Lehren," *Juristische Rundschau* 1949 3: 502-505.

3159 BELGION, HAROLD MONTGOMERY. *Epitaph on Nuremberg, a Letter Intended to have been sent to a Friend Temporarily Abroad.* London: Falcon Press, 1944. 96p. Rewritten as *Victors' Justice; a Letter Intended to have been sent to a Friend Recently in Germany.* Hinsdale, Illinois: Henry Regnery, 1949. 187p. Writing to his friend Daniel [no last name given], the author expresses the opinion that the Nuremberg IMT was an act of vengeance, and cites specific examples to show that the record of the victorious nations during and after World War II was not much better than that of those tried for war crimes. Deals with three possible conclusions: (1) nothing was to be gained by punishing Germany after World War I, (2) the assignment of war guilt was misleading and dangerous, and (3) the means of retribution against Germany following World War I were not sufficiently severe. Based on first-hand impressions and secondary sources; 87 notes.

3160 BENTON, WILBOURN E., and GEORG GRIMM (eds.). *Nuremberg: German Views of the War Trials.* Dallas: Southern Methodist University Press, 1955. 232p. Examines ideas on international criminal jurisdiction as reflected in articles by German professors and lawyers. Twelve essays include "The Nuremberg Trial against the Major War Criminals and International Law," by Hans Erhard, "The Nuremberg Judgment: Penal Jurisdiction over Citizens of Enemy States," by Karl-Heinz Lüders, and "Thoughts about Purpose and Effect of the Nuremberg Judgment," by Ra. Th. Klefisch. 354 notes. 2-page bibliography.

3161 BERNSTEIN, V.H. "Reunion in Warsaw: Remembering Nuremberg, Meeting of the Former Trial Correspondents," *Nation* 1967 204(January 23): 112-116.

3162 BIRMINGHAM, ROBERT L. "The War Crimes Trial: A Second Look," *University of Pittsburgh Law Review* 1962 24(1): 132-154. A general treatment of several war crimes trials. 74 notes.

3163 BRITISH PEOPLES PARTY. *Failure at Nuremberg, an Analysis of Trial, Evidence and Verdict.* London: Research Department of the British Peoples Party, 1946. 42p. The Russian invasion of Finland and the American attack on Hiroshima and Nagasaki were criminal acts. Discusses the indictment, the attitude of the British Bar, the court, documents, witnesses, the German-Soviet treaty, and the attitude of the press. Concludes that the trial by the IMT was invalid. Based on primary sources; undocumented, 1 photograph.

3164 CHAMBERLAIN, WILLIAM HENRY. "Don't call it Justice," *Forum* 1945 104 (December): 329-331.

3165 CIGLIANA, CARLO. "Luci ed Ombre a Norimbergo," *Rivista Militare* 1977 100(4): 99-103. Concludes that the major shortcoming of the Nuremberg IMT trial was in judging only those crimes committed by the Axis powers.

3166 CYPRIAN, TADEUSZ, and JERZY SAWICKI. *Nuremberg in Retrospect. People and Issues of the Trial.* Warsaw: Western Press Agency, 1967. 245p.

3167 DALY, EDWARD J. "War Crime Trials," *Connecticut Bar Journal* 1949 23(1): 2-10. Surveys the IMT trial and others.

3168 DAVIDSON, EUGENE. *The Nuremberg Fallacy: Wars and War Crimes since World War II*. New York: McMillan, [1973].

3169 DAVIDSON, EUGENE. "The Nuremberg Trials and One World, Issues and Conflicts," in George Alexander (ed.). *Studies in Twentieth Century American Diplomacy*. Lawrence: University of Kansas Press, 1959.

3170 DE MENTHON, FRANCOIS E. *Le Procès de Nuremberg. l'accusation française*. Paris: Office Français d'Information, 1946.

3171 DIMOCK, E.J. "Factual Outline of the Indictment of War Criminals," *American Bar Association Journal* 1945 31(December): 638-641, 646-647. Text of Articles 6-10 of the IMT and of the indictment.

3172 DOMAN, NICHOLAS R. "The Nuremberg Trials Revisited," *American Bar Association Journal* 1961 47(March): 260-264. 7 notes.

3173 EGBERT, LAWRENCE D. "L'Accusation américaine au tribunal militaire international," *Nouvelle Revue de Droit International Privé* 1946 13: 419-429.

3174 EITNER, LORENZ. "The Criminal State and its Servants: Reminiscences of the Nuremberg War Crime Trials," *Minnesota Review* 1963 3(2): 162-178.

3175 FOTH, C., and G. ENDER. "Twenty Years Later," *Law and Legislation in the German Democratic Republic* 1965 (2): 5-21.

3176 GALLUS, GALIENI. *Nuremberg and After*. Newton, Wales: Montgomeryshire, 1946. 31p.

3177 GIBB, ANDREW DEWAR. *Perjury Unlimited: A Monograph on Nuremberg*. Edinburgh: W. Green, 1954. 62p.

3178 GOLDSTEIN, ANATOLE. "New Concepts of Justice," *Congress Weekly, A Review of Jewish Interests* 1945 (November 2): 7-8. A comment on the indictment of the major war criminals at the Nuremberg IMT.

3179 GOODHART, ARTHUR L. "Questions and Answers Concerning the Nuremberg Trials," *International Law Quarterly* 1947 1(4): 525-531. A list of questions asked at public lectures - many of them implying criticism of the trials, and the author's answers.

3180 GORSKI, STEPHEN. *German Crimes Forgotten? Reflections on the Nuremberg Trial*. London: Polish Press Agency, 1946. 16p.

3181 GRAVEN, JEAN. "Vingt Ans après: La libération des prisonniers de Spandau," *Revue de Droit Pénal et de Criminologie* 1946-1947 27: 436-460.

3182 GRÜNDLER, GERHARD E., and ARNIM VON MANIKOWSKY. *Das Gericht der Sieger*. Oldenburg: Gehard Stalling, 1967. 288p.

3183 HAENSEL, CARL. "Der Ausklang von Nürnberg," *Neue Juristische Wochenschrift* 1949 2(10): 367-370. 36 notes.

3184 HAENSEL, CARL. "The Nuremberg Trial Revisited," De Paul Law Review 1964 13(2): 248-259. The Big Four, not the United Nations, prosecuted war criminals. The indictments were limited to crimes committed after the seizure of Austria in 1938. The trial distinguished between the Nazi party and the German people, but crimes committed by the Nazis against the German people were ignored. Deals with the arrest of euthanasia experts Werner Heyde (Dr. Fritz Sawade), Friederick Tillmann, Gerhard Bohne, and Hans Hevelmann, and the ensuing suicides of Heyde and Tillmann, the escape of Bohne, and the trial of Hevelmann. Claims that German law would have dealt more harshly with the criminals than did the laws under which they were prosecuted. Deals with American attempts to declare 6 Nazi organizations illegal, the composition of the IMT, and the possibility of conspiracy between Hitler and Stalin. Argues that the trial proceedings were fair, but that the legal foundations of the proceedings were questionable. The trial could be viewed as retaliatory, since the IMT had not a single German or even neutral member. Even though the German people had failed ethically and morally, their lack of resistance to their leaders should not be punished by victors administering a nonexistent international law. Based on primary and secondary sources; 22 notes.

3185 HANKEY, MAURICE P.A. Politics, Trials and Errors. Oxford: Penin-Hand, 1950. 150p. Chicago: Henry Regnery, 1950. Deals with war crimes and war crimes trials in both world wars. The author's purpose was to compile material to show that policies based on unworthy motives such as unconditional surrender and war crimes trials do not pay. This inventory of criticism against the trials makes much of Allied "deference to Soviet susceptibilities." Proposes a day of amnesty for prisoners convicted of war crimes other than sadism. A few secondary notes, no bibliography, 4-page index.

3186 HAZARD, JOHN N. "Drafting the Nuremberg Indictment," American Review of the Soviet Union 1947 8(2): 16-25.

3187 HOGAN WILLARD N. "War Criminals," South Atlantic Quarterly 1946 45(4): 415-424. Discusses the Nuremberg IMT and objections raised against it. Comments on a military tribunal hearing evidence on "crimes against peace," and laments that only victor nations served on the tribunal. The war crimes trials in Europe and the Far East were soundly conceived, considering the alternatives, which were to let war criminals go free or to execute them without formal indictments and open trials.

3188 HUBAND, CHARLES R. "Nuremberg Revisited," Manitoba Bar News 1959 31(3): 53-58.

3189 "International Hangings: Japanese War Criminals," Commonweal 1948 49(7): 165. Raises questions about the justice of the death sentences handed down at the Nuremberg and Tokyo IMT trials.

3190 INTERNATIONAL MILITARY TRIBUNAL (IMT), NUREMBERG. The Indictment. Nuremberg: Prepared by Public Relations, HQ CMD, IMT, [1945]. 13p.

3191 JACKSON, ROBERT H. "Nürnberg in Retrospect: Legal Answer to International Lawlessness," Canadian Bar Review 1949 27(7): 761-781, and in the American Bar Association Journal 1949

35(October): 813-816, 881-887. This address before the Canadian Bar Association at Banff, Alberta, on September 1, 1949, deals with the assumptions that have encouraged lawlessness and war: that every sovereign nation has a right to wage war, that courts must regard war as legal, that acts of war are acts of state for which leaders are not responsible, and that for obedience to superior orders an individual incurs no personal liability. The Nuremberg IMT trial challenged this concept of the law of nations. The cause of the war was Germany's ambition for conquest. Examines the justice of the trials, the St. James Declaration, and the United Nations War Crimes Commission, and analyzes the philosophical differences between the West and Russia. Jackson insists that neutral jurists would have been no more impartial than those who were selected to serve, even though German pride and nationalism objected to being judged by Russians. As early as 1935 Schacht was ordered to prepare the economy for war. In 1937 Hitler disclosed his plan to conquer Austria and Czechoslovakia. Jackson examines in depth Hitler's labor program and his persecution of Jews and concludes that the judges at Nuremberg were justified in the verdicts they reached. Undocumented; 1 photograph of Jackson.

3192 JACKSON, ROBERT H. "The Rule of Law among Nations," American Bar Association Journal 1945 31(June): 290-294. In this address to the American Society of International Law, the author insists that the world must seek viable alternatives to war. He rejects the "shibboleths" of "impairment of sovereignty" and "submission to foreign control." He refused to enter the controversy about what to do with war criminals, but stated that if in the future they were to be executed, it should be done not as a judicial act, but rather as a military or political act. Criticizes trials that have no genuine judicial process. He is not in principle opposed to war crimes trials, but they must be genuine trials. Undocumented.

3193 JAWORSKI, LEON. After Fifteen Years. Houston: Gulf, 1961. 154p. Colonel Jaworski served as Judge Advocate in a number of war crimes trials in Germany, some of which are discussed here for the first time. Topics covered include Hadamar, innoculations used to kill Jews, representatives of the United Nations War Crimes Commission, war criminals Herbert Messer, Emil Ludwig, Joseph Hartgen, as well as "Ashcan," the top-secret place of internment for Hermann Göring, Joachim von Ribbentrop, Wilhelm Keitel, et al, while they awaited trial. Undocumented.

3194 KEENAN, JOSEPH BERRY. "Observations and Lessons from International Criminal Trials," University of Kansas City Law Review 1949 17(2): 117-128.

3195 KEMPNER, ROBERT M.W. Das Dritte Reich im Kreuzverhör, aus den unveröffentlichen Vernehmungsprotokollen des Anklägers Robert M.W. Kempner. München: Bechtle, 1969. 300p. Reviews the trials of major war criminals through their testimony before the Nuremberg IMT. Records minutes from the interrogation of Hermann Göring, Johanna Wolf (Hitler's closest co-worker), Hugo Blaschke (Hitler's dentist), Martin Bormann's father-in-law, Hermann Göring's wife, Emmy, among others. The author was a prosecutor at the Nuremberg IMT. Based on primary sources.

3196 KEMPNER, ROBERT M.W. "The Nuremberg Trials as Sources of Recent German Political and Historical Materials," American Political Science Review 1950 44(2): 447-459. 21 notes.

3197 KONVITZ, MILTON R. Will Nuremberg Serve Justice," Commentary 1946 1(3): 9-15. Criticism of the IMT Charter and the indictment as violating basic conceptions of justice.

3198 KRANZBÜHLER, OTTO. "Nuremberg Eighteen Years Afterwards," De Paul Law Review 1965 14(2): 333-347. The author, Chief Counsel for Grand Admiral Karl Dönitz, Commander-in-Chief of the German Navy and successor to Hitler, is critical of nearly every aspect of the Nuremberg and subsequent war crimes trials. The trials were political, not judicial, and were used as a means of implementing American policy. Access to materials from foreign archives was denied to defense attorneys and frequently they were permitted to see only poorly translated English versions of documents rather than the original documents. Robert Jackson admitted that the purpose of the trial was not merely to punish those who had violated international law, but was to punish Germany and to set precedents for the future. The author argues that the notion that individuals are answerable to international law rather than national would undermine national legal systems. He discusses the vagueness of crimes against humanity or international "law," such as the Kellogg-Briand Pact. Wars in Korea, Viet Nam, Laos, Egypt, Cuba, and Israel prove that the Nuremberg trials did not outlaw war and that war guilt is to be assigned to all wars. Concludes that it is time for war crimes trials stemming from World War II to come to an end. Undocumented.

3199 KRANZBÜHLER, OTTO. Rückblick auf Nürnberg. Hamburg: Zeit Verlag, E. Schmidt, 1949. 25p. Reprint of a lecture presented at the University of Göttingen. Discusses the Nuremberg IMT, which sentenced 11 to death, imprisoned 7, and acquitted 3. Also deals with the American trials against 175 defendants. Covers historical, judicial, and political aspects of the trial.

3200 KRANZBÜHLER, OTTO. „Wert oder Unwert historischer Strafprozesse erötert am Nürnberger Beispiel," in „Möglichkeiten und Grenzen für die Bewältigung historischer und politischer Schuld in Strafprozessen," in Volume 19, Karl Foster (ed.). Studien und Berichte der Katholischen Akademie in Bayern. Würzburg: [no publisher given], 1962,

3201 KRAUS, HERBERT. "The Nuremberg Trials of the Major War Criminals: Reflections after Seventeen Years," De Paul Law Review 1964 13(2): 233-247. The author was defense counsel for Dr. Hjalmar Schacht, President of the Reichsbank and Minister of Economics, who was acquitted. The writer asserts that because of Heinrich Himmler's threats the counsels for the defense and the German public knew almost nothing of the atrocities committed by the Nazis. Discusses the moral and legal problems involved in Germany's role in the war, war crimes trials, extermination of Jews and the insane, criminal acts committed under orders of superiors, and the four indictments brought against the war criminals. The author writes critically of the legal foundations of the trial, calling into question particularly the notion that people live under and are subject to "international laws." When national and international laws are in contradiction, only national law is binding on a person. Rejects the whole "conspiracy" argument. Since only the victorious allies were represented on the court, they were the creators of the statutes and rules of law, as well as the prosecutors and judges. Concludes that if German law had been applied, there would have been less confusion among defendants and defense counsels. Based on memory and secondary sources; 13 notes.

3202 LAUTERN, MARK. Das letzte Wort über Nürnberg. Fassade und Sumpf in den Kriegsverbrecher-Prozessen. Buenos Aires: Dürer, 1950.

3203 "Majestic Justice," Christian Century 1946 63(42): 1238-1240. Argues that the Nuremberg IMT was fair and just.

3204 MARCUS, ROBERT S. "An Epilogue to Nuremberg," Congress Weekly, A Review of Jewish Interests 1949 (June 20): 5-7.

3205 MARTIN, GEORGE S. "Epilogue at Nuremberg," Free World 1946 12(3): 23-25. On the drama and essence of the last day of the Nuremberg IMT trial.

3206 MAUGHAM, VISCOUNT FREDERIC HERBERT. U. N. O. and War Crimes. London: John Murray, 1951. 143p. A former chancellor of Great Britain attempts to establish the principle that in any future war followed by trials and punishment of war criminals, the only persons who can justly be tried and convicted are those who are proved to have been guilty of the violation of the laws and usages of war. This view, which was adopted in the British zone of Germany, runs contrary to that accepted by the United Nations General Assembly and the United States. Discusses the Nuremberg Charter, defects in the charter as an instrument of justice, the trial and judgment, and subsequent trials. One chapter discusses trials in Germany after the Nuremberg IMT trial, while another deals with the relationship of the United Nations to the Charter of the IMT and the judgment at Nuremberg. Appendices contain excerpts from the Nuremberg charter and from Control Council Law No. 10 and a note on the review of sentences and on clemency in the American and British zones in Germany. 61 notes, no bibliography, no index.

3207 MAXWELL-FYFE, SIR DAVID (1st Earl of Kilmuir). Nuremberg in Retrospect: Being the Presidential Address of the President of the Holdsworth Club Birmingham: Holdsworth Club of the University of Birmingham. 1956.

3208 MELTZER, BERNARD D. "A Note on Some Aspects of the Nuremberg Debate," University of Chicago Law Review 1947 14(3): 455-469. Discusses many criticisms of the Nuremberg trial, particularly the charge of ex post facto law, the fairness of the trial, the concept of the crime of waging an aggressive war, and the restoration of law and order in Germany. 44 notes.

3209 MERLE, MARCEL. "Nuremberg vingt ans après," Revue de Droit Contemporain 1967 14(1): 11-18.

3210 MOMMSEN, WOLFGANG. "Die Akten der Nürnberger Kriegsverbrecherprozesse und die Möglichkeiten ihrer historischen Auswertung," Der Archivar 1950 3(1): 14-25.

3211 MORGAN, JOHN HARTMANN. "Nuremberg and After," Quarterly Review 1947 285(April): 318-336; (October):605-625.

3212 MORGENTHAU, HANS J., ERIC HULA, and MOORHOUSE F. X. MILLAR. "Views on Nuremberg: A Symposium," America 1946 76(December 7): 266-268.

3213 MUSZKAT, MARIAN. "Zum zehnjährigen Bestehen der Nürnberger Grundsätze," Neue Justiz 1955 9(20): 611-616. 11 notes.

3214 NASH, ARNOLD. 'The Nuremberg Trials," Christian Century 1946 63(39): 1148-1150. An evaluation of the IMT.

3215 NIEBUHR, REINHOLD. "Victors' Justice," Common Sense 1946 15(1): 6-9. Criticism of the Nuremberg IMT trial on the grounds that there was no international law which had defined the crimes charged and no legally constituted court that could adjudicate the charges. A general criticism of Allied policy toward Germany.

3216 "Note on the Nuremberg Trials," Law Quarterly Review 1946 62(July): 229-233. Commenting on the lack of understanding of the trial, the author defends the proceedings and stresses the difficulty of the task.

3217 PHLEGER, HERMAN. "Nuremberg - A Fair Trial? Dynamic Law" Atlantic Monthly 1946 177(4): 60-65.

3218 POLTORAK, ARKADII IOSIFOVICH, and N.S. LEBEDEVA. "25-Letie Nyurnbergskogo Proszessa [The 25th Anniversary of the Nuremberg Trial]," Voprosy Istorii 1971 (9): 85-106. The basic ideas of the trial of the major German war criminals by the Nuremberg IMT in 1946 have lost none of their significance in our time. Analyzing the Nuremberg documents as well as those of other trials of war criminals, the authors argues that the IMT was not merely judicium ad hoc, but played a part in the development of international law.

3219 POLTORAK, ARKADII I., and Y. ZAITSEV. Remember Nuremberg. Moscow: Foreign Languages Publishing House, [no date given, post 1952]. Original is in Russian. Soviet propaganda piece that focuses on various German acts that show similarities between Hitler and Konrad Adenauer. Some commentary on the Nuremberg IMT trial.

3220 QUINTANO RIPOLLÉS, ANTONIO. "Dix Ans après Nuremberg," Revue Internationale de Droit Pénal 1956 26: 45-57.

3221 RADIN, MAX. "Justice at Nürnberg," Foreign Affairs 1946 24(3): 369-384. Examines the 4 counts of the Nuremberg IMT indictment and concludes that it would have been better if the court had confined itself to war crimes and crimes against humanity and allowed crimes against peace to be dealt with in a different way by a different tribunal.

3222 RESTON, JAMES B., JR. "Is Nuremberg Coming Back to Haunt Us?" Saturday Review 1970 53(29): 14-17, 61.

3223 REUTER, PAUL. "Nürnberg 1946 - The Trial," Notre Dame Lawyer 1947 23(November): 76-97. Approves of the proceedings of the Nuremberg IMT trial, but criticizes the concept of collective guilt.

3224 RÜCKERL, ADALBERT, et al (eds.). NS-Prozesse nach 25 Jahren Strafverfolgung. Möglichkeiten - Grenzen - Ergebnisse. Karlsruhe: C.F. Müller, 1972. 224p. An anthology containing 6 essays by various writers. Topics covered include the status of research on war crimes trials, the murder of Jews in Poland, the crimes of the Einsatzgruppen in the Soviet Union, killings of prisoners in concentration camps, the argument of superior orders, and the statute of limitations on war crimes. Heavily documented, no bibliography, 6-page index of names.

3225 "Russia vs. Newsweek: How the Surviving Nuremberg War Criminals Are Living in Spandau Prison," Newsweek 1947 30(18): 36-38.

3226 SMIRNOV, LEV NIKOLAEVICH. Nürnberger Prozeß gestern und heute. Berlin: Staatsverlag der Deutschen Demokratischen Republik, 1966.

3227 SMITH, H.A. "The Nuremberg Trials," Free Europe 1946 13(162): 201-204. Argues that the trial was prejudiced against the defendants because the law which governed the trial was prepared by the prosecution. 1 note.

3228 TATGE, PAUL W. "The Nuremberg Trials: 'Victor's Justice?'" American Bar Association Journal 1950 36(March): 247-248.

3229 THORPE, GERALD L. "The Nuremberg Trials: Considerations and Suggestions," Intercom 1971 13(January-February): 33-35.

3230 VEALE, FREDERICK J.P. Advance to Barbarism: How the Reversion to Barbarism in Warfare and War-Trials Menaces Our Futures. Appleton, Wisconsin: C.C. Nelson, 1953. 305p. A new edition of a 1948 work under the pen name "A Jurist." Advances various objections to the Nuremberg IMT and points out many Russian atrocities that were as great as those perpetrated by Germany. War crimes trials remove all constraints from brutal and ruthless wars of the future. 2-page bibliography, index.

3231 VEALE, FREDERICK J.P. Advance to Barbarism: The Development of Total Warfare from Sarajevo to Hiroshima. London: Mitre, 1968. This criticism of war crimes trials was serialized in the Dublin Sunday Press.

3232 VEDOVATO, GIUSEPPE. Diritto Internazionale Bellico. Florence: G.C. Sansoni, 1946. 360p. The third part of this study deals with the punishment of war criminals. Comments critically on the London agreement and the Nuremberg indictment. The trial was a political reprisal.

3233 VOIGHT, F.A. "Nuremberg," Nineteenth Century and After 1946 140(November): 252-258. Critical appraisal of war crimes trials in general and the Nuremberg IMT in particular.

3234 WALSH, EDMUND A. "Comments and Corollaries," America 1946 76(November 9): 151-154.

3235 WATT, DONALD C. "Nuremberg Reconsidered," Encounter 1978 50(5): 81-87. Examines the origins and course of the Nuremberg IMT war crimes trial, based on a discussion of Werner Maser's Nürnberg: Tribunal der Sieger and Bradley F. Smith's Reaching Judgment at Nuremberg.

3236 WECHSLER, HERBERT. "Fortune Letters - Nürnberg Defended," Fortune 1947 35(4): 29-32.

3237 WYZANSKI, CHARLES E., JR. Whereas - a Judge's Premises: Essays in Judgment, Ethics, and the Law. Boston: Little, Brown, 1965. 312p. An anthology. "Nuremberg - A Fair Trial," pp. 164-179, and "Nuremberg in Retrospect," pp. 180-190, deal with the IMT. These essays appeared earlier as "Nuremberg: A Fair Trial? Dangerous Precedent," Atlantic Monthly 1946 177(4): 66-70; "Nuremberg in Retrospect," Atlantic Monthly 1946 178 (December): 56-59. Discusses arguments on the justice and fairness of the trial and concludes that even if it had not been held, it does not follow that war criminals should not have been punished. The outstanding accomplishment of the trial is that it crystalized the concept of the existence and enforceability of international criminal law.

N. SIGNIFICANCE OF THE IMT

3238 ALLEN, FLORENCE E. "Nuremberg Trial Implements World Law," Women Lawyers Journal 1948 34(Winter): 6-8, 26-28, 30.

3239 ARGÚAS, MARGARITA, and I. RUIZ MORENO. "Efectos sobre el derecho internacional de las decisiones de los tribunales con respecto a los criminales de guerra," Revista Peruana de Derecho Internacional 1947 7(25-26): 202-208.

3240 BALMER-BASILIUS, H.R. "Nürnberg und das Weltgewissen" Friedens-Warte 1946 46(5): 289-293.

3241 BERNAYS, MURRAY C. "Nuremberg: Its Vindication of Western Justice, its Profound Lessons in Moral Leadership, and its Deterrence to Future Aggression," Survey Graphic 1946 35(November): 390-391.

3242 BIAL, LOUIS C. "The Nurnberg Judgment and International Law," Brooklyn Law Review 1947 13(1): 34-49. Discusses the important points of the judgment and stresses the contributions of the trial in extending the scope of international law and in offering a solution to the problem of ex post facto law. 70 notes.

3243 BIRKETT, SIR NORMAN. "International Legal Theories Evolved at Nuremberg," International Affairs 1947 23(July): 317-325. Discusses some of the objections raised against the trials and analyzes such legal principles developed there as the crime of aggressive war, individual responsibility, and the rejection of the plea of superior orders.

3244 BROWN, JOHN MASON. "Nuremberg: The Age of Jackson (Part II)," Saturday Review of Literature 1946 29(34): 20-24.

3245 BULL, HENRY A. "Nurnberg Trial: Value to Civilization," Federal Rules Decisions 1947 7: 175-182. Report on the annual convention of the American Bar Association, Section on International Law.

3246 CALOYANNI, MÉGALOS A. "Le Procès de Nuremberg et l'Avenir de la justice pénale internationale," Revue de Droit International de Sciences Diplomatiques et Politiques 1946 24(3): 174-182. Examines the Nuremberg IMT trial and poses the question of the future of international law. Suggests that a United Nations commission study the question of an international code and criminal court.

3247 DE MENTHON, FRANCOIS. Le Procès de Nuremberg, son importance juridique et politique. Paris: Éditions du Mail, 1946. 29p.

3248 DOMAN, NICHOLAS R. "Political Consequences of the Nuremberg Trial," Annals of the American Academy of Political and Social Sciences 1946 246(July): 81-90. Comments on the legal-political aspects of a number of issues, among them individual responsibility and collective criminality, and discusses the effect of the proceedings on Germans.

3249 ECCARD, FRÉDÉRIC. "La Signification suprême du procès de Nuremberg," Revue de Droit International de Sciences Diplomatiques et Politiques 1946 24(2): 82-84.

3250 ECER, BOHUSLAV. "Lessons of the Nuremberg Trial," Central European Observer 1947 24(5): 70-71; 24(7)103-105.

3251 EULAU, HEINZ. "The Nuremberg War-Crime Trial: Revolution in International Law," New Republic 1945 113(20): 625-628.

3252 FALK, RICHARD A. "Nuremberg: Past, Present, and Future," Yale Law Journal 1971 80(7): 1501-1528. 81 notes.

3253 FARER, THOMAS J. "The Laws of War Twenty-five Years after Nuremberg," International Conciliation 1971(May): 1-54.

3254 FARER, THOMAS J. The Laws of War Twenty-five Years after Nuremberg. New York: Carnegie Endowment for International Peace, 1971.

3255 FRIED, HANS ERNST [JOHN ERNEST]. "The Great Nuremberg Trial," American Political Science Review 1976 70 (1): 192-197. A study of the content, significance, and use of the proceedings of the Nuremberg IMT. On the reissue of the 42-volume Trial of the Major War Criminals Before the International Military Tribunal, Nuremberg, November 14, 1945 - October 1, 1946, with a new Introduction by Gerhard L. Weinberg and Report of Robert H. Jackson on the International Conference on Military Trials. London: AMS Press, 1945. 9 notes.

3256 GLASER, STEFAN. "La Charte du tribunal de Nuremberg et les nouveaux principes du droit international," Schweizerische Zeitschrift für Strafrecht 1948 63: 13-38.

3257 HARTLMAYR, FRITZ. „Nürnberger Kriegsverbrecherprozeß und Völkerrecht," Österreichische Monatshefte 1946 1(8): 329-332.

3258 HARTMANN, E. „Probleme des traditionellen Völkerrechts im Urteil des Internationalen Militärgerichtshofes zu Nürnberg." Doctor of Law dissertation, Heidelberg University, 1952.

3259 HIRSCH, FELIX. "Lessons of Nuremberg," Current History 1946 11(62): 312-318.

3260 HONIG, FREDERICK. "Nuremberg: Justice or Vengeance?" World Affairs 1947 1(1): 79-88. Despite its imperfections, the Nuremberg IMT constituted an advance in international relations. 5 notes.

3261 HONIG, FREDERICK. "War Crimes Trials: Lessons for the Future," International Affairs 1950 26(4): 522-532.

3262 JACKSON, ROBERT H. "The Nuremberg Trial: An Example of Procedural Machinery for the Development of International Substantive Law," in Alison Reppy (ed). *David Dudley Field: Centenary Essays Celebrating One Hundred Years of Legal Reform*. New York: New York University School of Law, 1949.

3263 JACKSON, ROBERT H. "The Nuremberg Trial: Civilizations Chief Salvage from World War II," *Vital Speeches* 1946 13(December 1): 114-117.

3264 JACKSON, ROBERT H. "The Nuremberg Trial Becomes an Historic Precedent," *Temple Law Quarterly* 1946 20(2): 167-334. Survey of the concept, creation, and history of the IMT.

3265 JACKSON, ROBERT H. "The Significance of the Nuremberg Trials to the Armed Forces," *Military Affairs* 1946 10(4): 2-15. Personal observations on the Nuremberg IMT.

3266 JASPERS, KARL. "The Significance of the Nürnberg Trials for Germany and the World," *Notre Dame Lawyer* 1947 22(2): 150-160. The Nuremberg IMT trial was not yet concluded when Jaspers made this study, which is a portion of a longer work. In an attempt to counteract opposition existing in Germany to the trial, Jaspers concedes that World War II was undoubtedly started by Germany. The Nuremberg IMT trial actually deals with crime, not mere warfare. He examines five grounds on which many Germans challenged the lawfulness of the trial: (1) no war can be blamed entirely on one nation, (2) there should have been some Germans on the court, (3) there can be no crimes in the sphere of political sovereignty, (4) crime can be measured only on the basis of existing law, and (5) the might of the victors does not constitute law. Jaspers points out that the nation as a whole was not condemned for the crimes of a few. Though many genuine objections can be raised by what happened at Nuremberg, the trial points to a new world order which will redound to the benefit of Germany as well as the rest of the world. Undocumented; 2 informational notes.

3267 JESCHECK, HANS-HEINRICH. "Die Entwicklung des Völkerstrafrechts nach Nürnberg," *Schweizerische Zeitschrift für Strafrecht* 1957 72: 217-248.

3268 "Judgment Day at Nuremberg, World Law Takes a Long Stride Forward," *Senior Scholastic* 1945 49(November 12): 5-6.

3269 KELSEN, HANS. "Will the Judgment in the Nuremberg Trial constitute a Precedent in International Law?" *International Law Quarterly* 1947 1(2): 153-171. Contradicts Robert H. Jackson's argument that the rules of law applied at Nuremberg by the IMT had become a judicial precedent. Identifies formal and material conditions not fulfilled by the Nuremberg case that are a *sine qua non* of precedent-setting actions. First, such a system must establish a new rule of law, not merely apply a nonexistent rule of substantive law, which is what the IMT did. Examines ten arguments against the Nuremberg trial as a precedent-setting case. Complains that no Germans or neutrals were judges. Even worse, one of the nations which shared with Germany the "booty of the war waged against Poland" (the Soviet Union) was allowed to sit in judgment over Germany for the same crime it had committed. The vanquished were judged, but not all the criminals. The precedent established at Nuremberg was legislative, not judicial. Based on primary and secondary sources; 18 notes.

3270 KOHL, MICHAEL. "Die Nürnberger Prinzipien als Bestandteil des allgemeinendemokratischen Völkerrechts in ihrer Bedeutung für die Sicherung des Friedens," in Volume 2, Rudolf Arzinger, et al (eds.). *Deutschlandfrage und Völkerrecht*. 2 volumes. Berlin: Zentralverlag, 1962. 232, 243p. 44 notes.

3271 LA PRADELLE, ALBERT G. DE. "Le Procès des grands criminels de guerre et le développement du droit international," *Nouvelle Revue de Droit International Privé* 1947 14: 5-27.

3272 LA PRADELLE, ALBERT G. DE. "Une Révolution dans le droit pénal international," *Nouvelle Revue de Droit International Privé* 1946 13: 360-368.

3273 LAWRENCE, LORD JUSTICE GEOFFREY [Baron Oaksey]. *The Nuremberg Trials and the Process of International Law*. Birmingham: Holdsworth Club of the University of Birmingham, 1947.

3274 LIPPMANN, WALTER. "The Meaning of the Nuremberg Trial," *Ladies' Home Journal* 1946 63(June): 32, 188-190.

3275 MC MILLAN, JAMES. *Five Men at Nuremberg*. London: Harrap, 1985. 424p. A reassessment of the Nuremberg IMT trial in terms of its significance as an international legal precedent.

3276 PARKER, JOHN J. "The International Trial at Nuremberg: Giving Vitality to International Law," *American Bar Association Journal* 1951 37(July): 493-496, 549-555. 12 notes.

3277 REITHMULLER VACCARO, JULIO H. *El proceso de Nuremberg desde el punto de vista jurídico*. Santiago: Editorial Universitaria, 1962.

3278 SCHICK, FRANZ B. "The Nuremberg Trial and the Development of an International Criminal Law," *Juridical Review* 1947 59(3): 192-207. An international legal order in accord with the precepts of Nuremberg must be considered a modern utopia. Before creating an international criminal law applicable to individuals we should induce all states to submit their disputes to compulsory adjudication. 64 notes.

3279 SCHICK, FRANZ B. "The Nuremberg Trial and the International Law of the Future," *American Journal of International Law* 1947 41(4): 770-794. Believing that the desired preventive effect of the Nuremberg trial could take place only if the law of the future applied to victors and vanquished alike, the author finds little hope unless a permanent international criminal court is created with unqualified compulsory jurisdiction over states and individuals. Rejects the idea that Nuremberg created a legal precedent binding upon future courts. Examines the legality of the Nuremberg IMT trial.

3280 STEIN, LEO. "The Meaning of Nuremberg," *National Jewish Monthly* 1945 (December): 126-127.

3281 STOREY, ROBERT GERALD. "El Impacto de Nuremberg sobre el Derecho Internacional," *Revista Peruana de Derecho Internacional* 1948 8(27): 33-43.

3282 "The Results of Nuremberg," *New Republic* 1946 115(15): 467-468.

3283 TRAPP, ERWIN. Die kriegsrechtliche Bedeutung der Nürnberger Urteile. Düsseldorf: M. Triltsch, 1957.

3284 WASSERSTROM, RICHARD. "The Relevance of Nuremberg," Philosophy and Public Affairs 1971 1(1): 22-46.

3285 WECHSLER, HERBERT. Principles, Politics, and Fundamental Law: Selected Essays. Cambridge: Harvard University Press, 1961. 171p. Essay number 4, "The Issues of the Nuremberg Trial," pp. 138-157, deals with how the trial will be viewed in the future. This is a legal analysis that bypasses any discussion of any ex post facto aspect of the trial and concludes that it will stand as a "cornerstone in the house of peace." Read first at the American Historical Association annual meeting, on December 30, 1946. Published in the Political Science Quarterly 1947 621): 11-26. 8 notes.

3286 WITTENBERG, J.C. "De Grotius à Nuremberg: Quelques Réflexions," Revue Général de Droit International Public 1947 51(18): 89-112. Nuremberg can result in a new system of international law. 26 notes.

3287 WOODWARD, BEVERLY. "Nuremberg Law and U.S. Courts," Dissent 1969 16(2): 128-136. 11 notes.

O. THE UNITED NATIONS AND THE IMT

3288 AUSTRALIA. DEPARTMENT OF EXTERNAL AFFAIRS. "War Crimes," Current Notes on International Affairs 1945 16(7): 217-220. Outlines various steps leading up to the trial of major axis war criminals. Discusses the Moscow Declaration, actions being taken by the UNWCC, the London Agreement, the activities of the Australian War Crimes Commission, the Webb Report, and the establishment of Australian military tribunals to try Japanese war criminals apprehended by Australian military forces.

3289 BATHURST, M.E. "The United Nations War Crimes Commission," American Journal of International Law 1945 39(3): 565-570. Factual account of the events leading to the establishment of the Commission, its functions, organization, and composition.

3290 HOLBORN, LOUISE (ed.). War and Peace Aims of the United Nations. 2 volumes. Boston: World Peace Foundation, 1943, 1948. 730p. A collection of public speeches, documents, and reports of the Allies dealing with war aims. Much on war crimes, German responsibility for their crimes, and the agreement to prosecute them for these crimes.

3291 JACKSON, ROBERT H. "The United Nations Organization and War Crimes," American Society of International Law, Proceedings 1952 46: 196-204.

3292 MOUSSA, AMRE. "The Question of War Crimes in the United Nations," Revue Egyptienne de Droit International 1974 30: 91-97.

3293 RUSSELL, RUTH B. A History of the United Nations Charter: The Role of the United States. Washington: Brookings Institution, 1958.

3294 "The United Nations War Crimes Commission," International Law Quarterly 1947 1(1): 42-44. On the creation, history, and work of the UNWCC.

3295 UNITED NATIONS. Agreement by the Government of the United Kingdom of Great Britain and Northern Ireland, the Government of the United States of America, the Provisional Government of the French Republic and the Government of the Union of Soviet Socialist Republics for the Prosecution and Punishment of the Major War Criminals of the European Axis (and Charter of the International Military Tribunal), London, 8th August, 1945. London: HMSO, 1946. 31p. This was published as a government document by most of the Allied governments.

3296 UNITED NATIONS. INTERNATIONAL LAW COMMISSION. The Charter and Judgment of the Nürnberg Tribunal: History and Analysis. Memorandum submitted by the Secretary-General. Document A/CN.4/5. Lake Success: United Nations, 1949. 99p.

3297 UNITED NATIONS. WAR CRIMES COMMISSION. History of the United Nations War Crimes Commission and the Development of the Laws of War. London: HMSO, 1948. 592p. A detailed history of the origin and work of the War Crimes Commission, with background material on the laws of war and the concepts of war crimes, crimes against humanity, and crimes against peace. This volume, prepared by members of the United Nations War Crimes Commission to provide a record of their work, covers a wide range of subjects. The first chapters survey developments in the laws of war and the concept of war crimes before and during Wold War II. Chapters 6 and 7 describe the establishment and organization of the Commission and give a general historical survey of its activities. The following chapters deal largely with developments that led to the London Agreement and the IMT Charter, describing in detail conferences and discussions concerning specific counts and legal problems both prior and subsequent to the Nuremberg trials. Chapters 12 and 13 survey the arrangements made for the surrender of war criminals, and describe the machinery for the tracing and apprehension of war criminals, both on the national and international level. Chapter 14 gives an account of the movement for an international criminal jurisdiction from 1918 to the present, and describes the organization of the international and national courts for the prosecution of war criminals after World War II. The last chapter of the book describes the work of the Committee on Facts and Evidence of the UNWCC. Appendices include statistics on war criminals, a listing of noteworthy war criminals both in Europe and the Far East, and a bibliography of legal literature on the subject of war crimes.

3298 UNITED STATES - FRANCE - GREAT BRITAIN - SOVIET UNION. "Agreement for the Prosecution and Punishment of the Major War Criminals of the European Axis," pp. 257-258; Charter of the International Military Tribunal, pp. 258-264; "Unconditional Surrender of Japan," pp. 264-265. American Journal of International Law, Supplement 1945 39: 257-265.

3299 UNITED STATES, FRANCE, GREAT BRITAIN, SOVIET UNION. Agreement for the Prosecution and Punishment of the Major War Criminals of the European Axis, August 8, 1945. Reprinted in the American Journal of International Law, Supplement [Official Documents] 1945 39(October): 257-264.

3300 UNITED STATES. DEPARTMENT OF STATE. "United Nations Commission to Investigate War Crimes," Department of State Bulletin 1942 7(172): 797. October 10, 1942. A statement by President Roosevelt on the UNWCC and on individual responsibility for war crimes.

X
AMERICAN MILITARY TRIBUNALS (Non-IMT)

A. GENERAL WORKS

3301 "A Prosecutor's Memorandum in a War Crimes Trial," New Jersey Law Journal 1948 7(April 8): 129, 131, 133, 136.

3302 BEHLE, CALVIN A. "The War Crimes Trials," Nevada State Bar Journal 1948 13(2): 55-67. This is an account of the experiences of the author while he was on the staff of the United States War Crimes Office. Contains some statistics on American war crimes trials.

3303 BROOKS, WILLIS MONTFORD. "Precedent for the American War Crimes Trials," M.A. thesis, University of California, Los Angeles, 1947.

3304 FRATCHER, WILLIAM F. "Review by the Civil Courts of Judgments of Federal Military Tribunals," Ohio State Law Journal 1949 10(3): 271-300. 106 notes.

3305 GERMANY (Territory under Allied Occupation, 1945-1955. U.S. Zone). Military Governor. German and Military Government Courts 1946. Statistical Review. Special Report. January, 1947. [Berlin]: 1947. 25p.

3306 GERMANY (Territory under Allied Occupation, 1945-1955). U.S. Zone. Office of Military Government. Trial of Members of Criminal Organizations. [no city given]: Adjutant General, OMGUS, 194?. 48p.

3307 GOODMAN, LEO M. (comp.). Digest of Current Decisions of: 1. United States Military Government Court of Appeals. 2. District Courts, Land Bavaria. 3. British Control Commission Court of Appeals. 4. OMGUS Legal Division. 5. German Courts. Munich: 1949.

3308 GREEN, A. WIGFALL. "The Military Commission," American Journal of International Law 1948 42(4): 832-848. Discusses the history and legal authority of the military commission, 2 trials during the American revolution which were conducted by a military court, and trials by "councils of war", as military tribunals were called during the Mexican War. During the

Civil War the term "military commission" received statutory recognition. It was used as well during World War I. In 1942 President Franklin Roosevelt appointed a military commission to try 8 saboteurs. From 1941 to 1948 military commissions in the United States, France, Germany, Austria, Italy, Japan, and Korea tried people who violated the laws of war. Traces in detail the authority of military commissions, their constitutionality, the powers of the president, the articles of war, statutes other than articles of war, treaties, laws of war, and the appointment and jurisdiction of military commissions and their relation to local civil and criminal courts in occupied territories. Based largely on secondary sources; 13 notes.

3309 INGLIS, L.M. "The Occupation Courts in Germany," New Zealand Law Journal 1951 27(11): 172-175.

3310 KAPLAN, HAROLD L. "Constitutional Limitations on Trials by Military Commissions," University of Pennsylvania Law Review 1943 92(2): 119-149; 92(3): 272-294. History and general study of American trials by military commissions. 167, 94 notes.

3311 KOESSLER, MAXIMILIAN. "American War Crimes Trials in Europe," Georgetown Law Journal 1950 9(1): 18-112. The author, formerly an attorney for the War Crimes Group of the United States Army, asserts that the allied governments could not entrust to Axis courts the responsibility for trying criminals for crimes committed against Allies. The Americans held approximately 900 trials, including the Dachau trials and the twelve Nuremberg trials, involving over 3000 defendants. Half were held in Germany, the rest in Japan, Austria, Italy, the Philippines, China, and various Pacific islands. The Dachau trials were held generally as American army courts martial. Describes in detail differences and similarities between the Nuremberg and Dachau trials with respect to composition, purpose, charges, and sentencing. Examines jurisdictional bases of the Dachau trials, procedures and principles of evidence in the Dachau Trials, the indictment, prosecution and defense counsel, Anglo-American versus Continental procedures, review procedures, the Dachau law of evidence, the responsibility of individuals, forms of criminal participation, the plea of necessity, and habeas corpus review by the Supreme Court of the United States. Concludes that the Nuremberg and Tokyo trials established aggressive war as a category of international delinquency. Based on primary and secondary sources; 229 notes, 2 appendices on Regulations on Military Commissions and Regulation on Military Government Court.

3312 KOLANDER, MORRIS W. "War Crimes Trials in Germany," Pennsylvania Bar Association Quarterly 1947 18(3): 274-280. Surveys the war crimes trials in the American Zone. Describes the organization and procedures of the Intermediate Court and the General Military Government Court. 22 notes.

3313 MC CAULEY, WORTH B. "American Courts in Germany: 600,000 Cases Later," American Bar Association Journal 1954 40(December): 1041-1045.

3314 Memorandum by the Evangelical Church on the Question of War Crimes Trials before American Military Courts. Stuttgart: 1949.

3315 NOBLEMAN, ELI E. "A Lesson in Democracy: American Military Government Courts and the German People," *Military Government Journal* 1948 1(June): 6-8.

3316 NOBLEMAN, ELI E. "American Military Government Courts in Germany," *American Journal of International Law* 1946 40(4): 803-811. Nobleman, Criminal Investigator, Legal Officer, Chief of the German Courts Branch, and Chief of the Military Government Courts Branch, Legal Division, Office of Military Government of Bavaria, argues that it was in the courts that the German people realized their greatest loss of rights under the Nazi government. All German courts were suspended within occupied territories, beginning in September, 1944. Certain laws were abrogated and German ordinary and administrative courts were suspended. Summary, Intermediate, and General military government courts were established. Deals with the jurisdiction of these courts and examines their practical application as well as the relationship between American military courts and courts that would normally handle German civil matters. There was no means of appealing the judgment of a military government court. Based on various control laws, military government regulations (over 300 cited or alluded to in some way), and German criminal and civil court records; 53 notes.

3317 NOBLEMAN, ELI E. *American Military Government Courts in Germany: Their Role in the Democratization of the German People*. Washington: Provost Marshal General's School, Military Government Department for ORC Units, 1950. 261p. Deals with the legal bases for the establishment of occupational tribunals, American military government tribunals before World War II, American military tribunals in Germany during the war, civilian military government courts in Germany during the war, and military government courts as a basis for democracy. 9 photographs, 13 appendices, a table of 16 cases.

3318 NOBLEMAN, ELI E. "Military Government Courts: Law and Justice in the American Zone of Germany," *American Bar Association Journal* 1947 33(August): 851-852.

3319 NOBLEMAN, ELI E. "Procedure and Evidence in American Military Government Courts in the United States Zone of Germany," *Federal Bar Journal* 1947 8(January): 212-248.

3320 NOBLEMAN, ELI E. "The Administration of Justice in the United States Zone of Germany," *Federal Bar Journal* 1946 8(October): 70-97.

3321 UNITED STATES. OFFICE OF MILITARY GOVERNMENT, UNITED STATES (OMGUS). ADJUTANT GENERAL. *Trial of the Members of Criminal Organizations*. Berlin: OMGUS, 1947.

3322 UNITED STATES. OFFICE OF THE HIGH COMMISSIONER FOR GERMANY. "Epilogue to the War Crimes Trials," *6th Quarterly Report on Germany. January 1 - March 31, 1951*, pp. 40-53.

3323 WEBER, HELLMUTH VON. „Zur Auswirkung der Gesetzgebung der Besatzungsmächte auf das deutsche Strafgesetzbuch," *Süddeutsche Juristen-Zeitung* 1946 1(11/12): 238-240. 9 notes.

B. CONTROL COUNCIL TRIALS (12 "SUBSEQUENT PROCEEDINGS")

1. General Works

3324 ASCHENAUER, RUDOLF. Landsberg. Ein dokumentarischer Bericht von deutscher Seite. Munich: Stachus, 1951. 131p. Deals with the Dachau-Buchenwald trial in Landsberg in 1947. Part 1 discusses the ex post facto nature of laws under which war criminals were tried, appeals to the "higher authority" argument, and the Nuremberg death se~tences. Deals with testimony of questionable witnesses and discusses errors made at a number of trials, among them the Doctors' trial, the Milch trial, the Hostage trial, and the OKW (Reinecke) trial.

3325 BEHLING, KURT. "Die Schuldausprüche im Nürnberger Juristenurteil vom 4./5. Dezember 1947," Archiv des Völkerrechts 1950 2(August): 412-427.

3326 BOUMAL, J. "Les Jugements du tribunal militaire américain de Nuremberg," Revue de Droit Pénal et de Criminologie 1950 30(May): 844-861.

3327 CARTER, EDWARD F. "The Nürnberg Trials: A Turning Point in the Enforcement of International Law," Nebraska Law Review 1949 28(3): 370-386. Discusses some of the problems dealt with at the Nuremberg IMT in the course of subsequent trials. Considerable attention is paid the List (Hostage) case. Defends the fairness of the subsequent trials at Nuremberg, but disagrees with the notion that one could be guilty of the crimes of an organization by simply being a member of it. 50 notes.

3328 "Gutachten und Denkschriften über das IMT und die Nürnberger Nachfolgeprozesse," by Donnedieu de Vabres (June 25, 1949), Franz Exner (January 4, 1946), Gilbert Gidel (August 18, 1949), Carl Haensel (August 5, 1947), Erhard Heinke (January 28, 1947), Eric Kaufmann (October 27, 1948; July 15, 20, 1947), Theodor Klefisch (June 5, 1946; August 1947), Herbert Kraus (May 24, 1946; June 15, 1946; May 10, 1947; June 8, 1947; January 10, 1948; April 10, 1948; June 18, 1949), Günther Lummert (July 1947), Hermann Mosler (February 15, 1946; March 2, 1946; May 7, 1947), Ch. Rousseau (July 27, 1949), Eberhard Schmidt (November 1, 1946), Robert Servatius (February 15, 1946), Edward Wahl (May 21, 1948). These and others are located in the Institut für Völkerrecht, University of Göttingen.

3329 HALE, Winfield B. "Nuernberg War Crimes Tribunals," Tennessee Law Review 1949 21(1): 8-19.

3330 KNIERIEM, AUGUST VON. Nürnberg: rechtliche und menschliche Probleme. Stuttgart: Ernst Klett, 1953. 573p. Published in English as The Nuremberg Trials. Chicago: Henry Regnery, 1959. 561p. Focuses on the 12 Nuremberg trials of war criminals which followed the IMT trial. These trials lasted from the end of 1946 to the spring of 1949. Part I deals with the problems of substantive law, judicial organization, and procedural law. Part II discusses legal problems common to all the cases, especially punishability. Discusses the consciousness of wrong doing, conflict of duties, superior orders, state of necessity, and the consent of the person injured. Part III covers specific cases. General cases are presented with respect to problems of jurisdiction and procedure, the waging of war, occupation, and the treatment of prisoners. A section on industrialists cases discusses the Hague rules of land warfare and modern economic warfare, spoliation, employment of forced labor, and participation in a war of aggression. Appendix I contains the text of Control Council Law No. 10, a document intended to establish a uniform legal basis in Germany. Appendix II contains Military Government - Germany Ordinance No. 7, a document to provide for the establishment of military tribunals in Germany for trying and punishing war criminals. German edition also includes a list of abbreviations, 2-page bibliography of primary documents, 7-page bibliography of secondary sources. English edition contains 35 pages of notes.

3331 "Military Tribunals - Appointment of Judges at Nuremberg," American Bar Association Journal 1947 33(September): 896-897.

3332 "Nuremberg Trials Go On," New York Times Magazine 1947 (September 28): 12-13.

3333 SOTTILE, ANTOINE. "Un Peu Plus de Justice, S.V.P.! (À propos de certains verdicts et acquittements pronocés par les tribunaux militaires internationaux)," Revue de Droit International de Sciences Diplomatiques et Politiques 1948 26(3): 372-385. Criticizes the judgments in certain American trials, especially those of Ilse Koch, Krupp, and the General Staff.

3334 TAYLOR, TELFORD. Final Report to the Secretary of the Army on the Nuernberg War Crimes Trials under Control Council Law No. 10. Washington: GPO, August 15, 1949.

3335 TAYLOR, TELFORD. "Nuremberg Trials - Synthesis and Projection," Information Bulletin, Office of the U.S. High Commissioner for Germany 1949 (162): 3-6, 21-22, 24. Published in French as "Les procès de Nuremberg: Synthèse et vue d'avenir," Politiques Étrangère 1949 14(3): 207-218.

3336 TAYLOR, TELFORD. "Nuremberg Trials: War Crimes and International Law," International Conciliation 1949 (450): 241-371 [entire issue]. Concise account of the Nuremberg IMT trial and the Nuremberg trials under Control Law No. 10. The author, who was U.S. Chief of Counsel, points out how questions of law and procedure were handled by prosecutors, defense attorneys, and judges. Stresses the need for making people more aware of the contents of the Nuremberg record. Topics covered include origins and nature of war crimes trials, the London agreement, Control Council Law No. 10, the 12 Nuremberg trials under this law, and various legal problems. 257 notes.

3337 TAYLOR, TELFORD. "The Nuremberg War Crimes Trials: An Appraisal," Proceedings of the American Academy of Political Science 1949 23(May): 239-254.

3338 WEBER, HELLMUTH VON. „Der Einfluß der Militärstrafgerichtsbarkeit der Besatzungsmacht auf die deutsche Strafgerichtsbarkeit," Süddeutsche Juristen-Zeitung 1947 2(2): 65-70.

2. Trial Records

GERMANY (Territory Under Allied Occupation, 1945-. U.S. Zone). Military Tribunals. Trials of War Criminals before the Nuremberg Military Tribunals Under Control Council Law No. 10, Nuremberg, October 1946

– April 1949. Washington: GPO, 1949-1953. 15 volumes. Known as the "Green Series." In April 1949 judgment was handed down in the last of the 12 Nuremberg war crimes trials begun in October 1946 under Allied Control Council Law No. 10. Many political, industrial, professional, and military men were tried. The trials were conducted in English and German and were recorded. The 12 cases required 1200 days of court proceedings, and the records exceed 330,000 pages. These 15 volumes are the condensed record of these materials. Copies of the records of the 12 trials are available in the Library of Congress and the National Archives. Each trial record contains a detailed table of contents in lieu of an index. All volumes have photographs of courts, justices, defense counsels, and defendants. The contents of the 15 volumes are listed here by number, official name, and popular name, with the volume number identified.

Case 1, **Karl** Brandt, et al (**Medical** Case), Volumes 1 and 2. Case 2, **Erhard** Milch (**Milch** Case), Volume 2. Case 3, **Josef** Altstötter, et al (**Justice** Case), Volume 3. Case 4, **Oswald** Pohl, et al (**Pohl** Case), Volume 5. Case 5, **Friedrich** Flick, et al (**Flick** Case), Volume 6. Case 6, **Carl** Krauch, et al **I.G.** **Farben** Case), Volumes 7 and 8. Case 7, **Wilhelm** List, et al (**Hostage** Case), Volume 8, **Ulrich** Greifelt, et al (**RuSHA** Case), Volumes 4 and 5. Case 9, **Otto** Ohlendorf, et al (**Einsatzgruppen** Case), Volume 4. Case 10, **Alfried** Krupp, et al (**Krupp** Case), Volume 9. Case 11, **Ernst** von **Weizsäkker**, et al (**Ministries** Case), Volumes 12, 13, and 14. Case 12, **Wilhelm** von **Leeb**, et al (**High** Command Case), Volumes 10 and 11. Procedure, Volume 15.

3339 NUREMBERG MILITARY TRIBUNAL. Volume 1. **U.S.** vs. **Karl** Brandt, et al (**Medical** Case). 1004p. Volume 1 and Part of Volume 2 cover the first of the 12 cases. This has become known as the **Medical** Case because 20 of the 23 defendants were doctors, charged with performing medical experiments on human beings. Lists the defendants, the defense counsels, associate defense counsels, members of the prosecution, and members of the tribunal. Lengthy extracts from the argumentation and evidence offered by the prosecution and the defense. Much on the medical experiments, the Jewish skeleton collection, euthanasia, and 19 photographs from prosecution evidence.

3340 NUREMBERG MILITARY TRIBUNAL. Volume 2. The **Medical** Case and part of **U.S.** vs. **Erhard** Milch (Case 2, the **Milch** Case). 898p. Contains evidence and arguments on various aspects of the Medical Case, the ruling of the Tribunal, final pleas of the defendants, the judgment, and sentences. Contains the affirmation of the sentences by the Military Governor of the United States Zone of Occupation, appendices listing the witnesses, and an index of documents and testimony. The trial of Erhard Milch, a Field Marshal in the German Air Force, lasted from November 13, 1946, until April 17, 1947. Milch was charged with deportation of foreign nationals, enslavement, mistreatment of millions of people, and with performing medical experiments on people. Contains the indictment, names of members of the tribunal, prosecution and defense arguments, selections from the documents and testimony of witnesses, the judgment, petitions, affirmation of the sentence, and one index listing witnesses and another listing documents and testimony.

3341 NUREMBERG MILITARY TRIBUNAL. Volume 3. U.S. vs. Josef Altstötter, et al (Case 3, the Justice Case). 1236p. Called the Justice Case because all the defendants held positions either in the Reich system of justice, as officials of the Reich Ministry of Justice, or as judges or prosecutors of the Special Courts or the People's Courts. Introduction explains the case, lists members of the tribunal, the prosecution, and the defense, and gives the text of the indictment as well as the opening statements of the prosecution and defense. One section analyzes the general development of German law during the Nazi period. Another section deals with the evidence of the principal issues in the case. Concludes with final statements of the defendants, the opinion and judgment of the court, and confirmation of the sentences. One of the five appendices is a list of witnesses. Contains an index of documents and testimonies.

3342 NUREMBERG MILITARY TRIBUNAL. Volume 4. U.S. vs. Otto Ohlendorf, et al (Case 9, the Einsatzgruppen Case), and Sections 1-5 of U.S. vs Ulrich Greifelt, et al (Case 8, the RuSHA Case). 1185p. The Einsatzgruppen Case was the biggest murder trial in history. Ohlendorf and the other 23 defendants were commanders or subordinate officers of Special SS units which accompanied the German Army in its invasion of the Soviet Union in order to perform certain special "political" and "security" missions. These SS units were alleged to have killed approximately one million civilians and prisoners of war in the German occupied area of Russia. The second part of Volume 4 contains the first five sections of the RuSHA Case, which takes its name from the Rassen und Siedlungshauptamt (Race and Resettlement Office) of the SS. The 14 defendants were officials of SS branches concerned with the "racial" program.

3343 NUREMBERG MILITARY TRIBUNAL. Volume 5. U.S. vs. Ulrich Greifelt, et al (Case 8, the RuSHA Case), and U.S. vs. Oswald Pohl, et al (Case 4, the Pohl Case). 1237p. Pohl was the chief of the SS Wirtschafts-und Verwaltungshauptamt (WVHA). The other 17 defendants were officials of the same agency.

3344 NUREMBERG MILITARY TRIBUNAL. Volume 6. U.S. vs. Friedrich Flick, et al (Case 5, the Flick Case). 1268p. The Flick case was the first of the so-called industrialist cases tried in Nuremberg (Cases 5, 6, and 10). The 6 defendants were leading officials in the Flick company or its subsidiary companies and were charged with war crimes and crimes against humanity. The counts charged criminal conduct relating to slave labor, the spoliation of property in occupied France and the Soviet Union, the "organization" of Jewish industrial and mining properties, beginning in 1936. This charge was dismissed on the ground that the Tribunal did not have jurisdiction. Five indictments related to membership in and support of the SS.

3345 NUREMBERG MILITARY TRIBUNAL. Volumes 7-8. U.S. vs. Carl Krauch, et al (Case 6, the I.G. Farben Case). 1601p. and 1454p. The Farben Case involved slave labor and the plunder and expropriation of property in occupied countries. Contains charges relating to membership in and support of the SS.

3346 NUREMBERG MILITARY TRIBUNAL. Volume 9. U.S. vs. Alfried Krupp, et al. (Case 10, Krupp Case). 1539p. The trial of 12 officials of the Krupp company was the third and last of the so-called industrialist cases tried in Nuremberg. It lasted from August 16, 1947 to April 1, 1949. Gustav Krupp, the father of the first named defendant and the leading figure in the company until 1943, was not indicted, owing to physical and mental incapacity. The case contained charges relating to slave labor and to the plunder and expropriation of property in occupied countries and of crimes against the peace by participation in the planning and waging of aggressive war. These charges were all dismissed.

3347 NUREMBERG MILITARY TRIBUNAL. Volume 10. U.S. vs. Wilhelm von Leeb, et al. (Case 12, the High Command Case). Sections 1-7. 1308p. This case deals primarily with the activities of high-ranking German military leaders. Leeb and 12 of the other defendants indicted were field marshals or generals, and one was an admiral. All held high command and staff positions. The Tribunal found none of the defendants guilty of crimes against the peace, but did find 11 guilty of war crimes and crimes against humanity.

3348 NUREMBERG MILITARY TRIBUNAL. Volume 11. U.S. vs. Wilhelm von Leeb, et al (Case 12, the High Command Case). Sections 7-13. U.S. vs. Wilhelm List, et al (Case 7, The Hostage Case). 1332p. Most of the trial dealt with hostage or reprisal actions of one kind or another. The case was popularly known as the "Southeast Case," because most of the crimes were committed while the defendants were field commanders or chiefs of staff to field commanders in southeastern Europe. The Tribunal found 8 of the defendants who stood trial guilty and 2 not guilty.

3349 NUREMBERG MILITARY TRIBUNAL. Volumes 12, 13, 14. U.S. vs. Ernst von Weizsäcker, et al (Case 11, the Ministries Case, or Wilhelmstraße Case). 1330p., 1205p., 1270p. This was the longest of the 12 Nuremberg trials. Most of the 21 defendants were charged with crimes arising out of their duties as officials of the German government. Many of them held positions in organizations of the Nazi party. Three were Reich ministers. These 3 volumes represent less than 5 per cent of the total number of documents.

3350 NUREMBERG MILITARY TRIBUNAL. Volume 15. Procedure, Practices, and Administration. 1238p. Contains materials common to all the trials as well as selections from the record of each of the individual trials which bear directly upon the development of procedure, trial practice, the rules of evidence, and secondary matters. 20-page table of contents, 5-page introduction, 3-page index.

3. Indexes to Trial Records

3351 ARNDT, KARL (comp.). Alphabetical Index of all Witnesses and Defense Counsel heard in the 12 Nürnberg War Crimes Trials with Pages of the Official Transcripts of the Proceedings. Bremen: 1949. 171 lines.

3352 SERAPHIM, HANS-GÜNTHER (ed.). Indices zu den zwölf Nürnberger US-Militärgerichtsprozessen. Göttingen: Institut für Völkerrecht, 1950-1956. Each contains an explanatory essay.

3353 SERAPHIM, HANS-GÜNTHER (ed.). Sachindex zu den Urteilen der 12 Fälle. 3rd edition. Göttingen: Institut für Völkerrecht an der Universität Göttingen, 1954. Mimeograph.

3354 SERAPHIM, HANS-GÜNTHER. II. Sachindex zum Verfahren gegen Ernst Weizsäcker, u.a. (Fall XI, sogenannter "Wilhelmstrassen Prozeß). Göttingen: Institut für Völkerrecht an der Universität Göttingen, 1952. 278p. Mimeograph.

3355 SERAPHIM, HANS-GÜNTHER. III. A. Sachindex zum Verfahren gegen Wilhelm v. Leeb u.a. (Fall XII, sogenannter "OKW Prozeß)." Göttingen: Institut für Völkerrecht an der Universität Göttingen, 203p. Mimeograph.

3356 SERAPHIM, HANS-GÜNTHER. III. B und C. Personen- und Dokumentenindex zum Verfahren gegen Wilhelm v. Leeb u.a. (Fall XII, sogenannter "OKW Prozeß)." Göttingen: Institut für Völkerrecht an der Universität Göttingen, 1953. 56p. Mimeograph.

3357 SERAPHIM, HANS-GÜNTHER. Personenindex zum Verfahren gegen Friedrich Flick u.a. Teil IV A (Fall V). Göttingen: Institut für Völkerrecht an der Universität Göttingen, 1956. 231p. Mimeograph.

3358 SERAPHIM, HANS-GÜNTHER. Sach- und Dokumentenindex zum Verfahren gegen Friedrich Flick u.a. Teil B und C (Fall V). Göttingen: Institut für Völkerrecht an der Universität Göttingen, 1956. 248p. Mimeograph.

4. Specific Cases

a. Case 1. The Medical Case

3359 BADER, KARL S. "Umschau," Deutsche Rechts-Zeitschrift 1947 2(12): 401-402. Case 1: United States v. Karl Brandt, et al. 9 notes.

3360 BADER, KARL S. "Umschau," Deutsche Rechts-Zeitschrift 1946 1(5): 140-142.

3361 GOODMAN, ROGER (ed.). The First German War Crimes Trial: Chief Judge Walter B. Beals' Desk Notebook of the Doctors' Trial, held in Nuremberg, Germany, December 1946 to August 1947. 2 volumes. Salisbury, North Carolina: Documentary Publications, [1976].

3362 GRAHAM, ROBERT J. "The 'Right to Kill' in the Third Reich: Prelude to Genocide," Catholic Historical Review 1976 62(1): 56-76. On the Medical trial.

3363 GRAVEN, JEAN. "Le Procès des médecins nazis et les expériences pseudo-médicales: Esquisse d'une étude synthèse," Annals de Droit International Médical 1962 8: 11-75.

3364 GROSS, MARTIN. The Doctors. New York: Dell, 1967. 605p.

3365 "Indictment Case Number One - U.S. vs. Certain German Doctors," Florida Law Journal 1947 21(1): 15-22. The indictment in the Medical Case, signed by Telford Taylor.

3366 MITSCHERLICH, ALEXANDER, and FRED MIELKE. Das Diktat der Menschenverachtung. Der Nürnberger Ärzteprozeß und seine Quellen. Heidelberg: Lambert Schneider, 1947. 173p. Published in English as <u>Doctors</u> <u>of</u> <u>Infamy:</u> <u>The</u> <u>Story</u> <u>of</u> <u>the</u> <u>Nazi</u> <u>Medical</u> <u>Crimes</u>. New York: Henry Schuman, 1949. 172p. Contains a brief account of the Medical Case, the first of the 12 Nuremberg trials subsequent to the IMT trial. The decision to acquaint the German public more intimately with the facts of the case was made by members of the German Medical Commission, of which Dr. Mitscherlich was the head. Contains a note on medical ethics.

3367 MITSCHERLICH, ALEXANDER, and FRED MIELKE. <u>Medizin</u> <u>ohne</u> <u>Menschlichkeit.</u> <u>Dokumente</u> <u>des</u> <u>Nürnberger</u> <u>Ärzteprozesses</u>. Frankfurt am Main: S. Fischer, 1960, 1962.

3368 PLATTEN-HALLERMUND, ALICE. <u>Die</u> <u>Tötung</u> <u>Geisteskranker</u> <u>in</u> <u>Deutschland.</u> <u>Aus</u> <u>der</u> <u>deutschen</u> <u>Ärztekommission</u> <u>beim</u> <u>amerikanischen</u> <u>Militärgericht</u> <u>(Leiter</u> <u>Dr.</u> <u>Alexander</u> <u>Mitscherlich)</u>. Frankfurt am Main: Verlag der Frankfurter Hefte, 1948. 131p.

3369 SMITH, C.C. <u>Guide</u> <u>to</u> <u>the</u> <u>Documents</u> <u>that</u> <u>were</u> <u>admitted</u> <u>as</u> <u>Evidence</u> <u>for</u> <u>the</u> <u>Prosecution</u> <u>and</u> <u>Defense</u> <u>of</u> <u>the</u> <u>Nazi</u> <u>Doctors</u> <u>before</u> <u>the</u> <u>United</u> <u>States</u> <u>Military</u> <u>Tribunal</u> <u>at</u> <u>Nuremberg</u>. New York: 1955-1956.

3370 UNITED STATES. NATIONAL ARCHIVES AND RECORDS SERVICE. Microfilm Publications. Record Group 238. Pamphlet Describing M887. 46 rolls, Records of the United States Nuremberg War Crimes Trials. <u>United</u> <u>States</u> <u>of</u> <u>America</u> v. <u>Karl</u> <u>Brandt</u> et al. Case 1 of the 12 "subsequent" Nuremberg trials, known popularly as the Medical Case. November 21, 1946 - August 20, 1947. Washington: NARS, 1974. 14p. Lists 23 defendants, the charges against them, and the contents of each roll.

3371 WILLE, SIEGFRIED. "Grundsätze des Nürnberger Ärzteprozesses," <u>Neue</u> <u>Juristische</u> <u>Wochenschrift</u> 1949 2(10): 337.

b. <u>Case</u> <u>2.</u> <u>Milch</u> <u>Case</u>

3372 IRVING, DAVID. <u>The</u> <u>Rise</u> <u>and</u> <u>Fall</u> <u>of</u> <u>the</u> <u>Luftwaffe:</u> <u>The</u> <u>Life</u> <u>of</u> <u>Field</u> <u>Marshall</u> <u>Erhard</u> <u>Milch</u>. New York: Little, Brown, 1974. Deals in part with Case 2 of the Nuremberg 12.

3373 UNITED STATES. NATIONAL ARCHIVES AND RECORDS SERVICE. Microfilm Publications. Record Group 238. Pamphlet Describing M888. 13 rolls. Records of the United States Nuremberg War Crimes Trials. <u>United</u> <u>States</u> <u>of</u> <u>America</u> v. <u>Erhard</u> <u>Milch</u>. Case 2 of 12 "subsequent" Nuremberg trials, known popularly as the Milch or Luftwaffe Case. November 13, 1946 - April 17, 1947. Washington: NARS, 1974. 7p. Milch master-minded the 5-million-man slave labor recruiting program. The contents are identified by roll.

c. <u>Case</u> <u>3.</u> <u>Justice</u> <u>Case</u>

3374 BOBERACH, HEINZ (ed.). <u>Richterbriefe.</u> <u>Dokumente</u> <u>zur</u> <u>Beeinflussung</u> <u>der</u> <u>deutschen</u> <u>Rechtsprechung</u> <u>1942-1944</u>. Boppard am Rhein: Harald Boldt, 1975. 515p.

3375 <u>Das</u> <u>Nürnberger</u> <u>Juristenurteil.</u> <u>Allgemeiner</u> <u>Teil,</u> <u>Sonderveröffentlichungen</u> <u>des</u> <u>Zentral-Justizblattes</u> <u>für</u> <u>die</u> <u>Britische</u> <u>Zone</u>. Hamburg: Rechts- und Staatswissenschaftlicher Verlag, 1948. 64p. Annexes A1-A13, B1-B6, C1-C6. Special publications of the British Zone.

3376 Das Nürnberger Juristenurteil. Vollständige Ausgabe. Hamburg: 1948.

3377 FIGGE, ROBERT. "Die Verantwortlichkeit des Richters. Ein weiterer Beitrag zur Frage der strafrechtlichen Haftung der Richter für die Anwendung naturrechtswidriger Gesetze," Süddeutsche Juristen-Zeitung 1947 2(3/4): 179-184. Defends Nazi judges, exalts positive law, and denies the value of natural law and humanitarianism. 6 notes.

3378 HAAST, H.F. VON. "A Second Nuremberg Trial: Judges Tried for Subservience to the Fuhrer," New Zealand Law Journal 1948 24(5): 67-68. Some on the Justice trial.

3379 HAENSEL, CARL. "Das Urteil im Nürnberger Juristenprozeß," Deutsche Rechts-Zeitschrift 1948 3(2): 40-43. 9 notes.

3380 HANEY, GERHARD. "Friedensvertrag und Nürnberger Juristenurteil," Neue Justiz 1962 16(2): 54-59. 37 notes.

3381 JOHE, WERNER. Die gleichgeschaltete Justiz. Organisation des Rechtswesens und Politisierung der Rechtsprechung 1933-1945 dargestellt am Beispiel des Oberlandesgerichtsbezirks Hamburg. Frankfurt am Main: Europäische Verlagsanstalt, 1967.

3382 KAUL, FRIEDRICH KARL. Geschichte des Reichsgerichts: 1933-1945. Berlin: Akademie, 1971.

3383 KOESSLER, MAXIMILIAN. "Nazi Justice and the Democratic Approach: The Debasement of Germany's Legal System," American Bar Association Journal 1950 36(August): 634-638. 19 notes.

3384 KRAMER, G. The Influence of National Socialism on the Courts of Justice and the Police in the Third Reich. London: Weidenfeld and Nicolson, 1955.

3385 LA FOLLETTE, CHARLES M. Der Nürnberger Prozeß gegen führende Juristen des Dritten Reiches, Stuttgart: Stuttgarter Zeitung, 1948. 49p.

3386 LA FOLLETTE, CHARLES M. "Justice Case at Nuremberg," Information Bulletin [Office of the U.S. High Commissioner for Germany]. No. 138 (June 29, 1948), 9-12; No. 139 (July 13, 1948), 11-15; No. 140 (July 27, 1948), 15-20. Review of the case, with an opinion and speculations on its implications.

3387 RADBRUCH, GUSTAV. "Des Reichsjustizministeriums Ruhm und Ende, zum Nürnberger Juristen-Prozeß," Süddeutsche Juristen-Zeitung 1948 3(2): 57-64. Surveys the conduct of German Ministers of Justice from Joel to Frank, with special emphasis on Schlegelberger. In complete accordance with the Nuremberg IMT decision, but commends the heroism of judges who resisted Nazi justice. Undocumented.

3388 STAFF, ILSE. Justiz im Dritten Reich. Frankfurt am Main: Fischer-Bücherei, 1964. 265p. Much on the Justice Case.

3389 STEINIGER, P.A., and KAZIMIERZ LESZCZYŃSKI (eds.). Fall 3. Das Urteil im Juristenprozeß, gefällt am 4. Dezember 1947 vom Militärgerichtshof III der Vereinigten Staaten von Amerika. Berlin: VEB Deutscher Verlag der Wissenschaften, 1969. 320p. Examines the 9-month-long Justice trial, which resulted in the sentencing of 4 defendants to life imprisonment and 6 to shorter terms while 4 were acquitted. Defines the 4 counts of the indictment as they pertain to the Justice Case. Includes a chronological summary of documentation on the Night and Fog decree, and describes legal responsibility for the decree. Discusses crimes against Poles and Jews in connection with the decree, crimes against humanity, the blood bath of Sonnenburg, the legal basis for the judgment, Control Council Law No. 10, *ex post facto* law, the destruction of civil law as a crime against humanity, the conspiracy of criminal organizations, and concentration camps. Concludes with a review of 14 individual verdicts. Appendix lists the defendants and their sentences. 36 notes, 4-page index of names.

3390 SWEET, WILLIAM. "The Volksgerichtshof, 1934-1945," *Journal of Modern History* 1974 46: 314-329.

3391 THIELE-FREDERSDORF, HERBERT. „Das Urteil des Militärgerichtshofes Nr. III im Nürnberger Juristen-Prozeß," *Neue Juristische Wochenschrift* 1948 1(4): 122-126.

3392 UNITED STATES. NATIONAL ARCHIVES AND RECORDS SERVICE. Microfilm Publications. Record Group 238. Pamphlet describing M889, 53 rolls. Records of the United States Nuremberg War Crimes Trials. *United States of America* vs. *Josef Altstötter* et al. Case 3 of the 12 "subsequent" Nuremberg trials, known popularly as the Justice Case. February 17 - December 4, 1947. Washington: NARS, 1975. 12p. Includes 2 sets of 29 bound volumes, 1 in English, the other in German. There were 16 defendants, with each listed by name and position. The contents are identified by roll.

3393 WEINKAUFF, HERMANN, et al. *Die deutsche Justiz und der Nationalsozialismus.* 3 volumes. Stuttgart: Deutsche Verlags-Anstalt, 1968-1974.

3394 ZENTRAL-JUSTIZAMT FÜR DIE BRITISCHE ZONE. *Das Nürnberger Juristenurteil.* Hamburg: Rechts- und Staatswissenschaftlicher Verlag, 1948. 115p.

d. Case 4. The Pohl Case

3395 ARONSON, SHLOMO. *Reinhard Heydrich und die Frühgeschichte von Gestapo und SD.* Stuttgart: Deutsche Verlags-Anstalt, 1971. Contains some information on the Pohl case.

3396 BEYER, ALFRED. „Zum Tatbestand des Organisationsverbrechens. Unter Berücksichtigung des Urteils des amerikanischen MT. gegen Pohl und andere, vom 3. November 1947," *Spruchgerichte* 1948 2(April): 104-108. Examines the views of those who adopted Control Council Law No. 10, the judges in the Pohl case, and a trial in Hamm involving criminal organizations. The Nuremberg judges, contrary to the authors of Law No. 10 and the Hamm court, did not find that mere adherence to an organization in itself was a crime. The judgment in the Pohl case required that beyond mere membership, before a man could be guilty of a war crime he must have had a positive supporting attitude.

3397 SETTEL, ARTHUR. "Seven Nazis were Hanged. The Diary of a Witness," *Commentary* 1960 29(5): 1960: 369-379. Deals with the execution on June 7, 1951, of seven war criminals in Landsberg, Germany. They were Paul Blobel, Werner Braune, Erich

Naumann, Otto Ohlendorf, Oswald Pohl, Georg Schallermair, and Hans Schmidt.

3398 UNITED STATES. NATIONAL ARCHIVES AND RECORDS SERVICE. Microfilm Publications. Record Group 238. Pamphlet describing M890. 38 rolls. Records of the United States Nuremberg War Crimes Trials. United States of America vs. Oswald Pohl, et al. Case 4 of 12 "subsequent" Nuremberg trials, known popularly as the Pohl (SS) Case. January 13, 1947 - August 11, 1948. Washington: NARS, 1975. 12p. Contains the records of the trial of 18 defendants, all of whom are listed by position and rank. The contents are identified by roll.

3399 WARNER, ADOLPHE J. "What Case against the German Bankers?" Commercial and Financial Chronicle 1947 165(January 2): 4, 17.

e. Case 5. The Flick Case

3400 "A Travesty of Justice in the A.M.G. Tribunals," Nation 1948 166(8): 223-224. A letter to the editor critical of how Flick had escaped the gallows.

3401 Das Flick Urteil. Zusammenfassende Darstellung eines der Nürnberger Industrieprozesse. [no publication information given].

3402 DE WITT, DAVID S. "Military Tribunals for the Trial of War Criminals as International Courts," Michigan Law Review 1950 48(April): 881-883. The case of Flick v. Johnson. 13 notes.

3403 DROBISCH, KLAUS. "Flick und die Nazis," Zeitschrift für Geschichtswissenschaft 1966 14(3): 378-397.

3404 THIELEKE, KARL-HEINZ (ed.). Fall 5. Anklageplädoyer, ausgewählte Dokumente, Urteil des Flick-Prozesses, mit einer Studie über die "Arisierung" des Flick-Konzerns. Berlin: VEB Deutscher Verlag der Wissenschaften, 1965. 501p. The Flick trial was based on the assumption that large corporations promoted National Socialism and that preparations for war resulted from the exclusive control of German capital. Reviews the case against Friedrich Flick, Otto Steinbrinck, Konrad Kaletsch, Odilo Burkart, Bernhard Weiss, Hermann Terberger, and Alfred Rohde. The five charges against the coal manufacturer were using slave labor, plundering, crimes against humanity, financial support of the SS, and, in the case of Steinbrinck, membership in the SS. Discusses personal, private responsibility for war, superior orders, and the legitimacy of the Tribunal. Documents deal with weapons production, the Reich Coal Union (RVK), Reich Iron Union (RVE), forced labor, pillage, and the utilization of fascist terror organizations. Appendix 1 contains biographical sketches of leading company officials. Appendix 2 lists fascist laws, decrees, and ordinances for the implementation of Aryanization. 34 pages of notes, no bibliography.

3405 UNITED STATES. COURT OF APPEALS FOR THE DISTRICT OF COLUMBIA. Appeal No. 9883. "Brief for Appellees and Petition for Writ of Habeas Corpus," April 1, 1948. Deals with the appeal in the Flick case.

3406 UNITED STATES. NATIONAL ARCHIVES AND RECORDS SERVICE. Microfilm Publications. Record Group 238. Pamphlet describing M891. 42 rolls. Records of the United States Nuremberg War Crimes

Trials. United States of America vs. Friedrich Flick, et al. Case 5 of 12 "subsequent" Nuremberg trials, known popularly as the Industrialist Case. March 3 - December 22, 1947. Washington: NARS, 1975. 12p. Contains records of the trial of 6 defendants. Gives the names, locations, and nature of all the industrial companies involved. The contents are identified by roll.

f. Case 6. The Farben Case

3407 AMBRUSTER, HOWARD W. "Farben Nazis on Trial," Nation 1948 166(March 20): 321-323.

3408 AMBRUSTER, HOWARD W. "They Cheated the Gallows," Nation 1948 167(7): 176-178. Deals with officials of I.G. Farben.

3409 BORKIN, JOSEPH. The Crime and Punishment of I.G. Farben. New York: Free Press, 1978. 250p. History of the I.G. Farben corporation, an empire that enabled Germany to maneuver in the world of power politics. Describes Farben's exploitation of the chemical properties of Austria, Czechoslovakia, Poland, Norway, and France, and the building of a plant at Auschwitz for the production of oil and synthetic rubber. Discusses the World War I industrial complex, I.G. Farben's role in the preparation for World War II, its cartel partner, Standard Oil, as well as slave labor and mass murder. 19 pages of notes, 8-page index, 16 photographs.

3410 CLARK, DELBERT. "The Fabulous Farben Empire Faces Trial," New York Times Magazine 1947 (August 10): 12-13. 21 photographs.

3411 Das Urteil im IG-Farben Prozeß. Krefeld: 1948.

3412 Das Urteil im I.G.-Farben-Prozeß. Der vollständige Wortlaut mit Dokumentenanhang. Offenbach am Main: Bollwerk, 1948. Published in English as Judgment in the I.G. Farben Trial. Offenbach: Bollwerk, 1948. 184p. Trial held by OMGUS, Military Tribunal.

3413 "Disaster and Dishonor," Newsweek 1948 32(6): 27. On the sentencing of the directors of Farben and Krupp.

3414 DIX, HELLMUTH. "Die Urteile in den Nürnberger Wirtschaftsprozessen," Neue Juristische Wochenschrift 1949 2(17): 647-652. 65 notes.

3415 DU BOIS, JOSIAH E., and EDWARD JOHNSON. The Devil's Chemists: 24 Conspirators of the International Farben Cartel who manufacture Wars. Boston: Beacon, 1952. 374p. Published in England as Generals in Grey Suits: The Directors of the International "I.G. Farben" Cartel: Their Conspiracy Trial at Nuremberg. London: Bodley Head, 1953. 374p. Describes the extent of Farben's role in the production of gas for use in war and the manufacture of Cyclon B, which was used to exterminate prisoners at Auschwitz. Reviews the testimony of defendants on trial before the U.S. Military Tribunal No. 6 at Nuremberg. Contains a list of 23 defendants and their sentences (10 acquittals and a maximum sentence of 8 years), a letter by Judge Curtis G. Shake of the Tribunal to the Governor of Indiana recommending convicted defendant Max Ilgner for travel to the U.S. Appendices contain an organizational chart of I.G. Farbenindustrie A.G. (1938-1945), and biographical sketches of Farben defendants. Undocumented; 5-page index, 7 photographs.

3416 HEBERT, PAUL M. "The Nurnberg Subsequent Trials," *Insurance Counsel Journal* 1949 16(3): 226-232. The author served as Judge of U.S. Tribunal 6, which tried the IG Farben case. He gives a brief, factual account of the trials and notes that they focused attention on shortcomings in international law and furnished valuable material for future codification of such law.

3417 LOGAN ANDY. "Letter from Nuremberg," *New Yorker* 1947 23(December 27): 40, 42-47.

3418 RADANDT, HANS (ed.). *Fall 6. Ausgewählte Dokumente und Urteil des IG-Farben-Prozesses*. Berlin: VEB Deutscher Verlag der Wissenschaften, 1970. 325p. This East German publication charges that American imperialists would convict no criminal corporation, as reflected in the verdict of the case against the IG Farben Chemical Corporation. There would have been no war without Farben. Excerpts from 32 affidavits, memoranda, and letters pertaining to the Farben case. Discusses the legitimacy and composition of U.S. Military Tribunal 6. Appendix contains a list of the defendants and a brief history of their careers. 11 pages of notes, 11-page index of names and corporations.

3419 SASULY, RICHARD. *I.G. Farben*. New York: Boni and Gaer, 1947. 312p. An account of the rise of I.G. Farben, its political and economic role in Germany, its contribution to the plans for aggressive war, its relations with American business, and American occupation policy towards I.G. Farben, of which the author is critical. Appendix contains 49p. of documents.

3420 "The Farben Process," *Newsweek* 1947 30(10): 32, 35.

3421 THIELE-FREDERSDORF, HERBERT. „Das Urteil im I.G.-Farben-Prozeß," *Neue Juristische Wochenschrift* 1949 2(10): 376-377.

3422 UNITED STATES. NATIONAL ARCHIVES AND RECORDS SERVICE. Microfilm Publications. Record Group 238. Pamphlet describing M892. 113 rolls. Records of the United States Nuremberg War Crimes Trials. *United States of America* vs. *Carl Krauch*, et al. Case 6 of the 12 "subsequent" Nuremberg trials, known popularly as the IG Farben Case, or Industrialist Case. August 14, 1947 - July 30, 1948. Washington: NARS, 1977. 18p. Describes the records of the trial of 24 defendants charged with having launched an aggressive war. Lists defendants, their positions in various copies, and their sentences. The contents are identified by roll.

3423 VEICOPOULOS, NICOLAS. "Les Responsabilités des industriels dans la préparation de la guerre," *Revue de Droit International de Sciences Diplomatiques et Politiques* 1948 26(1): 53-62. Examines the role of IG Farben and Zaibatsu as supporters of the totalitarian regimes of Germany and Japan as shown from evidence presented as various war crimes trials. Stresses the need for effective control of world industries.

3424 WALENDY, UDO (ed.). *Auschwitz im IG-Farben Prozeß - Holocaust-Dokumente?* Vlotho an der Weser: Verlag für Volkstum und Zeitgeschichtsforschung, 1981. 404p. Collection of documents covering the IG-Farben corporation trial, which ended in 1948. Concentrates on the events at Auschwitz concentration camp and the extent of IG-Farben's involvement in the Holocaust. The editor maintains that the U.S. military tribunal did not justly try IG-Farben and that the trial was not designed to furnish evidence of the gassing of millions of Jews at Auschwitz-Birkenau. These documents are offered as evidence that IG-Farben was not responsible for the atrocities committed at Auschwitz. Contains documents offered as evidence by the prosecution, and testimony of defendants and witnesses. Appendices contain a list of the defendants at the trial and their sentences, as well as the text of Laws Nos. 9 and 10 of the Allied Council. 5-page index of names, no bibliography.

g. Case 7. Hostage Case

3425 Exposé des faits et jugement [du Tribunal Militaire Américain. les Etats-Unis d'Amérique contre Wilhelm List et consorts, accusés. Geneva: Comité International de la Croix-Rouge, [no date given]. 48p. Mimeograph.

3426 FISCH, ARNOLD G., JR. "Field Marshall Wilhelm List and the 'Hostages Case' at Nuremberg: An Historical Reassessment," Ph.D. dissertation, Pennsylvania State University, 1975. 236p. Abstracted in Dissertation Abstracts International 1975 36(4): 2360-A.

3427 SAWICKI, GEORGES. "Châtiment ou encouragement? (En marge du jugement du 19 février 1948, rendu par le Tribunal américain de Nuremberg, dans le procès intenté par les Etats-Unis contre Wilhelm List et co-accusés)," Revue de Droit International de Sciences Diplomatiques et Politiques 1948 26(2): 240-256. Criticism of the American handling of war crimes trials after the dissolution of the IMT. Discussion of the trial and judgment in the case of the German generals who directed the invasion of Greece and Yugoslavia and who later ruled these countries. 38 notes.

3428 UNITED STATES. NATIONAL ARCHIVES AND RECORDS SERVICE. Microfilm Publications. Record Group 238. Pamphlet describing M893. 48 rolls. Records of the United States Nuremberg War Crimes Trials. United States of America vs. Wilhelm List, et al. Case 7 of 12 "subsequent" Nuremberg trials, known popularly as the Hostage Case, sometimes called the Southeast Case. July 8, 1947 - February 19, 1948. Washington: NARS, 1974. 9p. Lists 12 defendants, their military positions, and the charges against them. Contents are identified by roll.

3429 ZÖLLNER, MARTIN, and KAZIMIERZ LESZCZYŃSKI (eds.). Fall 7. Das Urteil im Geiselmordprozeß, gefällt am 19. Februar 1948 vom Militärgerichtshof V der Vereinigten Staaten von Amerika. Berlin: VEB Deutscher Verlag der Wissenschaften, 1965. 250p. East German analysis of the 117-day trial of 10 German generals, including General Field Marshal Wilhelm List, for crimes against humanity from 1940-1945 in Yugoslavia, Greece, Albania, Norway, and Finland. The crimes included murder, mistreatment, deportation, and forced labor of prisoners of war and enemy citizens, pillage of public and private property, destruction of cities, and the murder of civilian hostages. Discusses the provisions of Control Council Law No. 10, ex post facto legislation, international treaties, and the violation of the Kellogg-Briand Pact. Deals with the status of Yugoslavia, Greece, and Norway, hostages and retaliation, and evidence at the trial. Summarizes the cases against each of the 10 generals. Appendices include a note on evidence provided by a Serbian military officer, chronologies of the resistance movements in Yugoslavia, Greece, and Albania, biographical sketches of the defendants, a list of documents used by the tribunal, a list prepared by Yugoslav civil courts of German generals who "deserved" execution, and a list of German generals who were not tried and subsequently became officers in the West German Army. 2-page bibliography, 9p. of notes, 9-page index of names, 5-page geographical index.

h. **Case 8. RuSHA Case**

3430 HAAG, JOHN. "National Socialism in Action: The RKFDV and the Alvensleben-Schönborn Estate Case," Historian 1964 26(2): 244-266. Some on the Ulrich Greifelt case, Case 8 of the Nuremberg 12. 44 notes.

3431 UNITED STATES. NATIONAL ARCHIVES AND RECORDS SERVICE. Microfilm Publications. Record Group 238. Pamphlet describing M894. 38 rolls. Records of the United States Nuremberg War Crimes Trials. United States of America vs. Ulrich Greifelt, et al. Case 8 of 12 "subsequent" Nuremberg trials, known popularly as the RuSHA (SS) Case. October 10, 1947 - March 10, 1948. Washington: NARS, 1973. 9p. Contains the records of the trial of 14 officers and deputies for a variety of war crimes. Lists the defendants by name and position. The contents are identified by roll.

i. **Case 9. Einsatzgruppen Case**

3432 ARNDT, ADOLF. "Zu den Einsatzgruppen-Prozessen," Neue Juristische Wochenschrift 1964 17(10): 486-488. 15 notes.

3433 GOLDSTEIN, ANATOLE, and MAXIMILIAN HURWITZ (eds.). Operation Murder. New York: World Jewish Congress, Institute of Jewish Affairs, 1949. 39p.

3434 LESZCZYŃSKI, KAZIMIERZ (ed.). Fall 9. Das Urteil im SS-Einsatzgruppenprozeß, gefällt am 10. April 1948 in Nürnberg vom Militärgerichtshof II der Vereinigten Staaten von Amerika. Berlin: Rütten and Loening, 1963. 259p. Examines the trial of 24 representatives of Einsatzgruppen A-D (July 25 to September 1947). Each Einsatzgruppe consisted of from 800 to 1200 men. Officers were recruited from the Gestapo, the SD, and the SS. Discusses the function and composition of the Einsatzgruppen, the authenticity of reports on them, and the extent of their enterprises. Deals with treatment of prisoners of war, methods of execution, the defense of necessity, the ideological basis for annihilation, and superior orders. Reviews individual cases of 22 defendants. Appendices contain a list of the verdicts, a comparison of ranks of the German prosecution. 7p. of notes, 3-page index of names, 2-page geographical index.

3435 MARCUS, ROBERT S. "The Greatest Murder Trial in History," Congress Weekly, A Review of Jewish Interests 1948 (May 14): 5-7.

3436 MUSMANNO, MICHAEL A. The Eichmann Kommandos. Philadelphia: Macrae Smith, 1961. 268p. Report on the Einsatzgruppen trial (September 1946 to April 1947). The author was an American naval officer and presiding judge. Discusses the military court, criticism of the Nuremberg trials, and the indictment against 24 defendants charged with the murder of more than one million people. Contains biographical information on Adolf Eichmann and the history of the Einsatzgruppen under him. The organization was made up of para-military units employed on the eastern front. Contains biographical sketches of 23 defendants, including Otto Ohlendorf, Heinz Jost, and Erich Jost. 2-page essay on source material.

3437 ROESEN, ANTON. "Rechtsfragen der Einsatzgruppen-Prozesse," Neue Juristische Wochenschrift 1964 17(4): 133-136; 17(24): 1111-1112. 25 notes.

3438 UNITED STATES. NATIONAL ARCHIVES AND RECORDS SERVICE. Microfilm Publications. Record Group 238. Pamphlet describing M895. 38 rolls. Records of the United States Nuremberg War Crimes Trials. United States of America vs. Otto Ohlendorf, et al. Case 9 of the 12 "subsequent" Nuremberg trials, popularly known as the Einsatzgruppen Case. September 15, 1947 - April 10, 1948. Washington: NARS, 1973. 11p. Lists 24 commanders and officers indicted, gives their ranks and positions, and discusses the 3 charges against them. The contents are identified by roll.

j. **Case 10. Krupp Case**

3439 ENGELMANN, BERNT. Krupp: Legenden und Wirklichkeit. Munich: Schneekluth, 1969.

3440 HEROLD, G.W. "Peculiar Case of Alfred Krupp," United Nations World 1953 7(April): 44.

3441 HONIG, FREDERICK. "German Industrialists on Trial," World Affairs 1948 2(April): 175-186. Short summary of the trial of German industrialists. Criticizes the trials, particularly the fact that the prosecution did not indict the corporations as distinct from the individual defendants and that none of the defendants was deprived of his property.

3442 KAUFMAN, JOSEPH W. "Krupp: What Price Expediency?" New Republic 1951 124(9): 15-16.

3443 MANCHESTER, WILLIAM. The Arms of Krupp, 1587-1968. Boston: Little, Brown, 1968. 1068p. A major study of Germany that contains a great deal on the Nuremberg IMT and the later trial, conviction, and imprisonment of Alfried Krupp.

3444 MASCHKE, HERMANN M. Das Krupp Urteil und das Problem der "Plünderung". Göttingen: Musterschmidt Wissenschaftlicher Verlag, 1951. 141p.

3445 MÜHLEN, NORBERT. Die Krupps. Frankfurt am Main: Scheffler, 1960.

3446 TAYLOR, TELFORD. "The Krupp Trial: Fact v. Fiction," Columbia Law Review 1953 53(2): 197-210. 89 notes.

3447 UNITED STATES. NATIONAL ARCHIVES AND RECORDS SERVICE. Microfilm Publications. Record Group 238. Pamphlet describing M896. 69 rolls. Records of the United States Nuremberg War Crimes Trials. United States of America vs. Alfried Krupp, et al. Case 10 of 12 "subsequent" Nuremberg trials, popularly known as the Krupp Case or Industrialist Case. August 16, 1947 - July 31, 1948. Washington: NARS, 1977. 12p. Lists the 12 defendants, gives their positions, and discusses related microfilmed records. The contents are identified by roll.

3448 WILMOWSKY, TILO VON. **Warum wurde Krupp verurteilt? Legende und Justizirrtum**. Stuttgart: Friedrich Vorwerk, 1950. 224p. Düsseldorf and Vienna: Econ-Verlag, 1962. 2nd edition. Number 10 of the Nuremberg 12 "subsequent" trials. The author, Alfred Krupp's brother-in-law, opposes the concept of collective guilt for National Socialist crimes. Maintains that Krupp's 1948 conviction before an American tribunal was an unjust political act arising out of war psychosis. This biography of Krupp deals with the history of the Krupp family's weapons factory from 1914 through the end of World War II, the German industrialist as a war criminal, and Krupp's plea of guilt in connection with forced labor in his factories. The book traces the wartime activities of Gustav Krupp and how his son became his "stand in" after the 1946 IMT dropped charges against him. Alfred Krupp was acquitted of some charges against him, but was convicted of plundering and using forced labor in his factories. Based on documents from Alfried Krupp's trial, no bibliography, 4 photographs.

k. **Case 11. Ministries Case**

3449 BOVERI, MARGARET. **Der Diplomat vor Gericht**. Berlin: Minerva, 1948. 88p. Report on the Wilhelmstrasse Trial of 18 Reichs diplomats who were tried by the American Military Tribunal at Nuremberg on November 3, 1947, for crimes against the peace. Concerned primarily with the case of Ernst von Weizsäcker, whom the author claims was innocent. Reviews documentation, testimony of witnesses, and the history of the German diplomatic corps. 6-page index of names, undocumented.

3450 DIRKSEN, HERBERT VON. **Moscow, Tokyo, London: Twenty Years of German Foreign Policy**. Norman: University of Oklahoma Press, 1952.

3451 HILL, LEONIDAS E. (ed.). **Die Weizsäcker-Papiere**. Berlin: Propyläen, 1974. 683p.

3452 HILL, LEONIDAS E. "The Wilhelmstrasse in the Nazi Era," **Political Science Quarterly** 1967 82(4): 546-570. 90 notes.

3453 KEMPNER, ROBERT M.W., and CARL HAENSEL (ed.). **Das Urteil im Wilhelmstrassen-Prozeß. Der amtliche Wortlaut der Entscheidung im Fall Nr. 11 des Nürnberger Militärtribunals gegen von Weizsäcker und andere, mit abweichender Urteilsbegründung, Berichtigungsbeschlüssen, den grundlegenden Gesetzesbestimmungen, einem Verzeichnis der Gerichtspersonen und Zeugen**. Munich: Alfons Bürger Verlag, 1950. 346p. Contains an overview of the judgment, an index to the literature of the case, a list of all the defendants, with a brief treatment of each, and a discussion of the various charges against them. Also discusses membership in criminal organizations.

3454 KORDT, ERICH. **Nicht aus den Akten. Die Wilhelmstrasse in Frieden und Krieg: Begebungen, Eindrücke, 1928-1945**. Stuttgart: Union Deutsche Verlagsgesellschaft. 1950. 441p.

3455 "Last Judgments," **Newsweek** 1949 33(17): 36, 38.

3456 LICHTEN, H.E. (ed.). **Das Urteil im Prozeß gegen die Wilhelmstraße**. Offenbach: 1949.

3457 MEDICUS, FRANZ A. **Das Reichsministerium des Innern: Geschichte und Aufbau.** Berlin: Junker und Dünnhaupt, 1940. 88p.

3458 RÖHL, J.C.G. "Higher Civil Service in Germany," *Journal of Contemporary History* 1967 2(3): 101-121.

3459 TILLMANN, H., and P. KIRCHEISEN (eds.). *Dokumente zum Wilhelmstrasseprozeß mit Auszügen aus dem Urteil und der Anklageschrift*. Berlin: Deutscher Verlag der Wissenschaften, 1970.

3460 UNITED STATES. NATIONAL ARCHIVES AND RECORDS SERVICE. Microfilm Publications. Record Group 238. Pamphlet describing M897. 173 rolls. Records of the United States Nuremberg War Crimes Trials. *United States of America* vs. *Ernst von Weizsaecker*, et al. Case 11 of 12 "subsequent" Nuremberg trials, known popularly as the Ministries Case. December 20, 1947 - April 14, 1949. Washington: NARS, 1979. 23p. There were 21 defendants, mostly high ranking public officials. List them by name and identifies their positions. Discusses related records that have been microfilmed. The contents are identified by roll.

3461 WEINBERG, GERHARD L. *The Foreign Policy of Hitler's Germany: Diplomatic Revolution in Europe, 1933-36*. Chicago: University of Chicago Press, 1970.

1. *Case 12. High Command Case*

3462 BETZ, HERMAN DIETER. *Das OKW und seine Haltung zum Landkriegsvölkerrecht im zweiten Weltkrieg*. Bamberg: Difo-Druck, 1970.

3463 CLARK, DELBERT. "Bubble, Bubble, Toil and Trouble," *Saturday Review of Literature* 1952 35(December 6): 29, 38.

3464 DOUGLAS, J.J. "High Command Case: A Study in Staff and Command Responsibility," *International Lawyer* 1972 6(4): 686-705.

3465 *Fall 12. Das Urteil gegen das Oberkommando der Wehrmacht, gefällt am 28. Oktober 1948 in Nürnberg vom Militärgerichtshof V der Vereinigten Staaten von Amerika*. Berlin: Rütten & Loening, 1960. 296p. Analysis of the High Command (OKW) case (November 28, 1947 to October 28, 1948) against 13 field marshals and generals. Reviews the 4 counts of the indictment, Control Council Law No. 10, international treaties, and the course of the proceedings. Describes the structure of the German military, the High Command of the Wehrmacht (OKW), air force (OKL), marines (OKM), and Heer (OKH). Discusses the defense of superior orders, hostages and retaliation, partisan warfare, and the responsibility for atrocities in the occupied zones. Contains sections on individual defendants outlining crimes committed, military position, and participation in war operations. Concludes with a list of the sentences handed down. 28 notes. 6 pages of facsimiles of orders issued by the OKW.

3466 "Guilty and Not Guilty: Thirteen Top German Commanders," *Newsweek* 1948 32(November 8): 27. Case 12 of the NMT trials.

3467 HEINZE, KURT, and KARL SCHILLING (comps.). *Die Rechtsprechung der Nürnberger Militärtribunale: Sammlung der Rechtsthesen der Urteile und gesonderten Urteilsbegründungen der dreizehn Nürnberger Prozesse*. Bonn: Girardet, 1952. 356p. Complete study of the 12 "subsequent" Nuremberg trials. Based on documentary sources; 11-page bibliography.

3468 HOBBS, MALCOLM. "Nürnberg's Indecent Burial," *Nation* 1949 169(December 3): 634-635.

3469 Procès verbal de l'audience du 27 octobre 1948, 9, 30 heures - 16, 30 heures du Tribunal Militaire Américain, sous la présidence du Judge John C. Young. Les Etats-Unis d'Amerique contre Wilhelm von Leeb et consorts, accusé. Nuremberg, Allemagne. [Geneva]: [Comité International de la Croix-Rouge], [no date given]. 123p. Mimeograph.

3470 RICHMAN, FRANK N. "Highlights of the Nurnberg Trials," Federal Rules Decisions 1948 7(February): 581-584. Short report on the organization and trial procedure of the American Military Tribunal at Nuremberg.

3471 UNITED STATES. NATIONAL ARCHIVES AND RECORDS SERVICE. Microfilm Publications. Record Group 238. Pamphlet describing M898. 69 rolls. Records of the United States Nuremberg War Crimes Trials. United States of America vs. Wilhelm Von Leeb, et al. Case 12 of 12 "subsequent" Nuremberg trials, known popularly as the High Command Case. November 28, 1947 - October 28, 1948. Washington: NARS, 1976. 14p. There were 14 general officers of the German military force indicted in this case for war crimes. Brief vita for each, with a list of their sentences. The contents are identified by volume.

C. WORKS ON DE-NAZIFICATION PROCEEDINGS

3472 BOYLE, KAY. The Smoking Mountain, Stories of Germany During the Occupation. London: 1952. New York: Knopf, 1963. Description of the Trial of Heinrich Baab.

3473 "Denazification," Social Research 1947 14(1): 59-74. A letter from a German, anti-Nazi lawyer. Contains a foreword by Alvin Johnson.

3474 "De-Nazification - Re-Nazification ('a farce,' 'a travesty,' 'a failure')," Wieber Library Bulletin 1949 3:1-3. A series of replies received by the journal from 3 competent observers on the scene.

3475 FITZGIBBON, CONSTANTINE. Denazification. New York: Norton, 1969. 222p.

3476 "German Churches and War Crimes Trials," Christian Century 1948 65(27): 677.

3477 GOLDMAN, FRANK. "The Failure of Denazification," National Jewish Monthly 1950 (July-August): 394-397.

3478 HERZ, JOHN H. "The Fiasco of Denazification in Germany," Political Science Quarterly 1948 63(4): 569-594. Discusses the technical and political difficulties involved in an effective denazification program. 114 notes.

3479 NAPOLI, JOSEPH F. "Denazification from America's Viewpoint," Annals of the American Academy of Political and Social Science 1949 (July): 115-123.

3480 PLISCHKE, ELMER. "Denazification Law and Procedure," American Journal of International Law 1947 41 (4): 807-827. 69 notes.

3481 RATZ, MICHAEL, et al. (comps.). Die Justiz und die Nazis: zur Strafverfolgung von Nazismus und Neonazismus seit 1945. Frankfurt am Main: Röderberg, 1979. 184p.

3482 ROTH, GÜNTHER, and KURT A. WOLFE. *The American Denazification of Germany. A Historical Survey and an Appraisal.* Columbus: Ohio State University, 1954-1955. 49p.

3483 SPERBER, HARRY N. "German Justice," *Congress Weekly, A Review of Jewish Interests* 1949 (March 7): 8-10. A denunciation of the methods used in German denazification courts. Examines the guilt of Franz von Papen and Hans Fritsche and comments on their crimes and punishments.

3484 STONE, SHEPARD. "I Had to Join - I Was Never a Good Nazi," *New York Times Magazine*, December 15, 1946: 12-13. A description of the denazification proceedings in the American Zone of Germany.

3485 UNITED STATES. DEPARTMENT OF STATE. *Germany 1947-1949: The Story in Documents.* State Department Publication No. 3556. Washington: GPO, 1950. 631p. Brief discussion of denazification and war crimes, with a chart summarizing the verdicts of the 12 "subsequent" Nuremberg trials (pp. 110-118). Some remarks and statistics on the Dachau trials.

3486 *War Crimes and Denazification in the US Zone of Germany (with Supplements).* New York: Institute of Jewish Affairs of the World Jewish Congress, 1948-1949. Mimeograph.

D. SABOTEURS CASE

3487 BATTLE, GEORGE GORDON. "Military Tribunals," *Virginia Law Review* 1942 29(3): 255-271. Saboteur's case (*Ex Parte Quirin*), 319 US 1 [1942]. 50 notes.

3488 CRAMER, MYRON C. "Military Commissions: Trial of the Eight Saboteurs," *Washington Law Review* 1942 17(4): 247-255.

3489 CUSHMAN, ROBERT E. "The Case of the Nazi Saboteurs," *American Political Science Review* 1942 36(6): 1082-1091.

3490 HYDE, CHARLES C. "Aspects of the Saboteur Cases," *American Journal of International Law* 1943 37(1): 89-91. Deals with a series of Supreme Court cases addressed to the problem of why a captured spy does not have the same rights as a captured soldier. The Court decided that a spy is an offender against international laws of war and is, therefore, subject to arrest, trial, and punishment by a military tribunal. The theoretical distinction is that a spy is a noncombatant. Based on secondary sources, 9 notes.

3491 KRAUS, ROSE. "Saboteurs and Military Justice," *St. John's Law Review* 1942 17(11): 29-34. 22 notes.

3492 M.L.C., JR. "The Military Commission in 1942," *Virginia Law Review* 1942 29(3): 317-338. On the Saboteurs case. 119 notes.

3493 "Military Trial of Saboteurs," *Indiana Law Journal* 1943 18(3): 246-247.

3494 SANDERS, JARED Y., JR. "Court Martial for Nazi Spies," *Congressional Record*, 77th Congress, 2nd Session. *Appendix* 88(9): A2685. July 9, 1942. Remarks by a Louisiana Congressman.

3495 SCHILLING, GEORGE T. "Constitutional Law - Saboteurs and the Jurisdiction of Military Commissions," Michigan Law Review 1942 41(3): 481-495. On the Saboteurs Case. 59 notes.

3496 UNITED STATES. NATIONAL ARCHIVES AND RECORDS SERVICE. FEDERAL REGISTER DIVISION. "Appointment of a Military Commission," Federal Register 1942 7(132): 5103 (July 7, 1942). Discusses a military commission appointed by President Roosevelt to try Ernst Peter Burger, George John Dasch, Herbert Hans Haupt, Henry Harm Heinck, Hermann Otto Neubauer, Edward John Kerling, Richard Quirin, and Werner Thiel. This was the first American war crimes trial conducted before the war ended.

E. ALBERT BURY AND WILHELM HAFNER TRIAL

3497 UNITED STATES. ARMY. THIRD ARMY HEADQUARTERS, GERMANY. United States v. Albert (Alfred) Bury and Wilhelm Hafner: Review of Proceedings in the First Trial of Germans before a Military Commission for Killing an American Aviator in Violation of the Laws of War. [no city given]: [no publisher given], 1945.

F. HADAMAR TRIAL

3498 KINTNER, EARL W. (ed.). Trial of Alfons Klein, Adolf Wahlmann, Heinrich Ruoff, Karl Willig, Adolf Merkle, Irmgard Huber, and Philipp Blum (The Hadamar Trial). London: William Hodge, 1949. 250p. Volume 4 of Maxwell-Fyfe (see Introduction). The trial was held in Wiesbaden in October 1945 before an American military commission for the trial of members of the staff of an institution near Hadamar, Germany, for the killing of Polish and Russian nationals in 1944 and 1945. The 7 German civilians were charged with killing more than 400 people at Hadamar by injections or poisonous drugs.

G. BORKUM ISLAND TRIAL

3499 HAMMERSTEIN, KURT WENTZEL. Landsberg, Henker des Rechts? Wuppertal: Abendland, 1952.

3500 KOESSLER, MAXIMILIAN. "Borkum Island Tragedy and Trial," Journal of Criminal Law and Criminology 1956 47(2): 183-196. 57 notes.

3501 UNITED STATES. NATIONAL ARCHIVES AND RECORDS SERVICE. Microfilm Publications. Record Groups 153 and 338. Pamphlet describing M1103. 7 rolls. Records of United States Army War Crimes Trials. United States of America vs. Kurt Goebell, et al. February 6 - March 21, 1946; and United States of America vs. August Haesiker, June 26, 1947. Washington: NARS, 1981. 12p. Both cases are concerned with the August 4, 1944, killing of 7 American airmen on the German island of Borkum in the North Sea. They are known popularly as the Borkum Island case. There were 22 Germans indicted, but only 15 were found and tried. Lists their verdicts and sentences and related trial records. The contents are identified by roll.

H. MALMÉDY TRIAL

3502 ASCHENAUER, RUDOLF. Der Malmédy-Fall 7 Jahre nach dem Urteil. Munich: [no publisher given], 1953. 10p. Published in English as Seven Years after the Malmedy Trail: An unsolved Problem endangering US Prestige in Europe. Miesbach: [no publisher given], 1953.

3503 ASCHENAUER, RUDOLF. Um Recht und Wahrheit im Malmédy-Fall. Eine Stellungnahme zum Bericht eines Untersuchungsausschusses des amerikanischen Senats in Sachen Malmédy-Prozeß. Nuremberg: Val. Höfling 1950. 34p. Discusses the Malmédy case and concludes that the defendants were judged guilty before the trial and that the trial itself was a sham, devoid of all American standards of justice.

3504 "Clemency: Malmedy Massacre," Time 1949 53(3): 19.

3505 DOENECKE, JUSTUS D. "Protest Over Malmedy: A Case of Clemency?" Peace and Change 1976 4(2): 28-33. Frederick J. Libby of the National Council for the Prevention of War campaigned for clemency for the German soldiers responsible for the Malmédy massacre of 1944, maintaining that the United States should apply to itself the same standards it applied to the Axis powers.

3506 DONIHI, ROBERT. "Occupation Justice," South Texas Law Journal 1955 1(4): 333-358. 76 notes. A general history of occupation justice, with emphasis on American courts in Germany.

3507 GLAZER, NATHAN. "The Method of Senator McCarthy: Its Origins, Its Uses, and Its Prospects," Commentary 1953 15(3): 244-256. On Malmédy hearings.

3508 GREIL, LOTHAR. Die Wahrheit über Malmedy. 3rd edition. Munich: Schild, 1958.

3509 GREVY, R. "La Répression des crimes de guerre en droit belge," Revue de Droit Pénal et de Criminologie 1947-1948 28: 806-823. Malmédy.

3510 "Hold Up Executions of 'Malmedy Germans,'" Christian Century 1949 66(13): 389.

3511 UNITED STATES. CONGRESS. SENATE. COMMITTEE ON ARMED SERVICES. Malmedy Massacre Investigation. Hearings before a Subcommittee of the Committee on Armed Services . . . Pursuant to S. Res. 42, Investigation of Action of Army with Respect to Trial of Persons Responsible for the Massacre of American Soldiers, Battle of the Bulge, Near Malmedy, Belgium, December 1944. 81st Congress, 1st Session, 2 parts. Washington: GPO, 1949.

3512 UTLEY, FREDA. "Malmedy and McCarthy," American Mercury 1954 79(November): 53-58.

3513 WEINGARTNER, JAMES J. Crossroads of Death, the Story of the Malmédy Massacre and Trial. Berkeley: University of California Press, 1979. 274p. The massacre of American soldiers by the Schutzstaffel in December 1944 captures "the essence of the Nazi evil." In a trial held by the U.S. Army in the spring and summer of 1946, all defendants were found guilty and over half were sentenced to death. No one was executed. By the end of 1956 the last convict had been released. Discusses the findings of the War Crimes Board of Review that the evidence was insufficient for conviction. Deals extensively with Wisconsin Senator Joseph McCarthy's participation in the trial. 2-page bibliography, 8-page index, 18 photographs.

3514 WHITING, CHARLES. Massacre at Malmédy: The Story of Jochen Peiper's Battle Group, Ardennes, December 1944. New York: Stein and Day, 1971. 198p. The story of Colonel Jochen Peiper, regimental commander in the German army. Describes one of the major massacres of World War II in December 1944. Brief examination of the Dachau trial proceedings and Peiper's sentence to death by hanging. Cites testimony of witnesses to the attack on American prisoners of war. 1-page bibliography, 17 photographs, 5 maps.

3515 ZIEMSSEN, DIETRICH. The Malmédy Trial: A Report Based on Documents and Personal Experiences. Munich: 1952. Der Malmédy Prozeß. [Munich]: Plesse, [no date given].

I. BUCHENWALD/DACHAU TRIAL

3516 "Death in the Sunshine," Time 1947 49(23): 31-32. Execution at the Landsberg Prison of Willi Frey.

3517 DENSON, WILLIAM D., et al. An Information Booklet on the Buchenwald Concentration Camp Case: The United States of America v. Josias Prince zu Waldeck et al., to Be Heard at Camp Dachau, Germany 11 April 1947. Dachau: 1947.

3518 GROSSMANN, KURT R. "The Trial of Ilse Koch," Congress Weekly, A Review of Jewish Interests 1950 (December 18): 7-9.

3519 KOESSLER, MAXIMILIAN. "The Ilse Koch Senate Investigation and Its Legal Problems on Double Jeopardy and res judicata," Missouri Law Review 1958 23(1): 1-23. 91 notes.

3520 "The Guilty: The Butchers of Buchenwald Hear the Stern Judgment of Civilization," Life 1947 23(8): 39. 4 photographs.

3521 UNITED STATES. CONGRESS. SENATE. COMMITTEE ON EXPENDITURES IN THE EXECUTIVE DEPARTMENTS. Conduct of Ilse Koch War Crimes Trial. Hearing before Investigations Subcommittee. 80th Congress, 2nd Session, pursuant to Senate Resolution 189, September 28 - December 9, 1948. Washington: GPO, 1949. Senate Report No. 1775. Several parts. Part 5, pp. 999-1279, particularly pp. 1197-1279, deal with the commutation of Koch's sentence from life to 4 years. Much on the testimony of high U.S. officials on Buchenwald and the original trial in Dachau, which lasted from April 11 to August 17, 1947. There were 30 defendants, including Ilse Koch.

3522 UNITED STATES. DEPARTMENT OF STATE. "Execution of Landsberg War Criminals," Department of State Bulletin 1951 24(625): 988. June 18, 1951. Press release on the execution at Landsberg prison of Oswald Pohl, Otto Ohlendorf, Erich Naumann, Paul Blobel, Werner Braune, Hans Schmidt, and George Schallermair.

3523 UNITED STATES. OFFICE OF THE HIGH COMMISSIONER FOR GERMANY. "Landsberg: A Documentary Report," Information Bulletin {HICCG, Berlin} 1951 (February): 3-8, 55-67. The full text of the decision of John J. McCloy regarding amnesty for German war criminals convicted by the Nuremberg Military Tribunals.

3524 Wieder Hinrichtungen in Landsberg? Munich: A. Girnth, 1951.

J. MISCELLANEOUS

3525 "Documents. The Case of Benjamin vs. Mayer: Krieger vs. Mittelmann," Congress Weekly, A Review of Jewish Interests 1950 (December 11): 12-14. Text of the decision rendered by the

Arbitration Tribunal under the auspices of the American Jewish Congress on the charges of B. Krieger against Major Mittelmann that the latter murdered Krieger's brother in a German concentration camp.

3526 UNITED STATES. NATIONAL ARCHIVES AND RECORDS SERVICE. Microfilm Publications. Record Groups 153 and 338. Pamphlet describing M1191. 2 rolls. Records of the United States Army War Crimes Trials. United States of America vs. Hans Joachim Georg Geiger, et al. July 9 - August 5, 1947. Washington: NARS, 1982. 14p. In this case 11 defendants were tried for crimes committed at Ebensee Outcamp of the Mauthausen concentration camp. Discusses jurisdiction for this case and the classes of 489 Army war crimes trials. Identifies the 11 defendants and discusses all trial records. The contents are identified by roll.

XI
ALLIED MILITARY TRIBUNALS AND NATIONAL TRIALS

A. GENERAL WORKS

3527 COWLES, WILLARD B. "Trials of War Criminals (Non-Nuremberg)," American Journal of International Law 1948 42(2): 299-319. Argues that there was adequate precedent in law for the Nuremberg IMT trial. Based on and in some ways a summary of 9 cases reported in Volume I of Law Reports of Trials of War Criminals The cases summarized are: (1) the Peleus case, (2) the murder of American "saboteurs" in Italy, (3) the execution without trial of a British flyer in the Netherlands, (4) hundreds of insane asylum murders, (5) the scuttling of German submarines in violation of the terms of surrender, (6) Japanese murder of American pilots, (7) German shooting of prisoners of war, (8) German lynching of prisoners of war, and (9) Zyklon B gas chamber murders. Based on primary and secondary sources; 20 notes.

3528 FOOT, MICHAEL [pseudonym, CASSIUS]. The Trial of Mussolini: Being a Verbatim Report of the First Great War Crimes Trial held in London Sometime in 1944 or 1945. London: V. Gollancz, 1943. 112p.

3529 KAUL, FRIEDRICH KARL. "Die westdeutsche Haltung zur Frage der Rechtshilfe durch sozialistische Staaten in Strafverfahren gegen nazistische Systemverbrecher," Zeitschrift für Geschichtswissenschaft 1968 16(1): 68-74. Rejects West German charges that socialist states have not cooperated in providing evidence in cases against Nazi criminals. Cites cases where legal aid from socialist countries has contributed to the conviction of Nazis, and reproduces a document dated December 23, 1964, from the North Rhine-Westphalian justice ministry showing that the West German government intentionally rejected cooperation by socialist governments. West Germans accused Poles and Czechs of withholding for political reasons evidence against war criminals. They admittedly rejected an exchange of legal documents with the Poles and Czechs on the ground that they had made accusations against West German judges and other government officials purely for political reasons. Based on court records; 10 notes.

3530 KIPPENBERGER, H.K. "War Criminals Trials Law Reports," New Zealand Law Journal 1947 23(12): 180-182. A Review of Law Reports of Trials of War Criminals, selected and prepared by the United Nations War Crimes Commission.

3531 MENZEL, EBERHARD. „Die ausländische Kriegsverbrechergesetzgebung (Polen, Norwegen, Niederlande)," Archiv des öffentlichen Rechts 1949 75: 424-452.

3532 NEUMANN, FRANZ. "The War Crimes Trials," World Politics 1949 2(October): 135-147. Brief inquiry into the significance of the war crimes trials for future research in the fields of international law and political science. Shows how research activities can be coordinated.

UNITED NATIONS WAR CRIMES COMMISSION (UNWCC). Law Reports of Trials of War Criminals, Selected and prepared by the United Nations War Crimes Commission. 15 volumes. London: HMPO, 1947-1949. This set contains law reports on 89 cases illustrating important questions of international and national law. The records of the Nuremberg IMT and the Tokyo IMT have not been included. Each report contains a summary of the debates, the judgment, and commentary on the most important questions of law. Each case contains a list of members of the tribunal, charges made against the defendants, the case for the prosecution and defense, closing statements, notes on the cases, and sentences. This and other basic information as well as appendices and indexes are found in the first 14 volumes.

3533 UNWCC. Law Reports. Volume 1, 1947, 127p. CASES 1-9. Reports of 6 cases tried by British military courts and 3 by American military commissions. These cases include crimes against prisoners of war, the killing of sailors attempting to escape from a torpedoed ship, use of poison gas on inmates of concentration camps, and killing by poison administered by medical personnel in a sanatorium. CASE 1. The Peleus Trial. Trial of Kapitanleutnant Heinz Eck and 4 others for killing members of the crew of the Greek steamship Peleus, which was sunk on the high seas. British Military Court for the trial of war criminals held at the War Crimes Court, Hamburg, October 17-20, 1945. CASE 2. The Dostler Trial. Trial of General Anton Dostler, Commander of the 75th German Army Corps, United States Military Commission, Rome, October 8-12, 1945, for shooting an unarmed prisoner of war. CASE 3. The Almelo Trial. Trial of Otto Sandrock and 3 others. British Military Court for the trial of war criminals, held at the Court House, Almelo, Holland, November 24-26, 1945, for killing a British soldier and a civilian. CASE 4. The Hadamar Trial. Trial of Alfons Klein and 6 others. United States Military Commission, appointed by the Commanding General, Western Military District, U.S.F.E.T., Wiesbaden, Germany, October 8-15, 1945, for killing allied civilians by means of injections. CASE 5. The Scuttled U-Boats Trial. Trial of Oberleutnant Gerhard Grumpelt. British Military Court held at Hamburg, Germany, February 12-13, 1946, for sinking a submarine in violation of the terms of surrender. CASE 6. The Jaluit Atoll Trial. Trial of Rear-Admiral Nisuke Masuda and 4 others of the Imperial Japanese Navy. United States Military Commission, United States Naval Air Base, Kwajalein Island, Kwajalein Atoll, Marshall Island, December 7-13, 1945, for shooting unarmed prisoners of war. CASE 7. The Dreierwalde Trial. Trial of Karl Amberger, formerly Oberfeldwebel. British Military Court, Wuppertal, Germany, March 11-14, 1946, for shooting unarmed prisoners of war. CASE 8. The Essen Lynching Trial. Trial of Erich Heyer and 6 others. British Military Court for the trial of war criminals, Essen, Germany, December 18-19, 21, 22, 1945, for killing unarmed prisoners of war. CASE 9. The Zyklon B. Trial. Trial of Bruno Tesch and 2 others. British Military Court, Hamburg, Germany, March 1-8, 1946, for the murder of interned allied civilians by means of poison gas.

3534 UNWCC. Law Reports. Volume 2, 1947, 156p. CASE 10. The Belsen Trial. Trial of Josef Kramer and 44 others. British Military Court, Lüneburg, September 17 to November 17, 1945, for killing civilians and mistreating military personnel in Belsen and Auschwitz concentration camps. This trial deals with the rise of concentration camps as instruments of terrorism and atrocity. There were more than 300 camps in territories occupied by Germany. Belsen was in Germany. Contains a chart identifying the names of the accused, the charges against them, their positions in the camps, verdicts, and sentences. 2-page index.

3535 UNWCC. Law Reports. Volume 3, 1948, 123p. CASES 11-20. A record of widely diverse cases held by various national and military courts all over the world. CASE 11. Trial of Kriminalassistent Karl-Hans Hermann Klinge. Eidsivating Lagmannsrett and Supreme Court of Norway, December 8, 1945, and February 27, 1946, for torture and other maltreatment of civilians. CASE 12. Trial of Kriminalsekretär Richard Wilhelm Hermann Bruns and 2 others. Eidsivating Lagmannsrett and the Supreme Court of Norway, March 20, and July 3, 1946, for torture. CASE 13. Trial of Robert Wagner, Gauleiter and Head of the civil government of Alsace during the occupation, and 6 others. Permanent Military Tribunal at Strasbourg April 23 to May 3, 1946, and Court of Appeal, July 24, 1946, for killing prisoners of war and deporting Jews and French nationals from Alsace. CASE 14. Trial of Gunther Thiele and Georg Steinert. United States Military Commission, Augsburg, Germany, June 13, 1945, for killing an American prisoner of war. CASE 15. Trial of Peter Back. United States Military Commission, Ahrweiler, Germany, June 16, 1945, for killing an unarmed American airman who had parachuted to earth. CASE 16. Trial of Albert Bury and Wilhelm Hafner. United States Military Commission, Freising, Germany, July 15, 1945, for killing an American prisoner of war. CASES 17 and 18. Trials of Anton Schosser, Josef Goldbrunner, and Alfons Jacob Wilm. United States Military Commissions at Dachau, September 14-15, 17, 1945, for killing a prisoner of war. CASE 19 Trial of Erich Killinger and 4 others. Dulag Luft Trial. British Military Court, Wuppertal, Germany, November 26 to December 3, 1945, for maltreatment of British prisoners of war. CASE 20. Trial of Yamamoto Chusaburo. British Military Court, Kuala Lumpur, January 30 to February 1, 1946, for killing a civilian for stealing rice.

3536 UNWCC. Law Reports. Volume 4, 1948, 130p. CASES 21-24. CASE 21. Trial of Tomoyuki Yamashita. United States Military Commission, Manila, October 8 to December 7, 1945, for responsibility for war crimes committed by his troops. Yamashita was condemned to death and his sentence was then appealed to the United States Supreme Court, where it was rejected as not being within that court's jurisdiction. United States Supreme Court judgment was delivered February 4, 1946. CASE 22.

The Abbaye Ardenne Trial. Trial of SS Brigadeführer Kurt Meyer. Canadian Military Court, Aurich, Germany, December, 10-28, 1945, for the shooting of prisoners of war by men under his command. CASE 23. Trial of Major Karl Rauer and 6 others. British Military Court, Wuppertal, Germany, February 18, 1946, for killing prisoners of war. CASE 24. Trial of Kurt Student. British Military Court, Lüneberg, Germany, May 6-10, 1946, for using prisoners of war as a screen for a German advance in Greece.

3537 UNWCC. Law Reports. Volume 5, 1948, 101p. CASES 25-34. These 10 cases deal with a type of crime summarily described as the denial of a fair trial. A general discussion of this theme is undertaken under the heading "Notes on the Case: The Criminal Aspect of the Denial of a Fair Trial," pp. 70-81. CASE 25. Trial of Lieutenant-General Shigeru Sawada and 3 others. United States Military Commission, Shanghai, February 27 to April 15, 1946, for denying a fair trial to American prisoners of war. CASE 26. Trial of Sergeant-Major Shigeru Ohashi and 6 others. Australian Military Court, Rabaul, March 20-23, 1946, for beheading 18 civilians for sabotage. CASE 27. Trial of Captain Eitaro Shinohara and 2 others. Australian Military Court, Rabaul, March 30 to April 1, 1946, for executing civilians without a fair trial. CASE 28. Trial of Captain Eikichi Kato. Australian Military Court, Rabaul, May 7, 1946, for the murder of 7 civilians without a trial. CASE 29. Trial of Karl Buck and 10 others. British Military Court, Wuppertal, Germany, May 6-10, 1946, for killing 6 British prisoners of war without a trial. CASE 30. Trial of Karl Adam Golkel and 13 others. British Military Court, Wuppertal, Germany, May 15-21, 1946, for killing 8 British prisoners of war. CASE 31. Trial of Werner Rohde and 8 others. Natzweiler Case. British Military Court, Wuppertal, Germany, May 29 to June 1, 1946, for killing 4 British women prisoners of war. CASE 32. Trial of Lieutenant General Harukei Isayama and 7 others. United States Military Commission, Shanghai, July 1-25, 1946, for killing American prisoners of war without a trial. CASE 33. Trial of General Tanaka Hisakasu and 5 others. United States Military Commission, Shanghai, August 13 to September 3, 1946, for killing an American prisoner of war. CASE 34. Trial of Hauptsturmführer Oscar Hans. Eidsivating Lagmannsrett, January 1947, and Supreme Court of Norway, August 1947, for killing 312 Norwegian patriots, 68 of whom were executed without a trial.

3538 UNWCC. Law Reports. Volume 6, 1948, 120p. CASES 35-36. CASE 35. Trial of Josef Altstötter and others. United States Military Tribunal, Nuremberg, February 17 - December 4, 1947, popularly known as the Justice Trial. The defendants were former German judges, prosecutors, and officials in the Ministry of Justice. All were charged with committing war crimes and crimes against humanity between September 1939 and April 1945. CASE 36. Trial of Gerhard Friedrich Ernst Flesch, SS Obersturmbannführer, Oberregierungsrat. Frostating Lagmannsrett, November to December, 1946 and Supreme Court of Norway, February 1948, for committing murder and torture in his capacity as Director of Public Prosecutions.

3539 UNWCC. Law Reports. Volume 7, 1948, 97p. CASES 37-42. CASE 37. Trial of Hauptsturmführer Amon Leopold Goeth, commandant of the forced labour camp near Cracow. Supreme National Tribunal of Poland, Cracow, August 27-31 and September 2-5, 1946,

Allied and National Trials 373

for genocide. CASE 38. Trial of Obersturmbannführer Rudolf Franz Ferdinand Hoess, commandant of the Auschwitz camp. Supreme National Tribunal of Poland, March 11-29, 1947, for genocide. CASE 39. Trial of Erhard Milch. United States Military Tribunal, Nuremberg, December 20, 1946, to April 17, 1947, for illegal medical experiments. CASE 40. Trial of Gustav Becker, Wilhelm Weber, Karl Schultz, and 17 others. Permanent Military Tribunal at Lyon, concluded July 17, 1947, for illegal arrest and ill-treatment of French civilians. CASE 41. Trial of Jean-Pierre Lex. Permanent Military Tribunal at Nancy, concluded May 13, 1946, for deporting 17 French families and looting their property. CASE 42. The Velpke Children's Home Case. Trial of Heinrich Gerike and 7 others. British Military Court, Brunswick, March 20 to April 3, 1946, for killing by willful neglect a number of Polish children.

3540 UNWCC. Law Reports. Volume 8, 1949, 92p. CASES 43-47. This volume deals mainly with what has come to be called the Hostages Trial. The Foreword contains a description of the illegality of hostage-taking as well as its practice in recent wars. CASE 43. Trial of General von Mackensen and General Maelzer. British Military Court, Rome, November 18-30, 1946, for killing 335 Italians in reprisal for the death of 32 German soldiers. CASE 44. Trial of Albert Kesselring. British Military Court, Venice, February 17 to May 6, 1947, same charge as CASE 43. CASE 45. Trial of Karl Bauer, Ernst Schrameck, and Herbert Falten. Permanent Military Tribunal at Dijon, completed October 18, 1945, for reprisal killing of 3 prisoners of war. CASE 46. Trial of Franz Holstein and 23 others. Permanent Military Tribunal at Dijon, completed February 3, 1947, for pillage and killing civilians. CASE 47. The Hostages Trial. Trial of Wilhelm List and 10 others. United States Military Tribunal, Nuremberg, July 8, 1947, to February 19, 1948, for reprisal killings by troops under their command.

3541 UNWCC. Law Reports. Volume 9, 1949, 94p. CASES 48-56. Most of these cases deal with crimes against property, which in principle are difficult to distinguish from crimes against the people who own the property. CASE 48. The Flick Trial. Trial of Friederick Flick and 5 others. United States Military Tribunal, Nuremberg, April 20 to December 22, 1947, for crimes against humanity and membership in criminal organizations. CASE 49. Trial of Hans Szabados. Permanent Military Tribunal at Clermont-Ferrand, judgment delivered on June 23, 1945, for killing hostages, destroying property, and pillage. CASE 50. Trial of Alois and Anna Bommer and their daughters. Permanent Military Tribunal at Metz, judgment delivered on February 19, 1947, for theft and receiving stolen goods. CASE 51. Trial of Karl Lingenfelder. Permanent Military Tribunal at Metz, judgment delivered on March 11, 1947, for destruction of a French World War I monument. CASE 52. Trial of Christian Baus. Permanent Military Tribunal at Metz, judgment delivered on August 21, 1947, for theft and abuse of confidence. CASE 53. Trial of Philippe Rust. Permanent Military Tribunal at Metz, judgment delivered on March 5, 1948, for illegal and abusive requisitioning. CASE 54. Trial of Karl-Heinz Moehle. British Military Court, Hamburg, October 15-16, 1948, for ordering the destruction of ships and their crews. CASE 55. Trial of Helmuth von Ruchteschell. British Military Court, Hamburg, May 5-21, 1947, for the prolongation of hostilities after the surrender of enemy troops. CASE 56. Trial of Otto Skorzeny and 9 others. General Military Government Court of the U.S. Zone of Germany, August 18 to September 9, 1947, for disguising themselves in American uniforms while fighting American soldiers.

3542 UNWCC. Law Reports. Volume 10, 1949, 181p. CASES 57-58. Two of the famous industrialist cases, involving the directors and managers of the Krupp organization and the chemical combine of I.G. Farben. Much on the exploitation of the resources of occupied countries. CASE 57. The I.G. Farben Trial. Trial of Carl Krauch and 22 others. United States Military Tribunal, Nuremberg, August 14, 1947, to July 19, 1948, for various war crimes. CASE 58. The Krupp Trial. Trial of Alfried Felix Alwyn Krupp von Bohlen und Halbach and 11 others. United States Military Tribunal, Nuremberg, November 17, 1947, to June 30, 1948, for war crimes, plunder and spoliation, and crimes involving prisoners of war and slave labor.

3543 UNWCC. Law Reports. Volume 11, 1949, 110p. All these trials deal with offenses against prisoners of war, based on the Geneva Conventions. CASE 59. Trial of Tanabe Koshiro. Netherlands Temporary Court-Martial, Macassar, February 5, 1947, for exposing 1200 Dutch, American, British, and Australian prisoners of war to acts of war. CASE 60. Trial of Martin Gottfried Weiss and 39 others. General Military Government Court of the United States Zone, Dachau, Germany, November 15 to December 13, 1945, for beating, starving, torturing, and killing prisoners of war at Dachau. CASE 61. Trial of Generaloberst Nickolaus von Falkenhorst. British Military Court, Brunswick, July 29 to August 2, 1946, for killing prisoners of war. CASE 62. Trial of Max Wielen and 17 others. Stalagluft III trial. British Military Court, Hamburg, Germany, July 1 to September 3, 1947, for killing prisoners of war. CASE 63. Trial of Lieutenant-General Kurt Maelzer. United States Military Commission, Florence, Italy, September 9-14, 1946, for exposing prisoners of war to acts of violence. CASE 64. Trial of Lieutenant-General Baba Masao. Australian Military Court, Rabaul, May 28 to June 2, 1947, for allowing his troops to commit acts of violence against prisoners of war. CASE 65. Trial of Tanaka Chuichi and 2 others. Australian Military Court, Rabaul, July 12, 1946, for ill treatment of prisoners of war. CASE 66. Trial of Franz Schonfeld and 9 others. British Military Court, Essen, June 11-26, 1946, for killing prisoners of war. CASE 67. Trial of Johannes Oenning and Emil Nix. British Military Court, Borken, Germany, December 21-22, 1945, for killing a prisoner of war. CASE 68. Trial of Hans Renoth and 3 others. British Military Court, Elten, Germany, January 8-10, 1946, for killing a prisoner of war. CASE 69. Trial of Arno Heering. British Military Court, Hannover, January 25-26, 1946, for mistreating prisoners of war. CASE 70. Trial of Willi Mackensen. British Military Court, Hannover, January 29, 1946, for a forced march of prisoners of war resulting in the death of 30 of them. CASE 71. Trial of Eberhard Schoengrath and 6 others. British Military Court, Burgsteinfurt, Germany, February 7-11, 1946, for killing a prisoner of war.

3544 UNWCC. Law Reports. Volume 12, 1949, 127p. CASE 72. The German High Command Trial. Trial of Wilhelm von Leeb and 13 others. United States Military Tribunal, Nuremberg, December 30, 1947, to October 28, 1948, deals with the responsibility of high-ranking officers of the German army for war crimes and crimes against humanity. The proceedings and evidence are voluminous, with 330 pages on the judgment alone. Discusses the question of whether military leaders were on the policy-making level.

3545 UNWCC. Law Reports. Volume 13, 1949, 152p. CASES 73-82. Contains records of minor trials as well as 2 involving genocide and the liability of parties to criminal organizations. CASE 73. Trial of Ulrich Greifelt and others. United States Military Tribunal, Nuremberg, October 10, 1947, to March 10, 1948, for genocide. CASE 74. Trial of Gauleiter Artur Greiser. Supreme National Tribunal of Poland, June 21 to July 7, 1946, for seizure of the free city of Danzig. CASE 75. Trial of Albert Wagner. General Military Government Tribunal of the French Zone of Occupation in Germany, judgment delivered on November 29, 1946, for slave labor and killing of escaped civilian prisoners. CASE 76. Trial of Washio Awochi. Netherlands Temporary Court-Martial at Batavia, Judgment delivered on October 25, 1946, for forcing Japanese women and girls into prostitution. CASE 77. Trial of Susuki Motosuke. Netherlands Temporary Court Martial at Amboina, judgment delivered on January 28, 1948, for denying fair trial to and execution of Indonesian natives. CASE 78. Trial of Wilhelm Gerbsch. Special Court in Amsterdam, First Chamber, judgment delivered on April 28, 1948, for ill treatment of and deportation of Dutch citizens. CASE 79. Trial of Shigeki Motomura and 15 others. Netherlands Temporary Court-Martial at Macassar, judgment delivered on July 18, 1947, for mass arrests, terrorism, and torture. CASE 80. Trial of Heinz Hagendorf. United States Intermediate Military Government Court at Dachau, Germany, August 8-9, 1946, for firing on American soldiers from an enemy ambulance displaying the Red Cross emblem. CASE 81. Trial of Erich Weiss and Wilhelm Mundo. United States General Military Government Court at Ludwigsburg, Germany, November 9-10, 1945, for killing a prisoner of war. CASE 82. Trial of Max Schmid. United States General Military Government Court at Dachau, Germany, May 9, 1947, for killing prisoners of war.

3546 UNWCC. Law Reports. Volume 14, 1949, 160p. CASES 83-89. CASE 83. Trial of Takashi Sakai. Chinese War Crimes Military Tribunal of the Ministry of National Defence, Nanking, China, judgment delivered on August 29, 1946, for killing and torturing Chinese civilians. CASE 84. Trial of Lothar Eisenträger and others. United States Military Commission, Shanghai, China, October 3, 1946, to January 14, 1947, for continuing to wage war against the United States after the unconditional surrender of Germany. CASE 85. Trial of Dr. Joseph Buhler. Supreme National Tribunal of Poland, June 17 to July 10, 1948, for mass murder and torture of Polish civilians. CASE 86. Trial of Hans Paul Helmuth Latza and 2 others. Eidsivating Lagmannsrett Court of Appeals and the Supreme Court of Norway, February 18, 1947, to December 3, 1948, for sentencing Norwegians to death without a free trial. CASE 87. Trial of Josef Hangobl. General Military Court, Dachau, Germany, October 17-18, 1945, for murder of unarmed soldiers in the act of surrender. CASE 88. Trial of Hans Albin Rauter. Netherlands Special Court in 's-Gravenhage (The Hague), judgment delivered on January 12, 1949, for persecution of Jews, deportation of Dutch civilians, slave labor, and pillage. CASE 89. Trial of Willy Zuehlke. Netherland's Special Court in Amsterdam, 1948, and Netherlands Special Court of Cassation, judgment delivered on December 6, 1948, for ill-treatment of Jewish prisoners.

3547 UNWCC. Law Reports. Volume 15, 1949, 216p. This volume summarizes and analyzes the trials reported in the previous 14

B. CONTROL COUNCIL LAW NO. 10

3548 BENJAMIN, HILDE. "Die Interzonentagung der Juristen der VVN in Schönberg von 20. bis 22. März 1948," *Neue Justiz* 1948 2(3): 56-58. Comments on Control Council Law No. 10 and related questions.

3549 CITRON, CURT. "Das Kontrollratsgesetz No. 10 [Control Law No. 10]," *Gegenwart* 1947 2(April 30): 23-24.

3550 COING, HELMUT. "Das Grundrecht der Menschenwürde, der Strafrechtliche Schutz der Menschlichkeit, und das Persönlichkeitsrecht des bürgerlichen Rechts," *Süddeutsche Juristen-Zeitung* 1947 2(12): 641-645. Points out that the German law showed some gaps in the protection of civil rights, some of which were being filled by Control Council Law No. 10. 21 notes.

3551 "Die Anwendung des Kontrollratsgesetzes Nr. 10 durch die deutschen Gerichte," *Deutsche Rechts-Zeitschrift* 1947 2(4): 111-118.

3552 "Die Kenntnis vom Unrecht der Organisationen," *Spruchgerichte* 1947 1(December): 71. Deals with Control Council Law No. 10. Concludes that the crime of membership is the crime of not leaving the organization, so that a knowledge of the obligation to leave is a condition of intentional infraction. The individual must recognize and evaluate the evil of the organization's activities.

3553 "Die Rechtsnatur der KRG Nr. 10," *Spruchgerichte* 1948 2: 267-269.

3554 FRATCHER, WILLIAM F. "American Organization for Prosecution of German War Criminals," *Missouri Law Review* 1948 13(January): 45-75. Describes the organization and functions of the United Nations War Crimes Commission, the American organization in Germany, the Central Registry of War Criminals and Security Suspects, the War Crimes Branch at Wiesbaden, and the American prosecution staff at Nuremberg. Describes the procedures adopted to enable German courts to try cases under Control Council Law No. 10. Appendix contains the text of Control Council Proclamation No. 3 and Control Council Law No. 10.

3555 GERMANY (Territory under Allied Occupation, 1945-). *Laws, Statutes, etc. Kontrollratsgesetz Nr. 10, erläutert von Herbert Kraus*. Hamburg: Rechts- und Staatswissenschaftlicher Verlag, 1948. 146p.

3556 GRAVESON, R.H. "Der Grundsatz 'nulla poena sine lege' und Kontrollratsgesetz No. 10," *Monatsschrift für Deutsches Recht* 1947 1(December): 278-281.

3557 HAENSEL, CARL. *Das Organisationsverbrechen. Nürnberger Betrachtungen zum Kontrollratsgesetz No. 10*. Munich: Biederstein, 1947. 61p. An analysis of those provisions of Control Council Law No. 10 concerning membership in criminal organizations. Discusses the Nuremberg IMT proceedings and judgment, the concept of conspiracy, and various aspects of proof and participation. International law leaves the judge considerable leeway.

3558 HODENBERG, HODO FREIHERR VON. "Zur Anwendung des Kontrollratsgesetzes Nr. 10 durch deutsche Gerichte," Süddeutsche Juristen-Zeitung 1947 2(March/Special Number): 113-124. Discusses the retroactive application of Control Law No. 10 and insists that this violated one of the fundamental principles of German law. This is true as well in cases involving denunciation. 9 notes.

3559 KATZENBERGER, K. "Das Recht der politischen Säuberung. Das Verhältnis des Nürnberger Urteils zum Befreiungsgesetz (U. S. Zone) und die aus dem Nürnberger Urteil für die Praxis der Spruchkammer sich ergebenden Konsequenzen," Süddeutsche Juristen-Zeitung 1948 3(1): 41-49. Deals with the relationship of the Nuremberg IMT judgment to Control Council Law No. 10. According to the former, knowledge of the criminal nature of the organization is to be assumed and may be disproved in individual cases. Argues that Directive No. 38 reconciles the differences between the judgment and the law and discusses the application of the law to individual cases. 14 notes.

3560 KRAUS, HERBERT. Kontrollratsgesetz Nr. 10. 1947. Hamburg: Rechts-und Staatswissenschaftlicher Verlag, 1947. 146p. Heavily annotated, with appendices containing 6 NMT documents on criminal organizations. Short bibliography, no index.

3561 LANGE, RICHARD. "Das Kontrollratsgesetz Nr. 10 in Theorie und Praxis," Deutsche Rechts-Zeitschrift 1948 3(5): 155-161. 69 notes.

3562 LANGE, RICHARD. "Kontrollratsgesetz Nr. 10 und deutsches Recht," Deutsche Rechts-Zeitschrift 1948 3(6): 185-193. 74 notes.

3563 LANGE, RICHARD. "Zum Denunziantenproblem," Süddeutsche Juristen-Zeitung 1948 3(6): 302-311. The author compares the trials of informers under Control Council Law No. 10 in different zones of occupation and recommends that the handling of these cases be made more uniform. 48 notes.

3564 "Law No. 10: Punishment of Persons Guilty of War Crimes, Crimes against Peace and against Humanity," Official Gazette of the Control Council for Germany 1946 3(January 31): 50-55.

3565 MELSHEIMER, ERNST. "Der Kampf der deutschen Justiz gegen die Naziverbrecher," Neue Justiz 1948 2(8): 126-131. Discusses the progress of the prosecution of war criminals under Control Law No. 10. Compares the practices in the Eastern and Western zones and praises the achievements in the Eastern zone.

3566 MEYER, R. "Das Kontrollratsgesetz Nr. 10 in der Praxis der deutschen Strafgerichte," Monatsschrift für Deutsches Recht 1947 1: 110-112.

3567 MITTELBACH, HANS. "Das Spruchgerichtsverfahren im Lichte der Urteile des amerikanischen Militärgerichtshofes Nr. II und III," Spruchgerichte 1948 2(April): 108-112. Discusses the consequences to be drawn from the judgments in the Pohl and Altstötter cases for the decisions of other cases tried under Control Council Law No. 10.

378 Allied and National Trials

3568 MOSLER, HERMANN. "Die Kriegshandlungen im rechtswidrigen Kriege," Jahrbuch für internationales und ausländisches öffentliches Recht 1948 2-3: 335-357. Commenting on the Kieler Garbe judgment and a judgment of OLG Dresden of March 21, 1947, the author concludes that even in a war of aggression measures taken in prosecution of war are irrelevant in terms of international law unless they violate principles of international law applicable after the beginning of the war. The application of Control Council Law No. 10 should be governed by this fundamental rule.

3569 RATZ, PAUL. "Über die völkerrechtlichen Grundlagen des Londoner Status vom 8. August 1945 und Kontrollratsgesetzes Nr. 10," Archiv des Völkerrechts 1952 3(May): 275-299.

3570 SCHÖNKE, ADOLF. "Grundsätzliche Strafmaß im Spruchgerichtsverfahren," Spruchgerichte 1948 2(March): 65-66.

3571 SCHÖNKE, ADOLF. "Grundsätzliche strafrechtliche Fragen des KRG 10 im ausländischen Schrifttum," Neue Juristische Wochenschrift 1948 1(18): 673-675.

3572 SCHULZE, HANS JOACHIM. Fragen zum "Allgemeinen Teil" des Kontrollratsgesetzes Nr. 10. Munich: 1960.

3573 STRUCKBERG, GEORG. "Zur Anwendung des Kontrollratsgesetzes Nr. 10," Deutsche Rechts-Zeitschrift 1947 2(9): 277-280. 20 notes.

3574 UTLEY, FREDA. The High Cost of Vengeance. Chicago: Henry Regnery, 1949. Hamburg, 1950.

3575 WERNER, WOLFHART. "Der Grundsatz 'nullum crimen, nulla poena sine lege' und die Anwendung des Gesetzes Nr. 10 des Alliierten Kontrollrats durch deutsche Gerichte," Spruchgerichte 1947 1(11): 25-30.

3576 WIMMER, AUGUST. "Rechtssicherheit und Rechtssicherungssätze im Strafrecht und Strafprozeßrecht als rechtsethisches Problem," Süddeutsche Juristen-Zeitung 1947 2(11): 594-599. Comment on Control Council Law No. 10. The principle "ignorance does not protect from punishment" and the maxim "nullum crimen sine lege" serve to assure legal security. The laws of punishment must be in accordance with the ethical order. 3 notes.

3577 WIMMER, AUGUST. "Unmenschlichkeitsverbrechen und deutschrechtliche Straftat in einer Handlung," Süddeutsche Juristen-Zeitung 1948 3(5): 253-258. Even though Control Council Law. No. 10 supersedes German penal law, German courts are still obligated to apply German law. Discusses differences between the American and British zones. 8 notes.

3578 WINKELMANN, PAUL. "Aufgaben der Staatsanwälte und Gerichte in den Verfahren nach dem Befehl Nr. 201," Neue Justiz 1947 1(August-September): 169-172. Discusses the duties of the state prosecutors and the German courts in procedures conducted under Decree No. 201. Special reference to paragraph 1, No. 5 of Directive No. 38 of the Allied Control Council, which left it to the commanding officers of the various zones to use German courts to enforce Control Council Law No. 10.

3579 ZECK, WILLIAM A. "Nuremberg: Proceedings Subsequent to Goering et al," North Carolina Law Review 1948 26(June): 350-389. The author was deputy chief of the Farben Trial team. He discusses the 12 "subsequent" trials, focusing on the composition of the tribunals, the substantive and legal aspects of the trials, and certain procedural matters. Discusses scope of Control Council Law No. 10. 126 notes.

C. AUSTRIA

3580 BRASSLOFF, F.L. "Austrian Justice on Trial," World Jewry 1966 (March-April): 9-10. On the trial of the Maurer brothers.

3581 "Das österreichische Kriegsverbrechergesetz 1947," Spruchgerichte 1948 2(December): 349-350.

3582 Der Hochverratsprozeß gegen Dr. Guido Schmidt vor dem Wiener Volksgericht. Die gerichtlichen Protokolle mit den Zeugenaussagen, unveröffentlichen Dokumenten, sämtlichen Geheimbriefen und Geheimakten. Vienna: Österreichische Staatsdruckerei, 1947. 697p. The complete documentary record of Schmidt's trial before the Landesgericht für Strafsachen als Volksgericht on February 27, 1947. Based on primary documents; 8-page index.

3583 FRIEDMAN, TUVIAH. Schupo-Kriegsverbrecher in Kolomea beim Verhör vor den Untersuchungsoffizieren in Wien. Haifa: Verband der ehemaligen Einwohner Von Kolomea in Israel, 1959. Mimeograph.

3584 FRIEDMAN, TUVIAH. Schupo-Kriegsverbrecher in Kolomea vor dem Wiener Volksgericht. Dokumentensammlung. Haifa: Verband der ehemaligen Einwohner Von Kolomea in Israel, 1957.

3585 FRIEDMAN, TUVIAH. Schupo-Kriegsverbrecher von Stryj vor dem Wiener Volksgericht. Haifa: Verband der ehemaligen Einwohner von Stryj in Israel mit Hilfe der Executive des Jüdischen Weltkongresses in Israel, 1957. 54p.

3586 FRIEDMAN, TUVIAH. Schupo- und Gestapo-Kriegsverbrecher von Stanislau vor dem Wiener Volksgericht. Haifa: Historisches Institut für Erforschung der Nazikriegsverbrechen, 1957. 83p. Mimeograph.

3587 GRUBER MICHAELIS, RUTH. "Austrian Justice - After a Fashion," Congress Weekly, A Review of Jewish Interests 1966 (December 19): 14-16. Argues that the murder sentence for brothers Wilhelm and Johann Maurer was light.

3588 HÖSS, RUDOLF. J'ai túe seulement 2.500.000 Personnes. Le Procès de Rudolf Hoess commendant d'Auschwitz (Varsavie 11 Mars-2 Avril 1947). Paris: Éditions de l'Amicale des Déportés d'Auschwitz, [no date given].

3589 LIEBESMAN-MIKULSKI, ABRAHAM. "Pro-Nazi Sentiments at the Maurer Trial," Yad Vashem Bulletin 1966 16: 58-59.

3590 SZECSI, MARIA, and KARL STADLER. Die NS-Justiz in Österreich und ihre Opfer. Vienna: Herold, 1962. 127p. Discusses reactions in Austria and Norway to Nazi control. Some on war crimes and crimes against the people of occupied nations.

D. BELGIUM

3591 BLEY, C. "Falkenhausen vor den Richtern," Frankfurter Hefte 1951 6(March): 159-168.

380 Allied and National Trials

3592 BREYMEIER, TH. „Die Bandenanklage im belgischen Kriegsverbrecherprozeß," Neue Juristische Wochenschrift 1950 3(7): 252-253.

3593 QUINTANO RIPOLLÉS, ANTONIO. "El proceso de von Falkenhausen ante el consejo de guerra de Bruselas," Revista Española de Derecho Internacional 1951 4(1): 161-164. 3 notes.

3594 RIGAUX, M., and P. E. TROUSSE. "La Qualification des crimes de guerre en droit pénal belge," Journal des Tribunaux 1948 63: 229-232.

3595 SLUZNY, M. "La Loi de 20 juin 1947 relative à la compétence des juridictions militaires en matière de crimes de guerre," Journal des Tribunaux 1947 62: 413-415.

3596 VOLKMANN, KURT. „Kriegsverbrecher-Verfahrung in Belgien," Neue Juristische Wochenschrift 1949 2(12): 455-456.

3597 WILLEQUET, J. "Le procès Falkenhausen," Revue d'Histoire de la Deuxième Mondiale 1951 1: 59-65.

3598 WOLF, JULES. Le Procès de Breendonk. Brussels: Larcier, 1973.

E. CANADA

3599 MC DONALD, BRUCE. The Trial of Kurt Meyer. Toronto: Clarke, Irwin, 1954. 216p.

F. CZECHOSLOVAKIA

3600 BIANCHI, LEONARD. "Hlavni Procesy S Ludaky Pred Narodnim Soudem V Bratislave V Letech 1945-1947 [Main Trials of Slovak Separatists in the National Court in Bratislava, 1945-1947]," Pravnehistoricke Studie 1977 20: 205-228. A study of Slovak clerical fascism and the punishment of its leaders after World War II. The author analyzes the trials of those accused of treason, racial persecution, destruction of pre-World War II Czechoslovak statehood, collaboration with Germany, and terrorism. 10 notes.

3601 DAXNER, IGOR. Ludáctvo pred Národnýn Súdom, 1945-1947. Bratislava: Vydavatel'stvo Slovneskej Akadémie Vied, 1961. The summary is in German.

3602 Justiz im Dienste der Vergeltung. Erlebnisberichte und Dokumente über die Rechtsprechung der tschechoslowakischen außerordentlichen Volksgerichte gegen Deutsche (1945-48). Munich: C. Wolf, 1962.

G. DENMARK

3603 BAY, CHRISTIAN. "Nürnberg-dommene under Debatt," Jus Gentium 1949 1(3): 254-273.

3604 THOMSEN, ERICH. Deutsche Besatzungspolitik in Dänemark 1940-1945. Düsseldorf: Bertelsmann Universitätsverlag, 1971. 277p. Deals with the terror of German occupation and control, Danish Jews, and the deportation of Danish policemen. 40p. of notes, bibliography, index.

H. FINLAND

3605 KUUSINEN, O. "The Trial of Finnish War Criminals," Information Bulletin 1945 6(18): 146-150.

3606 PROCOPÉ, HJALMAR J. Sowjetjustiz über Finnland. Prozeßakten aus dem Verfahren gegen die Kriegsverantwortlichen in Finnland. Zurich: Thomas, 1947. 325p.

3607 RAUTKALLIO, HANNU. "Suomen Sotasyylisyyskysymys ja Yhdysvallat Vuosina 1944-1945 [Finland's War Crimes Question and the United States, 1944-1945]," Historiallinen Aikakauskirja 1980 78(2): 128-141. From September 1944 to the end of 1945 the question of Finnish war crimes trials was approached with unusual moderation and gradualism by the Finnish government and the Soviet-British Control Commission for Finland. The government of the United States also favored moderation, although by the end of 1945 it began to view such trials as desirable in order to maintain Finnish political stability in the face of internal Finnish agitation. Based on United States State Department archives and Finnish monographs.

3608 SOINI, YRJÖ [pseudonym]. Kuin Pietari hiilivalkealla: Sotasyyllisyysasian vaiheet, 1944-1949 [Like Peter denying Christ: The phases of the question of war guilt - war responsibility - 1944-1949]. 2nd edition, Helsinki: Otava, 1956. 382p. Traces the development of the war responsibility trials which were forced on Finland by the Soviet Union. Concludes that the whole procedure was a travesty, that the guilty ones were in the Kremlin.

3609 STARKENBERG, OLOF. Kriegsansvarighetsprocessen i Finland. Stockholm: Utrikespolitiska institutet, 1946.

3610 TARKKA, JUKKA. "Paradokseja Sotasyyllisyyskysymyksesta [Paradoxes of the War Crimes Question]," Historiallinen Aikakauskirja 1980 78(3): 255-258. Criticizes Hannu Rautkallio's article, "Suomen Sotasyyllisyyskysymys ja Yhdysvallat Vuosina 1944-1945 [Finland's War Crimes Question and the United States, 1944-1945." Rautkallio distorted the international political background of Finland's decision in late 1945 to initiate war crimes trials.

I. FRANCE

3611 ABETZ, OTTO F. D'Une Prison. Paris: Amiot-Dumond, 1949. 313p. Complete study of the trial, sentencing, and execution of a collaborator who served as ambassador to occupied France.

3612 AUGE, THOMAS E. "Justice and Injustice: The French Collaboration Trials, 1944-1949," Ph.D. dissertation, University of Iowa, 1956. Abstracted in Dissertation Abstracts International 1957 17(12): 2986.

3613 AUJOL, JEAN LOUIS. Le Procès Benoist-Méchin (29 mai-6 juin 1947). Paris: Albin Michel, 1948.

3614 BISHOP, WILLIAM W., JR. "Judicial Decisions: The Case against Hermann Roechling and Others," American Journal of International Law 1949 43(1): 191-193. Decisions of the General Tribunal of the Military Government of the French Zone of Occupation in Germany, June 30, 1948. Roechling and 4 other

Nazi industrialists were tried under Control Council Law No. 10. Lists charges and sentences.

3615 BOULIER, JEAN. Les Juges nazis l'appareil d'état de la République Fédérale Allemande. Brussels: Éditions de l'Association internationale des Juristes Démocrates, 1962. 126p.

3616 BOURGET, PIERRE. Un certain Philippe Pétain. Paris: Castermann, 1966.

3617 CASSIN, RENÉ. "[France's participation in the decision to punish war crimes and in the activities of the United Nations Commission]," Panstwo i Prawo 1948 3(3): 105-110. Original is in Polish.

3618 CATHALA, PIERRE A.J. Face aux Réalités. Paris: Éditions du Triolet, 1948. 302p.

3619 CHAUDET, H. Le Procès Maurras. Lyon: Éditions de Savoie, 1945.

3620 COLE, HUBERT. Laval. A Biography. New York: Putnam, 1963. 314p.

3621 CRENESSE, P. Le Procès de Wagner. Paris: Office français d'édition, 1946.

3622 D'ORR, PAUL BARKSDALE. "The Trial of Marshal Pétain," Federal Rules Decisions 1949 8: 377-407.

3623 DEGAND, HENRI. "Les Jurisdictions françaises du gouvernement militaire en Allemagne Occupée," Revue juridique d'Alcase et de Lorraine 1947 28(November): 237-253. Describes the organization and competence of the tribunals, analyzes the sources of law for the inter-allied legislation, and explains the new methods adopted in the trials which differ from French procedure.

3624 DOBLHOFF, LILY. "Traitor or Patriot?" Commonweal 1949 50(19): 461-462. Deals with the Abetz trial in France.

3625 DONNEDIEU DE VABRES, HENRI. Traité de droit criminel et de legislation pénale comparée. 3rd edition. Paris: Recueil Sirey, 1947. 1059p. A textbook containing several chapters on French post-war legislation concerning collaboration and other war crimes. Chapters deal with the ex post facto nature of war crimes legislation, the functions of special courts instituted by the French Provisional Government, and recent developments in international penal law, including the Nuremberg IMT.

3626 DOUBLET, PIERRE H. La Collaboration, l'epuration, la confiscation, les reparations aux victimes de l'occupation. Exposé et commentaires suivis des principales ordonnances. Paris: R. Pichon, 1945. 283p. A study of the principal legislative provisions promulgated by the French Provisional Government dealing with collaboration, prosecution of collaborators, confiscation, reparations to the victims of the German occupation.

3627 EISELE, A. "Réflexions sur les procès des criminels de guerre en France," Revue de Droit Pénal et de Criminologie 1950 31 (December): 305-317.

3628 EISENMANN, CHARLES, and ALEX WEILL. "Le Tribunal français en Allemagne," Recueil Dalloz [Chronique] 1948 (19): 77-80. An examination of the ordinance of August 17, 1947.

3629 FABRE-LUCE, ALFRED. Le Mystère du Maréchal. Le Procès Pétain. Geneva: C. Bourquin, 1946. 198p. Account of the trial by a Pétain sympathizer. The author contends that the trial was purely political and that Charles de Gaulle could just as easily have been accused of acting outside the framework of the Republic.

3630 GIARDINI, CESARE. Il Processo Pétain. Milan: Rizzoli, 1947. 339p. A review of the Pétain trial. The author quotes extensively from the stenographic record and shows why in his opinion Pétain did not get a fair hearing.

3631 GLEISCHLÄGER, ROBERT. "Der Prozeß Frankreichs. Die Kriegsverbrecher von Oradour," Juristische Blätter 1953 75: 653-654.

3632 HOFSTETTER, ALBERT J. Les Tribunaux du Gouvernement Militaire en Zone Française d'Occupation en Allemagne. Freiburg-en-Brisgau: 1947. 167p.

3633 JAFFRÉ, YVES FRÉDÉRIC. Les Tribunaux d'exception, 1940-1962. Paris: Nouvelles Éditions Latines, 1963. 365p.

3634 JEANTET, GABRIEL. Pétain contre Hitler. Paris: Éditions de la Table Rond, 1966. Deals with the Pétain trial.

3635 JESCHECK, HANS-HEINRICH. "Kriegsverbrecherprozesse gegen deutsche Kriegsgefangene in Frankreich," Süddeutsche Juristen-Zeitung 1949 4(2): 107-116. On national trials held in France. 8 notes.

3636 JESCHECK, HANS-HEINRICH. "Zum Oradour-Prozeß," Juristenzeitung 1953 8(5): 156-157. The Oradour-sur-Glane massacre trial, 1953.

3637 JULIEN, M. La Loi du 15 septembre 1948 sur les crimes de guerre. Paris: Institut de Criminologie, 1952.

3638 KRUUSE, JENS. Oradour sur Glane. [Paris]: Fayard, 1969.

3639 LAVAL, PIERRE. Le Procès Laval. Compte rendu sténographique. Paris: A. Michel, 1946. 311p.

3640 LAVAL, PIERRE. The Diary of Pierre Laval. New York: Scribner, 1948. 240p. Diary, edited by Laval's daughter Josée.

3641 LUCHAIRE, JEAN, et al. Les Procès de Collaboration. Paris: Michel, 1948. 634p. The stenographic record of the trials of three prominent collaborators.

3642 LUTHER, HANS. "Zu den gegenwärtigen Kriegsverbrecherprozessen in Frankreich," Neue Juristische Wochenschrift 1954 7(10): 376-377.

3643 MAUNOIR, JEAN-PIERRE. La Réression des crimes de guerre devant les tribunaux français et allié. Geneva: Éditions Médecine et Hygiène, 1956. Thesis at the University of Geneva.

3644 MAUNOIR, JEAN-PIERRE. "Le Procès d'Oradour," Revue de Droit International 1953 31(April-June): 181-186.

3645 MEYROWITZ, HENRI. "Ein französisches Gutachten zu den Kriegsverbrecherprozessen in Frankreich," Deutsche Rechts-Zeitschrift 1950 5(17/18): 403-405. 5 notes.

3646 MEZGER, ERNST. "Französische Gesetze und Rechtsprechung über das Schicksal von Verträgen zwischen Franzosen und Deutschen aus der Zeit der deutschen Besatzung, 1940-1945," Nachrichten der Studiengesellschaft für privatrechtliche Auslandsinteressen 1950 9: 5-8.

3647 MEZGER, ERNST. "Schutz der Genfer Konvention für deutsche Kriegsgefangene unter Anklage wegen Kriegsverbrechens in Frankreich," Juristenzeitung 1951 6(11): 332-333.

3648 MICHEL, PAUL LOUIS. Le Procès Pétain. Paris: Éditions Médicis, 1945. 374p.

3649 MORELLET, CHARLES. Saint-Louis. Ou, La Justice sous les Chaines, 1944: Avant propos de Camille Chautemps. Paris: Éditions de L'Ermite, 1949.

3650 MORNET, A. Quatre Ans à Rayer de notre histoire. Paris: Self, 1949. 322p. Mornet served as attorney general at the trial of Pétain. In this work are reproduced notes he kept during the four years of German occupation as well as documents bearing on the activities of the Vichy collaborators.

3651 MOURET, G. Oradour, le crime, le procès. Paris: Plon, 1958.

3652 NAUD, ALBERT L. Pourquoi je n'ai pas défendu Pierre Laval. Paris: Fayard, 1948. 284p. A discussion of the trial of one of Laval's defense attorneys.

3653 NOGUÈRES, LOUIS. Le véritable procès du Maréchal Pétain. Paris: Librairie Arthème Fayard, 1955. 659p. The complete story of the political career and trial of the famous French collaborator. Discusses Pétain's relations with the Germans, English, Americans, and with Charles de Gaulle.

3654 "Otto Abetz in the Dock," Newsweek 1949 34(4): 30-31. Brief comment on the Abetz trial in France for looting art treasures, deporting French civilians to Germany, and persecuting Jews.

3655 PATIN, MAURICE. "La France et le jugement des crimes de guerre," Revue de Science Criminelle et de Droit Pénal Comparé 1951 6(3): 393-405.

3656 PAUCHOU, GUY, and PIERRE MASFRAND. Oradour-sur-Glane; Vision d'épouvante; ouvrage officiel du comité du souvenir et de l'association nationale des familles des martyrs d'Oradour-sur-Glane. Limoges: Charles - Lavauzelle et Cie., 1945.

3657 Procès du Maréchal Pétain. Paris: Imprimeries des Journaux Officials, 1945. 386p.

3658 ROY, JULES. Le grand Naufrage. [Paris]: René Julliard, 1966. Published in English as The Trial of Marshal Pétain. New York: Harper, 1968. 264p.

3659 SCHLUMBERGER, JEAN. Le Procès Pétain. Notes d'audiences. Blessures et séquelles de la guerre. Paris: Gallimard, 1949. 254p. Deals with Petain's wartime career, crimes alleged against him, and his famous and controversial trial. Undocumented.

3660 SCHWINGE, ERICH. "Angehörige der ehemaligen deutschen Wehrmacht und der SS vor französichen Militärgerichten," Monatsschrift für deutsches Recht 1949 3: 650-654.

3661 SERVUS JURIS [pseudonym]. Lettre ouverte à Messieurs les Présidents des cours de justice. Paris: A. Bonne, 1948.

3662 STITZER, K. Mordprozeß Oradour nach Prozeßberichten der "Humanité." Berlin: Dietz, 1954.

3663 TAEGE, HERBERT. Wo ist Kain? Enthüllungen und Dokumente zum Komplex Tulle ± Oradour. Bad Münder: Askania, 1981. 389p. Describes attacks by the SS on the towns of Tulle, Alsace, Oradour, and Vichy, France. Reveals the background of Alsace and other occupied territories and the effect of protests by the Alsatians on postwar trials. Discusses the Oradour trials of German soldiers in 1953. Those tried were sentenced to death by the French. Investigates the reopening of the trial in Germany without the benefit of French judicial records. Presents conflicting French literature on this theme. Appendix includes a letter from a French prison by an SS official to Field Marshal Gerd von Rundstedt. List of abbreviations, organizational breakdown of the German army of 1944, list of equivalent ranks of the Waffen SS and army officials. 3-page bibliography, 54 photographs.

3664 "Testimony of Abetz at Trial of Jean Luchaire," in Le Procès Collaboration, Fernand de Brinon, Joseph Darnand, Jean Luchaire, Compte Rendu Stenographie. Paris: Albion-Michel, 1948.

3665 "'The Butcher' Listens," Life 1954 36(10): 41-42. The trial of SS general Karl Oberg, known as the "Butcher of Paris." 8 photographs.

3666 "Tribunal Général de la zone française d'occupation siegeant à Rastatt affaire Tillessen," Journal Officiel du Commandement en Chef Française en Allemagne 1947 61(March 26): 606-636. Summary of the proceedings and judgment.

3667 "Tribunal général du gouvernement militaire de la zone française d'occupation à Rastatt: Procès des camps de concentration Nazis de Natzweiler, camps de Schomberg, Schorzingen, Spaichingen, Erzingen, Dautmergen," Journal Officiel du Commandement en Chef Français en Allemagne 1947 64(April 15): 653-666. Natzweiler trial, Rastatt, 1947.

3668 TRIBUNAL MILITAIRE PERMANENT DE PARIS. Dossiers des pièces de la procédure suivie contre le Général von Stülpnagel, Otto et autres, inculpés d'assassinats, complicité d'assassinats, pillage jugement no 556/1870 du 31 mai 1949. Paris: Tribunal Militaire Permanent de Paris, 1949.

3669 WALLACE, JOHN E. "Otto Abetz and the Question of a Franco-German Reconciliation, 1919-1939," Southern Quarterly 1975 13(3): 189-206. Examines the life and career of Heinrich Otto Abetz (1903-1958), German ambassador to occupied France, with special reference to activities leading to his trial in 1949 for war crimes. 75 notes.

3670 WARNER, GEOFFREY. Pierre Laval and the Eclipse of France. New York: Macmillan, 1968. London: Eyre & Spottiswoode, 1968. 461p. Complete biography of the infamous French collaborator. Much on his trial and execution. 14-page bibliography, index.

J. GERMANY

1. General

3671 ARNDT, ADOLF. "Status and Development of Constitutional Law in Germany," Annals of the American Academy of Political and Social Science 1948 260(November): 1-9. Discusses the status of Germany in the theory and practice of international law with special reference to the trials of Tilleson and Göring. Different paragraphs deal with the different zones of occupation.

3672 BLESSIN, G., et al. Bundes-Entschädigungsgesetze. Bundes-Ergänzungsgezetz zur Entschädigung für Opfer der nationalsozialistischen Verfolgung. Munich: Beck, 1954.

3673 BRAND, EMANUEL. "Prosecution of Nazi Criminals in West Germany, Austria, and East Germany in 1965-1966," Yad Vashem Bulletin 1967 (20): 14-29.

3674 BROCK-SHEPHERD, GORDON. "The Pursuit of Guilt: Germany's Final Roundup of War Criminals," Atlantic 1964 (September): 76-80.

3675 BRODZKA, HALINA. Nazi Judges in West Germany. Warsaw: Zachodnia Agencja Prasowa, 1963. 41p. Brief survey of the prosecution of Nazi war criminals published by the Federal Republic of Germany.

3676 "Closing the Loophole: Undetected German War Criminals Immune from Future Prosecution," Time 1969 94(July 18): 40.

3677 DOLLE, RENATE, and HORST RICHTER. "Die Anerkennungen der Urteile gegen Kriegs- und Naziverbrecher muß notwendiger Bestandteil eines Friedensvertrages mit Deutschland sein!" Staat und Recht 1955 8(5): 962-978.

3678 DORSEY, JOHN THOMAS. "The Courtroom Drama in Postwar Germany and America," Ph.D. dissertation, University of Illinois, Urbana-Champaign, 1979. Abstracted in Dissertation Abstracts International 1980 40(8): 4582-A.

3679 EUROPEAN COURT OF HUMAN RIGHTS. Affaire "Wemhoff". Strasbourg: Greffe de la Cour, Conseil de l'Europe, 1969. Deals with national war crimes trials in Germany after 1949.

3680 FINN, GERHARD. "Kriegsverbrecherprozesse in Deutschland. Über den unechten Antifaschismus," Deutschland Archiv 1979 12(7): 736-741. 15 notes, 1 table showing sentences of thousands of war criminals in Germany between 1945 and 1977.

3681 "From the Sentence against Concentration Camp Doctor Fischer Pronounced by the GDR Supreme Court on March 25, 1966," Law and Legislation in the German Democratic Republic 1966 (2): 51-63.

3682 GERMANY (DEMOCRATIC REPUBLIC). SUPREME COURT. Strafsache gegen Haase u.a. (Organisation Gehlen). Berlin(GDR): Zentralverlag, 1954.

3683 GERMANY (FEDERAL REPUBLIC). MINISTRY OF JUSTICE. Die Verfolgung nationalsozialistischer Straftaten im Gebiet der Bundesrepublik Deutschland seit 1945. Bonn: Deutscher Bundesverlag, 1964.

3684 Gewaltverbrechen. Dargestellt an Hand von 542 rechtskräftigen Urteilen deutscher Gerichte aus der Zeit von 1945-1975. Ulm: Oppitz, 1979. 380p. Diagrams, bibliography.

3685 GORZKOWSKA, JADWIGA, and ELZBIETA ZAKOWSKA. Nazi Criminals before West German Courts. Warsaw: Zachodnia Agencja Prasowa, 1965. 102p. Major topics covered include legislation on war crimes, criminals before Allied and West German courts, the West German record of prosecution, mitigating circumstances, extradition of war criminals, and statutes of limitation.

3686 GREEN, L.C. "Trials of Some Minor War Criminals," Indian Law Review 1950 4: 249-275.

3687 HELLENDALL, F. "Nazi Crime before German Courts - The Immediate Post-War Era," Wiener Library Bulletin 1970 24(20): 14-20. A review of the first few volumes of the series Justiz und NS-Verbrechen. Sammlung deutscher Strafurteile wegen nationalsozialistischer Tötungsverbrechen 1945-1966. Amsterdam: 1968-1970.

3688 HETLINGER, G. Die völkerrechtliche Verpflichtung der Staaten zur Bestrafung Einzelner und das materielle Strafrecht der Bundesrepublik Deutschland. Munich: Schön, 1965.

3689 HONIG, FREDERICK. "Criminal Justice in Germany Today: Crimes against Humanity before German Courts," Year Book of World Affairs 1951 5: 131-152.

3690 "I Knew I Did Nothing," Deals with former SS Officials Gertrud Slottke, Wilhelm Zoepf, and Wilhelm Harster," Newsweek 1967 69(8): 58.

3691 "Judging the Judges," Time 1967 90(2): 30, 32. On the trial of Hans Joachim Rehse, the first Nazi judge ever tried in a German Court. He was convicted of war crimes.

3692 "Justice Denied," Time 1972 100(19): 64-65. Deals with alleged delays in the trial of Nazi war criminals in West Germany.

3693 KOESSLER, MAXIMILIAN. "International Law on Use of Enemy Uniforms as a Stratagem and the Acquittal in the Skorzeny Case," Missouri Law Review 1959 24(1): 16-43. 95 notes.

3694 LANGBEIN, HERMANN. Im Namen des deutschen Volkes, Zwischenbilanz der Prozesse wegen nationalsozialistischer Verbrechen. Vienna: Europa, 1963. 205p. Report on legal proceedings against National Socialists from 1958-1963 before German and Austrian courts. Deals with mass destruction, concentration camps, and individual National Socialist crimes. Presents statistics of trials held and sentences handed down in these three categories. Appendix (pp. 147-197) lists post-1958 cases according to crime, date, and names of those indicted and their sentences. Based on primary sources; 106 notes, no bibliography.

3695 LANGBEIN, HERMANN. "The Nazi Criminals Stand Trial," *World Jewry* 1964 (March-April): 11-12. An assessment of German justice.

3696 LANGBEIN, HERMANN. "Trials Without Echo," *Yad Vashem Bulletin* 1966 19: 52-57. War crimes trials in Germany and Austria highlight the administration of justice in these countries but they are not being adequately reported in the press. The defendants tend to react most violently not when accused of mass murder, but when charged with having appropriated any of the victims' belongings. Every effort should be made to concentrate attention on war crimes trials. Illustrated.

3697 MARTINI, WINFRIED. *Die NS-Prozesse im ost-westlichen Spannungsfeld*. Pfaftenhoten: Imgau, 1969.

3698 ORMOND, HENRY. "Nazi Crime and German Law," *Wiener Library Bulletin* 1966 21(5): 16-21. A discussion of some of the problems in persecuting war criminals under German Law.

3699 PETERS, KARL. *Fehlerquellen im Strafprozeß. Eine Untersuchung der Wiederaufnahmeverfahren in der BRD*. Volume 1. Karlsruhe: 1970.

3700 SCHNEIDER, PETER, and HERMANN JOSEF MEYERS (eds.). *Rechtliche und politische Aspekte der NS-Verbrecherprozesse Kolloquium. 5 Vorträge von Fritz Bauer*. Mainz: Johannes-Gutenberg-Universität, 1968.

3701 SIEMSEN, K. „Über die strafrechtliche Verantwortlichkeit und die zivilrechtliche Haftung für politische Denunziationen aus der Nazizeit," *Geist und Tat* 1947 2(April): 25-27.

3702 SKORZENY, OTTO. *Geheimkommando Skorzeny*. Hamburg: Hansa Verlag Josef Toth, 1950.

3703 SONTAG, ERNST. „Die deutschen Spruchgerichte in der britischen Zone," *Friedens-Warte* 1950-1951 50: 51-64. 5 notes.

3704 "War Crimes Trials in Eastern Europe and Western Germany," *Wiener Library Bulletin* 1963 17: 5.

3705 WEINSCHENK, FRITZ. "Nazis Before German Courts - West German War-Crimes Trials," *International Lawyer* 1976 10(3): 515-529.

3706 WEIR, PATRICIA ANN LYONS. "The German War-Crimes Trials, 1949 to Present: Repercussions of American Involvement," Ph.D. dissertation, Ball State University, 1973. 563p. Abstracted in *Dissertation Abstracts International* 1974 34(8): 5086-A.

3707 WELLS, LEON W. "Recollections of a Witness," *Midstream* 1980 26(4): 40-43. The author relates his experiences as a witness at several German war crimes trials in the 1950's and 1960's, including that of Fritz G. Gebauer. Undocumented.

3708 WILKENS, E. *N.S.-Verbrechen, Strafjustiz, deutsche Selbstbesinnung*. Berlin: Lutherisches Verlagshaus Herbert Reuner, 1964.

3709 „Zur Rechtsprechung des Obersten Spruchgerichtshofes in Hamm. (Nochmals: Einheitliche Rechtsgrundlage.)," *Neue Juristische Wochenschrift* 1948 1(18): 685-686.

2. Hans Globke Trial, Berlin, 1963

3710 BOULIER, JEAN, et al. Der prozeß gegen Dr. Hans Globke (8-23.7 1963). Berlin: 1963.

3711 GERMANY (DEMOCRATIC REPUBLIC). SUPREME COURT. In the Name of the Peoples, in the Name of the Victims .... Excerpts From the Protocol of the Trial Held against Bonn State Secretary Hans Globke before the First Criminal Senate of the Supreme Court of the German Democratic Republic from July 8th to 23rd 1963 in Berlin. Berlin: Press Centre Globke Trial, 1963. 63p. Deals with war crimes and crimes against humanity. Contains opening addresses, extracts from the indictment, trial proceedings, a list of witnesses and victims, and the verdict and sentence. 63 notes.

3712 "Urteil des Obersten Gerichts der DDR gegen Dr. Hans Globke. Urteil vom 23. Juli 1963 - 1 Zst(I) 1/63," Neue Justiz 1963 17(15): 449-512.

3713 ZABOROWSKI, JAN. Dr. Hans Globke, the Good Clerk. Poznan: 1962.

3. Auschwitz Trials, Frankfurt am Main, 1963-1965

3714 AINSZTEIN, REUBEN. "The Auschwitz Trial," Midstream 1965 11(2): 3-22. Critical of so-called "German justice." West Germany has 960 judges and prosecutors who "helped establish Hitler's New Order."

3715 BAUER, F. Krigsforbrydere for domstolen: Med forord af S. Auswitz. Copenhagen: Westermann, 1945.

3716 BONHOFFER, EMMI. Zeugen im Auschwitz-Prozeß. [no city given]: Johannes Kiefel, [no date given]. Published in English as Auschwitz Trials: Letters from an Eyewitness. Richmond, Virginia: John Knox Press, 1967. 61p. A series of letters written by women who tended the witnesses at the Auschwitz trials. The author was Dietrich Bonhoeffer's sister-in-law.

3717 BRAND, EMANUEL. "Trials of Auschwitz Hangmen held from the End of the War until Now," Yad Vashem Bulletin 1964 15: 43-47.

3718 BULAWKO, HENRY. Le Procès d'Auschwitz n'a pas eu lieu. Paris: Presses du Temps Présent, 1965. 101p. Deals with restitution and punishment for war crimes in post-war years. Cites quotations from many European newspapers pertaining to crimes and punishment twenty years after the end of the war. Chapter 3 (pp. 33-44) discusses national trials held in the Federal Republic of Germany, which from 1945-1963 tried 12,982 Nazi war criminals. Gives the outcome of these trials and presents a breakdown of trials and sentences according to Allied zone. Chapter 4 (pp. 44-70) deals with accusations by Jews assembled in Paris at the 20th anniversary of their liberation from Auschwitz. Reviews reaction to the Frankfurt tribunal and its verdict convicting criminals of political crimes, in contrast to the four counts at Nuremberg. Chapter 5 (pp. 71-82) examines communications between Bonn and Jerusalem pertaining to this topic. Based on primary sources; 27 notes.

3719 HIRSCH, RUDOLF. Zeuge in Ost und West, aus dem Gerichtsalltag. Rudolstadt: VEB Greifenverlag, 1965. 334p. Memoirs of an anti-Fascist journalist at the Auschwitz trial. Deals with the search for and capture of Nazi war criminals. Extensive coverage of the trial, based primarily on the recollections of witnesses. Undocumented; 22 illustrations.

3720 HIRTHE, GUSTAV. "Zum Urteil im Auschwitz-Prozeß," Neue Justiz 1965 19(18): 568-572.

3721 KAUL, FRIEDRICH KARL. "About the Auschwitz Trials in Frankfurt/Main," Law and Legislation in the German Democratic Republic 1967 1: 65-72.

3722 KAUL, FRIEDRICH KARL. Auschwitz-Prozeß. Frankfurt am Main. Berlin: Komittee der Antifaschist, 1965. 105p.

3723 KULKA, ERICH. "Photographs as Evidence in the Frankfurt Court," Yad Vashem Bulletin 1965 17(December): 56. The album of photographs was found by Mrs. Lilly Zalmonovitz, who was deported from Carpatho-Russia to Auschwitz where she was selected to work in Germany. When liberated in 1945, she found the album in an abandoned attic in Nordhausen.

3724 LANGBEIN, HERMANN. "New Light on Auschwitz. Fresh Evidence Emerges at Frankfurt Trial," World Jewry 1965 (May-June): 14-15.

3725 LATERNSER, HANS. Die andere Seite im Auschwitz-Prozeß, 1963/65. Reden eines Verteidigers: Mit einer einführenden Untersuchung über die Prozeßführung. Stuttgart: Seewald, 1966. 454p. Covers the general procedures of the trial, and describes the prosecutors, defense attorneys, and witnesses. Chapter 2 (pp. 127-256) discusses a court session on fundamental questions of the Auschwitz trial held on June 10, 1965, in Frankfurt am Main. Chapter 3 (pp. 217-256) discusses the defense and trial of dentist Willi Frank, who was sentenced on July 1, 1965, to 7 years in prison for contributing to the deaths of over 1000 people. Chapter 4 (pp. 257-260) deals with the defense of dentist Willi Ludwig Schatz, who was acquitted on July 1, 1965, for lack of evidence. Chapter 5 (pp. 261-356) describes the defense of pharmacist Viktor Capesius, who was sentenced to 9 years imprisonment for contributing to the murders of at least 2000 people. Appendix contains the text of 31 documents on the Auschwitz trial. Based on primary sources; 6-page index, no bibliography.

3726 LINDQUIST, IRMELA, and JEREMY J. SHAPIRO. "The Auschwitz Trial and the Absence of Nemesis," Reconstructionist 1964 (June 26): 7-14.

3727 MULKA, ROBERT K.L. Der Auschwitzprozeß. Eine Dokumentation. 2 volumes. Vienna: Europa, 1965. 1029p. The trial of Mulke et at before the Schwurgericht, Frankfurt am Main.

3728 NAUMANN, BERND. Auschwitz. Bericht über die Strafsache gegen Mulka und andere vor dem Schwurgericht Frankfurt. Frankfurt am Main: Athenäum, 1965. 552p. Auschwitz: A Report on the Proceedings against Robert Karl Ludwig Mulka and Others before the Court at Frankfurt. New York: Praeger, 1966. London: Pall Mall, 1967. 433p. An account of the "show trial" held from 1963-1965 of 22 SS officers and officials who served at Auschwitz. Mulka, the main defendant, was adjutant to the camp commander, Rudolf Höß. The defendants were mostly "cold blooded" killers. Hannah Arendt's introduction covers some of the contemporary legal and political aspects of the trial as well as with puulic opinion.

3729 "Notes and Comments," New Yorker 1965 41(September 11): 41. On the sentences of an Auschwitz pharmacist and his comrades.

3730 ORMOND, HENRY. "Plädoyer im Auschwitz-prozeß," Gestern und Heute 1965 7 (Special Number).

3731 "Replik im Auschwitz-Prozeß," Frankfurter Hefte 1965 20(12): 827.

3732 SHNEIDERMAN, Samuel Loeb. "Auschwitz Trial in Frankfurt," Congress Weekly, A Review of Jewish Interests 1964 (January 13): 8, 13.

3733 "The Last Nazi Trial?" Newsweek 1979 94(22): 93-94. Trial of Kurt Lischka, Herbert Hagen, and Ernst Heinrichsohn for sending 73,000 French Jews to death in Auschwitz.

3734 "Urteil in der Strafsache gegen Helmrich Hermann Philipp Heilmann, Josef Kierspiel, Johann Mirbeth." Bremen: [no publisher], November 1953. 441p. Typescript. Deals with crimes in Auschwitz, Golleschau, and Obertraubling.

3735 WOETZEL, ROBERT K. "Reflections on the Auschwitz Trial," World Today 1965 21(11): 494-498.

4. Bishop Matthias Defregger Trial, 1969

3736 "Bishop Defregger Case," America 1969 121(3): 52; (5): 107.

3737 "The Bishop who was a Major," Time 1969 94(3): 63-64. Trial of Bishop Defregger, 1969. 1 photograph.

3738 "The Bishop's Burden," Newsweek 1969 74(7): 56-57. Deals with the massacre in the Italian village of Filetto di Camarda and the trial in Germany of Bishop Defregger. 2 photographs.

3739 "Under the Circumstances: M. Defregger Suspected Accomplice to Italian Atrocity," Newsweek 1969 74(July 12): 40.

5. Miscellaneous Trials

3740 "Anklageschrift (nach Voruntersuchung)." On the Ulm trial. Signed by Staatsanwalt Schüle and witnessed by Generalstaatsanwalt Nellmann. Ulm: [no publisher], June 25, 1957. 212p. Mimeograph.

3741 BRAND, EMANUEL. "The Lesson of the Treblinka Trial," Yad Vashem Bulletin 1965 17 : 49-53.

3742 DAS SCHWURGERICHT BEI DEM LANDESGERICHT NÜRNBERG-FURTH. "Anklageschrift gegen Franz Rademacher." Nuremberg: [no publisher], [1949]. 127p. Mimeograph.

3743 DAS SCHWURGERICHT BEI DEM LANDESGERICHT NÜRNBERG-FURTH. "Urteil gegen Franz Rademacher." Nuremberg: [no publisher], 1952. 151p. Mimeograph. Rademacher escaped.

3744 FRICKE, KARL WILHELM. "Geschichte und Legende der Waldheimer Prozesse," Deutschland Archiv 1980 13(11): 1172-1183. Deals with the trials in 1950 in East Germany of 3432 accused war criminals. 35 notes.

3745 "Germany: Who Is in the Dock?" *Newsweek* 1977 90(2): 43. On the Düsseldorf trial of 9 men and 5 women who ran the Maidanek "death factory."

3746 GERSH, GABRIEL. "Trial of a Nazi," *Jewish Digest* 1959 (March): 9-10. On the trial of neo-Nazi Wolfgang Hedler, condensed from *Congress Weekly, A Review of Jewish Interests*.

3747 GOLDSTEIN, ANATOLE. "The Germans Learn Fast," *Congress Weekly, A Review of Jewish Interests* 1952 (March 31): 8-9. On the Rademacher trial.

3748 KOREY, WILLIAM. "What Monument in Babi Yar?" *Saturday Review* 1968 (February 3): 18-19, 49. On a trial in Darmstadt.

3749 KUNZ, WOLFGANG. *Der Fall Marzabatto. Analyse eines Kriegsverbrecherprozesses*. Würzburg: Holzer, 1967. 92p. Analysis of the trial of Waffen-SS Major Walter Reder, which took place from October 19-30, 1951, in Bologna before an Italian military tribunal. Reder was indicted for violent crimes against private Italian citizens. Discusses the trial, the crimes and punishments, and problems with the Reder case in view of his Austrian citizenship. Based on primary sources; 6-page bibliography.

3750 "Murder by Marmalade: Trial of Former Nurses at the Oberwalde Insane Asylum in Brandenburg," *Time* 1965 85(March 19): 35.

3751 RASCHHOFER, HERMANN. *Der Fall Oberländer*. Tübingen: Fritz Schlichtenmayer, 1962. Published in English in 1964 by the same publisher as *Political Assassination: The Legal Background of the Oberländer and Stashinsky Cases*. 231p. Two prefaces to the English edition explain both cases. The trial of Professor Theodor Oberländer raised the question of whether a man who had worked in the Nazi party could later hold political office in the Federal Republic of Germany. English and French editions were enlarged by the addition of the Stashinsky Case, which threw light on the earlier Oberländer Case and which showed how modern nations, particularly the USSR, employed assassination as an extension of foreign policy. The English edition contains a list of judgments and court decisions used in the text and a list of sentences, decisions, statutes, and treaties quoted in the book. 296 notes, no bibliography, 3-page index.

3752 "The German Reaction to the Trial of 'The Raving Beast of Buchenwald,'" *World Jewry* 1958 (August): 16-17. The reference is to the trial of Martin Sommer, SS guard at Buchenwald.

3753 "The Innocents," *Nation* 1968 207(2): 36-37. Deals with the testimony of K. Kiesinger at the trial of Fritz Gebhard von Hahn in Bonn in 1968.

3754 "The Treblinka Trial. Eyewitness Reports," *World Jewry* 1965 (January-February): 9-10. The trial of Hermann Langbein and Miriam Novitch.

3755 "Trapping No. 3," *Newsweek* 1967 69(11): 63. Deals with the arrest of Franz Paul Stangl,"

3756 Urteil (Akten Zeichen Ks 2/57) in Strafsache Bernhard Fischer-Schweder et al. vor dem Schwurgericht in Ulm/Donau. Sitzung 29. August 1958. [no publication information given]. 503p. Multigraph. Mentions that the judgment is not yet legally binding in regard to all the defendants.

3757 VAN DAMM, H.G., and R. GIORDANO (eds.). KZ-Verbrecher vor deutschen Gerichten. Volume 1, Dokumente aus den Prozessen gegen Sommer (KZ Buchenwald) Sorge, Schubert (KZ Sachsenhausen) Unkelbach (Ghetto in Czenstochau). Frankfurt am Main: Europäische Verlagsanstalt, 1962.

3758 VAN DAMM, H.G., and R. GIORDANO (eds.). KZ-Verbrecher vor deutschen Gerichten. Volume 2, Einsatzkommando Tilsit, der Prozeß zu Ulm. Frankfurt am Main: Europäische Verlagsanstalt, 1966.

3759 "Witness for the Defense: Kiesinger in Bonn Courtroom," Time 1968 92(July 12): 24. On the trial of Fritz von Hahn in Bonn in 1968.

6. Court Decisions Under Control Council Law No. 10

3760 GERMANY. KAMMERN-GERICHT. "Urteil vom 17.5.1947 - 1 Ss 54/47," Neue Justiz 1947 1(6): 137-139. Prosecution for political reasons committed under the Nazis may be punished according to Control Council Law No. 10, even if the offense were not punishable under German law at the time.

3761 GERMANY. LANDESGERICHT FREIBERG. "Urteil vom 12.9.1947 - 1 Js 254/46," Monatsschrift für deutsches Recht 1948 2(April): 126-127. Denunciation is persecution in the sense of Control Council Law No. 10. Consciousness of unlawfulness and intent are necessary.

3762 GERMANY. LANDESGERICHT HAGEN, STRAFKAMMER III. "Urteil vom 4.8.1947 - 11 K.LS. 2/47," Monatsschrift für deutsches Recht 1948 2(March): 89-92. Relation of Article II, paragraph 4b of Control Council Law No. 10, and paragraph 4 of the decree of May 23, 1947 (regarding the removal of National Socialist encroachments on the administration of penal law) to paragraphs 59, 54 of the German Penal Code and paragraph 47 of the Military Penal Code.

3763 GERMANY. LANDESGERICHT KONSTANZ. "Urteil vom 28.2.1947 - Kls 3/47," Süddeutsche Juristen-Zeitung 1947 2(6): 337-345. Control Council Law No. 10 applied to acts committed before January 30, 1933. It created legal norms for crimes on the assumption that the punishable acts were regarded as crimes at the time they occurred, in view of the attitude of all civilized nations involved with them. The amnesty of March 21, 1933, was unconstitutional and therefore invalid. 2 notes.

3764 GERMANY. LANDESGERICHT KONSTANZ, 2. STRAFKAMMER. "Urteil vom 2.9.1947 - KLS 22/47," Monatsschrift für deutsches Recht 1947 1(December): 305-306. Deals with the punishability of an act of denunciation under Control Council Law No. 10.

3765 GERMANY. LANDESGERICHT SIEGEN. "Beschluß vfl. 8.5.1947 - 4 Js 80/46," Monatsschrift für deutsches Recht 1947 1(September): 203. The applicability of Control Council Law No. 10 in a case of denunciation.

3766 GERMANY. OBERLANDESGERICHT BRAUNSCHWEIG. "Urteil vom 28/29.11. 1947 - Ss 46/47," Süddeutsche Juristen-Zeitung 1948 3(5): 268-270. Crimes against humanity are in a state of ideal competition with violations of the German penal laws, even where an alternate indictment is admissible.

3767 GERMANY. OBERLANDESGERICHT BRAUNSCHWEIG. "Beschluß vom 26.2.1947 - Ss 7/47," Monatsschrift für deutsches Recht 1947 1(April): 37-38. Determination of the competence of German courts compared to military government courts.

3768 GERMANY. OBERLANDESGERICHT BRAUNSCHWEIG. "Beschluß vom 25.11.1947 - Ws 30/47," Monatsschrift für deutsches Recht 1948 2 April): 125. Persecution for political reasons is punishable as a crime against humanity if the action had inhuman consequences, regardless of the motives of the accused. Lack of an inhuman attitude and belief in the lawfulness of the National Socialist state are admitted as a defense in cases of denunciation.

3769 GERMANY. OBERLANDESGERICHT DRESDEN. "Urteil vom 21.3.1947 - 20.2.47," Neue Justiz 1947 1(4/5): 107-108. The provisions of the German penal law regarding maximum and minimum lengths of sentences are not valid in trials based on Control Law No. 10.

3770 GERMANY. OBERLANDESGERICHT DRESDEN. "Urteil vom 18.4.1947 - 20. 30/47," Neue Justiz 1947 1(4/5): 108. For crimes committed in the last days of the war, positive German law does not constitute a complete justification in the question of whether the act is to be considered inhuman.

3771 GERMANY. OBERLANDESGERICHT DRESDEN. "Urteil vom 16.5.1947 - 20. 18/47," Neue Justiz 1947 1(6): 139-140. Paragraph 3 of the law of juvenile court procedure of November 6, 1943, should be applied in criminal cases, according to Control Council Law No. 10.

3772 GERMANY. OBERLANDESGERICHT DRESDEN. "Urteil vom 16.5.47 - 21 18/47," Neue Justiz 1948 2(4/5): 25-26. An erroneous conception of the fundamental principles of humanity and of the unlawfulness of denouncing does not excuse the informer from penal responsibility, according to Control Council Law No. 10.

3773 GERMANY. OBERLANDESGERICHT DRESDEN. "Urteil vom 23.5.1947 - 20 58/47," Neue Justiz 1947 1(6): 139. In the case of crimes against humanity, duress in the sense of Paragraph 52 of the German Penal Code is to be considered only under special circumstances.

3774 GERMANY. OBERLANDESGERICHT DRESDEN. "Urteil vom 16.7.1947 - 21 ERKs 146/48," Neue Justiz 1948 2(7/8): 171. The denunciation of an anti-Fascist for suspicion of espionage in 1944 constitutes a crime against humanity.

3775 GERMANY. OBERLANDESGERICHT DRESDEN. "Urteil vom 12.9.47 - 20. 188/47," Neue Justiz 1947 1(8/9): 195-196. The denunciation of a foreign laboring woman by her "master" because of theft may constitute a crime against humanity.

3776 GERMANY. OBERLANDESGERICHT DRESDEN. "Urteil vom 12.9.1947 - 20 182/47," Neue Justiz 1947 1(11/12): 257. The punishment of a prisoner may constitute a crime against humanity even if a state of excitement were the reason for the act. The concept of crime against humanity does not demand that the perpetrator be a special type of inhuman personality.

3777 GERMANY. OBERLANDESGERICHT DRESDEN. "Urteil vom 6.2.1948 - 21 ERKs 8/47," Neue Justiz 1948 2(3): 55-56. An erroneous conception of love for the Fatherland cannot be considered sufficient cause for a reduction in sentences in crimes against humanity.

3778 GERMANY. OBERLANDESGERICHT DRESDEN. "Urteil vom 13.2.48 - 21 ERKs 39/47," Neue Justiz 1948 2(3): 56. The fact that the accused has not previously been convicted of a crime is not a mitigating factor in crimes against humanity.

3779 GERMANY. LANDESGERICHT DRESDEN. "Urteil vom 13.2.48 - 21 ERKs 6/47," Neue Justiz 1948 2(4/5): 86-87. The denunciation to the Gestapo of foreign workers by the owner of an enterprise because of slowness and carelessness can constitute a crime against humanity.

3780 GERMANY. OBERLANDESGERICHT DRESDEN. "Urteil vom 2.3.1948 - 21 ERKs 30/48," Neue Justiz 1948 2(4/5): 87. Deals with treatment of prisoners of war by foremen contrary to international law.

3781 GERMANY. OBERLANDESGERICHT DRESDEN. "Urteil vom 16.3.1948 - 21 ERKs 72/48," Neue Justiz 1948 2(4/5): 87-88. Deals with mistreatment of foreign civilians contrary to international law and participation in cruelties committed in concentration and labor camps.

3782 GERMANY. OBERLANDESGERICHT DRESDEN. "Urteil vom 11.5.48 - 21 ERKs 112/48," Neue Justiz 1948 2(6): 115. According to the concept of "inhumanity," it is sufficient that a criminal act violate the fundamental principles of the present state of human morality, according to Control Council Law No. 10,

3783 GERMANY. OBERLANDESGERICHT DRESDEN. "Urteil vom 1.7.1948 - 21 ERKs 130/48," Neue Justiz 1948 2(7/8): 169-171.

3784 GERMANY. OBERLANDESGERICHT DRESDEN. "Urteil vom 25.5.48 - 21 ERKs 121/48," Neue Justiz 1948 2(6): 115. Deals with the principal (Hauptschuldiger) according to Directive 38 and the accessory (Beihelfer), according to Control Council Law No. 10

3785 GERMANY. OBERLANDESGERICHT DÜSSELDORF. "Urteil vom 14.11.1947 - Ss 147-47," Süddeutsche Juristen-Zeitung 1948 3(6): 328-332; also in Monatsschrift für deutsches Recht 1948 2(April): 123-125. Deals with denunciation for political reasons, knowledge of illegality, and premeditation.

3786 GERMANY. OBERLANDESGERICHT GERA. "Urteil vom 3.3.1948 - 1 ERKs 34/48," Neue Justiz 1948 2(6): 115-116. Deals with the sanction of confiscation of property as provided in Part II of Article 9 of Directive No. 38, which should deprive those people of power who might endanger a democratic and peaceful development.

3787 GERMANY. OBERLANDESGERICHT HALLE. "Urteil vom 16.4.47 - Ss 22/47," Neue Justiz 1947 1(7): 166. If a violation of Control Council Law No. 10 constitutes at the same time an offense against provisions of the German Penal Code, competition of statutes exists.

3788 GERMANY. OBERLANDESGERICHT HAMBURG. "Urteil vom 18.6.47 - Ss 37/47," Süddeutsche Juristen-Zeitung 1948 3(1): 35-39. Also in Monatsschrift für deutsches Recht 1947 1(October): 241-243. Control Council Law No. 10 is equal to, not subsidiary to, Germany's penal code. It is valid because decreed by the Control Council, the supreme executive of the state, and it is not limited to acts of the civilian population.

3789 GERMANY. OBERLANDESGERICHT HAMM. "Beschluß vom 29.11.1947 - Ws 91/47," Monatsschrift für deutsches Recht 1948 2(March): 94. Deals with the objective and subjective elements of the offense of denunciation, according to Control Council Law No. 10.

3790 GERMANY. OBERLANDESGERICHT HAMM, 2 STRAFSENAT. "Beschluß vom 20.9.1948 - 2 Ws 83/48," Monatsschrift für deutsches Recht 1949 3(February): 121. An ancillary suit (Nebenklage) is not permissible, according to Control Council Law No. 10.

3791 GERMANY. OBERLANDESGERICHT KIEL. "Beschluß vom 3.10.1947 - Ws 67/47," Monatsschrift für deutsches Recht 1947 1(December): 307. Denunciation, according to Control Council Law No. 10, is punishable only if it constitutes an inhuman persecution for political reasons, and then only if the offender were aware of this at the time of his act.

3792 GERMANY. OBERLANDESGERICHT KIEL. "Urteil vom 26.3.47 -Ss 27/47," Süddeutsche Juristen-Zeitung 1947 2(6): 323-330. Also in Monatsschrift für deutsches Recht 1947 1(May): 69-75. The suspension of a penal law does not invalidate a past sentence under that law.

3793 GERMANY. OBERLANDESGERICHT SCHWERIN. "Urteil vom 14.7.74 -Ss 47/47," Neue Justiz 1947 1(7): 165-166. Paragraphs 47 and following of the German Penal Code are not the basis for dealing with the concept of participation, according to Control Council Law No. 10.

3794 GERMANY. OBERLANDESGERICHT STUTTGART, NEBENSITZ KARLSRUHE, 1. STRAFSENAT. "Urteil vom 13.5.1948 - Ss 33/48," Monatsschrift für deutsches Recht 1948 2(August): entire issue. Deals with the argument that acting on superior orders may be considered a mitigating factor in fixing penalties.

3795 GERMANY. OBERSTER GERICHTSHOF FÜR DIE BRITISCHE ZONE, COLOGNE. "Urteil vom 22.6.1948 - St S 8/48," Monatsschrift für deutsches Recht 1948 2(September): 303-304. Acting on conviction or from a sense of duty does not justify an action. Reprehensible and base motives are not required for an act to be a crime.

3796 GERMANY. OBERSTER SPRUCHGERICHTSHOF HAMM, 2. STRAFSENAT. "Beschluß vom 23.9.1947 - 2 Sp s1/47," Spruchgerichte 1947 1(December): 80. Deals with the criminal content of the crimes of organizations, the promotion of the criminal aims of the SS, and membership in the SS, both honorary and active.

3797 GERMANY. OBERSTER SPRUCHGERICHTSHOF HAMM, 2. SPRUCHSENAT. "Beschluß vom 10.10.1947," Spruchgerichte 1947 1(December): 81. Deals with the responsibility of the "Corps of Political Leaders" for the deportation of Jews. Concerned with a local group leader's knowledge of the slave labor program.

3798 GERMANY. OBERSTER SPRUCHGERICHTSHOF HAMM, 2. SPRUCHSENAT. "Beschluß vom 21.10.1947 (Spruchgericht Bielefeld - 2 Sp Ws 5/47)," Spruchgerichte 1947 1(December): 82. Deals with knowledge of the utilization of the "Corps of Political Leaders" for the execution of the slave labor program.

3799 GERMANY. OBERSTER SPRUCHGERICHTSHOF HAMM, 1. SPRUCHSENAT. "Urteil vom 14.10.1947 (Spruchgericht Benefeld-Bomlitz - Sp Ss 14/47)," Spruchgerichte 1947 1(December): 76. Deals with inhuman acts of the Gestapo, knowledge in the case of membership in a criminal organization, and the extent of knowledge. People who joined the organization voluntarily but who were prevented from resigning can plead duress but not compulsory membership. Reviews the reasons for sentencing by the court of appeal.

3800 GERMANY. OBERSTER SPRUCHGERICHTSHOF HAMM, 1. SPRUCHSENAT. "Urteil vom 21.10.1947 (Spruchgericht Bergedorf - Sp Ss 23/47)," Spruchgerichte 1947 1(December): 86. Deals with the significance of knowledge of crime in prewar times, crimes against humanity, crimes of organizations, slave labor programs, and the persecution of Jews. The accused had to have been conscious of the fact that a crime by an organization existed.

3801 GERMANY. OBERSTER SPRUCHGERICHTSHOF HAMM, 1. SPRUCHSENAT. "Urteil vom 21.10.1947 (Spruchgericht Stade - 1 Sp Ss 21/47)," Spruchgerichte 1947 1(December): 84. Deals with crimes of organizations, the "Corps of Political Leaders," the persecution of Jews, persecution for political reasons, knowledge of the events of November 1938, and the subjective elements of the offense.

3802 GERMANY. OBERSTER. SPRUCHGERICHTSHOF HAMM, 2. SPRUCHSENAT. "Beschluß vom 30.10.1947 - 2 Sp Ws 11/47," Spruchgerichte 1947 1(December): 82. Deals with the forcible transfer of a criminal police officer to the Gestapo and duress through prevention of his resignation.

3803 GERMANY. OBERSTER SPRUCHGERICHTSHOF HAMM, 2. SPRUCHSENAT. "Urteil vom 21.10.1947 (Spruchgericht Stade - Sps 18/47)," Spruchgerichte 1947 1(December): 79. On the inhuman acts of the "Corps of Political Leaders" concerning Germanization.

3804 GERMANY. SPRUCHGERICHTSHOF HAMM, 1. SPRUCHSENAT. "Urteil vom 28.10.1947 (Spruchgericht Recklingshausen - 1 Sp Ss 20/47)," Spruchgerichte 1947 1(December): 78. Deals with the significance of the organization chart contained in membership books, the so-called Einmann-Ämter (offices occupied by one man), crimes committed in the assumption of the position of the Amtsleiter, and the awareness of illegality in regard to the misdeeds of political leaders.

3805 GERMANY. OBERSTER SPRUCHGERICHTSHOF HAMM, 3. SPRUCHSENAT. "Urteil vom 14.1.1948 3 Sp Ss 105/47," Spruchgerichte 1948 2 (April): 114. Discusses coordination of crimes of organizations with the 3 parts of Paragraph 1 of the StGB (German Penal Code), continuity of action, and the possibility of review of penal sentences.

3806 GERMANY. SPRUCHGERICHT BIELEFELD. "Urteil vom 11.9.1947 - s Sps Ls 1042/47," Spruchgerichte 1947 1(December): 88. Deals with Paragraph 54 of the German Penal Code (StGB) and the failure to resign from the SS because of duress.

398 Allied and National Trials

3807 GERMANY. SCHWURGERICHT DRESDEN. "Urteil vom 7.7.47 - 1 Ks 58/47," Neue Justiz 1947 1(8/9): 193-195. Control Council Law No. 10 created an entirely new crime against humanity, which is a concept of mass crime based on the legal principles of civilized nations. Questions regarding knowledge, participation, and retroactivity should be considered according to the principles of German penal law.

3808 GERMANY. SPRUCHGERICHT HIDDESEN. "Urteil vom 27.8.1947 - 4 Sp Ls 12/47," Spruchgerichte 1947 1(September): 15. Comment on the judgment in Spruchgerichte 1947 1(December): 89. Deals with the crimes of the "Corps of Political Leaders," crimes of organizations, formulation of sentences, and reasons for the degrees of punishment.

3809 GERMANY. SPRUCHGERICHT HIDDESEN. "Urteil vom 7.10.1947 - 5p Sp Ls 134/47," Spruchgerichte 1947 1(December): 89.

3810 MENZEL, EBERHARD. "Die Rechtsnatur der Spruchgerichte und des von ihnen anzuwendenden Rechtes," Spruchgerichte 1949 3(February-March): 39-44.

3811 OFFENBERG, KARL. "Aus der Rechtsprechung des Obersten Spruchgerichtshofs," Spruchgerichte 1948 2(March): 71-74. Survey of the most important decisions of the Superior Court (Oberstes Spruchgericht) in Hamm. Summaries of 59 decisions, divided into questions of principle, nature of the crime of an organization, Tateinheit or Tatmehrheit, and membership.

K. GREAT BRITAIN

1. General Works

3812 Beweisdokumente für die Spruchgerichte in der britischen Zone. Hamburg: Dienstelle des Generalinspecteurs in der britischen Zone für die Spruchgerichte, 1947. 280p.

3813 FAIRFIELD, CICILY ISABEL [pseudonym, REBECCA WEST]. The New Meaning of Treason. New York: Viking, 1964. 374p. The first portion of the book deals with the treason trial of William Joyce, known as "Lord Haw Haw," and William Amery. In separate trials each was accused of treason for wartime broadcasts made from Germany.

3814 FOX, JOHN P. "The Jewish Factor in British War Crimes Policy in 1942," English Historical Review 1977 92(362): 82-106. Examines the formation of British foreign policy leading to participation in the Allied Declaration of December 17, 1942. A new principle of international law was formulated which dealt with all inhumane acts committed against any civilian population, before or during the war. The Foreign Office was reluctant to go beyond a call for retribution for war crimes. Neither did it want to include Jews as a specific category, citing lack of actual proof and the experience of World War I, after which reports of atrocities proved untrue. Pressured by world Jewish organizations and fearing public reaction to the lack of a pronouncement if stories of a deliberate German plan for wholesale extermination of the Jewish population proved true, the Foreign Office drafted the declaration condemning the general German policy of getting rid of useless Jews. Based on Foreign Office correspondence, parliamentary debates, memoirs, and newspaper reports; 61 notes.

3815 HOLSTE, HEINRICH. Einführung in das Verfahren vor den Gerichten der Kontrollkommission in der britischen Zone. Schloß Bleckede an der Elbe: Recht und Zeit, Rechtwissenschaftliche Studien zu Gegenwartsfragen, 1948. 108p.

3816 HONIG, FREDERICK. "Kriegsverbrecher vor englischen Militärgerichten," Schweizerische Zeitschrift für Strafrecht 1947 62: 20-33.

3817 "Justice for Germans? Case against the Field Marshalls," Newsweek 1948 32(14): 35. Trial of various generals and field marshalls, including von Rundstedt and von Manstein.

3818 KEETON, GEORGE WILLIAMS, and JOHN CAMERON (eds.). Trial of Gustav Rau, Otto Monsson, and William Smith; the Veronica Trial. New York: British Book Centre, [no date given]. London: Hodge, [no date given]. 248p.

3819 KOCH, EKHARD. "Ein Jahr Spruchgerichte," Zentral-Justizblatt für die britische Zone 1947 1: 109-110.

3820 KRAWINKEL, H. "Law in the British Zone of Germany," Current Legal Problems 1949 2: 245-257.

3821 LANGE, RICHARD. "Die Rechtsprechung des Obersten Gerichtshofes für die britische Zone zum Verbrechen gegen die Menschlichkeit," Süddeutsche Juristen-Zeitung 1948 3(11): 655-660. 6 notes.

3822 LIETZMANN, HEINRICH. "Die Strafgerichtsbarkeit der Kontrollkommission in der britischen Zone Deutschlands," Monatsschrift für deutsches Recht 1947 1(September): 183-186.

3823 "The British Court for War Criminals," Law Journal 1945 95(4257): 300. Note on the jurisdiction and procedure of the new British military court created by royal warrant.

3824 "The Last Defendant," Time 1949 54(26): 15. The trial of Field Marshal Fritz Erich von Manstein, Hamburg, 1949. 1 photograph.

3825 "The Legal Administration of Germany (British Zone)," Law Journal 1947 97(4245): 285.

3826 Trial of William Joyce. London: Hodge, 1946. 312p. A record of the trial of William Joyce at the Central Criminal Court. Contains a summary of the judgment and the full text of the judgment in the appeal to the House of Lords. Includes the text of the Treason Act of 1945 and the text of some of the wartime broadcasts made by Joyce from Germany.

3827 WADE, D.A.L. "A Survey of the Trials of War Criminals," Journal of the Royal United Services Institution 1951 96(581): 66-70. A brief survey of the nature and scope of the trials conducted by British military courts. 8 notes.

2. Peleus Trial, Hamburg, 1945

3828 CAMERON, JOHN (ed.). Trial of Heinz Eck, August Hoffman, Walter Weißpfennig, Hans Richard Lenz, and Wolfgang Schwender (The Peleus Trial). London: William Hodge, 1948. 247p. Volume 1 of Maxwell-Fyfe (see Introduction). [See UNWCC, Law Reports, Volume 1, Case 1]. The account of the trial of the crew of

400   Allied and National Trials

the German submarine U-852 for deliberately killing the surviving crewmen of the merchant ship Peleus. Most of the defendants were sentenced to death.

3. Dulag-Luft Trial, Wuppertal, 1945

3829 CUDDON, ERIC (ed.). Trial of Erich Killinger, Heinz Junge, Otto Boehringer, Heinrich Eberhardt, Gustav Bauer-Schlichtegroll (The Dulag-Luft Trial). London: William Hodge, 1952. 255p. Volume 9 of Maxwell-Fyfe (see Introduction). The trial of five German air force officers was held between November 26 and December 3, 1945, at Wuppertal before a British military court for the mistreatment of British prisoners of war at Dulag Luft, the name of the German air force interrogation center where Allied prisoners were taken for the purpose of gathering intelligence information. [See UNWCC, Law Reports, Volume 3, Case 19].

4. Belsen Trial, Lüneburg, 1945

3830 BENTWICH, NORMAN. "The Belsen Trial," Law Journal 1945 95 (4167): 394. Short commentary on the proceedings, showing that the trial was conducted with scrupulous fairness.

3831 EASTERMAN, ALEXANDER L. "Judgment Day for Belsen. First Trial of Nazi Criminals," World Jewry 1945 (November-December): 11-12.

3832 EASTERMAN, ALEXANDER L. "The Trial of German Hangmen," Congress Weekly, A Review of Jewish Interests 1945 (October 6): 9-10. The Lüneburg trial of 46 murderers of Belsen and Auschwitz.

3833 GORDEY, MICHEL. "Echoes from Auschwitz," New Republic 1947 117(25): 14-15.

3834 PHILLIPS, RAYMOND (ed.). Trial of Josef Kramer and Forty-four Others (The Belsen Trial). London: William Hodge, 1949. Volume 2 of Maxwell-Fyfe, (see Introduction), 749p. The 45 defendants were accused of mistreating and killing Allied nationals at Bergen-Belsen and Auschwitz. [See UNWCC, Law Reports, Volume 2, Case 10].

5. Velpke Baby Home Trial, Brunswick, 1946

3835 BRAND, GEORGE (ed.). Trial of Heinrich Gerika, Georg Hessling, Werner Noth, Hermann Muller, Gustav Claus, Richard Demmerich, Fritz Flint, and Valentina Bilien (The Velpke Baby Home Trial). London: William Hodge, 1950. Volume 7 of Maxwell-Fyfe, (see Introduction), 56p. Trial held March 20-April 3, 1946, at Brunswick before a British military court. The defendants were charged with neglecting and killing a number of Polish children at Velpke between May and December, 1944. [See UNWCC, Law Reports, Volume 7, Case 42].

6. Von Falkenhorst Trial, Hamburg, 1946

3836 "Falkenhorst: The Alibi," Newsweek 1945 25(21): 56. More on his attitude toward the war than on his trial.

3837 STEVENS, E.H. (ed.). Trial of Nikolaus von Falkenhorst, formerly Generaloberst in the German Army. London: William Hodge, 1949. Volume 6 of Maxwell-Fyfe, (see Introduction), 278p.

Trial held from July 20-August 2, 1946, at Hamburg before a British military court of General von Falkenhorst, the German commander-in-chief in Norway from 1940-1944. There were 9 charges against him, but basically he was tried for killing Allied prisoners of war. [See UNWCC, Law Reports, Volume 2, Case 61].

7. Natzweiler Trial, Wuppertal, 1946

3838 WEBB, ANTHONY M. (ed.). Trial of Wolfgang Zeuss, Magnus Wochner, Emil Meier, Peter Straub, Fritz Hartjenstein, Franz Berg, Werner Rohde, Emil Bruttel, Kurt aus dem Bruch and Harberg (The Natzweiler Trial). London: William Hodge, 1949. Volume 5 of Maxwell-Fyfe, (see Introduction), 233p. Trial held in May 1946 in Wuppertal before a British military court of 9 members of the staff of the Struthof-Natzweiler concentration camp for the execution on July 6, 1944, of 4 women employed by British military authorities while they were prisoners of the Germans. The women were killed by injections and were then cremated. It was suspected that they were alive and even conscious when placed in the ovens. The defense argued that it was legal to execute captured spies. [See UNWCC, Law Reports, Volume 5, Case 3].

8. Stalag-Luft III Trial, Dachau, 1947

3839 ANDREWS, ALLEN. Exemplary Justice. London: Harrap, 1976. 238p. Investigation into the murder of 50 allied officers as a deterrent to ten thousand prisoners in camps within Germany. In a mass breakout from Stalag Luft III, a prison camp at Sagan in Silesia, 79 officers escaped: 3 reached Great Britain, 76 were recaptured, and 50 of the 76 were shot on the personal order of Hitler. Based primarily on reports by survivors and British investigators. Some discussion of the Stalag Luft III trials at Nuremberg and Hamburg. Appendices contain biographical sketches of the victims, statements of the British Secretary for Foreign Affairs, a list of the Royal Air Force Special Investigation Branch Team, a list of the accused in order of seniority, the verdicts, and a chronology of the inquiry. 8-page index, 32 photographs, no bibliography.

9. Von Manstein Trial, Hamburg, 1947

3840 LEVERKUEHN, PAUL. Verteidigung Manstein. Hamburg: H.H. Nölke, 1950. 46p. Excellent, overall study of Von Manstein's trial.

3841 MANSTEIN, ERICH VON. Verlorene Siege. Bonn: Athenäum, 1955. 664p. Published in English as Lost Victories. Chicago: Henry Regnery, 1958.

3842 PAGET, REGINALD T. Manstein. Seine Feldzüge und sein Prozeß. Wiesbaden: Limes, 1951. 268p. Published in English as Manstein: His Campaigns and his Trial. London: William Collins, 1951. 239p. An account of the trial of Field-Marshal Erich von Manstein for war crimes committed by himself and men under his command in Poland and Russia. Manstein was found guilty and sentenced to 12 years in prison. The background material on his campaigns relates to his controversial trial, which many thought should never have been held. The author, a member of the defense, presents a sympathetic account. 3 appendices, index.

L. HUNGARY

3843 LÉVAI, JENÖ (EUGENE). "The War Crimes Trials Relating to Hungary," Hungarian Jewish Studies 1969: 252-296. Includes trials by Hungary's peoples tribunals and trials in other countries pertaining to Hungarian Jews.

3844 SZALAI, SÁNDOR. Jugements du peuple contre les criminels de guerre Hongrois. Budapest: Athenaeum, 1946.

M. ITALY

3845 "A Sunday Kind of Hate," Newsweek 1967 70(5): 43. The Italian village of Marzabotta votes to keep a German war criminal in prison.

3846 ALGARDI, ZARA. Processi ai Fascisti. Milan: Parenti, 1958. 284p. Testimonianze del tempo, Volume 30. Trials of Anfuso, Caruso, Graziani, and Borghese.

3847 ASSOCIAZIONE NAZIONALE PARTIGIANI D'ITALIA. Criminali alla sbarra: Il processo di Montemaggio. Siena: La Poligrafica, 1948. 90p. On the Siena trial.

3848 BONZITTI, NATALINO. "La cattura di un individuo all'estero in margine al caso Argoud," Rivista di Diritto Internationale 1965 48: 64-79. 46 notes.

3849 BORRINI, CARLO. Criminali di guerra italiani. Milan: IDOS, 1968.

3850 CAMPBELL, IAN. "Some Legal Problems arising out of the Establishment of the Allied Military Courts in Italy," International Law Review 1947 1: 192-206.

3851 CANEVARI, EMILIO (ed.). Graziani mi ha detto. Rome: Magi-Spinetti, 1947. 351p. Memoirs of an Italian marshal who was tried in Italy as a collaborator.

3852 "Il processo Graziani," Rivista Italiana di Diritto Penale 1949 2(1): 167-168.

3853 ITALY. TRIBUNALE MILITARA TERRITORIALE, ROME. Sentenza nella causa contro ... Data 20.7.1948. United States Library of Congress Microfilm, Law-97. Trial of Herbert Kappler in Rome in 1948.

3854 "Kesselring: Soft Soap," Newsweek 1945 25(21): 56.

3855 REPACI, A. Il processo Graziani. Milan: Instituto Nazionali per la Storia del Movimento di Liberazio in Italia, 1952.

3856 ROSSI, M. "Liberation Betrayed: Italian War Criminals," Nation 1949 168(March 26): 355-356.

3857 SCOTLAND, A.P. The Kesselring Case, Being a Representation of the Trial in Venice, Italy, Spring 1947. Bonn/Cologne: 1952.

3858 SMYTH, HOWARD MC GRAW. Secrets of the Fascist Era: How Uncle Sam obtained some of the Top-Level Documents of Mussolini's Period. Carbondale: Southern Illinois University Press, 1975.

3859 "The Missing Cancer Patient: Springing a Nazi War Criminal with Suitcase and Chivalry," Time 1977 110(9): 42-43. Deals with the 1948 trial in Rome of Herbert Kappler.

3860 "Urteil des italienischen Militärgerichts für den Bezirk Rom vom 20. Juli 1948 in Sachen Kappler," Archiv des Völkerrechts 1951-1952 3: 357-366.

3861 VASALLI, G. "Intorno al fondamento giurdico della punizione dei crimini di guerra," La Giustizia 1947 52(2): 618-626.

N. THE NETHERLANDS

3862 FRIEDMAN-VAN DER HEIDE, REINE. Drie Processen. Amsterdam: N.V. Amsterdamsche Boekien Courantmij, 1946. 144p.

3863 GODERIE, JAN. De Berschting van Oorlogsmisdadigers: Een karkaklerschets uit het process te Lueneburg, door den Nederlandschen oorlogscorrespandent, Jan Goderie. Gonda: N. v J. Mulder's Uitgmij, 1946. 99p.

3864 MAASS, WALTER B. The Netherlands at War. London: Abelard-Schumann, 1970.

3865 Processen. . . Max Blokzijl. Amsterdam: Uitgeverij Buyten en Schipperheyn, 1947. 96p. One of a series of war crimes trials reports published by the Rijksinstituut voor Oorlogsdocumentatie.

3866 RIJKSINSTITUUT VOOR OORLOGSDOCUMENTATIC. Het Process Christiansen. The Hague: Nijhoff, 1950.

3867 RIJKSINSTITUUT VOOR OORLOGSDOCUMENTATIC. Het Process Mussert. The Hague: Nijhoff, 1948.

3868 RIJKSINSTITUUT VOOR OORLOGSDOCUMENTATIC. Het Process Rauter. The Hague: Nijhoff, 1952.

3869 WARMBRUNN, WERNER. The Dutch under German Occupation, 1940-1945. Stanford: Stanford University Press, 1963.

O. NORWAY

3870 HAYES, PAUL M. Quisling: The Career and Political Ideas of Vidkun Quisling, 1887-1945. Bloomington: Indiana University Press, 1972. 368p.

3871 HEMMING-SJOBERG, A. Domen over Quisling. Stockholm: Natur och Kultur, 1946. 517p. An account of the trial of Quisling. Contains separate chapters on speeches by the defense and on the verdict.

3872 LOOCK, HANS-DIETRICH. Quisling, Rosenberg, und Terboven. Stuttgart: Deutsche Verlags-Anstalt, 1970. 587p.

3873 Straffesak mot Vidkun Abraham Lauritz Jonsson Quisling. Oslo: Utgitt pa offentlig bekostning av Eidsvating lagstols landsvikaveling, 1946.

P. POLAND

3874 BROSZAT, MARTIN. Nationalsozialistische Polenpolitik 1939 bis 1945. Schriftenreihe der Vierteljahrshefte für Zeitgeschichte.

Stuttgart: Deutsche Verlags-Anstalt, 1961. Frankfurt am Main: 1963. 200p.

3875 DATNER, SZYMON. "Opinia Bieglego w Procesie Szefa Referatu Zydowskiego w Bialostockim Gestapo (1942-1944), Fritza Gustawa Friedla [Opinion of an Expert at the Trial of Obersturmführer SS Fritz Gustav Friedel, Chief of the Jewish Department in Bialystok Gestapo, 1942-1944]," Biuletyn Zydowskiego Instytutu Historycznego w Polsce 1976 [no volume given](3) [whole number 9]: 41-58. In October 1949 action was taken before the Court of Appeal in Bialystok against Fritz Gustav Friedel, former chief of the Jewish Department in Bialystok. Doctor Szymon Datner, of the Jewish Historical Institute in Warsaw, delivered a report on Friedel's character and discussed his role in the extermination of approximately 130,000 Jews in February and August of 1943. Contains an abbreviated version of Datner's report. 32 notes.

3876 GUMKOWSKI, JANUSZ, and T. KULAKOWSKI. Zbrodniarze hitlerowscy przed Najwyzszym Trybunalem Narodowym. Warsaw: Wydawn Prawnicze, 1967.

3877 KWATERKO, A. "Trial of the Ghetto's Executioner. What was Revealed in the War Crimes Trial of the Nazi General in Command of Suppressing the Warsaw Ghetto Uprising Who was Condemned to Die," Jewish Life 1951 (October): 22-24. Deals with the trial of Stroop.

3878 MARK, B. "The Trial of Jürgen Stroop and Franz Konrad," Bleter far Geshikhte 1951 4(3): xii-xiii. English summary.

3879 POLISH INFORMATION CENTER (NEW YORK). Documents Relating to the Administration of Occupied Countries in Eastern Europe. New York: Polish Information Center, [see dates and pages below]. A series of pamphlets dealing with various aspects of War crimes committed in occupied areas. Those that deal most closely with war crimes are: (No. 1) The German Exploitation of Polish Forests, [no date], 10p. (No. 2) German Destruction of Cultural Life in poland. [1941], 23p. (No. 3) German Organization of Distribution in Poland, [no date given], 15p. (No. 4) German Persecution of Religious Life in Poland, [no date given], 29p. (No. 5) The Soviet occupation of Poland, [no date given], 46p. (No. 6) German Organization of Courts in the General Government of Poland, [no date given], 13p. (No. 7) German Iron and Steel Policies, [no date given], 18p. (Nos. 8 and 9) Extermination of the Polish People and Colonization by German Nationals, [1941], 46p.

3880 Process Iudobójey Amona Leopolda Goetha przed Najwyzszym Trybunalem Narodowym. Warsaw: Centralna Zydowska Komisja Historyczm w Polsce, 1947. The trial of Amon Leopold Goeth (the Treblinka trial), Cracow, 1947.

3881 SAWICKI, JERZY. "Law and the Demands of Justice," Poland of Today 1947 2(February): 4-7, 14.

3882 SAWICKI, JERZY. Vor dem polnischen Staatsanwalt. Berlin: Deutscher Militärverlag, [1962]. 287p. Trial of Bach Zelewski and others. All defendants and testimonies are listed in the contents.

Allied and National Trials   405

3883   Trial of Albert Forster, Polish Supreme National Tribunal, 5-
       29 April, 1948. [no publication information given]. Indictment
       of February 7, 1948, transcript of the proceedings, judgment.
       Mimeographed transcript.

3884   Trial of Rudolph F.F. Hoess, Polish Supreme National Tribunal.
       [no publication information given]. Indictment of February 11,
       1947. 98, 10p., mimeograph. Proceedings of March 11-28, 1947.
       1692p., typescript. Judgment of April 2, 1947. 59p., type-
       script.

3885   ZYLBERBERG, MICHAEL. "The Trial of Alfred Nossig - Traitor or
       Victim?" Wiener Library Bulletin 1969 23(15-16): 41-45. The
       reference is to the trial and execution by the Jewish under-
       ground of Nossig in Warsaw in 1943.

Q. RUMANIA

3886   UNITED STATES. OFFICE OF STRATEGIC SERVICES (OSS). Progress of
       Epuration under the Groza Government of Rumania. Washington:
       OSS Research and Analysis Branch no. 2957.1, 1945.

3887   UNITED STATES. OFFICE OF STRATEGIC SERVICES (OSS). The First
       War Criminal Trial in Rumania. Washington: OSS Research and
       Analysis Branch No. 2957.2, 1945.

R. USSR

3888   AINSZTEIN, REUBEN. "The Bandera-Oberlaender Case," Midstream
       1960 6(2): 17-25. Deals with Dr. Theodor Oberlaender's part in
       the 1941 Lvov massacre.

3889   BRAND, EMANUEL. "Nazi Criminals on Trial in the Soviet Union
       (1961-1965)," Yad Vashem Bulletin 1966 19: 36-44.

3890   DEAN, VERA M. "Russians take the Lead in Trying War Crimi-
       nals," Foreign Policy Bulletin 1943 23(10): 1-2.

3891   "Der Görlitzer Prozeß," Neue Justiz 1948 2(4/5): 89-90. Dis-
       cusses the trial on the basis of Order Number 201 of SMAD of
       August 16, 1947, by which Directive No. 38 of the KG had been
       put in force for the Soviet zone of occupation. The defendants
       were Dr. Bruno Malitz, last Nazi Kreisleiter, and Dr. Hans
       Meinshausen, last Nazi mayor of Görlitz.

3892   Deutsche Greuel in Rußland: Gerichtstag in Charkow. Vienna:
       Stern, [no date given]. Kharkov: 1943. 95p. Deals with the
       trial of Reinhard Retzlaff, et al, the Kharkov Trial.

3893   Documents relatifs au procès des anciens militaires de l'armée
       japonaise accusés d'avoir préparé et employé l'arme bactério-
       logique. Moscow: Éditions en langues étrangères, 1950.

3894   ECER, BOHUSLAV. The Lessons of the Kharkov Trial. London:
       Russia Today Society, 1944. 15p.

3895   FREY, GEORG. "Das Strafverfahren gegen deutsche Kriegsgefan-
       gene in der Sowjetunion," Osteuropa-Recht 1955 1(1): 31-37. 38
       notes.

3896   "Indictment in the Case of Former Servicemen in the Japanese
       Army . . . Charged with Preparing and Using Bacteriological
       Weapons . . . ," Current Digest of the Soviet Press 1950

1(52): 35-43. Contains the complete text of the story which appeared in the December 24 and 25, 1949, issues of *Pravda* and *Izvestia*, which told the story of the Khabarovsk trial. Discusses in detail the organization of special formations for preparing for and waging bacteriological warfare, experiments on live human beings, use of such warfare against China, preparation of such warfare against the Soviet Union, and personal responsibility of each of the defendants.

3897 KLADOV, IGNATII FEDOROVICH, et al. *The People's Verdict: A Full Report of the Proceedings at the Krasnodar and Kharkov German atrocity Trials*. London/New York: Hutchinson, 1944. Contains extracts from the records of the Krasnodar trial in July 1943, and the Kharkov trial in December 1943. 124p.

3898 LAUTERBACH, RICHARD E. "How the Russians Try Nazi Criminals," *Harper's* 1945 190(1141): 658-664. On the Kharkov trial.

3899 "Legal Proceedings on the War Crimes of the German Fascist-Usurpers in the Crimea and the Kuban," *Pravda*, November 13, 1947, and *Soviet Press Translations* 1948 3(3): 89-91. From *Pravda*, November 13, 1947.

3900 MAPEL, SIEGFRIED. *Die Entwicklung der Verfassungsordnung in der sowjetisch besetzten Zone Deutschlands von 1945 bis 1963*. Tübingen: 1964.

3901 MAURACH, REINHART. *Die Kriegsverbrecherprozesse gegen deutsche Gefangene in der Sowjetunion*. Hamburg: Arbeitsgemeinschaft vom Roten Kreuz in Deutschland, 1950. 96p.

3902 *Moscow Trial of 16 Polish Diversionists, June 18-21, 1945*. Soviet News, [1945]. 68p. On June 18, 1945, the Military Collegium of the Supreme Court of the Soviet Union began the trial of Leopold Okulicki and 15 others for subversive underground activity in the rear of the Red Army in the western regions of Byelorussia, the Ukraine, Lithuania, and Poland.

3903 NETTLE, PETER. "Inside the Russian Zone, 1945-1947," *Political Quarterly* 1948 19(3): 201-253.

3904 "Poor Misguided People," *Time* 1947 50(19): 30. Deals with the Sachsenhausen jailers. Sachsenhausen Trial, Berlin, 1947.

3905 *Prozeß in der Strafsache gegen die faschistischen deutschen Okkupanten und ihre Helfershelfer wegen ihre Bestialitäten im Gebiet der Stadt Krasnodar und des Krasnodarer Gans während der zeitweiligen Besatzung dieses Gebietes: Verhandelt am 14-17 juli 1943*. Moscow: Verlag für fremdsprachige Literatur, 1943.

3906 RODNEY, C.M. "The Trial of Sachsenhausen," *Central European Observer* 1947 24: 329-333. Sachsenhausen Trial, Berlin, 1947.

3907 SIGL, FRITZ (comp.). *Todeslager Sachsenhausen. Ein Dokumentarbericht vom Sachsenhausen-Prozeß*. Berlin: SWA-Verlag, 1948. 215p. Sachsenhausen Trial, Berlin, 1947.

3908 *The Case of the 16 Poles and the Plot for War on the U.S.S.R. as told in official Documents*. [New York]: National Council of American-Soviet Friendship, [1945]. 31p.

3909 The Trial in the Case of the Atrocities Committed by the German Fascist Invaders in the City of Kharkov and in the Kharkov Region, December 15-18, 1943. Moscow: Foreign Languages Publishing House, 1944. 83p. Translated from a report published in Pravda, December 16-20, 1943.

3910 U.S.S.R. SUPREME COURT. Trial of the Organizers, Leaders, and Members of the Polish Diversional Organizations in the Rear of the Red Army on the Territory of Poland, Lithuania, and the Western Regions of Byelorussia and the Ukraine, heard before the Military Collegium of the Supreme Court of the USSR, June 18-21, 1945. London/New York: Hutchinson, 1945. 239p. A verbatim report.

XII
ADOLF EICHMANN TRIAL

A. GENERAL

3911 ADLER, H.G. "In Sachen Adolf Eichmann," *Neue Politische Literatur* 1961 6: 975-983. 6 notes.

3912 AMERICAN JEWISH CONGRESS. COMMISSION ON INTERNATIONAL AFFAIRS. *The Eichmann Controversy: A Fact Sheet*. New York: June 17, 1960. 30p. Mimeograph.

3913 ANDERS, GÜNTHER. *Wir Eichmannsöhne. Offener Brief an Klaus Eichmann*. Munich: C.H. Beck, 1964. 75p. Bücher 20 Fragen unserer Zeit. "Schwarze Reihe."

3914 ARENDT, HANNAH. *Eichmann in Jerusalem: A Report on the Banality of Evil*. New York: Viking Press, 1963. Several editions reprinted between 1963 and 1979. Penguin, 1979. 312p. The 1979 edition is a revised enlargement of the account first published in 1963. Published in German as *Eichmann in Jerusalem. Ein Bericht von der Banalität des Bösen*. Munich: Piper, 1964. The author covered the 1961 Eichmann trial for the *New Yorker*. Covers Eichmann's various crimes against the Jewish people and the so-called three solutions: expulsion, concentration, and killing. It examines in detail deportations of Jews from Germany, Western Europe, the Balkans, and Central Europe, as well as the "killing centers" in the East. Traces the career of Eichmann from his birth in 1906 to his death in 1962. Contains a trial report and has as its main source the trial proceedings, which were delivered to the press in Jerusalem. The author concedes that the Eichmann trial, like the IMT at Nuremberg, was an *ex post facto* affair, but insists that the report analyzed here deals with nothing but the extent to which the court in Jerusalem succeeded in fulfilling the demands of justice. 5-page bibliography, 8-page index, undocumented. Randolph L. Braham's *The Eichmann Case: A Source Book* contains more than 250 reviews and criticisms of this work.

3915 BAUMANN, JÜRGEN. "Schuld und Verantwortung. Ein Beitrag zur juristischen Würdigung des Falles Eichmann," *Freiburger Rundbrief* 1962 14(53-56): 29-32.

3916 BEN-CHORIN, SCHALOM. "Adolf Eichmann. Menschlicher Gerichtsbarkeit entzogen," Europäische Begegnung 1962 2(7): 42-45.

3917 BÖLL, HEINRICH. "Befehl und Verantwortung. Gedanken zum Eichmann Prozeß," in Aufsätze, Kritiken, Reden. Cologne: Kieperheuer & Witsch, 1967.

3918 BONDY, FRANCOIS, and [KARL JASPERS]. "Karl Jaspers zum Eichmann-Prozeß," Der Monat 1961 13(152): 15-19. Also in French and Italian.

3919 BORINGE, BERNARD. "Eichmann," Historia 1960 (165): 155-161.

3920 BRAND, JOEL. Adolf Eichmann. Fabeln und Fakten. Frankfurt am Main: Ner Talmid, 1961.

3921 "Council for the Defense," Newsweek 1961 57(17): 56-57. 1 photograph.

3922 DAVID, ILANA. "Eichmann and the Young Israeli," Jewish Frontier 1961 28(4): 7-9 (Section 2).

3923 "Der Prozeß," Der Spiegel 1961 15(16): 20-30, 32. 12 photographs.

3924 "Documentary Evidence. Globke, Eichmann and Others," New Times 1960 (42): 13-18. Mostly on Eichmann. 2 photographs, 2 illustrations.

3925 EDEL, PETER. "Die Eichmannschaft und ihr Kommandant," Die Weltbühne 1960 15(24): 742-749.

3926 EICHMANN, ADOLF. "Meine Memoiren." Jerusalem, 1960. 127p. Handwritten. Document No. 1492 in the documentation prepared by the Sixth Bureau of the Police Headquarters of Israel.

3927 Eichmann. Das Gesicht im Spiegel Israels. Cairo: Informationsamt, 1961. 14p.

3928 "Eichmann and Justice: The 'Principle of Universality,'" Wiener Library Bulletin 1960 14(2): 21, 28.

3929 "Eichmann Is at Bay on Eve of Trial: An Intimate Study," Life 1961 50(15): 22-27. Pictorial report, with photographs by Gjon Milia.

3930 "Eichmann, Israel, und Wir," Kirche im Dorf 1961 22: 337-344.

3931 "Eichmann Names Accomplices," International Affairs 1961 7(8): 84-92; 7(9): 90-98; 7(10): 94-100.

3932 EPPLER, ELIZABETH E. "Eichmann's Aides on Trial," World Jewry 1964 (July-August): 9-10. Deals with the trial in Frankfurt of 2 of Eichmann's aides.

3933 FISZER, HENRYK. Eichmann. Materialien und Kommentare. Warsaw: Zachodnia Agencja Prasowa, [no date given].

3934 FUHRMANN, PETER. "Die Verantwortung Adolf Eichmanns," Politische Studien 1964 15(155): 310-319.

3935 HAMRIN, AGNE. Bokslut i Jerusalem [Balance in Jerusalem]. Stockholm: Bonnier, 1962. 224p.

3936 HANDLIN, OSCAR. "The Ethics of the Eichmann Case," Issues 1961 15(Winter): 1-8.

3937 HAREL, ISRAEL. The House on Garibaldi Street. New York: Viking, 1975. 296p.

3938 HAUSNER, GIDEON. "Can It Happen Again?" National Jewish Monthly 1962 76(10): 10a, 34-35.

3939 HAUSNER, GIDEON. Justice in Jerusalem. New York: Harper & Row 1966. 528p. New York: Schocken, 1968. Published in German as Gerechtigkeit in Jerusalem. Munich: Kindler, 1967. 760p. A justification of the Eichmann trial by the Attorney General of Israel, who was the chief prosecutor. The background materials present a general record of the "final solution," particularly where Eichmann was involved. Criticizes the Vatican and Pope Pius XII for their attitudes on the Jewish problem.

3940 HEIMAN, LEO. "Eichmann and the Arabs," Jewish Digest 1961 (June): 1-6.

3941 HELEN, JAMES JOHN, SISTER. "Eichmann and Buber:A Message of Responsibility," Commonweal 1962 76(15): 374-376.

3942 HERZBERG, ABEL J. Eichmann in Jerusalem. The Hague: B. Bakker, 1962. 204p.

3943 HESSE, FRITZ. Das Spiel um Deutschland. Munich: P. List, 1953. 443p.

3944 HILLEL, MARC. "Le dernier voyage d'Eichmann,"Constellation 1961 (153): 180-204.

3945 HILLEL, MARC, and RICHARD CARON. Operation Eichmann. Paris: Presses de la Cité, 1961. 187p.

3946 HILLRINGHAUS, F. HERBERT. "Eichmann, die Juden und wir," Die Kommanden 1961 15(9): 1-2.

3947 "How Israel Will Try Eichmann," Jewish Observer and Middle East Review 1960 (June 10): 14-15. Condensed in Jewish Digest 1960 (August): 18-22.

3948 "Il caso Eichmann al Consiglio di Sicurezza. Le richieste del Governo Argentino," Relazioni Internazionali 1960 24(27): 901-902.

3949 JASPER, G. "Eichmann," Judaica 1962 18(2): 65-104. A comprehensive review article.

3950 KATZ, SHLOMO. "Eichmann and the 'Liberal' Mentality," Midstream 1961 7(1): 64-67.

3951 KAUFMAN, G. "Eichmann's Israel," Time and Tide 1961 42(22): 891.

3952 KAUL, FRIEDRICH KARL. "Eichmann sagt aus," Die Weltbühne 1962 17(2): 38-46; 17(3): 76-82.

3953 KAZIN, ALFRED. "Eichmann and the New Israelis," The Reporter, 1961 (April 27): 24-25.

3954 KEMPNER, ROBERT M.W. Eichmann und Komplizen. Zurich/Stuttgart/Vienna: Europa, 1961. 452p. A complete history of Eichmann's career, with a country-by-country analysis of his deeds and methods of operation. Contains the complete minutes of the Wannsee Conference. Also done in Hebrew. Many documents, bibliography, index.

3955 LEWIS, FLORA. "Israel on the Eve of Eichmann's Trial," New York Times Magazine, April 9, 1961: 12, 101-103. 5 photographs.

3956 LINES, J. "Eichmann and His Bitter Harvest of Hate," American Mercury 1960 91(September): 127-130.

3957 MAYER, MILTON. "Eichmann in Israel," Progressive 1961 (April): 17-20.

3958 MAYER, REINHOLD. „Jad Vashem. Ein Beitrag aus Israel zum Eichmann-Prozeß," Deutsches Pfarrerblatt 1961 61: 325-327.

3959 MIKELLITIS, EDITH. „Der verlorene Sohn. Anmerkungen zum Fall Eichmann," Zeitschrift für Geopolitik 1961 32: 269-270.

3960 MURMELSTEIN, B. Terezin. Il ghetto-modello di Eichmann. Bologna: Cappelli, 1961. 239p.

3961 MUSMANNO, MICHAEL A. "Eichmann in Jerusalem: A Critique," Chicago Jewish Forum 1963 (Summer): 282-285.

3962 NORNENGAST, URDA. „Was geht in Jerusalem vor? Die weltgeschichtliche Bedeutung des Eichmann Prozesses," Zeitschrift für Geopolitik 1961 32: 270-271.

3963 NOXON, J. "The Eichmann Memoir," The Personalist 1961 43(3): 382-392.

3964 ORBACH, MAURICE. Does Eichmann Matter? London: London Committee for Inter-Racial Unity, 1960. 15p. Unity Pamphlet No. 2.

3965 PALMER, STUART. "Eichmann and Ourselves," Nation 1960 191(5): 91-92.

3966 PFLEIDERER, DIETRICH. „Eichmann und das Dritte Reich," Volkshochschule im Westen 1962 14(1): 47.

3967 PLAYFAIR, GILES. "Eichmann and the Problem of Justice," New Republic 1960 143(22): 15-17.

3968 PRITTIE, TERENCE. "Eichmann and the Germans," New Republic 1961 144(17): 5-6.

3969 ROBINSON, NEHEMIAH. Eichmann's Confederates and the Third Reich Hierarchy. New York: Institute of Jewish Affairs of the World Jewish Congress, 1961. 59p.

3970 SCHMIDT, REGINA, and EGON BECKER. Reaktionen auf politische Vorgänge. Drei Meinungsstudien aus der Bundesrepublik. Frankfurt am Main: Europäische Verlags-Anstalt, 1967. 160p.

3971 SEGALL, ARIE. "Books Around the Eichmann Trial," Yad Vashem Bulletin 1962 11: 29-35.

3972 ZAHN, GORDON C. "The Private Conscience and Legitimate Authority," Commonweal 1962 76(1): 9-13. Refers to the Eichmann trial and discusses collective versus individual guilt.

B. BIOGRAPHICAL AND SPECIAL STUDIES

3973 DE KONIG, INES. A Study of Adolf Eichmann (1906-1962). Adolf Hitler's Expert in Jewish Affairs. Newton, Massachusetts: [published by the author], 1964. 34p.

3974 "Dossier on Eichmann," World Jewry 1961 4(4): 32p. (Special Issue).

3975 EICHMANN, ADOLF. Eichmann par Eichmann. Paris: B. Grasset, 1970. 526p. Selections from the interrogations of Captain Avner Less.

3976 EICHMANN, ADOLF. Ich, Adolf Eichmann. Ein historischer Zeugenbericht. Leoni am Starnberger See: Druffel, 1980. 550p. Autobiography of Adolf Eichmann, edited and expanded upon by Rudolf Aschenauer, defense counsel for German soldiers before the allied tribunals and German courts. Information on Eichmann's role in the formation of Jewish policy, his denial of mass murder charges, and his admission to having participated in the deportation of Jews. Discusses his years in Germany after his flight and his plea of innocence. Appendices include essays on Eichmann's superiors and collaborators during his trial, commentary on documentation, questions and answers about the destruction of Jews. Documentation includes population statistics of Jews in Europe and the Soviet Union, the Korherr Report of 1943 (also known as "The Final Solution of the European Jewish Question"), and numerous reports and directives issued by top Nazi officials. The publishers state that this report was made by Eichmann 1955. 11-page index of names, cities, and organizations, 3p. of notes, 2-page bibliography, 8 photographs.

3977 Eichmann. Master of the Nazi Murder Machine. New York: World Jewish Congress, 1961. 32p. Also in Yiddish and Spanish.

3978 "Eichmann the 'Christian?'" America 1962 106(24): 814-815.

3979 HOLTHUSEN, HANS E. "Hannah Arendt, Eichmann und die Kritiker," Vierteljahrshefte für Zeitgeschichte 1965 13(2): 178-190. 14 notes.

3980 HULL, WILLIAM LOVELL. The Struggle for a Soul. Garden City: Doubleday, 1963. 175p. Published in German as Kampf um eine Seele. Gespräche mit Eichmann in der Todeszelle. Wuppertal: Sonne & Schild, 1964. 149p.

3981 KULCSAR, I.S., SHOSHANA KULCSAR, and LIPOT SZONDI. "Adolf Eichmann and the Third Reich," in Ralph Slorenko (ed.). Crime, Law, and Corrections. Springfield, Illinois: Charles C. Thomas, 1966. A psychiatric evaluation of Eichmann. German summary in Der Spiegel 1966 (47): 176-182.

3982 KÜSTERMEIER, R. "Der Mörder Eichmann und seine Ankläger," Der Gewerkschafter 1961 9(5): 13-15.

3983 MERTON, THOMAS. "A Devout Meditation in Memory of Adolf Eichmann," Ramparts 1966 (October): 8-10. Concludes, in light of

Eichmann's having been found sane by a psychiatrist, that the sane people are the most dangerous.

3984 MEYERHOFF, HANS. "Everyman's Eichmann," Nation 1962 194(20): Inside Cover.

3985 MONTFORT, FRANCOIS DE. Adolf Eichmann, levez-vous! Paris: Presses de la Cité, 1961.

3986 PEARLMAN, MOSHE. "Klement est Eichmann," Historia 1961 (176): 94-92.

3987 PUMPHREY, D. "Eichmann," Time and Tide 1961 42(16): 660-661.

3988 REYNOLDS, QUENTIN JAMES, EPHRAIM KATZ, and ZWY ALDOUBY. Minister of Death: the Adolf Eichmann Story. New York: Viking, 1960. 246p. Published in German as Der Bevollmächtigte des Todes. Der Fall Adolf Eichmann. Konstanz/Stuttgart: Diana, 1961. 253p. Also published in Dutch, Italian, and Portuguese.

3989 SERVATIUS, ROBERT. Verteidigung Adolf Eichmann: Plädoyer. Bad Kreuznach: Ferd. Harrach, 1961. 88p. Deals with Eichmann's trial, primarily with the indictment and the defense.

3990 SILVING, HELEN. "In re Eichmann: A Dilemma of Law and Morality," American Journal of International Law 1961 55(2): 307-358. 124 notes.

C. CRIMES

3991 "Adolf Eichmann und die 'Endlösung' der Judenfrage," Der Bürger 1960 10(4): 76-78. Eichmann's role in the "final solution."

3992 ALDOUBY, ZWY, and EPHRAIM KATZ. "Adolf Eichmann: Nazi Butcher," Look, August 2, 1960: 57-58, 61-63; August 16, 1960: 35-42.

3993 BETTELHEIM, BRUNO. "Eichmann; The System; the Victims," New Republic 1963 148(24): 23-33.

3994 BISS, ANDREAS. Der Stop der Endlösung - Kampf gegen Himmler und Eichmann in Budapest. Stuttgart: [no publisher given], 1966. 356p. An account of the author's and Kastner's dealings with Eichmann in an attempt to rescue Hungarian Jews.

3995 BRAHAM, RANDOLPH L. Eichmann and the Destruction of Hungarian Jewry. New York: Twayne Publishers for the World Federation of Hungarian Jews, 1961. 64p. Also in Hungarian.

3996 CENTRE DE DOCUMENTATION JUIVE CONTEMPORAINE. Le Dossier Eichmann et "la solution finale de la question juive." Paris: Éditions du Centre, 1960. 221p. Also published in Spanish.

3997 CLARKE, COMER. Eichmann: The Man and His Crimes. New York: Ballantine, 1960. 153p. Published in England as The Savage Truth. Eichmann: The Brutal Story of Hitler's Beast. London: World Distributors, 1960. 192p. Also published in Dutch, Swedish, and Portuguese.

3998 DONOVAN, JOHN. Eichmann, Man of Slaughter. New York: Avon, 1960. 109p.

414 Eichmann Trial

3999 DROST, PEITER N. *The Crime of State*. 2 volumes. Leyden: 1959.

4000 EASTERMAN, ALEXANDER L. "They did not aid Eichmann. Jews of Occupied Europe Repudiate Hannah Arendt's Slanders on the Martyred Victims of the Nazis," *World Jewry* 1963 (November-December): 9-12.

4001 EICHMANN, ADOLF. "I Transported them to the Butcher," *Life* 1960 (November 28): 19-24, 101-112; 1960 (December 5): 146-148.

4002 "Eichmann: Der Endlöser," *Der Spiegel* 1960 14(23): 32-33; 14(25): 20-33; 14(43): 37-41; 1961 15(26): 49-51; 15(53): 68-69; 1962 16(22): 51. Titles vary.

4003 EINSTEIN, SIEGFRIED. *Eichmann, Chefbuchhalter des Todes*. Frankfurt am Main: Röderberg, 1961. 184p.

4004 KASTNER, RUDOLF. *Der Kastner Bericht über Eichmann: Menschenhandel in Ungarn*. Munich: Kindler, 1961. 367p.

4005 KERMISCH, J. "Eichmann's Role in the Destruction of the Jews," *Yad Vashem Bulletin* 1961 10(April): 19-24. Also done in Hebrew.

4006 KIPPHARDT, HEINAR. *Joel Brand. Schauspiel*. Frankfurt am Main: Suhrkamp, 1965. 141p. The text of a play that deals with Eichmann's role in Hungary.

4007 KRZYZANOWSKA, ZOFIA, and HENRYK FISZER. *Little-Known Facts in the Criminal Career of Adolf Eichmann in Poland*. Washington: Embassy of the Polish People's Republic, 1961. 40p.

4008 KÜHNRICH, HEINZ. *Judenmörder Eichmann. Kein Fall der Vergangenheit*. Berlin(GDR): Dietz, 1961. 154p. Contains an account of Theresienstadt by Arnold Munter.

4009 LA GUARDIA GLUCK, GEMMA. "La Guardia's Sister - Eichmann's Hostage," *Midstream* 1961 7(1): 3-19.

4010 LÉVAI, JENÖ [EUGENE]. *Eichmann in Hungary. Documents*. Budapest: Pannonia, 1961. 294p. Also in French and German.

4011 LÉVAI, JENÖ (EUGENE). "The Hungarian Deportations in the Light of the Eichmann Trial," *Yad Vashem Studies* 1963 5: 69-103. 94 notes.

4012 LEVIN, MEYER. "Eichmann's Last Victim," *Coronet* 1961 (July): 98-107.

4013 PANETH, PHILIP. *Eichmann: Technician of Death*. New York: Robert Speller, 1960. 239p.

4014 PENDORF, ROBERT. *Mörder und Ermordete. Eichmann und die Judenpolitik des Dritten Reiches*. Hamburg: Rütten and Loening, 1961. 151p. Deals with the search for Eichmann, his various roles in the "final solution," and his life after the war.

4015 POLIAKOV, L[ÉON]. "Eichmann: Administrator of Extermination. The 'Definitive Solution of the Jewish Problem,'" *Commentary* 1949 7(5): 439-446.

4016 REYNOLDS, QUENTIN JAMES. "Adolf Eichmann, Henker von Millionen," Sie und Er 1961 37(January 5 - March 30): 1-13.

4017 [ROBINSON, NEHEMIAH]. Eichmann. Master of the Nazi Murder Machine. New York: World Jewish Congress, 1961. 32p.

4018 SCHROERS, Rolf. „Der banale Eichmann und seine Opfer," Merkur 1964 18(196): 578-583. 3 notes.

4019 SCHÜLE, ERWIN. „Endlösung - nach zwanzig Jahren. Von den Wannsee-Protokollen bis zum Eichmann Prozeß," Kommunität 1962 6: 97-108.

4020 WIGHTON, CHARLES. Eichmann: His Career and His Crimes. London: Oldhams Press, 1961. 288p. Also in Dutch.

D. PURSUIT AND APPREHENSION

4021 ARONÉANU, EUGÈNE. "L'Arrestation d'Eichmann et le droit international," Revue de Défense Nationale 1960 16(August-September): 1444-1456.

4022 BAR-ZOHAR, MICHEL. Les Vengeurs. Paris: Fayard, 1968. 315p. Published in English as The Avengers. New York: Hawthorn, 1968. 279p. Also available in Hebrew. The author claims that Eichmann's address in Argentina was supplied to Isser Harel, head of the Israeli Security Police and Intelligence Agency, by Dr. Fritz Bauer, chief prosecutor of the Hesse District in West Germany.

4023 ELLER, LILI. "The Day they caught Eichmann," Jewish Spectator 1960 (October): 17-19.

4024 FRIEDMANN, TUVYAH. The Hunter. London: A. Gibbs & Phillips, 1961. 299p. New York: Macfadden, 1961. 289p. An autobiographical account of the search for Eichmann and other war criminals.

4025 "La cattura di Eichmann. Chiarimenti di Israele all'Argentina," Relazioni Internazionali 1960 24(25): 830-831.

4026 PEARLMAN, MOSHE. The Capture and Trial of Adolph Eichmann. London: Weidenfeld and Nicolson, 1963. 666p. An expanded version of the earlier British publication The Capture of Adolf Eichmann. London: Wiedenfeld and Nicolson, 1961. 179p. Published in German as Die Festnahme des Adolf Eichmann. Frankfurt am Main: S. Fischer, 250p. Also done in French, Italian, Spanish, and Hebrew. Discusses Eichmann's capture, the diplomatic battle over custody, and courtroom proceedings. Excerpts portions of the interrogation of Eichmann in Jerusalem and reviews in detail evidence presented at the trial. An examination of Eichmann's cross-examination, and his responses to questions from the bench. Appendix contains the full text of the indictment. No bibliography, 22-page index.

4027 PENDORF, ROBERT. "Eichmanns letzte Jahre," Der Stern 1960 (June 25): 10-16.

4028 RODGERS, RAYMOND SPENCER. "Eichmann's Capture and Its Consequences," Saturday Night 1960 (October 1): 16-18.

4029 ROUSSEAU, CHARLES. "Affaire Eichmann: Arrestation et enlèvement en territoire argentin par des agents du gouvernement israélien d'un ressortissant allemand recherché pour crimes de guerre," Revue Général de Droit International Public 1960 64(4): 772-786. 37 notes.

4030 WIESENTHAL, SIMON. Ich jagte Eichmann. Tatsachenbericht. Gütersloh: Bartelsmann Lesering, 1961. Also in Hebrew.

E. PROSECUTION

4031 ALEXANDROV, VICTOR. Six Millions de morts. La Vie d'Adolf Eichmann. Paris: Librairie Plon, 1960. Also in Swedish.

4032 Another Witness Against Eichmann. Washington: Embassy of the Czechoslovak Socialist Republic, 1961. 2p. Deals with an eye-witness account by Dr. Eduard Taskier.

4033 AUERBACH, RACHEL. "Witnesses and Testimony in the Eichmann Trial," Yad Vashem Bulletin 1962 (11): 45-54. Also in Hebrew.

4034 CAPLAN, SAMUEL. "Six Million Prosecutors," Congress Bi-Weekly 1961 28(9): 5-7. The opening statement by Prosecutor Gideon Hausner in the trial of Eichmann.

4035 "Digest of Testimony at the Trial," Yad Vashem Bulletin 1962 (11): 60-76. Also in Hebrew.

4036 HAUER, MORDECAI. "Eye-Witness Report (Encounter with Eichmann)," Jewish Frontier 1963 (July): 29-30. The reference is to an encounter in Kasa (Slovakia).

4037 HEIMAN, LEO. "The Eichmann Trial: Witnesses for the Prosecution," Jewish Frontier 1961 28(4): 10-13.

4038 HÖSS, RUDOLF. Adolf Eichmann. Testimonio de Rudolf Hoess, commandant de exterminación de Auschwitz. Buenos Aires: Congreso Judio Mundial, Ejecutivo Sudamericano, 1960. 47p. Based on the autobiography of Höß.

4039 ISRAEL. GOVERNMENT PRESS OFFICE. Eichmann Trial - Witnesses for the Prosecution. Short Biographical Notes. Jerusalem: Government Press Office, 1961. 5p.

4040 ISRAEL. GOVERNMENT PRESS OFFICE. Trial of Adolf Eichmann. The Prosecution. Brief Biographies. Jerusalem: Government Press Office, 1961. 3p.

4041 ROSENNE, SHABTAI. 6,000,000 [i. e. Six Million] Accusers. Israel's Case Against Eichmann. The Opening Speech and Legal Arguments of Mr. Gideon Hausner, Attorney General. Jerusalem: Jerusalem Post, 1961. 316p. The original was in Hebrew. Also published in Italian, Russian, Spanish, German, and Hungarian.

4042 SCHAPPES, MORRIS U. "6,000,000 Prosecutors," Jewish Currents 1961 15(5): 3-4.

4043 SCHMORAK, DOV B. (ed.). Sieben Zeugen sagen aus im Eichmann-Prozeß. Berlin: Arani, 1962.

4044 "Six Million Accuse." An album of phonograph records based on the proceedings of the Eichmann trial cut by United Artist Records in 1963.

4045 WIESEL, ELIE. "Eichmann's Victims and the Unheard Testimony," Commentary 1961 32(6): 510-516.

4046 "Yes. We Knew Eichmann," Jewish Observer 1961 (March 24): 17-21. Some background stories of prosecution witnesses.

F. THE TRIAL

4047 ALLEMANN, FRITZ RENÉ. "Bücher über Eichmann. Der Prozeß warf seinen Schatten voraus," Der Monat 1961 13(152): 54-56. 8 notes.

4048 ALLON, DAFNA. "The Eichmann Trial," Jewish Frontier 1961 28(9): 16-20.

4049 "Anklage gegen Eichmann," Das Neue Israel 1961 13(9): Special Issue.

4050 AUERBACH, LUDWIG (ed.). Der Eichmann-Prozeß im Meinungsbild vom SBZ-Flüchtlingen. Munich: Infratest, 1961.

4051 AZPIAZU, I. DE. "The Trial of Adolf Eichmann in the Light of Christian Principles," Christian News from Israel 1961 12(2): 19-23.

4052 BAR-NATAN, MOSHE. "Background to the Eichmann Trial," Jewish Frontier 1961 28(5): 4-7.

4053 BAYNE, EDWARD ASHLEY. Israel's Indictment of Adolf Eichmann. Some Philosophical, Political, and Historical Aspects of the Israeli Action. New York: American University Field Staff, 1960. 20p. Southwest Asia Series, 1960 9(7).

4054 Behind the Eichmann Trial. New York: Community Relations Service, 1961. 6p. Reprinted from Senior Scholastic 1961 78(April 26): 12-15, 22.

4055 BENTWICH, NORMAN. "The Trial of Adolf Eichmann," Solicitor Quarterly 1962 1: 303-308.

4056 BILLIG, JOSEPH. "Le Procès Eichmann et les étapes de la solution de la question juive," Le Monde Juif 1961 16(24-25): 40-49.

4057 BLUMENTHAL, NACHMAN. "Eichmann Trial Throws New Light on History," Yad Vashem Bulletin 1962 11: 2-9.

4058 CASA, MAYOR. "Eichmann ou l'autre procès," Esprit [new series] 1961 29(6): 1109-1115.

4059 COHEN, NATHAN. Rechtliche. Gesichtspunkte zum Eichmann-Prozeß. Frankfurt am Main: Europäische Verlags-Anstalt, 1963. 92p.

4060 COMER, JOHN D. "The Eichmann Trial: Historic Justice?" Georgia Bar Journal 1961 23(4): 491-511. 22 notes.

4061 CUTLER, PHIL. "The Eichmann Trial," Canadian Bar Journal 1961 4(5): 352-371.

4062 DAVIS, ERNST. "Der Eichmann-Prozeß und die Rechtspflege in Israel," Deutsche Richterzeitung 1961 39: 250-352.

4063 DRAPER, G.I.A.D. "The Eichmann Trial: A Judicial Precedent," International Affairs 1962 38(4): 485-493.

4064 DÜRRENMATT, PETER. „Der Fall Eichmann," Reformatio. Evangelische Zeitschrift für Kultur und Kirche 1960 9: 387-388.

4065 EBAN, ABBA. "The Eichmann Trial in Retrospect," The Reporter 1962 26(13): 16-18.

4066 EICHMANN, ADOLF. Der Prozeß von Jerusalem. Düsseldorf: Econ, 1964. 336p.

4067 "Eichmann Goes on Trial," Saturday Review 1961 (April 8): 17-19, 49-50.

4068 "Eichmann on Trial," Polish Perspectives 1961 4(5): 3-7.

4069 EISENBERG, ALFRED. El caso Eichmann ante el derecho internacional. Montevideo: Comite Central Israelita, 1962. 23p. Based on a speech delivered to the Instituto Cultural Uruguayo-Israeli on October 26, 1951.

4070 FAWCETT, J.E.S. "Some Thoughts on the Eichmann Trial," The Lawyer 1961 4(3): 7-11. Reproduced in Atlas 1962 3(6): 446-448.

4071 FAWCETT, J.E.S. "The Eichmann Case," British Year Book of International Law 1962 38: 181-215. Heavily documented.

4072 GOLLANCZ, VICTOR. The Case of Adolf Eichmann. London: Victor Gollancz, 1961. 61p. A series of arguments offered by a British Jew to show why Eichmann should not have been executed. Argues that the 15-year search for Eichmann was a deplorable exercise and that his judicial murder was no different from German war crimes. Undocumented.

4073 GOLLANCZ, VICTOR. "The Case of Adolf Eichmann," Minnesota Review 1963 3(2): 257-262.

4074 GREEN, L.C. "The Eichmann Case," Modern Law Review 1960 23(5): 507-515.

4075 GRINGAUZ, SAMUEL. "The Case of Adolf Eichmann," Alliance Review 1961 15(35): 53-60.

4076 HALEVY-LEVY, I. "Trial of a Mass Killer," Jewish Life 1961 (June): 6-11.

4077 HALPERN, BEN. "Reflections on the Eichmann Trial," Jewish Frontier 1961 28(3): 30-35.

4078 HAUSNER, GIDEON. "Eichmann and His Trial," Saturday Evening Post 1962 235(39): 19-25; (40): 58-61; (41): 85-90.

4079 HAUSNER, GIDEON, et al. "The Eichmann Case. I. The Indictment," Midstream 1961 7(3): 3-13. Also in The New Leader 1961 (July 3): 12-15.

4080 HEIMAN, LEO. "Arabs Fear Eichmann Trial," National Jewish Monthly 1960 (August): 6-7.

4081 HEIZLER, R. "Eichmann vor Gericht," Die politische Meinung 1961 6: 85-90.

4082 IKOR, ROGER. "Le Procès Eichmann," Preuves 1961 (127): 29-32.

4083 "Israel-Eichmann-Prozeß. Das Labyrinth," Der Spiegel 1961 15(36): 46-52.

4084 ISRAEL. OFFICE OF INFORMATION. The Eichmann case before the United Nations Security Council. New York: [Israel Office of Information], 1960. 23p. I. Statement by Mrs. Golda Meir, Minister for Foreign Affairs of Israel. II. Excerpts from statements by members of the Security Council, June 22 and 23, 1960.

4085 ISRAEL. GOVERNMENT PRESS OFFICE. Trial of Adolf Eichmann. The Court. Brief Biographies. Jerusalem: [Israel Office of Information], 1961. 2p.

4086 JÄGER, HERBERT. "Betrachtungen zum Eichmann-Prozeß," Monatsschrift für Kriminologie 1962 45: 73-83. Also in Freiburger Rundbrief 1964 15(57-60): 47-52.

4087 KATZ, MILTON, and HERBERT WECHSLER. Does the Trial of Eichmann by Israel Serve the Cause of International Justice? New York: [no publisher given], 1961. 42p. Mimeographed transcript of the NBC Television program "The Nation's Future," April 8, 1961.

4088 KATZ, SHLOMO. "Hannah Arendt and the Eichmann Trial," Midstream 1963 9(3): 61-65. Revisionist history of the Holocaust, with examinations of Hannah Arendt by Ernst Simon, "A Textual Examination," Judaism 1963 12(4): 387-415, 19 notes; and Alexander Donat, "Empiric Examination," Judaism 1963 12(4): 416-435. 21 notes.

4089 KATZ, SHLOMO. "Notes on the Eichmann Case," Midstream 1960 6(3): 83-87.

4090 KAUL, FRIEDRICH KARL. Der Fall Eichmann. 2nd edition. Berlin: Verlag das Neue Berlin, 1963. 367p. Detailed study of the Eichmann case following his arrest, with some background material.

4091 KUSTER, REINHARD. "Zum Prozeß gegen Adolf Eichmann," Reformatio. Evangelische Zeitschrift für Kultur und Kirche 1961 10: 274-279.

4092 LANGENFASS, FRIEDRICH. "Der Eichmann-Prozeß und wir," Zeitwende, Neue Furche 1961 32(11): 721-725.

4093 LASOK, D. "The Eichmann Trial," International and Comparative Law Quarterly 1962 11(2): 355-374.

4094 "Le Vatican et le procès," Évidences 1961 13(89): 41-46.

4095 LEAVY, ZAD. "Eichmann: Murder Trial Without Precedent," Los Angeles Bar Bulletin 1961 36(4): 113-115, 135-141.

4096 LEAVY, ZAD. "Report from Jerusalem. The Eichmann Trial," Journal of the State Bar of California 1962 37(2): 243-261.

4097 LEAVY, ZAD. "The Eichmann Trial and the Rule of Law," American Bar Association Journal 1962 48(9): 820-825.

4098 LEBEDEV, A. "The Eichmann Trial: View of Oswiecim Survivors," New Times 1961 (17): 13-14.

4099 LINZE, DEWEY W. The Trial of Adolf Eichmann. Los Angeles: Holloway, 1961, 224p.

4100 LOWENBERG, HELMUTH. Notes on the Trial of Adolf Eichmann. New York: Foreign Affairs Department of the American Jewish Committee, 1961. Various pagination, mimeographed.

4101 MARTIN, BERNHARD. "Gedanken zum Eichmann-Prozeß in Jerusalem," Die neue Schau 1961 22: 178-179.

4102 MELO, ARTEMIO LUIS. "El caso Eichmann y la soberanía argentina," Revista de Derecho Internacional y Ciencias Diplomaticas 1960 8(17/18): 99-119.

4103 MILYUTIN, N. "The Eichmann Case – Further Developments," New Times 1961 (12): 13-15.

4104 MILYUTIN, N. "The Eichmann Trial," New Times 1961 (16): 13-14; (18): 18; (20): 10-11; (22): 19-20.

4105 "Murder Was Their Profession. Background to the Eichmann Trial," Wiener Library Bulletin 1961 15(1): 1-2.

4106 MUSMANNO, MICHAEL A. "The Objections in limine to the Eichmann Trial," Temple Law Quarterly 1961 35(1): 1-22.

4107 MUSZKAT, MARIAN. "The Problems of the Eichmann Trial," Yad Vashem Bulletin 1961 (10): 6-8. Also in Hebrew.

4108 NELLESSEN, BERND (ed.). Der Prozeß von Jerusalem: Ein Dokument. Düsseldorf: Econ, 1964. 336p. Documentary history of Eichmann's trial, with the testimony of over 2 dozen witnesses. Discusses the verdict and his execution. Undocumented; 2 indexes.

4109 PAPADATOS, PIERRE (PETER) A. "The Eichmann Trial," Bulletin of the International Commission of Jurists 1962 14(October): 13-19.

4110 PAPADATOS, PIERRE (PETER) A. The Eichmann Trial. New York: Frederick A Praeger, 1964. 129p. Published in French as Le Procès Eichmann. Geneva: Droz, 1964. 125p. Describes the law which was applied to the Eichmann case and discusses the main aspects of the Eichmann trial as a manifestation of international law, among them the impartiality of Israeli judges, the right of Israel to punish German war criminals, the abduction of the defendant, and the retroactivity of the Israeli law under which Eichmann was tried. Concludes with objections to the Eichmann judgment and a chapter on the struggle against genocide. Appendix contains the text of the indictment against Adolf Eichmann by the Attorney-General of Israel. 193 notes, 5-page bibliography.

4111 PEPPER, CURTIS G., and ROBERT MASSIE. "Eichmann on Trial," Newsweek 1961 57(16): 41-49.

4112 PERLZWEIG, MAURICE L. The Eichmann Trial and South America. New York: World Jewish Congress, 1961. 5p. Mimeograph.

4113 POLIAKOV, LÉON. "The Eichmann Trial," Commentary 1967 43(1): 86-90.

4114 POLIAKOV, LÉON. "The Eichmann Trial. The Proceedings," American Jewish Year Book 1962 63: 54-84.

4115 POTTECHER, FREDERIC. Grand procès. Powers, Adams, Eichmann. Paris: B. Arthaud, 1964. 340p.

4116 RASSINIER, PAUL. Le Véritable Procès Eichmann, ou les vainqueurs incorrigibles. Paris: Les Sept Couleurs, 1962. 252p. Published in German as Zum Fall Eichmann. Was ist Wahrheit? - oder - Die unbelehrbaren Sieger. Leoni am Starnberger See: Druffel, 1963. 248p. Part 1, "Nuremberg," pp.15-123, deals with the war from Stalingrad to Nuremberg, war crimes, crimes against the peace, crimes against humanity, and the Eichmann trial. Documented.

4117 RISSE, HEINZ THEO. "Der Eichmann-Prozeß und die Jugend in der Bundesrepublik," Freiburger Rundbrief 1961 13(50/52): 37-41.

4118 ROBINSON, JACOB. And the Crooked Shall be made Straight: The Eichmann Trial, the Jewish Catastrophe, and Hannah Arendt's Narrative. New York: Macmillan, 1965. 406p. The author was a prosecution consultant at the Eichmann trial. Deals with Eichmann's war crimes, the legal basis of the trial, the trial itself, Jewish behavior and resistance during the Holocaust, and the fate of Europe's Jews in a country-by-country survey. Defends Jewish behavior during the Holocaust.

4119 ROGAT, YOSAL. The Eichmann Trial and the Rule of Law. Santa Barbara: Center for the Study of Democratic Institutions, 1961. 44p. Discusses the purposes of the trial and international law and the trial. Concludes that Israel's action in administering international law was ambiguous, though not necessarily illegal.

4120 ROGAT, YOSAL. "The Measures Taken: The Eichmann Trial and the Rule of Law," The Second Coming Magazine 1962 1(3): 8-19.

4121 ROLIN, H. "Le Procès Eichmann," Journal des Tribunaux 1961 76(4320): 325-326.

4122 ROSENBERG, HAROLD. "The Trial and Eichmann," Commentary 1961 32(5): 369-381.

4123 RUSSELL, EDWARD F.L. [LORD RUSSELL OF LIVERPOOL]. The Trial of Adolf Eichmann. London: William Heinemann, 1962. American edition published as The Record, the Trial of Adolf Eichmann for his Crimes against the Jewish People and against Humanity. New York: Knopf, c.1962, 1963. 351p. Describes crimes committed by Adolf Eichmann, criminal conspiracy, the "final solution," and the Einsatzgruppen in Russia. Reviews Eichmann's testimony before the Israeli court and his final speeches. Concludes with an analysis of the judgment and sentence. Appendix I contains a list of SS ranks and their army equivalents. Appendix II is an essay on the defense of superior orders. No bibliography, 9-page index, 45 notes.

4124 SANTANDER, SILVANO. El gran proceso: Eichmann y el ante la Justicia. Buenos Aires: Ediciones Silva, 1961.

4125 TAYLOR, TELFORD. "Large Questions in the Eichmann Case," Revue de Droit International 1961 39: 46-52, and New York Times Magazine, January 22, 1961.

4126 "The Case of Adolf Eichmann," New Times 1960 (31): 7-11. 5 photographs.

G. TRIAL DOCUMENTS

4127 CARMEL, ISRAEL. "Hans Frank's Diary in the Eichmann Trial," Yad Vashem Bulletin 1961 (10): 19-24, (11): 35-36. This article is the outcome of the author's screening of the diary for the Eichmann trial. Also published in Hebrew.

4128 Die Ausnützung des Eichmann-Prozesses zur Diffamierung der BDR durch die östliche Propaganda und Agitation. Eine dokumentarische Zusammenstellung. Frankfurt am Main: VVN-Vereinigung der Verfolgten des Naziregimes, 1961.

4129 "Dokumentation zum Eichmann-Prozeß," Freiburger Rundbrief 1961 13(50-52): 55-66.

4130 Eichmann: Henker, Handlanger, Hintermänner. Eine Dokumentation. Berlin: Ausschuß für Deutsche Einheit, 1961.

4131 Full Text of Indictment of Adolf Eichmann in the District Court of Jerusalem of February 21, 1961. New York: Israel Office of Information, 1961. 13p. Mimeograph.

4132 GURI, HAIM. The Glass Cage: A Journal of the Eichmann Trial. New York: Orion, 1964. 288p. Le Cage de verre (journal du procès Eichmann. Paris: A. Michel, 1964. 167p. An Israeli poet-journalist describes his reactions to the trial and punishment of Eichmann.

4133 HAUSNER, GIDEON. "Text of the Indictment against Eichmann," American Jewish Year Book 1962 63: 120-131.

4134 ISRAEL. DISTRICT COURT OF JERUSALEM. Criminal Case No. 40/61. The Attorney General of the Government of Israel v. Adolf, the Son of Adolf Karl Eichmann. [Minutes of] Sessions 1-121. Jerusalem: 1961. 244 sections. Unpaged mimeograph. Washington: Microcard Editions, 1962. 65 microcards. Published in German as Strafakt 40/61. Der Generalstaatsanwalt des Staates Israel gegen Adolf Sohn des Adolf Karl Eichmann. Urteil. Jerusalem: 1961. Original is in Hebrew, also done in Yiddish and French. Contains legal arguments on the competence of Israel to try Eichmann (Sections 1-55), a biography of Eichmann (Sections 56-78), and a discussion of the "final solution" and Eichmann's role (Sections 79-80). Surveys Eichmann's entire career. Contains a section on the findings of fact in light of the indictment and on the judgment and death sentence.

4135 ISRAEL. POLICE HEADQUARTERS. SIXTH BUREAU. Adolf Eichmann. [Transcript of cross examination by Israeli police]. 6 volumes. Jerusalem: 1961.

4136 ISRAEL. POLICE HEADQUARTERS. SIXTH BUREAU. Eichmann. List of Documents Mentioned During Interrogation. [1960-1961]. 19p. Mimeograph. The documents pertaining to Eichmann's activities were submitted to get his reaction to them,

4137 ISRAEL. POLICE HEADQUARTERS. SIXTH BUREAU. ["List of documents and statements, 1960-1961"]. Unpaged mimeograph. Lists and abstracts 1656 documents selected and processed by the Israeli police. The origin, date, and subject matter are noted on the right column of each reference.

4138 ISRAEL. PUBLIC INFORMATION CENTRE. The Attorney-General of the Government of Israel v. Adolf, the Son of Adolf Karl Eichmann. 3 volumes. Jerusalem: Public Information Centre, Prime Minister's Office, 1961-1962.

4139 KERMISH, J. "Yad Vashem Archives Contribution to the Preparation of the Eichmann Trial," Yad Vashem Bulletin 1962 (11): 37-54. Also done in Hebrew.

4140 LANDAU, ERNEST (ed.). Der Kastner-Bericht über Eichmanns Menschenhandel in Ungarn. Munich: Kindler, 1961. 367p. A revised and enlarged edition of Rezso (Rudolph) Kasztner's Der Bericht des jüdischen Rettungskommittees aus Budapest 1942-1945. [Basel]: Vaadath Ezra Vehazalah Budapest, [1946]. 191p. The Kasztner version was used in the Eichmann trial as Exhibit T/1113.

4141 LANG, JOCHEN VON. Das Eichmann-Protokol. Tonbandaufzeichnungen der israelischen Verhöre. Berlin: Severin and Siedler, 1982. 276p. Includes 66 facsimiles of documents.

4142 "Le dossier Eichmann," Le Monde Juif 1960 15(21-22): 1-67 (Entire special issue).

4143 OPPENHEIMER, MAX (ed.). Eichmann und die Eichmänner. Dokumentarische Hinweise auf den Personenkreis der Helfer und Helfershelfer bei der Endlösung. Ludwigsburg: K.J. Schromm, 1961.

4144 POLIAKOV, LÉON (ed.). Le Procès de Jérusalem. Jugement et documents. Paris: Calmann-Lévy, 1963. 414p. A study of the Eichmann trial. Deals with various aspects of his career, including the deportation of Jews, the extermination camps, his official duties, and the defense at his trial. Includes several documents which deal with these topics.

4145 POLIAKOV, LÉON. "The Proceedings," American Jewish Year Book 1962 63: 54-84.

4146 SCHMORAK, DOV. B. Der Prozeß Eichmann. Dargestellt an Hand der in Nürnberg und Jerusalem vorgelegten Dokumente sowie der Gerichtsprotokolle. Vienna: Hans Deutsch, 1964. 437p. Deals with the complete official career of Eichmann, divided into 88 sections, most of them excerpts from the interrogation of and testimony of Eichmann. Uses numerous documents.

4147 SERVATIUS, ROBERT. Strafverfahren gegen Adolf Eichmann: AZ: District-Gericht Jerusalem 40/61; AZ: Supreme Court Jerusalem 336/61. Cologne: [no publisher given], 1963.

4148 "Trial of Adolf Eichmann." Jerusalem: 1961. Minutes of the trial, Official Transcript in English. Recorded on microfilm and mimeographed.

4149 WOLFMANN, ALFRED. Eichmannprozeß. Berichte aus Jerusalem. Düsseldorf: Deutscher Gewerkschaftbund, [1962]. 96p.

4150 YAD VASHEM. JERUSALEM. **Index of Exhibits Submitted to the District Court of Jerusalem. Criminal Case 40/61. The Attorney General v. Adolf Eichmann.** Jerusalem: [no publisher given], August 30, 1961. 84p. Lists both prosecution and defense documents and gives a synopsis of each.

4151 ZEIGER, HENRY A. (ed.). **The Case against Adolf Eichmann. Documents, Letters and Testimony.** New York: New American Library, 1960. 192p. Also in Hebrew, Italian, and Swedish.

H. VERDICT

4152 BAR-NATAN, MOSHE. "The Eichmann Verdict," **Jewish Frontier** 1962 29(1): 3-5.

4153 BAUMANN, JÜRGEN. "Gedanken zum Eichmann-Urteil," **Juristenzeitung** 1963 18(4): 110-121.

4154 "Eichmann condamné á mort," **Le Monde Juif** 1961 16(26-27): 19-31.

4155 "Eichmann Condemned to Death," **Hadassah Magazine** 1962 (January): 12-13, 19.

4156 "Eichmann Pays the Penalty," **Israel Digest** 1962 5(12): 1, 8.

4157 "Eichmann Trial Ended. Death Sentence Passed," **Israel Digest** 1961 4(26): 1-2, 4.

4158 GRAVEN, JEAN. "Comment juger le jugement Eichmann? Le bilan du procès," **Revue Internationale de Criminologie et de Police Technique** 1962 16(1): 19-60.

4159 KÜSTERMEIER, R. "Das Todesurteil," **Der Gewerkschafter** 1962 10(1): 11-12. On Eichmann.

4160 LISKOFSKY, SIDNEY. "The Eichmann Trial. The Judgment," **American Jewish Year Book** 1962 63: 104-119.

4161 MARTINI, WINFRIED. "Eichmann und die Todesstrafe," **Die dritte Gewalt** 1960 11(11): 6-7.

4162 MUSMANNO, MICHAEL A. **The Death Sentence in the Case of Adolf Eichmann: A Letter to His Excellency Itzhak Ben-Zvi, President of the State of Israel.** Pittsburgh: Supreme Court of Pennsylvania, 1962.

4163 SCHWARZENBERGER, GEORG. "The Eichmann Judgment," **Current Legal Problems** 1962 15: 248-265. 58 notes.

I. APPEAL

4164 "Eichmann Appeal Hearing Ends: No New Witnesses to Be Heard," **Israel Digest** 1962 5(8): 4-5, 8.

4165 ISRAEL. SUPREME COURT. **Adolf, the Son of Adolf Karl Eichmann v. the Attorney-General of the Government of Israel: Minutes of Session no. 1-7, March 22-May 29, 1962. Criminal Appeal No. 336.61.** Jerusalem: [no publisher given], 1962.

4166 ISRAEL. SUPREME COURT. Criminal Appeal No. 336/61. Adolf, Son of Adolf Karl Eichmann v. the Attorney General of the Government of Israel. Judgment. Jerusalem: [no publisher given], 1962. Original in Hebrew, also in Yiddish, French, and German.

4167 ISRAEL. SUPREME COURT. Judgment: Criminal Appeal in the Case of Adolf Eichmann v. the Attorney General. Jerusalem: Ministry of Justice, 1963. 116p. Summarizes Eichmann's trial, conviction, and appeal.

4168 LAPIDES, LEON. An Appeal to the District Court of Jerusalem. [no city given]: [no publisher given], 1961. 2p.

4169 SERVATIUS, ROBERT. Berufungsbegründung in der Berufungsstrafsache Adolf Eichmann gegen Generalstaatsanwalt. Cologne: [no publisher given], January 21, 1962. 18p. Typescript.

4170 SERVATIUS, ROBERT. Ergänzung der Berufungsbegründung vom 31. 1. 1962 in der Berufungsstrafsache Adolf Eichmann gegen Generalstaatsanwalt. Cologne: [no publisher given], February 15, 1962. 61p. Typescript. Published in English as Criminal Appeal of Adolf Eichmann v. Attorney General in Completing the Reasons of Appeal dated 31. 1. 1962. Jerusalem: [no publisher given], 1962. 61p. Mimeograph.

J. INTERNATIONAL LAW

4171 CARDOZO, MICHAEL H. "When Extradition Fails, Is Abduction the Solution?" American Journal of International Law 1961 55(1): 127-135. Deals with the Eichmann case in light of the alleged harboring by the United States of Andrija Artukovic, accused of being a Croatian war criminal. 48 notes.

4172 GASSMAN, BENJAMIN, and HERBERT WECHSLER. "Adolf Eichmann and the Law. Was His Trial by Israeli Court Justified?" Bar Bulletin 1962 19(3): 100-108.

4173 GIBBON, WILLIAM A. "Some Thoughts on the Eichmann Incident and the International Rule of Law," Manitoba Bar News 1960 32(4): 79-88.

4174 GREEN, LESLIE C. "Legal Issues of the Eichmann Trial," Tulane Law Review 1963 37(4): 641-684. Also available in French as "Aspects juridiques du procès Eichmann,' Annuaire Français de Droit International 1963 9: 150-190. 185 notes.

4175 GREEN, LESLIE C. "The Maxim nullem crimen, sine lege and the Eichmann Trial," British Year Book of International Law 1962 38: 457-471. Copiously annotated.

4176 HEAZLETT, ELIZABETH. "Eichmann - International Law?" University of Pittsburgh Law Review 1962 24(1): 116-132. 77 notes.

4177 KATZ, MILTON. "Eichmann: International Problem," Harvard Law Record 1961 32(3): 9-15.

4178 Le Jugement d'Eichmann. L'Opinion de juristes en droit international. Cairo: Administration de l'Information, [no date given]. 18p.

4179 LEO, GERHARD. "Internationale Aspekte des Eichmanns-Prozesses," Deutsche Außenpolitik 1961 6(12): 1447-1453.

4180 LIPSIC, RICARDO. *Principios elementales de derecho internacional en que se basa el proceso de Eichmann*. Buenos Aires: Centro de Estudios por el Adelanto de Derecho Internacional, 1961. 14p.

4181 LISKOFSKY, SIDNEY. "The Eichmann Case," *American Jewish Year Book* 1961 62: 199-208. Deals with the Security Council meeting on the dispute between Argentina and Israel on the abduction of Eichmann.

4182 MUSZKAT, MARIAN. "The Eichmann Trial - International Aspects," *Yad Vashem Bulletin* 1962 (11): 19-26. Also in Hebrew.

4183 WOETZEL, ROBERT K. "The Eichmann Case in International Law," *Criminal Law Review* 1962 (October): 671-682. 36 notes.

K. LEGALITY AND JURISDICTION

4184 AMERICAN JEWISH COMMITTEE. *The Eichmann Case. Moral Questions and Legal Arguments*. New York: [no publisher given], 1961. 7p.

4185 "American Jews Protest Against Israel," *Jewish Newsletter* 1960 16(13): 1-2. The American Council for Judaism criticizes Israel's claim to have the right to try Eichmann.

4186 BAADE, HANS W. "The Eichmann Trial: Some Legal Aspects," *Duke Law Journal* 1961 3(3): 400-420. 82 notes.

4187 HANDLIN, OSCAR. "Ethics & Eichmann," *Commentary* 1960 30(2): 161-162. A discussion of Jacob Robinson's article "Eichmann and the Question of Jurisdiction."

4188 MERON, THEODOR. *Public International Law Problems of the Jurisdiction of the State of Israel*. Paris: Éditions Techniques, 1961. 39p. Reprint of a work that appeared in English in *Journal du Droit International* 1961 88(4): 986-1063.

4189 OLIVER, COVEY. "Judicial Decisions Involving International Law. Jurisdiction of Israel to Try Eichmann. International Law in Relationship to the Israeli Nazi Collaboration (Punishment) Law," *American Journal of International Law* 1962 56(3): 805-845.

4190 PARSONS, GEORGE R., JR. "Israel's Right to Try Eichmann," *New Republic* 1961 144(12): 13-15.

4191 ROBINSON, JACOB. "Eichmann and the Question of Jurisdiction," *Commentary* 1960 30(1): 1-5. For a reaction to this article, see Oscar Handlin's "Ethics & Eichmann," and Robinson's reply to Handlin in *Commentary* 1960 30(2): 162-163. The discussion continued in the following 2 issues of the same journal. The original article was also published in Spanish.

4192 ROBINSON, NEHEMIAH. *Legality, Equity, and the Substantive Basis of the Eichmann Trial*. New York: Institute of Jewish Affairs of the World Jewish Congress, 1961. 10p.

4193 TREVES, VANNI E. "Jurisdictional Aspects of the Eichmann Case," *Minnesota Law Review* 1963 47(4): 557-592.

L. PUBLIC AND PRESS REACTIONS

4194 ALKALAY, DAVID. "World Opinion on the Eichmann Trial. Yugoslavia," Yad Vashem Bulletin 1962 (11): 84-86. Also in Hebrew.

4195 AMERICAN JEWISH COMMITTEE. The Eichmann Case in the American Press. New York: Institute of Human Relations Press, [no date given, after 1961]. 87p. Examines press reactions to the kidnapping of Eichmann, the matter of Israeli jurisdiction, the possibility of a fair trial, possible penalty, images of Eichmann, what the trial accomplished, reactions to the verdict, and approximately a dozen other topics.

4196 AMERICAN JEWISH CONGRESS. COMMISSION ON INTERNATIONAL AFFAIRS. The Opening of the Eichmann Trial: A Study of Press Reaction. New York: [American Jewish Congress], July 1961. 36p. Mimeograph.

4197 ARIEL, JOSEPH. "The Eichmann Trial in the Neo-Nazi Press," Yad Vashem Bulletin 1962 (11): 13-18. Also in Hebrew.

4198 [CAPRI, DANIEL]. "World Opinion on the Eichmann Trial. Italy," Yad Vashem Bulletin 1962 (11): 88-90. Also in Hebrew.

4199 CARMICHAEL, JOEL. "The Eichmann Case. II, Reactions in Germany," Midstream 1961 7(3): 13-27.

4200 D'HARCOURT, ROBERT. "Eichmann et l'opinion allemande," Revue de Paris 1961 68(6): 35-42.

4201 GLOCK, CHARLES Y., GERTRUDE J. SELZNICK, and JOE L. SPAETH. The Apathetic Majority: a Study based on public Responses to the Eichmann Trial. New York: Harper & Row, 1966, 1970. 222p. Volume 2 of a series based on a University of California 5-year study of anti-Semitism in the United States.

4202 ISRAEL. MINISTRY OF FOREIGN AFFAIRS. Eichmann in the World Press. Jerusalem: Ministry of Foreign Affairs, Information Division, 1961. 79p.

4203 KOL, A. "World Opinion on the Eichmann Trial. Czechoslovakia," Yad Vashem Bulletin 1962 11(April-May): 79-81. Also in Hebrew.

4204 KOPPEL, EDWARD JAMES. "Attitudinal and Informational Changes Precipitated by Local Newspaper Coverage of the Eichmann Trial," M.A. thesis, Stanford University, 1962. 161p.

4205 KOREY, WILLIAM. "Eichmann and the Socialist Press," Israel Horizons 1962 10(3): 8-12.

4206 KOREY, WILLIAM. "Reporting the Eichmann Case," Survey 1961 39(December): 17-28.

4207 LAMM, HANS (comp.). Der Eichmann-Prozeß in der deutschen öffentlichen Meinung. Eine Dokumentensammlung. Frankfurt am Main: Ner-Tamid, 1961. 73p. This collection of documents reflects German public reaction to the trial of Adolf Eichmann. Presents the opinion of the government, the parliamentary opposition, newspapers and magazines, churches, youth, and citizens of the Federal Republic of Germany. Discusses radio and television coverage and German journalists at the trial. Reprints 22 articles from leading German periodicals and lists books on the Eichmann trial published in Germany in 1961. Based on primary sources; 19 photographs.

4208 MELCHIOR, DAVID WERNER. "World Opinion on the Eichmann Trial. Scandinavia," Yad Vashem Bulletin 1962 (11): 86-87. Also in Hebrew.

4209 MUSZKAT, MARIAN. "Reactions to the Eichmann Trial," Yad Vashem Bulletin 1963 (13): 48-53. Also in Hebrew.

4210 RINGER, BENJAMIN B. The American Public and the Eichmann Trial. A Reanalysis of Data from the Gallup Poll of May, 1961. New York: American Jewish Committee, 1961. 22p. Mimeograph. The Gallup Poll results are included in an appendix.

4211 ROCKMAN, A. "World Opinion on the Eichmann Trial. Israel," Yad Vashem Bulletin 1962 (11): 95-96. Also in Hebrew.

4212 [ROTKIRCHEN, LIVIA]. "World Opinion on the Eichmann Trial. USA - Great Britain," Yad Vashem Bulletin 1962 (11): 91-93. Also in Hebrew.

M. SIGNIFICANCE

4213 AINSZTEIN, REUBEN. "After the Trial. Putting the Record Straight," Jewish Quarterly 1962 9(35): 18-20. Review essay on Edward F. L. Russell's The Record: The Trial of Adolf Eichmann for His Crimes against the Jewish People and against Humanity.

4214 BAUMINGER, ARYEH. "The Effect of the Eichmann Trial on Israeli Youth," Yad Vashem Bulletin 1962 (11): 9-12. Also in Hebrew.

4215 DE SOLA POOL, DAVID, and TAMAR DE SOLA POOL. "The Impact of the Eichmann Trial," Jewish Forum 1961 (November): 17-18.

4216 EBAN, ABBA. "Lessons of the Eichmann Trial," Jewish Spectator 1962 27(7): 7-9.

4217 ISERLES, ISRAEL. "Now that the Trial is Over," New Outlook 1962 5(1): 9-14. The Eichmann trial was the first instance in which the Nazi era was judged from the Jewish point of view.

4218 LEVI, ROBERT. "Some International Conclusions of the Eichmann Trial," Yad Vashem Bulletin 1962 (11): 26-29. Also in Hebrew.

4219 LEVIN, MEYER. "Eichmann: The Lesson Yet to be Learned," Congress Bi-Weekly 1962 29(1): 5-7.

4220 MATTHEWS, T.S. "The Meaning of the Eichmann Trial," Saturday Evening Post 1961 234(234): 32-33, 74-77. 6 photographs.

4221 PALMON, J.E. "Juristenbilanz des Eichmann-Prozesses," Geist und Tat 1961 16: 198-203.

4222 PETERS, KARL. "Gedanken eines Juristen zum Eichmann-Prozeß," in Kurt Ihlenfeld (ed.). Eckart Jahrbuch, 1961/2. Wilten: Eckart, 1961.

XIII
VIETNAM WAR
AND WAR CRIMES TRIALS

A. GENERAL WORKS

4223 BO NGOAI GIAO. *The Communist Policy of Terror*. Saigon: Ministry of Foreign Affairs, 1972.

4224 BOURNE, PETER G. *Men, Stress, and Vietnam*. Boston: Little, Brown, 1970.

4225 CAMACHO, PAUL R. *Post-War Crime and the Veteran Influence in Penal Populations*. Chestnut Hill, Massachusetts: Boston College, 1978. A study of Viet Nam war veterans incarcerated in a number of institutional facilities. Based on papers, letters, and inmate publications.

4226 DAVIDSON, A.L. "Vietnam: When Terror Is Not Statistics," *American Opinion* 1968 11(February): 73-84.

4227 FALK, RICHARD A. "Vietnam: The Final Deceptions," *Nation* 1975 200(19): 582-584.

4228 FALK, RICHARD A. "What We should learn from Vietnam," *Foreign Policy* 1970-1971 (1): 98-143. 6 notes.

4229 FRANCK, THOMAS M., and NIGEL S. RODLEY. "Legitimacy and Legal Rights of Revolutionary Movements with Special Reference to the Peoples' Revolutionary Government of South Viet Nam," *New York University Law Review* 1970 45(3): 679-694. 37 notes.

4230 GERASSI, JOHN. *North Vietnam: A Documentary*. Indianapolis: Bobbs-Merrill, 1968.

4231 HAVENS, CHARLES W. III. "Release and Repatriation of Vietnam Prisoners," *American Bar Association Journal* 1971 57(January): 41-44. 4 notes.

4232 JOINER, CHARLES A. *The Politics of Massacre: Political Processes in South Vietnam*. Philadelphia: Temple University Press, 1973.

4233 LACOUTURE, JEAN. "From the Vietnam War to an Indochina War," *Foreign Affairs* 1970 48(4): 617-628.

4234 MALLIN, JOY. _Terror in Viet Nam_. Princeton: Van Nostrand, 1966.

4235 MURPHY, CHARLES F., JR., and MULFORD Q. SIBLEY. "War In Vietnam: A Discussion," _Natural Law Forum_ 1967 13(12): 196-225.

4236 MURPHY, CORNELIUS F., JR. "Vietnam: A Study of Law and Politics," _Fordham Law Review_ 1968 36: 453-460. 23 notes.

4237 RAJAN, M.S., and T. ISRAEL. "The United Nations and the Conflict in Vietnam," _International Studies_ 1973 12(4): 511-540. 47 notes.

4238 RAMSEY, PAUL. "Is Vietnam a Just War?" _Dialogue_ 1967 6(Winter): 19-29.

4239 RAMSEY, PAUL. _The Just War, Force and Political Responsibility_. New York: Scribner's, 1968. Argues that insurgents have a responsibility to follow the rules of war, particularly since they initiate the violence.

4240 RUSSETT, BRUCE M. "Vietnam and Restraints on Aerial Warfare," _Ventures_ 1969 9(1): 55-61.

4241 SAHLINS, MARSHALL. "The Destruction of Conscience in Vietnam," _Dissent_ 1966 13(1): 36-62.

4242 SCHELL, JONATHAN. _The Military Half_. New York: Vintage, 1968. A basic sourcebook for American operations in Quang Ngai Province. First appeared in the _New Yorker_.

4243 SUMMERS, HARRY G., JR. _Vietnam War Almanac_. New York: Facts on File Publications, 1985. 413 p. Section on atrocities, 12-page bibliography.

4244 SYME, ANTHONY V. _Vietnam: The Cruel War_. London: Horwitz, 1966.

4245 ZAHN, GORDON C. _War, Conscience, and Dissent_. New York: Hawthorne Books, 1967.

B. INTERNATIONAL LAW

4246 ANDONIAN, JOSEPH K. "Law and Vietnam," _American Bar Association Journal_ 1968 54(May): 457-459. 5 notes.

4247 FALK, RICHARD A. "International Law and the United States Role in Viet Nam: A Response to Professor Moore," _Yale Law Journal_ 1966 75(6): 1095-1158. 148 notes.

4248 FALK, RICHARD A. "Law and Responsibility in Warfare: The Vietnam Experience," _Instant Research on Peace and Violence_ 1974 1: 1-13.

4249 FALK, RICHARD A. (ed.). _The Vietnam War and International Law_. 4 volumes. 633p., 1270p., 951p., 1051p. Princeton: Princeton University Press, 1968-1976. This anthology contains excerpts from approximately 200 speeches, journal articles, newspaper editorials, and documents. Deals in detail with legal issues, the laws of war, mistreatment of prisoners of war, the expansion of the war, prospects for settlement of the war, and war crimes. Each volume is separately indexed.

4250 FIRMAGE, EDWIN B. "Law and the Indo-China War: A Retrospective View," Utah Law Review 1974 1(Spring): 1-24. 89 notes.

4251 HOOKER, WADE S., JR., and DAVID H. SAVESTEN. "Geneva Convention of 1949: Application in the Vietnamese Conflict," Virginia Journal of International Law 1965 5: 243-265.

4252 MEEKER, LEONARD L. "Viet-Nam and the International Law of Self-Defense," Department of State Bulletin 1967 56(January 9): 54-63.

4253 MEYROWITZ, HENRI. "Le Droit de la guerre dans le conflict vietnamien," Annuaire Français de Droit International 1967 13: 153-201. 123 notes.

4254 MOORE, JOHN NORTON. "International Law and the United States Role in Viet Nam: A Reply," Yale Law Journal 1967 76(6): 1051-1094. 115 notes.

4255 MOORE, JOHN NORTON. "Law and Politics in the Vietnamese War: A Response to Professor Friedmann," American Journal of International Law 1967 61(4): 1039-1053. Discusses the complexities and oversimplifications of the Vietnam issue.

4256 MURPHY, CHARLES F., JR. "Indochina: Lingering Issues of Law and Policy," Duquesne Law Review 1971 10(2): 155-167. 38 notes.

4257 O'BRIEN, WILLIAM V. "The Law of War, Command Responsibility and Vietnam," Georgetown Law Journal 1972 60(February): 605-664. 135 notes.

4258 "The Geneva Convention and the Treatment of Prisoners of War in Vietnam," Harvard Law Review 1967 80(4): 851-868. 95 notes.

4259 WILSON, ANDREW. "The War in Vietnam: How Relevant are the Rules of War?" Current 1970 114(January): 3-6.

C. LEGALITY AND JUSTICE OF AMERICAN INTERVENTION

4260 ALDRICH, GEORGE H. "Comments on the Articles on the Legality of the United States Action in Cambodia," American Journal of International Law 1971 65(1): 76-77. Response to articles on the subject by Richard A. Falk and William D. Rogers, "The Constitutionality of the Cambodian Incursion," same issue, pp. 26-75. Defends American actions in Cambodia as legal and constitutional.

4261 ALFORD, NEILL H., JR. "The Legality of American Involvement in Vietnam: A Broader Perspective," Yale Law Journal 1966 75(7): 1109-1121. 24 notes.

4262 DEUTSCH, EBERHARD P. "Legality of the War in Vietnam," Washburn Law Journal 1968 7(2): 153-186. 125 notes.

4263 FALK, RICHARD A. The Six Legal Dimensions of the Vietnam War. Princeton: Center for International Studies, 1968. 53p. International law forbids the involvement and the battlefield practices of the United States in Vietnam. Discusses American war crimes and crimes against humanity. Based on secondary sources; 61 notes.

4264 FALK, RICHARD A. "U.S. in Vietnam: Rationale & Law," Dissent 1966 13(3): 275-284.

4265 FRIED, HANS ERNST [JOHN ERNEST]. Vietnam and International Law: The Illegality of United States Military Involvement. Flanders, New Jersey: O'Hare Books, 1967. 169p. Concludes that the United States violated international law by becoming involved in Vietnam and spells out the specific violations of a number of international accords. 9-page bibliography, 3-page topical index, 2-page name index.

4266 HENKIN, LOUIS. "Viet-Nam in the Courts of the United States: 'Political Questions,'" American Journal of International Law 1969 63(2): 284-289. Discusses the question of whether the United States acted within the terms of the charter of the United Nations and whether the president can exceed his constitutional authority in such cases. 17 notes.

4267 KAHIN, GEORGE M., and JOHN W. LEWIS. The United States in Vietnam. New York: Dell, 1969.

4268 LAWYERS COMMITTEE ON AMERICAN POLICY TOWARDS VIETNAM. Vietnam and International Law: An Analysis of the Legality of the U.S. Military Involvement. Flanders, New Jersey: O'Hare Books, 1967. 162p.

4269 LOBEL, WILLIAM N. "Legality of the United States' Involvement in Vietnam: A Pragmatic Approach," University of Miami Law Review 1969 23(4): 792-814. 182 notes.

4270 MESSING, JOHN H. "American Actions in Vietnam: Justifiable in International Law?" Stanford Law Review 1967 19(June): 1307-1336. 182 notes.

4271 MOORE, JOHN NORTON. Law and the Indo-China War. Princeton: Princeton University Press, 1972. 794p. Defends the United States in helping South Vietnam and discusses the principles of justice laid down at Nuremberg within the context of the war in Vietnam. 19-page bibliography.

4272 MOORE, JOHN NORTON. "The Lawfulness of Military Assistance to the Republic of Viet-Nam," American Journal of International Law 1967 61(1): 1-34. 64 notes.

4273 PARTAN, DANIEL G. "Legal Aspects of the Vietnam Conflict," Boston University Law Review 1966 46: 281-316. 126 notes.

4274 PAUST, JORDAN J. "Legal Aspects of the My Lai Incident: A Response to Professor Rubin," Oregon Law Review 1971 50(2): 138-152. 54 notes.

4275 PHAM VAN BAT, PHAM THAN VIN, and NGUYEN VAN HUONG. "Voina Vo V'Etname I Mezhdunarodno-Pravovaia Otvetstvennost' Amerikanskikh Agressorov [The War in Vietnam and the International Legal Responsibility of the US Aggressor]," Sovetskoe Gosudarstvo i Pravo 1972 (2): 64-73. Discusses legal problems in establishing responsibility for the Vietnam War, emphasizing the Nuremberg principle of personal responsibility for war crimes. American aggression in Vietnam differs from interimperialist wars in its objects and aims. Americans in Vietnam committed crimes of genocide, ecocide, and biocide. International law and humanity demand that the responsibility of the

U.S. imperialist aggressors be established and their crimes condemned.

4276 POSSONY, STEFAN T. *Aggression and Self-Defense: The Legality of U.S. Action in South Vietnam*. Philadelphia: University of Pennsylvania, Foreign Policy Research Institute, 1966. 123p. Discusses the "communist" war in South Vietnam, the American championing of international law, collective self-defense, and the American Constitution and United Nations Charter as they pertain to American involvement in Vietnam. North Vietnam violated international law in invading South Vietnam. Based on secondary sources; 87 notes.

4277 ROBERTSON, DAVID W. "Debate among American International Lawyers about the Vietnam War," *Texas Law Review* 1968 46(6): 898-913. 63 notes.

4278 SCHICK, FRANZ B. "Some Reflections on the Legal Controversies Concerning America's Involvement in Vietnam," *International and Comparative Law Quarterly* 1968 17(October): 953-995. 89 notes.

4279 SMYLIE, JAMES H. "American Religious Bodies, Just War, and Vietnam," *Journal of Church and State* 1969 11(3): 383-408.

4280 STANFORD WAR CRIMES STUDY GROUP. *The United States in Vietnam: A Preliminary Report of International Law and War Crimes*. Stanford: Stanford War Crimes Study Group, 1971. 22p. Anti-American diatribe that seeks to "outline the U.S. government's illegal and immoral waging of an aggressive war in Indochina and to document the everyday atrocities which are war crimes by all precedent of international agreements." Discusses various Hague conventions, Geneva accords, and the Nuremberg IMT trial. 119 notes, 1-page bibliography.

4281 "The War in Southeast Asia: A Legal Position Paper," *Gonzaga Law Review* 1970 6(1): 79-110. 161 notes.

4282 "The War in Southeast Asia: A Legal Position Paper," *New York University Law Review* 1970 45(June): 695-726. 161 notes.

4283 UNITED STATES DEPARTMENT OF STATE. OFFICE OF LEGAL ADVISER. "The Legality of United States Participation in the Defense of Viet Nam," *Yale Law Journal* 1966 75(7): 1084-1108. 14 notes.

4284 VELVEL, LAWRENCE R. "The War in Viet Nam: Unconstitutional, Justiciable, and Jurisdictionally Attackable," *University of Kansas Law Review* 1968 16: 449-503e. 260 notes.

4285 WORMUTH, FRANCIS D. "The Vietnam War: The President Versus the Constitution," *Occasional Paper for the Center for the Study of Democratic Institutions* 1968 1: 2-63.

4286 WRIGHT, QUINCY. "Legal Aspects of the Viet-Nam Situation," *American Journal of International Law* 1966 60(4): 750-769. 64 notes.

D. WAR CRIMES

1. General

4287 *American Crimes in Vietnam*. Democratic Republic of Vietnam [no city given]: [no publisher given], October 1966.

4288 ANDERSON, CHARLES R. *The Grunts*. Novato: Presidio, 1976. 208p. Deals with the Marine Corps in Vietnam. A socio-psychological explanation of why so many war crimes were committed.

4289 BEDAU, HUGO ADAM. "Genocide in Vietnam?" in Virginia Held, Sidney Morgenbesser, and Thomas Nagel (eds.). *Philosophy, Morality, and International Affairs*. London: Oxford University Press, 1974.

4290 BEDAU, HUGO ADAM. "Genocide in Vietnam? The Line Between Legal Argument and Moral Judgment," *Worldview* 1974 17(2): 40-45. Discusses international law and morality with regard to alleged genocide and war crimes committed by the United States in bombing raids in the Vietnam War.

4291 BEHAR, ABRAHAM. "I Bombardamenti di Objettiviv del Nord," *Il Porte* 1967 23(7/8): 897-913. Deals with the bombing of civilian objectives in North Vietnam.

4292 BO NGOAI GIAO, and VU THONG TIN BAO CHI. *U.S. War Crimes in North Viet Nam*. Hanoi: Foreign Languages Publishing House, 1966.

4293 BUCHOLZ, ERICH. "Der Kampf gegen Aggression und Kriegsverbrechen des USA-Imperialismus in Vietnam," *Staat und Recht* 1969 18(4): 505-518.

4294 CAREY, ALEX E. *Australian Atrocities in Vietnam*. Sydney: Gould, Convenor, Vietnam Action Campaign, 1968. 20p.

4295 CHAUMONE, CHARLES. "Analyse critique de l'intervention americaine au Vietnam," *Revue Belge de Droit International* 1968 (1): 61-93. This journal also bears the English title *Belgian Law Review*. 123 notes.

4296 D'AMATO, ANTHONY A., HARVEY L. GOULD, and LARRY D. WOODS. "War Crimes and Vietnam: The 'Nuremberg Defense' and the Military Service Register," *California Law Review* 1969 57 (5): 1055-1110. 32 notes.

4297 *Document Concerning the U.S. Chemical Warfare in South Vietnam*. [no city given]: South Viet Nam Committee for the Disclosure of the U.S. Imperialists' War Crimes in South Viet Nam, February 1970.

4298 FARER, THOMAS J., ROBERT G. GARD, and TELFORD TAYLOR. "Vietnam and the Nuremberg Principles: A Colloquy on War Crimes," *Rutgers Camden Law Journal* 1973 5(1): 1-78. 75 notes.

4299 FERENCZ, BENJAMIN B. "War Crimes and the Vietnam War," *American University Law Review* 1968 17(2): 403-423. 94 notes.

4300 *Genocide Crime in South Vietnam*. South Vietnam [no city given]: "Liberation" Editions, 1963. 32p. Report on toxic chemical spraying by the United States in South Vietnam during the early 1960s. Presents testimony from eyewitnesses in the Mekong Delta provinces, excerpts from radio reports defending experimentation with chemical products, and world wide protest against contamination by poisonous substances. Reprints a communiqué of the South Vietnam National Liberation Front on the chemicals used by the U.S.-Diem "clique." Contains a map of areas in the Mytho and Bentre provinces of South Vietnam which were affected by chemicals. Based on primary sources; undocumented, 5 photographs.

4301 HERMAN, EDWARD S. Atrocities in Vietnam: Myths and Realities. Philadelphia: Pilgrim Press, 1970. 104p. Summarizes 6 atrocity myths, among them that the governments supported in Vietnam by the United States committed fewer atrocities than did governments opposed by the United States. 245 annotations, 16-page appendix of 17 photographs.

4302 HERSH, SEYMOUR M. Chemical and Biological Warfare. America's Hidden Arsenal. Indianapolis: Bobbs-Merrill, 1968. 354p.

4303 KELMAN, HERBERT C. "War Criminals and War Resisters," Society 1975 12(4): 18-22. Discusses the moral failings of the American involvement in Indochina, particularly possible war crimes, and urges a universal unconditional amnesty for those who resisted on grounds of morality. Undocumented.

4304 KNOLL, ERWIN, and JUDITH NIES MC FADDEN (eds.). War Crimes and the American Conscience. New York: Holt, Rinehart and Winston, 1970. 208p. An edited transcript of the Congressional Conference on War and National Responsibility, which convened in Washington in early 1970. Topics covered include the ideals of Nuremberg, the lessons of My Lai, and the moral challenge of individual conscience. Five appendices contain documents dealing with the principles of Nuremberg, laws of land warfare, excerpts from the Yamashita Case, and the majority judgment of the Tokyo War Crimes Tribunal. Undocumented.

4305 KOLKO, GABRIEL. "War Crimes and the Nature of the Vietnam War," Journal of Contemporary Asia 1970 1(1): 5-14. Published in Italian as "Crimini di guerra e la natura della guerra americana nel Vietnam," Il Ponte 1970 26(2): 206-217. This survey of the types of warfare in Vietnam between 1961 and 1970 reveals "crimes of war systematically and daily committed." The only solution would be the immediate withdrawal of all American forces. 7 notes.

4306 LACOUTURE, JEAN. Vietnam: Between Two Truces. New York: Random House, 1966. 295p.

4307 LANE, MARK. Conversations with Americans. New York: Simon and Schuster, 1970. 247p. Focuses on American war crimes in Vietnam. In a guerrilla war there are no clearly drawn front lines, making it difficult to distinguish between soldiers and civilians. Because of this, many villages were destroyed and villagers killed. Discusses how American military training failed to prepare soldiers for the kind of war they would fight in Vietnam. Most of the book consists of interviews of American soldiers. Undocumented.

4308 LANG, DANIEL. Casualties of War. New York: McGraw-Hill, 1969; Random House, 1970. 121p. Originally published in the New Yorker 1969 (October 18): Appeared in England as Incident on Hill 192. Discusses war crimes committed by an unidentified American soldier in Vietnam. His crimes and those of his friends included rape and murder. Undocumented.

4309 LES 35 ORGANISATIONS DES ASSISES NATIONALES. Le Livre noir des crimes Américains au Vietnam. Paris: Fayard, 1970. 144p. Lists the various members of the periodical committee that assembled this work, which is part of a series entitled En toute liberté. Discusses chemical warfare in Vietnam, massive bombardments, massacres, the My Lai and similar incidents, and the social and psychological effects of the war. Light documentation.

4310 MELMAN, SEYMOUR. In the Name of America: The Conduct of the War in Vietnam by the Armed Forces of the United States as shown by Published Reports, Compared with the Laws of War Binding on the United States Government and on Its Citizens. Annandale, Virginia: Turnpike Press, 1968. 419p. This study was commissioned and published by "Clergy and Laymen Concerned about Vietnam." It contains commentaries and statements by various religious leaders on what they call the "erosion" of moral constraint in Vietnam. Contains an analysis of the laws of war, a summary of the principles laid down by the Nuremberg IMT, treatment of prisoners of war, use of gas in warfare, the destruction of villages, pillage, use of artillery, and defoliation. Mainly newspaper editorials and reports on the war.

4311 NEILANDS, J.B., et al. Harvest of Death: Chemical Warfare in Vietnam and Cambodia. New York: Free Press, 1972. 304p. An exhaustive study of "chemical aggression" in the war in Southeast Asia. 1-page bibliography, 8-page index, 9 appendices dealing with various official reports, and a glossary.

4312 NEINAST, WILLIAM H. "United States Use of Biological Warfare," Military Law Review 1964 (April): 1-45. 191 notes.

4313 New Facts: Phu Loi Mass Murder in South Viet Nam. Hanoi: Foreign Languages Publishing House, 1959.

4314 New War Crime in South Vietnam. Spraying by U.S. Planes of Toxic Chemicals. Hanoi: [no publisher given], 1963.

4315 NORDEN, ERIC. "American Atrocities in Vietnam," Liberation 1966 10(11): 14-27. 5 photographs.

4316 NORMAN, LLOYD. "Fighting a War where there are no Rules," Army 1971 21(February): 52-55. On war crimes in Vietnam.

4317 OBERLY, JAMES. Vietnam and the American War Crimes Dilemma: Independent Study. [no city given]: [no publisher given], 1971. 36p.

4318 PARKS, W. HAYS. "Crimes in Hostilities," Marine Corps Gazette 1976 60(8): 16-22; (9): 33-39. Part I reviews charges which resulted in the conviction of members of the United States Army and Marine Corps and Vietnamese for crimes against the Vietnamese. A Table lists various courts-martial convictions involving Vietnamese from 1965-1973, noting the offense, the branch of military service in which the accused served, and the number and classification of each offense. Part II discusses personnel shortages and quality of leadership.

4319 PHAM CUONG. "War Crimes and Genocide," Vietnamese Studies 1968 18/19(September): 275-302.

4320 "Punishment for War Crimes - Duty or Discretion?" Michigan Law Review 1971 69(7): 1312-1346. 205 notes. Written by an anonymous West Point graduate who was Special Security Assistant to the United States Commander in Viet Nam.

4321 SABURO, KUGAI. "The Root of U.S. War Crimes in Vietnam," No More Hiroshimas 1970 17(January 2): 1.

4322 SOUTH VIETNAM COMMITTEE TO DENOUNCE U.S. PUPPETS' WAR CRIMES. U.S. Puppet Massacres of the Population in South Vietnam (from 1965-1969). [no city given]: [no publisher given], 1969.

4323 The American Crime of Genocide in South Vietnam. South Vietnam [no city given]: Geh Phong Publishing House, 1968.

4324 The U.S. War of Aggression in Vietnam. A Crime against the Vietnamese People, against Peace and Humanity. Hanoi: Commission for Investigation of the American Imperialists War Crimes in Viet Nam, October 1966.

4325 TUCKER, ROBERT W. "Vietnam: The Final Reckoning," Commentary 1975 59(5): 27-34.

4326 UHL, MICHAEL. Vietnam: A Soldier's View. Wellington: New Zealand University Press, 1971. A pamphlet on atrocities.

4327 U.S. Imperialists' "Burn All, Destroy All, Kill All" Policy in South Vietnam. South Vietnam [no city given]: Giai Phong Liberations Editions, 1967.

4328 U.S. War Crimes in Viet Nam. Hanoi: Juridical Science Institute, State Commission of Social Sciences, 1968.

4329 VIETNAM (DEMOCRATIC REPUBLIC). U.S. War Crimes in Viet Nam. Hanoi: State Commission of Social Sciences, Juridical Science Institute, 1968.

4330 WEISBERG, BARRY. Ecocide in Indochina: The Ecology of War. San Francisco: Canfield, 1970. 241p. An anthology of more than 2 dozen contributions dealing with various aspects of the war in Vietnam. Focuses on chemical poisons, starvation, saturation bombing, and other atrocities. Heavily documented, 18-page bibliography, with end-chapter notes.

4331 WENNER, SCOTT J. "The Indochina War Cases in the United States Court of Appeals for the Second Circuit: The Constitutional Allocation of War Powers," New York University Journal of International Law and Politics 1974 7(1): 137-161. 181 notes.

4332 WHITE, RALPH. "Misperception of Aggression in Vietnam," Journal of International Affairs 1967 21(1): 123-140.

4333 ZABLOCKI, CLEMENT J. (ed.). "Chemical-Biological Warfare: U.S. Policies and International Effects," Part I, Hearings. Part II, Report. 1970. Prepared for the House Committee on Foreign Affairs, United States Congress.

4334 ZINN, HOWARD. Vietnam: The Logic of Withdrawal. Boston: Beacon, 1967. 131p. Much on American violence in Vietnam.

2. Ben Suc

4335 SCHELL, JONATHAN. The Village of Ben Suc. New York: A.A. Knopf, 1967. 132p. Appeared in slightly different form in the New Yorker. The story of Ben Suc during the Vietnam war, with emphasis on American war crimes. Unannotated; no table of contents, no bibliography, no index.

3. My Lai

4336 BARTHELMES, WES. "Mylai and the National Conscience - II: Cry, Our Beloved Country," Commonweal 1971 94(8): 186-187.

4337 BERGER, EDWARD, et al. "ROTC, Mylai, and the Volunteer Army," Foreign Policy 1971 1(Spring): 135-160.

4338 COOPER, NORMAN G. "My Lai and Military Justice - To What Effect?" Military Law Review 1973 59(Winter): 93-127.

4339 ESZTERHAS, JOSEPH. "The Massacre at Mylai," Life 1969 67(23): 36-45.

4340 FRENCH, PETER A. (ed.). Individual and Collective Responsibility: Massacre at My Lai. Cambridge: Schenkman, 1972. 207p. An anthology containing 8 essays and 8 documents. Among the topics covered is responsibility for the war crimes at My Lai. The documents include charges against Lt. William L. Calley, Jr., and the charter of the Nuremberg IMT. 3-page bibliography.

4341 GERBER, WILLIAM. "War Atrocities and the Law," Editorial Research Reports 1970 1(January 7): 3-20. 31 notes.

4342 GERSHEN, MARTIN. Destroy or Die: The True Story of Mylai. New Rochelle, New York: Arlington House, 1971.

4343 HAMMER, RICHARD. "My Lai: Did American Troops Attack the Wrong Place?" Look 1970 34(3): 60. Concludes that Medina and his men may have attacked the wrong hamlet as a result of confusing the names of a hamlet and a village.

4344 HERSH, SEYMOUR M. "My Lai 4: A Report on the Massacre and Its Aftermath," Harper's 1970 240(1440): 53-84.

4345 KARSTEN, PETER. Law, Soldiers, and Combat. Westport: Greenwood, 1978. 204p. Surveys the laws of war since ancient times and then focuses on the My Lai massacre, values and attitudes, and the problem of illegal orders and the crisis of conscience. Lt. William Calley and his men killed some 400-500 civilians. Four factors were important in their actions. First, their judgment was morally deficient in that they refused to distinguish between combatants and civilians. Second, their ethnocentricity caused them to devalue the Vietnamese. Third, fear, rage, and frustration of the Americans had developed as a result of their inability to close with the enemy and destroy them. Last and most important, the Americans suffered from poor leadership. Makes several recommendations on ways to eliminate war crimes, among them careful screening of recruits to identify in advance people disposed to criminal actions and giving soldiers more training in the laws of warfare. End-chapter notes and index.

4346 MC WILLIAMS, WILSON CAREY. Military Honor after My Lai. New York: Council on Religious and International Affairs, 1972. 70p. Special Studies No. 213.

4347 "My Lai Massacre: Grim Details, Unanswered Questions," Congressional Quarterly Weekly Report 1969 27(December 5): 2464-2473.

4348 NOVAK, MICHAEL. "My Lai and the National Conscience - I: The Battle Hymn of Lt. Calley . . . and the Republic," Commonweal 1971 94(8): 183-187.

4349 OPTON, EDWARD M., JR., and ROBERT DUCKLES. "Mental Gymnastics on Mylai," New Republic 1970 162(8): 14-16.

4350 OPTON, EDWARD M., JR., and ROBERT DUCKLES. My Lai: It Never Happened and Besides, They Deserved It. Berkeley: Wright Institute, 1970.

4351 PAULSON, STANLEY L., and JOHN S. BANTA. "The Killings at My Lai: 'Grave Breaches' Under the Geneva Conventions and the Question of Military Jurisdiction," Harvard International Law Journal 1971 12(2): 345-355. 52 notes.

4352 PAUST, JORDAN J. "After My Lai: The Case for War Crime Jurisdiction over Civilians in Federal District Courts," Texas Law Review 1971 50(1): 6-34. 107 notes.

4353 PAUST, JORDAN J. "My Lai and Vietnam: Norms, Myths, and Leadership Responsibility," Military Law Review 1972 57(Summer): 99-187. 324 notes.

4354 POIRIER, NORMAND. "An American Atrocity," Esquire 1969 72(2): 59-63, 132-134, 136-137, 140-141.

4355 ROWE, TERRY E. "Nevada Reacts to My Lai," Nevada Historical Society Quarterly 1974 17(Summer): 60-103.

4356 RUBIN, ALFRED P. "Legal Aspects of the My Lai Incident," Oregon Law Review 1970 49(April): 260-272. 20 notes.

4357 The My Lai Incident as a Case in Law," U.S. News and World Report 1969 67(25): 34-36. 4 photographs.

4358 THOMPSON, KENRICK S., et al. "Reactions to My-Lai: A Visual-Verbal Approach," Sociology and Social Research 1974 58(January): 122-129.

4359 "Who is Responsible for My Lai," Time 1971 97(March 8): 18-19.

4360 WINN, LARRY J. "My Lai: Birth and Death of a Rhetorical Symbol," Ph.D. dissertation, Indiana University, 1973. Abstracted in Dissertation Abstracts International 1974 34(4): 4466-A - 4467-A. 159p.

4361 ZOLL, DONALD ATWELL. "My Lai and the State of the Army," National Review 1971 23(39): 1112-1114.

4. Song My (Pinkville)

4362 CHOMSKY, NOAM. "After Pinkville," New York Review of Books, January 1, 1970: 3-14.

4363 FALK, RICHARD A. "Songmy: War Crimes and Individual Responsibility, A Legal Memorandum," Trans-Action 1970 7(3): 33-40. Examines responsibility for American war crimes in the Vietnam War. Efforts were made to suppress the revelation that war crimes had been committed. The Nuremberg principles and the Yamashita trial show that the American government and armed forces recognized the validity of international law governing the conduct of military forces. Using the Songmy incident as an example, the author suggests that we ascertain who issued orders for these incidents and punish those who carried them out. Political leaders who had knowledge of such practices and failed to act also bear responsibility.

4364 GRANGER, WILLIAM. "Pinkville Atrocity: That Was Our Orders," New Republic 1969 161(24): 16-17.

4365 "Great Atrocity Hunt: Murder at Songmy and the American Conscience," National Review 1969 21(December 16): 1252.

4366 HAMMER, RICHARD. One Morning in the War: The Tragedy at Son My. London: Hart-Davis, 1970. New York: Coward, Mc Cann, 1975. 207p.

4367 LELYVELD, JOSEPH. "The Story of a Soldier who refused to fire at Songmy," New York Times Magazine, December 14, 1969: 32-33.

4368 NORMAN, LLOYD. "The Killings at Song My," Newsweek 1969 74(23): 33-41. Discusses American war crimes in Vietnam.

4369 "Song My: A U.S. Atrocity?" Newsweek 1969 74(22): 35-37. Song My was not the first U.S. atrocity in Vietnam.

4370 "Tragedy at Song My: The Case Deepens," U.S. News and World Report 1970 68(March 30): 28.

5. Viet Cong Crimes

4371 BURNHAM, JAMES. "Hanoi's Special Weapons System," National Review 1966 18(32): 765.

4372 EPPRIDGE, BILL, and DON MOSER. "Vietcong Terror in a Village," Life 1965 59(September 3): 28-33, 68-70.

4373 FALACI, ORIANI. "An Interview with a Vietcong Terrorist," Look 1968 32(April 16): 36-42.

4374 HUBER, ROBERT J. "Communist Terror in South Vietnam," Congressional Record. 93rd Congress, 1st Session. House. Volume 119, Part 1. January 22, 1973, pp. 1767-1768.,

4375 "If North Vietnam 'Convicts' Captured U.S. Flyers - ," U.S. News and World Report 1966 61(5): 20-21. 2 photographs.

4376 LEVIE, HOWARD S. "Maltreatment of Prisoners of War in Vietnam," Boston University Law Review 1968 48: 323-359. 163 notes,

4377 RISNER, ROBINSON. The Passing of the Night: My Seven Years As a Prisoner of the North Vietnamese. New York: Random House, 1975. 267p. Much on the torturing of prisoners of war.

4378 ROLPH, HAMMOND M. "The Viet Cong: Politics at Gunpoint," Communist Affairs 1966 4(4): 3-13.

4379 "The Massacre of Dak Son," Time 1967 92(24): 32-34. Deals with the murder by the Vietcong of 252 Montagnards. 7 photographs.

4380 TREASTER, JOSEPH B. "Enemy is Said to Execute Hundreds in South Vietnam," Congressional Record. 93rd Congress, 2 Session. House. Volume 118, Part 21. August 4, 1972, pp. 26933-26934. Deals with incidents in Binh Dinyh province.

E. COVER-UP AND INVESTIGATION

4381 BROWNING, FRANK, and DOROTHY FORMAN (eds.). The Wasted Nations: Report of the International Commission of Enquiry into United States Crimes in Indochina, June 20-25, 1971. New York: Harper and Row, 1972. 346p. An anthology which contains approximately two dozen entries which deal with atrocities, napalm bombing, American aggression, and American war crimes in Vietnam. The concluding statement examines the International Commission of Enquiry in the U.S. Crimes in Indochina, held in Oslo, June 20-24, 1971.

4382 CITIZENS COMMISSION OF INQUIRY. The Dellums Committee: Hearings on War Crimes in Vietnam: An Inquiry into Command Responsibility in Southeast Asia. New York: Vintage, 1972. 335p. Following public revelation of the My Lai massacre Congressman Ronald V. Dellums endorsed a demand for a congressional investigation of American war crimes. This book examines American command responsibility in Vietnam, methods of military interrogation, and the conduct of the air war and so-called pacification in Vietnam. Undocumented.

4383 EWING, LEE. "Col. Anthony Herbert: The Unmaking of an Accuser," Columbia Journalism Review 1973 12(September-October): 8-14. Television's "60 Minutes" challenged many of Herbert's statements.

4384 GILES, BARBARA M. "My Lai and the Law: An Analysis of How International Law Relates to the Mylai Incident and Its Cover-up," Ph.D. dissertation, University of Tennessee, 1978. 178p. Abstracted in Dissertation Abstracts International 1978 39(6): 3816-A - 3817-A.

4385 GOLDSTEIN, JOSEPH, BURKE MARSHALL, JACK SCHWARTZ, and GEORGE C. HERRING (eds.). The My Lai Massacre and its Cover-Up: Beyond the Reach of the Law? The Peers Commission Report With a Supplement and Introductory Essay on the Limits of Law. New York: Free Press, 1976. 586p.

4386 HERSH, SEYMOUR M. Cover-Up: The Army's Secret Investigation of the Massacre at My Lai 4. New York: Random House, 1972. 305p. Based on official transcripts and documents compiled as a result of an extensive military investigation into the My Lai 4 cover-up. Traces the history of the cover-up from the initial disclosures to the final Pentagon investigation. 30 pages of notes, 7-page index.

4387 HERSH, SEYMOUR M. My Lai 4: A Report on the Massacre and its Aftermath. New York: Random House, 1970. 210p. Tells the story of the murder of all the inhabitants of a Vietnamese village and the subsequent trial of Lt. William L. Calley, Jr. for the murder of 102 of these people. The author traveled more than 50,000 miles seeking witnesses who could testify to the My Lai massacre. Deals with the massacre, the coverup, reactions in Vietnam, and reactions in the United States. Bibliographical essay traces the development of the case as newspaper reporters began telling the story and uncovering more and more evidence of the massacre. The author was awarded the George Polk Memorial Award and the Worth Bingham Prize in 1970 for his reporting of this story. Undocumented; based on interviews with the men in Charley Company who participated in the March 16, 1968, attack on My Lai 4. 22-page bibliographical essay, no index.

4388 HERSH, SEYMOUR M. "Reporter at Large: Peers Inquiry," *New Yorker* 1972 47(January 22): 34-69; (January 29): 40-71.

4389 "House Panel Charges 'Cover-up' of My Lai Massacre," *Congressional Quarterly Weekly Report* 1970 28(July 17): 1796-1797.

4390 JOHANSEN, ROBERT C. "U.S. War Crimes: The Guilt at the Top," *Progressive* 1971 35(6): 19-23.

4391 LANDO, BARRY. "The Herbert Affair," *Atlantic Monthly* 1973 231(5): 73-81.

4392 MAC MULLEN, DOUGLAS B., et al (eds.). *The My Lai Massacre and its Cover-Up: Beyond the Reach of the Law?* New York: Free Press, 1976. 586p.

4393 "Official U.S. Report on My Lai Investigation," *U.S. News and World Report* 1969 67(23): 78-79. 2 photographs.

4394 PEERS, WILLIAM R. *The My Lai Inquiry.* New York: Norton, 1979. 306p. General Peers conducted the official inquiry and in this book he analyzes the cover-up.

4395 RUSSELL, KENT A. "My Lai Massacre: The Need for an International Investigation," *California Law Review* 1970 58(3): 703-729. 156 notes.

4396 "The Herbert Case and the Record," *Army* 1972 22(February): 6-11.

4397 UNITED STATES. ARMY. *Report of the Department of the Army Review of the Preliminary Investigations Into the My Lai Incident (1970).* Washington: GPO, 1974.

4398 UNITED STATES. CONGRESS. HOUSE OF REPRESENTATIVES. COMMITTEE ON ARMED SERVICE. *Investigation of the My Lai Incident: Report under the Authority of House Resolution 105, July 15, 1970.* 91st Congress, 2nd Session. Washington: GPO, 1970.

4399 UNITED STATES. CONGRESS. SENATE. COMMITTEE ON FOREIGN RELATIONS. *Vietnam: Policy and Prospects, 1970.* Washington: GPO, 1970.

4400 VIETNAM (DEMOCRATIC REPUBLIC). *Commission for Investigation of the U.S. Imperialists' War Crimes in Vietnam.* Prague: Peace and Socialism Publishers, 1967.

4401 VIETNAM VETERANS AGAINST THE WAR. *The Winter Soldier Investigation: An Inquiry into American War Crimes.* Boston: Beacon Press, 1972. 188p. A 16-page appendix lists the participants in an investigation convened in Detroit, Michigan, on January 31 and February 1, 2, 1971, for the purpose of showing that the atrocities committed at My Lai were not an isolated incident. More than 100 veterans and 16 civilians testified to war crimes they had committed or witnessed. Undocumented.

F. WAR CRIMES TRIALS

1. *General*

4402 LEWY, GUENTER. "The Punishment of War Crimes: Have We Learned the Lessons of Vietnam?" *Parameters* 1979 9(December): 12-19.

4403 REEL, ADOLF FRANK. "Must we Hang Nixon Too?" Progressive 1970 34(March): 26-29.

4404 SHEEHAN, NEIL. "Should We Have War Crimes Trials? New York Times Book Review, March 29, 1971: 1-3, 30-34.

4405 "Tan Am Base Vietnam: Feb. 12 - 1000 Hrs.," Scanlan's 1970 1(April): 1-11. Deals with the trial of Lt. James B. Duffy.

4406 "Two Sides of Atrocity: Americans Committing Atrocities Receive Sentence," Time 1967 90(July 14): 38.

2. William Calley

4407 ABZUG, BELLA. "Lieutenant Calley - An Accessory to the Crime," Congressional Record. 92nd Congress, 1st Session. House. Volume 117, Part 8. April 6, 1971, pp. 9923-9824.

4408 ABRAHAMSEN, DAVID. "Is There a Bit of Calley in Us?" Look 1971 35(11): 76-77.

4409 ADAMS, BROCK. "The Calley Decision," Congressional Record. 92nd Congress, 1st Session. House. Volume 117, Part 8. April 6, 1971, p. 9886. Remarks on the trial and conviction of Calley.

4410 AUCHINCLOSS, ADOLF. "Who Else is Guilty?" Newsweek 1971 77 (15): 30-32. On William Calley. 6 photographs.

4411 C.M. 426402 CALLEY (1971): U.S. v Calley 46 CMR 1131 (ACMR, 1973). Lt. Calley was charged with the premeditated murder of a priest, a child, and 100 unnamed civilians, but was found guilty of the murder of only the priest, the child and 20 unnamed civilians.

4412 CALLEY, WILLIAM L. [as told to John Sack]. Lieutenant Calley: His Own Story. New York: Viking Press, 1971. 181p. Half this book appeared first in Esquire in different forms.

4413 "Calley and Company," New Republic 1971 164(15): 10-11.

4414 "Calley Case: U.S. Army Lieutenant Charged with Slaying of South Vietnamese Civilians," Newsweek 1969 724(November 24): 40.

4415 "Calley goes on Trial," Newsweek 1970 76(22): 16-17.

4416 "Calley's Defense," Newsweek 1970 76(25): 25-26.

4417 "Calley's Defense: Anger, Hate, Fear . . . Orders," Newsweek 1971 77(10): 51-52.

4418 "Command Influence," Newsweek 1970 75(5): 28. On Calley's pretrial hearing.

4418 EVERETT, ARTHUR, K. JOHNSON, and H. ROSENTHAL. Calley. New York: Dell, 1971. Written by 3 Associated Press reporters.

4420 GOLDSTEIN, JOSEPH. "The Meaning of Calley," New Republic 1971 164(19): 13-14.

4421 GREENHAW, WAYNE. The Making of a Hero: The Story of Lieut. William Calley, Jr. Louisville: Touchstone, 1971. 226p.

4422 "Guilty Minority: First U.S. War Crimes Trials to Come Out of Vietnam," *Time* 1968 91(January 5): 31-32.

4423 HAMMER, RICHARD. *The Court-Martial of Lt. Calley*. New York: Coward, McCann and Geoghegan, 1971.

4424 HATFIELD, MARK O. "Veterans' Testimony on Vietnam - need for Investigation," *Congressional Record*. 92nd Congress, 1st Session. House. Volume 117, Part 8. April 6, 1971, pp. 9947-10055.

4425 HEINL, ROBERT D., JR. "My Lai in Perspective: The Court-Martial of William L. Calley," *Armed Forces Journal* 1970 108(December 21): 38-39.

4426 KELMAN HERBERT C., and LEE H. LAWRENCE. "Assignment of Responsibility of the Case of Lt. Calley: Preliminary Report of a National Survey," *Journal of Social Issues* 1972 28(1): 177-212.

4427 KELMAN, HERBERT C., LEE H. LAWRENCE, and PETER KARSTEN (eds.). *American Response to the Trial of Lt. William L. Calley*. New York: Free Press, 1980. Analyzes public opinion about war crimes, particularly the My Lai massacre of 1968. Calley's conviction in 1971 was based on solid evidence, but the majority of Americans believed that he was used as a scapegoat for American involvement in Vietnam.

4428 LESHER, STEPHAN. "The Calley Case Re-Examined," *New York Times Magazine*, July 11, 1971: 6-7, 14-26.

4429 LUNARI, LUIGI. *Ma perche proprio a me? ovvero i contrattempi del tenente Calley*. Milan: S. Ghison, 1973.

4430 MERICK, W.S. "Massacre Trial - A Shift in the War?" *U.S. News and World Report* 1969 67(24): 23-28. On the Calley trial. 4 photographs.

4431 QUINN, ROBERT E., and WILLIAM H. DARDEN. "Opinion: United States v. William L. Calley, Jr.," *International Lawyer* 1974 8(July): 523-539.

4432 TIEDE, TOM. *Calley: Soldier or Killer?* New York: Pinnacle, 1971.

4433 UDALL, STEWART. "The Calley Conviction," *Congressional Record*. 92nd Congress, 1st Session. House. Volume 117, Part 8. April 6, 1971, pp. 9813-9815.

3. Howard B. Levy

4434 HOFFMAN, NICHOLAS VON. "Conviction of Captain Levy," *New Republic* 1967 156(24): 9-11.

4435 LANGER, ELINOR. "The Court-Martial of Captain Levy: Medical Ethics v. Military Law," *Science* 1967 156(3780): 1346-1350.

4. Ernest Medina

4436 MC CARTHY, MARY. *Medina*. New York: Harcourt Brace Jovanovich, 1972. 87p.

5. Bertrand Russell (Stockholm) Tribunal

4437 APTHEKER, HERBERT. "The Stockholm Conference on Vietnam," Political Affairs 1967 46(8): 47-56.

4438 BLOOMFIELD, LINCOLN P. The U.N. and Vietnam. New York: Carnegie Endowment for International Peace, 1968.

4439 COATS, KENNETH, et al. Prevent the Crime of Silence: Reports from the Sessions of the International War Crimes Tribunal Founded by Bertrand Russell. Baltimore: Penguin, 1971. On the Russell (Stockholm) Tribunal.

4440 DE WEERD, HARVEY A. Lord Russell's War Crimes Tribunal. Santa Monica: Rand Corporation, 1967.

4441 DUFFETT, JOHN (ed.). Against the Crime of Silence: Proceedings of the Russell International War Crimes Tribunal. New York/London: O'Hare, 1968. 662p. Also published as Stockholm and Copenhagen, 1967: Against the Crime of Silence: Proceedings of the Russell International War Crimes Tribunal. New York: Bertrand Russell Peace Foundation, 1968.

4442 DUFFETT, JOHN (ed.). We Accuse! A Report of the Copenhagen Session of the War Crimes Tribunal. London: Bertrand Russell Peace Foundation, 1968. 183p. A series of 11 essays on American war crimes in Vietnam. Among the topics covered are genocide, the Vietnamese "Gestapo," patterns of subversion, napalm, the bombing of Dai Lai, American intervention in Laos, and the findings of the Russell Tribunal that the government of the United States committed aggression against Vietnam, that there were deliberate, systematic, and large-scale bombings of civilian objectives in Vietnam, that there were repeated violations of the sovereignty of Cambodia, and that Australia, New Zealand, and South Korea were accomplices of the United States. Undocumented.

4443 IMQUECO, PETER, PETER WEISS, and KEN COATES (eds.). Prevent the Crime of Silence: Reports from the Sessions of the International War Crimes Tribunal, founded by Bertrand Russell. London: Allen Lane, the Penguin Press, 1971. 384p. An anthology of 39 essays on American war crimes in Vietnam. Contains a list of the members of the international War Crimes Tribunal and another of the reporters and witnesses appearing in the book. Light documentation.

4444 JACK, HOMER A. "Confrontation in Stockholm," War/Peace Report 1967 7(7): 7-9.

4445 JULIN, GOSTA. "Evidence at Stockholm: The Judges are Everywhere," Nation 1967 206(June 5): 712.

4446 LEVIN, BERNARD. "Bertrand Russell: Prosecutor, Judge and Jury," New York Times Magazine, February 19, 1967: 24-25, 55, 57, 60, 62, 67-68. 4 photographs.

4447 LYND, STAUGHTON. "The War Crimes Tribunal: A Dissent," Liberation 1967-1968 12(9-10): 76-79.

4448 RESTON, JAMES, JR. The Amnesty of John David Herndon. New York: McGraw-Hill, 1973. 146p. Herndon was a deserter from the U.S. Army who had been wounded in Vietnam and who lived in exile for two and a half years in France. This book tells his story in the context of the amnesty debate and the war crimes issue.

4449 ROSENWEIN, SAM. "International War Crimes Tribunal - Stockholm Session," Guild Practitioner 1967 26(4): 141-150; 1968 27(1): 22-29.

4450 RUSSELL, BERTRAND. War Crimes in Vietnam. London: George Allen & Unwin, 1967. 178p. Deals with American racism and war crimes in the Vietnam war. Covers the press in Vietnam, atrocities, American war crimes, the responsibility of the American people, and how the principles of the Nuremberg IMT fit in Vietnam. Undocumented; no index.

4451 RUSSELL, BERTRAND, and JEAN-PAUL SARTRE (eds.). Das Vietnam Tribunal oder Amerika vor Gericht. Hamburg: Rowohlt, 1970.

4452 RUSSELL, BERTRAND, and S. RUSSELL. War and Atrocity in Vietnam. London: Bertrand Russell Peace Foundation, 1964.

4453 SARTRE, JEAN-PAUL. Le Jugement final. Paris: Gallimard. 1968.

4454 SHEER, ROBERT. "Lord Russell," Ramparts, May 5, 1967: 16-23.

4455 TAKMAN, JOHN (ed.). Training Circular 3-16. Stockholm: [no publisher given], March 1970. Reprint of the manual, with the insignia of the United States placed on the front and a message describing the manual as "for war criminals by war criminals."

4456 TRIBUNAL RUSSELL. Le jugement de Stockholm (collection d'idées actuelles). Paris: Gallimard, 1967.

4457 TRIBUNAL RUSSELL II. Le jugement final (collection d'idées actuelles no. 164). Paris: Gallimard, 1968.

G. CAMBODIA

4458 BORK, ROBERT H. "Comments on the Articles on the Legality of the United States Action in Cambodia," American Journal of International Law 1971 65(1): 79-81. Argues that Nixon had full constitutional authority to wage war in Cambodia.

4459 CALDWELL, MALCOLM, and LEK TAN. Cambodia in the Southeast Asian War. New York/London: Monthly Review Press, 1973. 446p.

4460 FALK, RICHARD A. "The Cambodian Operation and International Law," American Journal of International Law 1971 65(1): 1-25. Argues that the American invasion of Cambodia was a blatant violation of international law. Based on secondary sources; 51 notes.

4461 HARGROVE, JOHN LAWRENCE. "Comments on the Articles on the Legality of the United States Action in Cambodia," American Journal of International Law 1971 65(1): 81-83.

4462 MOORE, JOHN NORTON. "Legal Dimensions of the Decision to Intercede in Cambodia," American Journal of International Law 1971 65(1): 38-75. Argues that the Cambodian incursion was legal and constitutional.

4463 ROGERS, WILLIAM D. "The Constitutionality of the Cambodian Incursion," American Journal of International Law 1971 65(1): 26-37. 30 notes.

4464 STEVENSON, JOHN R. "United States Military Action in Cambodia: Questions of International Law," Department of State Bulletin 1970 62(1617): 765-770. 23 notes.

XIV
MISCELLANEOUS

A. KOREAN WAR, 1950-1953

4465 "About that Report of Atrocities," Christian Century 1951 68(48): 1364.

4466 "Assembly Adopts Resolution on Atrocity by a Large Margin," United Nations Bulletin 1953 15(December): 571-579.

4467 "Atrocities in Korea - How Bad?" U.S. News and World Report 1953 34(May 1): 16-17.

4468 AUSTIN, WARREN R. "Charges of Atrocities in Korea called Propaganda to discredit U.N. Action," Department of State Bulletin 1951 25(631): 189-190. July 30, 1951.

4469 "Complaint of the Mass Murder of Korean and Chinese Prisoners of War by United States Armed Forces on the Island of Pongam," International Organization 1953 7(February): 54.

4470 "Do Liberals Condone War Crimes in Korea?" Saturday Evening Post 226(2): 10.

4471 LODGE, HENRY CABOT, JR. "Inclusion of Atrocities Question on General Assembly Agenda," Department of State Bulletin 1953 29(751): 685. November 16, 1953.

4472 "Korea, the Continuing Tragedy," Christian Century 1951 68(27): 790-791.

4473 LODGE, HENRY CABOT, JR. "Inclusion of Atrocities Items on General Assembly Agenda, Statements," Department of State Bulletin 1953 29(753): 757-758. November 30, 1953.

4474 "Question of Atrocities Committed by the North Korean and Chinese Communist Forces Against United Nations' Prisoners of War in Korea," International Organization 1954 8(February): 70-72.

4475 "Report of the Women's International Commission for the Investigation of Atrocities Committed by U.S.A. and Li Seung Man Troops in Korea" New Times Supplement 1951 (July 4): 1-19.

4476 "U.N. Commission on Korea Reports on Atrocities," Department of State Bulletin 1950 23(590): 649-650.

4477 UNITED NATIONS. GENERAL ASSEMBLY. "Question of Atrocities Committed by the North Korean and Chinese Communist Forces against United Nations Prisoners of War in Korea." Letter and documents, Agenda Item 74, 8th Session, 1953-1954. 100p. A compilation of statements and testimonies by witnesses and victims.

4478 UNITED STATES. ARMY. KOREAN COMMUNICATIONS ZONE. Extract of Interim Historical Report, Korean War Crimes Division, Cumulative to 30 June 1953. 87p. [no publication information given]. Copy in United States Army Military History Research Collection, Carlisle Barracks, Pennsylvania. Call Number DS 920.8 U52. Includes summaries of major incidents, case statistics, and photographs.

4479 UNITED STATES. CONGRESS. SENATE. COMMITTEE ON GOVERNMENT OPERATIONS. Korean War Atrocities . . . 2-4 December 1953. 3 parts. Washington: GPO, 1954. 228p. See also Committee's Report, same title, January 11, 1954. 27p.

4480 WHITE, WILLIAM L. The Captives of Korea: An Unofficial White Paper on the Treatment of War Prisoners; Our Treatment of Theirs; Their Treatment of Ours. Westport: Greenwood, 1957, 1979.

B. ALGERIAN CIVIL WAR, 1954-1962

4481 BEDJAOUI, MOHAMMED. Law and the Algerian Revolution. Brussels: International Association of Democratic Lawyers, 1961. 260p.

4482 BENABDALLAH, ABOGSSANAD, M. OUSSEDIK, and J. VERGÈS. Nuremberg pour l'Algérie. Paris: François Maspero, 1961.

4483 CLARK, MICHAEL K. Algeria in Turmoil: A History of the Rebellion. New York: Praeger, 1959. 466p.

4484 HORNE, ALISTAIR. A Savage War of Peace: Algeria 1954-1962. London: Macmillan, 1977. 604p.

4485 JONES, MERVYN. Ordeal: The Trial of Djamila Bouhired: Condemned to Death in Algiers, July 15th, 1957. London: Union of Democratic Control Publications, [no date given]. 15p. With the complete text of his speech for the defense by Jacques Vergès.

4486 JUREIDINI, PAUL A. Case Studies in Insurgency and Revolutionary Warfare: Algeria, 1954-1962. Washington: American University, Special Research Office, 1963.

4487 LEULLIETTE, PIERRE. St. Michael and the Dragon: Memoirs of a Paratrooper. Boston: Houghton Mifflin, 1964. 354p.

4488 PARET, PETER. French Revolutionary Warfare from Indochina to Algeria. The Analysis of a Political and Military Doctrine. New York: Praeger, 1964. 163p.

4489 SCHMITT, GASTON. Toute la vérité sur le procès Pucheau par un des juges. Paris: Plon, 1963.

C. PAKISTAN CIVIL WAR, BANGLADESH, 1972-1973

4490 ANLEY, HENRY. In Order to Die. London: Burke, 1955.

4491 DUTT, R. PALME. "India, Pakistan and Bangladesh," New World Review 1972 40(Winter): 10-17.

4492 HECHT, BEN. Perfidy. New York: Julian Messner, 1961. 281p. A critical appraisal of the Kastner case, with emphasis on the "perfidious" role played by members of the Mapai and the Jewish Agency.

4493 MEHRISH, BRIJESH NARAIN. War Crimes and Genocide: The Trial of Pakistani War Criminals. Delhi: Oriental, 1972. 1st edition. 349p. Discusses atrocities in Bangla Desh committed by the Pakistani army and the trial intended to be held in July 1972 of Pakistan's collaborators, the Razakars, and prisoners in the custody of the Government of India, including Pakistan's former president, General Yahka Khan, and Chief of Army Staff, General Tikka Khan, to be tried in absentia. Chapter 1 discusses the nature of international criminal law, the codification of the Nuremberg principles, and projects for an international criminal court. Chapter 2 provides a survey of proceedings and an appraisal of the judgment of the Leipzig, Nuremberg, Tokyo and Eichmann trials, among others. Chapter 3 analyzes the problems of admission of evidence, definition of crimes and of superior orders, and the problem of guilt. Discusses the composition of the tribunal, procedure for the trial, the defense of necessity, the pleas of the act of state, and the right of Bangla Desh to punish criminals. Appendices includes articles of the Hague Conventions of 1899 and 1907, the charter of the Nuremberg IMT, Control Council Law no. 10, a summary of the final judgment of the IMT for the Far East, a statistical table of the Nuremberg trials, and the text of the indictment against Adolf Eichmann. 10-page bibliography, 7-page index, 3 photographs.

4494 MORRIS-JONES, W.H. "Pakistan Post Mortem and the Roots of Bangladesh," Political Quarterly 1972 43(2): 187-200.

4495 PAUST, JORDAN J., and ALBERT P. BLAUSTEIN. Human Rights and the Bangladesh Trials: a Legal Memorandum to the People's Republic of Bangladesh on International Crime and Due Process (with Supporting Documents). New York: Editorial Correspondents, 1973 [temporary edition]. 236p. Analysis of human rights in the trial of war crimes. Discusses international criminal law and the problems of due process as they relate to the trial of those charged with genocide and other crimes against humanity. Deals specifically with the violation of human rights during the Indian-Pakistani-Bangladesh struggle. Part 1, pp. 1-50, contains a memorandum of law on the prospective Bangladesh trials. Part 2, pp. 51-74, contains key documents relating to the trials, including the International Crimes Act and the editor's comments on that act. Part 3, pp. 75-103, examines norms of due process. Part 4, pp. 104-234, consists of documents supporting the Bangladesh arguments and providing background data on the entire subject of war crimes. Based on primary sources.

D. MOZAMBIQUE MERCENARIES TRIAL, LUANDA, 1976

4496 BURCHETT, WILFRED, and DEREK ROEBUCK. The Whores of War: Mercenaries of Today. New York: Penguin, 1978.

E. EAST TIMOR

4497 UNITED STATES. CONGRESS. HOUSE OF REPRESENTATIVES. COMMITTEE ON INTERNATIONAL RELATIONS. Human Rights in East Timor and the Question of the Use of U.S. Equipment by the Indonesian Armed Forces, Hearing before the Subcommittees on International Organizations and on Asian and Pacific Affairs. 95th Congress, 1st Session. (March 23, 1977). 84p. Call Number Y4. In816: H8818. One of 29 volumes in a series on human rights, all of which are listed on pp. v and vi. All volumes pertaining to war crimes are abstracted in the present work. Discusses the situation in the Indonesian province of East Timor and war crimes against civilians. Based largely on testimony by refugees living in Portugal.

F. DERING-URIS CASE

4498 HILL, MAVIS M., and L. NORMAN WILLIAMS. Auschwitz in England. A Record of a Libel Action. London: MacGibbon and Kee, 1965. 293p. New York: Stein and Day, 1965. The story of the court case in a celebrated libel case in London brought by Dr. Wladislaw A. Dering against American author Leon Uris.

G. BETH-DIN TRIAL

4499 WAINWRIGHT, LOUDON S. "You Are the Man who killed my Brother," Life 1950 29(24): 132-134, 136, 138, 140, 142, 147-148, 150. An account of the Beth Dim trial of the Krieger-Mittelman case at the headquarters of the American Jewish Congress.

H. AFGHANISTAN-SOVIET UNION WAR, 1980

4500 ARNOLD, ANTHONY. Afghanistan. The Soviet Invasion in Perspective. Stanford: Hoover Institution Press, 1985. 179p. Some on Soviet terror tactics.

APPENDICES

PART 1
INTERNATIONAL MILITARY TRIBUNAL - NUREMBERG

APPENDIX 1

THE LONDON AGREEMENT FOR THE PROSECUTION AND PUNISHMENT
OF THE MAJOR WAR CRIMINALS OF THE EUROPEAN AXIS

Whereas the United Nations have from time to time made declarations of their intention that war criminals shall be brought to justice;

And whereas the Moscow Declaration of the 30th October, 1943, on German atrocities in Occupied Europe stated that those German officers and men and members of the Nazi Party who have been responsible for or have taken a consenting part in atrocities and crimes will be sent back to the countries in which their abominable deeds were done in order that they may be judged and punished according to the laws of these liberated countries and of the free Governments that will be created therein;

And whereas this Declaration was stated to be without prejudice to the case of major criminals whose offences have no particular geographical location and who will be punished by the joint decision of the Governments of the Allies;

Now therefore the Government of the United Kingdom of Great Britain and Northern Ireland, the Government of the United States of America, the Provisional Government of the French Republic and the Government of the Union of Soviet Socialist Republics (hereinafter called "the Signatories") acting in the interests of all the United Nations and by their representatives duly authorised thereto have concluded this agreement.

Article 1

There shall be established after consultation with the Control Council for Germany an International Military Tribunal for the trial of war criminals whose offences have no particular geographical location whether they be accused individually or in their capacity as members of organizations or groups or in both capacities.

Article 2

The constitution, jurisdiction and functions of the International Military Tribunal shall be those set out in the Charter annexed to this agreement, which Charter shall form an integral part of this Agreement.

Article 3

Each of the Signatories shall take the necessary steps to make available for the investigation of the charges and trial the major war criminals detained by them who are to be tried by the International Military Tribunal. The Signatories shall also use their best endeavors to make available for investigation of the charges against and the trial before the International Military Tribunal such of the major war criminals as are not in the territories of any of the Signatories.

Article 4

Nothing in this agreement shall prejudice the provisions established by the Moscow Declaration concerning the return of war criminals to the countries where they committed their crimes.

Article 5

Any Government of the United Nations may adhere to this agreement by notice given through the diplomatic channel to the Government of the United Kingdom, who shall inform the other signatory and adhering Governments of each such adherence.

Article 6

Nothing in this agreement shall prejudice the jurisdiction or the powers of any national or occupation court established or to be established in any Allied territory or in Germany for the trial of war criminals.

Article 7

This Agreement shall come into force on the day of signature and shall remain in force for the period of one year and shall continue thereafter, subject to the right of any Signatory to give, through the diplomatic channel, one month's notice of intention to terminate it. Such termination shall not prejudice any proceedings already taken or any findings already made in pursuance of this Agreement.

In witness whereof the Undersigned have signed the present Agreement.

Done in quadruplicate in London this 8th day of August, 1945, each in English, French, and Russian, and each text to have equal authenticity.

For the Government of the United Kingdom of Great Britain and Northern Ireland

                                                  JOWITT

For the Government of the United States of America

                                        ROBERT H. JACKSON

For the Provisional Government of the French Republic

                                             ROBERT FALCO

For the Government of the Union of Soviet Socialist Republics

                                         I. NIKITCHENKO
                                         A. TRAININ

APPENDIX 2

CHARTER OF THE NUREMBERG INTERNATIONAL MILITARY TRIBUNAL

I. Constitution of the International Military Tribunal

Article 1

In pursuance of the Agreement signed on the 8th August, 1945, by the Government of the United Kingdom of Great Britain and Northern Ireland, the Government of the United States of America, the Provisional Government of the French Republic and the Government of the Union of Soviet Socialist Republics, there shall be established an International Military Tribunal (hereinafter called "the Tribunal") for the just and prompt trial and punishment of the major war criminals of the European Axis.

Article 2

The Tribunal shall consist of four members, each with an alternate. One member and one alternate shall be appointed by each of the Signatories. The alternates shall, so far as they are able, be present at all sessions of the Tribunal. In case of illness of any member of the Tribunal or his incapacity for some other reason to fulfill his functions, his alternate shall take his place.

Article 3

Neither the Tribunal, its members nor their alternates can be challenged by the prosecution, or by the Defendants or their Counsel. Each Signatory may replace its member of the Tribunal or his alternate for reasons of health or for other good reasons, except that no replacement may take place during a Trial, other than by an alternate.

Article 4

(a) The presence of all four members of the Tribunal or the alternate for any absent member shall be necessary to constitute the quorum.

(b) The members of the Tribunal shall, before any trial begins, agree among themselves upon the selection from their number of a President, and the President shall hold office during that trial, or as may otherwise be agreed by a vote of not less than three members. The principle of rotation of presidency for successive trials is agreed. If, however, a session of the Tribunal takes place on the territory of one of the four Signatories, the representative of that Signatory on the Tribunal shall preside.

(c) Save as aforesaid the Tribunal shall take decisions by a majority vote and in case the votes are evenly divided, the vote of the President shall be decisive: provided always that convictions and sentences shall only be imposed by affirmative votes of at least three members of the Tribunal.

Article 5

In case of need and depending on the number of the matters to be tried, other Tribunals may be set up; and the establishment, functions, and procedure of each Tribunal shall be identical, and shall be governed by this Charter.

II. Jurisdiction and General Principles

Article 6

The Tribunal established by the Agreement referred to in Article I hereof for the trial and punishment of the major war criminals of the European Axis countries shall have the power to try and punish persons who, acting in the interests of the European Axis countries, whether as individuals or as members of organisations, committed any of the following crimes.

The following acts, or any of them, are crimes coming within the jurisdiction of the Tribunal for which there shall be individual responsibility:

(a) <u>Crimes against peace</u>: namely, planning, preparation, initiation or waging of a war of aggression, or a war in violation of international treaties, agreements or assurances, or participation in a common plan of conspiracy for the accomplishment of any of the foregoing;

(b) <u>War crimes</u>: namely, violations of the laws or customs of war. Such violations shall include, but not be limited to, murder, ill-treatment or deportation to slave labour or for any other purpose of civilian population of or in occupied territory, murder or ill-treatment of prisoners of war or persons on the seas, killing of hostages, plunder of public or private property, wanton destruction of cities, towns or villages, or devastation not justified by military necessity;

(c) <u>Crimes against humanity</u>: namely, murder, extermination, enslavement, deportation, and other inhumane acts committed against any civilian population, before or during the war; or persecutions on political, racial or religious grounds in execution of or in connection with any crime within the jurisdiction of the Tribunal, whether or not in violation of the domestic law of the country where perpetrated.

Leaders, organisers, instigators and accomplices participating in the formulation or execution of a common plan or conspiracy to commit any of the foregoing crimes are responsible for all acts performed by any persons in execution of such plan.

Article 7

The official position of Defendants, whether as Heads of State or responsible officials in Government Departments, shall not be considered as freeing them from responsibility or mitigating punishment.

Article 8

The fact that the Defendant acted pursuant to order of his Government or of a superior shall not free him from responsibility, but may be considered in mitigation of punishment if the Tribunal determines that justice so requires.

Article 9

At the trial of any individual member of any group or organisation the Tribunal may declare (in connection with any act of which the individual may be convicted) that the group or organisation of which the individual was a member was a criminal organisation.

After receipt of the Indictment the Tribunal shall give such notice as it thinks fit that the prosecution intends to ask the Tribunal to make such declaration and any member of the organisation will be entitled to apply to the Tribunal for leave to be heard by the Tribunal upon the question of the criminal character of the organisation. The Tribunal shall have the power to allow or reject the application. If the application is allowed, the Tribunal may direct in what manner the applicants shall be represented and heard.

Article 10

In cases where a group or organization is declared criminal by the Tribunal, the competent national authority of any Signatory shall have the right to bring individuals to trial for membership therein before national, military or occupation courts. In any such case the criminal nature of the group or organisation is considered proved and shall not be questioned.

Article 11

Any person convicted by the Tribunal may be charged before a national, military or occupation court, referred to in Article 10 of this Charter, with a crime other than of membership in a criminal group or organisation and such court may, after convicting him, impose upon him punishment independent of and additional to the punishment imposed by the Tribunal for participation in the criminal activities of such group or organisation.

Article 12

The Tribunal shall have the right to take proceedings against a person charged with crimes set out in Article 6 of this Charter in his absence, if he has not been found or if the Tribunal, for any reason, finds it necessary, in the interests of justice, to conduct the hearing in his absence.

Article 13

The Tribunal shall draw up rules for its procedure. These rules shall not be inconsistent with the provisions of this Charter.

III. Committee for the Investigation and Prosecution of Major War Criminals

Article 14

Each Signatory shall appoint a Chief Prosecutor for the investigation of the charges against and the prosecution of major war criminals.

The Chief Prosecutors shall act as a committee for the following purposes:

(a) to agree upon a plan of the individual work of each of the Chief Prosecutors and his staff,

(b) to settle the final designation of major war criminals to be tried by the Tribunal,

(c) to approve the Indictment and the documents to be submitted herewith,

(d) to lodge the Indictment and the accompanying documents with the Tribunal,

(e) to draw up and recommend to the Tribunal for its approval rules of procedure, contemplated by Article 13 of this Charter. The Tribunal shall have power to accept, with or without amendments, or to reject, the rules so recommended.

The Committee shall act in all the above matters by a majority vote and shall appoint a Chairman as may be convenient and in accordance with the principle of rotation: provided that if there is an equal division of vote concerning the designation of a Defendant to be tried by the Tribunal, or the crimes with which he shall be charged, that proposal will be adopted which was made by the party which proposed that the particular Defendant be tried, or the particular charges be preferred against him.

Article 15

The Chief Prosecutors shall individually, and acting in collaboration with one another, also undertake the following duties:

(a) investigation, collection and production before or at the Trial of all necessary evidence,

(b) the preparation of the Indictment for approval by the Committee in accordance with paragraph (c) of Article 14 hereof,

(c) the preliminary examination of all necessary witnesses and of the Defendants,

(d) to act as Prosecutor at the Trial,

(e) to appoint representatives to carry out such duties as may be assigned to them,

(f) to undertake such other matters as may appear necessary to them for the purposes of the preparation for and conduct of the Trial,

It is understood that no witness or Defendant detained by any Signatory shall be taken out of the possession of that Signatory without its consent.

IV. Fair Trial for Defendants

Article 16

In order to ensure fair trial for the Defendants, the following procedure shall be followed:

(a) The Indictment shall include full particulars specifying in detail the charges against the Defendants. A copy of the Indictment and of all the documents lodged with the Indictment, translated into a language which he understands, shall be furnished to the Defendant at a reasonable time before the Trial.

(b) During any preliminary examination or trial of a Defendant he shall have the right to give any explanation relevant to the charges made against him.

(c) A preliminary examination of a Defendant and his Trial shall be conducted in, or translated into, a language which the Defendant understands.

(d) A Defendant shall have the right to conduct his own defence before the Tribunal or to have the assistance of Counsel.

(e) A Defendant shall have the right through himself or through his Counsel to present evidence at the Trial in support of his defence, and to cross-examine any witness called by the Prosecution.

V. Powers of the Tribunal and Conduct of the Trial

Article 17

The Tribunal shall have the power

(a) to summon witnesses to the Trial and to require their attendance and testimony and to put questions to them,

(b) to interrogate any Defendant,

(c) to require the production of documents and other evidentiary material,

(d) to administer oaths to witnesses,

(e) to appoint officers for the carrying out of any task designated by the Tribunal including the power to have evidence taken on commission.

Article 18

The Tribunal shall

(a) confine the Trial strictly to an expeditious hearing of the issues raised by the charges,

(b) take strict measures to prevent any action which will cause unreasonable delay, and rule out irrelevant issues and statements of any kind whatsoever,

(c) deal summarily with any contumacy, imposing appropriate punishment, including exclusion of any Defendant or his Counsel from some or all further proceedings, but without prejudice to the determination of the charges.

Article 19

The Tribunal shall not be bound by technical rules of evidence. It shall adopt and apply to the greatest possible extent expeditious and non-technical procedure, and shall admit any evidence which it deems to have probative value.

Article 20

The Tribunal may require to be informed of the nature of any evidence before it is offered so that it may rule upon the relevance thereof.

Article 21

The Tribunal shall not require proof of facts of common knowledge but shall take judicial notice thereof. It shall also take judicial notice of official governmental documents and reports of the United Nations, including the acts and documents of the committees set up in the various Allied countries for the investigation of war crimes, and the records and findings of military or other Tribunals of any of the United Nations.

Article 22

The permanent seat of the Tribunal shall be in Berlin. The first meetings of the members of the Tribunal and of the Chief Prosecutors shall be held at Berlin in a place to be designated by the Control Council for Germany. The first trial shall be held at Nuremberg, and any subsequent trials shall be held at such places as the Tribunal may decide.

Article 23

One or more of the Chief Prosecutors may take part in the prosecution at each Trial. The function of any Chief Prosecutor may be discharged by him personally, or by any person or persons authorised by him.

The function of Counsel for a Defendant may be discharged at the Defendant's request by any Counsel professionally qualified to conduct cases before the courts of his own country, or by any other person who may be specially authorised thereto by the Tribunal.

Article 24

The proceedings of the Trial shall take the following course:

(a) The Indictment shall be read in court.

(b) The Tribunal shall ask each Defendant whether he pleads "guilty" or "not guilty."

(c) The Prosecution shall make an opening statement.

(d) The Tribunal shall ask the Prosecution and the Defence what evidence (if any) they wish to submit to the Tribunal, and the Tribunal shall rule upon the admissibility of any such evidence.

(e) The witnesses for the Prosecution shall be examined and after that the witnesses for the Defence. Thereafter such rebutting evidence as may be held by the Tribunal to be admissible shall be called by either the Prosecution or the Defence.

(f) The Tribunal may put any question to any witness and to any Defendant, at any time.

(g) The Prosecution and the Defence shall interrogate and may cross-examine any witness and any Defendant who gives testimony.

(h) The Defence shall address the court.

(i) The Prosecution shall address the court.

(j) Each Defendant may make a statement to the Tribunal.

(k) The Tribunal shall deliver judgment and pronounce sentence.

Article 25

All official documents shall be produced, and all court proceedings conducted, in English, French and Russian, and in the language of the Defendant. So much of the record and of the proceedings may also be translated into the language of any country in which the Tribunal is sitting, as the Tribunal considers desirable in the interests of justice and public opinion.

VI. Judgment and Sentence

Article 26

The judgment of the Tribunal as to the guilt or the innocence of any Defendant shall give the reasons on which it is based, and shall be final and not subject to review.

Article 27

The Tribunal shall have the right to impose upon a Defendant, on conviction, death or such other punishment as shall be determined by it to be just.

Article 28

In addition to any punishment imposed by it, the Tribunal shall have the right to deprive the convicted person of any stolen property and order its delivery to the Control Council for Germany.

Article 29

In case of guilt, sentences shall be carried out in accordance with the orders of the Control Council for Germany, which may at any time reduce or otherwise alter the sentences, but may not increase the severity thereof. If the Control Council for Germany, after any Defendant has been convicted and sentenced, discovers fresh evidence which, in its opinion, would found a fresh charge against him, the Council shall report accordingly to the Committee established under Article 14 hereof for such action as they may consider proper, having regard to the interests of justice.

VII. Expenses

Article 30

The expenses of the Tribunal and of the Trials shall be charged by the Signatories against the funds allotted for maintenance of the Control Council for Germany.

APPENDIX 3

NUREMBERG IMT MEMBERS AND ALTERNATE MEMBERS

France	Henri Donnedieu de Vabres
	Robert Falco
Soviet Union	I. T. Nikitchenko
	A. F. Volchkov
United Kingdom	Geoffrey Lawrence (President)
	William Norman Birkett
United States	Francis Biddle
	John J. Parker

APPENDIX 4

NUREMBERG IMT DEFENDANTS AND DEFENSE COUNSELS

Defendants	Defense Counsels
Hermann Göring	Otto Stahmer
Rudolf Hess	Günther von Rohrscheidt
	Alfred Seidl
Joachim von Ribbentrop	Fritz Sauter
	Martin Horn
Wilhelm Keitel	Otto Nelte
Ernst Kaltenbrunner	Kurt Kauffmann
Alfred Rosenberg	Alfred Thomas
Hans Frank	Alfred Seidl
Wilhelm Frick	Otto Pannenbecker

Defendants	Defense Counsels
Julius Streicher	Hanns Marx
Walther Funk	Fritz Sauter
Hjalmar Schacht	Rudolf Dix
	Herbert Kraus
Karl Dönitz	Otto Kranzbühler
Erich Raeder	Walter Siemers
Baldur von Schirach	Fritz Sauter
Fritz Sauckel	Robert Servatius
Alfred Jodl	Franz Exner
	Hermann Jahreiss
Martin Bormann	Friedrich Bergold
Franz von Papen	Egon Kubuschok
Arthur Seyss-Inquart	Gustav Steinbauer
Albert Speer	Hans Fläschner
Constantin von Neurath	Otto von Lüdinghausen
Hans Fritzsche	Heinz Fritz
	Alfred Schilf
Reich Cabinet	Egon Kubuschok
Leadership Corps	Robert Servatius
SS and SD	Ludwig Babel
	Horst Pelckmann
	Carl Haensel
	Hans Gawlik
SA	Georg Böhm
	Martin Loeffler
Gestapo	Rudolf Merkel
General Staff	Franz Exner
	Hans Laternser

APPENDIX 5

NUREMBERG IMT CHARGES, VERDICTS, AND SENTENCES

Figure 1. Counts of the Indictment

1. Conspiracy
2. Crimes Against Peace
3. War Crimes
4. Crimes Against Humanity

Figure 2. Extracts from the Nuremberg IMT Indictment

Count 1 - The Common Plan or Conspiracy

All the defendants, with divers other persons, during a period of years preceding 8th May, 1945, participated as leaders, organizers, instigators or accomplices in the formulation or execution of a common plan or conspiracy to commit, or which involved the commission of, Crimes against Peace, War Crimes, and Crimes against Humanity, as defined in the Charter of this Tribunal, and, in accordance with the provisions of the Charter, are individually responsible for their own acts and for all acts committed by any persons in the execution of such plan or conspiracy.

Count 2 - Crimes Against Peace

All the defendants with divers other persons, during a period of years preceding 8th May, 1945, participated in the planning, preparation, initiation and waging of wars of aggression, which were also wars in violation of international treaties, agreements and assurances.

Count 3 - War Crimes

All the defendants committed War Crimes between September, 1939, and 8th May, 1945, in Germany and in those countries and territories occupied by the German armed forces since 1st September, 1939, and in Austria, Czechoslovakia, and Italy, and on the High Seas . . . executed a common plan or conspiracy to commit War Crimes as defined in Article 6 (b) of the Charter.

The said War Crimes . . . constituted violations of international conventions, of internal penal laws and of the general principles of criminal law as derived from the criminal law of all civilized nations, and were involved in and part of a systematic course of conduct.

Count 4 - Crimes Against Humanity

All the defendants committed Crimes against Humanity during a period of years preceding 8th May, 1945, in Germany and all those countries occupied by the German armed forces since 1st September, 1939, and in Austria, Czechoslovakia, and Italy, and on the High Seas.

All the defendants, acting in concert with others, formulated and executed a common plan of conspiracy to commit Crimes against Humanity as defined in Article 6 (c) of the Charter. This plan involved, among other things, the murder and persecution of all who were suspected of being hostile to the Nazi Party and all who were or who were suspected of being opposed to the common plan alleged in Count 1.

The said Crimes against Humanity . . . constituted violations of international conventions, of internal penal laws, of the general principles of criminal law as derived from the criminal law of all civilized nations and were involved in and part of a systematic course of conduct.

Figure 3. Table of Counts, Verdicts, and Sentences

Defendants	Charges Counts				Verdicts Counts				Sentences
	1	2	3	4	1	2	3	4	
Göring	X	X	X	X	X	X	X	X	Death
Von Ribbentrop	X	X	X	X	X	X	X	X	Death
Keitel	X	X	X	X	X	X	X	X	Death
Jodl	X	X	X	X	X	X	X	X	Death
Rosenberg	X	X	X	X	X	X	X	X	Death
Frick	X	X	X	X		X	X	X	Death
Seyss-Inquart	X	X	X	X		X	X	X	Death
Sauckel	X	X	X	X			X	X	Death
Bormann	X		X	X			X	X	Death

Defendants	Charges				Verdicts				Sentences
	Counts				Counts				
	1	2	3	4	1	2	3	4	
Kaltenbrunner	X		X	X			X	X	Death
Frank	X		X	X			X	X	Death
Streicher	X			X				X	Death
Raeder	X	X	X	X	X	X	X		Life
Funk	X	X	X	X		X	X	X	Life
Hess	X	X	X	X	X	X			Life
Speer	X	X	X	X			X	X	20 years
Von Schirach	X			X				X	20 years
Von Neurath	X	X	X	X	X	X	X	X	15 years
Dönitz	X	X	X			X	X		10 years
Fritzsche	X		X	X					Acquitted
Von Papen	X	X							Acquitted
Schacht	X		X						Acquitted

APPENDIX 6

PRINCIPAL POSTS HELD BY NUREMBERG IMT DEFENDANTS

Martin Bormann
Hitler's Deputy
Head of the Chancellery of the Nazi Party

Karl Dönitz
Commander-in-Chief of the German Navy
Successor to Hitler

Hans Frank
Minister without Portfolio
Reichsleiter for Legal Affairs
Governor-General of Poland

Wilhelm Frick
Minister of the Interior
Plenipotentiary for Home Administration
Member of the Ministerial Council for the Defense of the Reich
Protector of Bohemia and Moravia

Hans Fritzsche
Chief of Radio Propaganda
Head of the German News Service
Plenipotentiary for the Political Organization of Radio in
  Greater Germany

Walter Funk
Government Press Chief
State Secretary in the Propaganda Ministry
Minister of Economics
Plenipotentiary for War Economy
President of the Reichsbank
Member of the Ministerial Council for the Defense of the Reich

Hermann Göring
  Early successor-designate to Hitler
  Air Minister and Commander in Chief of the Air Force
  Plenipotentiary for the Four-year Plan
  Chairman of the Ministerial Council for the Protection of the Reich
  President of the Reichstag

Rudolf Hess
  Deputy Führer and successor-designate after Göring
  Minister without portfolio
  Member of the Ministerial Council for the Defense of the Reich

Alfred Jodl
  Chief of the Operations Staff of the OKW
  Generaloberst

Ernst Kaltenbrunner
  Chief of the SS in Austria
  State Secretary for Security in Austria
  Chief of the German Security Police and Security Service (SD)
  Head of the RSHA in the Ministry of the Interior

Wilhelm Keitel
  Head of the OKW
  Member of the Ministerial Council for the Defense of the Reich
  Field Marshal

Robert Ley
  Leader of the Labor Front

Erich Raeder
  Commander-in-Chief of the German Navy

Alfred Rosenberg
  Head of the Foreign Department of the Nazi Party
  Reichsleiter for Ideology
  Minister for the Occupied Eastern Territories
  Editor of the *Völkischer Beobachter*
  Head of the Einsatzstab Rosenberg

Fritz Sauckel
  Gauleiter of Thuringia
  Minister of the Interior and Prime Minister of Thuringia
  Plenipotentiary for the Employment of Labor
  Manpower Chief under the Four-year Plan

Hjalmar Schacht
  Minister of Economics
  Plenipotentiary for War Economy
  President of the Reichsbank
  Minister without Portfolio

Arthur Seyss-Inquart
  Minister of the Interior and Chancellor of Austria
  Commissioner of the Netherlands
  Minister without Portfolio

Albert Speer
  Head of Organization Todt
  Minister for Armament and War Production
  Inspector-General of Roads and of Water and Power
  Plenipotentiary for Armaments under the Four-year Plan

Julius Streicher
  Gauleiter of Franconia
  Editor of <u>Der Stürmer</u>

Constantin von Neurath
  Foreign Minister
  Protector of Bohemia and Moravia
  Minister without Portfolio

Franz von Papen
  Vice-Chancellor of the Third Reich
  Ambassador to Austria
  Ambassador to Turkey

Joachim von Ribbentrop
  Ambassador to Great Britain
  Foreign Minister

Baldur von Schirach
  Leader of the Hitler Youth
  Governor and Gauleiter of Vienna

APPENDIX 7

NUREMBERG IMT OFFICIALS

Figure 1. American Prosecution Team

Chief Prosecutor	Justice Robert H. Jackson
Executive Trial Counsel	Col. Robert G. Storey
	Thomas J. Dodd
Associate Trial Counsel	Sidney S. Alderman
	Brig. Gen. Telford Taylor
	Col. John H. Amen
	Ralph G. Albrecht
Assistant Trial Counsel	Col. Leonard Wheeler, Jr.
	Lt. Col. William H. Baldwin
	Lt. Comdr. Whitney R. Harris
	Maj. William F. Walsh
	Maj. Hartley Murray
	Capt. Drexel A. Sprecher
	Lt. Thomas F. Lambert, Jr.
	Lt. Bernard D. Meltzer
	Walter W. Brudno
	Comdr. James Britt Donovan
	Lt. Col. Smith W. Brockhart, Jr.
	Maj. Frank B. Wallis
	Maj. Warren F. Farr
	Capt. Samuel Harris
	Lt. Henry K. Atherton
	Lt. Brady O. Bryson
	Dr. Robert M. W. Kempner, Defense/Prosecution Liaison Officer

Figure 2. American Documentary Evidence Preparation Team

```
Captain Seymour Krieger      Dr. Jacob Robinson
Lt. Brady Bryson             Lt. Kenyon
Lt. Frederick Felton         Dr. Derenberg
Isaac Stone                  Dr. Jacoby
            Hans Nathan
```

Figure 3. British Prosecution Team

```
Chief Prosecutor          Attorney General Sir Hartley Shawcross
Deputy Chief Prosecutor   Sir David Maxwell-Fyfe
Leading Counsel           G.D. Roberts
Junior Counsel            Lt. Col. J.M.G. Griffith-Jones
                          Col. Harry J. Phillimore
                          Maj. F. Elwyn-Jones
                          Airey Neave
                          Maj. J. Harcourt-Barrington
                          Wing. Comm. Peter Calvocoressi
Liaison Officer           Clement Freud
```

Figure 4. French Prosecution Team

```
Chief Prosecutors         François de Menthon
                          Auguste Champetier de Ribes
Deputy Chief Prosecutors  Charles Dubost
                          Edgar Faure
Assistant Prosecutor      Pierre Mounier
Chiefs of Sections        Charles Gerthoffer
                          Delphin Debenest
Assistant Prosecutors     Jacques-Bernard Herzog
                          Henry Delpech
                          Serge Fuster
                          Constant Quatre
                          Henri Monneray
```

Figure 5. Soviet Prosecution Team

```
Chief Prosecutor          Gen. R.A. Rudenko
Deputy Chief Prosecutor   Col. Y.V. Pokrovsky
Assistant Prosecutors     L.R. Shenin
                          M.Y. Raginski
                          N.D. Zorya
                          L.N. Smirnov
                          Col. D.S. Karev
                          Lt. Col. J.A. Ozol
                          Capt. V.V. Kuchin
```

PART 2
NUREMBERG MILITARY TRIBUNALS (NMT) (SUBSEQUENT CASES)

APPENDIX 8

NUREMBERG MILITARY TRIBUNAL
PROZESSE VOR AMERIKANISCHEN MILITÄRGERICHTSHÖFEN

(12 "SUBSEQUENT TRIALS")
(12 NACHFOLGEPROZESSE)

CASE 1

United States v. Brandt, et al
Medical Case

Prozeß gegen Wehrmachts- und SS-Ärzte
Ärzte-Prozeß

October 25, 1946 - August 20, 1947

Members of the Tribunal

Walter B. Beals	Presiding
Harold L. Sebring	Member
Johnson T. Crawford	Member
Victor C. Swearingen	Alternate

This case charged 24 defendants with performing medical experiments on concentration camp inmates and other living human subjects. Eight defendants were acquitted.

Defendants	Sentences	Commutations
Karl Brandt	Death	--------
Siegfried Handloser	Life	20 years
Oskar Schröder	Life	15 years
Karl Genzken	Life	20 years
Karl Gebhardt	Death	--------
Rudolf Brandt	Death	--------
Joachim Mrugowsky	Death	--------
Helmut Poppendick	10 years	Time served
Wolfram Sievers	Death	--------
Gerhard Rose	Life	15 years
Viktor Brack	Death	--------
Hermann Becker-Freyseng	20 years	10 years
Waldemar Hoven	Death	--------
Wilhelm Beiglböck	15 years	10 years
Herta Oberheuser	20 years	10 years
Fritz Fischer	Life	15 years

CASE 2

United States v. Erhard Milch
Milch Case

Prozeß gegen Erhard Milch
Milch-Prozeß

November 13, 1946 - April 17, 1947

Members of the Tribunal

Robert M. Toms	Presiding
Fitzroy D. Phillips	Member
Michael A. Musmanno	Member
John J. Speight	Alternate

Defendant	Sentence	Commutation
Erhard Milch	Life imprisonment	15 years

The defendant was charged with the exploitation of slave labor and with making medical experiments upon concentration camp inmates.

CASE 3

United States v. Josef Altstötter, et al
Justice Case

Prozeß gegen Justizbeamte
Juristen-Prozeß

January 4, 1947 - December 4, 1947

Members of the Tribunal

Carrington T. Marshall	Presiding (until June 19, 1947)
James T. Brand	Presiding (after June 19, 1947)
Mallory B. Blair	Member
Justin W. Harding	Alternate (Member after June 19, 1947)

This case charged 16 defendants with war crimes and crimes against humanity through the abuse of the judicial process and the administration of justice. Four defendants were acquitted.

Defendants	Sentences	Commutations
Franz Schlegelberger	Life	Medical parole
Herbert Klemm	Life	20 years
Curt Rothenberger	7 years	--------
Ernst Lautz	10 years	Time served
Wolfgang Mettgenberg	10 years	--------
Wilhelm von Ammon	10 years	Time served
Günther Joel	10 years	Time served
Oswald Rothaug	Life	20 years
Rudolf Öschey	Life	20 years
Josef Altstötter	5 years	--------

CASE 4

United States v. Pohl, et al
Pohl Case
Concentration Camps Case

Prozeß gegen Angehörige des Wirtschafts-
und Verwaltungshauptamtes der SS
Pohl-Prozeß

January 13, 1947 - December 3, 1947

Members of the Tribunal

Robert M. Toms   Presiding
Fitzroy D. Phillips   Member
Michael A. Musmanno   Member
John J. Speight

The Pohl Case charged 18 defendants with the administration of concentration camps or of economic enterprises of the SS conducted with slave labor. Three defendants were acquitted.

Defendants	Sentences	Commutations
Oswald Pohl	Death	-----
Franz Eirenschmalz	Death	9 years
Karl Sommer	Life	20 years
Karl Mummenthey	Life	20 years
August Frank	Life	15 years
Heinz Karl Fanslau	20 years	15 years
Georg Lörner	Life	15 years
Hans Lörner	10 years	Time served
Hans Baier	10 years	Time served
Hans Bobermin	15 years	Time served
Hermann Pook	10 years	Time served
Leo Volk	10 years	8 years
Erwin Tschentscher	10 years	Time Served
Max Kiefer	20 years	Time served
Hans Hohberg	10 years	Time served

CASE 5

United States v. Friedrich Flick, et al
Flick Case
Business Men Case

Prozeß gegen Friedrich Flick und leitende Angestellte
der Friedrich Flick KG
Flick-Prozeß

February 8, 1947 - December 22, 1947

Members of the Tribunal

Charles B. Sears   Presiding
Frank N. Richman   Member
William C. Christianson   Member
Richard D. Dixon   Alternate

This case charged 6 defendants with criminal conduct relating to slave labor, the spoliation of property in occupied France and the

Soviet Union, and the "Aryanization" of Jewish industrial and mining properties. Three of the defendants were acquitted.

Defendants	Sentences
Friedrich Flick	7 years
Otto Steinbrinck	5 years
Bernhard Weiss	2 1/2 years

CASE 6

United States v. Carl Krauch, et al
I. G. Farben Case

Prozeß gegen die Leiter der IG Farbenindustrie Aktiengesellschaft
IG-Prozeß

May 3, 1947 – July 30, 1947

Members of the Tribunal

Curtis Grover Shake	Presiding
James Morris	Member
Paul M. Herbert	Member
Clarence F. Merrill	Alternate

This case charged 24 leaders of I.G. Farben with spoliation of property in occupied countries and with participation in a slave labor program. Ten defendants were acquitted.

Defendants	Sentences
Carl Krauch	6 years
Georg von Schnitzler	5 years
Otto Ambros	8 years
Heinrich Bütefisch	6 years
Max Ilgner	3 years
Heinrich Oster	2 years
Hans Kugler	1 1/2 years
Hermann Schmitz	4 years
Fritz ter Meer	7 years
Ernst Bürgin	2 years
Paul Häfliger	6 years
Friedrich Jähne	1 1/2 years
Walter Dürrfeld	8 years

CASE 7

United States v. Wilhelm List, et al
Hostage Case

Prozeß gegen Generäle der Südostfront

May 10, 1947 – February 19, 1948

Members of the Tribunal

Charles F. Wennerstrum	Presiding
Edward F. Carter	Member
George B. Burke	Member

This case originally charged 12 generals assigned to southeastern
Europe with criminal disregard of the rules of warfare in respect
to the treatment of hostages and civilians. The case proceeded to
judgment against only 10 defendants, 2 of whom were acquitted.

Defendants	Sentences	Commutations
Wilhelm List	Life	----
Walter Kuntze	Life	----
Lothar Rendulic	20 years	10 years
Wilhelm Speidel	20 years	Time served
Helmuth Felmy	15 years	10 years
Ernst von Leyser	10 years	Time served
Hubert Lanz	12 years	Time served
Ernst Dehner	7 years	Time served

CASE 8

United States v. Ulrich Greifelt, et al
RuSHA Case

Prozeß gegen Angehörige des SS-Rasse- und
Siedlungshauptamtes (RuSHA) und anderer SS-Organisationen
RuSHA-Prozeß

July 1, 1947 - March 10, 1948

Members of the Tribunal

Lee B. Wyatt	Presiding
Daniel T. O'Connell	Member
Johnson T. Crawford	Member

The RuSHA Case charged 14 high officials in the Race and Settlement
Office of the SS Elite Guard and related offices with carrying out
systematic programs of genocide. Five defendants were acquitted,
and 5 were discharged as having served sufficient time before and
during the trial.

Defendants	Sentences	Commutations
Ulrich Greifelt	Life	-----
Rudolf Creutz	15 years	10 years
Herbert Hübner	15 years	Time served
Werner Lorenz	20 years	15 years
Heinz Brückner	15 years	Time served
Otto Hofmann	25 years	15 years
Richard Hildebrandt	25 years	-----
Fritz Schwalm	10 years	Time served

CASE 9

United States v. Otto Ohlendorf, et al
Einsatzgruppen Case

Prozeß gegen Ohlendorf und andere Führer von Einsatzgruppen
Einsatzgruppen-Prozeß

July 3, 1947 - April 10, 1948

Members of the Tribunal

Michael A. Musmanno   Presiding
John J. Speight   Member
Richard D. Dixon   Member

The Einsatzgruppen Case originally charged 23 officers of the SS Elite Guard who were in charge of the extermination squads with the murder of 2,000,000 people. The case proceeded to judgment against 22 defendants. One was discharged as having served sufficient time before and during the trial.

Defendants	Sentences	Commutations
Paul Blobel	Death	----
Ernst Biberstein	Death	Life
Walter Blume	Death	25 years
Werner Braune	Death	----
Walter Hänsch	Death	15 years
Woldemar Klingelhöfer	Death	Life
Erich Naumann	Death	----
Otto Ohlendorf	Death	----
Adolf Ott	Death	Life
Martin Sandberger	Death	Life
Heinz Hermann Schubert	Death	10 years
Willi Seibert	Death	15 years
Eugen Steimle	Death	20 years
Heinz Jost	Life	10 years
Gustav Nosske	Life	10 years
Waldemar von Radetzky	20 years	Time served
Erwin Schulz	20 years	15 years
Franz Six	20 years	10 years
Lothar Fendler	10 years	8 years
Felix Rühl	10 years	Time served
Eduard Strauch	Death	-----

Appendix 475

CASE 10

United States v. Alfried Krupp, et al
Krupp Case

Prozeß gegen Alfried Krupp
und leitende Angestellte der Friedrich Krupp AG
Krupp-Prozeß

August 16, 1947 - July 31, 1948

Members of the Tribunal

H. C. Anderson   Presiding
Edward James Daly   Member
William J. Wilkins   Member

The Krupp Case originally charged 12 executives of the Krupp industrial concern with using slave labor and with spoliation. The case proceeded to judgment against 11 defendants, 1 of whom was discharged as having served sufficient time before and after the trial.

Defendants	Sentences	Commutations
Alfried Felix Alwyn Krupp von Bohlen und Halbach	12 years and confiscation of all property	Time served and no confiscation
Ewald Oskar Löser	7 years	------
Eduard Houdremont	10 years	Time served
Erich Müller	12 years	Time served
Friedrich Wilhelm Heinrich Lehmann	6 years	Time served
Max Otto Ihn	9 years	Time served
Karl Adolf Ferdinand Eberhardt	9 years	Time served
Heinrich Leo Korschan	6 years	Time served
Friedrich von Bülow	12 years	Time served

CASE 11

United States v. Ernst von Weizsäcker, et al
Ministries Case
Wilhelmstrasse Case

Prozeß gegen Beamte des Auswärtigen Amtes
und andere Ministerien, SS-Führer und Wirtschaftler
Wilhelmstraßen-Prozeß

November 4, 1947 - April 13, 1949

Members of the Tribunal

William C. Christianson   Presiding
Leon W. Powers   Member
Robert F. Maguire   Member

The Ministries Case originally charged 21 defendants with playing an important part in the political and diplomatic preparation for war, with violation of international treaties, with economic spoliation, and with diplomatic implementation of the extermination program. The case proceeded to judgment against 19 defendants.

Defendants	Sentences	Commutations
Ernst von Weizsäcker	7 years	Time served
Ernst Bohle	5 years	-----
Ernst Wörmann	7 years	-----
Karl Ritter	4 years	-----
Edmund Veesenmayer	20 years	10 years
Hans Heinrich Lammers	20 years	10 years
Richard Darré	7 years	-----
Otto Dietrich	7 years	-----
Wilhelm Keppler	10 years	Time served
Walter Schellenberg	6 years	-----
Gottlob Berger	25 years	10 years
Lutz Schwerin von Krosigk	10 years	Time served
Emil Puhl	5 years	-----
Karl Rasche	7 years	-----
Paul Körner	15 years	10 years
Paul Pleiger	15 years	9 years
Hans Kehrl	15 years	Time served
Gustav Adolf Steengracht von Moyland	7 years	-----
Wilhelm Stuckart	3 years, 10 months, 20 days	

CASE 12

United States v. Wilhelm von Leeb, et al
High Command Case

Prozeß gegen höhere Offiziere des OKW,
des Heeres, der Kriegsmarine und der Luftwaffe
OKW-Prozeß

November 28, 1947 – October 28, 1948

Members of the Tribunal

John C. Young   Presiding
Winfield B. Hale   Member
Justin W. Harding   Member

The High Command Case originally charged 14 defendants who held command or staff positions in the armed forces with ordering the killing and mistreatment of prisoners of war and for deporting or abusing civilians in occupied areas. The case proceeded to judgment against 13 defendants. Two were acquitted, 1 was discharged as having served sufficient time before and during the trial.

Defendants	Sentences	Commutations
Wilhelm von Leeb	3 years	-----
Georg Karl Friedrich-Wilhelm von Küchler	20 years	12 years
Hermann Hoth	15 years	-----
Hans Reinhardt	15 years	-----
Hans von Salmuth	20 years	12 years
Karl Hollidt	5 years	-----
Karl von Roques	20 years	-----
Hermann Reinecke	Life	-----
Walter Warlimont	Life	18 years
Otto Wöhler	8 years	-----
Rudolf Lehmann	7 years	-----

APPENDIX 9

NMT SUMMARY OF VERDICTS

	Name	Indicted	Acquitted	Released	Death	Life	Prison	Released with time served
Case 1	Medical	24	8	0	7	5	4	0
Case 2	Milch	1	0	0	0	1	0	0
Case 3	Justice	16	4	2	0	4	6	0
Case 4	Pohl	18	3	0	3	3	9	0
Case 5	Flick	6	3	0	0	0	3	0
Case 6	Farben	24	10	1	0	0	11	2
Case 7	Hostage	12	2	2	0	2	6	0
Case 8	RuSHA	14	1	0	0	1	7	5
Case 9	Einsatz	23	0	1	14	2	5	1
Case 10	Krupp	12	1	0	0	0	10	1
Case 11	Ministries	21	2	0	0	0	18	1
Case 12	High Command	14	2	1	0	2	8	1
TOTALS		185	35	8	24	20	87	11

Source: UNITED STATES. DEPARTMENT OF STATE. Germany 1947-1949: The Story in Documents, p. 117. [Some were released from trial because of old age, illness, or suicide].

PART 3
INTERNATIONAL MILITARY TRIBUNAL FOR THE FAR EAST (IMTFE)

APPENDIX 10

IMTFE PROSECUTING NATIONS

1. Australia
2. Canada
3. China
4. France
5. India
6. The Netherlands
7. Philippines
8. New Zealand
9. Union of Soviet Socialist Republics
10. United Kingdom of Great Britain and Northern Ireland
11. United States of America

APPENDIX 11

IMTFE DEFENDANTS AND SENTENCES

1.	ARAKI, Sadao	Life imprisonment
2.	DOIHARA, Kenji	Death by hanging
3.	HASHIMOTO, Kingoro	Life imprisonment
4.	HATA, Shunroku	Life imprisonment
5.	HIRANUMA, Kiichiro	Life imprisonment
6.	HIROTA, Koki	Death by hanging
7.	HOSHINO, Naoki	Life imprisonment
8.	ITAGAKI, Seishiro	Death by hanging
9.	KAYA, Okinori	Life imprisonment
10.	KIDO, Koichi	Life imprisonment
11.	KIMURA, Heitaro	Death by hanging
12.	KOISO, Kuniaki	Life imprisonment
13.	MATSUI, Iwane	Death by hanging
14.	MATSUOKA, Yosuke	Died during trial
15.	MINAMI, Jiro	Life imprisonment
16.	MUTO, Akira	Death by hanging
17.	NAGANO, Osami	Died during trial
18.	OKA, Takasumi	Life imprisonment
19.	OKAWA, Shumei	Unfit for trial
20.	OSHIMA, Hiroshi	Life imprisonment
21.	SATO, Kenryo	Life imprisonment
22.	SHIGEMITSU, Mamoru	Seven years
23.	SHIMADA, Shigetaro	Life imprisonment
24.	SHIRATORI, Toshio	Life imprisonment
25.	SUZUKI, Teiichi	Life imprisonment
26.	TOGO, Shigenori	Twenty years
27.	TOJO, Hideki	Death by hanging
28.	UMEZU, Yoshijiro	Life imprisonment

APPENDIX 12

PRINCIPAL POSTS HELD BY IMTFE DEFENDANTS

Araki, Sadao
General
Army Minister, 1931-1934
Education Minister, 1938-1939

Doihara, Kenji
General
Commander-in-Chief, Japanese 5th Army in Manchuria, 1938-1940

Hashimoto, Kingoro
Colonel
Army General Staff, 1933
Propagandist

Hata, Shunroku
General
Commander-in-Chief, Expeditionary Force in Central China

Hiranuma, Kiichiro
Rightist Leader
Founder of Kokuhonsha
President, Privy Council, 1936-1939
Prime Minister, 1939

Hirota, Koki
Career Diplomat
Foreign Minister, 1933-1936
Prime Minister, 1936-1937

Hoshino, Naoki
President, Planning Board, 2nd Kenoe Cabinet
Chief Secretary and Minister without Portfolio, Tojo Cabinet

Itagaki, Seishiro
General
Chief of Staff, Kwantung Army, 1936-1937
War Minister, 1938-1939

Kaya, Okinori
Minister of Finance, 1937-1938, 1941-1944
President, North China Development Company, 1939-1941

Kido, Koichi
Education Minister, 1937
Welfare Minister, 1938
Home Minister, 1939
Privy Seal, 1940-1945

Kimura, Heitaro
General
Vice War Minister, 1941-1944

Koiso, Kuniaki
General
Chief of Staff, Kwantung Army, 1932-1934
Overseas Minister, 1939-1940
Prime Minister, 1944-1945

Matsui Iwane
General
Commander-in-Chief, Japanese Forces in Central China, 1937-1938

Matsuoka, Yosuke
Career Diplomat
Foreign Minister, 1940-1941

Minami, Jiro
General
War Minister, 1931
Commander-in-Chief, Kwantung Army, 1934-1936
Governor-General, Korea, 1936-1942

Muto, Akira
General
Chief, Military Affairs Bureau, War Ministry, 1939-1942
Field Commands, Dutch East Indies and the Philippines, 1943-1945

Nagano, Osami
Admiral
Navy Minister, 1936-1937
Chief of Naval General Staff, 1941-1944

Oka, Takasumi
Admiral
Chief, General and Military Affairs Bureau, Navy Ministry

Okawa, Shumei
Civilian
Alleged organizer of the Mukden Incident, 1931
Propagandist

Oshima, Hiroshi
Army officer
Military Attaché, Berlin, 1936
Ambassador to Germany, 1938-1939, 1941-1945

Sato, Kenryo
General
Chief, Military Affairs Bureau, War Ministry, 1942-1944

Shigemitsu, Mamoru
Career Diplomat
Foreign Minister, 1943-1945

Shimada, Shigetaro
Admiral
Navy Minister, 1941-1944

Shiratori, Toshio
Career diplomat
Ambassador to Italy, 1939

Suzuki, Teiichi
General
President, Cabinet Planning Board and Minister without Portfolio

Togo, Shigenori
Career diplomat
Ambassador to Germany, 1937
Ambassador to the Soviet Union, 1938
Foreign Minister, 1941-1942, 1945

Tojo, Hideki
General
Prime Minister and Army Minister, 1941-1944

Umezu, Yoshijiro
General
Commander, Kwantung Army and Ambassador to Manchukuo, 1939-1944

APPENDIX 13

IMTFE COUNSELS

Chief of Counsel

Joseph B. Keenan	United States

Associate Counsels

Judge Che-Chun Hsiang	China
Arthur S. Comyns-Carr	United Kingdom
Minister S. A. Golunsky	USSR
Maj. Gen. of Justice A. N. Vasilyev	USSR
Justice Alan J. Mansfield	Australia
Brig. Henry G. Nolan	Canada
Robert Oneto	France
Govinda Menon	India
Justice W. G. F. Borgerhoff-Mulder	The Netherlands
Brig. Ronald H. Quilliam	New Zealand
Major Pedro López	The Philippines

APPENDIX 14

IMTFE CHARGES, VERDICTS, AND SENTENCES

Figure 1. Counts of the Indictment

Count 1	Over-all conspiracy
Count 27	Waging war against China
Count 29	Waging war against the United States
Count 31	Waging war against the British Commonwealth
Count 32	Waging war against the Netherlands
Count 33	Waging war against France
Count 35	Waging war against the USSR at Lake Khassan
Count 36	Waging war against the USSR at Nomonhan
Count 54	Ordering, authorizing, and permitting atrocities
Count 55	Disregard of duty to secure observance of and prevent breaches of laws of war

Figure 2. Table of Counts, Verdicts, and Sentences

G - Guilty
A - Acquitted
0 - No finding made
(-) - No indictment

Count	1	27	29	31	32	33	35	36	54	55	Sentences
Araki	G	G	A	A	A	A	A	A	A	A	Life
Doihara	G	G	G	G	G	A	G	G	G	0	Hanging
Hashimoto	G	G	A	A	A	-	-	-	A	A	Life
Hata	G	G	G	G	G	-	A	A	A	G	Life
Hiranuma	G	G	G	G	G	A	A	G	A	A	Life
Hirota	G	G	A	A	A	A	A	-	A	G	Hanging
Hoshino	G	G	G	G	G	A	A	-	A	A	Life
Itagaki	G	G	G	G	G	A	G	G	G	0	Hanging
Kaya	G	G	G	G	G	-	-	-	A	A	Life
Kido	G	G	G	G	G	A	A	A	A	A	Life
Kimura	G	G	G	G	G	-	-	-	G	G	Hanging
Koiso	G	G	G	G	G	-	-	A	A	G	Life
Matsui	A	A	A	A	A	-	A	A	A	G	Hanging
Minami	G	G	A	A	A	-	-	-	A	A	Life
Muto	G	G	G	G	G	A	-	A	G	G	Hanging
Oka	G	G	G	G	G	-	-	-	A	A	Life
Oshima	G	A	A	A	A	-	-	-	A	A	Life
Sato	G	G	G	G	G	-	-	-	A	A	Life
Shigemitsu	A	G	G	G	G	G	A	-	A	G	7 years
Shimada	G	G	G	G	G	-	-	-	A	A	Life
Shiratori	G	A	A	A	A	-	-	-	-	-	Life
Suzuki	G	G	G	G	G	-	A	A	A	A	Life
Togo	G	G	G	G	G	-	-	A	A	A	20 years
Tojo	G	G	G	G	G	G	-	A	G	0	Hanging
Umezu	G	G	G	G	G	-	-	A	A	A	Life

PART 4
HOLOCAUST STATISTICS

APPENDIX 15

VARIOUS ESTIMATES OF JEWISH DEATHS

Table 1

Germany (1938 frontiers)	195,000
Austria	53,000
Czechoslovakia (1938)	255,000
Denmark	1,500
France	140,000
Belgium	57,000
Luxembourg	3,000
Norway	1,000
The Netherlands	120,000
Italy	20,000
Yugoslavia	64,000
Greece	64,000
Bulgaria (pre-1941 frontiers)	5,000
Roumania (pre-1940 frontiers)	530,000
Hungary (1938 frontiers)	200,000
Poland (1939 frontiers)	3,271,000
USSR (pre-1939 frontiers plus Baltic States)	1,050,000
Sub-Total	6,029,500
Less dispersed refugees	308,000
Total	5,721,500

Sources: Anglo-American Committee of Inquiry Regarding the Problems of European Jewry and Palestine, April 1946. Nora Levin. The Holocaust: The Destruction of European Jewry, 1933-1945. New York: Schocken, 1973. p. 715.

Table 2

Country	Number Killed	Percent Killed
Poland	3,000,000	90
Baltic countries	228,000	90
Germany/Austria	210,000	90
Slovakia	75,000	83
Greece	54,000	77
The Netherlands	105,000	75
Hungary	450,000	70
SSR White Russia	245,000	65
SSR Ukraine	900,000	60
Belgium	40,000	60
Yugoslavia	26,000	60
Roumania	300,000	50
Norway	900	50
France	90,000	26
Bulgaria	14,000	22
Italy	8,000	20

484 Appendix

Country	Number Killed	Percent Killed
Luxembourg	1,000	20
Russia	107,000	11
Total	5,933,900	67

Source: Lucy S. Dawidowicz. The War against the Jews, 1933-1945. New York: Holt, Rinehart and Winston, 1975. p. 544.

Table 3

Country	Number
Germany (boundaries of 1938)	130,000
Austria	58,000
Belgium	26,000
Czechoslovakia (boundaries of 1938)	245,000
France	64,000
Greece	58,000
Hungary and Carpatho-Ukraine	300,000
Italy	8,000
Latvia, Lithuania, Estonia	200,000
Luxembourg	3,000
The Netherlands	101,800
Norway	677
Poland (boundaries of 1938)	2,700,000
Roumania (boundaries prior to 1939)	220,000
USSR (boundaries prior to 1939)	800,000
Yugoslavia	54,000
Total	4,975,477

Source: Gerald Fleming. Hitler and the Final Solution. Berkeley: University of California Press, 1984. The original was in German.

Table 4

Country	Number Low	High
Germany (1938 frontiers)	160,000	180,000
Austria	58,000	60,000
Czechoslovakia (1938)	233,000	243,000
Denmark	<100	<100
France	60,000	65,000
Belgium	25,000	28,000
Luxembourg	3,000	3,000
Norway	700	700
The Netherlands	104,000	104,000
Italy	8,500	9,500
Yugoslavia	55,000	58,000
Greece	57,000	60,000
Roumania (pre-1940 frontier)	200,000	200,000
Hungary (1938 frontiers)	200,000	220,000

Country	Number	
	Low	High
Poland (1939 frontiers)	2,350,000	2,600,000
USSR (pre-1939 frontiers plus Baltic States)	700,000	750,000
Total	4,194,200	4,581,200

Source: Gerald Reitlinger. *The Final Solution, the Attempt to Exterminate the Jews of Europe, 1939-1945*. New York: Beechhurst Press, 1953.

Table 5

Country (prewar borders)	Number
Poland	2,850,000
USSR	1,500,000
Roumania	425,000
Hungary	200,000
Czechoslovakia	240,000
France	90,000
Germany	110,000
Austria	45,000
Lithuania	130,000
The Netherlands	105,000
Latvia	80,000
Belgium	40,000
Yugoslavia	55,000
Greece	60,000
Italy	15,000
Bulgaria	7,000
Denmark, Estonia, Norway, Luxembourg, Danzig	5,000
Total	5,957,000

Source: Jacob Lestchinsky. *Crisis, Catastrophe, and Survival: A Jewish Balance Sheet, 1941-1948*. New York: World Jewish Congress, 1948.

Table 6

Country	Number
Poland	up to 3,000,000
USSR	over 700,000
Romania	270,000
Czechoslovakia	260,000
Hungary	over 180,000
Lithuania	up to 130,000
Germany	over 120,000
Netherlands	over 100,000
France	75,000
Latvia	70,000
Yugoslavia	60,000
Greece	60,000
Austria	over 50,000
Belgium	24,000

Country	Number
Italy (including Rhodes)	9,000
Estonia	2,000
Norway	under 1,000
Luxembourg	under 1,000
Danzig	under 1,000
Total	5,100,100

Source: Raul Hilberg. 2 volumes. The Destruction of the European Jews. Revised and enlarged edition, New York/London: Holmes & Meier, 1985. II, 1220.

APPENDIX 16

ABSORPTION OF JEWISH REFUGEES, 1933-1943

Country	Number Admitted	Percentage
United States	190,000	23.5
Palestine	120,000	14.8
England	65,000	8.1
France	55,000	6.8
Netherlands	35,000	4.3
Belgium	30,000	3.7
Switzerland	16,000	1.9
Spain	12,000	1.4
Other European Countries	70,000	8.8
Argentina	50,000	6.2
Brazil	25,000	3.1
Bolivia	12,000	1.4
Chile	14,000	1.7
Uruguay	7,000	.8
Other Latin America Countries	20,000	2.4
China	25,000	3.1
Australia	9,000	1.1
South Africa	8,000	1.0
Canada	8,000	1.0
Other Countries	40,000	4.9
TOTAL	811,000	100.0

Source: Aryeh Tartakower and Kurt R. Grossman. The Jewish Refugee. New York: Institute of Jewish Affairs, 1944. p. 343.

PART 5
MISCELLANEOUS APPENDICES

APPENDIX 17

EQUIVALENT RANKS OF THE UNITED STATES ARMY,
THE GERMAN ARMY, AND THE WAFFEN-SS

[Ranks are approximate only]

UNITED STATES ARMY	GERMAN ARMY	WAFFEN-SS
No equivalent	Grenadier, Schütze	SS Mann
Private	Obergrenadier	SS Sturmmann
Private 1st Class	Gefreiter	SS Rottenführer
	Obergefreiter, Stabsgefreiter	
Corporal	Unteroffizier	SS Unterscharführer
Sergeant	Unterfeldwebel	SS Scharführer
Staff Sergeant	Feldwebel	SS Oberscharführer
Technical Sergeant	Oberfeldwebel	SS Hauptscharführer
Master Sergeant	Stabsfeldwebel	SS Sturmscharführer
2nd Lieutenant	Leutnant	SS Untersturmführer
1st Lieutenant	Oberleutnant	SS Obersturmführer
Captain	Hauptmann	SS Hauptsturmführer
Major	Major	SS Sturmbannführer
Lieutenant Colonel	Oberstleutnant	SS Obersturmbannführer
Colonel	Oberst	SS Standartenführer
No equivalent	No equivalent	SS Oberführer
Brigadier General	Generalmajor	SS Brigadeführer
Major General	Generalleutnant	SS Gruppenführer
Lieutenant General	General der Infanterie	SS Obergruppenführer
General	Generaloberst	SS Oberstgruppenführer
No equivalent	Generalfeldmarschall	Reichsführer-SS
No equivalent	Reichsmarschall	No equivalent
General of the Army	No equivalent	No equivalent

APPENDIX 18

INTERNATIONAL WAR CRIMES TRIBUNAL
(BERTRAND RUSSELL TRIBUNAL)
(STOCKHOLM TRIBUNAL)

Bertrand Russell	Honorary President
Jean-Paul Sartre	Executive President
Vladimir Dedijer	Chairman and President of Sessions

Tribunal Members

Wolfgang Abendroth	Lawrence Daly	Mahmud Ali Kasuri
Gunther Anders	Vladimir Dedijer	Sara Lidman
Mehmet Ali Aybar	Dave Dellinger	Kinju Morikawa
James Baldwin	Isaac Deutscher	Carl Oglesby
Lelio Basso	Haika Grossman	Shoichi Sakata
Simone de Beauvoir	Gisele Halimi	Laurent Schwartz
Lazaro Cardenas	Amado Hernandez	Peter Weiss
Stokely Carmichael	Melba Hernandez	

ABBREVIATIONS

A

ACJ	Allied Council for Japan
AFPAC	Air Force Pacific Air Command
AMG	Allied Military Government
ATIS	Allied Translator and Interpreter Section

B

BA KOBLENZ	Bundesarchiv Koblenz
BCOF	British Commonwealth Occupation Force
BDM	Bund Deutscher Mädel
BPP	Bavarian Political Police
BVN	Bund der Verfolgten des Naziregimes

C

CDJC	Centre de Documentation Juive Contemporaine
CID	[Dachau] Concentration Camp International Committee
CIE	Civil Information and Education [Section]
CIR	Consolidated Interrogation Report
CROWCASS	Central Registry of War Criminals and Security Suspects

D

DJ	Deutsches Jungvolk
DRF	Division of Research for the Far East

E

EC	Economic Case
ECAFE	Economic Commission for Asia and the Far East
EROA	Economic Rehabilitation of Occupied Areas

F

FEAC	Far Eastern Advisory Commission
FEC	Far Eastern Commission
FFDJF	Les Fils et Filles des Deportés Juifs de France
FTC	Federal Trade Commission

490 Abbreviations

G

GAO [United States] Government Accounting Office
GARIOA Government and Relief in Occupied Areas
GHQ General Headquarters
GPO Government Printing Office (United States)

H

HJ Hitlerjugend
HMPO His Majesty's Printing Office (Great Britain)
HMSO His Majesty's Stationery Office (Great Britain)

I

IDP International Defense Panel
IMG Internationaler Militärgerichtshof (IMT)
IMT International Military Tribunal (Nuremberg)
IMTFE International Military Tribunal for the Far East
IPR Institute of Pacific Relations
IPS International Prosecution Section
IRC International Red Cross
IRK Internationales Rotes Kreuz

J

JCP Japanese Communist Party
JM Jungmädelbund

K

KZ, KL Konzentrationslager (concentration camp)

L

L IMT Documents Collected in London
LARA Licensed Agency for Relief of Asia
LDP Liberal-Democratic Party

N

NARS National Archives and Records Service (United States)
NC Documents of German government agencies
NHK Nihon Hoso Kyokai (Japanese Broadcasting Corporation)
NMT Nuremberg Military Tribunal (American)
NO Nazi Organizations

O

OCCWC Office of the Chief of Counsel for War Crimes
OIR Office of Intelligence Research
OKH Oberkommando des Heeres (see glossary)
OKW Oberkommando der Wehrmacht (see glossary)
OMGUS Office of the Military Government United States
OSS Office of Strategic Services (now CIA)

P

PIO Public Information Office
PIR Preliminary Interrogation Report
PS Paris-Storey (American IMT Prosecution Documents)

R

R	Documents translated by Lt. Walter Rothschild
RKFDV	Reichskommisar für die Festung Deutschen Volkstums
RSHA	Reichssicherheitshauptamt (see glossary)
RuSHA	Rasse- und Siedlungshauptamt (see glossary)

S

SA	Sturmabteilung (see glossary)
SCAP	Supreme Commander for the Allied Powers
SD	Sicherheitsdienst (see glossary)
SEA	Staff Evidence Analysis
SOE	[British] Special Operations Executive [in France]
SS	Schutzstaffel (see glossary)
STALAG	Stammlager (see glossary)
SWNCC	State-War-Navy Coordinating Committee

U

UNRRA	United Nations Relief and Rehabilitation Administration

V

VVN	Vereinigung der Verfolgten des Naziregimes

W

WKB	Wehrbezirkskommando (see glossary)
WNRC	Washington National Records Center
WVHA	Wirtschafts- und Verwaltungshauptamt (see glossary)

Y

YIVO	YIVO Institute for Jewish Research

GLOSSARY

A

ABSCHNITT. Administrative subdistrict.

ABWEHR. The Intelligence Service of the German High Command, a military department. Taken over by the SS in 1944.

ABWEHRDIENST. Counter-espionage; military security service.

AKTION. Action, operation, undertaking.

ALLGEMEINE SS. General SS; main body of the pre-war SS, composed of part-time volunteers, all civilians. Most diplomats, top-level state employees, industrialists, lawyers, and doctors held high rank in the Allgemeine SS.

AMT. Office or Bureau.

ANSCHLUSS. Union or annexation, especially the annexation of Austria in 1938.

ARBEITSDIENSTFÜHRER. Leader of a paramilitary formation.

ARBEITSEINSATZ. Work replacement.

ARMEE. An army, field formation composed usually of at least two corps.

ARMEEKORPS (AK). An army corps, component of an army, usually composed of at least two divisions.

ARMEEOBERKOMMANDO (AOK). Army headquarters or headquarters staff.

AUFSEHER. Guard.

AUSCHWITZ. [Polish: Oswiecim]. The most notorious extermination camp. There was a central camp (Stammlager, Auschwitz 1), Birkenau (Auschwitz 2), and Manowic (Auschwitz 3).

AUSSENLAGER. Camp near large factories where inmates were employed.

AUSSENSTELLE (AST). Branch office.

AUSSIEDLUNG. Resettlement. The deportation of Jews to the ghettos of large cities or to annihilation camps.

AUSWÄRTIGES AMT. Foreign Office.

B

BANDE. Partisans, guerrilla band.

BARBAROSSA. Code name for the German invasion of the Soviet Union.

BAYERISCHE POLITISCHE POLIZEI (BPP). Bavarian Political Police, an organization dating from pre-Nazi times, infiltrated and then taken over by Heydrich and Himmler.

BEFEHLSHABER. Commander in Chief.

BEFEHLSHABER DER ORPO (BdO). Commander of Police in Occupied Territory.

BEFEHLSHABER DER SIPO (BdS). Commander of Security Police and Security Service in Occupied Territory.

BELZEC. A concentration camp near Lublin.

BEZIRK. District.

BIRKENAU. German name for Brzezinka (see AUSCHWITZ).

BLITZKRIEG. Lightening warfare.

BLOCKFÜHRER. SS in charge of barracks.

BUCHENWALD. Concentration camp.

C

CHEF. Chief, head, commander, superior.

CHELMNO. [German: Kulmhof]. Extermination camp near the Polish town of Kala.

D

DACHAU. Concentration camp.

DIENSTSTELLE. Duty station, bureau, command headquarters, administrative center.

E

EINSATZ. Commitment, employment, mission, task, special task, active duty.

EINSATZGRUPPE. Action Group, or Task Force, for special purposes. Special SS/SD execution team responsible for the liquidation of Jews.

EINSATZKOMMANDO. Einsatzgruppen were divided into a number of Kommandos. Execution squads.

EINWANDERUNGSZENTRALSTELLE (EwZ). Immigration central office.

EISERNES KREUZ (EK). Iron cross (military decoration).

ENDLÖSUNG. Final solution; refers to the extermination of the Jews.

ERGÄNZUNGSTELLE. Recruiting or replacement center.

ERSATZ. Replacement or reserve.

F

FALL GELB. Code name for the May 1940 attack on France and the Low Countries.

FALL ROT. Code name for the second phase of the Battle of France, June 1940.

FEINDNACHRICHTENABTEILUNG. Intelligence branch. See Ic.

FELDKOMMANDANTUR. Regional military government office.

FESTUNG. Fortress.

FÖRDERNDES MITGLIED (FM). Sponsoring member of the SS.

FREIKORPS. Free Corps; illegal military formations composed largely of World War I German soldiers active in postwar Germany.

FREIWILLIGE. Volunteers.

FÜHRER. Leader or officer.

FÜHRERBEFEHL. Order issued by Hitler.

FÜHRERERLASS. Decree or edict issued by Hitler.

G

GAU. Territorial division of the NSDAP (43 in all).

GAULEITER. Highest ranking Nazi official in a Gau. Responsible for political and economic activity as well as mobilization of labor and civil defense.

GEHEIME STAATSPOLIZEI (GESTAPO). Secret State Police. Originated in the Prussian Secret State Police, taken over by Göring in 1933. It became Department IV of the RSHA.

GENERALGOUVERNEMENT. Government-General; largest portion of German-occupied Poland.

GENERALKOMMANDO. Headquarters of an army corps.

GLEICHSCHALTUNG. Coordination; unification. The process of compulsory coordination by which Germany was brought under Nazi control.

GRUPPENSTAB. Group Staff.

H

HAUPTSCHARFÜHRER. Equivalent to master sergeant.

HAUPTSTURMFÜHRER. Equivalent to captain.

HEER. An army; the Army.

HEERESGRUPPE. Army group; field formation usually composed of at least two armies.

HITLERJUGEND (HJ). Hitler youth.

HÖHERER SS UND POLIZEI FÜHRER (HSSuPF). Sometimes written HSSPf. Higher SS and Police Leader. Commanding officer of SS and Police security forces, usually behind the front lines. Himmler's direct and senior representatives as chiefs of the SS and the police throughout the New Order.

I

Ic. Intelligence officer in a military headquarters or military formation.

IM AUFTRAG. By order.

IN VERTRETUNG. By proxy, deputy, representative.

INSPEKTION. Inspectorate.

INSPEKTOR DER ORPO (IdO). The equivalent of the BdO within the boundaries of Greater Germany.

INSPEKTOR DER SIPO (IdS). The equivalent of the BdS within the boundaries of Greater Germany.

K

KAMPFGRUPPE. Battle group.

KAMPFZEIT. Time of struggle; period during which the Nazis struggled to become the masters of Germany (1919-1933).

KAPO. Inmate in charge of work group. Derivation has been traced to Italian for head or chief, or to the anagram for Konzentrationslager-Arbeitpolizei. Kapos were frequently German prisoners.

KOMMANDOAMT DER WAFFEN-SS. Operational command headquarters of the Waffen-SS within the SS Führungshauptamt.

KOMMANDOSTAB RFSS. Headquarters of the Reichsführer SS while in the field.

KONZENTRATIONSLAGER (KZ or KL). Concentration camp.

KREIS. Administrative district of a Gau.

KREISLEITER. Head of a Kreis.

KRIEGSGEFANGENER. Prisoner of war.

KRIEGSMARINE. German Navy.

KRIMINALPOLIZEI (KRIPO). Criminal police. With the Gestapo, formed the Sipo.

LAGERFÜHRER SS. Camp commandant.

LAGERKOMMANDANT. Camp commandant.

LANDESGRUPPE. Nazi party organization in a country outside Germany.

LANDWEHR. Military reserve of men between ages 35 and 45.

LEBENSBORN. "Spring of life." SS maternity organization to promote Himmler's racial policies.

LEBENSRAUM. Living space. Additional territory desired by Germany for expansion.

LEGION. Legion, military formation composed of foreigners serving in the German armed forces.

LEIBSTANDARTE SS "ADOLF HITLER." Hitler bodyguard regiment.

LEITSTELLE. Control station.

LUFTWAFFE. German Air Force.

M

MARITA. Code name for the German invasion of Greece.

MAUTHAUSEN. Concentration camp organized in 1938.

N

NACHF[OLGER]. Successor.

NATIONALSOZIALISTISCHE DEUTSCHE ARBEITERPARTEI (NSDAP) (NAZI). National Socialist German Workers' Party, "Nazi" for short.

NEBENLAGER. Subsidiary or auxiliary camp, in the vicinity of central camp.

O

OBERABSCHNITT. SS district equivalent to a Wehrkreis.

OBERAUFSEHER. Head guard.

OBERBEFEHLSHABER DES HEERES (ObdH). Commander in chief of the Army.

OBERCAPO. Superior to a capo.

OBERKOMMANDO DES HEERES (OKH). Army High Command. Army General Staff.

OBERKOMMANDO DER WEHRMACHT (OKW). Armed Forces High Command. The combined services general staff.

OBERSTURMFÜHRER SS. SS equivalent to sergeant.

ORDNUNGSPOLIZEI (ORPO). Order Police. A branch of the uniformed police later incorporated into the SS.

ORGANIZATION TODT (OT). Military construction agency founded by Fritz Todt, Reich Minister for Armaments and Munitions until his death in 1942.

OSTLAND. Name for Baltic countries and White Russia.

OSTMARK. Name for Austria after its incorporation into the Third Reich.

OSTMINISTERIUM. Ministry of the East.

P

PANZER. Military tank.

PARTEIGENOSSE. Member of a party, generally the Nazi party during the Third Reich.

PRESSE- UND INFORMATIONSDIENST (PID). Press and Information Service, a cover under which the SD functioned in the last months of the Weimar Republic, which had proscribed it as a Nazi organization.

R

RASSE- UND SIEDLUNGSHAUPTAMT (RuSHA). SS main office for race and settlement.

REICHSARBEITSDIENST (RAD). Reich Labor Service, compulsory for young men.

REICHSDEUTSCHE. German citizens residing in Germany.

REICHSFÜHRER SS (RFSS). Reich Leader; highest rank in the SS. Held only by Himmler.

REICHSGESETZBLATT (RGBl). Reich Legal Gazette.

REICHSKOMMISSARIAT FÜR DIE FESTIGUNG DEUTSCHEN VOLKSTUMS (RKfDV). SS agency headed by Himmler for the "strengthening of Germanism." Concerned primarily with ethnic Germans.

REICHSMINISTERIUM DES INNEREN (RMdI). Minister of the Interior.

REICHSSICHERHEITSHAUPTAMT (RSHA). Reich Main Security Office, in which were coordinated all branches of the Nazi security service. Led by Reinhard Heinrich and later by Ernst Kaltenbrunner.

REICHSWEHR. The German armed forces from 1920-1935. Limited by the Treaty of Versailles to 100,000 men.

RITTERKREUZ. Knight's Cross.

S

SCHARFÜHRER. Equivalent to a sergeant lower grade.

SCHUPO. Abbreviation for Schutzpolizei.

SCHUTZSTAFFEL (SS). Protection Squad. Originally a small and elite corps of the NSDAP whose function was to act as Hitler's bodyguard. Known as the Black Shirts. Under the leadership of Himmler it developed into a state within a state. By the end of World War II it controlled the entire police machinery of the Nazi state, operated concentration camps throughout Europe, had a military arm known as the Waffen-SS, and owned and administered several huge business corporations. Contained the following sections: Allgemeine-SS, RSHA, Waffen-SS, and Totenkopfverbände.

SICHERHEITSDIENST (SD). Security and intelligence service of the SS. Founded by Heydrich in 1931 with the object of spying on both Nazi and non-Nazi organizations and people. Section VI of the RSHA.

SICHERHEITSPOLIZEI (SIPO). Name of the security police (Gestapo and Kripo) as opposed to the uniformed police (Orpo, Schupo, etc.). A component of the SS.

SIPPENHÄFTLING. Relative who stands in for another, usually for a prison sentence or execution.

SOBIBOR. Annihilation camp near Lublin. On October 14, 1943, the prisoners rebelled and destroyed the camp.

SONDERBEHANDLUNG. Special treatment. Used to denote killing.

SONDERKOMMANDO. Special command. Detail of inmates working in gas chambers and crematoria.

SS FÜHRUNGSHAUPTAMT (SSFHA). Main Leadership Office of the SS; operational headquarters of the SS established shortly after the beginning of World War II.

SS HAUPTAMT (SSHA). Main Office of the SS; principally concerned with administrative matters, recruiting, and ideological training.

(SS) TOTENKOPFSTANDARTEN. "Death's Head" (Skull) regiments; armed SS formations created at the beginning of the war to handle special police tasks. Disbanded in 1941, with most of the members being absorbed into field units of the Waffen-SS.

(SS) TOTENKOPFVERBÄNDE (SSTV). "Death's Head" formations; armed, full-time component of the SS during the prewar period, employed primarily in the guarding of political prisons and concentration camps.

(SS) TOTENKOPFWACHSTURMBANN. Designation for Death's Head guard battalions of the Waffen-SS, which guarded concentration camps and extermination camps during the war.

(SS) VERFÜGUNGSTRUPPE (SSVT). Full-time, militarized component of the SS in the prewar period; direct predecessor of the Waffen-SS.

(SS) WIRTSCHAFTS- UND VERWALTUNGSHAUPTAMT (WVHA). SS Main Economic and Administration Office; after March 1942 it was responsible for the operation of concentration camps.

STAMMLAGER (STALAG). Central camp for prisoners of war.

STANDARTE. SS or SA formation equivalent to a regiment.

STURM. SS or SA formation equivalent to a company.

STURMABTEILUNG (SA). Storm Troop, Hitler's paramilitary organization founded in 1921. Nazi Party militia. The SA launched Hitler's revolution in the streets. Its power waned after the Night of the Long Knives (June 30, 1934).

STURMBANN. SS or SA formation equivalent to a battalion.

T

TEILKOMMANDO. Detachment.

TOTENKOPF. "Death's Head" (Skull), a division of the Waffen-SS.

TREBLINKA. Annihilation camp in Poland. The camp was destroyed on August 2, 1943, by prisoners who revolted.

U

UNTERSTURMFÜHRER. The lowest ranking non-commissioned officer in the SS.

V

VERBINDUNGSSTAB. Liaison staff.

VERLAG. Publishing house.

VOLKSDEUTSCHE. Refers to ethnic or racial Germans or people of German "blood" but of non-German citizenship residing outside the Reich.

W

WAFFEN-SS. Military arm of the SS. Played a role for which it was not originally intended. It began as Hitler's bodyguard and later became an elite combat unit of the Wehrmacht. The longer the war went on the more the Waffen-SS became identified with the Army. Yet it did remain distinguishable from the Army; it retained a distinctively National Socialist character and never emerged entirely from its parent organization - the SS.

WEHRBEZIRK. Military recruiting subdistrict.

WEHRBEZIRKSKOMMANDO (WBK). Military recruiting subdistrict headquarters.

WEHRKREIS. Military district; in peacetime, equivalent to an army corps area.

WEHRKREISKOMMANDO. Military district headquarters.

WEHRMACHT. German armed forces, including of all branches of the military service.

JOURNALS AND OTHER PERIODICAL LITERATURE CONSULTED

A

Air Force Law Review
Air Force Magazine
Akron Law Review
Alliance Review
America
American Bar Association Journal
American Bar Association, Proceedings
American Foreign Service Journal
American Handbook of Psychiatry
American Heritage
American Historical Review
American Jewish Committee, Annual Report
American Jewish Historical Quarterly
American Jewish Year Book
American Journal of Economics and Sociology
American Journal of International Law
American Journal of International Law. Supplement
American Journal of Orthopsychiatry
American Journal of Psychiatry
American Journal of Sociology
American Legal News
American Mercury
American Perspective
American Philosophical Society, Proceedings
American Political Science Review
American Scholar
American Slavic and East European Review
American Society of Internation Law, Proceedings
American Sociological Review
American University Law Review
American Zionist
Annals de Droit International Médical
Annals de la Faculté de Droit d'Istanbul
Annals of the American Academy of Political and Social
  Science
Annuaire Français de Droit International
Annuaire Polonais des Affaires Internationales
Answer
Anti-Defamation League Bulletin
Arbor

Archeion
Archiv des öffentliches Rechts
Archiv des Völkerrechts
Archiv für klinische Chirurgie
Archivar
Archives of General Psychiatry
Archives of Neurology and Psychiatry
Archivmitteilungen
Armed Forces Journal
Armenian Review
Armored Cavalry Journal
Army
Army Information Digest
Ars Aecqui
Asia, merged with Free World and with Inter-American Monthly
  to form United Nations World
Atlantic Monthly
Außenpolitik
Australian Law Journal
Australian Quarterly
Ave Maria

B

Bar Bulletin
Beiträge zur Konfliktforschung
Belgium
Biuletyn Zydowskiego Instytutu Historycznego w Polsce
Bleter far Geshikhte
Boletín Jurídico Militar
Boston University Law Review
British Medical Journal
British Year Book of International Law
Brooklyn Law Review
Bulletin of Concerned Asian Scholars
Bulletin of International News
Bulletin of the Atomic Scientists
Bulletin of the International Commission of Jurists
Bürger

C

Cahiers du Monde Nouveau
Cahiers Politiques
California Law Review
California State Bar Proceedings
Canada's Mental Health
Canadian Bar Journal
Canadian Bar Review
Canadian Law Times
Canadian Yearbook of International Law
Case and Comment
Catholic Historical Review
Catholic Lawyer
Catholic World
Center Magazine
Central European History
Central European Observer
Ceskoslovensky Casopis Historicky
Changing World
Chicago Bar Record
Chicago Legal News
China Monthly

Christian Century
Christian Herald
Christian News from Israel
Civil War History
Civil War Times Illustrated
Civiltà Cattolica
Cleveland-Marshall Law Review
Collier's
Columbia Journal of Law and Social Problems
Columbia Journal of Transnational Law
Columbia Journalism Review
Columbia Law Review
Commentary
Commercial and Financial Chronicle
Common Cause
Common Sense
Commonweal
Commonwealth, Official Organ of the California Commonwealth Club
Communist Affairs
Confidential
Congress Bi-Weekly
Congress Weekly, A Review of Jewish Interests
Congressional Quarterly Weekly Report
Congressional Record
Connecticut Bar Journal
Contemporary Japan
Contemporary Jewish Record
Contemporary Review
Cornell Law Review
Coronet
Criminal Law Review
Current
Current Digest of the Soviet Press
Current History
Current Legal Problems
Current Notes on International Affairs

D

Danish Foreign Office Journal
Das Parlament
Das Parlament. Supplement
De Paul Law Review
Defense de l'Occident
Demokratie und Recht
Demokratyczny Przeglad Prawniczy
Department of State Bulletin
Der Monat
Der Weg
Deutsche Außenpolitik
Deutsche Juristenzeitung
Deutsche Rechts-Zeitschrift, merged with Süddeutsche Juristen-Zeitung to form Juristenzeitung
Deutsche Richterzeitung
Deutsche Rundschau
Deutsches Pfarrerblatt
Dialogue
Dicta
Die dritte Gewalt
Die neue Schau
Die politische Meinung
Dissent

Dissertation Abstracts International
Documenta Neerlandica et Indonesica de Morbis Tropicis
Documents
Duke Law Journal
Duquense University Law Review

E

Economisch en Sociaal Tijdschrift
Economist
Écrits de Paris
Editorial Research Reports
Eingriffe
Encounter
English Historical Review
Esprit
Esquire
Europa Archiv
Europäische Begegnung
European Observer
Évidence
External Affairs

F

Far Eastern Quarterly
Far Eastern Survey
Federal Bar Journal
Federal Register
Federal Rules Decisions
Fordham Law Review
Foreign Affairs
Foreign Policy
Foreign Policy Bulletin
Foreign Policy Reports
Fortnightly Journal
Fortnightly Review
Fortune
Forum
France Intérieure
France-Asie
Frankfurter Allgemeine Zeitung
Frankfurter Hefte
Free World, merged with Asia and with Inter-American Monthly to form United Nations World
Freiburger Rundbrief
Friedens-Warte

G

Gazette de Lausanne
Gegenwart
Geist und Tat
George Washington Law Review
Georgetown Law Journal
Georgia Bar Journal
German Foreign Policy
German Views
Gestern und Heute
Gewerkschafter
Gonzaga Law Review
Guistizia

H

Hadassah Magazine
Harper's
Harvard International Law Journal
Harvard Law Record
Harvard Law Review
Harvard Journal of Asiatic Studies
Headway in War-Time
Hibbert Journal
Historia
Historian
Historische Zeitschrift
Horna Nitra
Houston Law Review
Human Rights Review
Hungarian Jewish Studies
Hungarian Law Review
Huntington Library Quarterly

I

I.C.C. Practitioners' Journal
Idaho State Bar Proceedings
Il Politico
Illinois Law Review
Independent
Independent and Weekly Review
Indian Journal of International Law
Indian Law Review
Indian Yearbook of International Affairs
Indiana Law Journal
Information Bulletin
Instant Research on Peace and Violence
Insurance Council Journal
Inter-Allied Review
Inter-American Monthly, merged with Asia and with Free World to form United Nations World
Intercom
International Affairs
International and Comparative Law Quarterly
International Conciliation
International Journal of Group Psychotherapy
International Journal of Psychoanalysis
International Labour Review
International Law Association, Proceedings
International Law Quarterly
International Lawyer
International Organization
International Relations
International Review
International Studies
Iowa Law Review
Israel Annals of Psychiatry
Israel Horizons
Israel Law Review
Israel Magazine
Issues

J

Jahrbuch der Stadt Freiburg im Breisgau
Jahrbuch für internationales und ausländisches öffentliches Recht
Japan Interpreter
Jewish Currents
Jewish Digest
Jewish Forum
Jewish Frontier
Jewish Life
Jewish Newsletter
Jewish Observer and Middle East Review
Jewish Quarterly
Jewish Quarterly Review
Jewish Social Studies
Jewish Spectator
Jewish Yearbook of International Law
Journal des Tribunaux
Journal du Droit International
Journal of Abnormal and Social Psychology
Journal of Central European Affairs
Journal of Church and State
Journal of Contemporary Asia
Journal of Contemporary History
Journal of Contemporary Psychotherapy
Journal of Criminal Law and Criminology
Journal of International Affairs
Journal of Modern History
Journal of Personality Assessment
Journal of Public Law
Journal of Social Issues
Journal of Social Psychology
Journal of the American Institute of Criminal Law and Criminology
Journal of the American Judicature Society
Journal of the American Psychoanalytic Association
Journal of the Bar Association of the District of Columbia
Journal of the Royal United Services Institution
Journal of the State Bar of California
Journal Officiel du Commandement en Chef Française en Allemagne
Judaica
Judge Advocate Journal
Juridical Review
Juristenzeitung, formed by the merger of Süddeutsche Juristen-Zeitung with Deutsche Rechts-Zeitschrift
Juristische Blätter
Juristische Rundschau
Jus Gentium
Justice of the Peace

K

Kentucky Law Journal
Kentucky State Bar Journal
Knickerbocker Weekly
Kommanden
Kommunität
Komunikaty Mazursko-Warminskie
Kritische Justiz

L

L'Année Politique et Economique
La Vie Internationale
Labor and Nation
Labour Monthly
Ladies' Home Journal
Lancet
Law and Legislation in the German Democratic Republic
Law Journal
Law Library Journal
Law Notes
Law Quarterly Review
Lawyer
Lawyers Guild Practitioner
Lawyers Guild Review
Le Droit au Service de la Paix
Leo Baeck Institute Year Book
Les Temps Modernes
Leyte-Samar Studies
Liberation
Life
Literary Digest
Living Age
Look
Los Angeles Bar Bulletin
Louisiana Bar Journal
Louisiana Law Review
Louisiana State Bar Association Journal
Lutheran Outlook

M

Manchester Guardian
Manitoba Bar News
Marine Corps Gazette
Marine-Rundschau
Maryland Law Review
Maryland State Bar Association Report
Menschenrechte
Merkur
Message, Belgian Review
Miami Law Quarterly
Michigan Law Review
Michigan State Bar Journal
Mid-America
Middle Eastern Studies
Midstream, A Jewish Review
Militärgeschichte
Military Affairs
Military Government Journal
Military Law Review
Military Review
Minnesota Law Review
Miroir de l'Histoire
Mississippi Law Journal
Missouri Law Review
Modern Law Review
Monatsschrift für deutsches Recht
Monatsschrift für Kriminologie
Monde Juif
Montclair Journal of Social Science and Humanities

N

Nation
National Jewish Monthly
National Law Journal
National Lawyers Guild Practitioner
National Review
Natural Law Forum
Nebraska Law Review
Naval War College Review
Nebraska Law Review
Nederlandsch Tijdschrift voor International Recht
Neue Israel
Neue Juristiche Wochenschrift
Neue Justiz
Neues Deutschland
Nevada Historical Society Quarterly
Nevada State Bar Journal
New Commonwealth
New Commonwealth Quarterly
New England Journal of Medicine
New Europe
New Europe and World Reconstruction
New Jersey Law Journal
New Jersey State Bar Association Yearbook
New Leader
New Outlook
New Republic
New Statesman
New Times
New World Review
New York Law Journal
New York Review of Books
New York State Bar Association Bulletin
New York Times Magazine
New York University Journal of International Law and Politics
New York University Law Review
New Yorker
New Zealand Law Journal
News from Belgium and the Belgian Congo
News of Norway
Newsweek
Nineteenth Century and After
No More Hiroshimas
Norseman
North Carolina Law Review
North Dakota Bar Briefs
Notre Dame Lawyer
Nouvelle Revue de Droit International Pénal
Nove Obzory

O

Occasional Paper for the Center for the Study of Democratic Institutions
Official Gazette of the Control Council for Germany
Ohio Bar Association Report
Ohio State Law Journal
Oklahoma Bar Association Journal
Oregon Law Review

Österreichische Monatshefte
Österreichische Zeitschrift für öffentliches Recht
Osteuropa-Recht

P

Pacific Historical Review
Pakistan Horizon
Parade
Parameters
Patterns of Prejudice
Peace and Change
Peace News
Pennsylvania Bar Association Quarterly
Pennsylvania Law Journal Report
Personalist
Philadelphia Law Journal
Philippine Law Journal
Philosophy and Public Affairs
Philosophy, Morality and International Affairs
Poland of Today
Polish Perspectives
Polish Western Affairs
Political Affairs
Political Quarterly
Political Science Quarterly
Politique Étrangère
Politische Studien
Pranstwo i Prawo
Pravnehistoricke
Pravnik
Preuves
Proceedings of the American Society of Political Science
Proceedings of the American Society of International Law
Proceedings of the British Academy
Przegladu Zachodniego
Psyche
Psychiatric Quarterly
Psychiatric Quarterly Supplement
Psychoanalyse und Justiz
Psychoanalytic Forum
Psychohistory Review
Psychology Today
Public Opinion Quarterly

Q

Quarterly Journal of the Library of Congress
Quarterly Review

R

Ramparts
Readers Digest
Reconstructionist
Record
Recueil Dalloz
Recueil des Cours
Reformatio, evangelische Zeitschrift für Kultur und Kirche
Relazioni Internazionali
Reporter
République Française

510 Journals

Res Judicatae
Review of Politics
Revista de Derecho Internacional
Revista de Derecho Internacional y Ciencias Diplomaticas
Revista Española de Derecho Internacional
Revista Militare
Revista Peruana de Derecho Internacional
Revue Belge de Droit International
Revue d'Histoire de la Deuxième Guerre Mondiale
Revue de Défense Nationale
Revue de Droit International de Sciences Diplomatiques
  et Politiques
Revue de Droit International et de Législation Comparée
Revue de Droit International pour le Moyen-Orient
Revue de Droit Pénal et de Criminologie
Revue de Droit Pénal Militaire et de Droit de la Guerre
Revue de Paris
Revue de Science Criminelle et de Droit Pénal Comparé
Revue du Barreau de la Province du Québec
Revue Générale de Droit International Public
Revue Héllenique de Droit International
Revue Historique
Revue Internationale de Droit Pénal
Revue Internationale de la Croix-Rouge
Revue Pénitentiaire de Droit Pénal
Rivista di Psicologia Sociale
Rivista di Studi Politici Internazional
Rivista Italiana di Diretto Penale
Rotarian
Round Table
Rutgers Camden Law Journal

S

St. John's Law Review
St. Mary's Hospital Gazette
San Diego Law Review
Saturday Evening Post
Saturday Night
Saturday Review of Literature
Scanlan's
Scholastic
Schweizer Monatshefte
Schweizer Rundschau
Schweizerische Juristen-Zeitung
Schweizerische Zeitschrift für Psychologie und ihre
  Anwendung
Schweizerische Zeitschrift für Strafrecht
Science
Second Coming Magazine
Senior Scholastic
Sie und Er
Social Forces
Social Problems
Social Research
Societas
Society
Sociology and Social Research
Solicitor
Solicitor Quarterly
South
South Atlantic Quarterly
South Dakota Bar Journal

South Texas Law Journal
Southern Historical Society Papers
Southern Quarterly
Sovetskoe Gosudarstvo i Pravo
Soviet Press Translations
Soviet Russia Today
Soviet Studies
Soviet War News
Spiegel
Spirit of Czechoslovakia
Sprawy Miedzynarodowe
Spruchgerichte
Staat und Recht
Stanford Journal of International Studies
Stanford Law Review
State Bar Association Journal of California
Stato Moderno
Stern
Studies in Polish and Comparative Law
Süddeutsche Juristen-Zeitung, merged with Deutsche
 Rechts-Zeitschrift to form Juristenzeitung
Survey
Survey Graphic

T

Temple Law Quarterly
Tennessee Historical Quarterly
Tennessee Law Review
Texas Bar Journal
Texas Law Review
The Field, The Country Gentleman's Newspaper
Theological Studies
Theory and Practice
Tidsskrift for Rettsvitenskap
Time
Time and Tide
Town Meeting
Transactions of the Grotius Society
Tulane Law Review

U

United Nations Bulletin
United Nations Weekly Bulletin, changed titles frequently
United Nations World, a merger of Asia, Free World, and
 Inter-American Monthly
United States Naval Institute Proceedings
U.S. News and World Report
University of Chicago Law Review
University of Detroit Law Journal
University of Kansas Law Review
University of Kansas City Law Review
University of Miami Law Review
University of Pittsburgh Law Review
University of Richmond Law Review
University of Toronto Law Journal
University of Virginia Law Review
Utah Law Review

V

Ventures
Vereinte Nationen
Victimology, An International Journal
Vierteljahrshefte für Zeitgeschichte
Vietnamese Studies
Viewpoints Magazine
Virginia Journal of International Law
Virginia Law Review
Virginia Quarterly Review
Virginia State Bar Association Proceedings
Vital Speeches
Voks Bulletin
Volkshochschule im Westen
Voprosy Istorii

W

War/Peace Report
Washburn Law Journal
Washington and Lee Law Review
Washington Law Review and State Bar Journal
Washington University Law Quarterly
Watchman-Examiner
Wayne Law Review
Wehrwissenschaftliche Rundschau
Weltbühne
West Virginia Bar Association Report
Wiener Library Bulletin
William and Mary Law Quarterly
Wissenschaftliche Zeitschrift der Humboldt-Universität zu Berlin
Wojskowy Przeglad Prawniczy
Women Lawyer's Journal
World Jewry
World Politics
World Tomorrow
Worldview
Wyoming Law Review

Y

Yad Vashem Bulletin
Yad Vashem Studies
Yale Law Journal
Year Book of World Affairs
Yearbook of the United Nations
Yivo Annual of Jewish Social Science

Z

Zeitschrift für die Geschichte des Oberrheins
Zeitschrift für Geopolitik
Zeitschrift für Geschichtswissenschaft
Zeitschrift für Völkerrecht
Zeitwende
Zentral-Justizblatt für die britische Zone

INDEX OF AUTHORS, SUBJECTS, AND TOPICS

A

Abbaye Ardenne trial, 3536
Abel, Theodore, 1567, 2162
Abendroth, Wolfgang, (487)
Abetz, Otto, 1976, 3611, 3624, 3654, 3664, 3669
Abraham, Randolph L., 1510
Abrahams, Gerald, 2163
Abrahamsen, David, 4408
Abshagen, Karl Heinz, 1977
Abzug, Bella, 4407
Ackermann, Josef, 1978
Adam, George J., 789
Adam, Uwe Dietrich, 1459
Adams, Brock, 4409
Adams, William, 790
Adelsberger, Lucie, 1673-1675
Adler, Gerald J., 338
Adler, H.G., 979, 1310, 1494, 1568, 1676, 1948-1949, 3911
Adler, Marta, 1045
Adler, Selig, 1562
Afghanistan-Soviet Union war, 4500
Agus, Jacob B., 816
Ahmad, Feroz, 661
Ainsztein, Reuben, 1311-1312, 1940, 2164, 3714, 3888, 4213
Aks, Shammai, 1909
Albrecht, A.R., 2926
Albrecht, R.G., 2671, (467)
Alderman, Sidney S., 2672-2673, (467)
Alderson, William T., 778
Aldouby, Zwy, 3992
Aldrich, George H., 4260
Alekseev, Nikolaĭ Sergeevich, 2165-2166
Alexander, Charles A., 2727
Alexander, Edward, 1773, 1965

Alexander, Eva V., 2674
Alexander, Franz, 2167
Alexander, Leo, 817-820, 1008, 2378
Alexandrov, Georgiĭ N., 2168, 3070, 3155
Alexandrov, Victor, 4031
Alexandrowicz, Ignacy, 2404
Alfaro, Ricardo, 2927
Alford, Neill H., 4261
Algardi, Zara, 3846
Algazy, Joseph, 1313
Algerian civil war, 4481-4488
Alkalay, David, 1565, 4194
Allach, 1636
Allainmat, Henry, 1943
Allemann, Fritz René, 4047
Allen, Charles R., 2169, 2272, 2297
Allen, Florence E., 3238
Allen, Lafe Franklin, 2544, 2633
Allen, Maury, 2486
Allon, Dafna, 4048
Almelo trial, 3533
Almond, Nina, 1
Altmann, Erich, 1635
Altstötter, Josef, 3341, 3538, (470)
Alzin, Josse, see Alzinger, Joseph Adolphe
Alzinger, Joseph Adolphe, 2811
Amaudruz, G.A., 2675
Ambros, Otto, (472)
Ambruster, Howard W., 3407-3408
Amchan, Morris, 3156
Amen, John J., (467)
Ament, Susan G., 1280
American Association for a Democratic Germany, 1569
American Historical Association, 101, 2170

American Jewish Committee, 822, 4184, 4195
American Jewish Conference, 2405
American Jewish Congress, 3912; Commission on International Affairs, 4196
American Labor Party, 2406
American Military Tribunals (Nuremberg "subsequent" trials), 3339-3350, personnel of, 2245, (12), Appendix 8; summary of verdicts, Appendix 9
Améry, Jean, 1677
Amery, William, 3813
Amicale de Ravensbrück and Association des Déportées de la Résistance, 1910
Amicale Internationale de Neuengamme, 2, 1900
Ammon, Wilhelm von, (470)
Amnesty, 2323-2336, 2644-2650, 3523
Amos, Sheldon, 339
Anders, Günther, 3913, (487)
Anders, Karl, 1979
Anders, Wladyslaw, 1158
Anderson, C. Arnold, 2407, 4288
Anderson, H.C., (475)
Anderson, Jack, 2273
Andersonville, 605, 639
Andler, Charles Philippe Théodore, 491
Andonian, Joseph K., 4246
Andrews, Allen, 3839
Andrus, Burton C., 1980
Angell, Ernest, 510
Anglo-American Committee of Inquiry, 1248
Anley, Henry, 4490
Anspacher, John, 3022
Antelme, Robert, 1774
Antisemitism, 1305-1309, 2112
Antoni, E., 1801
Apenszlak, Jacob, 1532
Apitz, Bruno, 1775
Appleman, John Alan, 584
April, Nathan, 2979
Aptheker, Herbert, 4437
Arad, Yitzhak, 1286, 1521-1522
Aragezyan, Karen, 3088
Araki, Sadao, (478)-(479), (482)
Archer, William, 742
Archiv, Peter, 2171
Ardenne, R. [pseudonym], 1074
Arendt, Hannah, 1249, 2823, 3728, 3914, 4088
Arens, Richard, 638, 3023
Argúas, Margarita, 3239
Ariel, Joseph, 4197
Armenian-Turkish war crimes, 732-741
Armout, W.S., 340

Arndt, Adolf, 2980, 3024, 3432, 3671
Arndt, Ino, 1570
Arndt, Karl, 3351
Arnold, Anthony, 4500
Arnon, Joseph, 2812
Arolsen Archives, 223
Aronéanu, Eugène, 887, 930-936, 1571, 2172, 4021
Aronsfeld, C.C., 1314, 1447
Aronson, Shlomo, 1981, 3071, 3395
Arsenijevic, Drago, 492
Artukovic, Andrija, 2296
Artzt, G., 2165
Artzt, Heinz, 2350
Arzinger, R., 2173
Ascarelli, Attilio, 493
Aschenauer, Rudolf, 3157, 3324, 3502-3503
Ascherson, Neal, 2301
Asia, war crimes in, 1061-1073
Assmann, Kurt, 2174-2176
Associazione Nazionale Partigiani d'Italia, 3847
Aston, George Grey, 743
Atherton, Henry K., (467)
Auchincloss, Adolf, 4410
Auerbach, Hellmuth, 1315
Auerbach, Ludwig, 4050
Auerbach, Rachel, 1966, 4033
Aufricht, Hans, 4-5
Auge, Thomas E., 3612
Augstein, Rudolf, 3087
Aujol, Jean Louis, 3613
Auschwitz, 1276, 1635-1636, 1641, 1644, 1651, 1656-1657, 1669-1671, 1673-1753, 2103, 2353, 2822; trials at, 3714-3735
Ausschuß für deutsche Einheit, 1105
Austin, Warren R., 4468
Australia, 2502, 3288
Austria, Holocaust in, 1475-1477; war crimes trials, 3580-3590, 3694
Avins, Alfred, 419
Awochi, Washio, 3545
Aybar, Mehmet Ali, (487)
Aymar, Brandt, 585-586
Aziz, Philippe, 2177
Azpiazu, I. de, 4051

B

Baade, Hans W., 4186
Babel, Ludwig, (463)
Bach, Jürgen A., 1982
Back, Peter, trial of, 3535
Bader, Karl S., 3110, 3359-3360
Badkowski, Antoni, 1106
Baeck, Leo, 1950

Baer, Marcel de, 2178-2181, 2408
Baerwald, Hans, 2483
Baeyer, Walter Ritter von, 1009, 1429
Baier, Hans, (471)
Bailey, Gordon W., 801
Bailey, Sydney D., 563
Baird, Jay W., 587
Baker, Jack, 3073
Baker, Lillian, 1572
Balazs, André, 2946
Balch, Emily Greene, 6
Baldwin, James, (487)
Baldwin, Leonard H., (467)
Ball-Kaduri, K.J., 1495
Ballard, F., 687
Ballhorn, Franz, 1930
Ballis, William B., 341
Ballmann, Hans, 1573
Balmer-Basilius, H., 3240
Bandera-Oberländer trial, 3888
Banta, John S., 4351
Bar-Natan, Moshe, 1250, 4052, 4152
Bar-Zohar, Michel, 4022
Barbarossa, 2761, 2842
Barbie, Klaus, 2066, 2301, (8)
Barcikowski, Waclaw, 296
Bardèche, Maurice, 895, 2676-2677
Bardens, Dennis, 2813
Barkai, Meyer, 1126
Barocas, Carol B., 1430
Barocas, Harvey A., 1430
Barrett, Roger W., 380, 2841-2851, (297)
Barry, John V., 2409, 2929
Barski, Józef, 1052
Bartel, Walter, 1856
Barthel, Karl, 1574
Barthelmes, Wes, 4336
Bartlett, C.A. Hereshoff, 511
Bartolai, Sante, 1882
Bartolomeo Carlomagno, Roberto, 2410
Bassiouni, M.C., 342
Basso, A., 2411
Basso, Lelio, (487)
Basu, K.K., 2545
Bathurst, M.E., 3289
Battaglini, Ernesto, 1010
Battle, George Gordon, 802, 3487
Baudoin, R., 1944
Bauer, F., 2678, 3715
Bauer, Karl, 3540
Bauer, Yehuda, 109, 1296-1297, 1317, 1395, 1563
Bauer-Schlichtegroll, Gustav, 3829
Baum, Bruno, 1678, 1883
Baum, Phil, 3074
Baum, Rainer C., 1496

Baumann, J., 3075
Baumann, Jürgen, 3915, 4153
Bauminger, Aryeh, 4214
Baus, Christian, 3541
Baxter, Richard R., 343, 2981
Bay, Christian, 3603
Bayer, Theodore, 2412
Bayle, François, 1011
Bayles, William, 3111
Bayliss, Gwyn M., 7
Bayne, Edward Ashley, 4053
Beals, Walter B., (469)
Beauvoir, Simone de, (487)
Beck, Earl R., 1983
Becker, Gustav, 3539
Becker, Walter, 2351
Becker-Freyseng, Hermann, (469)
Beckmann, O., 1159
Bedau, Hugo Adam, 4289-4290
Bedjaoui, Mohammed, 4481
Bednarek, Irena, 8
Bednarz, L., 1796
Bednarz, Wladyslaw, 1797
Behar, Abraham, 4291
Behle, Calvin A., 3302
Behling, Kurt, 3158, 3325
Beiglböck, Wilhelm, (469)
Beimler, Hans, 1802
Belgion, Harold Montgomery, 3159
Belgium, 698, 742-749, 1074-1083, 1478-1479, 3591-3598,
Belina, Josef, 1084
Bellak, Giorgina, 1803
Belloni, G.A., 902
Bellot, Hugh Hale L., 297-299, 634, 688-691
Belsen trial, 3534, 3830-3834
Belzec, 1276, 1661, 1754-1755
Ben Suc, war crimes in, 4335
Ben-Chorin, Schalom, 3916
Benabdallah, Abogssanad, 4482
Benami, Shaddai, 2275
Bender, Bernhard (Colonel Ben-Salem), 2326
Beneš, Václav, 888, 2413-2414
Benjamin, D., 3076
Benjamin, Hilde, 3548
Benton, Wilbourn E., 3160
Bentwich, Norman, 344, 3830, 4055
Berben, Paul, 1804
Berber, Friedrich [Fritz], 230
Berezhkov, V., 2656
Berg, Franz, 3838
Berg, Mary, 1287
Bergamini, David, 2657
Bergen-Belsen, 1636, 1641, 1756-1770
Berger, Edward, 4337
Berger, Gottlob, (476)
Berger, Jacob, 420
Bergmann, Martin S., 1251
Bergold, Friedrich, (463)

516 Index

Bernadac, Christian, 1012, 1636, 1884, 1911-1912
Bernadotte [of Wisborg], Folke, 2184
Bernard, Henri, 2628, (13)
Bernard, Jean-Jacques, 1799
Bernays, Murray C., 2982-2983, 3241
Bernbaum, John A., 9
Bernstein, J., 1127
Bernstein, Victor H., 3112, 3161
Bertelsen, Aage, 1486
Bertrand, Charles-Auguste, 2679
Besier, Gerhard, 692
Bessie, Alvah Cecil, 1172
Best, S. Payne, 2111
Beth Dim trial, 4499
Bettelheim, Bruno, 1805-1806, 3993
Betz, Herman Dieter, 3462
Bevan, E.R., 754
Bewley, Charles, 1984
Bey, Naim, 733
Beyer, Alfred, 3396
Beyer, Stanley J., 2185
Bezwinska, Jadwiga, 1679-1680
Bezymenskiĭ, L[ev] A[leksandrovich], 1985-1987, 3077
Bial, Louis C., 2415, 3242
Bianchi, Leonard, 3600
Biberstein, Ernst, (474)
Bibliographies, 1-100
Bibliotheksverband der DDR, 214
Biddle, Francis B., 2680, 2824, 2897, (462)
Bieda, Tadeusz, 150
Bier, Jean-Paul, 1681
Bílek, Bohumil, 824
Billig, Joseph, 211, 1318-1320, 1487, 1497, 1575, 4056
Billinger, Karl, 1576
Billstein, Aurel, 980
Bird, Eugene K., 1988-1989
Birkenau, 1276
Birkenfeld, Günther, 1577
Birkett, William Norman, 2813, 2816, 3243, (462)
Birmingham, Robert L., 617, 3162
Bischoff, Friedrich, 1756
Bishop, Joseph W., 588
Bishop, William W., 272, 3614
Biss, Andreas, 3994
Bisschop, W.R., 903
Bissing, Friederich Wilhelm Freiherr von, 745
Blair, Mallory B., (470)
Blakeney, Ben Bruce, 2658
Blanchard, Carroll H., 16
Blaschke, Hugo, 3195
Blatter, Janet, 1252
Blaustein, Albert P., 17
Blayney, Michael S., 1253
Blessin, G., 3672

Blewett, George F., 2659
Bley, C., 3591
Bligh, David, 2276, 3078
Blobel, Paul, 3522, (474)
Bloch, Sam E., 1757
Bloom, Solomon F., 1533
Bloomberg, Marty, 18
Bloomfield, Lincoln P., 4438
Blum, Howard, 2277
Blume, Walter, (474)
Blumenthal, Nachman, 151, 1128, 1288-1289, 1321, 4057
Bo Ngoai Giao, 4223, 4292
Boberach, Heinz, 3374
Bobermin, Hans, (471)
Bock, Fedor von, 2032
Boehm, Eric H., 1950
Boehm, Max Hildebert, 2343
Boeringer, Otto, 3829
Bogusz, Józef, 1013, 1682
Bohle, Ernst, 2216, (476)
Böhm, Georg, (463)
Bohne, Gerhard, 3184
Boissarie, André, 923, 937
Boissier, Pierre, 264, 345
Böll, Heinrich, 3917
Bollmus, Reinhard, 2186
Bolzano, 1653
Bomerhausen, Christine, 981
Bommer, Alois, 3541
Bommer, Anna, 3541
Bonaparte, Napoleon, 634
Bondy, François, 3918
Bondy, Louis W., 1990
Bonhoffer, Emmi, 3716
Bonté, Florimond, 1322
Bonzitti, Natalino, 3848
Boohar, Charles W., 512
Booth, J.B., 755
Boozer, Jack S., 2187
Bor, Josef, 1951
Borchard, Edwin M., 273, 564
Borgerhoff-Mulder, W.G.F., (481)
Boringe, Bernard, 3919
Bork, Robert H., 4458
Borkin, Joseph, 3409
Bormann, Martin, 1985-1987, 2047, 2053, 2059, 2098, 2108, 2137, 2152, 2177, 2258, 2290, 2841, (463-465)
Bornstein, B., 1637
Borrini, Carlo, 3849
Borsum, Lise, 1913
Borwicz, Michel, 1053, 1129
Bosch, William J., 3113
Boselli, Aldo, 924
Bouard, Michel de, 1871, 1885
Boudkevitch, S.L., 2546, 2575
Boulier, Jean, 3615, 3710
Boumal, J., 3326
Bourget, Pierre, 3616
Bourne, Peter G., 4224
Boveri, Margaret, 3449

Bower, Francis, 1323
Bower, Graham J., 346
Bower, Robert J., 2898
Bowker, Archibald Edgar, 2814
Boyajian, Dickran H., 734, 1324
Boyakin, Jonathan, 1538
Boyd, Carl, 2547
Boyens, Armin, 1254, 3025
Boyle, Kay, 1431, 3472
Bracher, Karl Dietrich, 19
Brachmann, Botho, 3080
Brack, Viktor, (469)
Braham, Randolph L., 20-21, 3995
Brailsford, Henry N., 2188
Brand, Clarence, 347
Brand, Emanuel, 145, 2278, 3673, 3717, 3741, 3889
Brand, G., 569
Brand, George, 3835
Brand, James T., 595, 938, (470)
Brand, Joel, 3920
Brandenburg, 1647, 1649
Brandsma, Titus, 2811, 2821
Brandt, Karl, 2006, 3339, (469)
Brandt, Rudolf, (469)
Brassloff, F.L., 3580
Brauchitsch, Herman von, 2032
Brauer-Gramm, Hildburg, 626
Braun, A.Z., 1396
Braune, Werner, 3522, (474)
Breendonk, 1771-1772
Breetzke, E., 2352
Breitscheid, Rudolf, 756
Brennecke, Gerhard, 22
Breymeier, Th., 3592
Brierly, James Leslie, 274, 2984
Briggs, Herbert W., 275
Brines, Russell, 2490-2491
Bringmann, Fritz, 1054
Brissaud, André, 1991
Brito, J.G., 939
Broad, Perry, 1683
Brock-Shepherd, Gordon, 3674
Brockdorff, Werner, 2279
Brockhardt, Smith W., Jr., (467)
Brodzka, Halina, 3675
Brooks, Willis Montford, 3303
Bross, Werner, 1992
Broszat, Martin, 1578, 1684, 2389, 3874
Brown, A.W., 421
Brown, Allan Robert, 2548
Brown, Brendan Francis, 2549, 2563
Brown, Delmer M., 154
Brown, John Mason, 3244
Browne, Courtney, 1993
Browne, Waldo, 2681
Browning, Christopher R., 1325
Browning, Frank, 4381
Bruch, Elsa aus dem, 24
Bruch, Kurt aus dem, 3838
Brückner, Heinz, (473)

Brüdigam, Heinz, 25
Brudno, Walter W., (467)
Brügel, J.W., 693, 1370
Brungs, Bernard Joseph, 494
Bruns, Richard Wilhelm Hermann, trial of, 3535
Bruttel, Emil, 3838
Bryce, James, 735
Bryson, Brady O., (467)-(468)
Buchanan, Robert H., 1994
Buchenwald, 1635-1636, 1638, 1641, 1643, 1654-1655, 1659, 1667-1669, 1773-1795, 3757
Buchheim, Hans, 2379, 2389
Bucholz, Erich, 4293
Buck, Karl, trial of, 3537
Buhler, Joseph, 3546
Bulawko, Henry, 3718
Bulgaria, 662, 1480-1485
Bull, Henry A., 3245
Bullock, Alan, 1995
Bülow, Friedrich von, (475)
Bund der Verfolgten des Naziregimes, 1326
Burchett, Wilfred, 4496
Burg, J.G. [pseudonym], 3026
Bürgin, Ernst, (472)
Burke, George B., (472)
Burkhard, Hugo, 1638
Bürkner, Leopold, 2848
Burnham, James, 4371
Burns, Richard Dean, 26, 27, 2484
Bury, Albert, 3497; trial of, 3535
Busch, Richard, 940
Bütefisch, Heinrich, (472)
Butler, Ewan, 1996
Butler, Rohan, 144
Butow, Robert J., 1997
Butz, Arthur R., 1448
Bytwerk, Randall L., 1998

C

Cabala, Adam, 1857
Cadier, Henri, 1867
Cadoux, C.J., 757
Calderón Serrano, Ricardo, 825
Caldwell, Malcolm, 4459
Cale, Ruth, 1097
Calic, Edouard, 1999
Calley, William L., 4340, 4407-4433
Caloyanni, Mégalos A., 300-302, 2899, 3246
Calvocoressi, Peter, 2682, (468)
Camacho, Paul R., 4225
Cambodia, American action in, 4458-4464
Cameron, John, 3828
Campbell, Ian, 3850
Campbell, John C., 155

Campbell, Robyn Moore, Jr., 3027
Canada, war crimes trial, 3599
Canaris, Wilhelm, 1977, 1991, 2000
Canevari, Emilio, 3851
Capesius, Viktor, 3725
Caplan, Samuel, 4034
Capri, Daniel, 4198
Cardenas, Lazaro, (487)
Cardozo, Michael H., 4171
Carey, Alex E., 4294
Carjeu, P.M., 28, 3114
Carls, Hans, 1807
Carlston, Kenneth S., 1371-1372
Carmel, Israel, 4127
Carmichael, Joel, 4199
Carmichael, Stokely, (487)
Carmilly-Weinberger, Moshe, 1511
Carmon, Arye, 1255
Carnegie, A.R., 2985
Carnegie Endowment for International Peace, 29-30, 513, 674
Carp, Matatias, 1461
Carroll, Berenice A., 31
Carrouges, Michel, 1639
Carsten, Francis L., 791
Carter, Edward F., 3327, (472)
Cartier, Raymond, 2683
Carton de Wiart, H., 2190
Casa, Mayor, 4058
Case, Lynn M., 111
Cassin, René, 3617
Cassius [pseudonym for Michael Foot], 3528
Castle, John, 1685
Castrén, Erik, 348
Catel, Werner, 1014
Cathala, Pierre A., 3618
Caudhill, Watson G., 190
Cecil, Robert, 2191
Central Consistory of Jews in the People's Republic of Bulgaria, 1480
Central Registry of War Criminals and Security Suspects (CROWCASS), Berlin, 127-128
Centre de Documentation Juive Contemporaine, 3996
Centro di Documentazione Ebraica Contemporanea, Milano, 1518
Cermak, John F., 2280
Cetyński, Karol [pseudonym, Ka-Tzetnik 135 633], 1702, 1914
Chalufour, A., 2900
Chamberlain, William Henry, 3164
Champetier de Ribes, Auguste, (468)
Charley Company, war crimes of, 4387
Chart, K.S. Edmund, 1808

Chartock, Roselle, 1256
Chary, Frederick Barry, 1481
Chaudet, H., 3619
Chaumone, Charles, 4295
Chelmno, 1276, 1661, 1796, 1798
Chen, John H.M., 32
Cherniavskii, Iu.M., 1195
Chiang, Wen-Hsien, 1061
Chipman, Norton Parker, 639
Chkhikvadze, V., 514
Cho, Sung Yoon, 2550
Chodoff, Paul, 1579
Chomsky, Noam, 4362
Choumoff, Pierre Serge, 1886
Christiansen trial, 3866
Christianson, William C., (471), (475)
Chuichi, Tanaka, 3543
Churches, crimes against, 1056
Churchill, Peter, 1809
Churchill, Winston, 951
Ciano, Galeazzo, 149, 2827
Ciechanowski, Jan M., 1130
Cigliana, Carlo, 3165
Citron, Curt, 3549
Clark, Delbert, 3410, 3463
Clark, Michael K., 4483
Clarke, Comer, 3997
Claught, R., 1327
Clausnitzer, Martin, 3081
Cluent, Eduard, 803
Coats, Kenneth, 4439
Cockerham, William C., 515
Cohen, Elie A., 1580
Cohen, Laurence E., 515
Cohen, Marshall, 349, 516
Cohen, Nathan, 4059
Cohen, Robert A., 2281
Cohn, Ernst J., 826
Cohn, K., 941
Cohn, Norman, 1328
Coil, George L., 636
Coing, Helmut, 3550
Colas, Raymond, 2986
Colby, Elbridge, 694-695
Colditz, 1649
Cole, Hubert, 3620
Collaboration, 923-929, 3626, 3641, 3664
Collier, Cleveland E., 187
Collis, Robert, 1758
Colombos, C. John, 282
Colvin, Ian G., 2000
Comer, John D., 4060
Commissar Order, 480
Commission on the Responsibility of the Authors of War and on Enforcement of Penalties, 321
Commission on the Trial and Punishment of War Criminals, 2192

Committee of Anti-Fascist Resistance Fighters in the German Democratic Republic, 2353
Committee of the International Red Cross, 1581
Compiègne, 1671, 1799-1800
Comyns-Carr, Arthur S., 2551, 2634, (481)
Conférence des Commissions Historiques et des Centres de Documentation Juifs, 1257
Conlen, William J., 2987
Conot, Robert E., 2684
Conover, Helen F., 33-34
Conseil d'Administration du Mémorial Nationale du Fort de Breendonk, 1771
Constantinople, Demetrios S., 2193
Control Council Law No. 10, 3548-3579; German court decisions under, 3760-3811
Control Council Laws, (11)
Conway, John S., 156, 1056, 1299
Cook, Blanche Wiesen, 589
Cooper, Norman G., 4338
Cooper, Robert W., 2685
Cork, Lord, 422
Coste-Floret, Paul, 423
Cotter, Michael, 102
Cowles, Willard B., 322, 570, 2194, 2988, 3527
Craig, Gordon A., 3028
Cramer, Myron C., 2780, 2948, 3488
Crankshaw, Edward, 2373
Crawford, Fred Roberts, 1258, 1810
Crawford, Johnson T., (469), (473)
Creel, George, 2416-2417
Crelinsten, Ronald D., 494
Crenesse, P., 3621
Creutz, Ulrich, (473)
Crimes against humanity, 930-978
Criminal organizations, 2350-2371, 2373-2403
Crouchet, R., 2686
CROWCASS, see Central Registry of War Criminals and Security Suspects
Crystal Night, 2112
Cuddon, Eric, 3829
Cunningham, Owen, 595
Cushman, Robert E., 3489
Cutler, Phil, 4061
Cyprian, Tadeusz, 1108, 1116, 3082, 3166
Czech, Danuta, 1679-1680, 1686
Czechoslovakia, 1084-1091, 3600-3602
Czerniakow, Adam, 1290

D

D'Harcourt, Robert, 4200
D'Orr, Paul Barksdale, 3622
Dabrowska, Danuta, 1534
Dachau, 1636, 1638, 1649, 1653-1654, 1657, 1659, 1665, 1667-1669, 1801-1855
Daim, Wilfried, 2001
Dalby, Louise Elliott, 1778
Dallin, Alexander, 1173
Daly, Edward J., 3167, (475)
Daly, James J.A., 2518
Daly, Lawrence, (487)
Daniel, Aubrey M., III, 424
Daniel, J., 2419
Danieli, Yael, 1413, 1412
Darden, William H., 4431
Darré, Richard, (476)
Darville, Jacques, 1861
Datner, Szymon, 456, 3875
Daube, David, 425
Daum, F., 1640
Dautricourt, Joseph Y., 942-943, 1078-1079
David, Ilana, 3922
Davidson, Eugene, 2687, 3168-3169
Davidson, Shamai, 1414
Davies, Alan, 1305
Davis, Ernst, 4062
Davis, George B., 640
Davis, Lawrence P., 1515
Dawidowicz, Lucy S., 1259, 1300-1301
Daxner, Igor, 3601
De Coninck, L., 1813
De Gaulle, Geneviève, 1915
De Giulio, Anthony P., 426
De Konig, Ines, 3973
De Menthon, François E., 3170, 3247
De Voto, Andrea, 1582
De Witt, David S., 3402
Dean, Gideon, 1098
Dean, Gordon, 2195
Dean, Vera M., 2196, 3890
Debenest, Delphin, (468)
Dedijer, Vladimir, (487)
Defregger, Matthias, trial of, 3736-3739
Degand, Henri, 3623
Dehner, Ernst, (473)
Deker, Nikolai, 1558
Del Rosal Fernández, Juan, 944
Delarbre, Léon, 1641
Delarue, Jacques, 2374
Delfosse, Alphonse, 2153
Dellinger, Dave, (487)
Dellums Committee, 4382
Delpech, Henry, (468)
Delupis, Ingrid, 35

520 Index

Demant, Ebbo, 1687
Denazification trials, (7)
Denecke, Ludwig, 36
Denmark, Holocaust in, 1486
Denmark, war crimes trials, 3603-3604
Dennett, Raymond, 157, 2673
Denson, William D., 3517
Deportation, 979-1007, 2934
Des Pres, Terrence, 1583
Descheemaeker, Jacques, 2949
Deschner, Günther, 2002
Deschner, Karlheinz, 1584
Desmond, Charles S., 2154, 2420
Desroches, Alain, 2375
Deutsch, Harold C., 828
Deutsche Akademie der Künste, 1779
Deutscher, Irwin, 1780
Deutscher, Isaac, (487)
Deutsches Rundfunkarchiv, 2688
Deutschkron, Inge, 1585
Devito, Anthony, 2297
Devoto, Andrea, 40
Dickinson, Edwin D., 2930
Dickinson, George, 2502
Dickler, Gerald, 590
Dickmann, Fritz, 675
Didier, Friedrich, 2003
Diels, Rudolf, 2004
Dietrich, Otto, 2112, (476)
Dillon, J.V., 457
Dimitman, Eli Zachary, 1815
Dimock, E.J., 3171
Dimsdale, Joel E., 2127, 2197
Dinnerstein, Leonard, 1415
Dinstein, Yoram, 427
Diplomatic Conference for the Drawing up of a New Convention, 1057
Dirksen, Herbert von, 3450
Distel, Barbara, 1816
Dix, Hellmuth, 3414
Dix, Rudolf, (463)
Dixon, Richard D., (471), (474)
Djemal, Pasha, 736
Dobaczewska, Wanda, 1916
Doblhoff, Lily, 3624
Dockrill, Michael, 2756
Documents, and records by nation, 138-210; Holocaust, 1286-1295
Dodd, Thomas J., 2689, (467)
Doenecke, Justus D., 3505
Dohle, Horst, 1498
Doihara, Kenji, (478)-(479), (482)
Dolle, Renate, 3677
Doman, Nicholas R., 3172, 3248
Donat, Alexander, 1260, 1967
Donati, A., 2690
Donihi, Robert, 3506

Dönitz, Karl, 2005, 2012, 2032, 2070, 2101, 2113-2114, 2174 (463), (465)
Donnedieu de Vabres, Henri, 277, 303-304, 517, 1373, 2691-2693, 2901-2903, 3625, (462)
Donovan, James Britt, (467)
Donovan, John, 3998
Dora (Nordhausen), 1641, 1856-1860
Döring, Hans-Joachim, 1046-1047
Dorsey, John Thomas, 3678
Dostler trial, 3533
Double Tenth trial, 2505-2506
Doublet, Pierre H., 3626
Douglas, J.J., 3464
Dov, Levin, 1396
Dover Castle, 433
Downey, William G., 351-352, 1034
Drancy, 1671, 1861
Draper, G., 4063
Dreher, Eduard, 2355
Dreierwalde trial, 3533
Drinan, Robert F., 1261
Drobisch, Klaus, 1498, 3403
Drost, Peiter N., 3999
Du Bois, Josiah E., 3415
Du Prel, Max Freiherr, 1535
Dubost, Charles, 278, (468)
Duckles, Robert, 4350
Duff, Shiela Grant, 2007
Duffett, John, 4442
Dufournier, Denise, 1917
Duke, Marvin L., 428
Dulag-Luft trial, 3535, 3829
Dull, Paul S., 2621
Dulles, John Foster, 1374
Dumont-Wilden, L., 764
Dunbar, N.C.H., 353-355, 429-430
Dunn, Benjamin J., 2694
Dunn, J. Howard, 458
Dunn-Wasowicz, Krzysztof, 1947
Dupays, Paul, 2008, 2695-2698
Durand, Ch., 518
Durdenevsky, V., 2338
Dürrenmatt, Peter, 4064
Dürrfeld, Walter, (472)
Düsseldorf trial, 3745
Dutch, Oswald, 2009
Dutt, R. Palme, 4491
Dworzecki, Marc, 1642
Dyer, Brainerd, 641
Dyer, Gwynne, 737

E

Eagleton, Clyde, 571, 2421
East Timor, war crimes in, 4497
Easterman, Alexander L., 3831-3832, 4000
Eban, Abba, 4065, 4216

Ebensee, 1636
Eberhardt, Heinrich, 3829
Eberhardt, Karl A.F., (475)
Eccard, Frédéric, 3249
Ecer, Bohuslav, 2989, 3029, 3250, 3894
Eck, Heinz, 3828
Eck, Nathan, 1512
Eckardt, A. Roy, 1262
Eckardt, Alice L., 1262
Ecker, Fritz, 1817
Eckert, J., 3030
Edel, Peter, 3925
Edelman, Maurice, 2283
Edmunds, Sterling E., 356
Edwards, Charles Schaar, 357
Egbert, Lawrence D., 3173
Ehard, Hans, 2904
Ehrenburg, Ilya, 2699-2700
Ehrenzweig, A., 431
Ehrhardt, Helmut, 1329
Eichmann, Adolf, 3926, 3975-3976, 4001, 4066; bibliography, 20; trial of, 602, 617
Einsatzgruppen Case, Appendix 8
Einstein, Siegfried, 4003
Eirenschmalz, Franz, (471)
Eisele, A., 3627
Eisenberg, Alfred, 3869
Eisenberg, Azriel, 1263
Eisenmann, Charles, 3628
Eisenträger, Lothar, 3546
Eisner, Jack, 1416
Eitaro Shinohara trial, 3537
Eitinger, Leo, 1417-1418, 1586
Eitner, Lorenz, 3174
Eliach, Yaffa, 1587
Eliasberg, Wladimir C., 2701
Eller, Lili, 4023
Elwyn-Jones, F., (468)
Elyashiv, Vera, 1819
Emmet, Christopher, 3117
Ender, G., 3175
Endlösung, see Genocide
Engelmann, Bernt, 3439
Engelson, M., 279
Enser, Alfred G.S., 41-42
Eppler, Elizabeth E., 3932
Epstein, Helen, 1419
Epstein, N.B., 1423
Erhard, Hans, 2990
Erickson, Otto, 772
Erickson, Richard J., 43
Ermacora, F., 3084
Ernest, John [Hans Ernst Fried], 3255, 4265
Esgain, Albert J., 459
Esh, Shaul, 1330
Essen lynching trial, 3533
Estonia, concentration camps in, 1642
Eulau, Heinz, 3251

European Court of Human Rights, 3679
Euthanasia, 2386, 3184
Evrard, Jacques, 982
Ewing, Alfred C., 2422
Exner, Franz, 676, (463)
Extradition, 2337-2349
Eyck, Erich, 231

F

Fabre-Luce, Alfred, 3629
Fahey, James J., 896
Fairfield, Cicily Isabel [pseudonym, Rebecca West], 3813
Fairman, Charles, 2198, 2519
Falco, Robert, (455), (462)
Falk, Richard A., 519-521, 591, 897, 2702, 3252, 4227-4228, 4248-4249, 4260, 4264, 4460
Falk, Stanley L., 1062
Falkenhorst, Nikolaus von, 3543, 3836-3837
Falten, Herbert, 3540
Fanslau, Heinz Karl, (471)
Faramus, Anthony Charles, 1643
Farben, see I.G. Farben
Farer, Thomas J., 622, 3253-3254, 4298
Farnsworth, Clyde, 2199
Farr, Warren F., (467)
Farrell, John T., 664
Farrin, A., 522, 831
Fassina, P., 1759
Fattig, Richard C., 496
Faulkner, Stanley, 432
Faure, Edgar, 1035, (468)
Fawcett, J.E.S., 3085, 4070-4071
Fechner, Max, 2120
Federn, Ernst, 1588
Feig, Konnilyn G., 44-45, 1589
Feilchenfeld, Ernst Hermann, 460
Fein, Helen, 696, 1331
Feingold, Henry L., 1386-1387
Feis, Herbert, 323
Feldhaus, J. Gordon, 2520
Feldmann, Horst, 945
Felmy, Helmuth, (473)
Felton, Frederick, (468)
Fénelon, Fania, 1590, 1688
Fenwick, Charles G., 324, 697
Ferencz, Benjamin B., 305, 983, 2950, 4299
Fernández de la Mora, Gonzalo, 2703
Ferringer, Natalie Jean, 946
Fest, Joachim C., 2010-2011
Feuerbach, Walther, 1820
Feuerstein, Chester W., 1432
Figge, Robert, 3377
Filetto di Camarda, Italian village of, 3739

"Final solution," see Genocide
Finch, George A., 306, 433, 792, 1375, 2423, 2905, 2930
Fink, Clinton F., 31
Finland, war crimes trials, 3605-3610
Finn, Gerhard, 3680
Firmage, Edwin B., 4250
Fisch, Arnold G., 3426
Fischer, Fritz, (469)
Fischlschweiger, Hagen, 3031
Fishman, Jack, 2012
Fiszer, Henryk, 3933, 4007
Fitz Gibbon, Louis, 1161
Fitzgibbon, Constantine, 3475
Fixel, Rowland Wells, 2553
Fläschner, Hans, (463)
Fleischner, Eva, 1689
Fleming, Gerald, 1332
Flender, Harold, 1388
Flesch, Gerhard Friedrich Ernst, 3538
Flick, Friedrich, 3344; trial of, 3541, (471)-(472), Appendix 8
Flory, William E.S., 461
Flossenburg, 1637, 1646, 1665, 1862-1864
Foerster, Wolfgang, 2013
Foertsch, Hermann, 3032
Fogelman, Eva, 1434-1435
Foltz, David A., 677
Fonteneau, Homère, 1644
Foot, Michael R.D. [pseudonym, Cassius], 1821, 3528
Forbes, Gordon W., 2991
Forced labor, 979-1007
Foreman, Paul B., 1781
Forman, Benjamin, 622, 2992,
Forndran, Erhard, 2014
Forster, Albert, 3883
Forsythe, David P., 325
Fosmark, Johannes, 1591
Foster, Claude R., 1302
Foth, C., 3175
Fox, Galen C., 2554
Fox, Grace E., 1080
Fox, John P., 3814
Fraenkel, Ernst, 678
Fraenkel, Heinrich, 1354, 2055-2058
Fraenkel, Josef, 146, 1475
France, 326, 523, 832, 1592, 1690; depositories in, 211-213; documents and records, 141; Holocaust in, 1487-1493; World War I atrocities in, 750-752; World War II crimes against, 1092-1096
Franck, Thomas M., 4229
Franco Sodi, C., 2704
Frank, Anne, 2828, 2831
Frank, August, (471)

Frank, Hans, 2115-2116, 2123, 2218, (462), (465)
Frank, Karl-Hermann, 2015
Frank, Walter, 2012
Frank, Willi, 3725
Frankl, Victor E., 1593
Franklin, Mitchell, 2424
Franz Kursky Archives, (21)
Fraser, Lindley, 3033
Fratcher, William F., 3304, 3554
Freeman, Alwyn V., 265, 524, 1036
Frei, Bruno, 1875
French, Peter A., 4340
Fresnes, 1664
Fretard, Dominique, 2177
Freud, Clement, (468)
Freund, Paul A., 2154
Freundeskreis, 1901
Frey, Georg, 3895
Frey, Hans, 1939
Frey, Willi, 3516
Frick, Wilhelm, (462), (464)-(465)
Fricke, Karl Wilhelm, 3744
Fried, Hans Ernst [John Ernest], 525, 984-985, 3255, 4265
Friedel, Fritz Gustav, 3875
Friedlander, Henry, 1333
Friedman, Leon, 358
Friedman, Mrs. Philip, 76
Friedman, Philip, 46, 75, 1131, 1433, 1691-1692
Friedman, Saul S., 1264
Friedman[n], Tuvyah (Tuviah), 1132, 3583-3586, 4024
Friedman-van der Heide, Reine, 3862
Friedmann, Wolfgang, 359
Frischauer, Willi, 2016-2017
Fritsch, Werner von, 2032
Fritz, Heinz, (463)
Fritzsche, Hans, 2018, 2117, 2851, (463), (465)
Fritzsche, Hildegard, 2019
Fuchs, H.H., 859
Fuhrmann, Peter, 434, 3934
Funk, Arthur L., 47-48
Funk, Walther, 2020, 2068, 2255, (463), (465)
Funke, Manfred, 2021
Fuqua, Ellis E., 2521
Furman E., 1420
Fuster, Serge, (468)
Futch, Ovid L., 642
Fuz, G.C., 2285

G

Gabus, Eric, 904
Gade, Richard F., 1306
Galbe, José L., 833
Gallagher, Richard, 2705
Gallery, Daniel V., 898

Gallinger, August, 758
Gallus, Galieni, 3176
Ganoe, John T., 2522
Gar, Joseph, 46
García-Mora, Manuel R., 360, 526, 926, 947, 2340
Gard, Robert G., 4298
Garfunkel, L., 1559
Garlinski, Jozef, 1693
Garner, James W., 361-362, 759
Garrett, Richard, 462
Garse, Yvan van, 49-50
Gassman, Benjamin, 4172
Gault, P.F., 3060
Gawlik, Hans, (463)
Gebauer, Fritz G., 3707
Gebhardt, Karl, (469)
Gebhardt, Walther, 217
Gedziorowski, Tadeusz, 1822
Geheime Staatspolizei (Gestapo), 1981, 2373-2377, 2842, (463)
Geiger, Hans Joachim Georg, 3526
Geisel, Eike, 1766
Gelberg, Ludwig, 2951
Gendrel, Michel, 51
Generaldirektion der Bayerischen Staatlichen Bibliotheken, 218
Generalstaatsanwalt der DDR und Ministerium der Justiz der DDR, 827
Geneva Convention of 1949, 459, 2205, 4251
Genocide ("final solution," Endlösung), 1310-1369; convention, 1370-1383
Genton, J., 2706
Genzken, Karl, (469)
Gerassi, John, 4230
Gerber, William, 4341
Gerbsch, Wilhelm, 3545
Gerecke, Henry F., 2201
Gerhart, Eugene C., 2815
German General Staff, defense counsel for, (463)
Germany, British Zone, courts in, 3795; captured documents, 116; Control Council Law No. 10, German court decisions under, 3760-3811; Foreign Office, 679, 1162-1163; general works on, 142-143, 214-225; Holocaust in, 1494-1507; Ministry of Justice, 3683; Ministry of the Interior of Lower Saxony, 160; Reichsgericht, 805; Reich's Ministry for Occupied Eastern Territories, 1176; Supreme Court, 1175, 3682, 1; Territory under Allied occupation, 3305-3306, 3555
Gernet, M.N., 1177
Gersh, Gabriel, 3746

Gershen, Martin, 4342
Gerthoffer, Charles, (468)
Gestapo, see Geheime Staatspolizei
Geve, Thomas, 1436
Geyer, Curt, 762
Ghettos, war crimes in, 1126-1157
Giardini, Cesare, 3630
Gibb, Andrew Dewar, 3177
Gibbon, William A., 4173
Gibbons, Herbert Adams, 680
Gibbs, Philip, 700
Gibson, Hugh, 2827
Giebultowicz, Józef, 527
Giesing, E., 2202
Gilbert, Gustave M., 2203-2204, 2829
Gilbert, Martin, 1303, 1694
Giles, Barbara M., 4384
Gilman, Daniel C., 643
Gimbel, John, 219
Ginsburgs, George, 498
Giordano, R., 3758
Gisevius, Hans Bernd, 2118
Glahn, Gerhard von, 2993
Glaser, Stefan, 463, 528-531, 905-906, 2205, 2906, 3256
Glasgow, George, 2425
Glatstein, Jacob, 1265
Glazer, Nathan, 3507
Gleim, Leopold (Colonel Al-Naher), 2326
Gleina, 1655
Gleischläger, Robert, 3631
Glicksman, W., 1594
Globke, Hans, 2099, 3710-3713, 3924
Glock, Charles Y., 4201
Glueck, Sheldon, 572, 2206-2207, 2426-2427, 2994-2998
Goderie, Jan, 3863
Goebbels, Joseph, 201, 2034, 2045, 2069, 2080, 2082, 2090, 2097, 2119-2121
Goebell, Kurt, 3501
Goerdeler, Karl, 247
Goerlitz, Walther, 232
Goeth, Amon Leopold, 3880
Goguel, Rudi, 1110, 1498, 1902
Golczwewski, Frank, 2014
Goldbrunner, Josef, trial of, 3535
Goldhagen, Erich, 2022
Goldman, Frank, 3477
Goldman, Harvey A., 2999
Goldstein, Anatole, 948, 1307, 3178, 3433, 3747
Goldstein, Bernard, 1133
Goldstein, Joseph, 4385, 4420
Golkel, Karl Adam, 3537
Gollancz, Victor, 4072-4073
Golleschau, crimes in, 3734

Golunsky, S., 2555, (481)
Gómez Grajales, Octavio, 532
Goodhart, Arthur L., 907, 3000, 3179
Goodman, Leo M., 3307
Goodman, Roger, 3361
Göppinger, Horst, 1499
Gordey, Michel, 3833
Göring, Emmy, 2122, 3195
Göring, Hermann, 590, 1984, 1992, 1996, 2017, 2026, 2048, 2051, 2065, 2112, 2123, 2200, 2203, 2216, 2682, 2762, 2862, 3195, (462), (464), (466); trial of, 614
Goris, Jan Albert, 1081
Görlitz, Walter, 2023
Gorman, Robert N., 233
Gormley, W. Paul, 2952
Gorski, Stephen, 3180
Gorzkowska, Jadwiga, 3685
Gostner, Erwin, 1645
Gould, Harvey L., 4295
Goutel, Eric de, 2707
Graber, Doris Appel, 363
Graber, G.S., 2024
Graham, Robert J., 3362
Granet, M., 986
Granger, William, 4364
Grasshoff, Richard, 746
Graven, Jean, 949-950, 2708, 3001, 3181, 3363, 4158
Graveson, R.H., 3556
Gray, Leslie B., 2208
Great Britain, 144, 226-227, 702, 1016, 1037, 1782, 2428-2429, 2503-2504, 3118; Colonial Office, 701; Foreign Office, 681, 703; Ministry of Information, 834; Parliament, 704; Treasury, 705; House of Lords, 2430; Public Record Office, 103; War Office, 763
Greco-Bulgarian war, 662-663
Greece, Holocaust in, 1508-1509
"Green Series," (19)
Green, A. Wigfall, 3308
Green, Gerald, 1335
Green, L.C. [Leslie C.], 435, 2341, 2709, 3686, 4074, 4174-4175
Greenhaw, Wayne, 4421
Greenspan, Morris, 364
Gregory, S.S., 774
Gregory, Tappan, 2710-2711, 3002
Greifelt, Ulrich, 3342-3343, 3545, (473)
Greil, Lothar, 3508
Greiser, Artur, 3545
Grenfell, Russell, 436, 3034
Grevy, R., 3509
Grewe, Wilhelm Georg, 3061
Griffith-Jones, J.M.G., (468)

Griffiths, Richard, 2025
Grimm, George, 3160
Grimstadt, William N., 1450
Gringauz, Samuel, 4075
Grini, 1658, 1662
Gritzbach, Erich, 2026
Grobman, Alex, 1336
Groh, Franz, 2932
Gross, Feliks, 987
Gross, Leo, 908, 1500, 2432
Gross, Martin, 3364
Groß-Rosen, 1636-1637, 1865-1866
Grossman, Haika, (487)
Grossman, Wassili, 1968
Grossmann, Kurt R., 2323, 2433, 3518
Gruber Michaelis, Ruth, 3587
Gruber, Andreas, 2027
Grubsztein, Meir, 1397
Gruchmann, Lothar, 1017
Grunberger, Richard, 2382
Grundinsk, Ulrich, 2712
Gründler, Gerhard E., 3182
Grunheide, 1637
Gryn, Edward, 1878
Gsovski, Vladimir, 2856
Guderian, Heinz, 2028
Guelff, Richard, 2875
Guggenheim, Paul, 280
Guides, 101-117
Guilt and responsibility, 510-562, 3022-3059
Gumkowski, Janusz, 3876
Gummel', P., 1210
Gurewitsch, Brana, 1587
Guri, Haim, 4132
Gurs, 1669, 1867-1870
Gusen, 1636, 1639, 1653, 1871-1872
Gutman, Yisrael, 1536
Guttmann, T., 1546
Gutzwiller, Max, 3119
Guy, George F., 2524
Gypsies, crimes against, 1045-1051

H

Haag, E. van den, 835
Haag, John, 3430
Haas, Michael, 53
Haast, H.F. von, 3378
Hachworth, Green Haywood, 129
Hackel, Franz, 1873
Hadamar trial, 3533
Haensel, Carl, 2123, 2356, 2713, 3035, 3183-3184, 3379, 3453, 3557, (463)
Haesiker, August, 3501
Haffner, D., 1695
Haffner, Sebastian, 2029
Häfliger, Paul, (472)
Häfner, Heinz, 1429

Hafner, Wilhelm, 3497, trial of, 3535
Hagen, Herbert, 3733
Hagen, Louis, 2141
Hagen, Walter [pseudonym of Wilhelm Hoettl], 2384
Hagenbach, Peter von, 627-628
Hagendorf, Heinz, 3545
Hahn, Fritz Gebhard von, 3753, 3759
Hahnenfeld, G., 2714
Hájková, Dagmar, 1918
Hajsman, Jan, 1596
Halder, Franz, 2124, 2848
Hale, Winfield B., 3329, (476)
Halevy-Levy, I., 4076
Halimi, Gisele, (487)
Hall, Jerome, 533
Hall, Thomas van, 2155
Halleck, Henry Wager, 644
Halley, Fred G., 189
Halpern, Ben, 2715, 4077
Hamburger, Ernest, 592
Hamerow, Theodore S., 3036
Hammer, Ellen, 499
Hammer, Richard, 4343, 4366, 4423
Hammerstein, Kurt Wentzel, 3499
Hamrin, Agne, 3935
Hamsik, Dusan, 2030
Hanayama, Shinsho, 2496
Handlin, Oscar, 1398, 3936, 4187
Handloser, Siegfried, (469)
Haney, Gerhard, 3380
Hangobl, Josef, 3546
Hankey, Maurice P., 3185
Hannell, Salomea, 1291
Hannigan, Jane A., 52
Hanotoux, Gabriel, 775
Hans, Oscar, 3537
Hänsch, Walter, (474)
Hanson, John Frederick, 2507
Harari, Jacob, 1526
Harcourt-Barrington, J., (468)
Harding, Justin W., (470), (476)
Harding-Barlow, M., 2907
Hardman, Leslie, 1761
Harel, Israel, 3937
Hargrove, John Lawrence, 4461
Harris, Henry W., 2209
Harris, Samuel, (467)
Harris, Whitney R., 2716-2717, (467)
Harrison, Austin, 764
Harrower, Molly, 2210-2211, 2249
Harster, Wilhelm, 3690
Hart, Franklin A., 593
Hart, Herbert L.A., 534
Hart, Kitty, 1696-1697
Hart, S.T., 2031
Hart, W.E. [pseudomym], 2032
Harthauser, Wolfgang, 1041
Hartjenstein, Fritz, 3838

Härtle, Heinrich, 951, 2718
Hartlmayr, Fritz, 3257
Hartmann, E., 3258
Harukei Isayama trial, 3537
Haruzo, Sumida, 2505-2506
Harwood, Richard, 594, 1451
Hase, Hams Christoph von, 1018
Hashimoto, Kingoro, (478)-(479), (482)
Hasselbach, Hans Karl von, 2212
Hassell, Ulrich von, 2830
Hata, Shunroku, (478)-(479), (482)
Hatfield, Mark O., 4424
Hauer, Mordecai, 4036
Haulot, Arthur, 1823
Hauser, Ernest O., 2719
Hausner, Gideon, 2286, 3938-3939, 4078-4079, 4133
Hausser, Paul, 2383
Hauxhurst, H.A., 595
Havens, Charles W., 4231
Hayes, Paul M., 3870
Hazan, Edouard Tawfik, 3120
Hazard, John N., 889, 3186
Hearst, Ernest, 1337
Heartfield, John, 1762
Heazlett, Elizabeth, 617, 4176
Hebert, Paul M., 3416
Hebrew University, Jerusalem, 2933
Hecht, Ben, 4492
Hediger, Ernest S., 1038
Hedler, Wolfgang, 3746
Heering, Arno, 3543
Heffter, August W., 281
Heger, Heinz, 1646
Heiber, Helmut, 2033-2034, 2125
Heidelmeyer, Wolfgang, 952
Heiden, Louis (Louis Al-Hadj), 2326
Heilig, B., 1783
Heilmann, Helmrich Hermann Philipp, 3734
Heiman, Leo, 2287-2290, 3940, 4037, 4080
Heimann, Guido, 1452
Heimler, Eugene, 1784-1785
Heimpel, Hermann, 627-628
Heineman, John L., 2035
Heinl, Robert D., 4425
Heinrich, Walther, 2032
Heinrichsohn, Ernst, 3733
Heinze, Kurt, 2962, 3467
Heizler, R., 4081
Held, Virgina, 519, 4289
Helen, James John, Sister, 3941
Hellendall, F., 3687
Heller, Maxine Jacobson, 596
Heller, Paul, 1865
Hellman, Peter, 1698
Helman, Socrate, 1030-1032
Helweg-Larsen, Per, 1597

Hemming-Sjoberg, A., 3871
Hendry, Teressa, 2831
Henkin, Louis, 4266
Herbert, Anthony, 4383, 4391
Herbert, Paul M., (472)
Herisko, Ilona, 2835
Herman, Edward S., 4301
Hermann, Alfred, 1019
Hermann, Nanda, 1919
Hermann, R., 1024
Hermes, Ferdinand A., 535, 3037
Hernandez, Amado, (487)
Hernandez, Melba, (487)
Herold, G.W., 3440
Herre, Wybo P., 54
Hersch, Gisela, 55
Hersey, John, 1134
Hersh, Seymour M., 4302, 4344, 4386-4388
Hershey, Amos S., 365
Hershkovitch, Bendet, 1537
Herz, John H., 3478
Herzberg, Abel J., 1763, 3942
Herzog, Jacques-Bernard, 836-837, 953, 2720-2721, (468)
Herzog, Robert, 2036
Hess, Ilse, 2156-2157
Hess, P. Sales, 1824
Hess, Rudolf, 1988-1989, 2012, 2040, 2050, 2079, 2087, 2123, 2156-2157, 2243, 2255, 2841, 2851, 2860, (462), (465)-(466)
Hesse, Fritz, 3943
Hessel, Eugene A., 2515
Hesseltine, William Best, 645
Hessler, Curt A., 536
Heston, Leonard L., 2213
Heston, Renate, 2213
Hetlinger, G., 3688
Heuvel, J. van den, 747
Hevelmann, Hans, 3184
Heyde, Werner (Dr. Fritz Sawade), 3184
Heydecker, Joe J., 2722
Heydrich, Lina, 2126
Heydrich, Reinhard, 1977, 1999, 2002, 2004, 2015, 2024, 2030, 2041, 2071, 2107, 2111, 2267, 2373
Higgins, A. Pearce, 282
High Command Case, 3544, Appendix 8
High, Stanley, 3038
Hilberg, Raul, 1135, 1292, 1462, 1699,
Hildebrandt, Richard, (473)
Hill, Leonidas E., 2106, 3451-3452
Hill, Mavis M., 4498
Hillel, Marc, 3944-3945
Hiller, Kurt, 1647, 1825
Hillgruber, Andreas, 1338
Hillis, Newell D., 706
Hillringhaus, F. Herbert, 3946
Himmler, Heinrich, 1978, 1981, 2016, 2022, 2037, 2095, 2109, 2112, 2129, 2137, 2184, 2373
Hinrichs, Klaus, 1908
Hiranuma, Kiichiro, (478)-(479), (482)
Hirohito, 2064, 2641
Hirota, Koki, (478)-(479), (482)
Hirsch, Felix, 3259
Hirsch, Rudolf, 3719
Hirschbach, Frank, 56
Hirthe, Gustav, 3720
Hisakasu, Tanaka, 3537
Hitler, Adolf, 1995, 2011, 2029, 2033, 2038, 2094, 2102, 2110, 2133, 2158, 2171, 2202, 2212-2213, 2221, 2225, 2229, 2250
Hitler Youth (HJ), 2085-2086, 2220
Hobbs, Malcolm, 3468
Hobza, Antonín, 2434
Hodenberg, Hodo Freiherr von, 3558
Hoettl, Wilhelm (Willy) [pseudonym, Walter Hagen], 2384
Hoffman, August, 3828
Hoffman, Heinrich, 2038
Hoffman, Nicholas von, 4434
Hoffman, Stanley, 838, 1092
Hoffmann, Bedrich, 1598
Hoffmann, Gerhard, 839
Hoffmann, J.R., 891
Hofmann, Otto, (473)
Hofmannsthal, Emilio von, 3062
Hofstetter, Albert J., 3632
Hogan Willard N., 3187
Hohberg, Hans, (471)
Hohenstein, 1873
Hohenzollern, Kaiser Wilhelm, 772-788
Höhne, Heinz, 2385
Hohnstein, 1649
Holborn, Louise, 3290
Hollidt, Karl, (476)
Holls, Frederick William, 646
Holocaust, and the Nuremberg IMT, 1455-1458; bibliography of, 72; death statistics, Appendix 15; in Austria, 1475-1477; in Belgium, 1478-1479; in Bulgaria, 1480-1485; in Denmark, 1486; in Europe, 1459-1474; in France, 1487-1493; in Germany, 1494-1507; in Greece, 1508-1509; in Hungary, 1510-1517; in Italy, 1518-1520; in Lithuania, 1521-1525; in Poland, 1532-1545; in

Rumania, 1546-1550; in Slovakia, 1551-1556; in Thrace, 1557; in the Netherlands, 1526-1531; in the USSR, 1558-1561; in the United States, 1562-1564; in Yugoslavia, 1565-1566; Jewish resistance, 1395-1411; psychological aspects, 1429-1446; survivors, 1412-1428
Holste, Heinrich, 3815
Holstein, Franz, 3540
Holthusen, Hans E., 3979
Holtz, W., 954
Holzberg, Bryan, 2292
Holzhausen, Rudolf, 2857
Homma, Masaharu, 2507-2508, 2528, 2541-2543
Homosexuals, crimes against, 1041-1044
Homze, Edward L., 988
Honig, Frederick, 3260-3261, 3441, 3689, 3816
Honolka, Bert, 1020
Hooker, Wade S., 4251
Hoover, Glenn E., 574
Hoppe, Klaus, 1437, 1599
Horec, Jaromir, 1600
Horn, Martin, (462)
Horne, Alistair, 4484
Hornung, Walter, 1826
Horowitz, Irvin Louis, 1339
Horsky, Charles A., 597
Horwitz, Solis, 2556
Hoshino, Naoki, (478)-(479), (482)
Höß, Rudolf, 1700, 2127, 3539, 3588, 3884, 4038
Hossbach, Friederick, 537
Hostage Case, Appendix 8
Hostages, 491-509, 3540
Hoth, Hermann, (476)
Houdremont, Eduard, (475)
Housepian, Marjorie, 1340
Hoven, Waldemar, (469)
Howard, Kenneth A., 538
Howard, Toni, 2039
Hsiang, Che-Chun, (481)
Hsü, Shu-Hsi, 1063-1064
Huband, Charles R., 3188
Hubbert, Cecil F., 3121
Huber, John, 2723
Huber, Robert J., 4374
Hübner, Herbert, (473)
Hudes, Ted, 2435
Hufford, Harold E., 190
Hughes-Morgan, David, 437
Hugueney, Louis, 2953
Hula, Eric, 3212, 2436
Hull, William Lovell, 3980
Hungary, Holocaust in, 1510-1517; World War II crimes against, 1097-1102

Huong, Nguyen van, 4275
Huttenbach, Henry, 1501
Hutton, Joseph Bernard, 2040
Hyde, Charles C., 464, 1065, 2437, 2908, 2930, 3490
Hyde, H. Montgomery, 2816
Hyder, Elton M., 2557

I

I.G. Farben trial, 2353, 3542, Appendix 8
Ienaga, Saburo, 2660
Ihn, Max Otto, (475)
Ikor, Roger, 4082
Ilava, 1874
Ilgner, Max, 3309
Imqueco, Peter, 4443
Inglis, L.M., 3309
Institut für Geschichte an der deutschen Akademie der Wissenschaften zu Berlin, 3
Institute of Contemporary History and Wiener Library, 104
Institute of Jewish Affairs, 1463-1464
Inter-Allied Information Committee, London, 2438-2439
Inter-American Juridical Committee, 366
International Auschwitz Committee, 1701
International Committee for Penal Reconstruction and Development, 2440
International Conference on Prosecution of Nazi Criminals, 2441
International conferences and conventions, 321-336; and the IMT, 2926-2945
International Criminal Court, 296-320
International law, 266-267; works on, 272-295
International Military Tribunal (IMT), Nuremberg, 112, 584, 590, 594, 602, 608, 617, 619-620, 1455-1458, 2836, 3060-3069, (9), (11); charter of, (455)-(462); defendants, 2081, 2089; documents, (18ff.); indictment, (463)-(464); Rorschach tests of defendants, 2197, 2215, 2230; sentences, 3110-3154
International Military Tribunal for the Far East (IMTFE), 584, 2559, 2595, 2603-2627, (13); charges, verdicts, and sentences, Appendix 14; list of defendants and sentences, Appendix 11; defense counsels,

Appendix 13; list of prosecuting nations, Appendix 10
International Society of Military Law and the Laws of War, 2342
International Tracing Service, 1601-1602
Ireland, Gordon, 776, 2662
Irving, David, 3372
Isaacs, Harold Roberts, 138
Isayama, Harukei, 3537
Iserles, Israel, 4217
Isolani, Gertrud, 1868
Israel, documents and records, 145-148; District Court of Jerusalem, 4134; Government Press Office, 4039-4040, 4085; Ministry of Foreign Affairs, 4202; Office of Information, 4084; Police Headquarters, 4135-4137; Public Information Office, 4138; Supreme Court, Eichmann appeal, 4165-4167
Israel, T., 4237
Itagaki, Seishiro, (478), (479), (482)
Italy, 3853, documents and records, 149; Holocaust in, 1518-1520
Ivanov, Miroslav, 2041
Ivrakis, Solon Cléanthes, 367, 3003
Ivy, Andrew Conway, 1021
Iwamatsu, Shigetoshi, 1066

J

Jack, Homer A., 4444
Jackson, A.H., 234
Jackson, Robert H., 368, 520, 1465, 2154-2155, 2172, 2195, 2198, 2219, 2672, 2682, 2724-2725, 2815, 2861-2862, 2883, 2891-2892, 2909, 2935, 2987, 3004, 3191-3192, 3262-3265, 3291, (9), (455), (467)
Jackson, William E., 2497, 2841-2851, (297)
Jacob-Meyer, Wolfgang, 1123
Jacobs, Monty, 2296
Jacobsen, Hans-Adolf, 143, 2042, 2389
Jacobson, Jacob, 1953
Jacoby, Gerhard, 3124
Jaffe, Sidney E., 3005
Jaffré, Yves Frédéric, 3633
Jäger, Herbert, 840, 4086
Jagusch, Heinrich, 955
Jahn, Werner, 259
Jähne, Friedrich, (472)
Jahnke, K.H., 1827
Jahreiss, Hermann, (463)

Jakusch, Ruth, 1816
Jaluit Atoll trial, 3533
Janeczek, Edward J., 3125
Janowitz, Morris, 841
Janssen, Gregor, 2043
Japan, archives of, 228-229; bibliography, 97; research sources, 115
Jaranilla, Delfin, 2629
Jasper, G., 3949
Jaspers, Karl, 3039-3040, 3086-3087, 3266, 3918
Jaszai, Dezso, 2442
Jawischowitz, 1669
Jaworski, Leon, 466, 3193
Jeantet, Gabriel, 3634
Jennings, W. Ivor, 369
Jerome, Victor Jeremy, 2214
Jerusalem, Franz, 2357-2358
Jeruschalmi, Elieser, 1438
Jescheck, Hans-Heinrich, 539, 3267, 3635-3636
Jessup, Philip C., 2954
Jewish Black Book Committee, 1266, 1466
Jewish Committee for Theresienstadt, 1954
Jewish Documentation Center, Vienna, 2199
Jewish Historical Institute, 1341
Jobst, Valentine III, 842
Jochmann, Werner, 143
Jodl, Alfred, 83, 2044, 2123, 2148, 2762, (463)-(464), (466)
Jodl, Luise, 2044
Joel, Günther, (470)
Johanny, Karl, 2359
Johansen, Robert C., 4390
Johe, Werner, 3381
Johnson, Joseph E., 2673
Johnson, K., 4418
Joiner, Charles A., 4232
Jones, J. William, 647
Jones, Mervyn, 4485
Jong, Louis de, 1527
Joos, Joseph, 1828
Joseph, Charles Marie [pseudonym, Joseph Bédier], 707
Jost, Heinz, (474)
Jowett, (455)
Joyce, William (Lord "Haw Haw"), 3813, 3826
Jucovy, Milton E., 1251-1252
Juillard, E., 1603
Julien, M., 3637
Julin, Gosta, 4445
Junge, Heinz, 3839
Jureidini, Paul A., 4486
Justice Case, (470)
Justice trial, 3341, 3374-3394, 3538

K

Ka-Tzetnik 135 633 [pseudonym for Karol Cetyński], 1702, 1914
Kabeli, Isaac, 1508
Kahin, George M., 4267
Kahn, David, 220
Kahn, Leo, 2726
Kaiserswald, 1648
Kajima, Morinosuke, 2663
Kalnoky, Ingeborg, 2835
Kaltenbrunner, Ernst, 2135, 2762, 2841, 2846, (462), (465)-(466)
Kamenec, Ivan, 1551, 1907
Kamenetsky, Ihor, 1178
Kamin, Gerhard, 1786
Kaminski, Andrej, 1604
Kamps, Karl, 1764
Kanely, Edna M., 118
Kannapin, Hans-Eckhardt, 989
Kantor, Alfred, 1605
Kaplan, Chaim A., 2832
Kaplan, Harold L., 3310
Kaplanas, O., 1179
Kappler, Herbert, 3859
Karajian, Sarkis, 738
Karanikas, Démètre I., 3064
Karev, D.S., (468)
Karny, Miroslav, 1955
Karpenko, Z., 1180
Karr, Stephen David, 1439
Karsten, Peter, 4345, 4427
Karsten, Thomas L., 3127
Kastner, Rudolph (Rudolf), see Rezso Kasztner
Kasuri, Mahmud Ali, (487)
Kasztner, Rezso (Reszoe), 1097-1102, 1513, 4004, 4140
Kato, Eikichi, trial of, 3537
Katona, Paul, 2525
Katyn Woods, massacre, 594, 1158-1171, 2418
Katz, Josef, 1606
Katz, Milton, 4087, 4177
Katz, Robert, 500
Katz, Shlomo, 3950, 4088-4089
Katzenberger, K., 3006, 3559
Kauffmann, Kurt, (462)
Kaufman, G., 3951
Kaufman, Joseph W., 3442
Kaufman, Mary M., 2955
Kaufmann, Max, 1648
Kaul, Friedrich Karl, 765, 1703, 3089, 3382, 3529, 3721-3722, 3952, 4090
Kautsky, Benedikt, 1607
Kaya, Okinori, (478)-(479), (482)
Kazarian, Haigazn K., 739, 793-796
Kazin, Alfred, 3953

Keen, Maurice H., 370
Keenan, Joseph Berry, 2544, 2552, 2562-2563, 3194, (481)
Keeshan, Anne, 2727
Keeton, George Williams, 3818
Kehr, Helen, 57
Kehrl, Hans, (476)
Keitel, Wilhelm, 590, 2023, 2032, 2123, 2128, 2182, 2231, 2762, (462), (464), (466)
Kelley, Douglas M., 2215, 2836
Kellogg, Robert H., 648
Kelly, Joseph B., 371, 467
Kelman, Herbert C., 4303, 4426-4427
Kelsen, Hans, 283, 540-542, 2910-2911, 3065, 3269
Kempner, Robert M.W., 598, 1093, 1103, 1502, 2216, 2386, 2728-2729, 3195-3196, 3453, 3954, (467)
Kempski, Jürgen von, 3007
Kenner, Jacob, 1532
Kenny, John P., 2956
Kenrick, Donald, 1048
Keppler, Wilhelm, (476)
Kermisch, J., 1128, 4005, 4139
Kermish, J., see Kirmisch, J.
Kern, Erich [pseudonym of Erich Kernmayr]
Kern, Paul, 1903
Kernmayr, Erich [pseudonym, Erich Kern], 599, 1267
Kerr, Helen, 1308
Kersten, Felix, 2129, 2217
Kessel, Joseph, 2217
Kesselring, Albert, 2049, 2130, trial of, 3540, 3854, 3857
Kessemeier, Carin, 2045
Kessler, Leo, 1829
Kestenberg, Judith S., 1440
Khabarovsk trial, 2509-2514
Kharkov trial, 3892-3897, 3909
Kido, Koichi, (478)-(479), (482)
Kiefer, Max, (471)
Kiehl, Walter, 2046
Kierspiel, Josef, 3734
Killinger, Erich, 3535, 3829
Kimmich, Christoph, 106
Kimura, Heitaro, (478)-(479), (482)
Kintner, Earl W., 3498
Kippenberger, H.K., 3530, 3550
Kipphardt, Heinar, 4006
Kirchhoff, Hans, 1389
Kirchman, Charles V., 188
Kirchner, Carl, 2360-2361, 3128
Kisker, Karl Peter, 1429
Kladov, Ignatii Fedorovich, 3897
Klafkowski, Alfons, 575, 1111, 2957
Klaidman, Stephen, 2297
Klarsfeld, Beate, 1319

530 Index

Klarsfeld, Serge, 1319
Klausner, Carla L., 1279
Klausner, Israel, 1608
Kleffens, Eelco Nicolaas van, 1104
Klemm, Herbert, (470)
Klessmann, Cristoph, 2218
Klinge, Karl-Hans Hermann, trial of, 3535
Klingelhöfer, Woldemar, (474)
Klöß, Erhard, 2158
Knieriem, August von, 3330
Knoll, Erwin, 4304
Knox, Israel, 1265
Koch, Ekhard, 3819
Koch, Ilse, 3333, 3521
Kochba, Adina, 1528
Kodama, Yoshio, 2131-2132
Koehl, Robert L., 990, 2387
Koessler, Maximilian, 3311, 3383, 3500, 3519, 3693
Koestler, Arthur, 1876
Kogon, Eugen, 1609
Kohl, Michael, 3270
Köhler, Fritz, 2863
Kohn, Alan, 2298
Kohn, Stanislaw, 1136
Koht, Halvdan, 909
Koiso, Kuniaki, (478)-(479), (482)
Kojima, Noboru, 2564
Koki, Hirota, 2091
Kol, A., 4203
Kolander, Morris W., 3312
Kolb, Eberhard, 1765, 1787
Kolbe, Maximilian, 2822
Kolko, Gabriel, 521, 4305
Komarow, Gary, 543
Komitee der Antifaschistischen Widerstandskämpfer in der Deutschen Demokratischen Republik, 1920, 2388
Kondrates, Z., 1183
Königstein, 1649
Konrad, Franz, 3878
Konvitz, Milton R., 3197
Koo, Wellington, Jr., 1342
Koppel, Edward James, 4204
Korczak, Janusz, 2833
Kordt, Erich, 2837, 3454
Korean War, 4465-4480
Korey, William, 3748, 4205-4206
Korman, Gerd, 58, 1304
Korman, Shirley, 2297
Körner, Paul, (476)
Korovin, Eugene A., 372, 3041
Korschan, Heinrich Leo, (475)
Koshiro, Tanabe, 3543
Kosicki, Jerzy, 59
Kossak, Zofia, 1704
Kosso Edward, 1610
Kozhevnikov, F.I., 2958
Kozlowski, Waclaw, 59

Kramarz, H., 3129
Kramer, G., 3384
Kramer, Josef, 3543, 3830-3834
Krannhals, Hans von, 1137
Kranzbühler, Otto, 2730, 3198-3200, (463)
Kraske, Erich, 600
Krauch, Carl, 3345, 3422, 3542, (472)
Kraus, Herbert, 3130-3131, 3201, 3560, (463)
Kraus, Ota B., 1384, 1650, 1705
Kraus, Rose, 3491
Krausnick, Helmut, 1112, 1184, 2389
Krawinkel, H., 3820
Krebs, Albert, 2362
Krehbiel-Darmstadter, Maria, 1869
Kremer, Charles H., 2228
Kremers, Heinz, 1503
Kreslins, Janis A., 60
Krieger, B., 3525
Krieger, Seymour, 1467, (468)
Kropat, Wold-Arno, 1293
Krüger, Kurt, 2133
Krupp Case, Appendix 8
Krupp, Alfried, 3333, 3346; trial of, 3542, (475)
Krupp, Gustav, 2841
Kruuse, Jens, 3638
Krzyzanowska, Zofia, 4007
Kubuschok, Egon, (463)
Kuby, Erich, 1830
Kuchin, V.V., (468)
Küchler, Georg Karl Friedrich-Wilhelm, (476)
Kuci, Ali, 1823
Kuczynski, Jürgen, 991
Kudryavtsev, V., 2636
Kugelmass, Jack, 1538
Kugler, Hans, (472)
Kuhn, Arthur K., 501, 1377, 2526, 3008
Kühn, Günter, 1788
Kühnrich, Heinz, 1611, 4008
Kulcsar, I., 3981
Kulcsar, Shoshana, 3981
Kulischer, Eugene M., 992
Kulka, Erich, 1384, 1453, 1650, 1705-1706, 3723
Kunter, Erich, 1831
Kuntze, Walter, (473)
Kunz, Josef L., 284, 373, 468, 544, 1378
Kunz, Wolfgang, 3749
Kuper, Leo, 1343, 1441
Kupfer-Koberwitz, Edgar, 1832
Kurland, Philip B., 2219
Kurth, Gertrud M., 1504
Kurtha, Aziz Noomi, 469-470
Küster, Otto, 3061
Kuster, Reinhard, 4091

Küstermeier, R., 3982, 4159
Kuusinen, O., 3605
Kwaterko, A., 3877

L

L'Amicale des Anciens de Dachau, 1833
La Germonière, Paul, 2864
La Guardia Gluck, Gemma, 1921, 4009
La Coste, Raymond, 899
La Farge, John J., 3132
La Farge, Philippe, 51
La Follette, Charles M., 3385-3386
La Pradelle, Albert G. de, 777, 3271-3272
Lacconia, A., 1344
Lachs, Manfred, 374, 890, 2324, 2936
Laconia Affair, 2073
Lacouture, Jean, 4233, 4306
Lael, Richard L., 2527
Laeuen, Harald, 1113
Lagergemeinschaft Neuengamme, 1904
Lakshmanan, R., 3090
Lambert, Gilles, 1514
Lambert, Margaret, 139
Lambert, Thomas F., Jr., (467)
Lamm, Hans, 4207
Lammers, Hans Heinrich, (476)
Landau, A., 545
Landau, Ernest, 4140
Lande, Adolf, 3009
Landes, Daniel, 1336
Lando, Barry, 4391
Landsberg Prison, records of, 206
Landsberg, William H., 1379
Lane, Mark, 4307
Lang, Daniel, 4308
Lang, Jochen von, 2047, 4141
Lang, Serge, 2138
Langbein, Hermann, 843, 1612, 1651, 1676, 1707-1710, 3694-3696, 3724, 3754
Lange, Eitel, 2048
Lange, Horst, 993
Lange, Richard, 3561-3563, 3821
Langenfass, Friedrich, 4092
Langer, Elinor, 4435
Langhoff, Wolfgang, 1613
Langmaid, Janet, 57
Langsam, Walter Consuelo, 140
Lansing, Robert L., 565, 682
Lanz, Hubert, (473)
Lanzmann, Claude, 1652
Lapides, Leon, 4168
Laqueur, Walter, 1099, 1268, 1345, 2220
Larnaude, Fernand, 777

Lasic, Dusan, 1246
Laska, Lewis L., 649
Laska, Vera, 61, 1399
Lasok, D., 4093
Laternser, Hans, 2049, 2731, 3725, (463)
Latza, Hans Paul Helmuth, 3546
Lauer, Lawrence, 2912
Lauterbach, Richard E., 3898
Lautern, Mark, 3202
Lauterpacht, Hersch, 266, 375, 2443
Lautz, Ernst, (470)
Laval, Pierre, 3620, 3639-3640, 3652, 3670
Lavi, Theodore, 1548-1549
Law Reports, (19)
Lawrence, James F., 601
Lawrence, Lee H., 4426-4427
Lawrence, Lord Justice Geoffrey [Baron Oaksey], 2732, 3273, (462)
Lawyers Committee on American Policy Towards Vietnam, 4268
Lazard, Didier, 2733
Le Brethon, J., 1094
Le Chêne, Evelyn, 1888
Le Queux, William, 708
Le Vernet, 1875-1876
Lea, Luke, 778
Leasor, Thomas James, 2050
Leavy, Zad, 4095-4097
Lebed, Andrei, 1558
Lebedev, A., 4098
Lederer, Zdenek, 1956
Lee, Asher, 2051
Leeb, Johannes, 2722
Leeb, Wilhelm Ritter von, 2049, 3347-3348, 3544, (476)
Leers, Johannes von (Osman Amin von Leers), 2325
Lehmann, Friedrich, (475)
Lehmann, Rudolf, (476)
Leigh, Monroe, 2299
Leipzig trials, 800-815, 2242
Leitenberg, Milton, 27, 62
Leitner, Isabella, 1711
Lekschas, J., 3091
Lelewer, Georg, 2444
Lelyveld, Joseph, 4367
Lemkin, Raphael, 235, 1346-1351, 2221
Lener, Salvatore, 779, 956-957, 2735, 3010
Lengyel, Olga, 1712
Lenski, Mordecai, 1352
Lenz, Hans Richard, 3828
Lenz, Johann, 1834
Leo, Gerhard, 4179
Leonberg, 1637
Leonhardt, Hans, 3011
Lepsius, Johannes, 683
Lerner, Daniel, 2052

Lerner, Nathan, 3092
Lersner, Kurt von, 2343
Les Fils et Filles des Deportés Juifs de France (FFDJF), 1489
Lesher, Stephan, 4428
Lessner, Erwin, 3042
Leszczyński, Kazimierz, 3434
Leulliette, Pierre, 4487
Lévai, Jenö (Eugene), 1515, 3843, 4010-4011
Levasseur, G., 958
Leventhal, Harold, 3134
Leverkuehn, Paul, 3840
Levi, Primo, 1713
Levi, Robert, 4218
Levie, Howard S., 471, 4376
Levin, Bernard, 4446
Levin, Dov, 1523
Levin, Isaac, 1532
Levin, Meyer, 4012, 4219
Levin, Nora, 1353
Levit, S.E., 1186
Levy, Alan, 2300
Levy, Albert G.D., 307, 546
Levy, Howard B., 4436
Levy-Hass, Hanna, 1766
Lewanski, Richard C., 107-108
Lewanski, Rudolf J., 108
Lewe van Aduard, Evart Joost, 2485
Lewinska, Pelagia, 1714
Lewis, Flora, 3955
Lewis, George G., 472
Lewis, John R., 63
Lewis, John W., 4267
Lewy, Guenter, 438, 4402
Lex, Jean-Pierre, 3539
Ley, Robert, 2046, 2841, (466)
Leyrat, P. de, 910
Leyser, Ernst von, (473)
Liang, Yuen-Li, 308
Lichten, H.E., 3456
Lichtenburg, 1649
Lichtenstein, Heiner, 1879
Lichtheim, George, 1715
Liddell Hart, Basil H., 2222
Lidman, Sara, (487)
Liebesman-Mikulski, Abraham, 3589
Lietzmann, Heinrich, 3822
Lifton, Robert J., 521
Liggeri, Paolo, 1653
Lim, M., 2528
Lind, Jakov, 2737
Lindberg, Hugo, 2913
Lindenberger, Josef, 1855
Lindquist, Irmela, 3726
Lines, J., 3956
Lingenfelder, Karl, 3541
Lingens-Reiner, Ella, 1614, 1676
Linklater, Isabel Hilton, 2301
Linn, Edward, 1442
Linze, Dewey W., 4099

Lippe, Viktor von der, 2838
Lippert, David I., 602, 2959
Lippmann, Walter, 2987, 3274
Lipscher, Ladislav, 1552
Lipsic, Ricardo, 4180
Lischka, Kurt, 3733
Liskofsky, Sidney, 4160, 4181
List, Wilhelm, 2049, 3348, 3540, (472)-(473)
Litai, Chaim Lazar, 1138
Lithuania, Holocaust in, 1521-1525
Littell, Franklin H., 1269
Litten, Irmgard, 1654
Littlejohn, David, 2390
Littner, Jacob, 1139
Liu, James T.C., 2566, 2651
Lobel, William N., 4269
Lochner, L.P., 2119
Lodge, Henry Cabot, Jr., 4471, 4473
Loeb, Walter, 2445
Loeffler, Martin, (463)
Loehlein, W., 2225
Loesch, Karl C. von, 2343
Loewenstein, Karl, 236-237
Logan Andy, 3417
London International Assembly, 576, 2226; Commission on the Trial and Punishment of War Criminals, 2446
Loock, Hans-Dietrich, 3872
López, Pedro, (481)
Lord "Haw Haw," see William Joyce
Lorenz, Werner, (473)
Lörner, Georg, (471)
Lörner, Hans, (471)
Löser, Ewald Oskar, (475)
Lowenberg, Helmuth, 4100
Lowenthal, Zdenko, 1566
Lüders, Karl-Heinz, 547
Lüdinghausen, Otto von, (463)
Lütem, Ilham, 844
Luchaire, Jean, 3641, 3664
Ludwig, Emil, 577, 780
Lullies, Hildegard, 221
Lunari, Luigi, 4429
Lunau, Heinz, 2738
Lund, T.G., 3012
Lustgarten, Edgar, 1767
Luther, Hans, 3642
Lutz, Ralph Hasswell, 1
Lyman, Albert, 2537
Lynd, Staughton, 4447

M

M.L.C., Jr., 3492
Maass, Walter B., 3864
MacArthur, Douglas, 2331, 2541, 2644, (16)
MacMullen, Douglas B., 4392

Maccas, L., 710
Machleid, Wanda, 1922
Mackensen, Willi, 3543
Mackiewicz, Josef, 1166
Maelzer, Kurt, 3543
Maguire, Robert F., (475)
Mahan, Alfred Thayer, 327
Maidanek, 1276, 1644, 1656, 1877-1881, 2847, 3745
Maier, K., 2227
Mailman, Stanley, 2302
Major War Criminals of the European Axis, (453)-(455)
Malézieux, R., 2914
Malitz, Bruno, 3891
Mallal, Bashir, 2505
Mallin, Joy, 4234
Manchester, William, 3443
Manikowsky, Arnim von, 3182
Manila trial, 2515
Mann, Abby, 3135
Mann, Eric, 911
Mann, Peggy, 2228
Manner, George, 2447
Manning, Paul, 2053
Mansfield, Alan J., (481)
Manstein, Fritz Erich von 604, 2054, 2761, 3817, 3824, 3840-3842
Mant, A.K., 1022
Manvell, Roger A., 845, 1354, 2055-2058
Mapel, Siegfried, 3900
Marbaix, Edgar, 1772
Marcus, Robert S., 846, 3204, 3435
Margalot, Abraham, 1286
Margoshes, Samuel, 1265
Maridakis, Georges S., 603
Marin, Miguel A., 376
Mark, Bernard, 1140-1142, 1400, 3878
Markov, Kirill, 3093
Markov, M., 2567, 2664-2665
Markstadt, 1637
Maršálek, Hans, 1872, 1889-1891
Marshall, Bruce, 1655
Marshall, Carrington T., (470)
Marshall, Logan, 711
Martienssen, Anthony K., 2229
Martin, Bernhard, 4101
Martin, George S., 3205
Martínez, José Agustín, 604, 2739
Martini, Winfried, 3697, 4161
Martius, Georg, 3136
Marx, Hans, (463)
Marzabatto trial, 3749
Marzabotta, Italian village of, 3845
Masao, Baba, 3543
Maschke, Erich, 473
Maschke, Hermann M., 3444

Maser, Werner, 2740
Mason, Alpheus Thomas, 238, 2818
Mason, John B., 474
Mason, W. Wynne, 475
Massie, Robert, 4111
Massow, A.W., 1270
Masters, Anthony, 2819
Mastny, Vojtech, 1089
Masuda, Nisuke, 3533
Mathias, James H., 3127
Matkovski, Aleksandar, 1525
Matsui, Iwane, (478), (480), (482)
Matsuoka, Yosuke, (478), (480), (482)
Matthews, T.S., 4220
Matussek, Paul, 1615
Maugham, Viscount Frederic Herbert, 3206
Maunoir, Jean-Pierre, 3643-3644
Maurach, Reinhart, 3901
Maurel, Micheline, 1923
Mauthausen, 1636, 1639, 1643-1644, 1653, 1882-1889
Maxon, Yale Candee, 2601
Maxwell-Fyfe, David (1st Earl of Kilmuir), 2839, 3207, (468)
Maybaum, Ignaz, 1716
Mayda, Giuseppe, 2741
Mayer, Hellmuth, 2363
Mayer, Milton, 3957
Mayer, Reinhold, 3958
Mayer, S.L., 239
Mayevsky, V., 2510
Maynard, J.A., 2937
McAfee, B., 2568
McCarthy, Mary, 4436
McCauley, James, 3043
McCauley, Worth B., 3313
McCloy, John J., 2330, 3523
McConnell, G.R., 2742
McConnell, John R., 377
McDonald, Bruce, 3599
McDonald, James Grover, 712
McElroy, John, 650-651
McFadden, Judith Nies, 4304
McGinness, John R., 477
McGovern, James, 2059
McIntyre, Dina Ghandy, 617, 2743
McKeller, Peter, 1355
McKenzie, Walter I., 2569
McMillan, James, 3275
McWilliams, Wilson Carey, 4346
Mechanicus, Philip, 1973-1974
Mechelynck, Albert, 328
Medical Case, Appendix 8
Medical experiments, 2386
Medical war crimes, 1008-1033, 2103, 2187, 2705
Medicus, Franz A., 3457
Medina, Ernest, 4343, 4436
Meed, Vladka, 1143
Meek, Frank E., 2570

534 Index

Meeker, Leonard L., 4252
Meer, Fritz Ter, (472)
Mehrish, Brijesh Narain, 4493
Meier, Emil, 3838
Meier, Heinrich Christian, 1905
Meinshausen, Hans, 3891
Meir, Golda, 4084
Melchior, David Werner, 4208
Melchior, Marcus, 1091
Melen, Alexander-Czeslaw, 502
Melk, 1636
Melman, Seymour, 4310
Melo, Artemio Luis, 4102
Melodia, Giovanni, 1803
Melsheimer, Ernst, 3565
Meltzer, Bernard D., 3208, (467)
Menasche, Albert, 1717
Mendelsohn, John, 207-208, 1271, 1390, 2865-2866
Mendelssohn, Peter de, 2744, 2867
Mengele, Josef, 2103
Menges, Jan, 1023
Menkes, G., 1024
Menon, Govinda, (481)
Menten, Pieter, 2164
Menthon, François E. de, 847, (468)
Menzel, Eberhard, 3531, 3810
Mercury, Francis, 2707
Merick, W.S., 4430
Mérignhac, Alexandre G.J.A., 548, 713
Merkel, Rudolf, (463)
Merle, Marcel, 2745, 3209
Meron, Theodor, 4188
Merrill, Clarence F., (472)
Mertens, Pierre, 959-960
Merton, Thomas, 3983
Messing, John H., 4270
Metcalf, Lawrence E., 605
Mettgenberg, Wolfgang, (470)
Mewha, John, 472
Meyer, Kurt, 3536, 3599
Meyer, R., 3566
Meyer-Abich, Friedrich, 2364
Meyerhoff, Hans, 3984
Meyrowitz, Henri, 961, 3645, 4253
Mezger, Ernst, 3646-3647
Miaja de la Muela, Adolfo, 1356
Miale, Florence R., 2230
Michael, H.A., 1144
Michaelis, Meir, 1520, 2060
Michalka, Wolfgang, 2061
Michel, H., 212
Michel, Henri, 1428
Michel, Jean, 1858
Michel, Paul Louis, 3648
Michelet, Edmond, 1835
Michelon, Claude, 714
Michelsen, Andreas Heinrich, 808

Michie, Allan A., 578
Miège, A., 1024
Mielke, Fred, 1025-1026
Mignone, A. Frederick, 606
Mihan, George, 1039
Mikellitis, Edith, 3959
Mikulski, Jan, 1718
Milch Case, Appendix 8, (470), 3539; trial records of, 207
Milch, Erhard, 590, 2032, 2862, 3340, 3539, (470)
Milentijevich, Zoran, 1929
Milgram, Stanley, 439
Millar, Moorhouse F.X., 3212
Miller, Richard I., 378
Miller, Robert H., 3094
Miller, Robert W., 2538
Miller, Stuart C., 665
Milton, Sybil, 1252
Milyutin, N., 4103-4104
Minami, Jiro, (478), (480), (482)
Minco, Marga, 1529
Minear, Richard H., 2571, 2666
Ministries Case, Appendix 8
Minney, Rubeigh James, 1656
Mirbeth, Johann, 3734
Mirman, Léon, 715
Mitscherlich, Alexander, 1025-1026, 3366-3367
Mittelbach, Hans, 2365-2366, 2371, 3567
Mittermaier, Wolfgang, 962
Miwa Kai, 2572
Moczarski, Kazimierz, 2062
Moehle, Karl-Heinz, 3541
Mohraz, Jane E., 31
Mojonny, Gerardo Luigi, 478
Moldawa, Mieczyslaw, 1863, 1866
Moldawer, S., 1114
Molho, Michael, 1509
Moll, Otto E., 2063
Mollison, P., 1768
Moltmann, Günter, 241-242
Mommsen, Wolfgang, 3210
Monneray, Henri, 1468, 1490, 2868, (468)
Mönning, Richard, 64
Monsson, Otto, 3818
Montero, Mario, 2746
Montfort, François de, 3985
Moody, Samuel B., 2486
Moore, John Norton, 379, 4247, 4254-4255, 4271-4272, 4462
Moore, William Harrison, 285
Moorehead, Alan, 684
Morcinek, Gustav, 1657
Morellet, Charles, 3649
Morelli, Valeria, 1836
Morgan, John Hartmann, 716, 2960, 3211
Morgenbesser, Sidney, 519, 4289
Morgenstern, Felice, 2325

Morgenthau plan, 242
Morgenthau, Hans J., 3212
Morgenthau, Henry, Jr., 243
Morikawa, Kinju, (487)
Moringen, 1649
Moritz, Klaus, 1293
Morley, James W., 174
Mornet, A., 3650
Morris, James, 2747, (472)
Morris-Jones, W., 4494
Morsberger, Katharine M., 652
Morsberger, Robert E., 652
Morse, Arthur D., 1357
Morton, Louis, 65, 2487, 3044
Mosheim, Berthold, 1358
Mosler, Hermann, 244, 3568
Mosley, Leonard, 2064-2065
Mosse, George L., 1359
Mostar, Herrmann, 1837
Mostecky, Vaclav, 120
Motomura, Shigeki, 3545
Motosuke, Susuki, 3545
Moulis, Miloslav, 1790
Mounier, Pierre, (468)
Mouret, G., 3651
Moussa, Amre, 3292
Mouton, Martinus Willem, 267
Mozambique mercenaries trial, 4496
Mrugowsky, Joachim, (469)
Mueller, Gene A., 2231
Mühldorf, 1637
Mühlen, Norbert, 3445
Mulka, Robert K., 3727-3728
Müller, Erich, (475)
Müller, Filip, 1719
Müller, Werner, 1498
Müller-Payer, Albert, 848
Müller-Rappard, Ekkehart, 440
Müllerheim, Fritz, 1385
Mullins, Claude, 809-810
Mummenthey, Karl, (471)
Munch, Maurus, 1838
Mundo, Wilhelm, 3545
Munro, Hector A., 579-580, 892, 2232-2235, 2748, 3013
Münz, Max, 1482
Murawska, 1878, 1880
Murmelstein, B., 3960
Murphy, Brendan, 2066
Murphy, Charles F., 4235, 4256
Murphy, Cornelius F., 4236
Murray, Hartley, (467)
Murray, John Courtney, 912
Murray, Michael Patrick, 607
Musiol, Teodor, 1839
Musmanno, Michael A., 3436, 3961, 4107, 4162, (470)-(471), (474)
Mussert trial, 3867
Mussolini, Benito, 2060, 3528
Muszkat, Marian, 1115-1116, 2236, 2344-2345, 3095, 3213, 4106, 4182, 4209
Muto, Akira, (478), (480), (482)
My Lai, massacre and cover-up, 4381-4401; war crimes in, 4336-4361
Myerson, Moses Hyman, 2448

N

Nagano, Osami, (478), (480), (482)
Nagel, Thomas, 516, 519, 4289
Nainovitch, Isak, 1483
Namier, Lewis Bernstein, 2749
Nansen, Odd, 1658
Napoli, Joseph F., 3479
Napora, Paul Edward, 1720, 1769
Nartatez, M.C, 3014
Nash, Arnold, 3214
Nathan, Hans, (468)
National Lawyers Guild (National Executive Board), 2449
Natzweiler, 1636, 3537, 3667, 3838
Naud, Albert L., 3652
Naumann, Bernd, 3728
Naumann, Erich, 3522, (474)
Nazi Party, 245, 2191, 2362; Leadership Corps, 2842, (463); propaganda, 2084
Neave, Airey M.S., 2750-2751, (468)
Neilands, J.B., 4311
Neinast, William H., 4312
Nellessen, Bernd, 4108
Nelte, Otto, 2067, (462)
Nerlinger, Charles, 629
Nerone, F., 3015
Neshamit, Sara, 1145
Netherlands, Holocaust in, 1526-1531; World War II crimes against, 1103-1104
Netherlands Red Cross, Auschwitz, 1721-1726; Information Bureau, 1941
Nettle, Peter, 3903
Neue Breme, 1639
Neuengamme, 1636, 1658, 1900-1906
Neuhäusler, Johann, 1840
Neumann, Franz, 3139, 3532
Neumann, Inge S., 66
Neumann, Karl, 433
Neumann, Robert G., 2346
Neumark, 1670
Neuner, Robert, 913
Neurath, Constantin von, 590, 2012, 2035, 2255, (463), (465), (467)
Neurath, Paul Martin, 1659

Neusüss-Hunkel, Ermenhild, 2391
New York Public Library, the Research Library, 67
New York University School of Law Library Staff, 68
Newman, Judith Sternberg, 1727
Niebergall, Fred, 2869-2870
Niebuhr, Reinhold, 3215
Niedermeyer, Albert, 1027
Nikitchenko, I.T., 2682, (455), (462)
Nikitin, M.N., 1189
Nispen Tot Sevenaer, Carel Marie Otto van, 268, 503
Nix, Emil, 3543
Noakes, Jeremy, 1969
Noam, Ernst, 1293
Nobleman, Eli E., 3315-3320
Noguères, Louis, 3653
Nolan, Henry G., (481)
Nolte, Ernst, 1309
Norden, Eric, 4315
Nordhausen, 1636
Norgaard, Carl Aage, 286
Norman, Lloyd, 4316, 4368
Nornengast, Urda, 3962
Nossig, Alfred, 3885
Nosske, Gustav, (474)
Nothomb, Pierre, 748
Nouaille, Pierre, 2707
Novac, Ana, 1728
Novak, Michael, 4348
Novak, Vaclav, 1957
Nováky, 1907
Novitch, Miriam, 1049, 1146, 1401, 1942, 1970, 3754
Nowak, Kurt, 1028
Noxon, J., 3963
NSDAP, see Nazi Party
Nucéra, Louis, 1858
Nuremberg International Military Tribunal, see International Military Tribunal (IMT), Nuremberg
Nuremberg Military Tribunals, ("subsequent" trials), see American military tribunals
Nurick, Lester, 380
Nussbaum, Arthur, 381
Nyiszli, Miklos, 1402, 1729-1731
Nys, Ernest, 653

O

O'Brien, William V., 2961, 4257
O'Connell, Daniel T., (473)
Oberg, Karl, 3665
Oberheuser, Herta, (469)
Oberkommando Wehrmacht (OKW), 2851, Appendix 8
Oberländer, Theodor, 3751; trial of, 3753
Oberly, James, 4317

Obertraubling, crimes in, 3734
Oberwalde Insane Asylum trial, 3750
Occhi, Adamo Degli, 2752
OCCWC, see Office of the Chief Counsel for War Crimes
Oenning, Johannes, 3543
Oestreich, Paul H.A., 2068
Offenberg, Karl, 3811
Office of the Chief Counsel for War Crimes (OCCWC), (19)
Oglesby, Carl, (487)
Ohashi, Shigeru, 3537
Ohlendorf, Otto, 3342, 3522, (474); trial records, 208
Oka, Takasumi, (478), (480), (482)
Okawa, Shumei, (478), (480), (482)
Oliver, Covey, 4189
Oliver, H.D., 1484
Oneto, Robert, (481)
Oppenheim, Ralph, 1958
Oppenheimer, Max, 4143
Opton, Edward M., 4349-4350
Oradour-Sur-Glane, massacre of, 2418, 3636; trial, 3644, 3651, 3656, 3662-3663,
Oranienburg, 1635-1636, 1647
Orbach, Maurice, 3964
Ormond, Henry, 3698, 3730
Oscar, Friedrich (Olmes), 2873
Öschey, Rudolf, (470)
Oshima, Hiroshi, (478), (480), (482)
Oster, Heinrich, (472)
Österreichische Lagergemeinschaft Mauthausen, 1893
Ott, Adolf, (474)
Ottolenghi, Giacomo, 2238
Oussedik, M., 4482
Oven, Wilfred von, 2069
Ozol, J.A., (468)

P

Padfield, Peter, 2070
Paetel, Karl O., 69, 2392-2393
Paetzold, Kurt O., 245
Paget, Reginald T., 382, 3842
Paillard, Georges, 2071
Pakistan civil war, 4490-4495
Pal, Radhabinod, 2630-2631, 2660, 2666, 2668, 2915, (13), (16)
Palasti, Laszlo, 1516
Paley, Jeffrey, 3096
Palmer, Stuart, 3965
Palmon, J.E., 4221
Paneth, Philip, 4013
Pannenbecker, Otto, 2753, 2874, (462)
Panstwowe Museum, 1732

Paoli, Jules, 963
Paolini, F., 3016
Papadatos, Pierre (Peter) A., 287, 4109-4110
Papanek, Ernst, 1442
Papen, Franz von, 590, 2072, 2134, 2851, (463), (465), (467)
Papenburg, 1649, 1908
Pappalettera, Luigi, 1617
Pappalettera, Vincenzo, 1617
Paret, Peter, 4488
Paris Peace Conference, 329
Paris, Edmond, 1485
Parker, John J., 2263, 2754-2755, 2817, 3276, (462)
Parks, W. Hayes, 458, 549, 4318
Parliamentary Recruiting Service, 718
Parrish, Michael, 70
Parsons, George R., 383, 4190
Partan, Daniel G., 4273
Pascoli, Pietro, 1841
Paskins, Barries, 2756
Paston, David G., 441
Patin, Maurice, 3655
Paton, G.W., 581
Pauchou, Guy, 3656
Paulson, Stanley L., 3017, 4351
Paust, Jordan J., 4274, 4352-4353, 4495
Pavelic, Ante, 2296
Pawleczynska, Anna, 1733
Paxman, Jeremy, 849
Pétain, Philippe, 2025, 3616, 3622, 3629-3630, 3634, 3648, 3653, 3657-3659
Pearlman, Moshe, 3986, 4026
Peers, William R., 4394
Peillard, Léonce, 2073
Peisakhovich, 1191
Pelckmann, Horst, 2757, (463)
Peleus trial, 3527, 3533, 3828, (6)
Pella V., Vespasien (sometimes cited as Vespasien V.), 309-314, 927
Pendorf, Robert, 4014, 4027
Penkower, Monty N., 1391
Pentzlin, Heinz, 2074
Pepper, Claude D., 2450
Pepper, Curtis G., 4111
Peppers, Donald Alan, 550
Pergler, Charles, 893
Perl, Gisela, 1734
Perlmutter, Wayne, 2297
Perlzweig, Maurice L., 4112
Peters, Karl, 3699, 4222
Peterson, Agnes F., 2037, (xix-xx)
Peterson, Edward N., 2075
Petrow, Richard, 1959
Pfenniger, H.F., 850

Pfleiderer, Dietrich, 3966
Pham Cuong, 4319
Pham Van Bat, 4275
Pheleger, Hermann, 2758
Philippine insurrection, 664-673
Phillimore, Harry J., (468)
Phillimore, Walter G.P.F., 315
Phillips, C.P., 384
Phillips, Fitzroy D., (470-471)
Phillips, O.L., 1380
Phillips, Raymond, 3834
Phillipson, Coleman, 288, 385
Phleger, Herman, 3045, 3217
Piasente, Paride, 1660
Pic, Paul, 719
Piccigallo, Philip R., 2488-2489
Picciotto, Cyril M., 551
Pickthall, Marmaduke, 740
Pictet, Jean S., 330
Piekarz, Mendel, 71-73
Piggott, Francis S.G., 2825
Piggott, Francis T., 781
Pilch, Judah, 1272
Pilichowski, Czeslaw, 2304, 3097
Pilloud, Claude, 504
Pingel, Falk, 1618
Pinkus, Oscar, 1273
Pinkville (Song My), 4362-4370
Pinson, Koppel S., 1274
Pinter, István, 2305
Pisar, Samuel, 1735
Pius XII, Pope, 2451
Platten-Hallermund, Alice, 3368
Plauen, E.O., 2306
Playfair, Giles, 3967
Pleiger, Paul, (476)
Plischke, Elmer, 74, 3480
Poel, Albert van der, 1906
Pohl, Oswald, 3343, 3522, (471); case described, Appendix 8
Poirier, Normand, 4354
Pokrovsky, Y.V., (468)
Polakiewicz, Moses, 1532
Poland, 150-151, 1105-1125, 1147, 1167-1168, 1532-1545, 1619
Polevoĭ, Boris N., 608, 2759
Poliakov, Léon, 1360, 1469-1470, 1491-1492, 1736, 2760, 4015, 4113-4114, 4144-4145
Polish Government Information Center (New York), 1148, 3879
Poljokan, I., 552
Pollak, Stephen W., 2326
Poller, Walter, 1791
Pollock, Frederick, 442
Pollock, James K., 2239
Poltorak, Arkadiĭ Iosifovich, 2761-2762, 3218-3219
Polyansky, N.N., 2240, 2763
Pomeroy, William J., 666
Pompe, Cornelius A., 914
Pook, Hermann, (471)

Poppendick, Helmut, (469)
Pospieszalski, Karol Marian, 1798
Possony, Stefan T., 4276
Pottecher, Frederic, 4115
Potter, John Deane, 2076
Potter, Pitman B., 915
Powell, John W., 1067
Powers, Leon W., (475)
Präg, Werner, 1123
Prazak, J., 2030
Presseisen, Ernst L., 2077
Presser, Jacob, 1975, 1530
Preuss, Erich, 2394
Pridham, Geoffrey, 1969
Priepke, Manfred, 2078
Prince, Robert M., 1444
Prisoners of war, treatment of, 346, 456-490
Pritchard, R. John, 2503, 2626
Pritt, Denis N., 2241-2242, 3098
Prittie, Terence, 3968
Probst, H., 386
Procopé, Hjalmar J., 3606
Przybylski, Peter, 2327, 2764
Puchner, Otto, 222
Puhl, Emil, (476)
Pumphrey, D., 3987
Pupko, Bessy, 2297
Püschel, Wilhelm, 2765
Puxon, Grattan, 1048

Q

Quatre, Constant, (468)
Queneudec, Jean Pierre, 553
Quentin-Baxter, R.G., 2574
Quilliam, Ronald H., (481)
Quinn, Robert E., 4431
Quintano Ripollés, Antonio, 964, 3220, 3593
Quisling, Vidkun, trial of, 3871-3873

R

Rabinowitz, J., 1524
Rabus, Walter, 901
Radandt, Hans, 2367, 3418
Radbruch, Gustav, 965, 3387
Rademacher, Franz, 3742-3743
Radetzky, Waldemar von, (474)
Radin, Max, 269, 916, 2453, 3221
Radom, 1909
Raeder, Erich, 1994, 2012, 2032, 2135, 2175, (463), (465)-(466)
Raginskiĭ (Raginsky), Mark J., 1068, 2168, 2511, 2575-2576, 2653, 2667, (468)
Rajan, M., 4237
Rakoff, Vivian, 1422-1423
Rama Rao, T.S., 2668
Ramsey, Paul, 4238-4239

Rand, E., 1842
Rappaport, Emil S., 2766
Rasche, Karl, (476)
Raschhofer, Hermann, 3751
Rassinier, Paul, 1454, 1860, 4116
Ratz, Michael, 3481
Ratz, Paul, 3569
Rau, Gustav, 3818
Rauer, Karl, 3536
Rauschenbach, Gerhard, 2767
Rauter, Hans Albin, 3546; trial of, 3868
Rautkallio, Hannu, 3607
Ravensbrück, 1636, 1656, 1662, 1664, 1667, 1910-1928
Read, James Morgan, 685-686
Rector, Frank, 1042
Red Cross, 1929
Reder, Rudolf, 1754
Reder, Walter, 3749
Redish, Martin, 443
Redley, Adolphus G., 289
Reel, Adolf Frank, 2530-2531, 2534, 4403
Rees, John R., 2079, 2243
Rees, Joseph, 1800
Reeves, Jesse S., 290
Reference works, 127-137
Regent-Lechowicz, Maria, 3099
Rehmsdorf, 1655
Rehse, Hans Joachim, 3691
Reich Cabinet, defense counsel for, (463)
Reichenbach, 1649
Reichmann, Eva G., 1361
Reichssicherheitshauptamt (RSHA), 2374
Reik, Otto E., 851
Reimann, Viktor, 2080
Reinecke, Hermann, (476)
Reinhardt, Hans, (476)
Reipert, Fritz, 852
Reithmuller Vaccaro, Julio H., 3277
Reitlinger, Gerald, 480, 1362, 2395
Renault, Louis, 246, 388
Rendulic, Lothar, 609, (473)
Renoth, Hans, 3543
Repaci, A., 3855
Resettlement, 979-1007
Resich, Zbigniew, 966
Reston, James B., Jr., 3222, 4448
Retzlaff, Reinhard, 3892
Reut-Nicolussi, Eduard, 630
Reuter, Paul, 3142, 3223
Rey, Francis, 1095
Reynolds, Quentin James, 3988, 4016
Rezanoff, A.S., 722
Riasnoi, V.V., 1195

Index 539

Ribadeau Dumas, François, 2081
Ribbentrop, Annelies von, 2136
Ribbentrop, Joachim von, 590, 2061, 2123, 2136, 2248, 2762, (462), (464), (467)
Richman, Frank N., 3470, (471)
Riesenberger, Dieter, 2014
Riess, Curt, 2082
Riet, Victor van, 1894
Riga, ghetto of, 1670
Rigaux, M., 3594
Rigg, Robert B., 853
Rijksinstituut Voor Oorlogsdocumentatic, 3866-3868
Riley, Walter Lee, 2639
Ringelblum, Emanuel, 1149
Ringer, Benjamin B., 4210
Ringsted, H.V., 2768
Ringwood, Ona K.D., 2196
Ripley, Herbert S., 1072
Risner, Robinson, 4377
Risse, Heinz Theo, 4117
Ritter, Gerhard, 247
Ritter, Karl, (476)
Rix, Carl B., 291
Roberts, Adam, 2875
Roberts, G.D., (468)
Robertson, David W., 4277
Robin, Raymond, 248
Robinson, Jacob, 75-76, 109, 1275, 1455-1457, 3143, 4118, 4191, (468)
Robinson, Nehemiah, 610, 854, 2307, 3969, 4017, 4192
Rockman, A., 4211
Rodgers, Raymond Spencer, 4028
Rodley, Nigel S., 4229
Rodney, C.M., 3906
Roeder, M., 1737
Roesen, Anton, 3437
Rogat, Yosal, 4119-4120
Rogers, William D., 4260, 4463
Rohde, Werner, 3537, 3838
Rôheim, Géza, 389
Röhl, J.C.G., 3458
Rohrscheidt, Günther von, (462)
Rohwer, Jürgen, 1550
Roland, M., 967
Rolin, H., 4121
Röling, Bernard Victor A., 390, 611, 917, 2578, 2632, 2640, 2669, (13)
Rolph, Hammond M., 4378
Romanovskii, V.F., 1196
Romanowski, Wincenty, 1197
Romashkin, P.S., 855
Rome, M.E., 2769
Rommel, Erwin E.J., 2032
Roosevelt, Franklin D., 951, 3308
Roques, Karl von, (476)
Ros, André, 2431

Rose, Anna, 1960
Rose, Gerhard, (469)
Rosenberg, Alfred, 211, 249, 2031, 2083, 2123, 2137-2138, 2159-2161, 2186, 2191, (462), (464), (466)
Rosenberg, Harold, 4122
Rosencher, Henri, 1843
Rosenkrantz, Herbert, 1476
Rosenkrantz, J., 148
Rosenman, Samuel I., 250
Rosenne, Shabtai, 4041
Rosenthal, H., 4418
Rosenwein, Sam, 4449
Rossi, M., 3856
Rost, Nico, 1844-1846
Rostowski, Dieter, 1198
Rotenstreich, Nathan, 1298
Roth, Andrew, 2328
Roth, Günther, 3482
Roth, John K., 1276
Roth, S.J., 2329
Rothaug, Oswald, (470)
Rothchild, Sylvia, 1277
Rothe, Wolf Dieter, 1363
Rothenberger, Curt, (470)
Rotkirchen, Livia, 1553-1554, 4212
Rougerie, Claude, 2071
Rousseau, Charles, 4029
Rousset, David, 1096, 1621
Routier, Marcelle, 1688
Roux, J.A., 554, 3066
Rowe, Terry E., 4355
Rowley, Louis E., 767
Rowson, S.W.D., 2454
Roxburgh, Ronald F., 292
Roy, Jules, 3658
Rozanski, Zenon, 1738
Rozenblit, S., 2576, 2667
RSHA, see Reichssicherheitshauptamt
Rückerl, Adalbert, 856, 1661, 3224
Rühl, Felix, (474)
Rüter, C.F., 858-860, 2640
Rüter-Ehlermann, Adelheid L., 858-859
Rubenstein, Richard, 1294
Rubin, Alfred P., 4356
Rubin, Eli, 2770
Ruchteschell, Helmuth von, 3541
Rudenko, Roman A., 2888, 2893-2894, (468)
Rudnicki, Adolf, 1739
Ruff, V.H., 612
Ruhm von Oppen, Beate, 613
Ruiz Moreno, I., 3239
Rumania, Holocaust in, 1546-1550
Rundstedt, Gerd von, 2032, 3817
RuSHA Case, Appendix 8
Russ, William A., Jr., 654

Russell, Bertrand, 4437-4457, (487)
Russell, Edward F.L., 857, 1069, 4123
Russell, Kent A., 4395
Russell, Ruth B., 3293
Russell, S., 4452
Russett, Bruce M., 4240
Rust, Philippe, 3541
Rustin, Stanley, 1424
Rutman, Darrett B., 655
Ryan, Allan A., 2308
Ryan, Garry D., 188
Ryan, Marleigh, 115
Ryan, Michael D., 1403

S

SA, see Sturmabteilung
Sabbethai, K. (pseudonym), 2245
Sabille, Jacques, 1492
Saburo, Kugai, 4321
Sacharoff, Mark, 77
Sacharow, Valentin, 1895
Sachs, Henry, 1457
Sachsenburg, 1649
Sachsenhausen, 1640, 1646, 1658, 1665, 1930-1937, 3757, 3906-3907
Sack, Alexander N., 444-445, 555
Sadaichi, Gozawa, 2504
Sagarin, Edward, 585-586
Sagel-Grande, Irene, 859
Sahlins, Marshall, 4241
Sainsbury, Keith, 78
Saint-Clair, Simon, 1924
Sakai, Takashi, 3546
Sakakibara, Yasutake, 2517
Sakata, Shoichi, (487)
Sakowska, Ruta, 1150
Sakuda, Keiichi, 2500
Salaspils, 1636, 1938
Saldaña y Garcia Rubio, Quintiliano, 391
Salmuth, Hans von, (476)
Salomon, Michel, 2309
Salus, Grete, 1961
Salvesen, Sylvia, 1662
Salvin, Marina, 499
Sandberg, Moshe, 2840
Sandberger, Martin, (474)
Sanders, Jared Y., 3494
Sandmel, Samuel, 860
Sandor, Elo, 1874
Sandström, Emil, 2938
Sanguedolce, Joseph, 1848
Sankey, John S., 2455
Santander, Silvano, 4124
Sarker, Lotika, 293
Sarkissian, Arshag O., 723
Sartre, Jean-Paul, 1364, 4453, (487)
Sasuly, Richard, 3419

Sato, Kenryo, (478), (480), (482)
Sauckel, Fritz, 590, 2003, (463)-(464), (466)
Sauer, Paul, 1505
Sauer, Wilhelm, 861, 968, 3046
Saurel, Louis, 2771
Sausnitisa, K., 1938
Sauter, Fritz, (462)-(463)
Savesten, David H., 4251
Savran, Bella, 1434-1435
Sawacki, Jerzy, 1108
Sawada, Shigeru, trial of, 3537
Sawade, Fritz (Werner Heyde), 3184
Sawicki, Georges, 1116, 3427
Sawicki, Jerzy, 2772, 3166, 3881-3882
Sayre, Francis B., 862
Scanlon, Helen L., 79
Scanlon, Thomas, 516
SCAP, see Supreme Commander for the Allied Powers
Schacht, Hjalmar, 590, 1983, 2074-2075, 2139-2140, 2227, 2682, 2762, 2851, 2862, (463), (465)-(466)
Schadewaldt, Hans, 1124
Schafer, Mark, 928
Schaffer, Ronnld, 80
Schaible, Richard, 969-970
Schaick, F.L., 3018, 3018
Schallermair, George, 3522
Schappes, Morris U., 1404, 4042
Schatz, Willi Ludwig, 3725
Schätzel, Walter, 2246
Schatzker, Chaim, 1278
Schätzle, Julius, 1622, 1663
Scheel, Klaus, 2084
Scheffler, Wolfgang, 1471
Schell, Jonathan, 4242, 4335
Schellenberg, 2111, 2141, 2184, (476)
Schenck, Ernst von, 2138
Schenk, Reinhold, 392
Schiano, Vincent A., 2297
Schick, Franz B., 393, 929, 2916-2917, 3019, 3144, 3278-3279, 4278
Schickel, Alfred, 863
Schilf, Alfred, (463)
Schilling, George T., 3495
Schilling, Karl, 2962
Schindler, R., 3047
Schirach, Baldur von, 590, 2012, 2036, 2085-2086, 2142-2143, 2255, (463), (465), (467)
Schirach, Henriette von, 2143
Schirilla, László, 1058
Schirmer, D.B., 667
Schlachter, Gail, 81
Schlegelberger, Franz, (470)
Schleunes, Karl A., 1740

Schlögel, Anton, 2939
Schlumberger, Jean, 3659
Schmid, Jürg H., 394
Schmid, Max, 3545
Schmid, Richard, 1623
Schmidt, Dietmar, 1849
Schmidt, Ephraim, 1478
Schmidt, Gerhard, 1029
Schmidt, Hans, 3522
Schmidt, Mathias, 2247
Schmidt, Paul, 2773
Schmidt, Regina, 3970
Schmiedt, Shlomo, 1962
Schmitthenner, Walter, 1869
Schmitz, Hermann, (472)
Schmorak, Dov B., 4043, 4146
Schnabel, Reimund, 1850, 2396
Schneeberger, Ernst, 556
Schneider, Hans, 251
Schneider, Peter, 2376, 3700
Schneider, Rolf, 2876
Schnitzler, Georg von, (472)
Schochet, J., 1524
Schoenbaum, David L., 3101-3102
Schoenberner, Gerhard, 1472
Schoengrath, Eberhard, 3543
Scholz, Heinrich, 3048
Schönborn, Erwin, 2774
Schonfeld, Franz, 3543
Schönke, Adolf, 3570-3571
Schorsch, Ismar, 82
Schörzingen, 1636
Schosser, Anton, trial of, 3535
Schrameck, Ernst, 3540
Schramm, Hanna, 1870
Schröder, Oscar, (469)
Schroeder, Paul W., 2579
Schroers, Rolf, 4018
Schubert, Heinz Hermann, (474)
Schueller, George K., 2052
Schüle, Erwin, 4019
Schultz, Joseph P., 1279
Schultz, Karl, 3539
Schulz, Erich, 724
Schulz, Erwin, (474)
Schulze, Hans Joachim, 3572
Schulze-Wilde, Harry, 1043
Schumann, Horst, 2320
Schuster, George N., 3145
Schutter, Bart de, 83
Schütze, Heinrich Albrecht, 582
Schutzstaffel (SS), 69, 2037, 2378-2403, 2842, (463)
Schwalm, Fritz, (473)
Schwartz, Laurent, (487)
Schwarz, Solomon M., 1560
Schwarzenberger, Georg, 395, 3146, 4163
Schwarzwäller, Wulf, 2087
Schwelb, Egon, 331, 971
Schwender, Wolfgang, 3828
Schwengler, Walter, 2088

Schwerin von Krosigk, Lutz, 2089, (476)
Schwertfeger, B., 811
Schwinge, Erich, 3660
Scotland, A.P., 3857
Scott, James Brown, 783, 797
Screen, J.E.O., 84
Scuttled U-Boats trial, 3533
Seabury, Paul, 2248
Sears, Charles B., 2775, (471)
Sebald, William J., 2490
Sebba, Leslie, 1473
Sebring, Harold L., (469)
Segall, Aryeh (Arie), 110, 3971
Segalson, M., 1524
Seger, Gerhart, 1933
Sehn, Jan, 1741
Seibert, Willi, (474)
Seidl, Alfred, 2256, (462)
Selling, Lowell S., 864
Selzer, Michael, 1851, 2230, 2249
Semmler, Rudolf, 2090
Senesh, Hannah, 2819-2820
Seraphim, Hans-Günther, 583, 2877-2878, 3147, 3352-3358
Servatius, Robert, 3989, 4147, 4169-4170, (463)
Servus Juris [pseudonym], 3661
Settel, Arthur, 3022, 3397
Seyss-Inquart, Arthur, 590, (463)-(464), (466)
Shake, Curtis Grover, (472)
Shanghai, 1638, 2516
Shapiro, 1425, 2776
Shawcross, Hartley, 2154, 2888, 2895, (468)
Sheehan, Neil, 4404
Sheer, Robert, 4454
Sheerin, J.B., 865
Shenin, L.R., (468)
Shepard, William S., 656
Sherwin, Byron L., 1280
Shigemitsu, Mamoru, 640, 2665, (17), (478), (480), (482)
Shigeru Ohashi trial, 3537
Shinohara, Eitano, 3537
Shiratori, Toshio, (478), (480), (482)
Shirer, William L., 252
Shiroyama, Saburo, 2091
Shneiderman, Samuel Loeb, 1921, 3732
Shortis, F., 2821
Shotwell, James T., 566
Shtrigler, Mordecai, 1101
Shulman, Frank J., 97
Shuval, Judith T., 1445
Sibley, Mulford Quickert, 866-867, 4235
Sicherheitsdienst (SD), 2024, 2377, 2842 (463)

Siegert, Karl, 446
Siegrist, Ettor, 1852
Siekanowicz, Peter, 85
Siemers, Walter, (463)
Siemsen, K., 3701
Siene trial, 3847
Sievers, Wolfram, (469)
Siewert, Curt, 2092
Sigal, J.J., 1423
Sigl, Fritz, 3907
Sijes, B.A., 999, 1050, 1531
Silberschein, A., 1539
Silberstein, Jacob, 1855
Silkin, S.C., 2506
Silvergate, Jesse, 2940
Silving, Helen, 3990
Simon, Wichene, 1861
Simon, Ernst, 4088
Simon, S., 2777
Simon, Sam, 1624
Simonov, Konstantin, 1881
Sinclair, Upton, 2250
Singen (Hohentwiel), 1669
Sington, Derrick, 1770
Sinn, Dieter, 2093
Six, Franz, (474)
Skarzysko (Kamienna), 1939
Skorzeny, Otto, 3541, 3702; trial of, 3693
Sleeman, Colin, 2504, 2506
Sloan, F. Blaine, 294
Sloan, Jacob, 1102
Slooten, M. van, 798
Slorenko, Ralph, 3981
Slottke, Gertrud, 3690
Slovakia, Holocaust in, 1551-1556
Sluzny, M., 3595
Small, Melvin, 2580
Smead, Elmer E., 3067
Smirnov, Lev Nikolaevich, 2778, 3226, (468)
Smith, Bradley F., 2037, 2094-2095, 2779-2781
Smith, C.C., 3369
Smith, Delbert D., 482
Smith, H.A., 447, 3227
Smith, Jacob H., 673
Smith, James M., 649
Smith, Marcus J., 1853
Smith, Sydney, 1665
Smith, William, 3818
Smith, Willis, 2782
Smolen, Kazimierz, 1742
Smylie, James H., 4279
Smyth, Howard McGraw, 86, 3858
Snow, Edgar, 868
Snyder, Louis Leo, 130, 253
Snyder, Orville C., 614
Sobibor, 1276, 1661, 1940-1942
Sobotker, H., 2783
Sohn, Louis B., 2963
Soini, Yrjö [pseudonym], 3608

Sokolowski, Stanislaw, 8
Sola Pool, David de, 4215
Sola Pool, Tamar de, 4215
Sola Pool, Ithiel de, 2052
Solf, Waldemar A., 459, 615
Solow, Herbert, 2652
Sommer, Karl, (471)
Sommer, Martin, 3752
Song My (Pinkville), 4362-4370
Sonnenburg, 1649
Sontag, Ernst, 972, 2368, 3703
Sottile, Antoine, 316-317, 973, 2918, 3333
Sources and depositories, (17)
Spain, Ian, 2784
Spandau prisoners, 2039, 2223
Speek, Peter, 1001
Speer, Albert, 590, 2012, 2022, 2043, 2144-2145, 2247, 2255, 2862, (463), (465)-(466)
Speidel, Wilhelm, (473)
Speight, John J., (470)-(471), (474)
Spencer, Jack, 1256
Sperber, Harry N., 3483
Speyer, Paul, 869
Spier, Henry O., 87
Spiropoulos, Jean, 396, 2964
Sprecher, Drexel A., (467)
Springer, Hildegard, 2018
Spurlock, Paul E., 2539
SS, see Schutzstaffel
Stachura, Peter D., 88
Staff, Ilse, 3388
Stäglich, Wilhelm, 1743
Stahmer, Otto, (462)
Stalag Luft III trial, 3543, 3839
Stalin, Joseph, 951
Stanford War Crimes Study Group, 4280
Stangl, Franz Paul, 3755
Stapleton, Margaret L., 89
Starkenberg, Olof, 3609
Starr, Joshua, 1425
Starr, Merritt, 725
Stashinsky trial, 3751
Statutes of limitation on war crimes, 3070-3109
Staub, Hugo, 2167
Steakley, James D., 1044
Steengracht von Moyland, Gustav Adolf, (476)
Steimle, Eugen, (474)
Stein, George H., 2397
Stein, Leo, 3280
Steinbauer, Gustav, 2146, (463)
Steinberg, Lucien, 141, 1405, 1479
Steinbock, Johann, 1854
Steinbrinck, Otto, (472)
Steiner, Frederic, 1555
Steiner, Jean-François, 1971
Steinert, Georg, trial of, 3535

Steinert, Marlis G., 2096
Steiniger, P.A., 2879, 3389
Steinitz, Lucy Y., 1426
Steinmetz, Selma, 1051
Steinwender, Leonhard, 1792
Stendig, Jakob, 1295
Stenzel, Ernst, 254
Stephan, Werner, 2097
Stephens, Robert Greir, Jr., 2785
Stevens, E.H., 3837
Stevenson, John R., 4464
Stevenson, William, 2098
Stewart, John Hall, 635
Stewart, Potter, 2154
Stewart, William J., 90
Stillschweig, Kurt, 1365
Stimson, Henry L., 2919, 2251
Stipp, John L., 2880
Stitzer, K., 3662
Stöcker, Jakob, 2786
Stockholm Tribunal, 4437-4457
Stockhorst, Erich, 131
Stödter, Rolf, 397
Stöhr, Martin, 1281
Stone, Harlan, 238, 2531, 2818
Stone, Isaac, (468)
Stone, Julius, 398
Stone, R., 332
Stone, Shepard, 3484
Stoop, Bert, 3105
Storey, Robert Gerald, 616, 2787, 3020, 3281, (467)
Stowell, Ellery C., 399
Stransky, Jaroslav, 2456
Straub, Peter, 3838
Strauch, Eduard, (474)
Strauss, Herbert A., 91
Strauss, Walther, 1474
Strebel, Helmut, 2941
Strecker, Reinhard, 2099
Streicher, Julius, 1990, 1998, 2841, (463), (465), (467)
Streim, Alfred, 483
Streit, Christian, 484
Stri..ler, Mordchai, 1625
Strisower, Leo, 400
Stroop, Jürgen, 2062; trial of, 3877-3878
Struckberg, Georg, 3573
Strum, Harvey, 2251
Struthof (Natzweiler), 1943-1946
Strutz, Henry, 2101
Stuckart, Wilhelm, (476)
Student, Kurt, trial of, 3536,
Stülpnagel, Otto von, 726, 3668
Sturmabteilung (SA), 2842; defense counsel for, (463)
Stutthof, 1648, 1947
Styer, Wilhelm D., 2523, 2533
Submarine Warfare, World war II, 2174

"Subsequent," trials, see American military tribunals
Suhl, Yuri, 1406
Sullivan, James D., 2252, 2533
Summers, Harry G., 4243
Sund, Harald, 2253
Sündermann, Helmut, 2100
Superior orders, and necessity, 419-455
Supreme Commander for the Allied Powers (SCAP), 2331, 2517, 2534, 2540, 2581, 2596
Süßkind, W., 2788
Sutton, David Nelson, 2582-2583
Suzuki, Daisetz Teitaro, 2669
Suzuki, Teiichi, (478), (480), (482)
Sveshnikov, I., 1070
Swartz, Mary, 1366
Swearingen, Victor C., 2789, (469)
Sweet, William, 3390
Sybil, Milton, 1333
Sydnor, Charles W., 2398
Syme, Anthony V., 4244
Symonowicz, Wanda, 1925
Syrkin, Marie, 1282, 1407
Szabados, Hans, 3541
Szabo, Denis, 495
Szabó, László (Ladislao), 2305, 2310
Szalai, Sándor, 3844
Szalet, Leon, 1934
Szecsi, Maria, 3590
Szende, Stefan, 1125
Szilard, Leo, 2147
Szmaglewska, Seweryna, 1744
Szner, Zvi, 1408
Szondi, Lipot, 3981
Szony, David M., 1426
Szurlej, S., 401

T

Taege, Herbert, 3663
Taft, Donald R., 2457
Takayanagi, Kenzo, 2584
Takman, John, 4455
Talerico, Anthony, Jr, 448
Tallow, Adamin A., 557
Tanaka Hisakasu trial, 3537
Tarkka, Jukka, 3610
Tarnowska, Maria, 92
Tas, J., 1627
Tasjian, J.H., 799
Tatge, Paul W., 3228
Taubenschlag, Rafael (Raphael), 449
Taylor, Lawrence, 2541
Taylor, Telford, 175, 197, 402, 615, 618-621, 2682, 2790, 3334-3337, 3446, 4125, 4298, (467)

Teitgen, M., 3148
Temperley, Harold, 663
Tenenbaum, Joseph, 1745
Tennenbaum-Backer, Nina, 1151
Ternon, Yves, 1030-1032
Tesar, Ottokar, 974
Tesch, Bruno, 3533
Tharp, Paul A., 403
Theresienstadt, 1948-1964
Thiele, Gunther, trial of, 3535
Thiele-Fredersdorf, Herbert, 3391, 3421
Thieleke, Karl-Heinz, 3404
Thomas, A.J., Jr., 918
Thomas, Alfred, (462)
Thomas, Ann van Wynen, 918
Thomas, Daniel H., 111
Thomas, Georg, 255
Thomas, Gordon, 1392
Thomas, Jack, 1793
Thomas, W., 2256
Thompson, Harold Keith, 2101
Thompson, Kenrick S., 4358
Thompson, Larry, 2399
Thomsen, Erich, 3604
Thorne, Leon, 1427
Thorneycraft, E., 558
Thorpe, Gerald L., 2794, 3229
Thrace, Holocaust In, 1557
Thucydides, 631
Tidy, Henry Letheby, 1629
Tiede, Tom, 4432
Tillard, P., 1896
Tillion, Germaine, 1926
Tillmann, Friederick, 3184
Tillmann, H., 3459
Togo, Shigenori, (478), (480), (482)
Tojo, Hideki, 1993, 1997, 2547, (478), (481)-(482); trial of, 614
Tokayer, Marvin, 1366
Toland, John, 2102
Tomberg, Valentin, 295
Tomoyuki, Yamashita, 2076, 2518-2536, 2541-2543; trial of, 593, 604, 614, 3536, 4304; appeal of, 2252
Toms, Robert M., (470)-(471)
Torgersen, Rolf N., 2795
Totok, Wilhelm, 132
Touzalin, H. de, 3052
Toynbee, Arnold J., 256, 735, 741, 749, 752
Traĭnin[e], Aron Naumovich, 623, 2257, 2920, 2965-2966, 3053-3055, (455)
Trapp, Erwin, 3283
Treaster, Joseph B., 4380
Treblinka, 1276, 1661, 1965-1972, 2292, 3741, 3880
Treece, Patricia, 2822

Tregenza, Michael, 1755
Trevelyan, George Otto, 637
Treves, Vanni E., 4193
Trevor-Roper, Hugh R., 93, 2152, 2258
Tribunal Militaire Permanent de Paris, 3668
Tribunal Russell, 4456-4457
Trifa, Valerian, 2228
Triska, Jan F., 1630
Trofimenko, G., 486
Trousse, P.E., 3594
Truck, 1747, 2103
Truman, Harry S, (14)
Trunk, Isaiah, 1152-1153, 1409, 1541
Truyol y Serra, Antonio, 2921
Tsai, Paul Chung-Tseng, 2587
Tschentscher, Erwin, (471)
Tucker, Robert W., 4325
Turkey, 661
Turlington, Edgar, 1381
Turner, Robert K., 157
Tushins, J.W., 2922
Tushnet, Leonard, 1154, 1542

U

Udall, Stewart, 4433
Uematsu, Keita, 2588
Uhl, Michael, 4326
Uhlig, Heinrich, 450
Ullmann, Eduard, 1935
Ulm trial, 3740, 3758
Umadevi [pseudonym], 1155
Umemura, 2621
Umezu, Yoshijiro, (478), (481)-(482)
Underhill, L.K., 3021
Union für Recht und Freiheit, Prag, 1631
Union of Soviet Socialist Republics, 1172-1245, 2514; Holocaust in, 1558-1561; Supreme Court, 3910
United Artists, Phonograph of the Eichmann trial, 4044
United Nations, Committee For the Progressive Development of International Law and its Codification, 333; Committee of International Criminal Jurisdiction, 318; Committee on Human Rights, 2459; Communications and Records Division, 112-113, 121-123; Dag Hammarskjold Library, 124; Department of Public Information, 1382; documents and records, 152-153; General Assembly, 334, 487, 1383, 2349, 4447; Information Organization

Index 545

[Office], 505, 870, 871-872, 1003, 1283, 2460-2463; international criminal jurisdiction, 270; International Law Commission, 94, 153, 335-336, 404; Relief and Rehabilitation Administration, 1004; Secretary General, 2464-2467, 2491; Treaty Series, 133; War Crimes Commission (UNWCC), 113, 125-126, 134, 2259, 2321, (4); Law Reports, 3533-3547,
United States, Congress, 405, 624, 657, 669, 1169, 1666, 2260, 2311-2314, 2469-2470, 2493; Department of State, 159-173, 257, 506, 873, 875, 976, 1059-1060, 1367, 2261, 2331-2335, 2471, 2494, 2589-2590, 2597-2599, 2649-2650, 2670, 4283; Department of the Air Force, 406; Department of the Army, 407, 2602, 4397, Army Forces in the European Theater, 468, Far East Command, 158; documents and records, 154-210; Immigration and Naturalization Service (INS), 2316-2317; Library of Congress, 95, 507; National Archives and Records Service (NARS), 114, 176-185, 192-206, 1897, 2148, 2508, 3370; Naval War College, 210; Office of Military Government, 332; Office of the High Commissioner for Germany, 3322, 3523; Supreme Court, 2543; War Department, 258, 408-410, 488, 658
Université de Strasbourg, 1632
Uris, Leon, 1033
Utevskii, B.S., 1207-1208
Utitz, E., 1964
Utley, Freda, 3512, 3574
Utsch, Bert, 1936
Uyehara, Cecil H., 228
Uzhdavinis, V., 1209

V

Vagin, P.I., 1189
Valentin, Hugo, 1393
Vambery, Rustem, 2262, 2801, 2973
Van Damm, H., 3757-3758
Van Dyke, Jon M., 411
Vasalli, G., 3861
Vasek, Anton, 1556
Vasileva, Nadejda Slavi, 1557
Vasilyev, A.N., 1071, 2591-2592, 2653, (481)
Vassalli, G., 1010
Vatin, V., 1210

Vaughn, Richard, 632
Veale, Frederick J., 877, 3230-3231
Vedovato, Giuseppe, 2472, 3232
Veesenmayer, Edmund, 2216, (476)
Veicopoulos, Nicolas, 3423
Veidal, 1658
Velpke children's home trial, 3539, 3835
Velvel, Lawrence R., 4284
Venlo Incident, 2111
Vercel, Michel C., 3150
Vereinigung Österreichischer Bibliothekare, 224
Vergès, J., 4482
Vermehren, Isa, 1667
Vermeil, Edmond, 3056
Vermeylen, Pierre, 2473
Veronica trial, 3818
Versailles Treaty, 230, 2088
Vicar, G., 2885
Vichy, collaborators, 3650
Viereck, George S., 785
Vietnam War, bibliography, 27, 102; veterans against the war, 4401; Viet Cong, war crimes of, 4371-4380; Vietnam (Democratic Republic), 4400; war crimes trials, 587, 589, 619-620
Viéville, Lucien, 2707
Vin, Pham Than, 4275
Vogel, Rolf, 3107
Vogelsang, Reinhard, 2104
Vogt, Hannah, 3057
Voight, F.A., 3233
Volchkov, A.F., (462)
Volger, T., 451
Volk, Leo, (471)
Volkmann, Kurt, 3596
Vorlander, Herwart, 1946
Vormeier, Barbara, 1493
Voronkov, N.D., 1211
Vos, Jean de, 1005
Vu Thong Tin Bao Chi, 4292

W

Wade, D.A.L., 3827
Wadsworth, Lawrence W., 2593
Wagner, Albert, 3545
Wagner, Robert, trial of, 3535
Wainwright, Jonathan Mayhew, 2826
Wainwright, Loudon S., 4499
Waite, R.G., 2105
Wakin, Malham M., 271
Wald, George, 559
Waldheimer trial, 3744
Waldmann, Alfred, 919
Waldock, C.H.M., 920
Walendy, Udo, 3424
Walk, Joseph, 1506

Walkinshaw, Robert B., 625
Wall, Edgar, 2802
Wallace, John E., 3669
Walleitner, Hugo, 1864
Waller, Littleton, 673
Wallis, Frank B., (467)
Wallner, Peter, 1668
Waln, Nora, 2474
Walsh, Edmund A., 3234
Walsh, Moira, 3151
Walsh, William F., 2803, (467)
Walther, Hans Rudolf, 452
Waltzog, Alfons, 412
War Book Club, London, 96
War crimes, against Gypsies, 1045-1051; against homosexuals, 1041-1044; against Polist ghettos, 1126-1157; against the USSR, 1172-1245; aggression as, 902-922; Allied, 894-901; collaboration, 923-929; definition of, 867-890; economic, 1034-1040; general works on, 687-731; Katyn Woods massacre, 1158-1171; medical, 1008-1028; number of, (5ff.); slave labor, 2934; statutes of limitation, 3070-3109; victims, 1052-1060
War crimes trials, American, (8); British, (6); comparisons of 2 or more, 584-626; criticisms of, (22); Czechoslovakia, (8); early, 789-799; French, (6); general works on, 569-583; "parent cases," (8); statistics, 3311
War Criminals, amnesty, 2323-2336; definitions of, 2266; early, 753-771; executions delayed, 2261; extradition of, 2337-2349; general treatment, 2268-2269; judgment of, 2257; lists of, 127-128, 134; prosecution of, 2166-2168, 2237-2241; punishment of, 2163, 2179-2181, 2188-2190, 2192-2196, 2206-2209, 2226, 2404-2482; pursuit of, 2169, 2177, 2271-2322; surrender of, 2192; treatment of, 2232-2236
War, laws of, 338-418; renunciation of, 563-568
Ward, Robert E., 97
Warlimont, Walter, (476)
Warmbrunn, Werner, 3869
Warner, Adolphe J., 3399
Warner, Geoffrey, 3670
Warren, Charles, 2476
Warren, Earl, 2263
Wasilkowski, Cz, 545
Wasserstein, Bernard, 1410-1411

Wasserstrom, Richard, 560, 2804, 3284
Watkins, H.E., 2264
Watt, Donald C., 3235
Wauters, A., 1082
Webb, Anthony M., 3838
Webb, Herschel, 115
Webb, William F., 2643, (13)
Weber, Hans H., 18
Weber, Hellmuth von, 453, 2370, 3058, 3323, 3338
Weber, Werner, 259
Weber, Wilhelm, 3539
Weber, Wolfgang, 1788
Wechsler, Herbert, 3068, 3236, 3285
Weerd, Harvey A. de, 921
Wegerer, Alfred von, 260
Wehberg, Hans, 413
Weißpfennig, Walter, 3828
Weich, Maximilian von, 2049
Weimann, Karl-Heinz, 132
Weimar Republic, 231
Wein, Abraham, 1534
Weinberg, Gerhard L., 116, 3461
Weingartner, James J., 3513
Weinkauff, Hermann, 3393
Weinreich, Max, 1507
Weinschenk, Fritz, 3705
Weinstock, Eugene, 1794
Weinstock, Rolf, 1669
Weinzierl, Erika, 1477
Weir, Patricia Ann Lyons, 3706
Weis, George, 319
Weisberg, Barry, 4330
Weiss, Bernhard, (472)
Weiss, Erich, 3545
Weiss, Martin Gottfried, 3543
Weiss, Peter, (487)
Weiss, Reska, 1670
Weiss-Ruethels, A., 1937
Weissberg, Alexander, 1517
Weissmann Klein, Gerda, 1006
Weitzel, Rolf, 132
Weizsäcker, Ernst Heinrich von, 2106, 2149, 3349, (476)
Welch, Richard E., 672
Wellers, George, 1671, 1749, 1284
Wells, Leon W., 1543-1544, 3707
Welsch, Erwin K., 213, 225
Wendel, Hermann, 815
Wenger, Willo, 1898
Wenner, Scott J., 4331
Wennerstrum, Charles F., 595, (472)
Werner, Georges, 489
Werner, Wolfhart, 2371-2372, 3575
Werstein, Irving, 1156
West, Benjamin, 1561
West, Rebecca (Cicilly Isabel Fairfield), 3813

Westerbork, 1973-1975
Westerman, George F., 490
Westington, Mars McClelland, 633
Wharton, J.F., 561
Wheeler, Leonard, Jr., (467)
Wheeler-Bennett, John W., 567, 2805
White, Laura A., 659
White, Ralph, 4332
White, Thomas R., 2478
White, William L., 4480
Whiting, Charles, 3514
Whitman, Marjorie, 135
Whitney, Courtney, 2534
Wiart, H. Carton de, 2806
Wielen, Max, 3543
Wiener, Jan G., 2267
Wiener Library, 98, 227
Wiernik, Yankel, 1972
Wiesel, 1672, 4045
Wiesenthal, Simon, 1899, 2150-2151, 2199, 3108, 4030
Wighton, Charles, 2107, 4020
Wilde, H., 1633
Wilding-White, A.M., 2479
Wilensky, M., 1795
Wilhelm II, 786
Wilhelmstrasse Case, Appendix 8
Wilkens, E., 882, 3708
Wilkins, William J., (475)
Wille, Siegfried, 3371
Willequet, J., 3597
Williams, L. Norman, 4498
Williams, Roger M., 1750
Willis, James F., 769
Willis, William N., 787
Wilmowsky, Tilo von, 3448
Wilner, Alan M., 454
Wilson, Andrew, 4259
Wilson, George G., 414
Wilson, Thomas L., 660
Wimmer, August, 978, 3576-3577
Wind, Eduard de, 1751
Wind, Emmanuel de, 1446
Winkelmann, Paul, 3578
Winn, Larry J., 4360
Winner, Percy, 562
Winter, James, 2320
Winthrop, William W., 415
Wirtschafts- und Verwaltungshauptamt, 2386, 3343
Wirtz [Wirz], Henry, 639
Wistrich, Robert, 136
Wittenberg, J., 3286
Witts, Max Morgan, 1392
Wochner, Magnus, 3838
Woetzel, Robert K., 883, 2924, 2974, 3735, 4183
Wöhler, Otto, (476)
Wold, Terje, 884, 2268
Wolf, Jules, 1083, 2807, 3195, 3598

Wolf, Robert B., 2808
Wolf, Stewart, 1072
Wolfe, Kurt A., 3482
Wolfe, Robert, 209, 1458
Wolff, Ilse R., 99
Wolff, Theodor, 770
Wolfgang Scheffler, 1570
Wolfinger, Jarritus, 191
Wolfmann, Alfred, 4149
Woods, Larry D., 4295
Woodward, Beverly, 3287
Woodward, Ernest L., 144
Woolsey, L.H., 1040
Woolsey, Theodore S., 771
World Veterans Federation, 337
World Jewish Congress, British Section, 1285; Executive Committee, 2480; Institute of Jewish Affairs, 2481
World War I, bibliography, 30, 41; war guilt, 2888
World War II, bibliography, 42; documents, 103
Wörmann, Ernst, (476)
Wormser-Migot, Olga, 1634, 1428
Wormuth, Francis D., 4285
Wortley, B., 2975
Wright of Durley, Lord, 508
Wright, Quincy, 320, 416-418, 568, 788, 2482, 2536, 2809-2810, 2976-2977, 3059, 3069, 3154, 4286
Wright, Robert A.W., 2321
Wrong, Dennis H., 885
Wucher, Albert, 1368
Wulf, Josef (Joseph), 137, 261, 1157, 1469-1470, 1545, 2108
Wulfften Palthe, P.M. van, 1073
Würtenberger, Thomas, 455
WVHA, see Wirtschafts- und Verwaltungshauptamt
Wyatt, Lee B., (473)
Wykes, Alan, 2109
Wyman, David S., 1564, 1752
Wyzanski, Charles E., 3237

Y

Yad Vashem Jerusalem, 4150
Yahil, Leni, 1394
Yamamoto Chusaburo trial, 3535
Yamashita, see Tomoyuki, Yamashita
Yampolsky, Philip B., 2572
Yang, Lieu-Sheng, 509508
Ybarra, Thomas R., 786
Yisrael, Gutman, 1286
Yivo Institute, (21)
Yokohama trials, 2537-2540, (6)
Yokota, Kisaburo, 922
Young, George, 2269
Young, Gordon, 1996
Young, John, 229, (476)

Young, Kenneth Ray, 673
Young, Rowland L., 2322
Young-Bruehl, Elisabeth, 2823
Yrigoyen, Jaime, 2925
Yugoslavia, 1246-1247, 1565-1566

Z

Zablocki, Clement J., 4333
Zaborowski, Jan, 3713
Zachakel, Friedrich, 2400
Zahn, Gordon C., 3972, 4245
Zaide, Sonia Magbanua, 2626
Zaitsev, Y., 3219
Zak, Joel, 1855
Zakowska, Elzbieta, 3685
Zander, Jens-Peter, 2270
Zawodny, Januszk K., 117, 1170-1171
Zayas, Alfred M. de, 901
Zeck, William A., 3579
Zeiger, Henry A., 4151
Zelewski, Bach, 3882

Zeman, Zbynek A.B., 886
Zentner, Kurt, 262
Zentral-Justizamt für die britische Zone, 3394
Zentrale Stelle der Landesjustizverwaltungen, 1007
Zeuss, Wolfgang, 3838
Ziegler, Janet, 100
Ziemssen, Dietrich, 3515
Zimmels, Hirsch Jakob, 1369
Zimmermann, Ludwig, 263
Zinn, Howard, 4334
Zipfel, F., 2377
Zoepf, Wilhelm, 3690
Zoll, Donald Atwell, 4361
Zoller, Albert, 2110
Zöllner, Martin, 3429
Zorner, G., 1927
Zorya, N.D., (468)
Zourek, J., 2978
Zuehlke, Willy, 3546
Zumpe, L., 1928
Zyklon B trial, 3533
Zylberberg, Michael, 2834, 3885

Z 6464 W33 T87 1986
Tutorow, Norman E.
  War crimes, war criminals, and war crimes trials